AMERICAN GOVERNMENT

Roots and Reform

2020 Presidential Election Edition

Fourteenth Edition

Karen O'Connor

Jonathan N. Helfat Distinguished
Professor of Political Science, American University

Larry J. Sabato

University Professor and Robert Kent
Gooch Professor of Politics, University of Virginia

 Pearson

Content Management: Pam Chirls
Content Production: Rob DeGeorge,
Tina Gagliostro, Heather Pagano,

Product Management: Amy Wetzel
Product Marketing: Rachele Strober
Rights and Permissions: Ben Ferrini

Please contact https://support.pearson.com/getsupport/s/with any queries on this content.

Cover Image by Christophe BOISSON/123rf.com

Library of Congress Cataloging-in-Publication Data

Library of Congress Control Number: 2021907479

1 2021

Access Code Card
ISBN-10:   0-13-690036-4
ISBN-13: 978-0-13-690036-8

Rental Edition
ISBN-10:   0-13-690043-7
ISBN-13: 978-0-13-690043-6

Dedications

To Dolly, who at 86 followed politics, an addiction she bequeathed to me.

Karen O'Connor

To my Government 101 students over the years, who all know that "politics is a good thing."

Larry J. Sabato

Brief Contents

Meet the Authors   xii

To the Student   xiii

To the Instructor   xiv

Preface   xv

PART I   Foundations of Government

1 American Government: Roots, Context, and Culture   1

2 The Constitution   18

3 The Federal System   46

4 Civil Liberties   68

5 Civil Rights   101

PART II   Institutions of Government

6 Congress   134

7 The Presidency   166

8 The Executive Branch and the Federal Bureaucracy   190

9 The Judiciary   213

PART III   Political Behavior

10 Public Opinion and Political Socialization   242

11 Political Parties   261

12 Campaigns, Elections, and Voting   289

13 The News Media   328

14 Interest Groups   354

PART IV   Public Policy

15 Social and Economic Policy   379

16 Foreign and Defense Policy   406

Appendices

    I The Declaration of Independence   438
    II The Constitution of the United States of America   441
    III The Federalist Papers: Nos. 10, 51, 78   452

Glossary   461

Endnotes   478

Index   493

Contents

Meet the Authors ... xii
To the Student ... xiii
To the Instructor ... xiv
Preface ... xv
Acknowledgments ... xxii

PART I Foundations of Government

1 American Government: Roots, Context, and Culture ... 1

What Are the Roots of American Government? ... 2
   The Earliest Inhabitants of the Americas ... 2
   The First Colonists ... 3
   A Religious Tradition Takes Root ... 3
What Are the Functions of the American Government? ... 5
   Establishing Justice ... 6
   Ensuring Domestic Tranquility ... 6
   Providing for the Common Defense ... 7
   Promoting the General Welfare ... 7
   Secure the Blessings of Liberty ... 8
How Have the American People and Their Culture Changed Over Time? ... 8
   Size and Population Trends ... 8
   Racial and Ethnic Composition ... 9
   Issues of an Aging Population ... 10
   The Role of Religious Beliefs ... 11
   Family and Family Size ... 11
   Regional Growth and Expansion ... 12
Political Reform and Realities: How Are Things, Really? ... 13
   Conclusion and Review 17 • Learn the Terms 17 • Learn the Names 17

2 The Constitution ... 18

What Are the Roots of the U.S. Constitution? ... 20
   First Steps Toward Independence ... 21
   The First and Second Continental Congresses ... 22
   The Business of Independence ... 24
   Securing Foreign Alliances ... 24
   Preparing a Plan of Governance ... 25
What Are the Articles of Confederation? ... 25
   Problems Under the Articles of Confederation ... 26
   Rebellion in the States ... 26
How Was the U.S. Constitution Written? ... 27
   The Characteristics and Motives of the Framers ... 28
   The Virginia and New Jersey Plans ... 29
   Constitutional Compromises ... 30
   Unfinished Business: Selection of the President ... 31

What Are the Key Features of the U.S. Constitution? ... 32
   The Basic Principles of the Constitution ... 32
   The Structure of the Constitution ... 34
What Was the Process for Ratifying the U.S. Constitution? ... 37
   Federalists Versus Anti-Federalists ... 37
   The Federalist Papers, Publius, and Brutus ... 38
   Winning Support for the Constitution ... 39
   The Bill of Rights ... 39
Poltical Reform and Realities: How Does the Amendment Process Work? ... 40
   Formal Methods of Amending the Constitution ... 41
   Informal Methods of Amending the Constitution ... 42
   Conclusion and Review 44 • Learn the Terms 45 • Learn the Names 45

3 The Federal System ... 46

What Are the Roots of the Federal System? ... 47
   Types of Government ... 48
   Devising a Federal System ... 48
How Are the Powers of Government Divided By the Constitution? ... 49
   National Powers Under the Constitution ... 50
   State Powers Under the Constitution ... 50
   Concurrent Powers Under the Constitution ... 51
   Powers Denied Under the Constitution ... 51
   Interstate Relations Under the Constitution ... 52
   Local Governments Under the Constitution ... 52
How Has Federalism Evolved? ... 53
   Federalism and the Marshall Court ... 53
   The Civil War and Dual Federalism ... 55
   Cooperative Federalism and the Growth of National Government ... 59
Political Reform and Realities: How Are National and State Powers Really Balanced? ... 61
   The Influence of Federal Grants ... 63
   Federalism and the Supreme Court ... 65
   Conclusion and Review 66 • Learn the Terms 67 • Learn the Names 67

4 Civil Liberties ... 68

What Are the Roots of Civil Liberties and the Bill of Rights? ... 70
   The Incorporation Doctrine: The Bill of Rights Made Applicable to the States ... 71
   Selective Incorporation and Fundamental Freedoms ... 72
What Are the First Amendment Guarantees of Freedom of Religion? ... 73

The Establishment Clause 74
The Free Exercise Clause 75
What Are the First Amendment Guarantees of Freedom of Speech, Press, Assembly, and Petition? 77
Freedoms of Speech and of the Press 77
Protected Speech and Press 78
Unprotected Speech and Press 80
Freedoms of Assembly and Petition 81
What Does the Second Amendment Protect? 82
What Are the Rights of Criminal Defendants? 84
The Fourth Amendment and Searches and Seizures 84
The Fifth Amendment: Self-Incrimination and Double Jeopardy 85
The Fourth and Fifth Amendments and the Exclusionary Rule 87
The Sixth Amendment and the Right to Counsel 88
The Sixth Amendment and Jury Trials 88
The Eighth Amendment and Cruel and Unusual Punishment 89
What Is the Right to Privacy? 90
Birth Control 91
Abortion 92
Lesbian, Gay, Bisexual, Transgender, and Queer (LGBTQ) Issues 93
Political Reform and Realities: What Can Goverments Do About Covid-19, Racial Injustice, and Beyond? 94
The First Amendment 95
The Second Amendment 97
The Fourth Amendment 97
The Eighth Amendment 98
Conclusion and Review 99 • Learn the Terms 100 • Learn the Names 100

5 Civil Rights 101
What Are the Roots of American Civil Rights? 103
Slavery and Congress 104
The First Civil Rights Movements: Abolition and Women's Rights 104
The 1850s: The Calm Before the Storm 105
The Civil War and Its Aftermath: Civil Rights Laws and Constitutional Amendments 105
Civil Rights, Congress, and the Supreme Court 107
What was the Push for Equality, 1890–1954? 108
The Founding of the National Association for the Advancement of Colored People 109
The Suffrage Movement 109
Litigating for Equality 110
What Statutory Protections for Civil Rights Were and Continue to Be Enacted, 1955–Present? 113
School Desegregation After Brown 113
A New Movement for African American Rights 114
Formation of New Groups 115
The Civil Rights Act of 1964 116
A New Movement for Women's Rights 117
Other Statutory Remedies for Sex Discrimination 118
The Equal Rights Amendment 119

What Other Groups Have Mobilized for Rights? 120
Hispanic Americans 120
American Indians 123
Asian and Pacific Island Americans 125
The Lesbian, Gay, Bisexual, Transgender, and Queer (LGBTQ) Community 127
Americans with Disabilities 128
Political Reform and Realities: How Are Civil Rights Protected? 129
The Equal Protection Clause and Constitutional Standards of Review 129
Conclusion and Review 132 • Learn the Terms 132 • Learn the Names 133

PART II Institutions of Government

6 Congress 134
What Are the Roots and Structure of the U.S. Congress? 135
Constitutional Provisions That Define the Organization and Powers of Congress 136
How do Members of Congress Represent the American People? 138
Congressional Demographics 139
Representational Strategies 142
How do Members Stay in Congress? 142
Incumbency 143
Redistricting 143
How is Congress Organized? 145
Leadership in the House of Representatives 147
Leadership in the Senate 148
The Committee System 148
What Are the Powers of Congress? 151
The Law-making Function 151
The Budgetary Function 155
The Oversight Function 156
How Do Members of Congress Make Decisions? 158
Political Parties 158
Constituents 159
Colleagues and Caucuses 160
Interest Groups, Lobbyists, and Political Action Committees 160
Staff and Support Agencies 160
Political Reform and Realities: How Is Institutional Power Balanced? 161
Congress and the Executive 161
Congress and the Judiciary 162
Congress and the People 162
Conclusion and Review 164 • Learn the Terms 165 • Learn the Names 165

7 The Presidency 166
What Are the Roots of the Office of President of the United States? 168
Presidential Qualifications and Terms of Office 169
Rules of Succession 170

What Are the Constitutional Powers of the President?   171
  The Appointment Power   171
  The Power to Convene Congress   172
  The Power to Make Treaties   172
  The Veto Power   173
  The Power to Preside over the Military as
  Commander in Chief   174
  The Pardoning Power   175
How has Presidential Power Developed
and Expanded?   176
  Establishing Presidential Authority: The
  First Presidents   176
  Incremental Expansion of Presidential
  Powers: 1809–1933   177
  Creating the Modern Presidency   179
What is the Presidential Establishment?   179
  The Vice President   179
  The Cabinet   180
  First Ladies   181
  The Executive Office of the President (EOP)   182
  The White House Staff   182
How Do Presidents Lead?   182
  Presidential Leadership and Personality   182
  Going Public   183
How Does Public Opinion Affect Presidents?   184
Political Reform and Realities: What is the President's
Role as a Policy Maker?   185
  The President's Role in Proposing and Facilitating
  Legislation   185
  The Budgetary Process and Legislative
  Implementation   186
  Policy Making Through Executive Order   187
  Conclusion and Review   189 • Learn the Terms   189

8 The Executive Branch and the Federal Bureaucracy   190

What Are the Roots of the Federal Bureaucracy?   191
  The U.S. Civil War and the Growth
  of Government   193
  From the Spoils System to the Merit System   193
  Regulating Commerce   194
  The World Wars and the Growth of Government   195
How is the Federal Bureaucracy Formally Organized?   196
  Formal Organization   196
  Government Workers and Political Involvement   200
Who Are Bureaucrats?   200
  Profiling Bureaucrats   201
How does the Bureaucracy Work?   203
  Making Policy   205
Political Reform and Realities: How Can the Bureaucracy
Be Made Accountable?   207
  Executive Control   208
  Congressional Control   210
  Judicial Control   211
  Conclusion and Review   212 • Learn the Terms   212

9 The Judiciary   213

What Are the Roots of the Federal Judiciary?   214
  The Judiciary's Acts of 1789 and 1801 and
  the Creation of the Federal Judicial System   216
  The Marshall Court: *Marbury v. Madison* (1803)
  and Judicial Review   218
What is the Structure of the Federal Court System?   220
  The District Courts   220
  The Courts of Appeals   221
  The Supreme Court   221
How Are Federal Court Judges Selected?   222
  Who Are Federal Judges?   224
  Nomination Criteria   224
  The Confirmation Process   226
How Does the Supreme Court Make Decisions?   228
  Deciding to Hear a Case   228
  How Does a Case Survive the Process?   231
  Hearing and Deciding the Case   232
  Factors Influencing Judicial Decisions   235
Political Reform and Realities: How Much
Power Does the Court Have in Policy Making?   237
  Implementing Court Decisions   238
  The Roberts Court   239
  Conclusion and Review   241 • Learn the Terms   241 •
  Learn the Names   241

PART III Political Behavior

10 Public Opinion and Political Socialization   242

What Are the Roots of Public Opinion Research?   243
  The Earliest Public Opinion Research   244
  The Gallup Organization   245
  The American National Election Studies   245
  Pew Research Center   246
How Are Public Opinion Polls Conducted and Analyzed?   247
  Designing the Survey   247
  Selecting the Sample   247
  Contacting Respondents   248
  Analyzing the Data   249
  Shortcomings of Polling   250
What is Political Ideology?   251
  Types of Political Ideologies   252
  Problems with Ideological Labels   253
How Are Political Opinions Formed?   254
  Demographic Characteristics   254
  Family, Peers, and Education   256
  The Mass Media   257
  Cues from Leaders or Opinion Makers   257
  Political Knowledge   258
Political Reform and Realities: What Are the Effects
of Public Opinion on Politics?   258
  Conclusion and Review   260 • Learn the Terms   260

11 Political Parties 261

What Are the Roots of the Two-Party System? 263
    The Development of Political Parties, 1800–1824 263
    Jacksonian Democracy, 1824–1860 264
    The Golden Age, 1860–1932 264
    The Modern Era 265
    Citizen Support and Party Realignment 266
How Are American Political Parties Organized? 267
    The National Party 267
    State and Local Parties 269
    Informal Groups 270
What Are the Activities of American Political Parties? 271
    Running Candidates for Office 271
    Formulating and Promoting Policy 273
    Organizing Government 273
    Furthering Unity, Linkage, and Accountability 275
What Determines Party Identification? 276
    Political Socialization 277
    Group Identity 277
How Do Minor Parties Affect the American
Two-Party System? 281
    The Formation and Role of Minor Parties 282
    Barriers to Minor-Party Success 283
Political Reform and Realities: United or Divided? 283
    Causes of Polarization 283
    Consequences of Polarization 285
    Conclusion and Review 287 • Learn the Terms 288

12 Campaigns, Elections, and Voting 289

What Are the Roots of American Elections? 291
    Types of Elections 291
    Presidential Elections 294
    Congressional Elections 297
How Do Candidates Run for Office and Reach Voters? 300
    The Candidate 300
    The Campaign 302
    The Role of Conventions and Debates 304
    The Role of Media 305
How Are Elections Influenced By Campaign Finance
and Reform? 308
    Regulating Campaign Finance 308
    Sources of Campaign Funding 310
    Public Funds 314
What Are the Patterns in Voter Turnout and Choice? 314
    Party Identification and Ideology 315
    Income and Education 316
    Race and Ethnicity 317
    Gender and Age 318
    Religious Groups and Civic Organizations 319
    Candidate Traits and Issues 319

Political Reform and Realities: Mending the
Electoral Process 320
    Front-loading 320
    Electoral College 321
    Improving Voter Access and Participation 322
    Conclusion and Review 326 • Learn the Terms 327 •
    Learn the Names 327

13 The News Media 328

What Are the Roots of the News Media in
the United States? 330
    Print Media 331
    Radio News 333
    TV News 333
    Digital Media 335
How Do the News Media Cover Politics? 337
    How the Press and Public Figures Interact 337
    Covering the Presidency 338
    Covering Congress 339
    Covering the Supreme Court 339
How Do News Media Influence and News
Media Bias Affect Public Confidence? 340
    News Media Influence 340
    News Media Bias 341
    Public Confidence 343
What Rules Govern the News Media? 344
    Journalistic Standards 344
    Government Regulations 345
Political Reform and Realities: Current News Media Trends 347
    Corporate Ownership and Media Consolidation 347
    Narrowcasting 348
    Infotainment 349
    Experts and Pundits 351
    Citizen Journalists 351
    Conclusion and Review 353 • Learn the Terms 353

14 Interest Groups 354

What Are the Roots of American Interest Groups? 355
    National Groups Emerge (1830–1889) 356
    The Progressive Era (1890–1920) 357
How Did the Modern Interest Group State Develop? 358
    The Rise of Public Interest Groups 358
Why Do Interest Groups Form? 361
    Theories of Interest Group Formation 362
What Types of Interest Groups Exist? 363
    Public Interest Groups 363
    Economic Interest Groups 363
    Governmental Units 364
    Political Action Committees 364
What Do Interest Groups Do? 364
    Lobbying 365
    Election Activities 370

What Makes Interest Groups Successful? 372
  Leaders 373
  Funding and Patrons 374
  Members 374
Political Reform and Realities: How Are Interest
Groups and Lobbyists Regulated? 375
  Regulating Congressional Lobbyists 375
  Regulating Executive Branch Lobbyists 376
  Regulating Judicial Branch Lobbyists 376
  Conclusion and Review 377 • Learn the Terms 378 •
  Learn the Names 378

PART IV Public Policy

15 Social and Economic Policy 379

What Are the Roots of the Policy-making
Process? 381
  Theories of the Policy-making Process 382
  The Policy-making Cycle 384
What is the U.S. Fiscal Policy? 386
  The Foundations of Fiscal Policy 387
  The National Deficit and Debt 389
What is the U.S. Monetary Policy? 391
  The Federal Reserve System 391
  The Tools of Monetary Policy 391
What is the U.S. Health Policy? 392
  Medicare and Medicaid 393
  The Affordable Care Act 393
  Public Health 394
What is the U.S. Education Policy? 396
  Primary and Secondary Education 396
  Higher Education 397
What is the U.S. Social Welfare Policy? 398
  The Foundations of Social Welfare Policy 399
  Social Welfare Programs Today 399
Political Reform and Realities: Ongoing Challenges
in Social and Economic Policy Making 403
  Conclusion and Review 404 • Learn the Terms 405

16 Foreign and Defense Policy 406

What Are the Roots of U.S. Foreign and Defense Policy? 408
  Isolationism in the Early Republic 408
  The United States as an Emerging Power 409
  World War I and the Interwar Years 410
  World War II and Its Aftermath 411
  The Cold War: Containment and Deterrence 412
  The Post–Cold War World 414
  September 11, 2001, and the War on Terror 415
How Does the United States Make Foreign and
Defense Policy Decisions? 417
  The Constitution 417
  The Executive Branch 418
  Congress 420
  The Judiciary 422
  Interest Groups and Political Parties 423
What Are the Contemporary Challenges in Foreign
and Defense Policy? 424
  The International Context 424
  Trade 426
  Terrorism 427
  Nuclear Weapons 429
  Global Climate Change 431
Political Reform and Realities: A Global System in Flux 431
  China 432
  Russia 432
  Europe 433
  The Middle East and North Africa (MENA) Region 434
  Conclusion and Review 436 • Learn the Terms 437

Appendices

  I The Declaration of Independence 438
  II The Constitution of the United States of America 441
  III The Federalist Papers: Nos. 10, 51, 78 452

Glossary 461

Endnotes 478

Index 493

Meet the Authors

Karen O'Connor is the Jonathan N. Helfat Distinguished Professor of Political Science and the Founder and Director Emerita of the Women & Politics Institute at American University. Before coming to American University, Professor O'Connor taught political science for seventeen years at Emory University in Atlanta, Georgia, where she was the first woman to receive the university's highest teaching award. She has been recognized by several associations as the most outstanding woman in political science and public administration as well as by the Southern Political Science Association (SPSA) for her contributions to the discipline. She has served on the American Political Science Association (APSA) and SPSA councils and as chair of the Law and Courts and Women and Politics Research sections of the APSA.

Larry J. Sabato is the founder and director of the University of Virginia Center for Politics. A Rhodes Scholar, Professor Sabato has taught tens of thousands of students in his career at Oxford University, Cambridge University, and the University of Virginia. At the University of Virginia, he has received every major teaching award, including the university's highest honor, the Thomas Jefferson Award. In 2013, Professor Sabato won an Emmy award for the documentary *Out of Order*, which he produced to highlight the dysfunctional U.S. Senate, and in 2014, he received a second Emmy award for the PBS documentary based on his *New York Times* bestseller *The Kennedy Half-Century*. Professor Sabato directs the Crystal Ball Web site, which has an unparalleled record of accuracy in predicting U.S. elections. For more information, visit http://www.centerforpolitics.org.

As you open this book, you may be asking yourself, "What possible impact could the Framers of the Constitution—long gone—have on my life in the twenty-first century?" Why is learning about history important to the study of politics today? And how are the ideas of the Framers relevant for understanding modern political issues such as health care, immigration, and abortion rights? We believe that without knowing the history—the roots—of our government, we won't understand how movements for political change—or reform—came to pass.

As students of the American political process, it can be challenging to identify what is really important and how government truly affects your lives. It is tempting to get caught up in key terms and definitions and miss the major themes that prevail—not only in the American political system, but also around the world.

People like you are still the cornerstone of the political process, something we may forget from time to time. But your vote counts, and executing your rights as a citizen of the United States by taking the time to vote is an important facet of American life that has changed over time to include nearly all citizens, regardless of gender or race.

We hope you will challenge prevailing notions about politics, ideas that suggest government is bloated, inefficient, wasteful, and only for old people. We hope you will come to see that politics can be a good thing, and that government is only able to represent the interests of those who actively pursue their own voice. To this end, we challenge you to identify the issues that affect your everyday lives—education, health care, the economy, just to name a few—and take every opportunity to make your voices heard. Just as the Framers' decisions in crafting a constitution live on in American political institutions, every decision made by policy makers today will have a lasting impact on your lives tomorrow.

To the Instructor

- This country was founded with the express purpose of welcoming immigrants with open arms, providing safe haven from persecution in native lands. Could the Framers have foreseen tough immigration laws like those considered by the Court in *Arizona* v. *United States* (2012)?

- The Framers saw Congress as a body with limited powers. But modern members of Congress balance the roles of lawmaker, budgeter, and policy maker while also acting as representatives of their district, state, party, and sometimes their race, ethnicity, or gender. How does this affect their behavior?

- The Twenty-Sixth Amendment lowered the voting age to 18. Today, young people are becoming increasingly civically aware and engaged. Could the Framers ever have anticipated how demographic changes would affect public policy?

American Government: Roots and Reform provides students with a historical context for understanding modern-day events and legislation. By drawing on more than 250 years of the American political experience, the text aids instructors and students in making comparisons between past and present. In so doing, it helps students realize that some of the challenges we face in American politics today are not new—they are simply new to us. Further, it emphasizes that by learning from the experiences of our predecessors, we may be better able to address these problems efficiently and effectively.

As instructors of American government and politics, we are faced with an increasingly challenging dilemma—persuading students to invest in the American political system at a time when trust in government is at all-time lows, and disillusionment is the norm. But as we well know, this task is perhaps more important than ever. Our students live in a rapidly changing political landscape, in which both the identity of America and its role in the world are dramatically challenged and altered. We explore issues the Framers could never have envisioned and how the basic institutions of governments have changed in responding to these new demands.

Our philosophy remains the same as always—roots and reform. By providing students with information about the roots of government and by explaining why it is important, they come to understand how their participation influences policy reforms today. And we hope students will come to see that politics can be, and most often is, a good thing.

Every chapter in this text uses history to serve three purposes: first, to show how institutions and processes have evolved to their present states; second, to provide some of the color that makes information memorable; and third, to provide students with a more thorough appreciation of the fact that our government was born amid burning issues of representation and power—issues that continue to smolder today. A richer historical texture helps to explain the present.

With roots and reform providing the foundation from which all topics and concepts in this book are discussed, the text is divided into four parts. Part I, Foundations of Government, covers the American government's roots, context, and culture. Through a discussion of the Constitution, it considers those broad concepts associated with government in the United States: the federal system, civil liberties, and civil rights. Part I sets the stage for the coverage in Part II, Institutions of Government, which introduces students to the institutions of government through its discussion of Congress, the presidency, the executive branch and the federal bureaucracy, and the judiciary. Political Behavior, Part III, delves into the ideas and processes that make democracy what it is: public opinion and political socialization, political parties, elections and voting, the campaign process, the news media, and interest groups. Part IV, Public Policy, rounds out the coverage with detailed discussions of domestic policy, economic policy, and foreign and defense policy. Coverage in these chapters makes use of the most current data and debates to frame discussions of health care, energy and the environment, education, and the United States' role on the global political stage.

PEDAGOGICAL FEATURES

- **Special chapter sections** highlight the text's emphasis on the importance of the history of American government as well as the dynamic cycle of reassessment that allows the United States to continue to evolve.

- **New photos** capture major events from the last few years, of course, but also illustrate politics' relevance; they show political actors and processes as well as people affected by politics, creating a visual narrative that enhances rather than repeats the text. Historical photos further illustrate how the past informs the present. Each photo caption includes a critical thinking question.

- **Key terms** related to the chapter content are defined throughout the text to help students identify new and important concepts and again in a comprehensive glossary.

- A focus on **qualitative literacy** helps students analyze, interpret, synthesize, and apply visual information—skills essential in today's world. We receive information from the written and spoken word, but knowledge also comes in visual forms. We are used to thinking about reading text critically, but we do not always think about "reading" visuals in this way. A focus on qualitative literacy encourages students to think about the images and informational graphics they will encounter throughout this text as well as those they see every day in the newspaper, in magazines, on the Web, on television, and in books. Critical thinking questions assist students in learning how to analyze visuals.

  - **Tables** consist of textual information and/or numerical data arranged in tabular form in columns and rows. Tables are frequently used when exact information is required and when orderly arrangement is necessary to locate, and in many cases, to compare the information. All tables in this edition include questions and encourage critical thinking.

- **Charts, graphs, and maps** depict numerical data in visual forms. Examples that students will encounter throughout this text are line graphs, pie charts, and bar graphs. Line graphs show a progression, usually over time (as in how the U.S. population has grown over time). Pie charts (such as ones showing population demographics) demonstrate how a whole (total American population) is divided into its parts (different racial and ethnic groups). Bar graphs compare values across categories, showing how proportions are related to each other (as in how much money each party raised in presidential election years). Bar graphs can present data either horizontally or vertically. All charts and graphs in this edition are based on questions that encourage critical thinking.

- Some of the most interesting commentary on American politics takes place in the form of **political cartoons**. The cartoonist's goal is to comment on and/or criticize political figures, policies, or events. The cartoonist uses several techniques to accomplish this goal, including exaggeration, irony, and juxtaposition. For example, the cartoonist may point out how the results of governmental policies are the opposite of their intended effects (irony). In other cartoons, two people, ideas, or events that do not belong together may be joined to make a point (juxtaposition). Knowledge of current events is helpful in interpreting political cartoons.

CONTENT UPDATES

While this edition stays true to its historical approach and emphasis on currency, the overall content of the book has been significantly streamlined and shortened for greater readability and ease of comprehension.

- As always, we strive to present a currency unparalleled by any other book in the market. *American Government: Roots and Reform* includes updated examples, figures, and tables that draw on experiences in American government in the here and now that are relevant to students' lives. At the same time, the book's historical approach has been strengthened with new opening vignettes and key examples. A better understanding of how American government has developed over time is a critical dimension that makes the content interesting to students.

- The entire book has been updated with examples and data from Trump's presidency, including Trump's second impeachment, which came in the aftermath of the 2021 Capitol insurrection. It also covers the appointment of Amy Coney Barrett to the Supreme Court, the latest decisions from the Court, the 2020 election results, and the evolution of the Black Lives Matter movement after the killing of George Floyd. Naturally, the COVID-19 pandemic looms large, and the book aims to understand how the public health crisis has challenged American politics and society.

- **Chapter 1** includes new 2021 coverage on these topics: the death of Justice Ruth Bader Ginsburg and Trump's appointment of Amy Coney Barrett to the Supreme Court, the latest debates on the Affordable Care Act, updated immigration figures and the detention of migrants along the border with Mexico, the investigation of Russian meddling in the 2016 election, and the episodes of police brutality against African American communities that led to increased activism such as the Black Lives Matter movement. The chapter also explores the COVID-19 pandemic in relation to American demographics to illustrate how difficult it is to solve a crisis when the nation is politically divided. Four figures have been updated with the latest available data: Figure 1.3 "How Has the Percentage of

Immigrants as a Proportion of the U.S. Population Changed over Time?", Figure 1.4 "How Does Population Correlate with Representation?", Figure 1.5 "What Is Your Religious Preference: Protestant, Roman Catholic, Jewish, Another Religion, or No Religion?", and Figure 1.6 "Do Americans Have Confidence in American Institutions?"

- **Chapter 2** now includes a greater emphasis on the French contributions to the War of Independence and the radical ideas that contributed to the American Declaration of Independence and the Constitution. It also covers contemporary political episodes that have affected constitutional precedents, such as the adoption of technology in elections and the impact of COVID-19 on the 2020 election.

- **Chapter 3** is updated with examples of how local, state, and federal government worked together to fight the COVID-19 crisis. The chapter also explores the idea of progressive federalism, which encourages friction between the states and the federal government. President Trump's decision to withhold grants to "sanctuary cities" offers a case in point. Finally, the chapter updates many images to illustrate public debates over confederate monuments, the historic election of Kamala Harris as vice president, and the leadership of Anthony Fauci as director of the National Institute of Allergy and Infectious Diseases.

- **Chapter 4** now features Trump administration policies and the consequence for civil liberties, including free speech, the rights of convicted felons, individual privacy, and access to health care. It also updates the evolving constitutional precedents set by the Supreme Court, citing recent cases decided on the freedom of religion, obscenity and the Internet, illegal searches in schools, and sexuality as a protected characteristic in employment law. A major update comes with regard to the pandemic and the constitutionality of stay-at-home orders, mask mandates, protests, and health privacy. The rising tensions between police and the African American community receives fresh treatment with a new section devoted to the search and seizure clause of the Fourth Amendment as it relates to the killing of George Floyd. Figure 4.1 "How Strong Are Your State's Gun Laws?" has been updated to reflect the latest available data.

- **Chapter 5** is updated with coverage of African American history, including slavery in the colonial period, lynching in the Jim Crow era, and a broader range of civil rights organizations that led the freedom struggle in the 1950s and 1960s. The chapter also updates with reference to organizations dedicated to civil rights of Hispanic people and the origins of the Native American civil rights movement. Recent decisions like the Supreme Court's ruling in favor of the Trump travel ban on majority-Muslim nations highlight the tensions over race, immigration, and religion in contemporary society, as does President Trump's characterization of COVID-19 as the "Asian flu." President Biden's reversal of Trump's ban on transgender military personnel exemplifies the ongoing efforts toward LGBTQ inclusivity.

- **Chapter 6** includes the latest results from the 2020 elections and the rise in young, women, minority, and LGBTQ congresspeople. Greater emphasis is given to those congresspeople most regularly appearing in the news, such as the four Democratic congresswomen known as "The Squad." It also updates on the appointment of Amy Coney Barrett to the Supreme Court, the insurrection at the Capitol in January 2021, and the second impeachment trial of Donald Trump. Figure 6.1 "How Well Does the House of Representatives Reflect the American People?", Figures 6.4A and 6.4B "What Is the Partisan Composition of the 117th Congress?", Figure 6.5 "What Were the Committees of the 117th Congress?", and Figure 6.6 "What Do Americans Think About Congress?" have been updated to reflect the latest available data.

- **Chapter 7** includes new coverage of President Trump's last two years in office, the USMCA trade agreement, the withdrawal from JCPOA, the Paris Agreement, the WHO, and the president's hospitalization with COVID-19. The chapter also examines Congress's attempt to limit presidential powers through the Constitution's emolument clause, the War Powers resolution, and the two impeachment trials. And it discusses the 2020 election of President Joe Biden and Vice President Kamala Harris, highlights the diversity of the Biden/Harris Cabinet, and features a section on First Lady Dr. Jill Biden.

- **Chapter 8** contains updates with President Trump's use of the Cabinet as political theatre, particularly the president's propensity to oust Cabinet members in tweets on social media. The chapter also covers the Republican-controlled Senate's decision to fill federal judiciary posts before bureaucracy positions. Coverage of the tensions between the bureaucracy and the president also includes specific treatment of the attorney general's role as government investigator, and the disagreements over combatting the COVID-19 pandemic. Figure 8.1 "What Agencies Rate Well in Public Opinion?", Figure 8.2 "Who Works in the Federal Executive Branch?", and Figure 8.4 "Who Are Federal Workers?" have been updated with the latest data.

- **Chapter 9** is updated to include coverage of cases heard in 2019–2020, President Trump's appointment of Amy Coney Barrett to replace Ruth Bader Ginsburg, and President Biden's promise to appoint an African American woman to the court if a vacancy comes up. A new section on the "Roberts Court" details the most important cases heard since John Roberts became chief justice in 2005, and the chapter examines the first live-streamed Supreme Court cases heard over the Internet due to the COVID-19 pandemic. Figure 9.1 "How Is the American Judicial System Structured?", Figure 9.3 "Who Are Federal Judges?", and Table 9.2 "Who Are the Justices of the Supreme Court in December 2020?" have been updated with the latest data.

- **Chapter 10** includes the latest available information on 2020 elections, as well as broader analysis of public opinion polls with the addition of the Pew Research Center as a key organization that collects these data. The chapter also explores the way the Trump presidency disrupted traditional ideological boundaries between the major political parties. Contemporary issues like the COVID-19 pandemic and the removal of Confederate monuments offer insights into the effect of public opinion on policy making. Figure 10.1 "How Many Americans Are Familiar with the Green New Deal?", Figure 10.2 "How Successful Are Presidential Election Polls?", Figure 10.3 "What Does a Tracking Poll Look Like?", Figure 10.4 "What Are Americans' Political Ideologies?", Figure 10.6 "How Do Demographic Characteristics Affect Public Opinion?", and Table 10.1 "How Are Participants Recruited for the American Trends Panel?" have been updated with the latest numbers.

- **Chapter 11** includes an update on the 2020 elections, President Biden's victory, and the Democratic Party's growing popularity with suburban voters. There is further coverage on local political parties and how they interact with national party structures. Figure 11.4 "How Much Money Do Parties Raise?", Figure 11.5 "How Much Has Public Trust in Government Declined?", Figure 11.8 "How Polarized Are American Political Parties?", and Table 11.1 "What Do Party Platforms Say?" have been updated with new data.

- **Chapter 12** has been thoroughly updated with the latest available results, photos, and data from the 2020 elections, the Trump campaign's legal challenges to state results, the popularity of mail-in ballots, and the virtual party conventions. The chapter also explores the recent efforts to recall elected officials, the expanded role of social media in campaigns, the changing impression of the Electoral College, minorities' and women's access to political power, and the trends in youth participation. Figure 12.1 "How Did Joe Biden and Kamala Harris Win the

Electoral College?", Figure 12.2 "What Are the Reelection Rates over the Years?", Table 12.1 "How Does the President Affect Congressional Elections?", Figure 12.4 "How Is a Campaign Staff Organized?", Table 12.2 "What Are the Contribution Limits for the 2019–2020 Federal Elections?", Figure 12.6 "How Has Campaign Financing Changed over Time?", Figure 12.7 "How Do Super PACs Allocate Their Campaign Contributions", Figure 12.8 "How Has the Racial and Ethnic Composition of Voters Changed?", Figure 12.9 "When Do States Choose Their Nominee for President?", and Table 12.4 "What Ballots Do States Use?" now include the latest data.

- **Chapter 13** has been substantially updated with a new introduction on the 2020 elections and COVID-19, which sets the scene for the importance of media in politics. The rise of Internet radio and the decline of print media is featured, along with several new sections on the changing business model for media companies, podcasting, the lack of coverage of the Supreme Court, comparisons of political ideologies in social media, misinformation surrounding COVID-19, and the growing trend of media consolidation. Figure 13.1 "Where Do Americans Get their Political Views?", Figure 13.2 "How Is News Consumption Changing?", Figure 13.3 "How Does Partisanship Relate to Public Confidence in the Media?", Figure 13.5 "What Are the Criteria for Allocating Free Broadcast Time and/or Free Printed Advertisement Space to Political Parties?", Figure 13.6 "Are Televised Debates Between Candidates or Party Representatives Normally Conducted?", and Figure 13.7 "Where Do News Audiences Fit on the Political Spectrum?" are updated with the most recent numbers.

- **Chapter 14** includes new coverage related to radical interest groups associated with the Capitol insurrection in 2021, such as the Proud Boys and QAnon. The chapter also explores the rising representation of Catholics on the Supreme Court, as well as President Joe Biden's and Speaker of the House Nancy Pelosi's Catholic faith. The top lobbying groups of 2020 are featured in this chapter, as are the largest PAC contributors to the 2020 election. Several figures have been updated with the latest available data, including Figure 14.1 "Where Is Union Membership Highest?", Figure 14.2 "How Many Lobbyists Are There? How Much Do They Spend?", and Figure 14.3 "How Much Money Do Top PACs Spend on National Elections?"

- **Chapter 15** begins with a revised introduction about the Affordable Care Act explaining why Republicans failed to repeal Obamacare. The chapter also features the 2018 Tax Cuts and Jobs Act, the impact of COVID-19 on the federal budget and deficit, the rising stock market value in 2020, and the unemployment figures during the pandemic. The chapter speculates on President Biden's policy plans for the following four years. Figure 15.2 "How Does the Federal Government Raise and Spend Money?" has been updated with the latest available data.

- **Chapter 16** has been updated to include coverage of important developments during the Trump administration, including the defeat of ISIS in the Middle East, the U.S. Space Force, the USMCA agreement, and the expectation that President Biden will take a different position on many policies such as JCPOA, the Paris Climate accords, and relations with American partners in Europe and the Middle East.

INTERACTIVE FEATURES

Revel improves results by empowering students to actively participate in learning. More than a digital textbook, Revel delivers an engaging blend of author content, media, and assessment. With Revel, students read and practice in one continuous experience—anytime, anywhere, on any device. A wealth of student and instructor resources and materials can be found within Revel, such as the following:

- **Current Events Bulletins** feature author-written articles that put breaking news and current events into the context of American government. For example, students can start Chapter 4 with "How Absolute Is the Right to Free Speech?" and Chapter 6 with "What Is the Role of Congress in Policing the President?"

- **Interactive Figures and Maps** feature Social Explorer technology and provide updates for the latest data and clickable hot spots with pop-ups of images and captions. For example, when learning about the 2020 election campaigns and results, students can explore an interactive map of the United States that details voting laws and voter turnout by state.

- **Newsclips and Historical Videos** bring to life chapter contents and key moments in American government. For example, students can watch one of the 2020 presidential debates between President Donald Trump and then-former Vice President Joe Biden and contrast it with the 1960 debate between Senator John F. Kennedy and Senator Richard Nixon.

- **Pearson Originals for Political Science** are compelling stories about contemporary issues. These short-form documentaries contextualize the complex social and political issues impacting the world today. In addition to helping students better understand core concepts, Pearson Originals inspire students to think critically as empowered citizens who can inspire social and political change. Explaining complex political issues in a simplified and entertaining way, Pearson Originals for Political Science help students become informed members of society. Videos include "Marijuana and Federalism: Who's in Charge?"; "Who Should Be Allowed to Call Themselves 'American'?"; and "What Is the Emoluments Clause and Why Should I Care About It?"

- **Pearson's Politics Hidden in Plain Sight** video series does exactly that—provides students with concrete examples of how politics influences the activities of their daily lives—from using their cell phones to going to a convenience store—in ways they likely had not previously noticed.

- **Shared Media Activities** allow instructors to assign and grade both prewritten and their own prompts that incorporate video, visuals, and weblinks. Prewritten assignments around the Pearson Originals for Political Science videos are also available.

- **Interactive Tables** give students the opportunity, after viewing the information in a table, to check their understanding of the connections.

- **Key Term Flashcards** conclude each chapter and review important concepts, names to know, events, and court cases.

- **End-of-Section and End-of-Chapter Assessment Questions** allow instructors and students to track progress and get immediate feedback.

- **Integrated Writing Opportunities** help students reason more logically and write more clearly. Each chapter offers three types of writing prompts that measure comprehension and critical thinking:

  - **Journal Prompts** provide students with an opportunity to write short answers in response to the learning objectives in each section. Journal prompts are not graded and can be used as a note-taking feature for readers. In addition, select Social Explorer visualizations are now followed up with a journal prompt to encourage data literacy and deeper analysis.

  - **Shared Writing Prompts** encourage students to address multiple sides of a comparative issue by sharing their own views and responding to each other's viewpoints, encouraging all students to expand their thinking to countries beyond the borders of the United States.

- **Essay Prompts** are from Pearson's Writing Solutions, where instructors can assign both automatically graded and instructor-graded prompts. Writing Solutions is the best way to develop and assess concept mastery and critical thinking through writing. Writing Solutions provides a single place within Revel to create, track, and grade writing assignments; access writing resources; and exchange meaningful, personalized feedback quickly and easily to improve results.

INSTRUCTOR AND STUDENT RESOURCES

Make more time for your students with instructor resources that offer effective learning assessments and classroom engagement. Pearson's partnership with educators does not end with the delivery of course materials; Pearson is there with you on the first day of class and beyond. A dedicated team of local Pearson representatives will work with you to not only choose course materials but also integrate them into your class and assess their effectiveness. Our goal is your goal—to improve instruction with each semester.

Pearson is pleased to offer the following resources to qualified adopters of *American Government*. Several of these supplements are available to instantly download from Revel or on the Instructor Resource Center (IRC); please visit the IRC at www.pearsonhighered.com/irc to register for access.

- **TEST BANK** Evaluate learning at every level. Reviewed for clarity and accuracy, the Test Bank measures this material's learning objectives with multiple-choice questions. You can easily customize the assessment to work in any major learning management system and to match what is covered in your course. Word, PDF, and Blackboard versions are available on the IRC, and Respondus versions are available on request from www.respondus.com.

- **MYTEST** This powerful assessment generation program includes all of the questions in the Test Bank. Quizzes and exams can be easily authored and saved online, and then printed for classroom use, giving you ultimate flexibility to manage assessments anytime and anywhere. To learn more, visit www.pearsonhighered.com/mytest.

- **INSTRUCTOR'S RESOURCE MANUAL** Create a comprehensive roadmap for teaching classroom, online, or hybrid courses. Designed for new and experienced instructors, the Instructor's Manual includes learning objectives, lecture and discussion suggestions, activities for in or out of class, research activities, participation activities, and suggested readings, series, and films as well as a Revel features section. Available within Revel and on the IRC.

- **LECTURE POWERPOINTS** Make lectures more enriching for students. The accessible PowerPoint presentations include full lecture outlines and photos and figures from the book. Available within Revel and on the IRC.

Acknowledgments

The authors would like to thank those who reviewed the text at the various stages of revision; they gave generously of their time and expertise and we are, as always, in their debt.

Karen O'Connor thanks the thousands of students in her American Government courses at Emory and American Universities who, over the years, have pushed her to learn more about American government and to have fun in the process. She especially thanks Jonathan and Robin Helfat for their generous support of her scholarly work. Her former students, too, have contributed in various ways to this project, especially Linda Mancillas at Georgia Gwinnett College, John R. Hermann at Trinity University, Sue Davis at Denison University, and Laura van Assendelft at Mary Baldwin College. She also thanks Professor Kent Miller for his ongoing review of the text.

For previous editions, Alixandra B. Yanus of High Point University offered invaluable assistance, unflagging support, friendship, and a keen eye to the latest trends in footwear—a must in a profession known for sensible shoes. First, as a student at American University, where she won the President's Award for Outstanding Research, and next at the University of North Carolina at Chapel Hill, her fresh perspectives on politics and ideas about things of interest to students, as well as her keen eye for the typo, her research abilities, and her unbelievably hard work have continually made this a much better book. She stepped up to be an invaluable contributor, bringing enthusiasm and the viewpoint of a newly minted PhD and an outstanding, devoted classroom teacher to the book. She remains a dear friend.

Karen further acknowledges the help and encouragement of Steve Gilbert, Beth Mutha, Jerry Share, Christina Stayeas, and Armistead Williams III. She also is appreciative of the constant companionship of Penny Louise, who asks for nothing more than any dog would, and keeps Karen (and often "Aunt Ali") from going crazy as we work to keep this book current and student-friendly; and her brother, TR, who starts her Sundays with a Starbucks mixture of soy that actually doesn't taste that bad.

Last, but certainly not least, Karen needs to recognize the support of her daughter, Meghan O'Connor McDonogh. She grew up with this book and considers Eric Stano, our editor during her college and doctoral studies, to be a quasi big brother, which sometimes frightens Karen. And despite her vow never to teach or coach, she does both at The Catholic University of America, proving that old adage that the apple sometimes does not fall far from the tree.

Particular thanks goes to Ray Smith, who tackled the revisions of the chapters on domestic and economic policy as well as the rapidly shifting landscape of foreign and defense policy for this edition. Our continued thanks go to Christopher Simon at the University of Utah, Glenn Hastedt of James Madison University, Steven Koven at the University of Louisville, Daniel S. Papp of Kennesaw State University, and Kiki Caruson of the University of South Florida, whose earlier work on policy content continues to serve as a strong foundation.

Larry J. Sabato would like to acknowledge the 15,000-plus students from his University of Virginia Introduction to American Politics classes over more than thirty-five years and the many student interns at the UVA Center for Politics who have offered valuable suggestions and an abundance of thoughtful feedback. A massive textbook project like this one needs the very best assistance an author can find, and this author was lucky enough to find some marvelously talented people. Carah Ong Whaley worked tirelessly to research the new edition and weave together beautifully constructed sections on recent American politics. Her attention to detail and editor's eye have refined many chapters and improved the overall flow. As always, the staff of the University of Virginia Center for Politics and a team of extraordinary interns contributed in many important ways toward the successful completion of this volume, including chief of staff Ken Stroupe and communications director Kyle Kondik. Their commitment to excellence is also obvious in their work for the Center's Crystal Ball Web site (www. centerforpolitics.org/crystalball)—a very useful resource in completing this volume.

In the now many years we have been writing this book, we have been blessed to have been helped by many people at Pearson. For this edition, managers Pamela Chirls and Amy Wetzel have responded to our fiery personalities and endless ideas with a few tricks—and a whole lot of enthusiasm—of their own. Rob DeGeorge brought a flexibility and efficiency to the process; and doing all the behind-the-scenes work that too often goes underappreciated, Heather Pagano, Tom Pauken, and David Chodoff brought their editorial know-how, good humor, patience, enthusiasm, and careful eye to our content.

Finally, the authors wish to thank the many professors and researchers who provided detailed feedback on how to improve content, especially John Kincaid at Lafayette College. Additionally, we thank many other colleagues for their invaluable input during professional conferences and Pearson-sponsored events. They gave generously of their time and expertise and we are, as always, in their debt.

O'Connor - American Government: Roots and Reform, 2018 edition Sharolyn Stauffer, Western Wyoming Community College; Robert H. Bruhl, University of Illinois at Chicago; Steven J Wallace, Technical College of the Lowcountry; Professor Julie L. Hershenberg, J.D., M.A., M.P.T., Collin College; Domenic Maffei, Caldwell University; Steve B. Lem, Kutztown University; David Z. Kanaan, San Diego State University

Spring 2018 Revel Editorial Workshops Christopher Hallenbrook, Bloomsburg University; Ben Christ, Harrisburg Area Community College; Laci Hubbard–Mattix, Spokane Falls Community College–Pullman; Shobana Jayaraman, Savannah State University; Jeneen Hobby, Cleveland State University; John Arnold, Midland College; Reed Welch, West Texas A&M; Amanda Friesen, IUPUI; Thomas Ambrosio, North Dakota State; Ted Vaggalis, Drury University; Coyle Neal, Southwest Baptist University; Hanna Samir Kassab, Northern Michigan University; Julie Keil, Saginaw Valley State University; Henry Esparza, University of Texas at San Antonio; Sierra Powell, Mount San Antonio College; Edgar Bravo, Broward College; Alicia Andreatta, Angelina College; Robert Sterken, The University of Texas at Tyler; Jessica Anderson, University of Louisiana Monroe; Pat Frost, San Diego Miramar College; Scott Robinson, Houston Baptist University; Cessna Winslow, Tarleton State; Carrie Currier, Texas Christian University; Paul Jorgensen, University of Texas Rio Grande Valley; Steve Lem, Kutztown University; Meng Lu, Sinclair Community College; James Pearn, Southern State Community College; Blake Farrar, Texas State University; Carlin Barmada, NVCC; Michael Chan, California State University, Long Beach; Mehwish Sarwari, SUNY Buffalo State; Daniel Tirone, Louisiana State University; Richard Haesly, California State University, Long Beach; Hyung Park, El Paso Community College; Jesse Kapenga, UTEP; Stephanie A. Slocum–Schaffer, Shepherd University; Augustine Hammond, Augusta University; Shawn Easley, Cuyahoga Community College; Darius Smith, Community College of Aurora; Robert Glover, University of Maine; Carolyn Cocca, State University of NY, College at Old Westbury; Benjamin Arah, Bowie State University; Ahmet Turker, Pima Community College; Eric Loepp, UW–Whitewater; Holly Lindamod, University of North Georgia; Denise Robles, San Antonio College; Asslan Khaligh, Alamo–San Antonio College; Brandy Martinez, San Antonio College; Andrew Sanders, Texas

A&M University, San Antonio; Mohsen Omar, Northeast Lakeview College; Heather Frederick, Slippery Rock University; Heather Rice, Slippery Rock University; Leslie Baker, Mississippi State University; Jamie Warner, Marshall University; Will Jennings, University of Tennessee; Arjun Banerjee, University of Tennessee, Knoxville; Jonathan Honig, University of Tennessee; Rachel Fuentes, University of Tennessee, Knoxville; Andrew Straight, University of Tennessee, Knoxville; Margaret Choka, Pellissippi State Community College; Christopher Lawrence, Middle Georgia State University; LaTasha Chaffin, College of Charleston; Jeff Worsham, West Virginia University; Cigdem Sirin–Villalobos, University of Texas at El Paso; Lyle Wind, Suffolk Community College; Marcus Holmes, College of William & Mary; Kurt Guenther, Palm Beach State College; Kevin Wagner, Florida Atlantic University; Eric Sands, Berry College; Shari MacLachlan, Palm Beach State College; Sharon Manna, North Lake College; Tamir Sukkary, American River College; Willie Hamilton, Mt. San Jacinto College; Linda Trautman, Ohio University–Lancaster; Dr. William H, Kraus, Motlow State Community College; Kim Winford, Blinn College; Lana Obradovic, University of Nebraska at Omaha; Doug Schorling, College of the Sequoias; Sarah Lischer, Wake Forest University; Ted Clayton, Central Michigan University; Steven Greene, North Carolina State University; Sharon Navarro, University of Texas at San Antonio; Curtis Ogland, San Antonio College; Henry Esparza, UT San Antonio; Mario Salas, UTSA; Robert Porter, Ventura College; Will Jennings, University of Tennessee; Haroon Khan, Henderson State University; Brenda Riddick, Houston Community College; Julie Lantrip, Tarrant County College; Kyle C. Kopko, Elizabethtown College; Kristine Mohajer, Austin Community College (ACC); Dovie D. Dawson, Central Texas College; Joycelyn Caesar, Cedar Valley College; Daniel Ponder, Drury University

APSA TLC 2018 Mujahid Nyahuma, Community College of Philadelphia; Tahiya Nyahuma, NCAT; Christopher Lawrence, Middle Georgia State University; Jason Robles, University of Colorado; Tim Reynolds, Alvin Community College; Marilyn C. Buresh, Lake Region State College; Frances Marquez, Gallaudet University; Natasha Washington, Liberal Arts and Communications; Jonathan Honig, University of Tennessee–Knoxville; Ayesha Ahsanuddin, University of Tennessee–Knoxville; Arjun Banerjee, University of Tennessee–Knoxville; Jesse R. Cragwall, Tusculum College and Pellissippi State Community College; Ms. Amnah H. Ibraheem, University of Tennessee–Knoxville; Karl Smith, Delaware Technical Community College; Richard Waterman, University of Kentucky; Peggy R. Wright, ASU–Jonesboro; Christopher Hallenbrook, Bloomsburg University; Eric Loepp, UW–Whitewater; Robert Glover, University of Maine; Heather Rice, Slippery Rock University; Shawn Easley, Cuyahoga Community College; Benjamin Arah, Bowie State University; Andrew Straight, University of Tennessee; Rachel Fuentes, University of Tennessee at Knoxville; Stephanie A. Slocum–Schaffer, Shepherd University; Will Jennings, University of Tennessee

APSA 2017 Jooeun Kim, Georgetown; Leonard L. Lira, San José State University; Abigail Post, University of Virginia; Jamilya Ukudeeva, Chabot College; Shannon Jenkins, University of Massachusetts–Dartmouth; Matthew Platt, Morehouse College; Sara Angevine, Whittier College; Andy Aoki, Augsburg University; Stephen Meinhold, University of North Carolina–Wilmington; Manoutchehr Eskandari–Qajar, Santa Barbara City College; Clayton Thyne, University of Kentucky; Alice Jackson, Morgan State University; Mark Rom, Georgetown University; Krista Wiegand, University of Tennessee; Geoffrey Wallace, University of Washington; Precious Hall, Truckee Meadows Community College; Patrick Larue, University of Texas at Dallas; Margot Morgan, Indiana University Southeast; Patrick Wohlfarth, University of Maryland; Christian Grose, University of Southern California; Clinton Jenkins, George Washington University; Jeffrey W. Koch, US Air Force Academy and SUNY Geneseo; Albert Ponce,

Diablo Valley College; Justin Vaughn, Boise State University; Joe Weinberg, University of Southern Mississippi; Cindy Stavrianos, Gonzaga University; Kevan M. Yenerall, Clarion University; Katherine Barbieri, University of South Carolina; Elsa Dias, Metropolitan State University of Denver; Maria Gabryszewska, Florida International University; Erich Saphir, Pima Community College; Mzilikazi Kone, College of the Desert; Mary McHugh, Merrimack College; Joel Lieske, Cleveland State University; Joseph W. Roberts, Roger Williams University; Eugen L. Nagy, Central Washington University; Henry B. Sirgo, McNeese State University; Brian Newman, Pepperdine University; Bruce Stinebrickner, DePauw University; Amanda Friesen, IUPUI; LaTasha Chaffin, College of Charleston; Richard Waterman, University of Kentucky

MPSA 2018 Adam Bilinski, Pittsburg State University; Daniel Chand, Kent State University; Agber Dimah, Chicago State University; Yu Ouyang, Purdue University Northwest; Steven Sylvester, Utah Valley University; Ben Bierly, Joliet Junior College; Mahalley Allen, California State University, Chico; Christian Goergen, College of DuPage; Patrick Stewart, University of Arkansas, Fayettville; Richard Barrett, Mount Mercy University; Daniel Hawes, Kent State University; Niki Kalaf–Hughes, Bowling Green State University; Gregg R. Murray, Augusta University; Ryan Reed, Bradley University; Kimberly Turner, College of DuPage; Peter Wielhouwer, Western Michigan University; Leena Thacker Kumar, University of Houston–DTN; Debra Leiter, University of Missouri Kansas City; Michael Makara, University of Central Missouri; Ola Adeoye, University of Illinois–Chicago; Russell Brooker, Alverno College; Dr. Royal G. Cravens, Bowling Green State University; Vincent T. Gawronski, Birmingham–Southern College; Benjamin I. Gross, Jacksonville State University; Matthew Hitt, University of Northern Colorado; Megan Osterbur, New England College; Pamela Schaal, Ball State University; Edward Clayton, Central Michigan University; Ali Masood, California State University, Fresno; Joel Lieske, Cleveland State University; Patrick Wohlfarth, University of Maryland; Steven Greene, NC State; Will Jennings, University of Tennessee; Haroon Khan, Henderson State University; Kyle Kopko, Elizabethtown College; Hyung Lae Park, El Paso Community College; Linda Trautman, Ohio University–Lancaster

WHAT HAPPENED WHEN EUROPEANS REACHED THE AMERICAS?

Attitudes in the United States toward explorers such as Christopher Columbus, featured above, have shifted sharply in recent decades. Columbus once was heralded for "discovering" the Americas, and a federal holiday still honors him each October. Nevertheless, several states and the District of Columbia have chosen to rename the holiday. In 1989, South Dakota renamed it Indigenous Peoples' Day. In 2019, the District of Columbia did the same. Other cities and states have opted to call it Native American Day. However, emphasis has been placed increasingly on the negative impacts of foreign explorers and residents on native peoples and broader critiques of European colonialism.

CRITICAL THINKING QUESTION: *Does your city, town, or state observe Columbus Day or has it adopted Indigenous Peoples' Day or Native American Day?*

AMERICAN GOVERNMENT: ROOTS, CONTEXT, AND CULTURE

LEARNING OBJECTIVES

1.1   Trace the origins of American government.

1.2   Explain the functions of American government.

1.3   Analyze the changing characteristics of the American public.

1.4   Characterize changes in Americans' attitudes toward and expectations of government.

n 1492, Christopher Columbus, with the support of the king and queen of Spain, landed in the Bahamas on his journey to find a quicker water route to India and its riches. Believing he had landed in India, he named the native peoples *Indians*. After the news of Columbus's expedition, other explorers sponsored by Spain, such as Hernando de Soto and Juan Ponce de León, traveled west looking for gold, furs, and rich soil. Adventurers such as John Cabot and Sir Francis Drake from England and Giovanni da Verrazano, an Italian sponsored by France, soon launched their own expeditions.

These early explorers were not interested in establishing permanent residences. The monarchies supporting them wanted to claim native lands and their possible riches for themselves. Spain, France, and England more than welcomed the gold, furs, and new agricultural products, which greatly enlarged their respective national treasuries.

As nations began to compete for lands, Pope Alexander VI, who claimed all lands for God and thus the Roman Catholic Church, issued a proclamation in 1494 that drew a north/south line through the Western Hemisphere, giving the west to Spain and the east to Portugal. Spain occupied settlements in Florida, eventually the entire Southwest, and the lands from Louisiana to Montana, in what later became known as the Louisiana Purchase.

By the mid-1500s, France, Holland, and Great Britain were actively engaged in exploring North America. French fur trappers moved throughout what is now the eastern parts of Canada and established a settlement in Quebec. To facilitate trade, trappers knew that they had to establish good working relationships with several Indigenous tribes. In sharp contrast, the Spanish enslaved American Indians and treated them with brutality. It wasn't too long before France, Holland, and Great Britain recognized the potential offered by the New World and sought to seek land previously claimed by Spain.

● ● ●

In this text, we explore the American political system through a historical lens. This perspective allows us to analyze the ways that the ideas and actions of a host of different Americans—from European explorers, to American Indians, to colonists, to the Framers of the Constitution as well as the global citizens of today—have affected how our **government**—the formal vehicle through which policies are made and affairs of state are conducted—works.

government
The formal vehicle through which policies are made and affairs of state are conducted.

WHAT ARE THE ROOTS OF AMERICAN GOVERNMENT?

1.1 Trace the origins of American government.

Much has changed since the earliest explorers and settlers came to the New World. The people who live in America today differ greatly from those early inhabitants. In this section, we lay the groundwork for the study of the United States today by looking at the earliest inhabitants of the Americas, their initial and ongoing interactions with European colonists, and how new Americans continually build on the experiences of the past to create a new future.

The Earliest Inhabitants of the Americas

By the time the first colonists arrived in what is now known as the United States, indigenous peoples had been living from coast to coast for more than 30,000 years. Most historians and archaeologists believe that these peoples migrated from present-day Russia through the Bering Strait into North America and then dispersed throughout the American continents. Some debate continues, however, about where they first appeared and whether they crossed an ice bridge from Siberia or arrived on boats from across the Pacific. Other peoples came from the Southern Hemisphere and settled in the Southwest.

The indigenous peoples were not a homogeneous group; their cultures, customs, languages, and values varied widely, as did their political systems. The Iroquois League of Nations, made up of 5 northeastern tribes, had a confederacy type of governmental structure in which the tribes acted together concerning issues of mutual interest and ceased warring with each other in a somewhat loose league of friendship.

FIGURE 1.1 WHAT DID TRIBAL DISTRIBUTION LOOK LIKE BEFORE EUROPEAN
SETTLEMENT?

The first peoples of North America were extremely diverse, with hundreds of different cultures, languages, and traditions dispersed across North America before the arrival of European settlers. This map reveals many of the largest tribal nations on what is now U.S. soil.

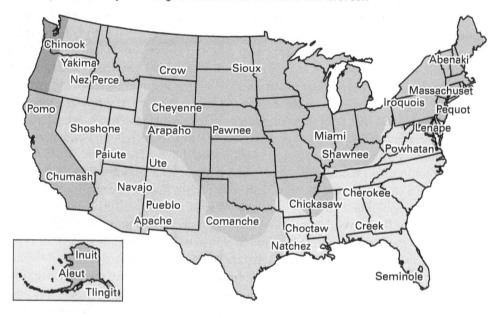

The number of these indigenous peoples, who lived in all parts of what is now the United States, is impossible to know for certain. Estimates by scholars, however, range from 100 million people to many more. These numbers quickly diminished as colonists brought with them to the New World a range of diseases to which the indigenous peoples had not been exposed. In addition, warfare with the European settlers as well as within tribes not only killed many American Indians but also disrupted previously established ways of life. And, European settlers continually displaced American Indians, pushing them south and westward as they created settlements and, later, colonies (see Figure 1.1).

The First Colonists

Unlike early explorers, colonists journeyed to North America for a variety of reasons. Many wealthy Englishmen and other Europeans left home seeking to enhance their fortunes. With them came a host of laborers who hoped to find their own opportunities for riches. In fact, commerce was the most common initial reason for settlement in North America.

The first permanent English settlement was established in Jamestown, Virginia, in 1607 by a joint stock company seeking wealth in the New World. In 1619, the first enslaved people arrived there, along with the first women. In 1609, employees of the Dutch New Netherland Company settled along the Hudson and lower Delaware Rivers, calling the area New Netherlands. Later, in 1626, the Dutch West India Company purchased Manhattan Island from an Indigenous tribe and established trading posts all along the Hudson River. Both Fort Orange, created in 1614, in what is now Albany, New York, and New Amsterdam, New York City's Manhattan Island, were populated not by colonists but by salaried employees of the company. Among those who flocked to New Amsterdam (renamed New York in 1664) were settlers from Holland, Finland, Germany, and Sweden. The varied immigrants also included free Black people, mainly from the British Isles, where they served as sailors. This ethnic and racial mix created its own system of cultural inclusiveness that continues to make New York City and its citizenry unique today (see Figure 1.2).

A Religious Tradition Takes Root

In 1620, just thirteen years after the Jamestown settlement, a group of Protestants known as Puritans left Europe, having been ejected earlier from England for their strict religious

FIGURE 1.2   WHAT DID COLONIAL SETTLEMENT LOOK LIKE BEFORE 1700?

Prior to 1700, pockets of colonial settlement existed along the east coast of what became the United States, from present-day Virginia to what is now Maine. These settlements were divided among a number of colonial powers, including the English in the northeast and around the Chesapeake Bay, the Dutch in what is present-day New York, and the Swedes, largely in present-day Delaware. The settlements of three colonial powers—the English, Dutch, and Swedish—are illustrated in this figure:

Mayflower Compact

Document signed by the men on the *Mayflower*, creating an agreement to set up a government and be subject to its rules and laws.

Roger Williams

Seventeenth-century religious and political leader who was expelled by Puritans in Massachusetts and then established the colony of Providence Plantations that later became Rhode Island.

Anne Hutchinson

Seventeenth-century political leader and thinker who supported religious liberty.

Thomas Hooker

A minister who believed that Puritans were too narrow-minded. He founded the colony of Connecticut where all men were given the right to vote, regardless of religious views or property qualifications.

William Penn

Quaker leader and supporter of religious tolerance who founded Pennsylvania.

beliefs. They sailed on the *Mayflower*, destined for Virginia; however, they found themselves off course and landed instead in Plymouth, in what is now Massachusetts. Their arrival in Massachusetts in 1620 is considering a founding moment for the nation. These new settlers differed from those in Virginia and New York, who saw their settlements as commercial ventures. Adhering to Calvinist religious beliefs, the Puritans (also called Pilgrims, a term used to describe religious travelers) came instead as families bound together by a common belief in the powerful role of religion in their lives. They believed the Old Testament charged them to create "a city on a hill" that would shine as an example of righteousness. To help achieve this goal, they enforced a strict code of authority and obedience, while simultaneously stressing the importance of individualism. While aboard the *Mayflower*, all men on the ship signed the **Mayflower Compact**, which was modeled after English town charters. In it, they pledged to create laws and to abide by those laws while living in accordance with the Christian faith. Puritanism and its variants were not the only religious beliefs practiced in the New World. The Swedes brought Lutheranism with them as they settled along the Delaware River after they failed to find a way across the Western Hemisphere to the Pacific Ocean.

Soon, the ideas at the core of these strict puritanical values faced challenges. In 1631, Puritan minister **Roger Williams** arrived in the Boston, Massachusetts Bay Colony. He preached extreme separation from the Church of England and even questioned the right of Europeans to settle on Indigenous lands. He believed that the Puritans went too far when they punished settlers who deviated from their strict code of morality, arguing that it was God, not people, who should punish individuals for their moral shortcomings. These "heretical views" prompted local magistrates to banish him from the colony in 1635. In 1636, Williams founded a new colony: Providence Plantations. Providence, now the capital of present-day Rhode Island, was named for "God's merciful Providence," which Williams believed had allowed his followers to find a place to settle.

A later challenge to the Puritans' religious beliefs came from midwife **Anne Hutchinson**. She began to share her view that the churches established in the Massachusetts Bay Colony had lost touch with the Holy Spirit and challenged the views of male-dominated religious authorities. Many of her followers were women who were attracted to her progressive ideas on the importance of religious tolerance, as well as on the equality and rights of women. Authorities in Massachusetts tried Hutchinson for blasphemy for her views and banished her from the colony. She and her followers joined Roger Williams and eventually settled in Portsmouth, Rhode Island, which became a beacon for those seeking religious toleration and popular—as opposed to religious—sovereignty.

Thomas Hooker, too, soon found himself at odds with the Calvinist Puritans in the Massachusetts Bay Colony. Hooker believed they were too narrow-minded; in his view, all men should have the right to vote regardless of religious views or property qualifications. He and his supporters relocated to the new colony of Connecticut in 1636, where they developed a settlement at Hartford. Hooker's words inspired the drafting of the Connecticut Constitution, a representative form of government and closest of any colonies to the eventual Constitution of the United States, along with a Bill of Rights.

Later colonies in the New World were established with religious tolerance in mind. In 1632, King Charles I granted a well-known English Catholic, George Calvert, the first Lord Baltimore, a charter to establish the Catholic colony of Maryland in the New World. In 1681, King Charles II bestowed upon **William Penn** a charter giving him sole ownership of a vast area of land just north of Maryland. The king called the land Pennsylvania, or Penn's Woods. Penn, a Quaker, eventually also purchased the land that is present-day Delaware. In this area, Penn launched what he called "the holy experiment," attracting other persecuted Europeans, including German Mennonites and Lutherans, and French Huguenots. The survival of Penn's colony is largely attributable to its ethnic and religious diversity.

Massacre of Anne Hutchinson.

Hulton Archives/Getty Images

WHAT ARE THE FUNCTIONS OF THE AMERICAN GOVERNMENT?

1.2 Explain the functions of American government.

From Jamestown to the founding period in the 1760s, examples of governance abounded in the colonies. Eventually from the 1600s until the 1750s, the thirteen colonies were of two types: the Royal and the Proprietary. Royal colonies operated by grants from the king with colonial profits going directly into his coffers. Proprietary colonies were begun with grants from the king to conduct business at a profit for the corporation and the king. All of the colonies were eventually tied to England and were greatly influenced by English law. Most of the colonies' respective forms of government varied over time, as is the case in the states today. All but two colonies had three branches of government: (1) a governor appointed by the king or the owners of the colony; (2) a council, appointed by the governor; and, (3) an assembly elected by the people (that is, White men and usually, but not always, property owners). Governors yielded enormous powers in the name of the king, who ruled by Divine Right. He could veto acts of the assemblies, had command of militias, and appointed many to key posts in the judiciary as well as local and state law enforcement officials.

Councils operated more like the British House of Lords. Their members were usually men of high status who were well connected politically. They acted as advisers to the governors and often functioned as the highest court in the colonies.

Assemblies were elected by the people. Technically, they were the chief law-making bodies, but their acts could be overruled by the governor or the king. The key power of these elected assemblies was the power of the purse, as they were the sole entities entrusted with allocating taxes. For decades, the king and the colonists were in conflict over the taxing power of the elected assemblies, which ultimately led to the Revolutionary War, as discussed in Chapter 2. Moreover, each colony, except Pennsylvania and Georgia, had a two-house legislature.

The colonies also had judicial systems that generally followed systems in place today. Justices of the peace, appointed by the governor, were at the lowest rung of the judicial ladder and heard only petty civil cases. Next were county courts that heard civil and criminal matters. The highest court was made up of the governor and his council.

Within each of the colonies, a system of local governments existed. First, there were plantations, as in the case of Jamestown. There were small compact communities, often called townships, settled around churches. Men met several times a year to discuss issues of concern, lay taxes, pass local laws, and elect officers such as the town clerk, assessors, and treasurer.

Many of the early systems of governance, from the creation of the Virginia House of Burgesses to the adoption of colonial institutions, contained a Bill of Rights. These enumerated a list of liberties and rights that could not be infringed upon by any government. Thus, a set, shared group of principles about government and its proper function emerged.

The people who settled in colonial America were a diverse lot. They were driven to settle in the New World for a variety of reasons, including religious freedom and economic gain. Thus, when the colonists declared independence from Great Britain in 1776, it was no easy task to devise a system of government that served all of these citizens' interests. Initially, each colony considered itself an independent state. To fight the Revolutionary War against the British, they agreed upon a confederate form of government—used by many Indigenous tribes—described within the Articles of Confederation (see Chapter 2). Eventually, leaders fashioned a political system with the people at the center of power. Many citizens, however, were uncomfortable with calling this new system a **democracy** because it conjured up fears of the people and mob rule. They instead preferred the term **republic**, which implied a system of government in which the interests of the people were represented by more educated or wealthier citizens who were responsible to those who elected them. Today, the words *democracy* and *republic* often are used interchangeably. Yet, in the United States, we still pledge allegiance to our "republic," not our democracy.

After winning the war with Great Britain, the Articles proved unworkable to guide a new nation. Thus, as discussed in Chapter 2, a new constitution was soon written and adopted by most of the colonies. Its guiding principles stated that government should: (1) establish justice; (2) ensure domestic tranquility; (3) provide for the common defense; (4) promote the general welfare; and (5) secure the blessings of liberty upon all of its citizens. Each of these goals is still relevant today and often challenging for governments at all levels to provide.

Establishing Justice

One of the first tasks expected of any government is the creation of a system of laws allowing individuals to abide by a common set of principles. Societies adhering to what is called the **rule of law** allow for the rational dispensing of justice by acknowledged legal authorities. Thus, the Constitution authorizes Congress to create a federal judicial system to dispense justice. The Bill of Rights contains several amendments geared toward the administration of justice, including the right to a trial by jury, the right for those charged with crimes to be informed of the charges against them, and the right to be tried in a courtroom presided over by an impartial judge and a jury of one's peers.

In 2020, as protesters around the nation took to the streets in anger about the killing of Black Americans George Floyd, Breonna Taylor and others, shouts of "No Justice, No Peace" rang out from the crowds and members of **Black Lives Matter**. In their wake, cities, states, and the House of Representatives moved to pass laws to ensure that many citizens, especially Black people, could get "justice" in the legal system.

Ensuring Domestic Tranquility

As we discuss throughout this text, the role of governments in ensuring domestic tranquility is a subject of much debate and especially since the period between 1715 and 1789 is known as the **Enlightenment**. Originating in Europe, the Enlightenment was a period of time in which political philosophers believed that liberty and domestic tranquility went hand in hand and required tolerance of individual differences. They especially criticized the role of religion and political abuses and rejected the role of an all-powerful monarch as antithetical to a peaceful society. In crises, however, even adherents of the Enlightenment thought governments at all levels could take extraordinary measures to contain threats of terrorism from abroad as well as from within the United States. To that end, governments are

democracy
A system of government that gives power to the people, whether directly or through elected representatives.

republic
A government rooted in the consent of the governed; a representative or indirect democracy.

rule of law
The set of principles and ideals that posits that all people and institutions are subject to the law that is fairly applied and enforced.

Black Lives Matter
An organized movement for racial justice in America advocating for non-violent protest and civil disobedience. It began in 2013, after a police officer was acquitted of killing Trayvon Martin, a Black teenager. Subsequent deaths of Black men and women at the hands of police officers have sparked continued protests.

Enlightenment
A philosophical movement in eighteenth-century Europe; its adherents advocated liberty and tolerance of individual differences, decried religious and political abuses, and rejected the notion of an absolute monarch.

WHAT DID THE DISTRICT OF COLUMBIA'S MAYOR DO IN RESPONSE TO PRESIDENT DONALD J. TRUMP'S USE OF FORCE TO CLEAR D.C. STREETS OF PROTESTERS?

In the wake of President Trump's use of force to clear peaceful protestors from in front of the White House, DC Mayor Muriel Bowser had BLACK LIVES MATTER painted in bright yellow within eyesight of the White House and renamed the area BLACK LIVES MATTER Plaza.

designed to ensure our safety. Local governments have police forces, states have national guards, and the federal government has both the armed services and the ability to call up state militias to quell any threats to order. All were on display as protests spread around the nation in 2020. Safety, in this case pertaining to the worldwide coronavirus (COVID-19) pandemic, also placed huge strains on the capacities of governments to provide supplies, testing, and health care to all 331 million Americans. Individuals were also asked to self-quarantine and governments issued travel bans and safety requirements, such as the wearing of masks and banned large public gatherings, among other restrictions.

Providing for the Common Defense

Historically, nearly all governments have been responsible for the safety and defense of their citizens against threats of foreign aggression. In fact, in the early years of the republic, many believed that the major function of government was to protect the nation from foreign threats, such as the British invasion of the United States in the War of 1812, the continued problem of piracy on the high seas, and the Civil War. The Constitution calls for the president to be commander in chief of the armed forces, and Congress has the authority to raise an army. The defense budget continues to be a considerable and often controversial proportion of all federal outlays, as new internal and external threats abound in the United States, whether mass shootings, foreign intervention in our elections, or the COVID-19 pandemic. The mayor of Washington, D.C., for example, complained loudly when President Donald J. Trump ordered state militias from around the country to quell what the president considered to be riots in the District.

Promoting the General Welfare

Most governments, at least democratic ones, operate to make people's lives better. The concept of what is "better" has evolved over time. When the Framers added "promoting the general Welfare" to their list of key governmental functions, they never envisioned how governmental involvement at all levels would expand so tremendously. In fact, promoting the general welfare initially was more of an ideal than a mandate. Over time, though, our notions of what governments should do have expanded along with governmental size to include Social Security, Medicare, the building of federal interstate highways, and funding for local public schools. However, the proper scope of government in an individualistic society such as the United States is a source of much disagreement and debate among Americans and among their elected representatives. There was, however, at least initially, bipartisan agreement in Congress on the need for trillions of dollars in aid to workers and businesses affected by the pandemic as the economy appeared, at times, in freefall and unemployment reached record highs.

Securing the Blessings of Liberty

Liberty is a word that has had many meanings over time. Liberty generally means that individuals can act as they wish so long as no others are harmed, and it often sets up conflict between individuals as well as individuals with their government. Liberty allows citizens, with but few exceptions, to criticize the government and to petition it when they disagree with its policies or have a grievance. People can act as they wish so long as their actions don't infringe on the rights of others. This freedom to criticize and to petition is perhaps the best way to "secure the Blessings of Liberty."

Some commentators argue that liberty is in peril, racism and bigotry rear their ugly heads, and regional differences make building consensus on issues often impossible. While New York, for example, placed the state on virtual lockdown to stem the spread of COVID-19, many southern states remained open, creating huge spikes in the number of cases. In states such as Texas and Florida, some frustrated citizens challenged the right of government to enforce mask wearing, social distancing, and orders to shelter in place, and many businesses argued their liberty was being infringed upon by drastic government measures. These restrictions also affected voting rights. Many states moved to mail ballots for the first time; others opened voting centers for early voting. Still, as Americans went to the polls or cast their ballots remotely in record numbers, COVID-19 positive tests began to increase in record numbers. Then President-elect Joe Biden's first official act after his victory was announced was to establish his own task force on the coronavirus. After President Trump had campaigned openly flaunting local and state rules that were usually followed by virus outbreaks, Biden wanted to make it clear that some liberties would have to take second place to the overall health of the nation.

HOW HAVE THE AMERICAN PEOPLE AND THEIR CULTURE CHANGED OVER TIME?

1.3 Analyze the changing characteristics of the American public.

All of the functions of government noted above played a major role and continue to do so in how Americans live amidst a changing American culture that has become more, not less, divided along a variety of factors that often influence one's policy preferences and political ideology. Among these frequently interrelated factors are America's size and population, its racial and ethnic composition, population trends, family and family size, issues of an aging population, the role of religion, and regional growth.

Size and Population Trends

One major factor is simply the size of the nation as it has grown in land mass westward and in population. For example, California, the most populous state, was not even a dream of the Founders. Nor were the far-off lands of Alaska and Hawai'i.

One year after ratification of the U.S. Constitution, fewer than 4 million people lived in the thirteen states. Most of those people shared a single language and a Protestant-Christian heritage, and those who voted were White male property owners. The Constitution mandated that the number of members of the House of Representatives should not exceed one for every 30,000 people and set the size of the first House at sixty-five members.

As the nation grew westward, hundreds of thousands of new immigrants, mostly White, came to America, often in waves, fleeing wars, famine, or political unrest, or simply in search of a better life. Although the geographic size of the United States has remained stable since the addition of Alaska and Hawai'i as states in 1959, the population has grown to over 331 million inhabitants. As a result of this population growth, most people today feel far removed from the national government and their

FIGURE 1.3 HOW HAS THE PERCENTAGE OF IMMIGRANTS AS A PROPORTION OF THE U.S. POPULATION CHANGED OVER TIME?

As this figure shows, immigration was highest in the mid-1800s to around 1910. Then amidst wars and other social upheaval including the Great Depression, the proportion of immigrants plummeted until passage of the Immigration and Nationality Act was passed in 1965 opening the way for a new wave of immigration.

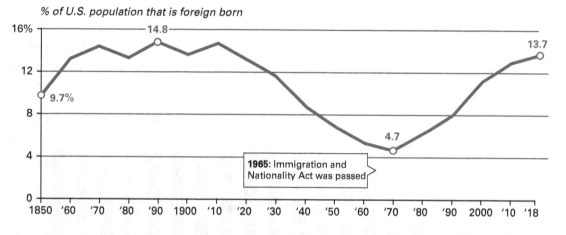

elected representatives (see Figure 1.3). It is also increasingly apparent that some feel threatened by the racial or religious attributes of new immigrants, although waves of immigrants from China and the Irish in the 1800s also drew protests and suspicions.

Racial and Ethnic Composition

The racial and ethnic composition of the American population has changed constantly as new people arrived from various regions—Western Europeans fleeing religious persecution in the 1600s to early 1700s; enslaved people brought in chains from Africa in the mid- to late 1700s; Chinese laborers arriving in California to work on the railroads following the Gold Rush in 1848; Irish Catholics settling in the Northeast to escape the potato famine in the 1850s; northern and eastern Europeans from the 1880s to 1910s; and, most recently, South and Southeast Asians, Cubans, Mexicans, and refugees from South and Central America, among others.

Today, slightly more than 13 percent of Americans can be classified as immigrants. According to the PEW Research Center, the United States has more immigrants than any other nation. More than 40 million people now living in the United States were born in another nation. In 2018, immigrants accounted for 13.7 percent of the population; however, in 1890, immigrants made up a record percent of the American people: 14.8 percent, as compared to a low of 4.7 million in 1970.

Immigration was a key issue in Donald J. Trump's election to the presidency in 2016. He promised his supporters that he would build a wall to keep the influx of immigrants on the southern border out of the country. Interestingly, although President Trump promised that a wall between the United States and Mexico would be built with Mexico paying for it, ultimately about 400 miles of wall were constructed. Far more attention, however, turned to the Trump administration's treatment of asylum seekers, especially the separation of parents and children. The week before the November election, most major news outlets covered the fact that hundreds of parents of children in U.S. custody could not be located, bringing back the specter of children held in cages that early on in the administration had been the norm.

Immigration has led to significant alterations in American racial and ethnic composition. The balance in America has changed dramatically over the past fifty years, with the proportion of Hispanic people* overtaking Black people as the second largest racial or ethnic group. The Asian American population, moreover, is now the fastest growing minority group in the United States. The majority of babies born in the United States are now members of a minority group, a fact that will have a significant

---

* In this text, we have made the decision to refer to those of Spanish, Latin American, Mexican, Cuban, and Puerto Rican descent as Hispanic instead of Latinx. Although this label is not accepted universally by the community it describes, Hispanic is the term used by the U.S. government when reporting federal data.

FIGURE 1.4   HOW DOES POPULATION CORRELATE WITH REPRESENTATION?

The population of the United States has grown dramatically since the nation's founding. A larger geographic area, immigration, and living longer have contributed to this trend. The size of the House of Representatives, however, has not kept pace with this expansion, so that members have, on average, 711,000 people in their congressional districts.

SOURCE: U.S. Census Bureau Population Projections, www.census.gov.

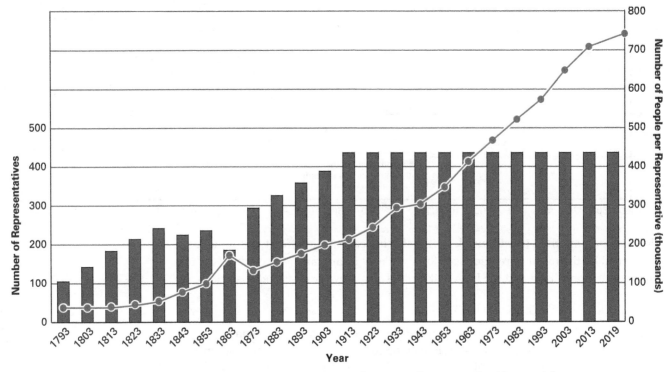

■ Number of Representatives   ━●━ Number of People per Representative (thousands)

White privilege

The societal benefits, some obvious and many not, believed to be afforded to White persons over persons of color in many societies.

impact not only on the demographics of the American polity but also on how America "looks." It is a fact that has not been lost on those who fear dilution of White America and the potential loss of what some term **White privilege**.

In states such as California, Hawai'i, New Mexico, and Texas, members of minority groups already are the majority of residents. Nevada, Maryland, and Georgia are soon to follow. In a generation, minorities are likely to be the majority in America. Issues concerning immigration of Mexican and Central and South American individuals were often brought up during the 2020 presidential election.

During the Trump administration, although the number of foreign-born individuals only went up slightly, where they came from changed dramatically. The share of immigrants born in Mexico plummeted due in part to the percentage of persons coming into the United States from the Caribbean and Latin America.

Issues of an Aging Population

Just as the racial and ethnic composition of the American population is shifting, so too is the average age. "For decades, the U.S. was described as a nation of the young because the number of persons under the age of twenty greatly outnumber[ed] those sixty-five and older," but this is no longer the case.[1] Because of changes in patterns of fertility, life expectancy, and immigration, the nation's age profile has altered drastically. At the founding of the United States, the average life expectancy was thirty-five years; today, it is nearly eighty years, although studies show that White Americans aged twenty to sixty have experienced a significant increase in death rates. Heart failure deaths among Black men aged thirty-five to sixty-four are critically high; moreover, from 2010 to 2017, the greatest jump in death rates, 29 percent, was among those aged twenty-five to thirty-four.[2] What are called "excessive deaths" occurred in Indiana, Kentucky, Ohio, and Pennsylvania. Explanations include rapidly rising suicide rates and illnesses and deaths related to drug addiction and alcohol abuse, diabetes, and obesity.[3] Widespread opioid abuses are central to this problem, with many government agencies seeking to limit their use. The risk of dying from a drug overdose from 1999 to 2017 increased by 486 percent for men and 357 percent for women.[4] At the same time, several states and the District of Columbia have legalized marijuana, which some critics view as a gateway drug to other, often harder, substances.

Deaths from COVID-19 initially disproportionately hit Black people and Hispanics. Lack of access to quality health care and high rates of contributing causes such as diabetes and stress were blamed.

Of course, individual refusals to comply with the Centers for Disease Control and Prevention (CDC) precautions including wearing masks, maintaining strict social distancing, and bans on groups of ten or fifty depending upon the circumstances, added to concerns about new daily highs of positive tests that began just before the 2020 election and continued to grow at alarming rates.[5]

An aging population places a host of costly demands on the government. An aging America imposes a great financial burden on working Americans, whose proportion in the population is rapidly declining. These changes could potentially pit younger people against older people and result in dramatic cuts in benefits to the elderly and increased taxes for younger workers. Moreover, the elderly often vote against programs favored by younger voters, such as increases to public education spending. At the same time, younger voters are less likely to support issues important to seniors, such as Medicare and Social Security benefits.

The Role of Religious Beliefs

As we have discussed throughout this chapter, many of the first settlers came to America to pursue their religious beliefs free from governmental intervention. Although these early immigrants were members of a number of different churches, nearly all identified with Christian sects. Moreover, they viewed the American Indians' belief systems, which included multiple gods, to be savage and unholy. Records exist of early Jewish colonists as well as Muslims from Africa being enslaved and brought to the New World, but the numbers of early Americans practicing these faiths were small in comparison to Christian settlers.[6] Thus, references to Christianity and Christian values permeate American social and political systems.

While many citizens view the United States as a Christian nation, a great number of religious groups—including Jews, Buddhists, Hindus, and Muslims—have established strong roots in this country. With this growth have come different political and social demands.[7] For example, some American Jews continually work to ensure that America's policies in the Middle East favor Israel, while some Muslims demand more support for a Palestinian state. When President Trump fulfilled a campaign promise and moved the U.S. embassy from Israel's capital city, Tel Aviv, to Jerusalem, many American Jews were irate, while evangelical Christians cheered the move.[8]

As revealed in Figure 1.5, the percentage of Americans identifying as Protestant has fallen dramatically over time. Catholics, Christians, and others have remained relatively stable but, anecdotally, attendance at, and giving to, the Catholic Church has seen sharp declines in the wake of scandal after scandal involving Catholic priests. Perhaps the most interesting finding in Figure 1.5 is how the number of individuals not identifying with any religion has gone up dramatically, with about the same percentage of "nones" as Catholics. Yet, it is rare to see a politician or elected member of government not identify with some religion, and nearly all are sworn in using some form of holy book such as the Bible or Qur'an, although that is simply by tradition.

Family and Family Size

In the past, familial gender roles were clearly defined. White women did housework and men worked in the fields. Large families were imperative; children were a source of cheap farm labor. Industrialization and knowledge of birth control methods, however, began to put a dent in the size of American families by the early 1900s. No longer needing children to work for survival of the household, couples began to limit family size.

FIGURE 1.5 WHAT ARE AMERICANS' RELIGIOUS PREFERENCES?

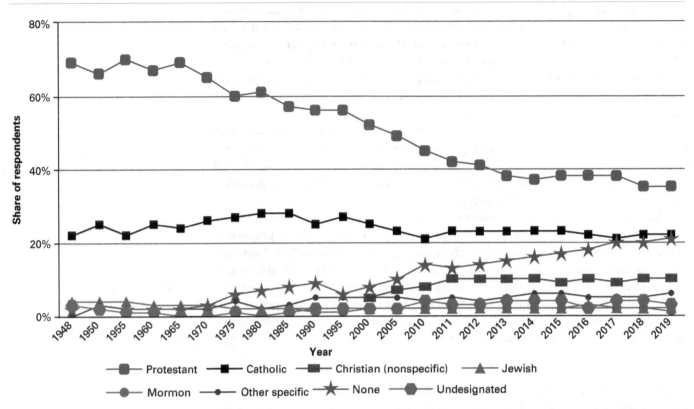

In 1949, 49 percent of those polled thought that four or more children constituted the "ideal" family size; today, most Americans believe that having no children or two children at most is "best." In 1940, nine of ten households were traditional family households. Today, 27 percent of children under eighteen live with just one of their parents; the vast majority of those live with their mother.[9] Moreover, nearly 28 percent of all households consist of a single person, a trend that reflects, in part, the aging American population and declining marriage rate. According to the Pew Research Center, only half of all adults in the nation are married.[10] The "families" polled in the 1940s were conventional ones that no longer exist in the large proportions found in earlier decades. Now, same-sex couples often have children. The number of unmarried teenage mothers has declined, and the greatest growth in women having babies is among women over forty, an age long ago considered too old for motherhood.[11]

Even the institution of marriage has undergone tremendous change. Since the U.S. Supreme Court's decision *Obergefell* v. *Hodges* (2015), same-sex marriage is legal in all states.[12] These changes in composition of households, lower birthrates, marriage, and the prevalence of single-parent families affect the kinds of demands people place on government. Single-parent families, for example, may be more likely to support government-subsidized day care or after-school programs.

Regional Growth and Expansion

Regional sectionalism emerged almost immediately in the United States. Settlers from the Virginia colony southward largely focused on commerce. Those seeking various forms of religious freedom populated many of the settlements from the mid-Atlantic to the Northeast. That search for religious freedom also came with puritanical values, so that New England evolved differently from the South in many aspects of culture.

Sectional differences continued to emerge as the United States developed into a major industrial nation and waves of immigrants with various religious traditions and customs entered the country, often settling in areas where other immigrants from their homeland already lived. For example, thousands of Scandinavians flocked to Minnesota, and many Irish settled in the urban centers of the Northeast, as did many Italians and Jews. All brought with them unique views about numerous issues and varying demands on government as well as different ideas about the role of government. Subsequent generations have often handed down these political views, and many regional differences continue to affect public opinion today. As examples, online retail giant Amazon's search for a second corporate headquarters, issues such as how state laws treat members of the LGBTQ communities (with restrictions far more common in southern states) have undergone strict scrutiny.

One of the most long-standing and dramatic regional differences in the United States is that between the South and the North. During the Constitutional Convention, most Southerners staunchly advocated for a weak national government. While the Civil War was later fought largely over the issue of slavery, which many Northerners opposed, it also was in part due to basic philosophical differences about government. As we know from modern political polling, the South continues to lag behind the rest of the nation in supporting civil rights and by keeping statues honoring Confederate generals, while still favoring return of power to the states and downsizing the national government.

The West, too, has always appeared unique compared with the rest of the United States. Populated first by those seeking free land and then by many chasing dreams of gold, the American West has often been characterized as "wild." Its population today is a study in contrasts. Some people have moved there to avoid city life and have an anti-government bias. Other Westerners are attracted to the region's abundant sunshine and natural resources and seek governmental solutions to problems like drought and environmental degradation.

Significant differences in attitude also arise in rural versus urban areas. Those who live in rural areas are much more conservative than those in large cities. One need only look at a map of the vote distribution in recent presidential elections to see stark differences in candidate appeal. Democratic candidates have carried almost every large city in America; Republicans have carried most rural voters as well as most of America's heartland.[13]

POLITICAL REFORM AND REALITIES: HOW ARE THINGS, REALLY?

1.4 Characterize changes in Americans' attitudes toward and expectations of government.

As the American population has changed over time, so has the American political process. **Politics** is the study of who gets what, when, and how—the process by which policy decisions are made. The evolving nature of the American citizenry deeply affects this process. Competing demands often lead to political struggles, which create winners and losers within the system. A loser today, however, may be a winner tomorrow in the ever-changing world of politics. The political ideologies of those in control of Congress, the executive branch, and state houses also have a huge impact on who gets what, when, and how.

Nevertheless, shared American values continue to bind citizens together. Many Americans share the common goal of achieving the **American Dream**—an American ideal of a happy and successful life in which education, freedom, and home ownership are core elements. Although manifestations of the American Dream have changed over time, it often includes wealth, a house, a better life for one's children, and, for some, the opportunity to grow up to be president. Many voters for President **Donald J. Trump** in 2016 saw the American Dream falling from their or their children's grasp.

In roughly the first 150 years of our nation's history, the federal government had few responsibilities, and citizens had few expectations of it beyond national defense, printing money, and collecting tariffs and taxes. The state governments were generally far more powerful than the federal government in matters affecting the everyday lives of Americans.

As the nation and its economy grew in size and complexity, the federal government took on more responsibilities such as regulating some businesses, providing poverty relief, and inspecting food. With these new roles come greater demands on government, although many citizens often do not realize how much they depend on government

politics
The study of who gets what, when, and how—or how policy decisions are made.

American Dream
An American ideal of a happy, successful life, which often assumes wealth, a house, and a better life for one's children.

Donald J. Trump
The 45th president, a Republican, elected in 2016, serving only one term; first candidate elected without prior political or military experience; an experienced businessman.

FIGURE 1.6   DO AMERICANS HAVE CONFIDENCE IN AMERICAN INSTITUTIONS?

The line graph below shows the percentages of Americans declaring they have a "great deal" or "quite a lot" of confidence in American institutions. Note the sharp declining trend of trust in all political institutions. It is easy to conclude that few Americans have confidence in any institutions or industries.

SOURCE: *Gallup, https://news.gallup.com/poll/1597/confidence-institutions.aspx.*

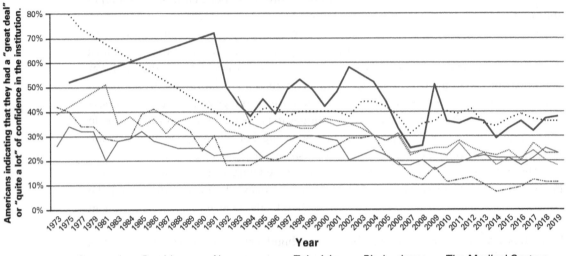

--- Congress — Presidency ···· Newspapers — Television — Big business ···· The Medical System

programs, whether income tax deductions for home mortgages, subsidies for the high costs of heating (in northern states) or cooling (in southern states), or grants to support the distribution of COVID-19 vaccinations.

The debate over the repeal of the Affordable Care Act, often called Obamacare, is illustrative of the conflicts individuals experience in terms of how much government they want. Most Americans were happy to see that their medical insurance provider was forced to extend medical coverage to their children until they were twenty-six. Appeals to force insurers to cover preexisting conditions, however, were greeted with mixed results—often based on the perspectives of those who had (or had friends or family) with preexisting conditions that could have left them without insurance or coverage for medical treatment for life-threatening conditions.

The issue of insurance coverage became especially critical as COVID-19 raged on at the same time the Trump administration filed briefs at the Supreme Court arguing that the Affordable Care Act was unconstitutional.

Today, many Americans are skeptical of government, and they lack faith in the country's institutions (see Figure 1.6). These concerns make it even easier for citizens to blame the government for all kinds of woes—personal as well as societal—or to fail to credit it for those things it does well. Many Americans, for example, enjoy a remarkably high standard of living, and much of it is due to governmental programs and protections.[14]

While Americans have little faith in institutions, they also believe that trust in each other has declined as partisanship and political acrimony are at the highest levels we have seen in years, and whether or not to wear a face mask becomes a political issue. The 2016 presidential campaign was particularly divisive, as name-calling, bullying, and "alternative facts" came into vogue. Adding to distrust of government was the fact that many "facts" uttered by Donald J. Trump and then checked by the *Washington Post* proved to be unfounded. Hillary Clinton was also not immune from making false or "pants-on-fire" claims during the campaign, but her tally fell far short of those made by Trump. By Election Day 2020, the *Washington Post* found that the president had spoken or tweeted over 20,000 lies averaging over 50 false or misleading claims a day.

The Women's March on Washington, D.C., in 2017, which saw participation in all fifty states and across six continents, was estimated to attract far more protesters than President Trump's inauguration did attendees the day before. Also, in 2017, after another deadly mass shooting in a school in the United States (this time in Parkland, Florida), many students finally said, "Enough." They used social media to enhance their voices, called on legislatures to strengthen gun control laws, and organized a national march on Washington, D.C., to draw attention to the fact that they were future voters. Other marches for the environment, science, students against guns, and even a Tax Day protest urging the president to release his tax returns (as all presidents since 1976 have done), may signal a new burst in political activity unseen in years gone by on both sides. The nationwide marches against police brutality and Confederate statuary may just be the tip of the iceberg of what is to come.

By 2018, we also learned conclusively that the Russian government participated in a massive effort to use Facebook and other forms of social media to push voters toward Donald J. Trump. Americans, for the first time and on a pervasive level, were bombarded with false news designed to further influence their political leanings. With no way of sorting through the flood of misleading information, the preexisting political loyalties of many were only strengthened. Democratic women, in particular, motivated by the March and outraged by some of the president's behavior toward women, in 2018 ran for elective office at the local, state, and national level turning advocacy into action. Black women, in particular, were not only an ultra-stable Democratic voting bloc, they also won seats at all levels of government in record numbers. So many Black women, for example, won new seats in the House of Representative that their numbers gave Democrats back the majority and made Nancy Pelosi the Speaker of the House. Their victories did not translate to winning over the Senate in 2018.

Thus, through 2020, Republicans and conservatives controlled the Senate and the Supreme Court, offering little to no check on the powers of the president. One of the highlights of President Trump's first one hundred days was the fairly easy confirmation of Judge Neil Gorsuch to the Supreme Court. Trump was presented with another critical opportunity when Justice Anthony Kennedy, often the swing voter on many 5–4 decisions of the Court, opted to retire. In contentious hearings involving charges of sexual assault, Trump's second nominee, Judge Brett Kavanaugh, was confirmed.

The death of Justice Ruth Bader Ginsburg, an unlikely pop icon, on September 18, 2020, stunned the nation although the justice had been ill for several years. With voting already underway in some states, President Trump promised to name her replacement quickly and the Senate Majority Leader Mitch McConnell (R-KY) vowed to approve his nominee, Judge Amy Coney Barrett, a former clerk to the Court's once most conservative justice, Antonin Scalia. Her appointment solidified the conservative majority on the Court for decades to come as the president could claim that accomplishment and the filling of about one-third of the federal court judgeships. The nomination of Barrett was a well-attended White House event where nary a mask was to be found. It also reinforced the idea, held by many medical experts, that the president was flaunting CDC guidelines as well as the recommendations of his own coronavirus task force. Within a short time, it was clear that it had become a super spreader event and even the president, first lady, and their young son fell ill with the virus.

Women's rights activists found no friend in Justice Barrett and they were concerned about the president's continued emphasis on repealing Obamacare, abolishing coverage for preexisting conditions in the time of a worldwide pandemic, ending the extension of medical coverage to age twenty-six for those whose parents had insurance, and ending all coverage for contraceptives.

Along with members of Black Lives Matter (BLM) and myriad other local, state and national social justice groups, the murders of George Floyd and Breonna Taylor set off protests throughout the United States. For many, especially as the virus was causing fear, unemployment, and hitting minority groups hardest, the death of Floyd was simply the match of a latent fire as more and more examples of murdered Blacks came to light and the president pushed back on even peaceful marchers. As a call came from civil rights leaders, President Trump went back to appearing to condone the actions of those arguing that no systematic discrimination existed in the United States and that monuments to Confederate generals were fitting acknowledgments of their service. He approved of Confederate flags, berated

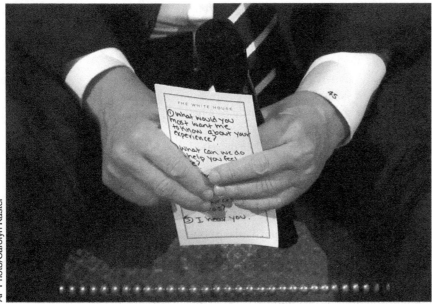

WHY IS IT IMPORTANT THAT PRESIDENTS SHOW EMPATHY?

Here, President Donald J. Trump holds notes prompting empathetic questions during a listening session with survivors of gun violence after the deadly school shootings in Parkland, Florida, that left seventeen students and staff dead. His staff recognized that it was vital that the president convey comforting words in a crisis or after some horrible occurrence. Comforting did not come naturally to the 45th president.

professional athletes for supporting BLM and speaking out on long standing racial acts, both large and small, encountered by many Blacks on a daily basis.

This insensitivity certainly mobilized moderate and progressive voters in 2020 contributing to the defeat of Donald J. Trump making him one of the few one-term presidents in American history. President Trump governed like no other and appeared to draw energy nearly unparalleled in a 74-year-old man from crowds and their adulation after a bout of COVID-19. Ultimately, nearly 5 million more voters said no to his brand of governance turning to Joe Biden, the oldest president ever to take office, joined by Vice President Kamala Harris, the first woman to hold that position as well as the first Black, Indian, and Jamaican to hold the office. Many expect the days of tweets, drama, and a revolving door of advisors will soon be evident.

In this text, we present you with the tools needed to understand how our political system has evolved and to understand changes yet to come. Approaching the study of American government and politics with an open mind should help you become a better citizen. We hope that you learn to ask questions; to comprehend how various issues have come to be important; and to see why a particular law was enacted, how it was implemented, and whether it needs reform. We further hope that you will learn not to accept at face value everything you see on the TV news, hear on the radio, or read on social media, especially in the blogosphere and Twitterverse. Work to understand your government and use your vote and other forms of participation to help ensure that your government works for you.

We recognize that the discourse of politics has changed dramatically, most notably in the unprecedented events surrounding the 2016 and 2020 presidential elections. There is no doubt that politics often appears to have devolved into a nasty sport, a fact that has led many voters to question what government does for them. Many breathed a sigh of relief when the news of Joe Biden's and Kamala Harris's election did not produce angry protests around the nation even though windows were shuttered around major cities in anticipation of mass protests on either side. Instead, many people took to the streets to celebrate. Sadly, violence did rock the Capital on January 6, 2021, as the election of the Biden/Harris ticket was being finalized.

We hope that Americans will pay increasing attention to our democracy and consider carefully what we want from government. We challenge you to consider how government regulations and policies affect your life. For example, after graduation, do you plan to stay on your parent's health insurance? Do you believe poor people should get housing and food assistance? Do you believe in climate change, and should we, as a country, take steps to reduce pollution? It is easier than ever before to become informed about the political process and to get involved in campaigns and elections.

We believe that a thorough understanding of the workings of government will allow you to question and think about the political system—the good parts and the bad—and decide for yourself whether proposed changes and reforms are advantageous or disadvantageous. Equipped with such an understanding, we hope you will become better informed and a more active participant in the political process and remain aware of the possibilities and limitations of government as we enter a period where after two years, the House of Representatives may begin to assert itself in the policy process and curtail or stall the implementation of policy positions favored by President Trump.

CONCLUSION AND REVIEW

What Are the Roots of American Government?

1.1 Trace the origins of American government.

American government is rooted in the cultures and experiences of early European colonists as well as interactions with the indigenous populations of the New World. The first colonists sought wealth. Later, Pilgrims came for religious freedom. The colonies set up systems of government that differed widely in terms of form, role, and function. As the colonies developed, they sought more independence from the British monarchy.

What Are the Functions of the American Government?

1.2 Explain the functions of American government.

The functions of American government include establishing justice, ensuring domestic tranquility, providing for the common defense, promoting the general welfare, and securing the blessings of liberty.

How Have the American People and Their Culture Changed over Time?

1.3 Analyze the changing characteristics of the American public.

Several characteristics of the American electorate can help us understand how the system continues to evolve and change. Among these are changes in size and population, racial and ethnic composition, population trends, age, the role of religion, and regional growth.

Political Reform and Realities: How Are Things, Really?

1.4 Characterize changes in Americans' attitudes toward and expectations of government.

Shifts in population have created controversy in the American electorate throughout America's history. Americans have high and often unrealistic expectations of government, yet often fail to appreciate how much their government actually does for them. Americans' failing trust in institutions also explains some of the dissatisfaction among the American electorate.

LEARN THE TERMS

American Dream	government	rule of law
Black Lives Matter	Mayflower Compact	White privilege
democracy	politics	
Enlightenment	republic	

LEARN THE NAMES

Anne Hutchinson	Roger Williams	William Penn
Donald J. Trump	Thomas Hooker	

AP Photo/Charles Tasnadi

HOW MANY CONSTITUTIONAL AMENDMENTS HAVE ADDRESSED VOTING?

Many constitutional amendments have addressed voting rights. Above, President Richard M. Nixon signs the Twenty-Sixth Amendment, which guaranteed eighteen-year-olds the right to vote in all elections. Today, in the wake of school shootings, many are calling on Congress to pass an amendment to lower the voting age to sixteen.

CRITICAL THINKING QUESTION: *What are the pros and cons of allowing those 16 years of age and older to vote?*

THE CONSTITUTION

LEARNING OBJECTIVES

2.1   Identify the causes of the American Revolution and the ideals on which the United States and the Constitution are based.

2.2   Identify the components of the Articles of Confederation and the reasons for their failure.

2.3   Outline the issues resolved by compromise during the writing of the Constitution.

2.4   Describe the framework for government expressed in the Constitution.

2.5   Outline the arguments for and against ratification of the Constitution.

2.6   Describe the processes by which the Constitution can be amended.

At age eighteen, all American citizens are eligible to vote in state and national elections. This has not always been the case. It took an amendment to the U.S. Constitution—one of only seventeen that have been added since the ratification of the Bill of Rights in 1791—to guarantee the vote in national elections to those younger than twenty-one years of age.

In 1942, during World War II, Representative Jennings Randolph (D–WV) proposed a constitutional amendment that would lower the voting age to eighteen, believing that since young men were old enough to be drafted, go to war, and fight and die for their country, they also should be allowed to vote. He continued to reintroduce his proposal during every session of Congress. In 1954, President **Dwight D. Eisenhower** endorsed the idea in his State of the Union Address. Presidents Lyndon B. Johnson and Richard M. Nixon—men who had also called upon the nation's young men to fight on foreign shores—echoed his appeal.[1]

During the 1960s, the campaign to lower the voting age took on a new sense of urgency as the draft sent hundreds of thousands of young men to fight in the unpopular war in Vietnam, where thousands of men and women were killed in action. "Old Enough to Fight, Old Enough to Vote" was one popular slogan of the day. By 1970, four states—the U.S. Constitution allows states to set the eligibility requirements for their voters—had lowered their voting ages to eighteen. Later that year, Congress passed legislation lowering the voting age in national, state, and local elections to eighteen.

The state of Oregon immediately challenged the constitutionality of that law in court, arguing that the *Constitution* (see Appendix III) did not give Congress the authority to establish a uniform voting age in state and local government elections. The U.S. Supreme Court agreed.[2] The decision from the divided Court meant that those under age twenty-one could vote in national elections but that the states were free to prohibit them from voting in state and local elections. The decision presented the states with a logistical nightmare. States setting the voting age at twenty-one would be forced to keep two sets of voter registration books: one for voters twenty-one and over and one for voters under twenty-one.

Jennings Randolph, by then a senator from West Virginia, reintroduced his proposed amendment to lower the national voting age to eighteen.[3] Within three months of the Supreme Court's decision, Congress sent the proposed Twenty-Sixth Amendment to the states for their ratification. The required three-fourths of the states approved the amendment within three months, making its adoption on June 30, 1971, the quickest in the history of the constitutional amending process. In the aftermath of the 2018 Parkland, Florida, school shooting and subsequent march on Washington, D.C., by high school students around the nation, many called for lowering the voting age to sixteen. *The New York Times*, for example, noted that several countries, including Argentina, Austria, and Brazil, allow sixteen-year-olds to vote and that their voter turnout is significantly higher than that of older Americans. The District of Columbia was the first to allow sixteen- and seventeen-year-olds to register to vote in national elections.

Dwight D. Eisenhower

Thirty-fourth president of the United States (1953–1961). Also a general like George Washington, he served as the Supreme Commander of the Allied Expeditionary Force in Europe during World War II.

• • •

The Framers never intended the U.S. Constitution to be easily changed. They made the amendment process time consuming and difficult, and the Twenty-Sixth Amendment continues to be an anomaly. Over the years, thousands of amendments—including those to prohibit child labor, provide equal rights for women, grant statehood to the District of Columbia, balance the federal budget, and ban flag burning—have been debated or sent to the states for approval, only to die slow deaths. Only twenty-seven amendments have made their way into the Constitution. What the Framers wrote in Philadelphia has continued to work, in spite of increasing demands on and dissatisfaction with our national government. Although Americans often clamor for reform, perhaps they are happier with the system of government created by the Framers than they realize. The ideas that went into the making of the Constitution and the ways its interpretation has evolved to address the problems of a growing and changing nation form the core of our discussion in this chapter.

WHAT ARE THE ROOTS OF THE U.S. CONSTITUTION?

2.1 Identify the causes of the American Revolution and the ideals on which the United States and the Constitution are based.

Beginning in the early seventeenth century, colonists came to the New World, settling in what were to become the original thirteen colonies. Often, they sought a new start on a continent where land was plentiful or saw business opportunities to be gained in the New World. Others wished to escape religious persecution. The economic, ethnic, and religious diversity of the settlers in the New World complicated the question of how best to rule the new colonies. British colonists agreed that the king ruled by Divine Right, but those monarchs allowed the colonists significant liberties in terms of self-government, religious practices, and economic organization. For 140 years, this system worked fairly well.[4] By the early 1750s, however, after a century and a half of physical separation from Europe, development of colonial industry and relative self-governance by the colonies led to weakening ties with—and loyalties to—the Crown.

Benjamin Franklin

A brilliant inventor and senior statesman at the Constitutional Convention who urged colonial unity as early as 1754, twenty-two years before the Declaration of Independence.

As early as 1754, at the urgings of Pennsylvanian **Benjamin Franklin**, more than twenty representatives from the Mid-Atlantic and northern colonies met in Albany, New York. The chief concern of those present in Albany was their role in the French and Indian War being fought in the colonies between the French and English with the majority American Indians as French allies. The American phase of what was called the Seven Years' War was fought from 1754 to 1763. On one side were the French and French Canadian colonists. American colonists fought alongside British soldiers. Various Indian tribes fought on the sides of the British or French. Although those in attendance were concerned about the war and how it was financed, the resultant Albany Plan of Union, which called for the colonies to unite, was rejected by the states. Eventually, bits of it found their way into the Articles of Confederation.

To justifiy taxing the colonies, the British relied upon on an economic theory called mercantilism. Followers of **mercantilism** believe that a nation's wealth is increased through the development of commercial industry and a favorable balance of trade. From 1650 until well into the 1700s, Britain retained strict controls on colonial imports and exports, believing it critical to export more goods than it imported as a way of increasing the gold and silver in its treasury. The British found it difficult to enforce these policies, however, and the colonists, seeing little self-benefit in their operation, widely ignored them. They were also loyal to England.

mercantilism

An economic theory designed to increase a nation's wealth through the development of commercial industry and a favorable balance of trade.

Many of the most oppressive British traditions—feudalism, a rigid class system, and absolute adherence to the authority of the king—were absent in the colonies. Land was abundant. The guild and craft systems that severely limited entry into many skilled professions in Great Britain were not part of life in the colonies because individuals could freely pursue skilled crafts. And, although religion was central to the lives of most colonists, no single state church existed, so the colonists did not follow the British practice of compulsory tithing (giving a fixed percentage of one's earnings to the state-sanctioned and state-supported church).

To raise money to pay for the French and Indian War as well as the expenses of administering the colonies, Parliament enacted the Sugar Act in 1764, one year after it won the war. This act placed taxes on sugar, wine, coffee, and other products commonly exported to the colonies. A postwar colonial depression heightened resentment of the tax. Major protest, however, failed to materialize until imposition of the Stamp Act by the British Parliament in 1765. This law required that all paper items—from playing cards to books—bought and sold in the colonies carry a stamp mandated by the Crown. The colonists feared this act would establish a precedent for the British Parliament not only to control commerce in the colonies but also to raise revenues from the colonists without approval of the colonial governments. The political cry "no taxation without representation" rang out across the colonies. To add insult to injury, in 1765, Parliament passed the Quartering Act, which required colonists to furnish barracks or provide living quarters within their own homes for British troops.

Most colonists, especially those in New England, where taxes hit merchants hardest, were outraged. Men throughout the colonies organized the Sons of Liberty and women formed the Daughters of Liberty. Protests against the Stamp Act were violent and loud. Riots, often led by the Sons of Liberty, broke out. In Boston, an angry mob burned the colonial governor's home and protesters threatened British stamp agents charged with collecting the tax. The outraged colonists also organized a boycott of goods needing the stamps as well as a boycott of British imports.

First Steps Toward Independence

In 1765, at the urging of **Samuel Adams**, nine of the thirteen colonies sent representatives to a meeting in New York City where they drafted a detailed list of Crown violations of the colonists' fundamental rights. The Stamp Act Congress was the first official joint political meeting, with representatives of nine of the thirteen colonies in attendance, and the first step toward creating a unified nation. Attendees defined what they thought to be the proper relationship between colonial governments and the British Parliament. They ardently believed that Parliament had no authority to tax them without colonial representation in that body, yet they still remained loyal to the king, although they sent three petitions arguing against "the very burdensome restrictions." The British, however, believed that direct representation of the colonists was impractical; that members of Parliament represented the best interests of all the British, including the colonists, who were British subjects; and that Parliament had absolute authority to tax the colonists.

The Stamp Act Congress and its petitions to the Crown did little to stop the onslaught of taxing measures. Parliament did, however, repeal the Stamp Act and revise the Sugar Act in 1766, largely because of the uproar made by British merchants who were losing large sums of money as a result of the boycotts. Rather than appeasing the colonists, however, these actions emboldened them to increase their resistance. In 1767, Parliament enacted the Townshend Acts, which imposed duties on all kinds of colonial imports, including tea. Responses from the Sons and Daughters of Liberty were immediate. Protesters announced another boycott of tea, and almost all colonists gave up their favorite drink in a united show of resistance to the tax and British authority.[5] Tensions continued to run high, especially after the British sent 4,000 troops to Boston. On March 5, 1770, British troops opened fire on an unruly mob that included disgruntled dockworkers, whose jobs had been taken by British soldiers, and members of the Sons of Liberty, who were taunting the soldiers and throwing objects at British sentries stationed in front of the Boston Customs House where taxes were collected. The troops killed five colonists, including **Crispus Attucks**, a free Black American and the first American to die in the early days of unrest before the Revolutionary War, in what became known as the Boston Massacre. The Massacre and Paul Revere's pro-colonialist engraving are credited with transforming public opinion. Following this confrontation, the British Parliament lifted all duties except those on tea. The tea tax, however, continued to be a symbolic irritant. To keep this revolutionary fervor going, in 1772, at the suggestion of Samuel Adams, colonists created the Committees of Correspondence to keep each other abreast of developments with the British.

Meanwhile, despite dissent in Britain over treatment of the colonies, Parliament passed another tea tax designed to shore up the sagging sales of the East India Company, a British exporter of tea. The colonists' boycott had left that trading company with more than 18 million pounds of tea in its warehouses. To rescue British merchants

traveler1116/Getty Images

WHY WAS SAMUEL ADAMS IMPORTANT?

Samuel Adams (1722–1803), cousin of President John Adams, was an early leader against the British and loyalist oppressors. He played a key role in developing the Committees of Correspondence and was active in Massachusetts and colonial politics. Today, he is known for the beer that bears his name, which is ironic, considering he bankrupted his family's brewery business.

Samuel Adams

A founder of the Committees of Correspondences, a key way colonists communicated with each other.

Crispus Attucks

A Black American and first American to die in what became known as the Boston Massacre in 1770.

WHAT REALLY HAPPENED AT THE BOSTON MASSACRE?

Paul Revere's famous engraving of the Boston Massacre played fast and loose with the facts. While the event occurred on a cold winter's night, the engraving features a clear sky and no ice or snow. Crispus Attucks, the Revolution's first martyr, was a Black American, although the engraving depicts him as a White man seen lying on the ground closest to the British soldiers. Popular propaganda such as this engraving—and even dubbing the incident a "massacre"—did much to stoke anti-British sentiment in the years leading up to the Revolutionary War.

MPI/Archive Photos/Getty Images

from disaster, in 1773, Parliament passed the Tea Act, which granted a monopoly to the financially strapped East India Company to sell tea imported from Britain. This act allowed the company to funnel business to American merchants loyal to the Crown, thereby undercutting dissident colonial merchants who could sell only tea imported from other nations. This practice drove down the price of tea and hurt colonial merchants who were forced to buy tea at higher prices from other sources.

When the next shipment of tea from Britain arrived in Boston, the colonists responded by throwing the Boston Tea Party; other colonies held similar tea parties up and down the eastern coast. King George III flew into a rage upon hearing of the actions of his disloyal subjects. "The die is now cast," the king told his prime minister. "The colonies must either submit or triumph."

King George III's first act of retaliation was to persuade Parliament to pass the Coercive Acts of 1774. Known in the colonies as the Intolerable Acts, they contained a key provision calling for a total blockade of Boston Harbor, cutting off Bostonians' access to many foodstuffs until restitution was made for the tea. Another provision reinforced the Quartering Act. It gave Massachusetts's royal governor the authority to house British soldiers in the homes of Boston citizens, allowing Britain to send an additional 4,000 soldiers in a show of force.

The First and Second Continental Congresses

The British could never have guessed how the cumulative impact of these actions would unite the colonists. The Committees of Correspondence spread the word, and the people of Boston received food and money from all over the colonies. The tax itself was no longer the key issue; now the extent of British authority over the colonies presented the far more important question. At the request of the colonial assemblies of Massachusetts and Virginia, all but Georgia's colonial assembly agreed to select a group of delegates to attend a continental congress authorized to communicate with the king on behalf of the now-united colonies.

The First Continental Congress, comprising fifty-six delegates from all of the colonies but Georgia, met in Philadelphia from September 5 to October 26, 1774. The colonists had yet to think of breaking with Great Britain; at this point, they simply wanted to iron out their differences with the king. By October, they had agreed on a series of resolutions to oppose the Coercive Acts and to establish a formal organization to boycott British goods. The Congress also drafted a Declaration of Rights and Resolves, which called for colonial rights of petition and assembly, trial by peers, freedom from a standing army, and the selection of representative councils to levy taxes. The Congress further agreed that if the king did not capitulate to its demands, it would meet again in Philadelphia in May 1775.

King George III refused to yield, tensions continued to rise, and a Second Continental Congress was deemed necessary. Before it could meet, fighting broke out on April 19, 1775, at Lexington and Concord, Massachusetts, with what was later called "the shot heard 'round the world." Eight colonial soldiers, called Minutemen, were killed, and 16,000 British troops besieged Boston.

When the Second Continental Congress convened in Philadelphia on May 10, 1775, delegates were united by their increased hostility to Great Britain. In a final attempt to avert conflict, the Second Continental Congress adopted the Olive Branch Petition on July 5, 1775, asking the king to end hostilities. King George III rejected the petition and sent an additional 20,000 troops to quell the rebellion; he labeled all in attendance traitors to the king and subject to death. The king's refusal to even look at the petition was the equivalent of signing an act of war. It crystallized in the minds of many colonists the need for a clean break with Great Britain. The Congress also decided to raise an army with Virginian George Washington as its commander in chief.

In January 1776, **Thomas Paine**, an English-born political theorist, issued (at first anonymously) *Common Sense*, a pamphlet paid for by Benjamin Franklin that forcefully argued for independence from Great Britain. In frank, easy-to-understand language, Paine denounced the corrupt British monarchy and offered reasons to break with Great Britain. "The blood of the slain, the weeping voice of nature cries 'Tis Time to Part,'" wrote Paine. *Common Sense*, widely read throughout the colonies, helped to change minds in a very short time. In its first three months of publication, *Common Sense* sold 120,000 copies—one for every thirteen people in the colonies.

Common Sense galvanized the American public against reconciliation. On May 15, 1776, Virginia became the first colony to call for independence. On June 7, 1776, Richard Henry Lee rose to move "that these United Colonies are, and of right ought to be, free and independent States, and that all connection between them and the State of Great Britain is, and ought to be, dissolved." His three-part resolution—which called for (1) independence from Great Britain; (2) the formation of foreign alliances; and (3) preparation of a plan of governance—triggered hot debate among the delegates. A proclamation of independence from Great Britain constituted treason, a crime punishable by death. Although six of the thirteen colonies had already instructed their delegates to vote for independence, the Second Continental Congress was suspended to allow its delegates to return home to their respective colonial legislatures for final instructions. Independence was not a move the colonists took lightly.

Thomas Paine

The influential writer of *Common Sense*, a pamphlet that advocated for independence from Great Britain.

WHAT WAS *COMMON SENSE*?

Written by Thomas Paine with financial support from Benjamin Franklin, the case for separating with Great Britain was laid out in clear, easy-to-read terms in a short pamphlet to convince colonialists that a break with it was the only course.

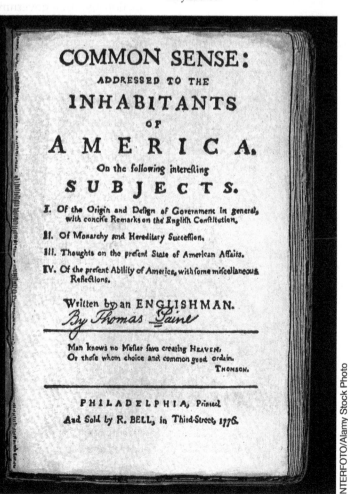

COMMON SENSE:
ADDRESSED TO THE
INHABITANTS
OF
AMERICA.
On the following interesting
SUBJECTS.

I. Of the Origin and Design of Government in general, with concise Remarks on the English Constitution.

II. Of Monarchy and Hereditary Succession.

III. Thoughts on the present State of American Affairs.

IV. Of the present Ability of America, with some miscellaneous Reflections.

Written by an ENGLISHMAN.
By Thomas Paine

Man knows no Master save creating HEAVEN,
Or those whom choice and common good ordain.
THOMSON.

PHILADELPHIA, Printed.
And Sold by R. BELL, in Third-Street, 1776.

Thomas Jefferson
Principal drafter of the Declaration of Independence; second vice president of the United States; third president of the United States from 1801 to 1809. Co-founder of the Democratic-Republican Party created to oppose Federalists.

Declaration of Independence
Document drafted largely by Thomas Jefferson in 1776 that proclaimed the right of the American colonies to separate from Great Britain.

Jean-Jacques Rousseau
Swiss-born philosopher, writer, and political theorist who influenced the French Revolution and the formation of modern governments.

John Locke
An English philosopher and physician, widely regarded as one of the most influential of Enlightenment thinkers and commonly known as the "Father of Liberalism."

social contract theory
The belief that governments exist based on the consent of the governed.

The Business of Independence

When delegates returned to Philadelphia, they set about dealing with each of the three prongs of Richard Henry Lee's resolution by creating several working committees. As to the first point, severing ties with Great Britain, the Committee of Five (Chair **Thomas Jefferson**, John Adams, Benjamin Franklin, Robert Livingston, and Robert Sherman) began work on the **Declaration of Independence** (see Appendix I), which drew heavily on the works of the Enlightenment period. On July 2, 1776, twelve of the thirteen colonies (with New York abstaining) voted for independence. Two days later, on July 4th, the Second Continental Congress voted to adopt the Declaration of Independence. On July 9, 1776, the document, now with the approval of New York, was read aloud in Philadelphia.[6]

THE DECLARATION OF INDEPENDENCE, in simple but eloquent language, set out the reasons for separation of the colonies from Great Britain. Most of its stirring rhetoric drew heavily on the works of seventeenth- and eighteenth-century political philosophers, particularly the French Enlightenment theorist **Jean-Jacques Rousseau** and the English philosopher **John Locke**. Locke's (as well as Rousseau's) theory of natural liberty and equality and his advocacy of **social contract theory**, which holds that governments exist based on the consent of the governed, heavily influenced Jefferson, who was credited with primary authorship of the Declaration. According to Locke, people agree to set up governments largely for the protection of property rights, to preserve life and liberty, and to establish justice. Furthermore, argued Locke, individuals who give their consent to be governed have the right to resist or remove rulers who deviate from those purposes. Such a government exists for the good of its subjects and not for the benefit of those who govern. Thus, rebellion is the ultimate sanction against a government that violates the rights of its citizens.

It is easy to see the colonists' debt to John Locke. In Jefferson's stirring language, the Declaration of Independence proclaims:

> We hold these truths to be self-evident, that all men are created equal, that they are endowed by their Creator with certain unalienable Rights, that among these are Life, Liberty and the pursuit of Happiness.

Jefferson and others in attendance at the Second Continental Congress wanted to have a document that would stand for all time, justifying their break with Great Britain and clarifying their notions of the proper form of government. So, the Declaration continued:

> That to secure these rights, Governments are instituted among Men, deriving their just powers from the consent of the governed. That whenever any Form of Government becomes destructive of these ends, it is the Right of the People to alter or abolish it, and to institute new Government, laying its foundation on such Principles and organizing its Powers in such form, as to them shall seem most likely to effect their Safety and Happiness.

After its stirring preamble and the enumeration of the wrongs suffered by the colonists under British rule, its final words are apt. All pertain to the denial of personal rights and liberties, many of which would later be guaranteed by the U.S. Constitution through the Bill of Rights. It, and the Articles of Confederation that were drawn up by the Second Continental Congress, were the bases by which the Revolutionary War was fought.

Securing Foreign Alliances

While some members were busy writing the Declaration, others sought to secure relationships with nations other than Great Britain. The Declaration itself, by definition, allowed the Second Continental Congress to seek foreign allies. It reached out to France, sending Benjamin Franklin as its envoy; without French support, the colonists in all likelihood would not have won the Revolutionary War. In fact, the Marquis de Lafayette of France led thousands of American soldiers, including the Siege at Yorktown, as a general.

Lake County Museum/Archive Photos/Getty Images

WHAT DID THE DECLARATION OF INDEPENDENCE PROCLAIM?

The Declaration of Independence states that all individuals have the right to life, liberty, and the pursuit of happiness. The bell that hung from the tower of the Pennsylvania State House in Philadelphia, Pennsylvania, rang loudly as this Declaration was read; today it is known as the "Liberty Bell."

The French also supplied the Continental Army, under the direction of General George Washington, with arms and clothing. Spain and the Netherlands also gave support to the new United States of America during the war, as did Russia, Norway, Denmark, and Portugal, but in much more limited ways. All were united in their hatred of Great Britain and its colonial policies affecting the United States as well as colonies around the world.

Preparing a Plan of Governance

The British had no written constitution. Delegates to the Second Continental Congress were attempting to codify many arrangements that had never before been expressed in legal terminology. Thus, a committee of delegates sat down to draft a document creating a new government necessary to wage war and unite the colonies. The resultant Articles reflect the unique political culture of the colonies. We define political culture as commonly shared attitudes, behaviors, and core values about how government should operate.

WHAT ARE THE ARTICLES OF CONFEDERATION?

2.2 Identify the components of the Articles of Confederation and the reasons for their failure.

In late 1777, the Second Continental Congress adopted the **Articles of Confederation** and presented the Articles to the colonies for ratification. The Articles created a loose "league of friendship" between the thirteen sovereign, or independent, colonies (some that even called themselves separate countries). The Articles created a type of government called a confederation or confederacy, one quite common among the Indian tribes. The national government in a confederacy is weaker than the sum of its parts, and the states often consider themselves independent nation-states linked together only for limited purposes such as national defense. The Articles of Confederation included the following:

Articles of Confederation
The compact between the thirteen original colonies that created a loose league of friendship, with the national government drawing its powers from the states.

- A national government with a congress empowered to make peace, coin money, appoint officers for an army, control the post office, and negotiate with Indian tribes
- Each state's retention of its independence and sovereignty, or ultimate authority, to govern within its territories
- One vote in the legislature, the Congress of the Confederation, for each state regardless of size

- The vote of nine states to pass any measure (a unanimous vote for any amendment)
- The selection and payment of delegates to the Congress by the states

The Articles, finally ratified by all thirteen states in March 1781, fashioned a government that reflected the political culture and philosophy of the times.[7] Although it had its flaws, the government under the Articles of Confederation saw the nation through the Revolutionary War. However, once the British surrendered in 1781 and the new nation found itself no longer united by the war effort, the national government quickly fell into chaos.

Problems Under the Articles of Confederation

Critical Period

The chaotic period from 1781 to 1789 after the American Revolution during which the former colonies were governed under the Articles of Confederation.

Historians refer to the chaotic period from 1781 to 1789, when the former colonies were governed under the Articles, as the **Critical Period**.[8] The Congress of the Confederation rarely could assemble the required quorum of nine states to conduct business. Even when they did meet, states found it difficult to agree on any policies. To raise revenue to pay off war debts and run the government, Congress proposed various land, poll, and liquor taxes. But, since it had no specific power to tax, all these proposals were rejected. At one point, Congress was even driven out of Philadelphia (then the capital of the new national government) by its own unpaid army.

Although the national government could coin money, it had no resources to back up the value of its currency. Continental dollars were worth little, and trade between states grew chaotic as some of them began to coin their own money. Another weakness was that the Articles of Confederation did not allow Congress to regulate commerce among the states or with foreign nations. As a result, individual states attempted to enter into agreements with other countries, and foreign nations were suspicious of trade agreements made with the Congress of the Confederation.

Fearful of a chief executive who would rule tyrannically, the drafters of the Articles made no provision for an executive branch of government that would be responsible for executing, or implementing, laws passed by the legislative branch. Instead, the president was merely the presiding officer at meetings. The Articles of Confederation, moreover, had no provision for a judicial system to handle the growing number of economic conflicts and boundary disputes among the individual states. Several states claimed the same lands to the west, and Pennsylvania and Virginia went to war with each other.

The Articles' greatest weakness, however, was its failure to provide for a strong central government. Although states had operated independently before the war, during the war they acceded to the national government's authority to wage armed conflict. Once the war was over, however, each state resumed its sovereign status and was unwilling to give up rights, such as the power to tax, to an untested national government. Consequently, the government could not force states to abide by the provisions of the second Treaty of Paris, signed in 1783, which officially ended the Revolutionary War. For example, states passed laws to allow debtors who owed money to Great Britain to postpone payment. These actions violated the treaty. Still, the Articles did foster some successes. Improvements were made in transportation and communication. The establishment of a national postal service also helped foster a sense of some nationality that went beyond state borders.

Rebellion in the States

Before concerned states and individuals could take action to strengthen the government, new unrest broke out in America. In 1780, Massachusetts adopted a constitution that appeared to favor the interests of the wealthy. Property-owning requirements barred the lower and middle classes from voting and holding office. And, as the economy of Massachusetts declined, banks foreclosed on the farms of many Massachusetts Continental Army veterans, who were still waiting for promised bonuses that the national government had no funds to pay. The last straw came in 1786, when the Massachusetts

North Wind Picture Archives/Alamy Stock Photo

WHAT WAS THE RESULT OF SHAYS'S REBELLION?

With Daniel Shays in the lead, a group of farmers who had served in the Continental Army marched to Springfield, Massachusetts, to stop the state court from foreclosing on the veterans' farms. The rebellion illustrated many of the problems of the national government under the Articles of Confederation and is widely thought to have influenced the proceedings of the Constitutional Convention.

legislature enacted a new law requiring the payment of all debts in cash. Frustration and outrage at the new law incited Daniel Shays, a former Continental Army captain, and 1,500 armed, disgruntled farmers to march to the government arsenal in Springfield, Massachusetts. This group obstructed the entrance to the state court located there, thus preventing the court from foreclosing on the mortgages on the protestors' farms.

The Congress of the Confederation immediately authorized the secretary of war to call for a new national militia. Congress made a $530,000 appropriation for this purpose, but every state except Virginia refused to pay. The governor of Massachusetts then tried to raise a state militia, but because of the poor economy, the commonwealth's treasury lacked the necessary funds to support his action. A militia finally was assembled after frantic attempts to collect private financial support. By February 4, 1787, this privately paid force ended what was called **Shays's Rebellion**. The failure of the Congress to muster an army and quell the rebellion provided a dramatic example of the weaknesses inherent in the Articles of Confederation and shocked the nation's leaders into recognizing the new national government's inadequacies. It finally prompted several states to join together and call for a convention in Philadelphia in 1787.

Shays's Rebellion

A rebellion in which an army of 1,500 disgruntled and angry farmers led by Daniel Shays marched to Springfield, Massachusetts, and forcibly restrained the state court from foreclosing mortgages on their farms.

HOW WAS THE U.S. CONSTITUTION WRITTEN?

2.3 Outline the issues resolved by compromise during the writing of the Constitution.

On February 21, 1787, in the throes of economic turmoil and with domestic tranquility gone haywire, the Congress called for a Constitutional Convention in Philadelphia for "the sole and express purpose of revising the Articles of Confederation." However, many delegates who gathered in sweltering Philadelphia on May 25, 1787, were prepared to take potentially treasonous steps to preserve the union. On the first day of the convention, delegates from Virginia proposed fifteen resolutions creating an entirely new government (later known as the Virginia Plan). Their enthusiasm, however, was not universal. Many delegates considered these resolutions to be in violation of the convention's charter. They proposed the New Jersey Plan, which took greater steps to preserve the Articles.

These proposals met heated debate on the convention's floor and resulted in several compromises. Although the delegates had established the basic structure of the new government, the work of the Constitutional Convention was not complete. Remaining differences were resolved through a series of compromises, and less than one hundred days after the meeting convened, the Framers had created a new Constitution to submit to the electorate for its approval.

The Characteristics and Motives of the Framers

The fifty-five delegates who attended the Constitutional Convention labored long and hard that summer. Owing to the high stakes of their actions, they conducted all of the convention's work behind closed doors. **George Washington** of Virginia, who commanded the U.S. army during the Revolutionary War, was unanimously elected the convention's presiding officer. He cautioned delegates not to reveal details of the convention even to family members. The delegates agreed to accompany Benjamin Franklin of Pennsylvania to all of his meals. They feared that the normally gregarious gentleman might get carried away with the mood or by liquor and inadvertently let news of the proceedings slip from his tongue.

All of the delegates to the Constitutional Convention were White men; they often are called the "Founding Fathers." This text generally refers to them as the Framers because their work provided the framework for the new government of the United States. The Framers brought with them a vast amount of political, educational, legal, and business experience. Clearly, they were an exceptional lot who ultimately produced a brilliant **constitution**, or document establishing the structure, functions, and limitations of a government.

Debate about the Framers' motives filled the air during the ratification struggle and has provided grist for the mill of historians and political scientists over the years. In his *Economic Interpretation of the Constitution of the United States* (1913), Charles A. Beard argued that the 1780s were a critical period not for the nation as a whole, but rather for business owners who feared that a weak, decentralized government could harm their economic interests.[9] Beard argued that merchants wanted a strong national government to promote industry and trade, to protect private property, and to ensure payment of the public debt—much of which was owed to them. Therefore, according to Beard, the Constitution represents "an economic document drawn with superb skill by men whose property interests were immediately at stake."[10] Many would say the same today (see Figure 2.1).

By the 1950s, Beard's view had fallen into disfavor when other historians were unable to find direct links between wealth and the Framers' motives for establishing the Constitution. Others faulted Beard's failure to consider the impact of religion and individual views about government.[11] In the 1960s, however, another group of historians began to argue that social and economic factors were, in fact, important motives for supporting the Constitution. In 1969, Gordon S. Wood's *The Creation of the American Republic* resurrected this debate. Wood deemphasized economics to argue that major social divisions explained different groups' support for (or opposition to) the new Constitution. He concluded that the Framers were representative of a class that favored order and stability over some of the more radical ideas that had inspired the American Revolutionary War and the break with Britain.[12] With the founding of the Tea Party as a caucus in Congress in 2010, a faction in that group argued that it was critical to go back to the Framers' intentions as one of limited government and to remove any powers from the national government that are not specifically discussed in the Constitution.

George Washington

Widely considered the "Father of the Nation," he was the commander of the revolutionary armies; served as the presiding officer of the Constitutional Convention and as the United States' first president from 1789 to 1797.

constitution

A document establishing the structure, functions, and limitations of a government.

FIGURE 2.1   WHO WERE THE FRAMERS?

The Framers of the Constitution spent a summer in Philadelphia in nearly complete secrecy, drafting the nation's supreme code of laws. But who were these men? They came from varied jobs, cultures, and viewpoints; most men were enslavers, many were lawyers, and others had little political experience. These differences influenced many of the compromises seen in the final version of the Constitution.

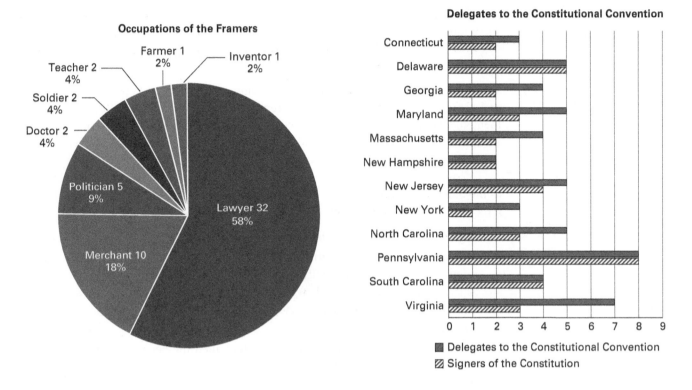

The Virginia and New Jersey Plans

The less populous states were concerned with being lost in any new system of government in which states were not treated as equals regardless of population. It is not surprising, therefore, that a large state and then a small one, Virginia and New Jersey, respectively, weighed in with ideas about how the new government should operate.

The **Virginia Plan** called for a national system based heavily on the European nation-state model, wherein the national government derives its powers from the people and not from the member states.

Its key features included the following:

- Creation of a powerful central government with three branches—legislative, executive, and judicial
- A two-house legislature with one house elected directly by the people, the other chosen from among persons nominated by the state legislatures
- A legislature with the power to select the executive and the judiciary
- An executive selected by the legislature to execute the laws passed by Congress

In general, delegates from smaller states such as New Jersey and Connecticut were comfortable with the arrangements under the Articles of Confederation. These states offered another model of government, the **New Jersey Plan**. Its key features included the following:

- Strengthening the Articles, not replacing them
- Creating a one-house legislature with one vote for each state and with representatives chosen by state legislatures
- Giving Congress the power to raise revenue from duties on imports and from postal service fees

Virginia Plan

A proposed framework for the Constitution favoring large states. It called for a bicameral legislature, which would appoint executive and judicial officers.

New Jersey Plan

A framework for the Constitution proposed by a group of small states; it called for a one-house legislature with one vote for each state, a Congress with the ability to raise revenue, and a Supreme Court appointed for life.

- Creating an executive branch of multiple persons elected by Congress
- Creating a national Supreme Court with members appointed for life by the executive

Constitutional Compromises

The Virginia and New Jersey Plans necessitated serious compromise. Three of these were particularly important. Below, we discuss the Great Compromise, which concerned the form of the new government; the issue of slavery; and the Three-Fifths Compromise, which dealt with representation.

THE GREAT COMPROMISE   The most serious disagreement between the Virginia and New Jersey Plans concerned state representation in Congress. When a deadlock loomed, Connecticut offered its own compromise. Representation in the lower house would be determined by population, and each state would have an equal vote in the upper house. Again, a stalemate occurred.

A committee to work out an agreement soon reported back what became known as the **Great Compromise**. Taking ideas from both the Virginia and New Jersey Plans, it recommended the following:

- A two-house, or bicameral, legislature.
- In one house of the legislature (later called the House of Representatives), representatives would number fifty-six—no more than one representative for every 30,000 inhabitants. The people would directly elect those representatives.
- That house would have the power to originate all bills for raising and spending money.
- In the second house of the legislature (later called the Senate), each state would have an equal vote, and state legislatures would select the representatives.
- In dividing power between the national and state governments, national power would be supreme.[13]

The Great Compromise ultimately met with the approval of all states in attendance. The smaller states were pleased because they received equal representation in the Senate; the larger states were satisfied with the proportional representation in the House of Representatives. The small states then would dominate the Senate, while the large states would control the House. But because both houses had to pass any legislation, neither body could dominate the other.

THE ISSUE OF SLAVERY   Slavery, which formed the basis of much of the southern states' cotton economy, was one of the thorniest issues for the Framers to tackle. To reach an agreement on the Constitution, the Framers had to craft a compromise that balanced southern commercial interests with comparable northern concerns about the evils of slavery. Eventually, the Framers agreed that Northerners would support continuation of trading enslaved people for twenty more years, as well as a twenty-year ban on taxing exports to protect the cotton trade, while Southerners consented to a provision requiring only a majority vote on navigation laws. The Framers also gave the national government the authority to regulate foreign commerce and agreed that the Senate would have the power to ratify treaties by a two-thirds majority, which assuaged the fears of southern states, which made up more than one-third of the nation.

THE THREE-FIFTHS COMPROMISE   One major conflict had yet to be resolved: how to determine state population with regard to representation in the House of Representatives. Enslaved people could not vote, but the southern states wanted them included in the determination of population numbers. After considerable dissension, the delegates decided that population for purposes of representation and the apportionment of direct taxes would be calculated by adding the "whole Number of Free Persons" to "three-fifths of all other Persons." "All other Persons" was the delegates' euphemistic way of referring to enslaved people. Known as the **Three-Fifths Compromise**, this highly

Great Compromise

The final decision of the Constitutional Convention to create a two-house legislature, with the lower house elected by the people and powers divided between the two houses; also made national law supreme.

Three-Fifths Compromise

Agreement reached at the Constitutional Convention stipulating that three-fifths of the total number of enslaved people in each state was to be counted for purposes of determining population for representation in the U.S. House of Representatives.

Artokoloro/Alamy Stock Photo

WHY WAS SLAVERY SUCH AN IMPORTANT ISSUE AT THE CONSTITUTIONAL CONVENTION?

WHY WAS SLAVERY SUCH AN IMPORTANT ISSUE AT THE CONSTITUTIONAL CONVENTION?

Even at the time of the writing of the Constitution, many Americans struggled to reconcile moral, legal, and economic views on the institution of slavery. Some of the Framers, including Alexander Hamilton, Benjamin Franklin, and John Jay, supported abolition. Others, especially those living in the South, objected to efforts to abolish slavery. Although the Constitution ultimately banned the importation of enslaved people in 1808, the institution was allowed to continue well into the nineteenth century. Here, the horrors of enslaved people being sold at auction in Virginia during the 1800s is depicted. In many cases, enslaved families were separated.

political deal ensured that the South would hold 47 percent of the House—enough to prevent attacks on slavery but not so much as to foster the spread of slavery northward. It also enshrined slavery into the Constitution.

Unfinished Business: Selection of the President

The Framers next turned to fashioning an executive branch. While they agreed on the idea of a one-person executive, they could not settle on the length of the term of office or on the procedure for choosing the chief executive. With Shays's Rebellion still fresh in their minds, the delegates feared putting too much power, including selection of a president, into the hands of the lower classes. At the same time, representatives from the smaller states feared that selection of the chief executive by the legislature would put additional power into the hands of the large states.

Amid these fears, the Committee on Unfinished Portions conducted its sole task: ironing out problems and disagreements concerning the office of chief executive. The committee recommended that the presidential term of office be fixed at four years instead of seven, as had been proposed earlier. The committee also made it possible for a president to serve more than one term.

In addition, the Framers created the **Electoral College** as a mechanism for selecting the chief executive of the new nation. The Electoral College system gave individual states a key role because each state would choose electors equal to the number of representatives it had in the House and Senate. Those electors, in turn, would vote for the presidential candidate receiving the greatest number of popular votes in their states. This step was a vague compromise that removed election of the president and vice president from both the Congress and the people and placed it in the hands of electors whose method of selection would be left to the states. As **Alexander Hamilton** noted in *Federalist No. 68*, the Framers fashioned the Electoral College to avoid the "tumult and disorder" they feared could result if the masses were allowed to vote directly for president.

In drafting the new Constitution, the Framers also took care to provide for removal of the chief executive. The House of Representatives assumed the sole responsibility of investigating and charging a president or vice president with "Treason, Bribery, or other high Crimes and Misdemeanors." A majority vote then would result in issuing articles of impeachment against the president or vice president. In turn, the Senate took on the sole responsibility of trying the president or vice president on the charges

Electoral College

The system established by the Constitution through which the president is chosen by electors from each state, which has as many electoral votes as it has members of Congress.

Alexander Hamilton

A key Framer who envisioned a powerful central government, co-authored *The Federalist Papers*, and served as the first secretary of the treasury. He was killed by Vice President Aaron Burr in a duel.

issued by the House. To convict and remove the president or vice president from office required a two-thirds vote of the Senate. The chief justice of the United States was to preside over the Senate proceedings in place of the vice president (that body's constitutional leader) to prevent any conflict of interest on the vice president's part.

WHAT ARE THE KEY FEATURES OF THE U.S. CONSTITUTION?

2.4 Describe the framework for government expressed in the Constitution.

The U.S. Constitution's opening line, "We the People," ended, at least for the time being, the question of the source of the government's power: it came directly from the people. The Constitution then explained the need for the new outline of government; "in Order to form a more perfect Union" indirectly acknowledged the weaknesses of the Articles of Confederation in governing a growing nation. Next, the optimistic goals of the Framers for the new nation were set out—to "establish Justice, insure domestic Tranquility, provide for the common defence, promote the general Welfare, and secure the Blessings of Liberty to ourselves and our Posterity"—followed by the formal creation of a new government: "do ordain and establish this Constitution for the United States of America."

On September 17, 1787, the delegates approved the Constitution. While the completed document did not satisfy all delegates, of the fifty-five delegates who attended some portion of the meetings, thirty-nine ultimately signed it. The sentiments uttered by Benjamin Franklin probably well reflected those of many others: "Thus, I consent, Sir, to this Constitution because I expect no better, and because I am not sure that it is not the best."[14]

The Basic Principles of the Constitution

Montesquieu

The French baron and political theorist who first articulated the concept of separation of powers with checks and balances.

The structure of the proposed new national government owed much to the writings of the French philosopher **Montesquieu** (1689–1755), who advocated distinct functions for each branch of government, called *separation of powers*, with a system of *checks and balances* between each branch. Another French philosopher, Jean-Jacques Rousseau, added the notion that the power of the government should come from the people. The Constitution's concern with the distribution of power between states and the national government also reveals the heavy influence of political philosophers as well as the colonists' experience under the Articles of Confederation.[15]

FEDERALISM   The question before and during the convention concerned how much power states would give up to the national government. Given the nation's experiences under the Articles of Confederation, the Framers believed that a strong national government was necessary for the new nation's survival. However, they were reluctant to create a powerful government after the model of Great Britain, the country from which they had just won their independence. The colonists did not even consider Great Britain's unitary system. Instead, they fashioned a way, now known as a federal system, to divide the power of government between a strong national government and the individual states, with national power being supreme. **Federalism** was based on the principle that the federal, or national, government derived its power from the citizens, not the states, as the national government had done under the Articles of Confederation.

federalism

The distribution of constitutional authority between state governments and the national government, with different powers and functions exercised by both.

Opponents of this system feared that a strong national government would infringe on their liberty. But, supporters of a federal system argued that a strong national government with distinct state governments could, if properly directed by constitutional arrangements, actually be a source of expanded liberties and national unity. The Framers viewed the division of governmental authority between the national government and the states as a means of checking power with power, and providing the people with double security against governmental tyranny. Later, the passage of the Tenth Amendment, which stated that powers not given to the national government were reserved to the states or the people, further clarified the federal structure.

SEPARATION OF POWERS   **Separation of powers** is simply a way of parceling out power among the three branches of government. Its three key features are:

1. Three distinct branches of government: the legislative, the executive, and the judicial.
2. Three separately staffed branches of government to exercise these functions.
3. Constitutional equality and independence of each branch.

As illustrated in Figure 2.2, the Framers carefully created a system in which the functions of making, enforcing, and interpreting laws were assigned to independent branches of government. Only the legislature has the authority to make laws; the chief executive enforces laws; and the judiciary interprets them. Moreover, initially, members of the House of Representatives, members of the Senate, the president, and members of the federal courts were selected by, and therefore responsible to, different constituencies.

The Framers could not have foreseen the intermingling of governmental functions that has since evolved. In Article I of the Constitution, the legislative power is vested in Congress. But the president also has a role in the legislative process; for a bill to become law, he must sign the legislation. If he disagrees with the content of a bill, he may veto the legislation, although a two-thirds vote in Congress can override his veto. He may also issue legally binding executive orders. Judicial interpretation also helps to clarify the language or implementation of legislation enacted through this process.

So, instead of a pure system of separation of powers, a symbiotic, or interdependent, relationship among the three branches of government has existed from the beginning. Or, as one scholar has explained, there are "separated institutions sharing powers."[16] While Congress still is entrusted with making the laws, the president, as a single person who can easily capture the attention of the media and of the electorate, retains tremendous power in setting the agenda and proposing legislation. And although the Supreme Court's major function is to interpret the Constitution,

separation of powers
A way of dividing the power of government among the legislative, executive, and judicial branches, each staffed separately, with equality and independence of each branch ensured by the Constitution.

FIGURE 2.2   WHAT IS THE SEPARATION OF POWERS, AND HOW DO CHECKS AND BALANCES WORK UNDER THE U.S. CONSTITUTION?

Drawing inspiration from Montesquieu, the Framers crafted a political system of checks and balances and separation of powers. Each of the three branches—executive, legislative, and judicial—has distinct powers, and each branch has powers that intersect with the powers of each of the other branches. This system prevents any one branch from becoming too powerful.

Legislative Checks on the Executive
Impeach the president
Reject legislation or funding the president wants
Refuse to confirm nominees or approve treaties*
Override the president's veto by a two-thirds vote

Executive Checks on the Legislative
Veto legislation
Call Congress into special session
Implement (or fail to implement) laws passed by Congress

Judicial Checks on the Legislative
Rule federal and state laws unconstitutional

Judicial Checks on the Executive
Declare executive branch actions unconstitutional
Chief justice presides over impeachment trials

Legislative Checks on the Judicial
Change the number and jurisdiction of federal courts
Impeach and remove federal judges
Propose constitutional amendments to override judicial decisions

Executive Checks on the Judicial
Appoint federal judges
Refuse to implement decisions

Rob Hill/Fotolia

Vacclav/Fotolia

trekandphoto/Fotolia

* This power belongs to the Senate only.

HOW DOES CHECKS AND BALANCES WORK?

At an angry White House meeting, it appeared that President Trump, according to some sources, experienced a "meltdown" after the House passed a bipartisan condemnation of his order to remove U.S. soldiers from Syria. At this October 16, 2019 meeting, the president called the Speaker of the House "a third rate politician" and she and other Democratic leaders then exited the White House immediately after Pelosi rose to point out to the president that the principle of checks and balances required congressional approval involving massive troop movements.

checks and balances

A constitutionally mandated structure that gives each of the three branches of government some degree of oversight and control over the actions of the others.

Article I

Vests all legislative powers in the Congress and establishes a bicameral legislature, consisting of the Senate and the House of Representatives; it also sets out the qualifications for holding office in each house, the terms of office, the methods of selection of representatives and senators, and the system of apportionment among the states to determine membership in the House of Representatives. Its numbering as Article I and the extensive attention to its powers make it clear that the Congress was to be the most important political actor in the new government.

enumerated powers

The powers of the national government specifically granted to Congress in Article I, section 8, of the Constitution.

necessary and proper clause

The final paragraph of Article I, section 8, of the Constitution, which gives Congress the authority to pass all laws "necessary and proper" to carry out the enumerated powers specified in the Constitution; also called the "elastic clause."

its decisions affecting criminal procedure, reproductive rights, health care, and other issues have led many critics to charge that it has surpassed its constitutional authority and has become, in effect, a law-making body.

CHECKS AND BALANCES The separation of powers among the three branches of the national government is not complete. The powers of each branch (as well as the powers of the two houses of the national legislature and the powers between the states and the national government) are also used to check those of the other two governmental branches. The power of each branch of government is checked, or limited, and balanced because the legislative, executive, and judicial branches share some authority, and no branch has exclusive domain over any single activity. The creation of this system, **checks and balances**, allowed the Framers to minimize the threat of tyranny from any one branch. Thus, for almost every power granted to one branch, the Framers established an equal control in the other two branches.

The Structure of the Constitution

The document finally signed by the Framers condensed numerous resolutions into a preamble and seven separate articles remedying many of the deficiencies within the Articles of Confederation (see Table 2.1). The first three articles established the three branches of government, defined their internal operations, and clarified their relationships with one another. The Framers technically considered all branches of government equal, yet some initially appeared more powerful than others. The order of the articles, as well as the detail contained in the first three, reflect the Framers' concern that these branches of government might abuse their powers. The four remaining articles define the relationships between the states, declare national law to be supreme, and set out methods of amending and ratifying the Constitution.

ARTICLE I: THE LEGISLATIVE BRANCH **Article I** vests all legislative powers in the Congress and establishes a bicameral legislature, consisting of the Senate and the House of Representatives. It also sets out the qualifications for holding office in each house, the terms of office, the methods of selection of representatives and senators, and the system of apportionment among the states to determine membership in the House of Representatives.

One of the most important sections of Article I is section 8. It carefully lists those powers the Framers wished the new Congress to possess. These specified, or **enumerated powers**, contain many key provisions that had been denied to the

TABLE 2.1 HOW DO THE ARTICLES OF CONFEDERATION AND THE U.S. CONSTITUTION COMPARE?

	Articles of Confederation	Constitution
Formal name of the nation	The United States of America	Not specified, but referred to in the Preamble as "the United States of America"
Legislature	Unicameral, called Congress	Bicameral, called Congress, divided into the House of Representatives and the Senate
Members of Congress	A delegation between two and seven members per state	Two senators per state, representatives apportioned according to population of each state
Voting in Congress	One vote per state delegation	One vote per representative or senator
Appointment of members	All appointed by state legislatures in the manner each legislature directed	Representatives elected by popular vote; senators appointed by state legislatures (which was switched to direct election by the Seventeenth Amendment of 1913)
Term of legislative office	One year	Two years for representatives; six years for senators
Term limit for legislative office	No more than three years in any six years	None
When Congress is not in session	A Committee of States had the full powers of Congress	The president of the United States can call on Congress to assemble
Chair of legislature	President of Congress	Speaker of the House of Representatives; vice president is president of the Senate
Executive	None; the "president" was simply presiding officer of Congress	President
National judiciary	Maritime judiciary established—other courts left to states	Supreme Court established as well as other federal courts Congress deems necessary
Adjudicator of disputes between states	Congress	Supreme Court
New states	Admitted upon agreement of nine states (special exemption provided for Canada)	Admitted upon agreement of majority of Congress
Amendment	When agreed upon by all states	When agreed upon by two-thirds of Congress and three-fourths of the states
Navy	Congress authorized to build a navy; states authorized to equip warships to counter piracy	Congress authorized to build a navy; states not allowed to keep ships of war
Army	Congress to decide on size of force and to requisition troops from each state according to population	Congress authorized to raise and support armies
Power to coin money	United States and the states	United States only
Taxes	Apportioned by Congress, collected by the states	Levied and collected by Congress
Ratification	Unanimous consent required	Consent of nine states required

Continental Congress under the Articles of Confederation. A final, general clause authorizing Congress to "make all Laws which shall be necessary and proper for carrying into Execution the foregoing Powers" completes Article I. The **necessary and proper clause** is the basis for the **implied powers** that Congress uses to execute its other powers.

ARTICLE II: THE EXECUTIVE BRANCH **Article II** vests the executive power, that is, the authority to execute the laws of the nation, in a president of the United States. Section 1 sets the president's term of office at four years and explains the Electoral College. It also states the qualifications for office and describes a mechanism to replace the president in case of death, disability, or removal from office. Article II also limits the presidency to natural-born citizens. The powers and duties of the president are set out in section 3. Among the most important of these are the president's role as commander in chief of the armed forces, the authority to make treaties with the consent of the Senate, and the authority to "appoint Ambassadors, other public Ministers and Consuls, the Judges of the Supreme Court, and all other Officers of the United States." From these powers presidents have claimed **inherent powers**, allowing them to take broad-reaching authority not specified in the Constitution, from using the National Guard to integrate state schools over the deviance of state governors, to sending the National Guard to keep peace in cities where President Donald J. Trump determined that racial protests were beyond the control of Democratic mayors or governors.

implied powers

The powers of the national government derived from the enumerated powers and the necessary and proper clause.

Article II

Vests the executive power, that is, the authority to execute the laws of the nation, in a president of the United States; section 1 sets the president's term of office at four years, explains the Electoral College, states the qualifications for office, and describes a mechanism to replace the president in case of death, disability, or removal from office.

inherent powers

Powers that belong to the president because they can be inferred from the Constitution.

WHAT POWER DOES THE PRESIDENT HAVE REGARDING LAWS?

Article I of the Constitution obliges the president of the United States to approve or reject bills passed by both the House of Representative and the Senate. Here, President Biden signs the $1.9 trillion COVID relief bill into law.

Pool/Getty Images

Article III

Establishes a Supreme Court and defines its jurisdiction.

Article IV

Mandates that states honor the laws and judicial proceedings of other states. Article IV also includes the mechanisms for admitting new states to the union. *See also* "full faith and credit clause."

full faith and credit clause

Section of Article IV of the Constitution that ensures judicial decrees and contracts made in one state will be binding and enforceable in any other state.

Article V

Specifies how amendments can be added to the Constitution.

Article VI

Contains the supremacy clause, which asserts the basic primacy of the Constitution and national law over state laws and constitutions. *See also* "supremacy clause."

supremacy clause

Portion of Article VI of the Constitution mandating that national law is supreme over (that is, supersedes) all other laws passed by the states or by any other subdivision of government.

Article VII

Sets forth the procedures for the newly minted U.S. Constitution to be ratified by the states.

ARTICLE III: THE JUDICIAL BRANCH   **Article III** establishes a Supreme Court and defines its jurisdiction. During the Philadelphia meeting, the smaller states feared that a strong unelected judiciary would trample on their liberties. Thus, the Framers permitted Congress to establish lower national courts but did not require them. State courts and the national court system would exist side by side with distinct areas of authority. Federal courts had authority to decide cases arising under federal law and the U.S. Constitution. The U.S. Supreme Court also assumed the power to settle disputes between states or between a state and the national government. Ultimately, it was up to the Supreme Court to determine what the provisions of the Constitution actually meant.

ARTICLES IV THROUGH VII   The remainder of the articles in the Constitution attempted to anticipate problems that might occur in the operation of the new national government as well as its relation with the states. **Article IV** begins with what is called the **full faith and credit clause**, which mandates that states honor the laws and judicial proceedings of other states. Article IV also includes the mechanisms for admitting new states to the union.

Article V specifies how amendments can be added to the Constitution. The Bill of Rights, which added ten amendments to the Constitution in 1791, was one of the first items of business when the First Congress met in 1789.

Article VI contains the supremacy clause, which asserts the basic primacy of the Constitution and national law over state laws and constitutions. The **supremacy clause** provides that the "Constitution, and the laws of the United States" as well as all treaties are to be the supreme law of the land. Without the supremacy clause and the federal courts' ability to invoke it, the national government would have little actual enforceable power; thus, many commentators call the supremacy clause the linchpin of the entire federal system.

Mindful of the potential problems that could occur if church and state were too enmeshed, the Framers specified in Article VI that no religious test shall be required for holding any office. This mandate is strengthened by the separation of church and state guarantee that became part of the Constitution when the First Amendment was ratified.

Article VII, the seventh and final article of the Constitution, concerns the procedures for ratifying the new Constitution: nine of the thirteen states would have to agree to, or ratify, its new provisions before it would become the supreme law of the land.

WHAT WAS THE PROCESS FOR RATIFYING THE U.S. CONSTITUTION?

2.5 Outline the arguments for and against ratification of the Constitution.

While delegates to the Constitutional Convention labored in Philadelphia, the Congress of the Confederation continued to govern the former colonies under the Articles of Confederation. The day after the delegates signed the Constitution, the secretary of the Convention left for New York City, then the nation's capital, to deliver the official copy of the document to the Congress. He also took with him a resolution of the delegates calling upon each of the states to vote on the new Constitution. Anticipating resistance from representatives in the state legislatures, however, the Framers required the states to call special ratifying conventions to consider the proposed Constitution.

The Congress of the Confederation immediately accepted the work of the convention and forwarded the proposed Constitution to the states for their votes. It was by no means certain, however, that the states would adopt the new Constitution. From the fall of 1787 to the summer of 1788, debate over the proposed Constitution raged around the nation. State politicians understandably feared a strong central government. Farmers and other working-class people feared a distant national government. And those who had accrued substantial debts during the economic chaos following the Revolutionary War feared that a new government with a new financial policy would plunge them into even greater debt. The public in general was very leery of taxes—these were the same people who had revolted against the king's taxes. At the heart of many of their concerns lay an underlying apprehension of the massive changes that a new system would create. Favoring the Constitution were wealthy merchants, lawyers, bankers, and those who believed that the new nation could not continue to exist under the Articles of Confederation.

Federalists Versus Anti-Federalists

During the debate over whether to ratify the Constitution, those who favored the new strong national government chose to call themselves **Federalists**. They were well aware that many people still generally opposed the notion of a strong national government. They did not want to risk being labeled nationalists, so they tried to get the upper hand in the debate by nicknaming their opponents **Anti-Federalists**. As noted in Table 2.2, Anti-Federalists argued that they simply wanted to protect state governments from the tyranny of a too powerful national government.[17]

Federalists and Anti-Federalists participated in the mass meetings held in state legislatures to discuss the pros and cons of the new plan. Tempers ran high at these meetings, and fervent debates were discussed at town hall meetings and published in

Federalists
Those who favored a stronger national government and supported the proposed U.S. Constitution; later became the first U.S. political party.

Anti-Federalists
Those who favored strong state governments and a weak national government; opposed ratification of the U.S. Constitution.

TABLE 2.2 WHAT WERE THE DIFFERENCES BETWEEN FEDERALISTS AND ANTI-FEDERALISTS?

	Federalists	Anti-Federalists
Who were they?	Property owners, landed rich, merchants of Northeast and Mid-Atlantic	Small farmers, shopkeepers, laborers
Political philosophy	Elitist; saw themselves and those of their class as most fit to govern (others were to be governed)	Believed in the decency of "the common man" and in participatory democracy; viewed elites as corrupt; sought greater protection of individual rights
Type of government favored	Powerful central government; two-house legislature; upper house (six-year term) further removed from the people, whom they distrusted	Wanted stronger state governments (closer to the people) at the expense of the powers of the national government; sought smaller electoral districts, frequent elections, referendum and recall, and a large unicameral legislature to provide for greater class and occupational representation
Alliances	Pro-British, anti-French	Anti-British, pro-French

newspapers, which played a powerful role in the adoption process. Just two days after the convention's end, in fact, the *Pennsylvania Packet* printed the entire Constitution. Other major papers quickly followed suit. Soon, opinion pieces on both sides of the adoption issue began to appear around the nation, often written under pseudonyms such as "Caesar," "Brutus," or "Constant Reader," as was the custom of the day.

The Federalist Papers, Publius, and Brutus

One name stood out from all the rest: "Publius" (Latin for "the people"). Between October 1787 and May 1788, eighty-five essays written under that pen name routinely appeared in newspapers in New York, a state where ratification was in doubt. Alexander Hamilton and **James Madison** wrote most of them. Hamilton, a young, fiery New Yorker born in the British West Indies, wrote fifty-one; Madison, a Virginian who later served as the fourth president, authored twenty-six; jointly, they penned another three. **John Jay**, also of New York, and later the first chief justice of the United States, wrote five of the pieces. These eighty-five essays became known as ***The Federalist Papers***.

Today, *The Federalist Papers* are considered masterful explanations of the Framers' intentions as they drafted the new Constitution. At the time, although they were reprinted widely, they were far too theoretical to have much impact on those who would ultimately vote on the proposed Constitution. Dry and scholarly, they lacked the fervor of much of the political rhetoric then in use. *The Federalist Papers* did, however, highlight the reasons for the new government's structure and its benefits. These musings of Madison, Hamilton, and Jay continue to stand as the clearest articulation of the political theories and philosophies that lie at the heart of our Constitution.

Forced on the defensive, Anti-Federalists responded to *The Federalist Papers* with their own series of letters written under the pen names "Brutus" and "Cato," two ancient Romans famous for their intolerance of tyranny. These letters (actually essays, sixteen in total) undertook a line-by-line critique of the Constitution, as did other works. In *Brutus I*, for example, Anti-Federalists harkened back to the Critical Period, questioning the need for a strong national government.

Anti-Federalists argued that a strong central government would render the states powerless.[18] They stressed the strengths granted to the government under the Articles of Confederation and maintained that the Articles, not the proposed Constitution, created a true federal system. Moreover, they believed that the strong national government would tax heavily, that the U.S. Supreme Court would overwhelm the states by invalidating state laws, and that the president eventually would have too much power as commander in chief of a large and powerful army.[19]

In particular, Anti-Federalists feared the power of the national government to run roughshod over the liberties of the people. They proposed that the taxing power of Congress be limited, that the executive be curbed by a council, that the military consist of state militias rather than a national force, and that the jurisdiction of the Supreme Court be limited to prevent it from reviewing and potentially overturning the decisions of state courts. But their most effective argument concerned the absence of a bill of rights in the Constitution. James Madison answered these criticisms in *Federalist Nos. 10* and *51* (see Appendix III). In *Federalist No. 10*, Madison pointed out that the voters would not always succeed in electing "enlightened statesmen" as their representatives. The greatest threat to individual liberties would therefore come from factions within the government that might place narrow interests above broader national interests and the rights of citizens. While recognizing that no form of government could protect the country from unscrupulous politicians, Madison argued that the organization of the new government would minimize the effects of political factions. The great advantage of a federal system, Madison maintained, was that it created the "happy combination" of a national government too large for any single faction to control and several state governments that would be smaller and more responsive to local needs. Moreover, he argued in *Federalist No. 51* that

James Madison

A key Framer often called the "Father of the Constitution" for his role in conceptualizing the federal government. Co-authored *The Federalist Papers*; served as secretary of state; served as the fourth U.S. president from 1809 to 1817.

John Jay

A member of the Founding generation who was the first chief justice of the United States. A diplomat and co-author of *The Federalist Papers*.

The Federalist Papers

A series of eighty-five political essays written by Alexander Hamilton, James Madison, and John Jay in support of ratification of the U.S. Constitution.

the proposed federal government's separation of powers would prohibit any one branch from either dominating the national government or violating the rights of citizens.

Winning Support for the Constitution

Debate continued in the thirteen states as votes were taken from December 1787 to June 1788, in accordance with the ratifying process laid out in Article VII of the proposed Constitution. Three states acted quickly to ratify the new Constitution. Two small states, Delaware and New Jersey, voted to ratify before the large states could rethink the notion of equal representation of the states in the Senate. Pennsylvania, where Federalists were well organized, was also one of the first three states to ratify. Massachusetts assented to the new government but tempered its support by calling for an immediate addition of amendments, including one protecting personal rights. New Hampshire became the crucial ninth state to ratify on June 21, 1788. This action completed the ratification process outlined in Article VII of the Constitution and marked the beginning of a new nation. But New York and Virginia, which at that time accounted for more than 40 percent of the new nation's population, had not yet ratified the Constitution. Thus, the practical future of the new nation remained in doubt.

Hamilton in New York and Madison in Virginia worked feverishly to convince delegates to their state conventions to vote for the new government. In New York, sentiment against the Constitution ran high. In Albany, fighting broke out over ratification and resulted in injuries and death. When news of Virginia's acceptance of the Constitution reached the New York convention, Hamilton was able to convince a majority of those present to follow suit by a margin of three votes. Both states also recommended the addition of a series of structural amendments and a bill of rights.

North Carolina and Rhode Island continued to hold out against ratification. Both had recently printed new currencies and feared that values would plummet in a federal system that authorized the Congress to coin money. On August 2, 1788, North Carolina became the first state to reject the Constitution on the grounds that no Anti-Federalist amendments were included. Soon after, in September 1789, owing much to Anti-Federalist pressure for additional protections from the national government, the first Congress submitted the Bill of Rights to the states for their ratification. North Carolina then ratified the Constitution by a vote of 194–77. Rhode Island, the only state that had not sent representatives to Philadelphia, remained out of the new nation until 1790. Finally, under threats from its largest cities to secede from the state, the legislature called a convention that ratified the Constitution by only two votes (34–32)—one year after George Washington became the first president of the United States.

The Bill of Rights

Once the Constitution was ratified, elections took place. When Congress convened, it immediately sent a set of amendments to the states for ratification. An amendment authorizing the enlargement of the House of Representatives and another to prevent members of the House from raising their own salaries failed to garner favorable votes in the necessary three-fourths of the states. The remaining ten amendments, known as the **Bill of Rights**, were ratified by 1791 in accordance with the procedures set out in the Constitution. Sought by Anti-Federalists as a protection for individual liberties, they offered numerous specific limitations on the national government's ability to interfere with a wide variety of personal liberties, some of which many state constitutions had already guaranteed. These include freedom of expression, speech, press, religion, and assembly, guaranteed by the First Amendment. The Bill of Rights also contains numerous safeguards for those accused of crimes. The Ninth Amendment notes that these enumerated rights are not inclusive, meaning they are not the only rights to be enjoyed by the people, and the Tenth Amendment states that powers not given to the national government are reserved by the states or the people.

Bill of Rights
The first ten amendments to the U.S. Constitution, which largely guarantee specific rights and liberties.

POLTICAL REFORM AND REALITIES: HOW DOES THE AMENDMENT PROCESS WORK?

2.6 Describe the processes by which the Constitution can be amended.

The Framers did not want to fashion a government subject to the whims of the people. Therefore, they made the formal amendment process a slow one to guard against impulsive amendment of the Constitution. In keeping with this intent, only seventeen amendments have been added since the Bill of Rights were ratified in 1791 (see Table 2.3). However, informal amendments, prompted by judicial interpretation, cultural and social change, and technological change, have had a tremendous impact on the Constitution.

TABLE 2.3 WHAT ARE THE AMENDMENTS TO THE U.S. CONSTITUTION?

Constitutional amendments have mostly been enacted during four distinct historical periods, often separated by decades and associated with major upheavals in American history. Amendments also mostly deal with only four major themes: 1) federalism and states' rights; 2) the role and powers of Congress or the presidency; 3) civil liberties or civil rights; or 4) voting and elections. (Only two amendments have ever directly created public policy, one by establishing Prohibition and the other repealing it.) The amendments have also had widely varying levels of historical significance.

Number and Year	Historical Era	Main Topic of Amendment	Main Area of Impact
1 (1791)	**Founding Era (1791–1804)**	Free expression and religion	Civil liberties
2 (1791)		Right to bear arms	Civil liberties
3 (1791)		Quartering of troops	Civil liberties
4 (1791)		Unreasonable search and seizure	Civil liberties
5 (1791)		Rights of the accused	Civil liberties
6 (1791)		Rights of the accused	Civil liberties
7 (1791)		Rights of the accused	Civil liberties
8 (1791)		Cruel and unusual punishment	Civil liberties
9 (1791)		Other rights of the people	Civil liberties
10 (1791)		Rights of the states or the people	Federalism
11 (1795)		Immunity of states to lawsuits	Federalism
12 (1804)		Electoral College	Voting and elections
13 (1865)	**Civil War Era (1861–1870)**	Ending slavery	Civil rights
14 (1868)		Equal protection of the law	Civil rights
15 (1870)		Voting on the basis of race	Voting and elections
16 (1913)	**Progressive Era (1890–1933)**	Federal income tax	Federalism
17 (1913)		Direct election of senators	Voting and elections
18 (1919)		Prohibition on sale of alcohol	Public policy
19 (1920)		Voting on the basis of sex	Voting and elections
20 (1933)	**Corrections (1933–1951)**	Start of presidential and congressional terms	Public policy
21 (1933)		Repeal of prohibition	Congress and presidency
22 (1951)		Two-term limit for presidents	Voting and elections
23 (1961)	**Civil Rights Era (1954–1971)**	Electoral votes for Washington, DC	Voting and elections
24 (1964)		Ban on poll taxes	Voting and elections
25 (1967)		VP as acting president (also outlier)	Congress and presidency
26 (1971)		Voting for 18-year-olds	Voting and elections
27 (1992)	***Outlier (1992)***	Congressional pay raises	Congress and presidency

TABLE 2.4 WHAT ARE THE CONSTITUTIONAL AND POLITICAL DIMENSIONS OF ENACTING A CONSTITUTIONAL AMENDMENT?

Although Article V provides a number of options for amending the Constitution, one main route is generally used. The constitutional requirements and political realities of this usual route are presented here.

How are the parts of government involved?	What constitutional support is required?	What are the political implications?
House	Proposal by vote of ⅔ of all members	This is a supermajority of 288 out of 435 members, requiring at least some bipartisan support.
Senate	Proposal by a vote of ⅔ of all members	This is a supermajority of 67 out of 100 members, requiring at least some bipartisan support.
States	Ratification by a vote of ¾ of the state legislatures	This is a supermajority of at least 38 out of 50 states. A simple majority must vote for ratification in each of the state's legislative chambers. This requires at least some bipartisan support across multiple parts of the country.
Presidents and governors	Presidents and governors play no formal institutional role.	Presidents and governors may offer their political support or opposition. They may also influence how the provisions of an amendment are later applied in practice.
Federal and state courts	The courts may not review or strike down an amendment.	In any future rulings, all courts are bound by the provisions of an amendment. They may be called on to interpret an amendment's legal meaning and impact.

Formal Methods of Amending the Constitution

Article V of the Constitution creates a two-stage amendment process: proposal and ratification. The Constitution specifies two ways to accomplish each stage. As explained in Table 2.4, amendments to the Constitution can be proposed by (1) a vote of two-thirds of the members in both houses of Congress; or (2) a vote of two-thirds of the state legislatures specifically requesting Congress to call a national convention to propose amendments. The second method has never been used.

The ratification process is fairly straightforward. When Congress votes to propose an amendment, the Constitution specifies that the ratification process must occur in one of two ways: (1) a favorable vote in three-fourths of the state legislatures; or (2) a favorable vote in specially called ratifying conventions in three-fourths of the states. Since ratification of the Constitution, however, only one ratifying convention has been called.

The intensity of efforts to amend the Constitution has varied considerably, depending on the nature of the change proposed. Whereas the Twenty-First Amendment took only ten months to ratify, the Equal Rights Amendment (ERA) was

WHAT IS THE STATUS OF THE ERA?

On February 13, 2020, members of the House, under the leadership of Speaker Nancy Pelosi, reintroduced the ERA without a deadline for the ratification. Here, she is surrounded by members of Congress, including bill sponsor Carolyn Maloney (D-NY) (far left).

dpa picture alliance/Alamy Stock Photo

introduced in every session of Congress from 1923 until 1972, when Congress finally voted favorably for it. Even then, years of lobbying by women's groups were insufficient to garner necessary state support. By 1982, the congressionally mandated date for ratification, only thirty-five states—three short of the number required—had voted favorably on the amendment.[20] Yet, it has been reintroduced in every session of Congress since. In the wake of the massive Women's March the day after Trump's inauguration, many resolved to make a new push for an ERA. Their tactics were two-fold. First, the House voted to remove the 1982 deadline for its ratification when it was three states short of ratification. In 2017, Nebraska ratified the amendment and Illinois followed suit in 2018. In early 2020, Virginia became the thirty-eighth state to ratify the amendment, technically becoming the last state necessary to do so.

At President Donald J. Trump's State of the Union address in 2020, Democratic women wore white suits and dresses while sporting green ERA pins, symbolic of woman suffrage and its 100th Anniversary and to press their support for the ERA. (Vice President Kamala Harris wore white on that occasion and at her first appearance as vice-president elect.)

With Democrats in the majority in the Senate, the extension or the second tactic is possible, one urged by Justice Ruth Bader Ginsburg, who said she "would like to see a new beginning."[21] The Trump Justice Department released an opinion that states ratifying the amendment were too late, and Alabama, Louisiana, South Dakota, sued in federal court to block the amendment. The next course of action is to try to repeat the whole ratification process without a deadline for approval.

The failed battles for the ERA as well as other amendments, including one to prohibit child labor and another to grant statehood to the District of Columbia, underscore how difficult it is to amend the Constitution. Thus, unlike the constitutions of individual states or many other nations, the U.S. Constitution rarely has been amended.

Informal Methods of Amending the Constitution

The formal amendment process is not the only way the Constitution has been altered over time. Judicial interpretation, cultural and social change, and the growth of technology also have had a major impact on how the Constitution has evolved.

JUDICIAL INTERPRETATION   As early as 1803, the Supreme Court declared in *Marbury* v. *Madison* that federal courts had the power to nullify acts of the nation's government when the courts found such acts to conflict with the Constitution.[22] Over the years, this check on the other branches of government and on the states has increased the authority of the Court and significantly altered the meaning of various provisions of the Constitution. This fact prompted President Woodrow Wilson to call the Supreme Court "a constitutional convention in continuous session," a role demonstrated by recent decisions in civil liberties, civil rights, and economic regulation.

Today, some analysts argue that the original intent of the Framers—as evidenced in *The Federalist Papers*, as well as in private notes taken by James Madison at the Constitutional Convention—should govern judicial interpretation of the Constitution.[23] Others argue that the Framers knew a changing society needed an elastic, flexible document that could adapt to the ages.[24] In all likelihood, the vagueness of the document was purposeful. Those in attendance in Philadelphia recognized that they could not agree on everything and that it was wiser to leave interpretation to future generations. This view, however, has turned nominations to the federal courts into political footballs. The Republican-controlled Senate, for example, refused to even hold hearings on Barack Obama's nominee to the Supreme Court of the United States, allowing the seat to lie vacant for more than a year. After Donald J. Trump's inauguration, he quickly nominated conservative Judge Neil Gorsuch to the Court and then Judge Brett Kavanaugh, another avowed conservative. This appeared to give the conservatives on the Court a majority. Then, as the 2020 election began, the death of liberal Justice Ruth Bader Ginsburg allowed the president to nominate Judge Amy Coney Barrett to

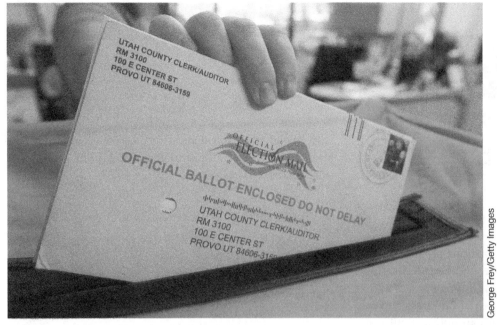

CAN VOTING BE HACKED?
According to researchers, the diverse types of voting—electronic and paper—continue to be vulnerable to hacking as well as simply not working, causing long lines at the polls. During the 2020 presidential election, nearly half of voters submitted absentee or mail-in ballots.

the High Court before Justice Ginsburg was even buried. Hearings were held quickly, and Barrett's nomination was passed by the full Senate on a 52–48 vote in the affirmative. This now six-member conservative majority could greatly alter a host of policies favored by more liberal administrations and even Courts in the past.

SOCIAL AND CULTURAL CHANGE Even the most far-sighted of those in attendance at the Constitutional Convention could not have anticipated the vast changes that have occurred in the United States. For example, none could have imagined that a Black man would one day become president of the United States or a Black woman of Indian and Jamaican descent would become the vice president. Likewise, few of the Framers could have anticipated the devastation that a global pandemic could play in the United States as millions were affected and hundreds of thousands died while cries for an end to systemic racism were raised all around the nation.

THE CHALLENGES OF TECHNOLOGICAL CHANGE Ongoing technological advances continue to create new questions related to privacy and free speech rights under the Constitution. To what extent can private companies regulate Internet access and traffic speeds? Under what circumstances should online speech be regulated? Can our electoral systems be compromised by foreign or domestic interference in the conduct of elections and voting? Government reports clearly indicate that Russians tried to interfere in the 2016 presidential election. In the wake of the COVID-19 epidemic, numerous technological challenges to voting quickly became needed. Some state legislatures changed their laws to allow voters to cast absentee ballots via the U.S. Postal Service at the same time that the president appeared to be encouraging slower mail times and challenging the legality of mailed ballots. Many states and localities also opened up voting centers early with strict social distancing requirements, mask requirements, and regular disinfecting of voting booths. All of these changes, in part because of, or in spite of the increasing spread of COVID-19, led to the highest voter turnout rates and the most votes cast in the history of the United States.

Government access to private online communication and personal electronic devices is another issue testing the flexibility of the Constitution. In 2014, the U.S. Supreme Court addressed the scope of protection for digital information seized from a cell phone. A unanimous Court found that a warrant was needed before the phone could be searched.[25] In 2018, the Court issued a divided opinion that cell phone records from cell towers over a period of time as long as four months could not be used by law enforcement officials unless a search warrant was first obtained.[26]

CONCLUSION AND REVIEW

What Are the Roots of the U.S. Constitution?

2.1 Identify the causes of the American Revolution and the ideals on which the United States and the Constitution are based.

Settlers came to the New World for a variety of reasons, but most of these early inhabitants remained loyal to Great Britain and considered themselves subjects of the king. Over the years, as new generations of Americans were born on colonial soil, those ties weakened. A series of taxes levied by the British Crown ultimately led colonists to convene the Second Continental Congress and to declare their independence. American political culture emphasizes several key values, including liberty, equality, majority rule, and individualism.

What Are the Articles of Confederation?

2.2 Identify the components of the Articles of Confederation and the reasons for their failure.

The Articles of Confederation (1781) created a loose league of friendship between the new national government and the states. Numerous weaknesses in the new government quickly became apparent. Among the major flaws were Congress's inability to tax or regulate commerce, the absence of an executive to administer the government, the lack of a strong central government, and no judiciary.

How Was the U.S. Constitution Written?

2.3 Outline the issues resolved by compromise during the writing of the Constitution.

When weaknesses of the Articles of Confederation became apparent, the states called for a meeting to reform them. The Constitutional Convention (1787) threw out the Articles of Confederation and fashioned a new, more workable form of government. The U.S. Constitution resulted from a series of compromises, including those over representation, issues involving large and small states, slavery, and how to determine population. The delegates also made compromises on how members of each branch of government were to be selected. They created the Electoral College to give states a key role in the selection of the president.

What Are the Key Features of the U.S. Constitution?

2.4 Describe the framework for government expressed in the Constitution.

The proposed U.S. Constitution created a federal system that drew heavily on Montesquieu's ideas about separation of powers. These ideas concerned a way of parceling out power among the three branches of government. A system of checks and balances also prevented any one branch from having too much power.

What Was the Process for Ratifying the U.S. Constitution?

2.5 Outline the arguments for and against ratification of the Constitution.

The drive for ratification became a fierce fight between Federalists and Anti-Federalists. Federalists lobbied for the strong national government created by the Constitution; Anti-Federalists favored greater state power.

Political Reform and Realities: How Does the Amendment Process Work?

2.6 Describe the processes by which the Constitution can be amended.

The Framers did not want the whims of the people to sway the government unduly. Therefore, they designed a deliberate two-stage, formal amendment process that required approval on both federal and state levels; this process has rarely been used. However, informal amendments, prompted by judicial interpretation, cultural and social changes, and technological change, have had a tremendous impact on the Constitution.

LEARN THE TERMS

Anti-Federalists
Article I
Article II
Article III
Article IV
Article V
Article VI
Article VII
Articles of Confederation
Bill of Rights
checks and balances

constitution
Critical Period
Declaration of Independence
Electoral College
enumerated powers
federalism
Federalists
full faith and credit clause
Great Compromise
implied powers
inherent powers

mercantilism
necessary and proper clause
New Jersey Plan
separation of powers
Shays's Rebellion
social contract theory
supremacy clause
The Federalist Papers
Three-Fifths Compromise
Virginia Plan

LEARN THE NAMES

Alexander Hamilton
Benjamin Franklin
Crispus Attucks
Dwight D. Eisenhower
George Washington

James Madison
Jean-Jacques Rousseau
John Jay
John Locke
Montesquieu

Samuel Adams
Thomas Jefferson
Thomas Paine

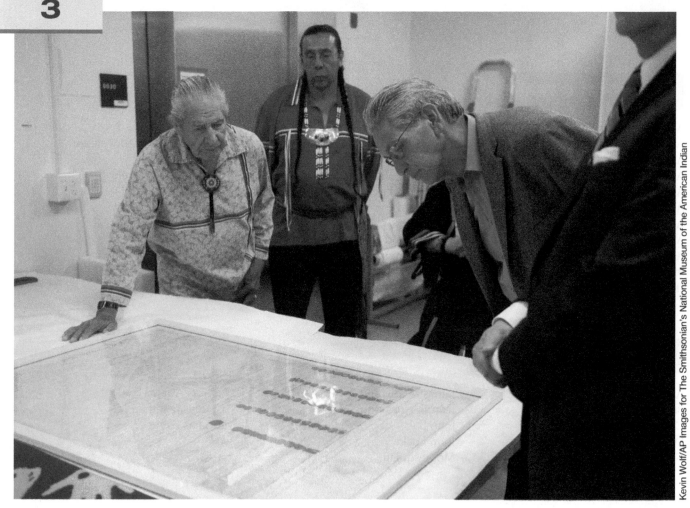

HOW DID NATIVE AMERICANS GOVERN THEMSELVES?

The governing structure of the Iroquois Confederacy, which was located mainly in what is today's New York State, has been acknowledged as one of a number of sources for the writing of the Articles of Confederation, which created a confederated, not federal, form of government. Above, at an exhibition at the Smithsonian Institution, tribal leaders view a 1794 treaty between the United States and the Iroquois nation.

CRITICAL THINKING QUESTION: *Why did the Framers reject a confederated form of government? If given the opportunity to select it over a federal system, what form of government would Americans favor today?*

THE FEDERAL SYSTEM

LEARNING OBJECTIVES

3.1 Trace the roots of the federal system and distinguish it from other types of government.

3.2 Explain the constitutional foundations for federalism.

3.3 Trace the evolution of federalism, from ratification to the present.

3.4 Analyze the impact of federalism on the relationships among national, state, and local levels of government.

The millions of American Indians living throughout most parts of what is now the United States during colonial times were divided into as many as 600 tribes. Tribes had distinct lineages, languages, cultures, and structures of government, as well as regional differences. Each tribe believed in its sovereignty, which bound its members to its ideals and authority. Similar to the principles that found their way into the Constitution of the United States of America, the power of elected officials came directly from the people.

Unlike the United States, however, tribes operated by consensus. Principles of majority rule were foreign to American Indians. All decisions made by those in authority were based on political and religious beliefs with no differentiation between the two.

Common troubles and the need to often create a united front to prevent Europeans from taking their lands led a group of tribes on the East Coast to create a **confederation**, a political structure in which power is granted to a central authority by its individual components—in this case, each sovereign tribe or nation. Called the Iroquois Confederacy, the Mohawk, Oneida, Onondaga, Cayuga, and Seneca created this structure to protect themselves from outside threats, including those posed by warring Indian confederations.

The Iroquois Confederacy's constitution, called the "Great Binding Law," included a Council of Fifty with seats apportioned by population and status. While women could not vote, in many tribes the oldest woman held the key position of selecting those who would represent her tribe at the Council. The Great Binding Law also created a system of checks and balances, an approach to governing that is a key feature in how the U.S. government is structured.

confederation
Type of government in which the national government derives its powers from the states; a league of independent states.

• • •

Like the Great Binding Law of the Iroquois Confederacy, the U.S. Constitution binds a diverse array of governments at the national, state, and local levels. The Constitution lays out the duties, obligations, and powers of national and state governments; states establish and charter local governments. Throughout American history, crises, historical evolution, public opinion, and judicial interpretation continually have reshaped these relationships. All of these forces have had a tremendous influence on policy decisions affecting your daily life. Because there is only one national government, for example, you do not need a passport to travel from Texas to Oklahoma. Only one national currency exists, as does a national minimum wage, although states and cities may set higher hourly wages. The laws of various states, however, exhibit many differences. The age at which you may marry is a state issue, as are laws governing divorce, child custody, and criminal justice, including how—or whether—the death penalty may be applied. Local governments often set liquor or smoking laws. Other policies and programs, such as waging war and air traffic regulation, lie solely within the province of the national government. In areas such as education, however, national, state, and local governments work together in a system of shared powers. The COVID-19 pandemic put issues of federalism, including the powers of local, state, and the national governments, at the center of many controversies, including mask wearing and social distancing. Some states even imposed a fourteen-day quarantine on persons coming from several states with high infection rates.

WHAT ARE THE ROOTS OF THE FEDERAL SYSTEM?

3.1 Trace the roots of the federal system and distinguish it from other types of government.

The Framers drafted the U.S. Constitution at a time when many citizens and political theorists were beginning to question the source of government's power. The Framers drew upon their struggles under the British crown to fashion a new system of government, where power was divided between sovereign states and the national government, and the ultimate source of power lay with the people. Creating a strong national government

TABLE 3.1 HOW DID ARISTOTLE CLASSIFY THE TYPES OF GOVERNMENTS?

Rule by	In Whose Interest	
	Public	**Self**
One	Monarchy	Tyranny
The Few	Aristocracy	Oligarchy
The Many	Polity	Democracy

SOURCE: *Aristotle, Politics 3, 7.*

but maintaining a role for the states and the people, was important to the Framers because state and local governments predated the existence of the national government in every one of the thirteen colonies. Even the earliest settlers in the New World realized that rules or laws were necessary to keep order within communities.

Types of Government

Early Greek theorists such as Plato and Aristotle tried to categorize governments by who participates, who governs, and how much authority those who govern enjoy. As reflected in Table 3.1, in a true **monarchy**, absolute power is vested in but one person who ascends to the role of king or queen, or in the case of Vatican City, the pope, who rules the nation as head of state as well as the head of government. Very few true monarchies remain; Brunei, Oman, and Vatican City are notable examples. Great Britain is a constitutional monarchy. The prime minister, the head of the House of Commons, informs the queen or king of its actions; the monarch has no say in actual policy decisions, but may offer guidance. In Vatican City, Pope Francis rules over the tiny city-state located within Rome, Italy. Other monarchs are expected to rule benevolently on behalf of their subjects, but that is not always the case. Another form, an **aristocracy**, is a government in which a small group of individuals govern for the perceived good of all. **Totalitarianism** is a type of government that Aristotle considered rule by "tyranny." Tyrants, such as Adolf Hitler, often come to power by coups, uprisings, or tainted elections and rule their countries to benefit themselves. In tyrannical or totalitarian systems, the leader exercises unlimited power, and individuals have no personal rights or liberties. Generally, the rule of these systems tends to be based on a particular religion or orthodoxy, an ideology, or a personality cult organized around a supreme leader. An **oligarchy**, in contrast, occurs when a few people rule in their own interest. In an oligarchy, wealth, social status, military position, or achievement dictates participation in government. Many commentators refer to Vladimir Putin's leadership in Russia as an example of this type of government.

Aristotle called rule of the many for the benefit of all citizens a "polity" and rule of the many to benefit themselves a "democracy." The term *democracy* derives from the Greek words *demos* ("the people") and *kratia* ("power" or "authority") and may apply to any system of government that gives power to the people, either directly, or indirectly through elected representatives. Of the more than 190 countries in the world today, 123 claim to be some form of democracy.

Devising a Federal System

American colonists rejected a system with a strong ruler, such as the British monarchy, when they declared their independence. They feared replicating the landed and titled system of the British aristocracy and viewed the formation of a republican form of government as far more in keeping with their values. In a republican form of government, authority is ceded to elected representatives who make decisions on behalf of those who elected them.

The United States became the first country to adopt a **federal system** of government (although the word "federal" never appears in the U.S. Constitution). The Framers designed this system, wherein the national and state governments share power and

monarchy

A form of government in which power is vested in hereditary kings and queens who govern the entire society.

aristocracy

A government in which a small group of individuals govern for the perceived good of all.

totalitarianism

A form of government in which power resides in leaders who rule by force in their own self-interest and without regard to rights and liberties.

oligarchy

A form of government in which the right to participate depends on the possession of wealth, social status, military position, or achievement.

federal system

System of government in which the national government and state governments share power and derive all authority from the people.

FIGURE 3.1 WHAT IS THE SOURCE OF GOVERNMENTAL AUTHORITY?

The source of governmental authority varies between federal, unitary, and confederate systems. Having experienced the challenges of both unitary and confederate systems, the Framers of the Constitution chose a federal system, in which the power of both state and national governments derives from the people.

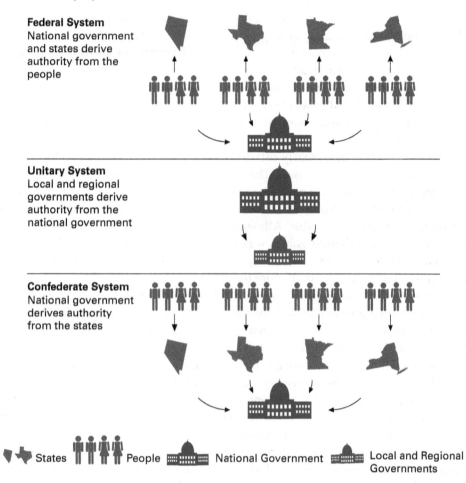

Federal System
National government and states derive authority from the people

Unitary System
Local and regional governments derive authority from the national government

Confederate System
National government derives authority from the states

States   People   National Government   Local and Regional Governments

derive all authority from the people, to remedy many of the problems experienced under the Articles of Confederation. Under the Articles, the national government derived all of its powers from the states, similar to the Iroquois Confederacy's relationship to its constituent tribes. In the colonies, this arrangement led to a weak national government often unable to respond to even localized crises, such as Shays's Rebellion.

The new system of government also had to be different from the unitary system found in Great Britain, where local and regional governments derived all of their power from a strong national government (see Figure 3.1). Having been under the rule of British kings, whom they considered tyrants, the Framers feared centralizing power in one government or institution. Therefore, they made both the state and the federal governments accountable to the people. While the governments shared some powers, each government was supreme in some spheres.

HOW ARE THE POWERS OF GOVERNMENT DIVIDED BY THE CONSTITUTION?

3.2 Explain the constitutional foundations for federalism.

The U.S. Constitution spells out a division of power between the national and state governments. Some powers are expressly assigned to the national government, while others are given to the states. The two governments share some powers, while others are denied to both the national and state governments. No powers, however, are given to local governments. Local governments lack sovereign authority and must be chartered by the state governments.

National Powers Under the Constitution

All of the powers specifically stated in Article I, section 8, of the Constitution are called *enumerated powers*. Chief among these exclusive powers of the national government are the authorities to coin money, conduct foreign relations, provide for an army and navy, and declare war. In addition, Article I, section 8, contains the necessary and proper clause (also called the elastic clause), which gives Congress the authority to enact laws "necessary and proper" for exercising any of its enumerated powers. These powers derived from enumerated powers and the necessary and proper clause are known as *implied powers*.

The Constitution also clearly set out the federal government's right to collect duties and excises (a form of taxes). The Framers wanted to avoid the financial problems experienced by the national government under the Articles of Confederation. If they wished to create a strong new national government, they had to make its power to raise revenue unquestionable. Allowing the new national government to collect tariffs, or taxes on imported goods, was one way to assert this power. And giving the national government the exclusive power to do so eliminated the financial wars between states that had occurred under the Articles.

Article VI of the Constitution underscores the notion that the national government is supreme in situations of conflict between state and national law. It declares that the U.S. Constitution, the laws of the United States, and its treaties are "the supreme Law of the Land; and the Judges in every State shall be bound thereby."

In spite of this explicit language, the courts have consistently been called on to clarify the meaning of the supremacy clause. In 1920, for example, Missouri sought to prevent a U.S. game warden from enforcing the Migratory Bird Treaty Act of 1918, which prohibited the killing or capturing of many species of birds as they made their annual migration across the international border from Canada to parts of the United States.[1] Missouri argued that the Tenth Amendment, which reserved a state's powers to legislate for the general welfare of its citizens, allowed Missouri to regulate hunting. But, the Court ruled that since the treaty was legal, it must be considered the supreme law of the land (see the discussion of *McCulloch* v. *Maryland* [1819] later in this chapter).

State Powers Under the Constitution

Because states held all the power at the time the Constitution was written, the Framers felt no need, as they did for the new national government, to list and restate all of the powers of the states, although some are specified throughout the Constitution. Article I of the U.S. Constitution notes that each state is entitled to two senators, and it leaves to the states the times, places, and manner of national elections. Thus, the states may enact their own restrictions on who can and cannot vote so long as those restrictions are constitutional. Article II requires that each state appoint electors to vote for president. And, Article IV guarantees each state a "Republican Form of Government," meaning one that represents the citizens of the state.

Not until the **Tenth Amendment**, the final part of the Bill of Rights, were the states' powers described in greater detail: "The powers not delegated to the United States by the Constitution, nor prohibited by it to the States, are reserved to the States respectively, or to the people." These powers, often called the states' **reserved powers**, include the ability to legislate for the public health, safety, and morals of their citizens. Today, the states' rights to legislate under their reserved powers provide the rationale for laws passed regarding access to bathrooms for transgender persons and

Tenth Amendment
The final part of the Bill of Rights that defines the basic principle of American federalism in stating that the powers not delegated to the national government are reserved to the states or to the people.

reserved powers
Powers reserved to the states by the Tenth Amendment that lie at the foundation of a state's right to legislate for the public health and welfare of its citizens.

FIGURE 3.2   HOW IS GOVERNMENTAL POWER DISTRIBUTED IN THE FEDERAL SYSTEM?

The Constitution divides power between the national and state governments. It gives the national government a list of enumerated powers, while many state powers are captured in the reserved powers clause of the Tenth Amendment. The national and state governments also share some powers, known as concurrent powers.

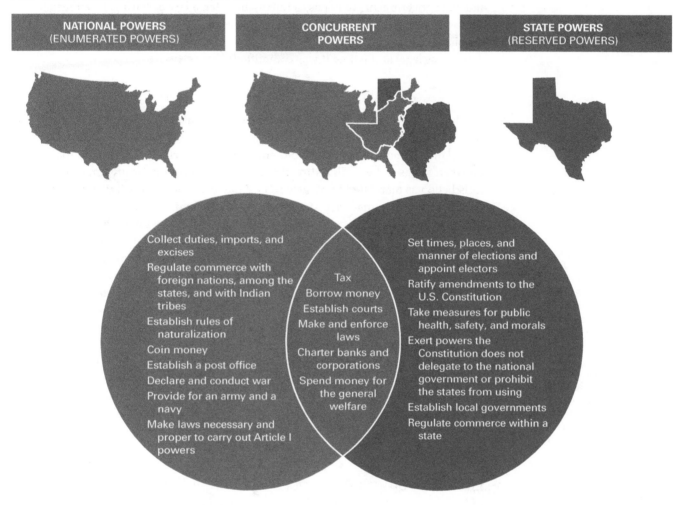

NATIONAL POWERS
(ENUMERATED POWERS)

CONCURRENT POWERS

STATE POWERS
(RESERVED POWERS)

Collect duties, imports, and excises

Regulate commerce with foreign nations, among the states, and with Indian tribes

Establish rules of naturalization

Coin money

Establish a post office

Declare and conduct war

Provide for an army and a navy

Make laws necessary and proper to carry out Article I powers

Tax
Borrow money
Establish courts
Make and enforce laws
Charter banks and corporations
Spend money for the general welfare

Set times, places, and manner of elections and appoint electors

Ratify amendments to the U.S. Constitution

Take measures for public health, safety, and morals

Exert powers the Constitution does not delegate to the national government or prohibit the states from using

Establish local governments

Regulate commerce within a state

restrictions on abortion providers, to give but two examples. Reserved powers also form the basis for state criminal laws, including those concerning the death penalty. As long as the U.S. Supreme Court continues to find the death penalty not in violation of the U.S. Constitution, the states may impose it, whether by lethal injection, gas chamber, electric chair, hanging, or firing squad.

Concurrent Powers Under the Constitution

As revealed in Figure 3.2, national and state powers overlap. The area in which the systems overlap represents **concurrent powers**—powers shared by the national and state governments. States already had the power to tax; the Constitution extended this power to the national government as well. Other important concurrent powers include the rights to borrow money, establish courts, charter banks, and spend money for the general welfare. Due to concurrent powers, most individuals must file both state and federal tax returns.

concurrent powers

Powers shared by the national and state governments.

Powers Denied Under the Constitution

Article I of the Constitution explicitly denies some powers to the national government or states. Congress, for example, is barred from favoring one state over another in regulating commerce, and it cannot lay duties on items exported from any state.

Article I also prohibits the national government from granting titles of nobility, and government employees may not accept salaries or gifts from foreign heads of state.

State governments (as well as the national government) are denied the authority to take arbitrary actions affecting constitutional rights and liberties. Neither national nor state governments may pass a bill of attainder, a law declaring an act illegal without a judicial trial. The Constitution also bars national and state governments from passing *ex post facto* laws, those that make an act punishable as a crime even if the action was legal at the time it was committed.

Interstate Relations Under the Constitution

In addition to delineating the relationship between states and the national government, the Constitution provides a mechanism for resolving interstate disputes and facilitating relations among states. To avoid any sense of favoritism, it arranges for disputes between states to be settled directly by the U.S. Supreme Court under its original jurisdiction as mandated by Article III (see the discussion of the judiciary). Moreover, Article IV requires that each state give "Full Faith and Credit . . . to the public Acts, Records, and judicial Proceedings of every other State." The full faith and credit clause ensures that judicial decrees and contracts made in one state will be binding and enforceable in another, thereby facilitating trade and other commercial relationships. Article IV also contains the privileges and immunities clause, guaranteeing that the citizens of each state have the same rights as citizens of all other states. In addition, Article IV includes the extradition clause, which requires states to extradite, or return, criminals to states where they have been convicted or are to stand trial.

To facilitate relations among states, Article I, section 10, clause 3, of the U.S. Constitution sets the legal foundation for interstate cooperation in the form of interstate compacts, contracts between states that carry the force of law. Currently, more than 200 interstate compacts exist. While some deal with rudimentary items such as state boundaries, others help states carry out their policy objectives and administrative functions.[2] For example, the Driver License Compact facilitates nationwide recognition of licenses issued in the respective states.

Local Governments Under the Constitution

Local governments have no express power under the U.S. Constitution. A description of the relationship between states and local governments comes from Judge John F. Dillon, who in 1868 articulated a premise known as **Dillon's Rule**. Dillon's Rule states that all local governments—whether towns, villages, cities, counties, or some other form—do not have any inherent sovereignty and instead must be authorized by state governments, which can create or abolish them.

Local governments, therefore, need a **charter**—a document that, like a constitution, specifies the basic policies, procedures, and institutions that are acceptable to the state legislature. States issue charters that establish the authority and procedures defining a municipality, and all amendments to these charters require approval by state governments. The responsibilities of local governments described in these charters vary widely and include public health and safety, education, jobs, zoning land, and assistance to those in need. Local governments are of several types, as highlighted in Figure 3.3.

COUNTIES   Counties are the basic administrative units of local government. Every state has counties, although in Louisiana they are called parishes, and in Alaska, boroughs. With few exceptions, counties have very broad responsibilities and are used by state governments for welfare and environmental programs, courts, elections, and the registration of land, births, deaths, and party affiliations.

MUNICIPALITIES   Municipalities are city governments created in response to the emergence of relatively densely populated areas. Some of the most intense struggles

Dillon's Rule

A premise articulated by Judge John F. Dillon in 1868 that states that local governments do not have any inherent sovereignty and instead must be authorized by state governments that can create or abolish them.

charter

A document that, like a constitution, specifies the basic policies, procedures, and institutions of local government. Charters for local governments must be approved by state legislatures.

FIGURE 3.3   HOW MANY GOVERNMENTS EXIST IN THE UNITED STATES?

Nearly 90,000 governments exist in the United States. Most of these governments are at the local level and divided among municipal governments, towns, and special districts such as school districts. The most common form of government is the special district.

SOURCE: U.S. Census Bureau, www2.census.gov/govs/cog/g12_org.pdf

1	U.S. government
50	State governments
89,004	Local governments
3,031	County
19,522	Municipal (city)
16,364	Townships
12,884	School districts
37,203	Special districts
89,055	**TOTAL**

among governments within the United States are over the boundaries, scope of authority, and sources of revenue for municipal governments. County and municipal boundaries may overlap. State actions have merged city and county into a consolidated government in several areas, including San Francisco, California; Denver, Colorado; Honolulu, Hawai'i; and Jacksonville, Florida.

TOWNS   The term is used today to refer to smaller communities, often run by a mayor and town council. The definition of a town varies considerably from state to state. In some states, towns and municipalities may be virtually indistinguishable, while other states set specific restrictions on the size of each type of government.

SPECIAL DISTRICTS   Among forms of government, special districts are the most numerous. A special district is a local government restricted to a particular function. These districts exist for services such as libraries, sewage, water, and parks and are governed through a variety of structures. One reason for the proliferation of special districts is the desire to avoid restrictions on funds faced by municipalities or other jurisdictions.

School districts, the most common form of special districts, exist to provide free public education to students. They frequently cross town lines for purposes of practicality. They have their own budgets and must persuade those without children in a district to agree to help fund schools and extracurricular programs through referenda. Most school districts also receive assistance from states or the federal government for some specialized programs.

HOW HAS FEDERALISM EVOLVED?

3.3 Trace the evolution of federalism, from ratification to the present.

The nature of federalism, including its allocation of power between the national government and the states, has changed dramatically over the past 200 years. Much of this change has resulted from rulings of the U.S. Supreme Court, which has played a major role in defining the nature of the federal system. Other changes have resulted from major crises throughout American history.

Federalism and the Marshall Court

Few Supreme Courts have had a greater impact on the federal–state relationship than the one headed by Chief Justice **John Marshall** from 1801 to 1835. In a series of decisions, he and his associates carved out an important role for the Court in defining the balance of power between the national government and the states. Three rulings in the early 1800s, *McCulloch* v. *Maryland* (1819), *Gibbons* v. *Ogden* (1824), and *Barron* v. *Baltimore* (1833), were particularly important.

DEFINING NATIONAL POWER: *McCULLOCH v. MARYLAND* (1819)   **McCulloch v. Maryland (1819)** was the first major Supreme Court decision to define the relationship between the national and state governments. In 1816, Congress chartered the Second Bank of the United States. (The charter of the First Bank had been allowed to expire.) In 1818, the Maryland state legislature levied a tax requiring all banks not chartered by Maryland (that is, the Second Bank of the United States) to: (1) buy stamped paper from the state on which their bank notes were to be issued; (2) pay the state $15,000 a year; or, (3) go out of business. James McCulloch, the head cashier of the Baltimore branch of the Second Bank of the United States, refused to pay the tax, and Maryland brought suit against him. After losing in a Maryland state court, McCulloch appealed the decision to the U.S. Supreme Court by order of the U.S. secretary of the treasury. In a unanimous opinion, the Court answered the two central questions presented to it: (1) Did Congress have the authority to charter a bank? and, (2) if it did, could a state tax it?

John Marshall

The longest-serving Supreme Court Chief Justice, Marshall served from 1801 to 1835. Marshall's decision in *Marbury* v. *Madison* (1803) established the principle of judicial review.

McCulloch v. Maryland (1819)

Supreme Court ruling that upheld the power of the national government and denied the right of a state to tax the federal bank, using the Constitution's supremacy clause. The Court's broad interpretation of the necessary and proper clause paved the way for later rulings upholding expansive federal powers.

DOES CONGRESS HAVE THE RIGHT TO CHARTER A BANK?
In *McCulloch* v. *Maryland* (1819), the U.S. Supreme Court ruled that Congress did have this power. Pictured, the Bank of the United States.

Chief Justice John Marshall's answer to the first question—whether Congress had the right to establish a bank or another type of corporation—continues to stand as the classic exposition of the doctrine of implied powers and as a statement of the authority of a strong national government. Although the word "bank" does not appear in the Constitution, the Constitution enumerates powers that give Congress the authority to levy and collect taxes, issue a currency, and borrow funds. From these enumerated powers, Marshall found, it was reasonable to imply that Congress had the power to charter a bank, which could be considered "necessary and proper" to the exercise of its aforementioned enumerated powers.

Marshall next addressed whether any state government could tax a federal bank. To Marshall, this was not a difficult question. The national government depended on the people, not the states, for its powers. In addition, Marshall noted, the Constitution specifically called for the national law to be supreme. "The power to tax involves the power to destroy," wrote the chief justice.[3] Thus, the state tax violated the supremacy clause because individual states cannot interfere with operations of the national government, whose laws are supreme.

AFFIRMING NATIONAL POWER: *GIBBONS* v. *OGDEN* (1824) Shortly after *McCulloch*, the Marshall Court had another opportunity to rule in favor of a broad interpretation of the scope of national power. *Gibbons* **v.** *Ogden* **(1824)** involved a dispute that arose after the New York state legislature granted to Robert Fulton the exclusive right to operate steamboats on the Hudson River.[4] Simultaneously, Congress licensed a ship to sail on the same waters. By the time the case reached the Supreme Court, it was complicated both factually and procedurally. Suffice it to say that both New York and New Jersey wanted to control shipping on the lower Hudson River. But *Gibbons* actually addressed one simple, very important question: What was the scope of Congress's authority under the commerce clause? The states argued that "commerce," as mentioned in Article I, should be interpreted narrowly to include only direct dealings in products. In *Gibbons*, however, the Supreme Court ruled that Congress's power to regulate interstate commerce included the power to regulate commercial activity as well, and that the commerce power had no limits except those specifically found in the Constitution. Thus, New York had no constitutional

Gibbons **v.** *Ogden* **(1824)**
Supreme Court ruling that upheld broad congressional power to regulate interstate commerce. The Court's broad interpretation of the Constitution's commerce clause paved the way for later rulings upholding expansive federal powers.

Departure of the Clermont on her First Voyage

IllustratedHistory/Alamy Stock Photo

authority to grant a monopoly to a single steamboat operator, an action that interfered with interstate commerce.[5]

LIMITING THE BILL OF RIGHTS: *BARRON* v. *BALTIMORE* (1833) One of Chief Justice Marshall's last major cases on the federal–state relationship was *Barron* v. *Baltimore* (1833). In 1833, the Court addressed the issue of whether the due process clause of the Fifth Amendment applied to actions of the states.[6] John Barron, a Baltimore businessman, ran a successful docking business off the city's wharf. As the city entered a period of extensive construction, dirt, sand, and silt drifted to his section of the wharf, making it unusable as a harbor. Barron sued the city and state for damages, arguing that the city took his lands "without just compensation," as guaranteed by the Fifth Amendment of the U.S. Constitution. The Marshall Court ruled that Barron had no federal claim because enumerated rights contained in the Bill of Rights applied only to the national government.[7]

The Civil War and Dual Federalism

In the early to mid-1800s, a national crisis began over the division of power between the states and the federal government. One major battleground in this struggle was the issue of slavery, which the pro-states' rights southern states fought to maintain. In contrast, the northern states, where commercial and manufacturing interests were more powerful, favored greater national power. Chief Justice **Roger B. Taney**, who succeeded John Marshall, saw the Court as an arbiter of those competing state and nationalist views. Chief Justice Taney and the Court also began to articulate further the notions of concurrent power and **dual federalism**. Dual federalism posits that having separate and equally powerful state and national governments is the best constitutional arrangement. Adherents of this theory typically believe the national government should not exceed its constitutionally enumerated powers, and, as stated in the Tenth Amendment, all other powers are—and should be—reserved to the states or to the people.

NULLIFICATION While the courts worked to carve out the appropriate roles for each level of government in the federal system, the political debate over states' rights swirled in large part over what is called **nullification**, the belief in the right of a state to declare a federal law void. The question of nullification arose in 1828, when the national government enacted a tariff act, most commonly referred to as the "Tariff of Abominations," that raised duties on raw materials, iron, hemp, and flax and reduced protections against imported woolen goods. Vice President **John C. Calhoun** opposed the bill because it badly affected his home state of South Carolina. Not only did South Carolinians have to pay more for raw materials because of the tariff law, but it was also becoming increasingly difficult for them to sell their dwindling crops abroad for a profit.

Barron v. Baltimore (1833)
Supreme Court ruling that, before the Civil War, limited the applicability of the Bill of Rights to the federal government and not to the states.

Roger B. Taney
Supreme Court chief justice who served from 1835 to 1864. Taney supported slavery and states' rights in the pre-Civil War era.

dual federalism
The belief that having separate and equally powerful levels of government is the best arrangement, often referred to as layer-cake federalism.

nullification
The belief in the right of a state to declare void a federal law.

John C. Calhoun
A politician and political theorist from South Carolina who supported slavery and states' rights in the pre-Civil War era and served as vice president from 1825 to 1832.

Calhoun theorized that the federal government functioned merely as the agent of the states (the people and the individual state governments) and that the Constitution was simply a compact providing instructions on how the agent was to act. Thus, according to Calhoun, the U.S. Supreme Court could not pass judgment on the constitutional validity of acts of Congress. Calhoun posited that if the people of any individual state did not like an act of Congress, they could hold a convention to nullify that act. If a state contested an act, the law would have no force until three-fourths of all the states ratified an amendment expressly giving Congress that power. Then, if the nullifying state still did not wish to be bound by the new provision, it could secede, or withdraw, from the Union.

THE *DRED SCOTT* DECISION   Debate over nullification only forestalled debate on the inevitable slavery issue. By the 1850s, the country could wait no longer. In cases such as *Dred Scott* v. *Sandford* (1857), the Court tried to manage the slavery issue by resolving questions of ownership, the status of fugitives from slavery, and slavery in the new territories.[8]

Dred Scott was born into slavery about 1795. In 1833, his original enslavers sold him to a family in Missouri. Later, he tried to buy his freedom. His ability to take this action was questioned, so abolitionists gave money to support a test case seeking Scott's freedom. They believed his prior residence with a family living in free states and the Wisconsin Territory, which prohibited slavery, made Scott a free man, even though he now lived in a state where slavery was legal, Missouri. In 1857, after many delays, the U.S. Supreme Court ruled 7–2 that Scott was not a citizen of the United States. "Slaves," said the Court, "were never thought of or spoken of except as property." The Court also

Dred Scott **v.** *Sandford* **(1857)**

Supreme Court decision that ruled the Missouri Compromise unconstitutional and denied citizenship rights to enslaved Black people. *Dred Scott* heightened tensions between the pro-slavery South and the abolitionist North in the run-up to the Civil War.

Dred Scott

Named plaintiff in major Supreme Court case in which the Court concluded enslaved people were property—not persons.

HOW WERE NEWLY ARRIVED NORTHERNERS PERCEIVED BY SOUTHERNERS AFTER THE CIVIL WAR?

This cartoon, called "The Man with the (Carpet) Bags," by Thomas Nast, the most acclaimed cartoonist of the times, depicts the resentment of Southerners after the Civil War toward Northerners who flooded the South seeking riches to be had from federal funds allotted to rebuilding the South.

Tomas Nast/Library of Congress Prints and Photographs Division

found that Congress lacked the authority to ban slavery in the territories. In so doing, this decision narrowed the scope of national power, while it enhanced that of the states. Eventually, however, no form of federalism could accommodate the existence of slavery, and the nation marched toward inevitable war with itself.

THE CIVIL WAR AND RECONSTRUCTION   The **Civil War** forever changed the nature of federalism. The concepts of nullification and dual federalism, as well as their emphasis on the role of the states, were destroyed at that time along with the South's attempt at forming a new nation.

The war was fought on American soil from 1861 to 1865 after the election of the first president from the Republican Party, **Abraham Lincoln**, in 1860. Lincoln had run on a platform pledged to banning slavery in all new territories. By January 1861, before Lincoln first took office, seven southern states had announced their **secession** from the United States to form the Confederate States of America. The first six states to secede had populations of nearly 50 percent enslaved people. Eventually the new nation, never recognized as such by any other country, included eleven states, with many men living in the southern parts of Union states also taking up arms for the Confederacy and against the Union.

The war had many causes, including slavery, which Southerners viewed as critical to the maintenance of their agricultural economy. The institution of slavery appalled most Northerners. This chasm over slavery was a highlight of many of the cultural, social, and political differences that had grown between the North and South since the ratification of the Constitution and Bill of Rights. It continues today as many people clamor for the removal of statues of Southern Civil War generals whose actions in taking up arms against the United States of America were actually treasonous and therefore punishable by death but for pardons granted them by Presidents Lincoln and Andrew Johnson.

The war left 620,000 dead and more wounded. The South was decimated by battles and General William Tecumseh Sherman's famous March to the Sea in which the Union Army, beginning in Atlanta, Georgia, leveled fields, infrastructure, homes, and cities, setting fire all the way to Savannah. The Civil War remains the bloodiest war ever fought by the United States. When the war ended, many Southerners bristled as a host of constraints were placed on those who had taken up arms against the Union or had helped in the Confederate war effort. They were equally outraged by the abolition of slavery and its consequences.

Most historians date the **Reconstruction** period as beginning at the end of the Civil War and lasting until 1877. President Lincoln had made it clear to his advisers that he wished a gentle way to deal with the vanquished states, as did his successor, **Andrew Johnson**, who became president after Lincoln's assassination. Their wishes were ignored. Former Confederate states were required to "reconstruct," or adopt new state constitutions approved by the nationalist Congress in Washington, D.C., and endure a range of punishments for their actions.

The elections of 1866, the first after the war, barred former Confederates from voting. Radical Republicans were able to win most key races, vowing to set up a labor-dependent economy using the U.S. Army and freedmen, formerly enslaved people, along with thousands of Northerners seeking new opportunities in the vanquished South. Called "carpetbaggers," they came south for a variety of reasons, including to be politicians, since nearly all Southern men had taken up arms against the Union, and therefore were legally disenfranchised.

The actions of this new breed of politician helped facilitate passage of the Thirteenth, Fourteenth, and Fifteenth Amendments to the Constitution, creating a profound change in the reunited nation's concept of federalism.

Civil War

The military conflict from 1861 to 1865 in the United States between the Northern forces of the Union and the Southern forces of the Confederacy. Over 600,000 Americans lost their lives during this war.

Abraham Lincoln

Sixteenth president of the United States, the first elected Republican president, who served from 1861 to 1865. Lincoln, who led the Union during the Civil War, was assassinated in 1865 by a Confederate sympathizer, John Wilkes Booth.

secession

A unilateral assertion of independence by a geographic region within a country. The eleven southern states making up the Confederacy during the Civil War seceded from the United States.

Reconstruction

The period from 1865 to 1877 after the Civil War, in which the U.S. militarily occupied and dominated the eleven former states of the Confederacy.

Andrew Johnson

Seventeenth president of the United States, a Republican, who served from 1865 to 1869. Johnson had served as Abraham Lincoln's vice president and became president after Lincoln's assassination.

WHY ARE CONFEDERATE MONUMENTS SO CONTROVERSIAL?

This mammoth mural, carved in stone, memorializes and glorifies leaders of the Confederacy from left to right: President Jefferson Davis, and Generals Robert E. Lee and Stonewall Jackson. All of them were traitors to the Union and actively engaged in treason. Located within a park owned by the state of Georgia, critics say it is a daily affront to Black Americans.

Horizon International Images Limited/Alamy Stock Photo

After the Civil War, the Supreme Court often stepped in to limit state powers in favor of a stronger national government. The Court also recognized the need for national involvement in projects such as railroad construction, canal building, and the development of new technology such as the telegraph.[9] Beginning in the 1880s, the Court allowed Congress to regulate many aspects of economic relationships, such as outlawing monopolies, a type of regulation formerly considered to exist exclusively in the realm of the states. By the 1890s, passage of laws such as the Interstate Commerce Act and the Sherman Anti-Trust Act allowed Congress to establish itself as the supreme player in a growing national economy.

This role was enhanced by the ratification of the Sixteenth and Seventeenth Amendments during the early twentieth century. The **Sixteenth Amendment** gave Congress the power to levy and collect taxes on incomes without apportioning them

Sixteenth Amendment

Amendment to the U.S. Constitution that authorized Congress to enact a national income tax.

HOW DID THE ROLE OF THE NATIONAL GOVERNMENT CHANGE AFTER THE CIVIL WAR?

The competition of the construction of the coast-to-coast transportation system such as the transcontinental railroad, shown here, was a much-celebrated event in nineteenth-century America. Transportation lines and telecommunications systems that stretched across multiple state boundaries necessitated a greater role for the national government. Such changes helped to doom dual federalism, which dominated for the first one hundred years of the nation's history.

Underwood Archives/ Getty Images

among the states. The revenues taken in by the federal government through taxation of personal income "removed a major constraint on the federal government by giving it access to almost unlimited revenues."[10] The **Seventeenth Amendment**, ratified in 1913, similarly enhanced the power of the national government at the expense of the states. This amendment terminated the state legislatures' election of senators and placed their election in the hands of the people. With senators no longer directly accountable to the state legislatures, states lost their principal protectors in Congress.

Cooperative Federalism and the Growth of National Government

While the ratification of the Sixteenth and Seventeenth Amendments set the stage for expanded national government, the catalyst for dual federalism's demise was a series of economic events that ended in the cataclysm of the Great Depression:

- Throughout the 1920s, bank failures were common.
- In 1921, the nation experienced a severe slump in agricultural prices.
- In 1926, the construction industry went into decline.
- In the summer of 1929, inventories of consumer goods and automobiles were at an all-time high.
- On October 29, 1929, stock prices, which had risen steadily since 1926, crashed, taking with them the entire national economy—and thus began the Great Depression.

Despite the severity of these indicators, Presidents **Calvin Coolidge** and **Herbert Hoover** took little action, believing that the national depression comprised an amalgamation of economic crises better dealt with by state and local governments. It would take the election of President **Franklin D. Roosevelt (FDR)** in 1932 to both respond to this crisis and forever change the relationship between state and national governments. To create these changes, Roosevelt proposed a program of relief, recovery, and reform known as the **New Deal**.

In the first few weeks of the legislative session after FDR's inauguration, Congress passed a series of acts creating the new federal agencies and programs proposed by the president. These new agencies, often known by their initials, created what many termed an "alphabetocracy." Among the more significant New Deal programs were the Federal Housing Administration (FHA), which provided federal financing for new home construction; the Civilian Conservation Corps (CCC), a work relief program for farmers and homeowners; the Social Security Administration (SSA), which provided government support to retired wage earners; and, the National Recovery Administration (NRA), which imposed restrictions on production in agriculture and many industries while also providing subsidies to farmers.

New Deal programs forced all levels of government to work cooperatively with one another. Local governments, especially those of cities, were embraced as equal partners in an intergovernmental system for the first time and became players in the national political arena because many members of Congress wanted to bypass state legislatures, where urban interests usually were underrepresented. FDR also relied on big-city Democratic political machines to turn out voters to support his programs.

Those who feared these unprecedented changes in the federal system quickly challenged the constitutionality of the programs. And, at least initially, the U.S. Supreme Court often agreed with them. Through the mid-1930s, the Court continued to rule that certain aspects of New Deal programs went beyond the authority of Congress to regulate commerce. FDR's frustration with the Court prompted him to suggest what ultimately was nicknamed his "Court-packing plan." Knowing he could

Seventeenth Amendment
Amendment to the U.S. Constitution that made senators directly elected by the people, removing their selection by state legislatures.

Calvin Coolidge
Thirtieth president of the United States, a Republican, who served from 1923 to 1929.

Herbert Hoover
Thirty-first president of the United States, a Republican, who served from 1929 to 1933 during the start of the Great Depression.

Franklin D. Roosevelt (FDR)
Thirty-second president, a Democrat, who served from 1933 to 1945. FDR's leadership took the United States through the Great Depression and World War II.

New Deal
The political program enacted by President Franklin D. Roosevelt in the 1930s that greatly expanded the role of the federal government to combat the effects of the Great Depression.

HOW DID FDR'S PUBLIC ACTIONS CHANGE CONCEPTIONS OF FEDERALISM?

This cartoon illustrates FDR's difficulties garnering support from the Supreme Court for the economic and social programs he believed were necessary to end the Great Depression. To coerce support from the Court to transform the federal–state relationship, FDR proposed his Court-packing plan, which was met with great opposition. The plan, however, seemed to convince a majority of justices to overturn the Court's earlier decisions and to support the constitutionality of New Deal programs.

do little to change the minds of those already on the Court, FDR suggested enlarging its size from nine to thirteen justices. This plan would have given him the opportunity to pack the Court with a majority of justices predisposed toward the constitutional validity of the New Deal.

Even though Roosevelt was popular, the Court-packing plan was not.[11] Congress and the public expressed outrage over even the suggestion of tampering with an institution of government. But the Court appeared to respond to this threat. In 1937, it reversed its series of anti–New Deal decisions, concluding that Congress (and therefore the national government) had broad authority to legislate in any area as long as what was regulated affected commerce in any way. The Court also upheld the constitutionality of most of the massive New Deal relief programs, including the National Labor Relations Act of 1935, which authorized collective bargaining between unions and employees;[12] the Fair Labor Standards Act of 1938, which set a national minimum wage; and, the Agricultural Adjustment Act of 1938, which provided crop subsidies to farmers.[13] Congress then used these newly recognized powers to legislate in a wide range of areas, including maximum hour laws and regulation of child labor.

The New Deal dramatically changed the federal system. Most political scientists likened the federal system before the 1930s to a layer cake: in most policy areas, each level or layer of government—national, state, and local—had clearly defined powers and responsibilities. By contrast, the metaphor of marble-cake federalism refers to what political scientists call **cooperative federalism**, a term that describes the intertwined relations among the national, state, and local governments that began during this period (see Figure 3.4). States began to take a secondary, albeit important, cooperative role in the scheme of governance, as did many cities.

cooperative federalism

The intertwined relationship between national, state, and local governments that began with the New Deal; often referred to as marble-cake federalism.

FIGURE 3.4 HOW HAS THE FEDERAL–STATE RELATIONSHIP EVOLVED?

The balance of power between the national and state governments has evolved over time. In the early years of the new republic, the nation maintained a system of dual federalism, often referred to as "layer cake" federalism. This relationship transformed into a "marble cake" form of federalism known as cooperative federalism during the 1930s with the passage of FDR's New Deal programs. This image illustrates the changing national–state relationship, building on the cake metaphor. President Donald J. Trump was somewhat unusual. He claimed broad presidential authority yet let states and local governments set their own rules regarding COVID-19 restrictions. He did, however, disregard pleas from Washington, D.C., Mayor Muriel Bowser concerning the use of national and state guards in D.C. during the early days of protest in the aftermath of the killing of George Floyd, a Black man, by a White police officer in Minneapolis, Minnesota.

PROGRESSIVE FEDERALISM

The modern relationship between the states and federal government is both cooperative and coercive, depending on the issue area.

THE GREAT SOCIETY

One of the hallmarks of President Lyndon B. Johnson's Great Society program was offering federal financial aid to states in the form of grants-in-aid.

GROWING NATIONAL INTERVENTION IN THE ECONOMY

The needs of a growing and more technologically advanced nation required the intervention of the national government in economic affairs, such as regulating business and constructing roads, railroads, and ports.

DUAL FEDERALISM

The division of national and state powers envisioned by the Framers; each government had separate spheres of authority dictated by the Constitution.

NEW FEDERALISM AND THE DEVOLUTION REVOLUTION

Republican President Ronald Reagan and Republicans in Congress demanded that the national government return some administrative authority to state governments.

THE NEW DEAL AND COOPERATIVE FEDERALISM

The Great Depression and the New Deal signaled the beginning of a new era in federalism where the state and national governments worked together to address a broad array of policy issues, including job creation, health, and welfare.

CIVIL WAR AND RECONSTRUCTION

The Civil War and the defeat of the states'-rights South began to alter the division of power between state and national governments.

2010s | 1980s | 1960s | 1930s | 1880s | 1860s | 1800s

POLITICAL REFORM AND REALITIES: HOW ARE NATIONAL AND STATE POWERS REALLY BALANCED?

3.4 Analyze the impact of federalism on the relationships among national, state, and local levels of government.

As we have seen throughout this chapter, attempting to find equilibrium between the powers and responsibilities of national and state governments is one of the greatest challenges of a federal system. While the interdependent relationship of the state

WHAT WILL SHAPE VICE PRESIDENT KAMALA HARRIS'S VIEWS ON FEDERALISM?

As a former locally elected San Francisco District Attorney, the elected California State Attorney General, and a U.S. senator, Harris brings a deep understanding of the federal system both good and bad.

progressive federalism

A pragmatic approach to federalism that views relations between national and state governments as both coercive and cooperative.

Barack Obama

The first Black president of the United States, a Democrat, who served as the forty-fourth president from 2009 to 2017. Senator from Illinois from 2005 to 2008; member of the Illinois Senate from 1997 to 2004.

HOW HAS DR. FAUCI'S ROLE CHANGED?

Dr. Anthony Fauci was a leading and visible member of President Trump's Coronavirus Task Force headed by Vice President Mike Pence. As President Trump downplayed the seriousness of the pandemic, Trump took to attacking Fauci. President Joe Biden named Fauci his Chief Medical Advisor to work to solve pandemic issues.

and national governments characterized by cooperative federalism can be an advantageous way to solve large-scale problems, it may also ask both the states and the national government to do things they are not necessarily equipped to do. State governments, for example, may struggle with redistributive policies such as health care exchanges or the testing associated with the "No Child Left Behind" Act.

The relative strengths of the national and state governments continue to evolve today; finding a way to utilize these strengths is the aim of **progressive federalism**. Advocates of progressive federalism, such as former President **Barack Obama**, view the relationship between the states and the national government as both coercive and cooperative.[14] The form taken by the relationship depends chiefly on the political environment at each level of government. The best and first option is when the federal government is able to reach consensus and establish a national standard. However, failing the national government's ability to enact a particular proposal, national policy makers may embrace states' efforts to address that policy issue, particularly when those in power agree with the outcome of the state policy-making process. This approach allows policy makers to achieve their goals gradually and encourages states to act as what U.S. Supreme Court Justice Louis Brandeis called laboratories of democracy.[15] In 2020, the pandemic caused by the novel coronavirus, or COVID-19, however, required coordination between local, state, and the national governments, as well as international actors such as the World Health Organization (WHO). President Trump, however, terminated the United States' relationship with WHO by withdrawing funding based on his belief that it failed to act quickly enough in response to COVID-19. He also handed over control of restrictions to local and state governments. He also handed over control to state and local governments, leading to dissimilarity in rules and regulations. Even in cities or states where masks were required, President Trump refused to wear a mask, nor did he ask so of his supporters to wear them.[16]

The COVID-19 pandemic also brought about expansive change in the power of governors. Governor Andrew Cuomo's (D–NY) daily briefings drew national attention as he used his authority to lock down the state. Mayors also took on more authority as they ordered distancing requirements and created phased openings, reopenings, and reclosings. President Joe Biden is taking a much more federalist approach to controlling the pandemic, which had killed nearly 300,000 people by the time he took office. He and his task force on the virus went to work on multiple forms of remedies and rules from vaccines to public safety measures as his election was announced in mid-November.[17]

FIGURE 3.5 HOW DO FEDERAL GRANTS HELP STATE GOVERNMENTS?

Finances are one very important tool that the national government uses to influence state policy. On average, approximately one-third of state revenues come from the federal government, which means that states are highly dependent on the national government for financial solvency.

SOURCE: 2017 data from the Pew Charitable Trusts, www.pewtrusts.org.

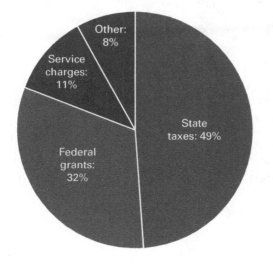

Other: 8%

Service charges: 11%

State taxes: 49%

Federal grants: 32%

Here, we explore two major factors that influence the relative balance of power between the state and national governments. First, we consider the role that finances play in creating and resolving national–state conflict and cooperation. We also consider the continuing role of the Supreme Court as the umpire of the federal system.

The Influence of Federal Grants

Until the 1960s, the national government constructed most federal grant programs in cooperation with the states, with emphasis on assisting the states in fulfilling their traditional responsibilities to protect the health, welfare, and, safety of their citizens. Today, however, the national government provides grants from its general revenues to states, local governments, nonprofit organizations, and even individuals (see Figure 3.5). These programs range from grants to support state programs that aid needy families to Pell grants that give college students help to fund their educations to federal payments to supplement unemployment checks to assist those who lost their jobs due to COVID-19. These grants are given for a number of purposes, including: (1) providing state and local governments with additional funds; (2) setting national standards for national problems such as clean air and water; and, (3) attempting to financially equalize rich and poor states and localities. Federal grants are of three major types: (1) categorical grants; (2) block grants; and, (3) programmatic requests.

CATEGORICAL GRANTS **Categorical grants** are grants for which Congress appropriates funds for *specific* purposes. About 90 percent of federal aid monies go to categorical grants. These grants became more prominent in 1964, when President **Lyndon B. Johnson (LBJ)** launched his **Great Society** program, which included what LBJ called a "War on Poverty." Categorical grants allocate federal dollars by a precise formula, often based on population. They are subject to detailed conditions imposed by the national government. Often, they are made available on a matching basis; that is, states must contribute money to match federal funds, although the national government may pay as much as 90 percent of the total. Categorical grants may be used by the national government to alter states' policy priorities or to coerce states to adopt particular policy objectives. With large sums of money at stake, states will often neglect

categorical grants
Grants that appropriate federal funds to states for a specific purpose.

Lyndon B. Johnson (LBJ)
Thirty-sixth president of the United States, a Democrat, who served from immediately following the death of President John F. Kennedy in 1963 to 1969. LBJ led the nation during the civil rights era and the Vietnam War.

Great Society
Reform program begun in 1964 by President Lyndon B. Johnson that was a broad attempt to combat poverty and discrimination through urban renewal, education reform, and unemployment relief.

FIGURE 3.6   WHERE CAN SANCTUARY CITIES, COUNTIES, OR STATES BE FOUND?

As Figure 3.6 shows, sanctuary areas are largely clustered on the east and west coasts, along with Colorado and counties within Iowa.

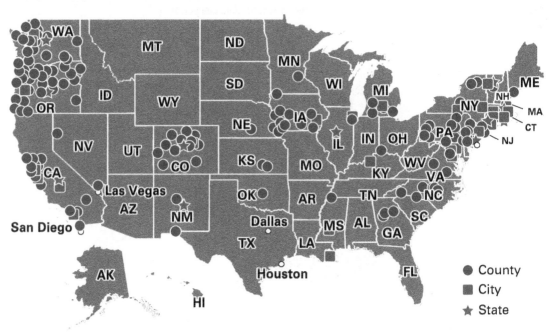

their own wants and needs to follow the leadership of the national government. One exception has been the case of "sanctuary cities." Early in the Trump administration, Attorney General Jeff Sessions announced that he would cut off federal funds allocated to cities for enhanced community policing unless they cooperated with federal immigration law enforcement officers and provided them access to city jails, among other measures. Los Angeles sued, and a federal court ruled that withholding funds was unconstitutional. As of November 2020, there were eleven sanctuary states, hundreds of sanctuary cities, and even more cities and counties who simply refused to comply with federal law, risking their federal funding.[18]

Ronald Reagan

Fortieth president of the United States, a Republican, who served from 1981 to 1989. Reagan led the nation through the end of the Cold War, and his leadership led to a national shift toward political conservatism.

block grant

A large grant given to a state by the federal government with only general spending guidelines.

BLOCK GRANTS   In 1981, former California Republican Governor **Ronald Reagan** became president, pledging to advance what he called New Federalism and a return of power to the states. The hallmark of this action was the consolidation of many categorical grants into fewer, less-restrictive **block grants**—large amounts of money given to states with only general spending guidelines. Many of these went to education and health care. Perhaps not surprisingly, block grants continue to be popular with governors, who often urge the consolidation of even more programs into block grants.

PROGRAMMATIC REQUESTS   Informally known as *earmarks*, programmatic requests became the norm after earmarks were banned in 2011. They are federal funds designated for special projects within a state or congressional district that direct specific exemptions from taxes or mandated fees. Federal funds have been provided for special projects since the first Congress, but the use of these grants exploded in the past two decades. Programmatic requests are not competitively awarded, and have thus become very controversial owing to the use of paid political lobbyists who try to secure federal funds for their clients, be they states, cities, universities, or nonprofit groups. Members of Congress also attempt to secure these funds to bring programs and economic development back to their home districts.

Federalism and the Supreme Court

The U.S. Supreme Court has always played an important role as the umpire of the federal system. When governmental powers, especially those of the state and national governments, come into conflict, it is the Court's job to determine which government is supreme. From the 1930s until the 1980s, the Court made its federalism decisions largely outside of the public eye. While the Court under Chief Justice **Earl Warren** in the 1950s and 1960s attracted a great deal of attention, it was largely for the justices' decisions on civil rights and liberties issues, not the Court's decisions on the balance of power between the state and national governments. Through the process of incorporation, which bound state governments to the provisions of the U.S. Constitution, however, many of these decisions had the result—intended or not—of expanding federal power at the expense of subnational units. Still, it is important to note that the votes of any justices in federalism cases are not easily explainable. In cases involving states' rights as well as important civil rights or civil liberties, one can never be certain which issue is controlling. For example, when a justice deliberates over a case involving the right of states to pass gender preference bathroom laws—one in which a justice must consider whether the issue falls within the exclusive power of the states or under the national constitutional right to privacy—which issue informs their decision?

THE REHNQUIST COURT Beginning in the late 1980s, the Court's willingness to allow Congress to regulate in a variety of areas waned. According to one observer, the federalism decisions made by the Court under Chief Justice **William H. Rehnquist** in the 1980s and 1990s were "a reexamination of the country's most basic constitutional arrangements."[19] The Court's decisions largely agreed with the Republican states' rights view supported by advocates of New Federalism.

THE ROBERTS COURT In 2005, following the death of Chief Justice Rehnquist, President George W. Bush appointed Chief Justice John Roberts to head the Supreme Court. In its early years, the Roberts Court appeared reluctant to address high-profile federalism cases. Today, the Court has become a willing participant in the federalism debate, deciding a series of visible cases related to the balance of national and state power. The Roberts's Court's approach to federalism has shied away from the Rehnquist Court's strict interpretation of New Federalism. Unlike earlier cases, most of the Roberts's Court cases have involved issues of preemption and the largely dormant commerce clause. In several cases where the conservative majority of the Court has reviewed state economic regulation under the states' police powers, it has balanced states rights in the federal system with that of Congress guided by cases decided in the pre-New Deal era that limited the scope of the commerce clause. In one of its major federalism cases, *Shelby County v. Holder* (1965), for example, the Court struck down as unconstitutional key sections of the Voting Rights Act of 1965.[20] The majority found that the continued imposition of preclearance reporting requirements concerning any voting law changes on some states (basically those in the South) and not on others violated the equal protection clause because states were not all treated equally. In this ruling and other cases including those involving issues such as immigration, redistricting, same-sex marriage, and the Affordable Care Act (Obamacare),[21] the Court came down on the side of the national government. It is reasonable, however, that with three new conservative Republican appointees on the Court, to expect a return to a more states' rights tradition as the Biden administration seeks to assist states deal with the pandemic and racially biased policing.

Earl Warren

Served as Chief Justice of the Supreme Court from 1953 to 1969. The Warren Court was noted for its major constitutional shifts on issues such as defendants' rights and the desegregation of southern schools.

William H. Rehnquist

Served first as an Associate Justice and Chief Justice from 1972 until 2005. He was a strong supporter of state's rights within the federal system.

Shelby County v. Holder **(2013)**

Court ruled that preclearance of election changes cannot be applied to just certain states previously found to curtail or inhibit minority voting thus overruling a key provision of the Voting Rights Act.

CONCLUSION AND REVIEW

What Are the Roots of the Federal System?

3.1 Trace the roots of the federal system and distinguish it from other types of government.

Aristotle classifies the types of governments according to who rules, and in whose interest. Types of governments include monarchy, totalitarianism, aristocracy, oligarchy, polity, confederacy, and democracy. Fears about mob rule and the vast size of the United States led the Framers to create a republican democracy that relies on the role of representatives to filter citizens' viewpoints.

How Are Powers of Government Divided by the Constitution?

3.2 Explain the constitutional foundations for federalism.

The national government has both enumerated and implied powers under the Constitution. National and state governments share an additional group of concurrent powers. Other powers are reserved to the states or the people, or expressly denied to both governments. The powers of the national government are ultimately declared supreme. Local governments are not expressly mentioned in the Constitution but are formed when state governments delegate their sovereign authority.

How Has Federalism Evolved?

3.3 Trace the evolution of federalism, from ratification to the present.

Dual federalism was characterized by a system of separate but equally powerful state and national governments. This system was exemplified by states' authority to regulate issues such as slavery, evident in the doctrine of nullification and the Supreme Court's decision in *Dred Scott* v. *Sanford* (1857). The Civil War changed forever the nature of federalism. The notion of equally powerful but separate national and state governments met its demise in the wake of the Great Depression. Franklin D. Roosevelt's New Deal ushered in an era of cooperative federalism, in which the powers of the national and state and local governments became more integrated, working together to solve shared problems.

Political Reform and Realities: How Are National and State Powers Really Balanced?

3.4 Analyze the impact of federalism on the relationships among national, state, and local levels of government.

The balance of power between the state and national governments may be affected by a number of factors. The federal government provides money to states in a number of ways, including categorical grants, block grants, and programmatic requests. The Supreme Court also plays an important role as the umpire of the federal system. The 1980s ushered in an era of New Federalism, in which President Ronald Reagan and Republican representatives in Congress sought to return power to the states. Progressive federalism, an approach that views the relationship between the states and the national government as both cooperative and coercive, gained ground during President Barack Obama's two terms in office. President Donald J. Trump's approach to federalism departed significantly from President Obama's. President Joe Biden is expected to revert to "Obama-like" federalism, especially in dealing with COVID-19 and helping states remedy policing issues.

LEARN THE TERMS

aristocracy
Barron v. *Baltimore* (1833)
block grant
categorical grants
charter
Civil War
concurrent powers
confederation
cooperative federalism
Dillon's Rule

Dred Scott v. *Sandford* (1857)
dual federalism
enumerated powers
federal system
Gibbons v. *Ogden* (1824)
Great Society
McCulloch v. *Maryland* (1819)
monarchy
New Deal
nullification

oligarchy
progressive federalism
Reconstruction
reserved powers
secession
Seventeenth Amendment
Shelby County v. *Holder* (2013)
Sixteenth Amendment
Tenth Amendment
totalitarianism

LEARN THE NAMES

Abraham Lincoln
Andrew Johnson
Barack Obama
Calvin Coolidge
Dred Scott

Earl Warren
Franklin D. Roosevelt (FDR)
Herbert Hoover
John C. Calhoun
John Marshall

Lyndon B. Johnson (LBJ)
Roger B. Taney
Ronald Reagan
William H. Rehnquist

North Wind Picture Archives

HOW DID THE *ZENGER* CASE EXPAND FREEDOM OF THE PRESS?

The 1734 case of *The Crown* v. *Zenger* strengthened the core principle of freedom of the press that information that is true and not libelous may be published even if it insults those in power. In this illustration, the right of Zenger to make truthful accusations against the British governor of New York is defended in court by his lawyer.

CRITICAL THINKING QUESTION: *As you read this chapter, do you see particular civil liberties in need of greater (or less) protection?*

CIVIL LIBERTIES

LEARNING OBJECTIVES

4.1 Explain the roots of civil liberties in the Constitution and their development in the Bill of Rights.

4.2 Distinguish between the establishment and the free exercise clauses of the First Amendment.

4.3 Outline the First Amendment liberties and limitations on the freedoms of speech, press, assembly, and petition.

4.4 Describe the Second Amendment's guarantee of the right to bear arms.

4.5 Outline the constitutional rights of defendants and the issues involved in protecting defendants' liberties as guaranteed by the Bill of Rights.

4.6 Explain the origins and significance of the right to privacy.

4.7 Evaluate how civil liberties have been affected by the simultaneous arrival of COVID-19 and racial unrest in the United States.

On May 11, 1732, Colonel William Cosby arrived in what is now New York City to become the Province of New York's new royal governor. The Province of New York included what are now the states of New York, New Jersey, Vermont, Delaware, and parts of several other northeastern states. Nothing in the historical record indicates that Cosby was anything other than an angry, power-hungry, corrupt fool. After watching the new governor's actions and petty politics, which included rigging elections and dismissing the chief justice of the New York Court and replacing him with an old crony, John Peter Zenger, a German immigrant, decided to begin publication of the *New York Weekly Journal* in autumn 1733. His goal? Spread the news of the governor's actions around the province.

Zenger, an expert printer, solicited columns and news articles from a stable of authors. At that time, however, it was a crime to write or publish criticisms of any public officials or government—even if the accusations were true. Upon publication of articles criticizing Cosby, the governor issued a proclamation condemning the "scandalous, virulent, false and seditious reflections" contained in the paper. On Cosby's orders, the sheriff jailed Zenger. Two grand juries refused to indict Zenger as requested by the province's attorney general. Stymied, Cosby instructed that Zenger be arrested by information, meaning a judge issued a warrant for Zenger's arrest charging him with seditious libel. It was yet another highly unpopular move by the governor. Zenger was sent to New York's Old City Jail, and bond was set so high that he was unable to make bail. Thus, he ended up staying in jail for nearly a year.

The tale gets worse for Zenger. During what became his first trial, both of his lawyers were disbarred at the direction of the governor. Thus, they could no longer represent Zenger. At his second trial, however, gasps were heard around the courtroom as his new lawyer, thirty-eight-year-old Andrew Hamilton, the most famous attorney in the colonies (no relation to Alexander Hamilton), rose to announce his representation of Zenger.

The presiding judge who saw that Zenger would not reveal the names of the authors of the "libelous" articles, thought the case was cut-and-dried. Zenger did not deny publishing the articles, and they definitely criticized Cosby. But Hamilton had not earned his reputation for nothing.

Appealing directly to the twelve empaneled jurors, he argued that governments should not be allowed to punish those who published truthful criticism about public officials. How could public officials be held accountable if the hands of the press were tied, Hamilton asked the jury.

At the end of Hamilton's closing arguments, the judge directed the jury to find Zenger guilty. Within ten minutes after it retired, the jury came back and rendered a "not guilty" verdict, freeing Zenger. This decision, *The Crown v. Zenger* (1735), set an important standard for civil liberties that found its way into colonial and state constitutions and, eventually, the Bill of Rights. Early on, colonists realized how important freedom of the press was to a free flow of ideas in what was to become the new republic.

• • •

Civil liberties are the personal guarantees and freedoms that government usually cannot abridge, by law, constitution, or judicial interpretation. As guarantees of "freedom to" action, they place limitations on the power of the government to restrain or dictate an individual's actions. **Civil rights**, in contrast, provide freedom from arbitrary or discriminatory treatment (treating someone differently based on a variety of characteristics, including race, religion, gender, or—in many cases—gender orientation) by government or individuals.

Questions of civil liberties often present complex problems. We must decide how to determine the boundaries of speech and assembly and how much control over our personal liberties we give to police or other law enforcement officials. Moreover,

civil liberties
The personal guarantees and freedoms that the government cannot abridge by law, constitution, or judicial interpretation.

civil rights
The government-protected rights of individuals against arbitrary or discriminatory treatment by governments or individuals.

during times of war and social unrest, it is important to consider the liberties accorded to those who oppose war or are suspected of anti-government activities.

Resolution of civil liberties questions often falls to the judiciary, which must balance the competing interests of the government and the people. However, in cases such as the U.S. Supreme Court's decision to uphold President Trump's executive order to ban nationals from five majority-Muslim countries from entering the United States (in what many called a Muslim ban), a majority of the Court deferred to presidential action even where religious liberties seemed to be curtailed. In this chapter, we explore the various dimensions of civil liberties guarantees contained in the U.S. Constitution and the Bill of Rights.

WHAT ARE THE ROOTS OF CIVIL LIBERTIES AND THE BILL OF RIGHTS?

4.1 Explain the roots of civil liberties in the Constitution and their development in the Bill of Rights.

In 1787, most state constitutions explicitly protected a variety of personal liberties, such as freedoms of speech and religion, freedom from unreasonable searches and seizures, and trial by jury. The new federal system established by the Constitution would redistribute power between the national government and the states. Without an explicit guarantee of specific civil liberties, could the national government be trusted to uphold the freedoms already granted to citizens by their states?

Recognition of the increased power of the new national government led Anti-Federalists to stress the need for a bill of rights. Anti-Federalists and many others were confident they could control the actions of their own state legislators, but they did not trust the national government to protect civil liberties.

The notion of including a bill of rights in the Constitution was not popular at the Constitutional Convention. When George Mason of Virginia suggested adding such a bill to the preface of the proposed Constitution, representatives unanimously defeated his resolution.[1] In subsequent ratification debates, Federalists argued that a bill of rights was unnecessary, putting forward three main arguments in opposition:

1. A bill of rights was unnecessary in a constitutional republic founded on the idea of popular sovereignty and inalienable, natural rights. Moreover, most state constitutions contained bills of rights, so federal guarantees were unnecessary.

2. A bill of rights would be dangerous. According to Alexander Hamilton in *Federalist No. 84*, since the national government was one of enumerated powers (that is, it had only the powers listed in the Constitution), "Why declare that things shall not be done which there is no power to do?"

3. A national bill of rights would be impractical to enforce. Its validity would largely depend on public opinion and the spirit of the people and government.

Some Framers, however, came to support the idea. After the Philadelphia convention, James Madison conducted a lively correspondence with Thomas Jefferson about the need for a national bill of rights. Jefferson supported such guarantees far more quickly than did Madison. But the reluctant Madison soon found himself in a close race against James Monroe for a seat in the House of Representatives in the First Congress. The district was largely Anti-Federalist. In an act of political expediency, Madison issued a new series of public letters similar to *The Federalist Papers*, in which he vowed to support a bill of rights. Once elected to the House, Madison made good on his promise and became the prime author of the Bill of Rights. Still, he considered Congress to have far more important matters to handle and viewed his work on the Bill of Rights as "a nauseous project."[2]

With fear of political instability running high, Congress worked quickly to approve Madison's draft. The proposed Bill of Rights with twelve amendments was sent to the states for ratification in 1789, the same year the first Congress convened. By 1791, the states had approved the first ten of its amendments.

The *Bill of Rights* contains numerous specific guarantees against encroachment by the national government, including those of free speech, press, and religion. The Ninth and Tenth Amendments, favored by the Federalists, note that the Bill of Rights is not exclusive.

The **Ninth Amendment** makes clear that the Bill of Rights' listing of rights does not mean that others do not exist. This amendment played a critical role when the Supreme Court began to address the constitutionality of state laws prohibiting contraceptives, surely nothing the Framers were thinking about as they neared completion of the Bill of Rights. The *Tenth Amendment* reiterates that powers not delegated to the national government are reserved to the states or to the people.

Ninth Amendment

Part of the Bill of Rights that makes it clear that enumerating rights in the Constitution or Bill of Rights does not mean that others do not exist.

The Incorporation Doctrine: The Bill of Rights Made Applicable to the States

The Framers intended the Bill of Rights to limit the national government's power to infringe on the rights and liberties of the citizenry. Thus, in *Barron* v. *Baltimore* (1833), the Supreme Court ruled that the Bill of Rights limited only the actions of the U.S. government and not those of the states.[3] In 1868, however, the **Fourteenth Amendment** was added to the U.S. Constitution. Its language suggested that some or even all protections guaranteed in the Bill of Rights might be interpreted to prevent state infringement of those rights. Section 1 of the Fourteenth Amendment reads: "No State shall . . . Deprive any person of life, liberty, or property, without due process of law." Questions about the scope of "life" and "liberty" as well as the meaning of the phrase "due process of law" continue even today to engage legal scholars and jurists.

Until nearly the turn of the twentieth century, the Supreme Court steadfastly rejected numerous arguments for interpreting the Fourteenth Amendment's **due process clause** in such a way as to make various provisions in the Bill of Rights applicable to the states. In 1897, however, the Court began to increase its jurisdiction over the states by holding them to what was termed a **substantive due process** standard. This new standard required states to prove that their laws constituted a valid exercise of their power to regulate the health, welfare, or public morals of citizens.[4] Interference with state power, however, was rare, and states passed **sedition laws** that made it illegal to speak or write any political criticism that threatened to diminish respect for the government, its laws, or public officials. States anticipated that the U.S. Supreme Court would uphold the constitutionality of these laws. When Benjamin Gitlow, a member of the Socialist Party, printed a manifesto in which he urged workers to overthrow the U.S. government, he was convicted of violating a New York state law that prohibited such advocacy. Although his conviction was upheld, in *Gitlow* v. *New York* (1925), the justices noted that states were not completely free to limit forms of political expression, saying,

> For present purposes we may and do assume that freedom of speech and of the press—which are protected by the First Amendment from abridgment by Congress—are among the *fundamental personal rights and "liberties"* protected by the due process clause of the Fourteenth Amendment from impairment by the states [emphasis added].[5]

Gitlow, with its finding that states could not abridge free speech protections, was the first decision to clearly articulate the **incorporation doctrine**. It also enunciated the belief that some "personal rights" and "liberties" were so fundamental that they required special protection from the states. This was clarified in *Near* v. *Minnesota*

Fourteenth Amendment

One of three major amendments enacted after the Civil War, extending the "privileges and immunities of citizenship" and "equal protection of the law" to all U.S. citizens. None of these rights or liberties could be taken without the "due process" of law.

due process clause

Clause contained in the Fifth and Fourteenth Amendments, which over the years has been construed to guarantee a variety of rights to individuals.

substantive due process

Judicial interpretation of the Fifth and Fourteenth Amendments' due process clauses. Protects citizens from arbitrary or unjust state or federal laws.

sedition laws

Laws that make it illegal to speak or write any political criticism that threaten to diminish respect for the government, its laws, or public officials. State sedition laws were overturned in the 1925 *Gitlow* v. *New York* Supreme Court decision.

incorporation doctrine

An interpretation of the Constitution holding that the due process clause of the Fourteenth Amendment requires state and local governments to guarantee the rights stated in the Bill of Rights.

selective incorporation
A judicial doctrine whereby most, but not all, protections found in the Bill of Rights are made applicable to the states via the Fourteenth Amendment.

fundamental freedoms
Those rights defined by the Court as essential to order, liberty, and justice and therefore entitled to the highest standard of review.

Warren Court
The period in Supreme Court history during which Earl Warren served as chief justice (1953–1969), noted for its many rulings expanding civil liberties and civil rights.

Earl Warren
Chief Justice (1953–1969) who presided over a Court that moved progressively to the left on civil liberties and civil rights issues.

(1931), when the U.S. Supreme Court further developed this doctrine by holding that a state law violated the First Amendment's freedom of the press.[6]

Selective Incorporation and Fundamental Freedoms

By 2021, the Supreme Court has made nearly all specific guarantees in the Bill of Rights applicable to the states through the due process clause of the Fourteenth Amendment as shown in Table 4.1. Historically, the Court used **selective incorporation** to limit the rights of states by protecting against abridgment of **fundamental freedoms**. These freedoms—defined by the Court as essential to order, liberty, and justice—are subject to the Court's most rigorous standard of review. The liberal **Warren Court**, led by Chief Justice **Earl Warren**, was responsible for ten of the decisions listed in Table 4.1.

The Court set out the rationale for selective incorporation in *Palko v. Connecticut* (1937).[7] Frank Palko was charged with first-degree murder for killing two Connecticut police officers, found guilty of a lesser charge of second-degree murder, and sentenced to life imprisonment. Connecticut appealed. Palko was retried, found guilty of first-degree murder, and sentenced to death. Palko then appealed his second conviction, arguing that it violated the Fifth Amendment's prohibition against double jeopardy because the due process clause of the Fourteenth Amendment had made the Fifth Amendment applicable to the states.

TABLE 4.1 HOW HAS SELECTIVE INCORPORATION MADE THE BILL OF RIGHTS APPLICABLE TO THE STATES?

Amendment	Right	Date	Case Incorporated
I	Speech	1925	*Gitlow v. New York*
	Press	1931	*Near v. Minnesota*
	Assembly and petition	1937	*DeJonge v. Oregon*
	Free exercise of religion	1940	*Cantwell v. Connecticut*
	Establishment of religion	1947	*Everson v. Board of Education*
	Petition	1963	*Edwards v. South Carolina*
II	Bear arms	2008/2010	*D.C. v. Heller/McDonald v. City of Chicago*
III	No quartering of soldiers		Not incorporated
IV	No unreasonable searches by state governments	1961	*Mapp v. Ohio*
	Requirements for a warrant	1964	*Aguilar v. Texas*
V	Just compensation for seized property	1897	*Chicago, B&O R.R. Co. v. Chicago*
	Self-incrimination	1964	*Malloy v. Hogan*
	Double jeopardy	1969	*Benton v. Maryland*
	Grand jury indictment		Not incorporated
VI	Public trial and notice of accusations	1948	*In re Oliver*
	Right to counsel	1963	*Gideon v. Wainwright*
	Confrontation of hostile witnesses	1965	*Pointer v. Texas*
	Impartial jury	1966	*Parker v. Gladden*
	Speedy trial	1967	*Klopfer v. North Carolina*
	Compulsory process to obtain witness testimony	1965	*Washington v. Texas*
	Criminal trial	1968	*Duncan v. Louisiana*
	Right to jury selected from residents of states and district where crime committed		Not incorporated
VII	Civil jury trial		Not incorporated
VIII	No cruel and unusual punishment	1962	*Robinson v. California*
	No excessive bail	1971	*Schilb v. Kuebel*
	Protection against excessive fines		Not incorporated

What did he mean, the prohibition on double jeapardy isn't "implicit in the concept of ordered liberty"?

You lost.

stus.com

Stuart Rees/Stu's Views

WHEN DID THE COURT FIRST ARTICULATE THE DOCTRINE OF SELECTIVE INCORPORATION?

In *Palko* v. *Connecticut* (1937), the Court found that Palko's retrial in a murder case was constitutional even though it was double jeopardy. At that time (and since overruled) the Court did not believe that protections from state retrial of cases (double jeopardy) were **NOT** sufficiently important to warrant strict scrutiny.

The Supreme Court disagreed. It ruled that the due process clause bound states only to those rights that were "of the very essence of a scheme of ordered liberty." The Fifth Amendment's double jeopardy clause was not, in the Court's view, among these rights. The Court overruled that decision in 1969.[8]

Today, selective incorporation requires states to respect freedoms of press, speech, and assembly, among other liberties. The Court has not incorporated other guarantees, such as those contained in the Third, Fifth, and Seventh Amendments (housing of soldiers, grand jury indictments, and jury trials in civil cases), because it has yet to consider them sufficiently fundamental to national notions of liberty and justice. When such laws involving fundamental freedoms are challenged, the Supreme Court evaluates their constitutionality by using a standard called **strict scrutiny**. This requires that the challenged law must advance a compelling government interest and be narrowly written in the least restrictive way to achieve its goals. At that time (and since overruled) the Court did not believe that protections from the state retrial of the cases (double jeopardy) were not sufficiently important to warrant strict scrutiny.

WHAT ARE THE FIRST AMENDMENT GUARANTEES OF FREEDOM OF RELIGION?

4.2 Distinguish between the establishment and the free exercise clauses of the First Amendment.

The **First Amendment** to the Constitution begins, "Congress shall make no law respecting an establishment of religion, or prohibiting the free exercise thereof." This statement sets the boundaries of governmental action. The **establishment clause** directs the national government not to sanction an official religion. The **free exercise clause** ("or prohibiting the free exercise thereof") guarantees citizens that the national government will not interfere with the practice of their religion. These guarantees, however, are not absolute and can come into conflict, creating a difficult job for the courts. As the Supreme Court observed in 1940, the First Amendment "embraces two concepts—freedom to believe and freedom to act. The first is absolute. Thoughts cannot be regulated. In contrast, conduct remains subject to regulation by all levels of government."[9] This was the case in *Masterpiece Cakeshop* v. *Colorado Civil Rights Commission* (2018) in which a baker, Jack Phillips, refused to bake a wedding cake for a same-sex couple, claiming that doing so would violate

strict scrutiny
A heightened standard of review used by the Supreme Court to determine the constitutional validity of a challenged practice. Legislation affecting the fundamental freedoms of speech, assembly, religion, and the press as well as suspect classifications are automatically accorded this level of review.

First Amendment
Part of the Bill of Rights that imposes a number of restrictions on the federal government with respect to civil liberties, including freedom of religion, speech, press, assembly, and petition.

establishment clause
The first clause of the First Amendment; it directs the national government not to sanction an official religion.

free exercise clause
The second clause of the First Amendment; it prohibits the U.S. government from interfering with a citizen's right to practice his or her religion.

his religious belief that gay marriage is a sin. The Court ruled that the state commission had singled out Phillips, violating his protected rights to exercise or act upon his religious beliefs, thus allowing personal faith-based actions, however discriminatory, to be protected by the First Amendment.

The Establishment Clause

The U.S. Constitution's separation of church and state has always generated controversy in American politics. A majority of Americans clearly value the moral teachings of their respective religions. U.S. coins are embossed with "In God We Trust." The U.S. Supreme Court asks for God's blessing on the Court at the beginning of every session. Every session of the U.S. House and Senate begins with a prayer, and both the House and Senate have their own chaplains. Through the years, the Court has been divided over the interpretation of the establishment clause. Does this clause erect a total wall between church and state, as favored by Thomas Jefferson, or does it allow some governmental accommodation of religion?

Until recently, the Court's basic rule for dealing with church–state questions was the *Lemon* test. This three-part test is named for **Lemon v. Kurtzman (1971)**.[10] According to the *Lemon* test, a practice or policy is constitutional under the establishment clause if it meets three criteria:

1. Has a legitimate secular purpose
2. Neither advances nor inhibits religion
3. Does not foster an excessive government entanglement with religion

One practice that clearly violates the *Lemon* test is prayer in public schools. In **Engel v. Vitale (1962)**, for example, the Court ruled that the recitation of a brief nondenominational prayer drafted by the local school board in public school classrooms was unconstitutional.[11] One year later, in *Abington School District v. Schempp* (1963), the Court ruled that state-mandated Bible reading or recitation of the Lord's Prayer in public schools was also unconstitutional.[12] The Court has also prohibited prayer at other public school events, such as graduations and sporting events.[13] Many public schools, however, continue to ignore that mandate.

In **Santa Fe Independent School District v. Doe (2000)**, the Rehnquist Court ruled that a student elected by the student body to act as chaplain who delivered an overtly Christian prayer over the loudspeaker system before each varsity football game violated the First Amendment's establishment clause. While the lawsuit was pending, the school district allowed students to vote on permitting nonsectarian, student-led prayer. Mormon and Catholic families continued to challenge the old and new policies. The Court agreed with the parents, finding that the policies violated the establishment clause and ruling that the prayer was public, not private, speech.[14]

Lemon v. Kurtzman **(1971)**

The Supreme Court created a three-part test for examining the constitutionality of religious establishment issues.

Engel v. Vitale **(1962)**

Court case in which the recitation of a brief, nondenominational prayer drafted by the school board was unconstitutional because it violated the First Amendment's religious establishment clause.

Santa Fe Independent School District v. Doe **(2000)**

Supreme Court decision that even nondenominational prayers made part of public-school gatherings violate the establishment clause of the First Amendment.

ARE CHILDREN STILL EXPECTED TO PRAY IN PUBLIC SCHOOLS?

School prayer is just one of the thorny questions the Supreme Court has addressed under the establishment clause. While prayer in public schools was once quite common, since the 1960s the Court has usually decided against this practice, even when it is student-led. Despite Court rulings, many educational institutions maintain this practice. Pictured is a soccer team praying before practice.

H. Mark Weidman Photography/Alamy Stock Photo

The Court, however, has allowed a wide variety of other church–state entanglements. For example, the use of public buildings for religious worship[15] and governments providing textbooks, computers, and other instructional materials to students at religious schools are allowed.[16] As recently as 2020, the Court also permitted governments to offer students vouchers to attend private or religious schools.[17] And, student fees at public universities may be used to fund the activities of religious organizations, so long as those groups allow members of a variety of faiths.[18]

Establishment issues, however, do not always focus on education. The Court has used the *Lemon* test to rule that a privately donated courthouse display, which included the Ten Commandments and 300 other historical documents illustrating the evolution of American law, violated the First Amendment's establishment clause.[19] In 1928, the citizens of Bladensburg, Maryland, erected a 140-foot cross, placing it in a public traffic circle, to honor its 48 men killed in World War I. The statue was maintained by the state since its erection. In a 7–2 opinion in 2019, striking down the challenge to the cross as violation of the establishment clause, the justices stressed that the cross was old and was dedicated in a multi-faith ceremony. Importantly, Justice Samuel A. Alito rejected using the *Lemon* test, noting that *Lemon* has not been a workable "framework" for deciding First Amendment cases and that it offered little consistent guidance to lower courts as to its application.[20]

The Free Exercise Clause

The free exercise clause of the First Amendment proclaims that "Congress shall make no law . . . prohibiting the free exercise [of religion]." Although the free exercise clause of the First Amendment guarantees individuals the right to be free from governmental interference in the exercise of their religion, this guarantee, like other First Amendment freedoms, is not absolute. For example, in the first case where the Supreme Court interpreted the Constitution's protection of the free exercise clause, ***Reynolds* v. *United States* (1878)**, at issue

***Reynolds* v. *United States* (1878)**

Supreme Court ruling that plural marriages could be banned by federal law and that prohibiting such practices did not violate the free exercise clause of the First Amendment.

HOW RIGID IS THE WALL BETWEEN CHURCH AND STATE?

The Peace Cross, or Bladensburg World War I Memorial, was commissioned by the American Legion to commemorate the 49 servicemen from Prince George's County, Maryland, who died during the war. Although early on some claimed that publicly funded maintenance of the cross breached the wall separating church and state, in 2019 the Supreme Court ruled that the cross could remain on public land and did not violate the establishment clause of the U.S. Constitution, further easing the height of the wall between church and state.

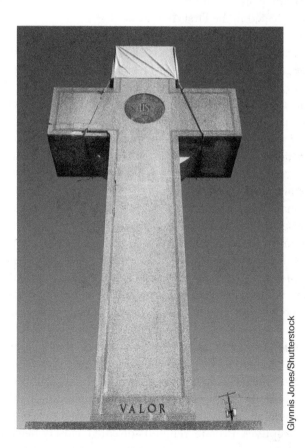

Glynnis Jones/Shutterstock

was the constitutionality of the federal Morrill Anti-Bigamy Act, which prohibited all marriages with more than one wife. It was part of the Church of Jesus Christ of Latter Day Saints (Mormons) doctrine that men were commanded to take more than one wife. The Church decided to make a test case challenging the federal law. Thus, after one of its members was convicted for having more than one wife, the Supreme Court ruled that the free exercise clause protects any religious belief but not action. The Court examined the history of religious freedom in the United States, quoting from Thomas Jefferson, who wrote about the distinction between religious belief and action. According to Jefferson, a keen advocate of erecting a wall between church and state, "Belief lies solely between man and his God"; thus, "the legislative powers of the government reach actions only." Plural marriages were abhorrent to the majority, and as actions, could be outlawed by Congress.[21]

In the area of free exercise, the Court often has had to confront questions of "What is a god?" and "What is a religious faith?"—questions that theologians have grappled with for centuries. In 1965, for example, in a case involving three men who were denied conscientious objector deferments during the Vietnam War because they did not subscribe to "traditional" organized religions, the Court ruled unanimously that belief in a supreme being was not essential for recognition as a conscientious objector.[22] Thus, the men were entitled to the draft deferments because their views paralleled those who objected to war and who belonged to traditional faiths.

Wisconsin v. Yoder (1972)

Supreme Court ruling that a state compulsory school attendance law violated the free exercise clause as it applied to the Amish, who believed education beyond the eighth grade was harmful to their children, who they did not want to be further exposed to the influences outside their insular community.

In *Wisconsin v. Yoder* (1972), the Supreme Court ruled that a Wisconsin law, which required that all children attend school until at least the age of sixteen, was unconstitutional as it applied to the Amish, who wished to remove their children from school after the eighth grade. The Amish argued that their children would be exposed to worldly values unacceptable to their faith and that their children learned what they needed to be productive members of their Amish communities. The Court agreed, noting how peaceable the Amish community was and its particular restrictions allowed boys and girls the opportunity to learn skills not necessarily needed by others, such as responsibilities for home and farm life. Thus, the law violated the Amish's free exercise of religion as protected in the First Amendment.[23]

In contrast, the Court has ruled that prisoners can be denied access to religious services provided the action was "reasonably related to penological interests."[24] Lawful free exercise curtailments by the government as a result of this 1987 ruling include denying Muslim prisoners access to religious services for security reasons. Thus, the U.S. Supreme Court has interpreted the Constitution to mean that governmental interests can outweigh free exercise rights in some situations, as was the case in a 2020 decision where the Court tackled the issue of whether teachers who work at church-run schools could use federal anti-discrimination laws against their employers. In a 7–2 decision, the Court ruled that church-run schools could discriminate against teachers for any reason. One of the plaintiffs was fired after revealing she had breast cancer; another, a teacher who refused to retire. They originally filed their claims under the federal Americans with Disabilities Act and the federal Civil Rights Act of 1964's prohibition on age discrimination, respectively. The Court found that to allow the claims to go forward would infringe on private religious schools' ability to discharge their mission and violate the free exercise clause.[25]

Oregon Employment Division v. Smith (1990)

Supreme Court decision that a state could deny unemployment benefits to American Indian employees who tested positive for peyote, which was categorized as an illegal drug, even though it was part of an age-old religious ceremony of the Native American Church. The Court found that this state action was not a violation of the free exercise clause.

In *Oregon Employment Division v. Smith* (1990), the Court found that an Oregon law denying American Indians' claims for unemployment benefits after they tested positive for using peyote was constitutional. Peyote, a hallucinogenic drug, had long been used in religious ceremonies of the Native American Church.[26]

Outrage prompted Congress, three years later, to pass the Religious Freedom Restoration Act (RFRA).[27] While the Court has limited some sections of the act, in 2006 the act was used to protect the use of hallucinogenic drugs in religious ceremonies.[28] More recently, RFRA successfully was used to challenge the constitutionality of the Affordable Care Act's provisions requiring employer-sponsored health plans to include coverage for contraceptives. Private, religious-oriented, closely held companies thus could opt out of coverage for their female employees if the employer has religious objections to the use of contraceptives.[29] This decision was expanded in 2020 when the Court ruled that the types of employers that could stop provision of contraceptives for women could be expanded to universities and publicly traded companies.[30]

WHAT ARE THE FIRST AMENDMENT GUARANTEES OF FREEDOM OF SPEECH, PRESS, ASSEMBLY, AND PETITION?

4.3 Outline the First Amendment liberties and limitations on the freedoms of speech, press, assembly, and petition.

The Supreme Court has, to varying degrees, scrutinized the remaining guarantees protected by the First Amendment. During times of war, for example, the Court generally has allowed Congress and the chief executive extraordinary leeway in limiting First Amendment liberties, including the aforementioned free exercise and establishment clauses. Below, we provide historical background and current judicial interpretations of the liberties of speech, press, assembly, and petition.

Freedoms of Speech and of the Press

A democracy depends on a free exchange of ideas, and the First Amendment shows that the Framers were well aware of this fact. Historically, one of the most volatile issues of constitutional interpretation has centered on the First Amendment's mandate that "Congress shall make no law . . . abridging the freedom of speech or of the press." As with the establishment and free exercise clauses of the First Amendment, the Court has not interpreted speech and press clauses as absolute bans on government regulation. This leeway in interpretation has led to thousands of cases seeking both broader and narrower judicial interpretations of the scope of these clauses in the First Amendment. Over the years, the Court has employed a hierarchical approach in determining what governments can and cannot regulate, with some liberties getting greater protection than others. Generally, the Court has granted thoughts the greatest protection and actions or deeds the least. Words have fallen somewhere in the middle, depending on their content and purpose.

THE ALIEN AND SEDITION ACTS   When the states ratified the First Amendment in 1791, it was considered to protect against **prior restraint** of speech or expression—meaning to guard against the prohibition of speech or publication before the fact. Faced with increasing criticism of the Federalist government by Democratic-Republicans in 1798, the Federalist Congress, with President John Adams's blessing, enacted the **Alien and Sedition Acts**. These acts banned any criticism of the Federalist government by the growing numbers of Democratic-Republicans informally headed by Thomas Jefferson. Although the law clearly flew in the face of the First Amendment's ban on prior restraint, the Adams administration successfully prosecuted, and partisan Federalist judges imposed fines and jail terms on, at least ten Democratic-Republican newspaper editors. The Alien and Sedition Acts became a major issue in the 1800 presidential election campaign, which led to the election of Jefferson, a vocal opponent of the acts. Upon taking office, Jefferson quickly pardoned all who had been convicted under their provisions. The newly elected majority Democratic-Republican controlled Congress allowed the acts to expire before the Federalist-controlled U.S. Supreme Court had an opportunity to rule on the constitutionality of these First Amendment infringements, although commentators (then and now) viewed them as unconstitutional.

SLAVERY, THE CIVIL WAR, AND RIGHTS CURTAILMENTS   After the public outcry over the Alien and Sedition Acts, the national government largely refrained from regulating speech. But, in its place, the states, which were not yet bound by the Bill of Rights through selective incorporation, began to prosecute those who published articles critical of governmental policies. In the 1830s, at the urging of abolitionists, those

prior restraint
Constitutional doctrine that prevents the government from prohibiting speech or publication before the fact; generally held to be in violation of the First Amendment.

Alien and Sedition Acts
Laws passed in 1798 that allowed the imprisonment and deportation of aliens considered dangerous and criminalized false statements against the government.

who sought an end to slavery, the publication or dissemination of any positive information about slavery became a punishable offense in the North. By contrast, in the South, supporters of slavery enacted laws to prohibit publication of any anti-slavery sentiments. Southern postmasters, for example, refused to deliver northern abolitionist newspapers, a step that amounted to censorship of the U.S. mail.

During the Civil War, President Abraham Lincoln took several steps that violated the First Amendment. He convinced Congress to make it unlawful to print any criticisms of the national government or of the Civil War, effectively suspending the First Amendment's free press protections. Lincoln went so far as to order the arrest of several newspaper editors critical of his conduct of the war and ignored a decision written by Chief Justice Roger Taney, sitting as a circuit court judge, that said that jailing editors indefinitely was unconstitutional.[31] Eventually, upon conclusion of the war, the Supreme Court ruled that Lincoln's actions were unconstitutional.

WORLD WAR I AND ANTI-GOVERNMENTAL SPEECH   The next major efforts to restrict freedom of speech and the press did not occur until Congress, at the urging of President Woodrow Wilson during World War I, passed the Espionage Act in 1917. The government successfully prosecuted nearly 2,000 Americans for violating its various provisions, especially those urging resistance to the draft or distributing anti-war leaflets. In *Schenck* v. *U.S.* **(1919)**, the Supreme Court upheld the Espionage Act, ruling that Congress had a right to restrict speech "of such a nature as to create a clear and present danger that will bring about the substantive evils that Congress has a right to prevent."[32] Under this clear and present danger test, the circumstances surrounding an incident are important. Anti-war leaflets, for example, may be permissible during peacetime, but during World War I they were considered too dangerous because they posed the possibility of encouraging more opposition to the war.[33]

Still, for decades, the Supreme Court wrestled with what constituted a danger. Finally, in *Brandenburg* v. *Ohio* (1969), the Court fashioned a new test for deciding whether the government could regulate certain kinds of speech: the **direct incitement test**. Now, the government could punish the advocacy of illegal action only if "such advocacy is directed to inciting or producing imminent lawless action and is likely to incite or produce such action."[34] The requirement of "imminent lawless action" makes it more difficult for the government to punish speech and publication and is consistent with the Framers' notion of the special role played by these elements in a democratic society.

Protected Speech and Press

The expression of ideas through speech and the press is a cornerstone of a free society. In line with this thinking, the U.S. Supreme Court has accorded constitutional protection to a number of aspects of speech and the press, even though the content of such expression may be objectionable to some citizens or the government. Here, we discuss the implications of these protections with respect to prior restraint, symbolic speech, and hate speech.

LIMITING PRIOR RESTRAINT   As was the case with the Alien and Sedition Acts, although Congress attempted to limit speech before the fact as early as 1798, the U.S. Supreme Court did not take a firm position on this issue until the 1970s. In *New York Times Co.* v. *U.S.* **(1971)**, also called the *Pentagon Papers* case, the Court ruled that the U.S. government could not block the publication of secret Department of Defense documents illegally furnished to the *Times* by anti-war activists.[35] In 1976, the U.S. Supreme Court went even further, noting in *Nebraska Press Association* v. *Stuart*, a case that involved a challenge to the actions of a state court judge who barred press reports of an ongoing trial, that any attempt by the government to prevent expression carried "'a heavy presumption' against its constitutionality."[36]

Schenck **v. U.S. (1919)**
Supreme Court ruling that upheld the federal Espionage Act, which outlawed resistance against the draft or distributing anti-war leaflets, saying they presented a "clear and present danger" to the conduct of war.

direct incitement test
Test articulated by the Supreme Court in *Brandenburg* v. *Ohio* (1969) holding that the First Amendment protects advocacy of illegal action unless imminent lawless action is intended and likely to occur.

New York Times Co. **v. U.S. (1971)**
Supreme Court decision that the U.S. government could not block the publication of secret Department of Defense documents illegally furnished to the *Times* by anti-war activists. Also called the *Pentagon Papers* case.

In June and July 2020, President Trump sought to bar publication of two books highly critical of him: former National Security Adviser John Bolton's *The Room Where It Happened: A White House Memoir* and his niece Mary L. Trump's *Too Much and Never Enough: How My Family Created the World's Most Dangerous Man*.[37] He took his fight to the federal courts, where his arguments that Bolton's book revealed classified information and Trump's book violated a nondisclosure agreement were insufficient to rise to the high bar in prior restraint cases.[38]

SYMBOLIC SPEECH   In addition to the general protection accorded to pure speech, the Supreme Court has extended the reach of the First Amendment to **symbolic speech**, a means of expression that includes symbols or signs. In the words of Justice John Marshall Harlan, these kinds of speech are part of the "free trade in ideas."[39] Perhaps the most visible example of protected symbolic speech is the burning of the American flag as an expression of protest.

symbolic speech
Symbols, signs, and other methods of expression generally considered to be protected by the First Amendment.

The Supreme Court first acknowledged that symbolic speech was entitled to First Amendment protection in *Stromberg v. California* (1931).[40] In that case, the Court overturned a communist youth camp director's conviction under a state statute prohibiting the display of a red flag, a symbol of support for communism and opposition to the U.S. government. In a similar vein, the right of high school students to wear black armbands to protest the Vietnam War was upheld in *Tinker v. Des Moines Independent Community School District* (1969).[41]

In 2007, however, the Court appeared less willing to support the standards established in *Tinker*. In a case commonly referred to as "Bong Hits 4 Jesus," the Court ruled that a student's free speech rights were not violated when a school suspended him for displaying what the Court characterized as a "sophomoric" banner at an Olympic torch relay parade.[42]

HATE SPEECH   In the 1990s, a particularly thorny First Amendment issue emerged as cities and universities attempted to prohibit what they viewed as hate speech, or any communication that belittles a person or group on the basis of individual characteristics. In *R.A.V. v. City of St. Paul* (1992), a St. Paul, Minnesota, ordinance that made it a crime to engage in speech or action likely to arouse "anger," "alarm," or "resentment" on the basis of race, color, creed, religion, or gender was challenged. The Court ruled 5–4 that a White teenager who burned a cross on a Black family's front lawn, thereby committing a hate crime under the ordinance, could not face charges under that law because the First Amendment prevents governments from "silencing speech on the basis of its content."[43] In 2003, after much criticism, the Court narrowed this definition, ruling that state governments could constitutionally restrict cross burning when it occurred with the intent of racial intimidation.[44]

Meanwhile, over 350 public colleges and universities have banned speech or conduct that creates or fosters an intimidating, hostile, or offensive environment on campus.[45] A high proportion of private schools have done so as well. Since the spring semester of 2017, minority students at several colleges and universities experienced racist attacks, which are growing at an alarming rate nationwide. At American University in Washington, D.C., for example, several bananas were found hanging from nooses around campus, targeting the installation of the first female Black student as president of the Student Government Association. And, when members of several White supremacist groups marched at the University of Virginia in Charlottesville to protest the removal of a statue commemorating Confederate General Robert E. Lee, riots broke out between marchers and liberal counterprotesters, one of whom was killed. As the nation watched in horror, President Trump created even more controversy by commenting that there were good people on both sides in Charlottesville.

It is important to remember that in the United States—unlike in many other countries—federal law does not restrict hate speech. An interesting development that relates to the reaches of the free speech clause involves political apparel. For decades, most states or localities banned any form of political expression, such as campaign buttons, stickers, or shirts, not only from polling places but also within varying levels of measurable distance surrounding them. In 2018, the Supreme Court ruled that a Minnesota law that banned all political apparel at a polling site was unconstitutionally overbroad.[46] Also, while up till now the actions of White supremacist groups have formed the basis of recent Court definitions of hate speech, charges by conservative commentators that young activists in the Occupy Wall Street and Black Lives Matter (BLM) movements have participated in hate speech suggest a new chapter in arguments over what constitutes problematic speech. These comments, of course, were made prior to the nationalization and normalization of the BLM movement in 2020.

Unprotected Speech and Press

Although the Supreme Court has allowed few governmental bans on most types of speech, some forms of expression lack protection. In 1942, the Supreme Court set forth the rationale by which it would distinguish between protected and unprotected speech. According to the Court, libel, slander, fighting words, and obscenity are not protected by the First Amendment because "such expressions are no essential part of any exposition of ideals, and are of such slight social value as a step to truth that any benefit that may be derived from them is clearly outweighed by the social interest in order and morality."[47]

libel
False written statement that defames a person's character.

slander
Untrue spoken statements that defame the character of a person.

LIBEL AND SLANDER   **Libel** is a false written statement that defames the character of a person. If the statement is spoken, it is **slander**. In many nations—such as Great Britain, for example—suing someone for libel is relatively easy. In the United States, however, the standards of proof reach much higher. A person who believes that he or she has been a victim of libel must show that the statements made were untrue. Truth is an absolute defense against the charge of libel, no matter how painful or embarrassing the revelations.

Individuals whom the U.S. Supreme Court considers "public persons or public officials" often find it even more difficult to sue for libel or slander. *New York Times Co.* v. *Sullivan* (1964) was the first major libel case considered by the Supreme Court.[48] An Alabama state court found the *Times* guilty of libel for printing a full-page advertisement accusing Alabama officials of physically abusing Black people during various civil rights protests. (Civil rights activists, including former First Lady Eleanor Roosevelt, paid for the ad.) The Supreme Court overturned the conviction and established that a finding of libel against a public official could stand only if "actual malice," or a knowing disregard for the truth, was shown. Later, the Court ruled that even intentional infliction of emotional distress was not sufficient grounds for proving libel.[49]

fighting words
Words that "by their very utterance inflict injury or tend to incite an immediate breach of peace." Fighting words are not subject to the protections of the First Amendment.

FIGHTING WORDS   In 1942, the Court stated that **fighting words**, or words that "by their very utterance inflict injury or tend to incite an immediate breach of peace," are not subject to the protections of the First Amendment.[50] Federal and state governments can therefore regulate fighting words, which include "profanity, obscenity, and threats."

OBSCENITY   In *Miller* v. *California* (1973), the U.S. Supreme Court set out a test that continues to form the modern basis for defining obscenity. The justices concluded that lower courts must ask "whether the work depicts or describes, in a patently offensive way, sexual conduct specifically defined by state law" and "whether the work, taken as a whole, lacks serious literary, artistic, political, or scientific value." The Court also noted that local standards might affect its assessment of obscenity, under the rationale that what the citizens of New York City find acceptable might not be the case in Maine or Mississippi.[51]

Time and contexts clearly have altered the Court's and, indeed, much of America's perceptions of what works are obscene. But the Supreme Court has allowed communities great leeway in drafting statutes to deal with obscenity and, even more importantly, other forms of questionable expression. The Court, for example, has allowed some states to ban totally nude erotic dancing, concluding that statutes of this nature furthered a substantial governmental interest in creating order in society and regulating morals therefore did not violate the First Amendment. Other states continue to allow this practice.

The Internet, however, poses a particular challenge to the *Miller* test. Applying local standards is almost impossible in this context, since users in one state may easily access information generated in another state. Congress and the Supreme Court have struggled, in particular, to regulate the transmission of obscene or "harmful" materials over the Internet to anyone under age eighteen. In one of the early efforts to stop Internet pornography, in 1996, Congress passed the Communication Decency Act to protect minors from unsuitable information contained on the Internet. It criminalized any transmission or posting of "obscene" or "indecent" messages or information that depicts or describes "sexual or excretory activities or organs." In ***Reno v. ACLU (1997)***, the Supreme Court found that both the First and Fifth Amendments were violated because its regulations were, in effect, content-based regulations of free speech. Moreover, since prior Court decisions had made distinctions against obscenity (not protected), and pornography (protected), the act's provisions were overly broad and unconstitutional.[52] However, in 2019 the Court upheld the constitutionality of part of the PROTECT Act (2003), which outlawed the sale or transmission of child pornography.[53]

Freedoms of Assembly and Petition

"Peaceful assembly for lawful discussion cannot be made a crime," Chief Justice Charles Evans Hughes wrote in *DeJonge v. Oregon* (1937), which incorporated the First Amendment's freedom of assembly clause.[54] Despite this clear assertion, the fundamental freedoms of assembly and petition have been among the most controversial, especially in times of war and in 2020 over issues of race. As with other First Amendment liberties, the Supreme Court often has become the arbiter between the freedom of the people to express dissent and government's authority to limit controversy in the name of national security, as discussed later in this chapter.

The freedoms of assembly and petition relate directly to those of speech and the press because the freedom to assemble hinges on peaceful conduct. If the words spoken or actions taken at any event cross the line of constitutionality, the First

Reno **v.** *ACLU* **(1997)**
Supreme Court ruling that found a federal law prohibiting transmission of pornography via the Internet to minors was unconstitutionally broad and violated the First Amendment.

BSR Agency/Getty Images

HOW DO WE USE OUR RIGHT TO ASSEMBLE?

The First Amendment rights to assembly and petition are often seen in the form of protests, marches, and rallies. A number of high-profile killings by police of unarmed Black teenagers and adults have sparked both lawful peaceful protests and unlawful riots in cities across the United States, often with Black Lives Matter leaders playing an important role in peaceful protests.

Amendment may no longer protect events such as parades or protests. Absent that protection, leaders and attendees may be subject to governmental regulation and even arrest, incarceration, or civil fines.

The U.S. Supreme Court has rarely addressed the question of the right to petition the government. But in 2010, the Court heard a case questioning the constitutionality of Washington State's Public Records Act. This law allowed the government to release the names of citizens who had signed a petition in support of a ballot initiative that would have banned gay couples from adopting children. The plaintiffs who signed the "Preserve Marriage, Protect Children" petition did not want their names released because they feared harassment. The Court, however, ruled that disclosure of these names did not violate the First Amendment.[55]

WHAT DOES THE SECOND AMENDMENT PROTECT?

4.4 Describe the Second Amendment's guarantee of the right to bear arms.

During colonial times, the colonists' distrust of standing armies was evident. Most colonies required all White men to keep and bear arms, and deputized these men to defend their settlements against American Indians and European powers. The colonists viewed these local militias as the best way to keep order and protect liberty.

The Framers added the Second Amendment to the Constitution to ensure that Congress could not pass laws to disarm state militias. This amendment appeased Anti-Federalists, who feared that the new Constitution would abolish the right to

FIGURE 4.1 HOW STRONG ARE YOUR STATE'S GUN LAWS?

The Giffords Law Center to Prevent Gun Violence, a liberal advocacy group, annually ranks the fifty states based on the strength of what they call "smart gun laws." These include running background checks on purchasers, limiting bulk firearms purchases, and requiring a permit for concealed weapons. In 2020, the group ranked California as maintaining the strongest gun laws.

SOURCE: Data from the Giffords Law Center to Prevent Gun Violence, www.gunlawscorecard.org.

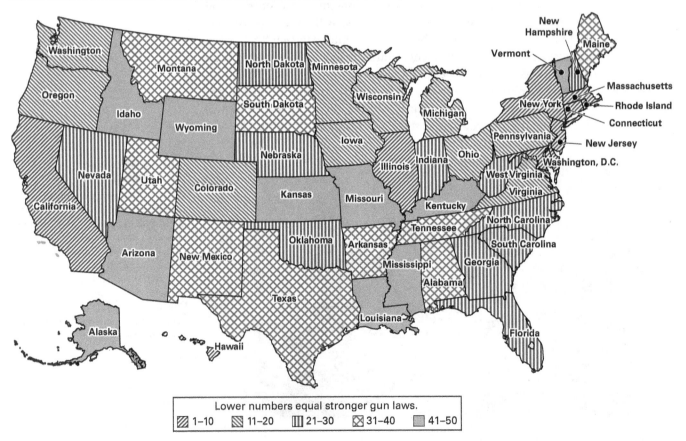

WHAT SHOULD BE PROTECTED BY THE SECOND AMENDMENT?
As school shootings become more commonplace, the extent of gun rights is increasingly called into question. The March for Our Lives, depicted here before the Minnesota State Capitol, was a student-led demonstration in support of gun control legislation. The main protest took place March 24, 2018, in Washington DC, with hundreds of sibling events around the country. The movement continues, with the goal of pushing Congress to finally pass significant gun control reforms.

"keep and bear arms." It also preserved an unstated right—the right to revolt against governmental tyranny. Through the early 1920s, few state statutes were passed to regulate firearms (and, generally, these laws dealt with banning possession of firearms by formerly enslaved people).

In 1934, Congress passed the National Firearms Act. This was in response to the explosion of organized crime in the 1920s and 1930s that occurred after the **Eighteenth Amendment** prohibited the sale of alcohol. Organized crime families became notorious for shooting anyone who tried to stop the profitable illegal sales of alcohol. To quell this dangerous unintended consequence of the amendment, the act imposed taxes on automatic weapons and sawed-off shotguns. In *U.S. v. Miller* (1939), a unanimous Court upheld the constitutionality of the act, stating that the Second Amendment was intended only to protect a citizen's right to own ordinary militia weapons, which did not include sawed-off shotguns.[56]

For nearly seventy years following *Miller*, the Court did not directly address the Second Amendment. Then, in *D.C. v. Heller* (2008), the Court offered some clarification, ruling that the Second Amendment protected an individual's right to own a firearm for personal use in Washington, D.C.[57] In light of the Court's ruling, the D.C. City Council adopted new gun control laws requiring gun registration and prohibiting assault weapons and large-capacity magazines. A U.S. District Court ruled that these laws were valid and within the scope of the *Heller* decision.[58] In 2010, in **McDonald v. City of Chicago (2010)**, the Supreme Court broadened the ownership rights in *Heller* to include citizens of all states. It also incorporated the Second Amendment (see Figure 4.1).[59] In the aftermath of these decisions, states across the nation have acted to pass all sorts of laws allowing citizens to carry weapons. In many states, for example, it is lawful for college students to carry licensed concealed weapons to class.

The scope of what should be protected by the Second Amendment remains an extremely contentious issue. In the wake of mass shootings in Las Vegas and at Marjory Stoneman Douglas High School in Parkland, Florida, there were new calls to limit the sale of AR-15 rifles (military-style, semiautomatic weapons). Student-led protests spurred a national march on Washington by high school students and their supporters seeking limits on the purchase of some types of guns. But as school shootings become increasingly commonplace, little action has been made legislatively to limit their sales. The powerful National Rifle Association (NRA) has effectively lobbied lawmakers at the local, state, and national levels to prevent what it views as any attack on Second Amendment rights as the nation's collective attention turned to the COVID-19 pandemic and a discussion of longstanding racially discriminatory policing.

Eighteenth Amendment
A 1913 amendment that created the nationwide prohibition on alcoholic beverages; it was repealed in 1933 by the Twentieth Amendment.

***McDonald* v. *City of Chicago* (2010)**
Supreme Court decision that the Second Amendment, which guarantees a citizen's right to "keep and bear arms," applies to state and local governments.

WHAT ARE THE RIGHTS OF CRIMINAL DEFENDANTS?

4.5 Outline the constitutional rights of defendants and the issues involved in protecting defendants' liberties as guaranteed by the Bill of Rights.

Article I, section 9, of the Constitution guarantees a number of rights and liberties for persons accused of federal crimes. Among those are writs of *habeas corpus*, or court orders in which a judge requires authorities to prove that they are holding a prisoner lawfully and that allow the prisoner to be freed if the government's case does not persuade the judge. In addition, *habeas corpus* rights imply that prisoners have a right to know what charges are being made against them.

Article I of the Constitution also prohibits *ex post facto* **laws**, which make an act punishable as a crime even if the act was legal at the time it was committed. Article I also prohibits bills of attainder, laws declaring an act illegal without a judicial trial.

The Fourth, Fifth, Sixth, and Eighth Amendments supplement these rights with a variety of procedural guarantees, often called **due process rights**. In this section, we examine how the courts have interpreted and applied these guarantees in an attempt to balance personal liberties and national safety and security. We also look at some policing issues that have hampered the due process rights of many marginalized groups.

The Fourth Amendment and Searches and Seizures

The **Fourth Amendment** to the Constitution protects people from unreasonable searches by the national government and, through incorporation, state governments. The purpose of this amendment was to deny national authorities the right to conduct general searches of private property. Thus, without a warrant, searches are limited to (1) the person arrested; (2) things in plain view of the accused person; and (3) places or things that the arrested person could touch or reach or that otherwise could easily be in the arrestee's immediate control. In situations where individuals would reasonably have some expectation of privacy—such as houses or offices—police must obtain a search warrant that defines the scope of the search from a "neutral and detached magistrate" prior to conducting a more extensive search that is based on probable cause that a crime has been committed. Those seeking a warrant must also show that criminal activity is ongoing and based on more than a law enforcement officer's "hunch." In 1968, in *Terry* **v.** *Ohio* **(1968)**, the Court ruled that the Fourth Amendment was not violated if a police officer stops someone if they have a reasonable suspicion that the person has committed, is committing, or is about to commit a crime and the officer has a reasonable belief that the suspect "may be armed and dangerous."[60] In 2014, however, the Court loosened requirements in deciding 6–3 that one person may give permission for a house search if the objector to the search is removed from the house.[61] In 2018, the Court also ruled that police must obtain a warrant to monitor an individual's cell phone information over a period of time.[62]

Cars, however, have proven problematic in relation to searches by the authorities. Although an individual has an expectation of privacy in their own vehicle, cars "can quickly be moved out of the locality or jurisdiction in which the warrant must be sought."[63] Border patrol agents, therefore, have great leeway in pulling over suspicious motorists.[64] Also, courts do not require search warrants in possible drunk driving situations.[65] Police must also allow citizens access to their vehicles during a search,[66] and they may not implant GPS tracking devices on criminal suspects' vehicles without a warrant.[67] In 2018, the Court clarified the issue further. It ruled that a warrantless police search of a motorcycle housed on private property under a tarp near a residence did not meet its earlier stated reasons for allowing warrantless searches of cars (or motorcycles).[68]

Warrantless searches may occur under several other circumstances. No warrant is necessary if police suspect that someone is committing or is about to commit a crime. In these cases, "reasonable suspicion" presents sufficient justification for stopping a

---

ex post facto law

Law that makes an act punishable as a crime even if the action was legal at the time it was committed.

due process rights

Protections drawn from the Fourth Amendment and the Bill of Rights. Due process may be procedural, ensuring fair treatment, or substantive, protecting fundamental rights.

Fourth Amendment

Part of the Bill of Rights that protects people from unreasonable searches and seizures of their persons, houses, papers, and effects without a warrant from a judge, among other guarantees. Items found pursuant to an illegal search are to be prevented from use at trial according to what is called the *exclusionary rule*.

Terry v. Ohio (1968)

Supreme Court decision that the Fourth Amendment is not violated if a police officer, acting on a reasonable suspicion, stops someone that they suspect is armed and dangerous and about to commit a crime.

suspect—a much lower standard than probable cause.[69] Police, for example, use reasonable suspicion to justify so-called limited "stop and frisk" searches. In these searches, law enforcement agents stop pedestrians and search for weapons or contraband. Questions, however, have been raised about racial bias in these searches, which occur far more often to Black and Hispanic people.

For example, on May 25, 2020, George Floyd, a forty-six-year-old Black man, was arrested by Minneapolis, Minnesota, police after a convenience store clerk called 911 saying Floyd had passed a counterfeit 20-dollar bill. As four police officers attempted to put him into a police car, he told the officers that he was claustrophobic. This exchange ended up with Floyd on the ground. Cell phone footage of the incident showed that an officer placed his knee on Floyd's neck for nearly eight minutes while Floyd cried out, "I can't breathe!" numerous times and bystanders urged the police to stop and call for an ambulance. The last three minutes of the video show Floyd motionless and not breathing as the officers continued to hold down the handcuffed man.[70]

Reaction to the video was nearly immediate. Protests began in Minneapolis and soon spread around the nation. The Black Lives Matter movement was reenergized as Black, White, and Brown persons of all ages marched chanting, "Black Lives Matter" and "I Can't Breathe!" all over the United States. In some places, they tried with varying degrees of success to topple statues of Confederate generals, forcing new, and sometimes uncomfortable, discussions of race discrimination in all of its forms, including the targeting of Black men for arrest and systematic racism in policing.[71]

If the police obtain consent for a search from an individual, no warrant is necessary. Warrantless searches also are permissible in places where citizens cannot reasonably expect privacy. For example, under the open fields doctrine first articulated by the Supreme Court in 1924, if you own a field, and even if you post "No Trespassing" signs, the police can search your field without a warrant to see if you are engaging in any type of illegal activity.[72] Similarly, firefighters can enter your home to fight a fire without a warrant. But if they decide to investigate the cause of the fire, they must obtain a warrant before they reenter.[73] Public school officials can search a student's purse, bookbag, or locker. In *New Jersey v. T.L.O.* (1985), a school official searched a student's purse looking for cigarettes and found a small amount of marijuana. Her lawyer moved to exclude the search as unconstitutional under the Fourth Amendment. The question then became, as the case moved to the Supreme Court, does the exclusionary rule, which prohibits the introduction of illegally seized items for use in court, apply to school officials in public schools? The answer was a clear yes.[74]

The Fifth Amendment: Self-Incrimination and Double Jeopardy

The **Fifth Amendment** provides a variety of guarantees protecting those charged with a crime. It requires, for example, that persons accused in the most serious cases first be subject to a grand jury investigation. A **grand jury** is a group of citizens charged with determining whether enough evidence exists for a case to go to trial.

The Fifth Amendment also states that "No person shall be . . . compelled in any criminal case to be a witness against himself." "Taking the Fifth" is shorthand for exercising one's constitutional right not to self-incriminate. The Supreme Court has interpreted this guarantee to be "as broad as the mischief against which it seeks to guard," finding that criminal defendants do not have to take the stand at trial to answer questions, nor can a judge make mention of their failure to do so as evidence of guilt.[75] Moreover, prosecutors cannot imply that a defendant who refuses to take the stand must be guilty or have something to hide.

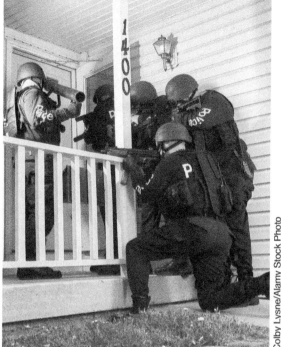

Colby Lysne/Alamy Stock Photo

WHEN ARE NO-KNOCK WARRANTS JUSTIFIED?

The increased use of no-knock warrants stems from the country's "war on drugs," allowing law enforcement to enter a property without immediate prior notification of the residents. Nationwide protests in response to the police killing of Breonna Taylor have led to calls to end such warrants, which conflict with an individual's rights and are claimed to involve racial bias.

New Jersey v. T.L.O. (1985)
Supreme Court case that decided that public school officials can search a student's items without violating the Fourth Amendment.

Fifth Amendment
Part of the Bill of Rights that imposes a number of restrictions on the federal government with respect to the rights of persons suspected of committing a crime. It provides for indictment by a grand jury and protection against self-incrimination, and it prevents the national government from denying a person life, liberty, or property without the due process of law. It also prevents the national government from taking property without just compensation.

grand jury
A group of citizens charged with determining whether enough evidence exists for a case to go to trial. Guaranteed by the Fifth Amendment.

This right not to incriminate oneself also means that prosecutors cannot use as evidence in a trial any of a defendant's statements or confessions that were not made voluntarily or after a lawyer is requested. As is the case in many areas of law, however, judicial interpretation of the term "voluntary" has changed over time.

In earlier times, it was not unusual for police to beat defendants to obtain their confessions. In 1936, however, the Supreme Court ruled that convictions for murder based solely on confessions given after physical beatings were unconstitutional.[76] Police then began to resort to other measures for forcing confessions. Defendants, for example, faced questioning for hours on end with no sleep or food, or threats of physical violence until they were mentally beaten into giving confessions. In other situations, police threatened family members. In one case, authorities told a young mother accused of marijuana possession that her welfare benefits would be terminated and her children taken away if she failed to talk.[77]

***Miranda* v. *Arizona* (1966)**

Landmark Supreme Court ruling holding that the Fifth Amendment requires individuals arrested for a crime to be advised of their right to remain silent and to have counsel present.

***Miranda* v. *Arizona* (1966)** was the Supreme Court's first response to coercive efforts used to obtain confessions. On March 3, 1963, an eighteen-year-old girl was kidnapped and raped on the outskirts of Phoenix, Arizona. Ten days later, police arrested Ernesto Miranda, a poor, mentally disturbed man with a ninth-grade education. In a police-station lineup, the victim identified Miranda as her attacker. Police then took Miranda to a separate room and questioned him for two hours. At first, he denied guilt. Eventually, however, he confessed and wrote and signed a brief statement describing the crime and admitting his guilt. At no time did police tell him that he did not have to answer any questions or that he could have an attorney present.

After Miranda's conviction based on his admission of guilt, his case was appealed on the grounds that his Fifth Amendment right not to incriminate himself had been violated because the police had coerced his confession. Writing for the Court, Chief Justice Earl Warren, himself a former district attorney and a former California state attorney general, noted that because police have a tremendous advantage in any

WHY WAS ERNESTO MIRANDA IMPORTANT TO THE DEVELOPMENT OF DEFENDANTS' RIGHTS?

Even though Ernesto Miranda's confession was not admitted as evidence at his retrial, the testimonies of his ex-girlfriend and the victim were enough to convince the jury of his guilt. He served nine years in prison before he was paroled. After his release, he routinely sold autographed cards inscribed with the *Miranda* rights now read to all suspects. In 1976, four years after his release, Miranda was stabbed to death during a card game. Two *Miranda* cards were found on his body, and the person who killed him was read his *Miranda* rights upon his arrest.

Matt York/Associated Press

interrogation situation, the law must grant criminal suspects greater protections. A confession obtained in the manner of Miranda's was not truly voluntary; thus, the justices concluded it was inadmissible at trial.

To provide guidelines for police to implement *Miranda*, the Court mandated that "Prior to any questioning, the person must be warned that he has a right to remain silent, that any statements he does make may be used as evidence against him, and that he has a right to the presence of an attorney, either retained or appointed."[78] In response to this mandate from the Court, police routinely began to read suspects what are now called their *Miranda* **rights**, a practice you undoubtedly have seen repeated over and over in movies and TV police dramas.

Although the **Burger Court** did not enforce the reading of *Miranda* rights as vehemently as had the Warren Court, Chief Justice **Warren E. Burger**, Warren's successor, acknowledged that they had become an integral part of established police procedures.[79] The more conservative Rehnquist and Roberts Courts, however, have been more willing to weaken *Miranda* rights, allowing coerced confessions and employing much more flexible standards for the admission of evidence.[80]

The Fifth Amendment also mandates, "nor shall any person be subject for the same offense to be twice put in jeopardy of life or limb." This **double jeopardy clause** protects individuals from being tried twice for the same crime in the same jurisdiction. Thus, if a jury finds a defendant not guilty of a murder, the defendant cannot be retried in that jurisdiction for the murder even if new information supporting a guilty verdict is discovered. But if a defendant was tried in a state court, he or she could still face charges in a federal court or vice versa. This provision is relatively clear and embedded in the law; the Court has heard little litigation on this issue in the past fifty years. In 2016, however, in the first case heard by the U.S. Supreme Court for its 2016–17 term, the Court ruled in a double jeopardy case that an individual could not be tried for the same crime in both Puerto Rico and in federal court, because Puerto Rico is a United States territory.[81]

The Fourth and Fifth Amendments and the Exclusionary Rule

In *Weeks* v. *U.S.* (1914), the U.S. Supreme Court adopted the **exclusionary rule**, which bars the use of illegally seized evidence at trial. Thus, although the Fourth and Fifth Amendments do not prohibit the use of evidence obtained in violation of their provisions, the exclusionary rule is a judicially created remedy to deter constitutional violations. In *Weeks*, for example, the Court reasoned that allowing police and prosecutors to use the "fruits of a poisonous tree" (evidence obtained in an illegal search) would only encourage that activity.[82] The Court, however, did not opt to incorporate the exclusionary rule into the list of actions barred to the states.

In balancing the need to deter police misconduct against the possibility that guilty individuals could go free, the Warren Court decided that deterring police misconduct was more important. In **Mapp v. Ohio (1961)**, the Warren Court ruled "all evidence obtained by searches and seizures in violation of the Constitution, is inadmissible in a state court."[83] This historic and controversial case put law enforcement officers on notice that if they violated any constitutional rights in the search for evidence, their efforts would be for naught because federal or state trials could not accept tainted evidence.

In 1976, the Court noted that the exclusionary rule "deflects the truth-finding process and often frees the guilty."[84] Since then, the Court has carved out a variety of limited "good faith exceptions" to the exclusionary rule, allowing the use of tainted evidence in a variety of situations, especially when police have a search warrant, and in good faith, conduct the search on the assumption that the warrant is valid. Since the purpose of the exclusionary rule is to deter police misconduct, and in this situation no police misconduct exists, the courts have permitted introduction of the seized evidence at trial. Another exception to the exclusionary rule is "inevitable discovery." Courts may allow illegally seized evidence if such evidence would likely have been discovered in the course of continuing an investigation.

Miranda **rights**
Statements required of police that inform a suspect of their constitutional rights protected by the Fifth Amendment, including the right to an attorney provided by a court if the suspect cannot afford one.

Burger Court
The period in Supreme Court history during which Warren Burger served as chief justice (1969–1986).

Warren E. Burger
Fifteenth chief justice of the United States. Served from 1969 to 1986. Was a well-known critic of the liberal Warren Court and moved the Court to the right on key civil rights and civil liberties issues.

double jeopardy clause
Part of the Fifth Amendment that protects individuals from being tried twice for the same offense in the same jurisdiction.

exclusionary rule
Judicially created rule that prohibits police from using illegally seized evidence at trial.

Mapp **v.** *Ohio* **(1961)**
Court ruling that made the "fruits" of all searches conducted illegally inadmissible in court.

The Sixth Amendment and the Right to Counsel

Sixth Amendment

Part of the Bill of Rights that sets out the basic requirements of procedural due process for federal courts to follow in criminal trials. These include speedy and public trials, impartial juries, trials in the state where the crime was committed, notice of the charges, the right to confront and obtain favorable witnesses, and the right to counsel.

Gideon **v.** *Wainwright* **(1963)**

Unanimous Supreme Court decision that criminal defendants who cannot afford an attorney are guaranteed one by the Sixth Amendment.

The **Sixth Amendment** guarantees to an accused person "the Assistance of Counsel in his defense." In the past, this guarantee meant only that an individual could hire an attorney to represent him or her in court. Since a criminal defence can be costly, this provision gave little assistance to many, who could not afford a lawyer, found themselves on trial. Recognizing this, Congress required federal courts to provide an attorney for defendants who could not afford one. Capital cases, in which the death penalty is a possibility, were the first to require this provision;[85] eventually, poor people were guaranteed legal counsel in all federal criminal cases.[86] The Court also began to expand the right to counsel to some state offenses but did so in a piecemeal fashion that gave the states little direction. Given the high cost of legal counsel, this ambiguity often made it cost-effective for the states not to provide counsel at all.

These ambiguities came to an end with the Court's decision in *Gideon v. Wainwright* **(1963)**.[87] Clarence Earl Gideon, a fifty-one-year-old drifter, was charged with breaking into a Panama City, Florida, pool hall and stealing beer, wine, and some change from a vending machine. At his trial, he asked the judge to appoint a lawyer for him because he was too poor to hire one. The judge refused, and Gideon was convicted and given a five-year prison term for petty larceny. The case against Gideon had not been strong, but as a layperson unfamiliar with the law, trial practice, and procedure, he was unable to point out its weaknesses.

The apparent inequities in the system that had resulted in Gideon's conviction continued to bother him. Eventually, he requested some paper from a prison guard, consulted books in the prison library, and then drafted and mailed a writ of *certiorari* to the U.S. Supreme Court, asking it to overrule his conviction.

In a unanimous decision, the Supreme Court agreed with Gideon and his court-appointed lawyer, Abe Fortas, a future associate justice of the Court. Writing for the Court, Justice Hugo Black explained, "Lawyers in criminal courts are necessities, not luxuries." Therefore, the Court concluded, the state must provide an attorney to indigent defendants in felony cases. Underscoring the importance of counsel, the jury acquitted Gideon when he was retried with a lawyer to argue his case.

The Burger and Rehnquist Courts gradually expanded the *Gideon* rule. The justices first applied this standard to cases that were not felonies[88] and, later, to many cases in which probation and future penalties were possibilities. In 2008, the Court also ruled that the right to counsel began at the accused's first appearance before a judge.[89]

The issue of legal representation also extends to questions of competence. Various courts have held that lawyers who fell asleep during trial, failed to put forth a defense, or were drunk during the proceedings were "adequate." In 2005, however, the Supreme Court ruled that the Sixth Amendment's guarantees required lawyers to take reasonable steps to prepare for their clients' trial and sentencing, including examination of their prior criminal history.[90]

The Sixth Amendment and Jury Trials

The Sixth Amendment (and, to a lesser extent, Article III of the Constitution) provides that a person accused of a crime shall enjoy the right to a speedy and public trial by an impartial jury—that is, a trial in which a group of the accused's peers act as a fact-finding, deliberative body to determine guilt or innocence. It also gives defendants the right to confront witnesses against them. The Supreme Court has held that jury trials must be available if a prison sentence of six or more months is possible.

Impartiality is a requirement of jury trials that has undergone significant change, with the method of jury selection being the most frequently challenged part of the process. Historically, lawyers had used peremptory challenges (those for which no cause needs to be given) to exclude women and minorities from juries, especially in certain types of cases. In 1954, however, the U.S. Supreme Court ruled that Hispanics were entitled to a jury trial that included other Hispanics.[91] In 1986, the Court ruled that the use of peremptory challenges specifically to exclude Black jurors violated the equal protection clause of the Fourteenth Amendment.[92] In 1994, the Court extended its ruling to discrimination in jury selection on the basis of gender.[93]

The right to confront witnesses at trial also is protected by the Sixth Amendment. However, this right is not absolute. The testimony of a six-year-old alleged child abuse victim via one-way closed-circuit TV, for example, is permissible.[94] In this case, the child was questioned out of the presence of the defendant, who was in communication with his defense and prosecuting attorneys. The defendant, along with the judge and jury, watched the testimony.

The Eighth Amendment and Cruel and Unusual Punishment

Among its protections, the **Eighth Amendment** prohibits "cruel and unusual punishments," a concept rooted in the English common-law tradition. Today, the United States is the only western nation to put people to death for committing crimes. Not surprisingly, tremendous state-by-state differences exist in the imposition of the death penalty. Texas leads the nation in the number of executions each year. In July 2020, the federal government carried out its first execution in nearly twenty years.[95]

The death penalty was in use in all colonies at the time they adopted the U.S. Constitution, and its constitutionality went unquestioned. In fact, in two separate cases in the late 1800s, the Supreme Court ruled that deaths by public shooting[96] and electrocution were not "cruel and unusual" forms of punishment in the same category as "punishments which inflict torture, such as the rack, the thumbscrew, the iron boot, the stretching of limbs and the like."[97]

Recently, the Court has addressed the imposition of state laws in which juveniles may be sentenced to life imprisonment without any opportunity for parole. In 2016, by a 6–3 vote, the Court ruled that its 2012 decision limiting life sentences for juveniles was retroactive.[98] President Barack Obama weighed in on cruel and unusual punishment by prohibiting federal prisons from putting juveniles in solitary confinement.

MODERN QUESTIONS OF CONSTITUTIONALITY In the 1960s, the NAACP (National Association for the Advancement of Colored People) Legal Defense and Educational Fund (LDF), believing that Black people received the death penalty more frequently than members of other groups, orchestrated a carefully designed legal attack on its constitutionality. Public opinion polls revealed that in 1971, on the eve of the LDF's first major death sentence case to reach the Supreme Court, public support for the death penalty had fallen below 50 percent. With the timing just right, in *Furman v. Georgia* (1972), the Supreme Court effectively put an end to capital punishment, at least in the short run.[99] The Court ruled that because the death penalty often was imposed in an arbitrary manner, it constituted cruel and unusual punishment in violation of the Eighth and Fourteenth Amendments. Following *Furman*, several state legislatures enacted new laws designed to meet the Court's objections to the arbitrary nature of the sentence. In 1976, in *Gregg v. Georgia* (1976), the Supreme Court ruled 7–2 that Georgia's rewritten death penalty statute specifying under what situations the death penalty could be imposed was constitutional.[100]

This ruling did not deter the NAACP LDF from continuing to bring challenges to the death penalty to the Court. In 1987, a 5–4 Court ruled that imposition of the death penalty—even when it appeared to discriminate against Black people—did not violate the equal protection clause.[101] The Court noted that even if statistics show clear discrimination, reversal of an individual sentence required demonstration of racial discrimination in that particular case.

Four years later, a case involving the same defendant produced an equally important ruling on the death penalty and criminal procedure. In the second case, the Court held that new issues could not be raised on appeal, even if some state error existed. The case, *McCleskey v. Zant* (1991), produced new standards designed to make the filing of

Eighth Amendment
Part of the Bill of Rights that states: "Excessive bail shall not be required, nor excessive fines imposed, nor cruel and unusual punishments inflicted."

***Furman* v. *Georgia* (1972)**
Supreme Court decision that ended capital punishment in the United States based on the fact that it was applied in an arbitrary manner within and across the states that had a death penalty and could be considered cruel and unusual punishment in violation of the Eighth and Fourteenth Amendments.

***Gregg* v. *Georgia* (1976)**
Supreme Court decision that found Georgia's new statutory requirements specifying a range of crimes that could be considered for possible death sentences to be acceptable.

Beth A. Keiser/Associated Press

HOW DO STATES VARY IN THEIR APPLICATION OF THE DEATH PENALTY?

A growing number of states have formally or informally objected to the use of the death penalty as a means of punishment for felony crimes. While many human rights activists praise these decisions, others—such as the families of victims of violent crime—are more hesitant to offer support. Here, Anthony Porter (far left), who had been wrongfully convicted and sentenced to death row, celebrates his release with some of the Northwestern University students whose research helped to set him free.

repeated appeals much more difficult for death-row inmates.[102] In 2016, voters in Nebraska and Oklahoma approved measures allowing the death penalty.

Although as recently as 2008 the Supreme Court has upheld the constitutionality of the death penalty by lethal injection,[103] it has made some exceptions. The Court, for example, has exempted two key classes of people from the death penalty: those with intellectual disabilities and those under the age of eighteen.[104] The question of how to put an inmate to death is now coming to the fore. When Arkansas announced in 2017 that it planned to put eight inmates to death in quick succession because the drugs the prisons used to kill people were soon to expire, lawsuits rained down on the state. Manufacturers of the drugs charged that the state acquired the drugs illegally. Critics charged that problems with a three-drug cocktail made its administration cruel and unusual punishment. Nevertheless, the Supreme Court has upheld its usage and at 2 a.m., July 14, 2020, in a 5–4 unsigned opinion, the Court allowed the execution of Daniel Lewis Lee after a U.S. District Court judge issued a preliminary injunction against the scheduled execution saying that the use of a single drug could result in "extreme pain and needless suffering." The Supreme Court lifted the injunction, noting that pentobarbital had been used in over 100 state executions "without incident."[105]

PROTECTING THE WRONGFULLY CONVICTED   At the state level, some officials have publicly questioned the application of the death penalty. In 1999, a class project by Northwestern University students unearthed information that led to the release of thirteen men on Illinois's death row. Before leaving office in January 2003, that state's governor commuted the sentences of 167 death-row inmates, giving them life in prison instead. This action constituted the single largest anti–death-penalty action since the Court's decision in *Gregg*, and it spurred a national conversation on the death penalty, which, in recent polls, has seen its lowest levels of support since 1978. Twenty-one states and the District of Columbia have abolished the death penalty.

In another effort to verify that those on death row are not there in error, several states offer free DNA testing to death-row inmates. Inmates in other states may file a civil rights lawsuit seeking DNA testing.[106] The U.S. Supreme Court recognized the potential exculpatory power of DNA evidence in *House* v. *Bell* (2006). In this case, the Court ruled that a Tennessee death-row inmate who had exhausted other federal appeals was entitled to an exception to more stringent federal appeals rules because DNA and related evidence suggested his innocence.[107]

WHAT IS THE RIGHT TO PRIVACY?

4.6 Explain the origins and significance of the right to privacy

To this point, we have discussed rights and freedoms that have been derived from *specific* guarantees contained in the Bill of Rights. However, the U.S. Supreme Court also has given protection to rights not enumerated specifically in the Constitution. Although silent about the **right to privacy**, the Bill of Rights contains many indications that the Framers expected some areas of life to be off-limits to governmental regulation. The liberty to practice one's religion guaranteed in the First Amendment implies the right to exercise private, personal beliefs. The guarantee against unreasonable searches and seizures contained in the Fourth Amendment similarly suggests that persons are to be secure in their homes and should not fear that police will invade their homes without cause. As early as 1928, Justice Louis Brandeis hailed privacy, an unenumerated right, as "the right to be left alone—the most comprehensive

right to privacy

The right to be left alone; a judicially created principle encompassing a variety of individual actions protected by the penumbras cast by several constitutional amendments, including the First, Third, Fourth, Ninth, and Fourteenth Amendments.

WHAT WAS THE OUTCOME OF *GRISWOLD* V. *CONNECTICUT* (1965)?

In this photo, Estelle Griswold (left), executive director of the Planned Parenthood League of Connecticut, and Cornelia Jahncke, its president, hold up their local newspaper announcing "High Court Rules Birth Control Law Unconstitutional." *Griswold* v. *Connecticut* (1965) invalidated a Connecticut law that made selling contraceptives or disseminating information about contraception to married couples illegal.

of rights and the right most valued by civilized men."[108] Not until 1965, however, did the Court attempt to explain the origins of this right.

Birth Control

Today, most Americans take access to birth control for granted. Grocery stores sell condoms, most college health centers give them away, and TV stations air ads for them. Other forms of birth control from pills to implants to intrauterine devices also are advertised on TV, in magazines, and online. Acceptance of and easy access to birth control, however, was not always the case. Many states often barred the sale of contraceptives to minors, prohibited the display of contraceptives, or even banned their sale altogether, even to married couples. One of the last states to do away with these kinds of laws was Connecticut. It outlawed the sale of all forms of birth control and even prohibited physicians from discussing it with their married patients until the Supreme Court ruled its restrictive laws unconstitutional.

Griswold v. *Connecticut* (1965) involved a challenge to the constitutionality of an 1879 Connecticut law prohibiting the dissemination of information about and/or the sale of contraceptives.[109] In *Griswold*, seven justices decided that various portions of the Bill of Rights, including the First, Third, Fourth, Ninth, and Fourteenth Amendments, cast what the Court called "penumbras" (unstated liberties on the fringes or in the shadow of more explicitly stated rights), thereby creating zones of privacy, including a married couple's right to plan a family. Thus, the Connecticut statute was ruled unconstitutional because it violated marital privacy, a right the Court concluded could be read into the U.S. Constitution through interpreting several amendments.

Later, in 1972, the Court expanded the right to privacy to include the right of unmarried individuals to have access to contraceptives. "If the right of privacy means anything," wrote Justice William J. Brennan Jr., "it is the right of the individual, married or single, to be free from unwarranted governmental intrusion into matters so fundamentally affecting a person as the decision to bear or beget a child."[110] The questions of who and how contraceptives, as well as abortion, should be paid for came to the forefront with the passage of the Affordable Care Act. Many conservative employers, as well as religious institutions (mostly Roman Catholic), sued the federal government, saying that they should be exempt from the act's requirement that employers provide free contraceptives to their employees. The law allowed companies to opt out of the contraceptive guarantee by simply signing a document noting their objections. In *Burwell* v. *Hobby Lobby* (2014), the Supreme Court ruled that closely held (often family) businesses were exempt from the contraceptive mandate because it violated the Religious Freedom Restoration Act.[111] Once elected, President Donald J. Trump signed a far-reaching religious liberty executive order extending the *Hobby Lobby* decision and guaranteeing that associations such as the Little Sisters of the Poor, a Roman Catholic group of nuns, would be protected from paying contraceptive insurance coverage. In 2020, the Supreme Court addressed the legality of the Trump regulations. In a 7–2 decision, the Court ruled that the regulations narrowing the Affordable Care Act's (Obamacare) contraceptive coverage mandate requiring employers to provide free contraceptives in their health plans were permissible.[112] This decision expanded the range of employers exempt from the act to private employers who have religious or moral objections to contraception.[113]

Abortion

In the early 1960s, two instances of birth-related tragedies occurred. Many European women who had taken the drug thalidomide while pregnant gave birth to severely deformed babies, and, in the United States, a nationwide measles epidemic resulted in the birth of babies with major health problems. The medical establishment's view that rates of abortions were on the rise and the growing women's rights movement combined with these tragedies to put pressure on the legal and medical establishments to support laws guaranteeing a woman's access to a safe and legal abortion.

By the late 1960s, fourteen states had voted to liberalize their abortion policies, and four states decriminalized abortion in the early stages of pregnancy. But many women's rights activists wanted more. They argued that the decision to carry a pregnancy to term was a woman's fundamental right. In 1973, in one of the most controversial decisions ever handed down, seven members of the Supreme Court agreed with this position.

The woman whose case became the catalyst for pro-choice and pro-life groups was Norma McCorvey, an itinerant circus worker. The mother of a toddler she was unable to care for, McCorvey could not leave another child in her mother's care. So, she decided to terminate her second pregnancy. McCorvey turned to two young Texas lawyers who were aiming to challenge Texas's restrictive statute and were looking to bring a lawsuit with just such a plaintiff. McCorvey, who was unable to obtain a legal abortion, later gave birth and put the baby up for adoption. Nevertheless, she allowed her lawyers to proceed, with her as their plaintiff. Her lawyers used the pseudonym Jane Roe for McCorvey in their challenge of the Texas law as enforced by Henry Wade, the district attorney for Dallas County, Texas.

When the case finally came before the Supreme Court, Justice Harry A. Blackmun, a former lawyer at the Mayo Clinic, one of the best hospitals in America, relied heavily on medical evidence to rule that the Texas law violated a woman's constitutionally guaranteed right to privacy, which, he concluded, included her decision to terminate a pregnancy. Writing for the majority in *Roe* v. *Wade* (1973), Blackmun divided pregnancy into three stages. In the first trimester, a woman's right to privacy gave her an absolute right (in consultation with her physician), free from state interference, to terminate her pregnancy. In the second trimester, the state's interest in the health of the mother gave it the right to regulate abortions, but only to protect the woman's health. Only in the third trimester—when the Court decided that the fetus becomes potentially viable—did the Court find that the state's interest in potential life outweighed a woman's privacy interests. Even in the third trimester, however, the Court ruled that abortions to save the life or preserve the health of the mother were legal.[114]

Roe v. *Wade* unleashed a torrent of political controversy. Pro-life groups, caught off guard, scrambled to recoup their losses in Congress. Representative Henry Hyde (R–IL) persuaded Congress to ban the use of Medicaid funds for abortions for poor women, and the Supreme Court upheld the constitutionality of the Hyde Amendment in 1977 and again in 1980.[115] The issue soon became political—it was incorporated into the Republican Party's platform in 1980—and quickly polarized both major political parties.

Roe v. *Wade* (1973)

Supreme Court ruling that found that a woman's right to an abortion was protected by the right to privacy that could be implied from specific guarantees found in the Bill of Rights applied to the states through the Fourteenth Amendment.

Since *Roe* v. *Wade*, well-organized pro-life groups have attacked the right to an abortion and its constitutional underpinnings in the right to privacy. The administrations of Ronald Reagan and George H. W. Bush strongly opposed abortions, and their Justice Departments regularly urged the Court to overrule *Roe*. They came close to victory in *Webster* v. *Reproductive Health Services* (1989).[116] In *Webster*, the Court upheld state-required fetal viability tests in the second trimester, even though these tests increased the cost of an abortion considerably. The Court also upheld Missouri's refusal to allow abortions to be performed in state-supported hospitals or by state-funded doctors or nurses. Perhaps most noteworthy, however, was that four justices seemed willing to overrule *Roe* v. *Wade*.

After *Webster*, states began to enact more restrictive legislation. In *Planned Parenthood of Southeastern Pennsylvania* v. *Casey* (1992), the Court wrote that Pennsylvania could limit abortions as long as its regulations did not pose "an undue burden" on pregnant women. The narrowly supported standard, by which the Court upheld a twenty-four-hour waiting period and parental consent requirements, did not overrule *Roe* but clearly limited its scope. *Casey* lowered the standard of review from strict scrutiny—used for fundamental freedoms—to a far lower **undue burden test**.[117]

In the 1990s, pro-choice Democratic President Bill Clinton and the Republican-controlled Congresses repeatedly clashed on the issue of abortion rights. In 1996 and again in 1998, Congress passed and sent to President Clinton a bill to ban—for the first time—a specific procedure used in late-term abortions. The president repeatedly vetoed the federal Partial Birth Abortion Ban Act. In 2003, however, Republican control of the White House and both houses of Congress overruled his veto. Pro-choice groups immediately filed lawsuits challenging the constitutionality of this law. In a 5–4 decision, *Gonzales* v. *Carhart* (2007), the Supreme Court upheld the federal act, even though it contained no exceptions for the health of the mother.[118] Observers viewed this ruling as a significant step toward reversing *Roe* v. *Wade* altogether.

The Court's decision in *Gonzales* empowered states to enact abortion regulations with new gusto. In 2013, Texas enacted legislation that required clinic physicians to have admitting privileges to local hospitals and required clinics to meet the same standards as ambulatory surgical centers. With only eight justices on the Court, five members found that these provisions of the Texas law imposed an undue burden on women seeking an abortion and thus were unconstitutional. The majority noted that the closures of Texas clinics, which would have left no clinics in West Texas, an area larger than California, would mean "fewer doctors, longer waiting times, increased crowding, and significantly greater travel distances, all of which, when taken together, burden a woman's right to choose."[119] The ruling in *Whole Woman's Health* v. *Hellerstedt* (2016) called into question similar laws in twenty-six states and the more than 250 restrictions enacted by state and local governments that currently are being litigated in the courts, putting it on a par with *Roe* and *Casey* in its impact on legal access to abortion.

In 2020, many Court observers were shocked when the Court struck down a Louisiana law, nearly identical to the Texas statute, by a 5–4 vote applying the undue burden test.[120] Had the law been upheld, only one clinic could have remained open. In 2021, however, by a 6–3 vote, the Court found a similar state law constitutional with all three Trump appointees in the majority.

Lesbian, Gay, Bisexual, Transgender, and Queer (LGBTQ) Issues

First, a note on terminology. Initially, LGBT was used to denote lesbian, gay, bisexual, and transgender individuals. Then, a Q was added, making it LGBTQ with Q standing for Queer or Questioning (as in one's sexual orientation). LBGTQIA adds I (intersex) and A (referring to asexual). Here, we use LGBTQ in discussing the civil liberties and civil rights of this large, diverse community.

Not until 2003 did the U.S. Supreme Court rule that an individual's constitutional right to privacy, which provided the basis for the *Griswold* (contraceptives) and *Roe*

undue burden test

A standard set by the Supreme Court, in the *Casey* case in 1992, that narrowed *Roe* v. *Wade* and allowed for greater regulation of abortion by the states.

AP Photo/David J. Phillip

WHICH CASE LED TO GREATER DISCUSSION OF GAY RIGHTS ISSUES?

Tyron Garner (left) and John Geddes Lawrence (center), the plaintiffs in *Lawrence v. Texas* (2003), are shown here with their attorney. The ruling in this case proved to be a huge victory for advocates of gay and lesbian rights, as it deemed anti-sodomy laws unconstitutional. Following this decision, states began to debate laws related to marriage and other rights for same-sex couples.

(abortion) decisions, prevents states from criminalizing private sexual behavior. This monumental decision invalidated the laws of fourteen states.

In *Lawrence v. Texas* (2003), six members of the Court overruled its decision in *Bowers v. Hardwick* (1986), which had upheld anti-sodomy laws. They found the Texas law unconstitutional; five justices found it violated fundamental privacy rights.[121] Justice Sandra Day O'Connor agreed that the law was unconstitutional, but concluded it was an equal protection violation. More recently, privacy rights have been invoked concerning the availability of public bathrooms to transgender persons. Many states allow transgender people to select a bathroom or locker room based on their gender identity. Some cities and states, however, have passed laws barring people from using bathrooms that do not match their biological gender. North Carolina, for example, passed such a law in 2016 that led the National Basketball Association to withdraw its All-Star game from the state; the National College Athletic Association also moved playoff games in several sports out of the state in protest. Lesbian, bisexual, gay, and transgender rights are discussed further in Chapters 3 and 5.

Many Court watchers were stunned by the Court's decision in June 2020 that concluded that lesbians, gays, bisexuals, and transgender persons were protected from discrimination by their employers. The conservative Chief Justice John G. Roberts Jr. and Trump-appointee Associate Justice Neil Gorsuch joined with four liberal justices to find that the Civil Rights Act of 1964's prohibition of discrimination "because of sex" included gay and transgender employees.[122]

POLITICAL REFORM AND REALITIES: WHAT CAN GOVERMENTS DO ABOUT COVID-19, RACIAL INJUSTICE, AND BEYOND?

4.7　Evaluate how civil liberties have been affected by the simultaneous arrival of COVID-19 and racial unrest in the United States.

The year 2020 will stand out as being the most challenging in history globally and more specifically in the United States. The novel coronavirus, called COVID-19, which first originated in a market in Wuhan, China, created a global pandemic as millions were infected and hundreds of thousands died of the disease for which medical experts had little ammunition. The first reported symptoms appear to have occurred on December 8, 2019, thus the -19 designation. Much-needed supplies, including masks, protective medical gear, and ventilators, were in short supply in the early months of 2020. This highly infectious disease created strains on the medical system of the United States, the individual states, and localities. Moreover, many of the actions taken by governments at all levels involved some restrictions of civil liberties.

As the virus led some elected officials to take the dramatic steps of basically closing down cities such as New York and Seattle, Washington, many Americans found themselves out of work, and unemployment claims eventually reached numbers not seen since the Great Depression of 1929. Moreover, in the United States, the disease attacked Black people and Hispanics in far greater percentages, reflecting decades of disparate health access in America. While the disease raged on in the United States, the pandemic had other unforeseen consequences. When a video first appeared showing the death of George Floyd, a Black male, under the knee of a police

David Smith/Alamy Stock Photo

HOW DID GEORGE FLOYD'S DEATH SPARK A RACIAL INJUSTICE MOVEMENT?

In May 2020, after being handcuffed and pinned to the ground by a White officer's knee on his neck, George Floyd, a Black man, died. Floyd's death spurred nationwide protests against police brutality and racism. This mural, covering storefront windows in Santa Monica, California, protests the murder.

officer in Minneapolis, Minnesota, riots broke out in that city. Although over the years the deaths of unarmed Black men and woman at the hands of police officers often attracted short-term public attention and local protest, George Floyd's vivid cries of "I can't breathe!" as he lay dying shocked the conscience of America at a time when many were at home, out of work or school. Additionally, as school district after school district began to close nationwide when schools, colleges, and universities shuttered their doors and went to online learning, additional economic and social disparities were revealed; lines at food banks went on for miles and parents struggled to educate their children at home, whether or not they had Wi-Fi or Internet access. It was a confluence of factors that no one could have predicted, although the Obama administration actually left a plan to handle a pandemic for the incoming Trump administration, but it was discarded. It was chaos never before seen in America. Below are only some examples of how governmental reactions to COVID-19 and disparate racial policing became the political realities and challenges for reform in 2020 and beyond.

The First Amendment

FREE EXERCISE OF RELIGION One of the first measures that elected officials took as the coronavirus spread unevenly around the nation was to prohibit meetings of more than one hundred persons; soon that number decreased to fifty and then to ten. As schools closed, so did businesses and restaurants. Immediately affected were most religious establishments. It was impossible for churches, temples, synagogues, and other places of worship to meet not only the decreased size of group meetings but also safe distancing guidelines that called for spacing people six feet apart to prevent spreading the virus. Most churches complied immediately and went to online streaming of services. While there was some pushback, and persons accustomed to the comradery and comfort of worshipping with others expressed displeasure with these measures, nearly all complied. Some congregations held the equivalent of drive-in movies, with congregants spaced out in their vehicles. One of the largest evangelical churches in the nation, with around 30,000 in-person congregants every Sunday in the suburbs of Atlanta, Georgia, announced in early July 2020 that it would not hold any in-person services until 2021. Thus, for the millions accustomed to worship, receiving communion or other blessings, the practice, or free exercise, of their religion was severely altered.

While most major denominations complied with local or state stay-at-home orders, over 1,500 federal and state lawsuits were initiated in many states, including California, Louisiana, and Virginia.[123] The Trump administration actually supported these moves. The Justice Department said that social-distancing requirements discriminated against houses of worship, and the chair of the White House's Coronavirus Task Force, Vice President Mike Pence, said that "he couldn't be more proud of the department" for its actions.[124]

FREEDOM OF EXPRESSION   The wearing of masks as a way to stem the virus first was recommended by the Centers for Disease Control and Prevention (CDC) and became mandatory in some states and localities. As the virus appeared to spike again, particularly in states that had more lax mandates, hospitals met their capacities in July and August and some localities mandated masks. Big-box stores, including Walmart, Home Depot, Lowe's, Target, and grocery chains, soon mandated masks. Some in the twittersphere who believed that the virus was a fiction or that mask requirements violated their First Amendment rights refused to wear them, leading to violent encounters. President Trump initially refused to wear a mask or widely encourage their use—and held large superspreader political rallies that were held in violation of local mask or social-distancing rules or regulations.

Some commentators argued that "forcing an individual to wear face masks arguably does implicate your fundamental right to free expression," as one Idaho Law School professor said.[125] In Washington state, the nonprofit Freedom Foundation filed a lawsuit in state court arguing the actions of the governor and secretary of health ordering "every person in Washington state (to) wear a face covering that covers their nose and mouth when in any indoor or outdoor public setting" violated their free speech rights, among other liberties.[126]

Ironically, some states have had face-covering ordinances on their books for years, largely to target the Ku Klux Klan's use of face coverings during racist assemblies to conceal their identities.[127] More recently, some states have proposed, and even enacted, face-covering restrictions after early Black Lives Matter, Alaska pipeline, or anti-facist (Antifa) protests.[128] For example, a New York anti-mask provision made it a crime punishable by fifteen days in jail for two or more masked persons to gather in a public place (unless a specific exception is made). The police used the provision to imprison Occupy Wall Street protesters in 2011.[129] Government regulations requiring face coverings or masks to prevent disease spread are exempted from such laws.

SYMBOLIC SPEECH   Some also compared the decision whether or not to wear a mask to symbolic speech, largely protected by the First Amendment. Slogans such as "I Can't Breathe," "No Justice, No Peace," and "Black Lives Matter" appeared on clothing and masks worn by thousands of protesters in the spring, summer, and fall of 2020. While fringe groups of White supremacists viewed those slogans as the kind of "fighting words" prohibited by Supreme Court decisions, their arguments received little traction.

FREEDOM OF ASSEMBLY AND ASSOCIATION   Freedom of assembly and association were tested by COVID-19 and mass racial protests. After a few nights of riots took place in many cities protesting the death of George Floyd, Black Lives Matter and other civil rights and liberties organizations pleaded with their supporters to engage in peaceful protest. Thousands heeded their calls. While social distancing rules were often broken, nearly all protesters wore masks, often using them to amplify their concerns and anger in the kind of peaceful protest envisioned by the drafters of the Bill of Rights.

Many Americans were thus shocked when on June 14, 2020, Attorney General William Barr used members of the National Guard, Secret Service, federal Park Police, and other law enforcement officers in riot gear whose uniforms carried no identification to remove peaceful protesters who had amassed in Lafayette Square,[130] directly across the street from the White House. President Trump wanted the square cleared so that he could walk safely from the White House to St. John's Church, located on the square, to hold up a Bible and lash out at protesters as he praised those who favored law and order.[131] According to a video timeline posted by the *Washington Post*,[132] supported by a congressional investigation into the use of tear gas and rubber bullets on the protesters, the actions taken by law enforcement violated their constitutional rights to freedom of assembly and association.[133]

Similar concerns were voiced when President Trump ordered members of the National Guard and other federal officers to pick up protesters in Portland, Oregon. Service personnel were in unmarked uniforms, and protesters were thrown into unmarked vans and taken to various locations around the city with no charges filed against them or arrests made. These actions by the administration were unprecedented, even as the president announced that he would take control over other cities governed by Democratic mayors. The Democratic mayor of Portland, as well as Oregon's Democratic governor, strongly assailed this unprecedented use of federal power. While President Trump labelled the protesters "anarchists," the mayor claimed that the presence of federal officers served only to inflame the protesters.[134]

The Second Amendment

As COVID-19 made its way to the United States, the issue of the utility of wearing face masks was hotly debated. Initially, the CDC made no recommendations for their use by anyone other than health care workers on the front lines in hospitals, clinics, and nursing homes. Stay-at-home orders, with the closing of nearly all facilities and institutions, also quickly became a flash point for some conservatives who believed the government had overstepped its authority. Democratic Michigan Governor Gretchen Whitmer quickly became the target of protesters on the political right when she extended a stay-at-home order after Michigan's cases of the virus continued to trend upward rapidy. The "American Patriot Rally" was quickly organized and called for the reopening of all state businesses. Armed with signs proclaiming, "GIVE ME GOVT DISTANCING," and many carrying guns, protesters entered the State House in a show of force. They wore no masks, nor did they social distance. Michigan state law allows the open carry of guns in the building, including the House and Senate galleries. Some lawmakers wore bulletproof vests as gun-toting protesters yelled, "This is the people's house; you cannot lock us out!" Two decades ago, few individuals could have predicted that an angry cadre of fully armed individuals could make this kind of show of force in a state capitol building or later plan to kidnap the governor. But decisions expanding what many believe are constitutionally the protected rights to bear arms have come from the Supreme Court of the United States, making the protests that occurred in Michigan legal. President Trump even tweeted words of encouragement, including "LIBERATE MICHIGAN."[135]

The Fourth Amendment

In part, the Fourth Amendment protects individuals from unreasonable searches and seizures. However, President Trump used the force of the federal military to snatch and detain nonviolent protesters in Washington, D.C.; Portland, Oregon; and elsewhere in the name of keeping the peace. President Trump believes that large cities and states, nearly all run by Democratic mayors, were not doing enough to stem the tide of racial protests in their respective jurisdictions that were triggered by the murder of George Floyd and of several other Black women and men.

While Fourth Amendment issues were raised in the context of racial protesting, the amendment also had an effect on how local and state laws and regulations to stop the spread of COVID-19 were put in place. If the government, for example, requires you to shutter your business, is such a policy an unreasonable seizure of your property and/or profits? Should personnel in hospitals or stores make social distancing or the wearing of a mask required before service or entry? Is what is called "disease surveillance," including the taking of temperatures, violative of the Fourth Amendment? What is or is not "reasonable" in the context of the amendment is key. There is a burden that governments must weigh when announcing restrictions and conditions on travel, work, and school.

South Korea was the first nation to use digital surveillance by using cell-phone location data as its scientists and policy makers sought to track transmission of COVID-19.[136] This usage soon was discussed in the United States as a way to trace what proportion of the population was actually obeying shelter-in-place rules. The CARES Act, which included trillions of dollars for economic relief caused by the pandemic, also contained a proviso requiring the CDC to develop a way to collect data about the virus, and many cities offer voluntary contact tracing apps for cell phones.

Because the Supreme Court ruled in 2018 that the government can force wireless carriers to give up information on their clients to law enforcement officials, the tracing of spatial information from GPS coordinates could possibly pass constitutional muster, given the facts of any particular case.[137]

The Eighth Amendment

COVID-19 appears to flourish on cruise ships, in nursing homes, and in prisons. In the context of prisons, a question has arisen as to whether or not confinement to a COVID-19-infected prison is "cruel and unusual punishment" forbidden by the Eighth Amendment, especially when imprisonment is for nonviolent offenses. Several of President Trump's advisers who were convicted of violating campaign finance laws argued that they should be released from prison or be allowed to postpone their incarceration dates. With over 2 million inmates in U.S. prisons, proximity to those with the disease is a near certainty. Some commentators argued that the virus is not only "cruel," it is also unusual in that it is a pandemic known to thrive in prisonlike conditions.[138]

At least one federal district judge agreed that prison conditions produce situations that violate the Eighth Amendment. In *Nellson* v. *Barnhart and the U.S. Federal Bureau of Prisons*, an ongoing class-action lawsuit brought by Nellson, who is in custody in a U.S. prison, against the warden and the Federal Bureau of Prisons, the judge found that a lack of testing; protective garments, including face masks; and social distancing conditions were "cruel and unusual punishments" violative of the Eighth Amendment.[139] Scores of challenges to prison conditions, already subject to hundreds of cases challenging other common conditions prior to the pandemic, are likely to be filed in state and federal courts until the Supreme Court decides to weigh in on what constitutes cruel and unusual punishment in a time of pandemic.

CONCLUSION AND REVIEW

What Are the Roots of Civil Liberties and the Bill of Rights?

4.1 Explain the roots of civil liberties in the Constitution and their development in the Bill of Rights.

Most of the Framers originally opposed the Bill of Rights. Anti-Federalists, however, continued to stress the need for a bill of rights during the drive for ratification of the Constitution, and some states tried to make their ratification contingent on the addition of a bill of rights. Thus, during its first session, Congress sent the first ten amendments to the Constitution, the Bill of Rights, to the states for their ratification. Later, the addition of the Fourteenth Amendment allowed the Supreme Court to apply most of the amendments to the states through a process called selective incorporation.

What Are the First Amendment Guarantees of Freedom of Religion?

4.2 Distinguish between the establishment and the free exercise clauses of the First Amendment.

The First Amendment guarantees freedom of religion. The establishment clause, which prohibits the national government from establishing a religion, does not generally allow prayer in schools. However, the Court has held that many forms of aid are constitutionally permissible. The Court has also allowed some governmental regulation of religious practices under the free exercise clause.

What Are the First Amendment Guarantees of Freedom of Speech, Press, Assembly, and Petition?

4.3 Outline the First Amendment liberties and limitations on the freedoms of speech, press, assembly, and petition.

Historically, one of the most volatile subjects of constitutional interpretation has been the First Amendment's mandate that "Congress shall make no law . . . abridging the freedom of speech or of the press." As with the establishment and free exercise clauses of the First Amendment, the Court has not interpreted the speech and press clauses as absolute bans against government regulation. The Supreme Court has ruled against prior restraint, thus protecting freedom of the press. The Court has also protected symbolic speech and hate speech.

Areas of speech and publication unprotected by the First Amendment include libel, fighting words, and obscenity. The freedoms of peaceable assembly and petition are directly related to the freedoms of speech and the press.

What Does the Second Amendment Protect?

4.4 Describe the Second Amendment's guarantee right to bear arms.

Initially, the right to bear arms was envisioned in terms of state militias. Over the years, states and Congress have enacted various gun ownership restrictions with little Supreme Court interpretation. However, the Court ruled in *D.C.* v. *Heller* (2008) and *McDonald* v. *City of Chicago* (2010) that the Second Amendment protects an individual's right to own and carry a firearm.

What Are the Rights of Criminal Defendants?

4.5 Outline the constitutional rights of defendants and the issues involved in protecting defendants' liberties as guaranteed by the Bill of Rights.

The Fourth, Fifth, Sixth, and Eighth Amendments provide a variety of procedural guarantees to individuals accused of crimes. The Fourth Amendment prohibits unreasonable searches and seizures. The Fifth Amendment protects those who have been charged with crimes. It mandates the use of grand juries in cases of serious crimes. It also guarantees that "no person shall be compelled to be a witness against himself." Finally, the Fifth Amendment's double jeopardy clause protects individuals from being tried twice for the same crimes in the same jurisdiction. The Court's interpretation of the Sixth Amendment's guarantee of "assistance of counsel" stipulates that the government provide counsel to defendants unable to pay for it in cases subject to prison sentences. The Sixth Amendment also requires an impartial jury. The Court's current view is that the Eighth Amendment's ban against "cruel and unusual punishments" does not bar imposition of the death penalty.

What Is the Right to Privacy?

4.6 Explain the origins and significance of the right to privacy.

The right to privacy is a judicially created right carved from the penumbras (unstated liberties implied by more explicitly stated rights) of several amendments, including the First, Third, Fourth, Ninth, and Fourteenth Amendments. The Court has found statutes that limit access to birth control, prohibit abortion, and ban homosexual acts to be unconstitutional under this right. The Court has abandoned its use of privacy doctrine standards dealing with abortion and adopted an undue burden standard.

Political Reform and Realities: What Can Governments Do About COVID-19, Racial Injustice, and Beyond?

4.7 Evaluate how civil liberties have been affected by the simultaneous arrival of COVID-19 and racial unrest in the United States.

The COVID-19 pandemic not only created strains on the medical system, but led to some cities being closed down, many Americans placed out of work, and schools moving to online learning, all with the economically disadvantaged affected in far greater percentages. Meanwhile, the killing of George Floyd led to local protest and attracted public attention to the ongoing problem of unarmed Black men and women being killed by police officers. Both the pandemic and protests affected a wide range of civil liberties, when authorities instated stay at home orders, distancing guidelines, size limits on gatherings, and the wearing of masks.

LEARN THE TERMS

Alien and Sedition Acts
Burger Court
civil liberties
civil rights
direct incitement test
double jeopardy clause
due process clause
due process rights
ex post facto law
Eighteenth Amendment
Eighth Amendment
Engel v. *Vitale* (1962)
establishment clause
exclusionary rule
Fifth Amendment
fighting words
First Amendment
Fourteenth Amendment
Fourth Amendment

free exercise clause
fundamental freedoms
Furman v. *Georgia* (1972)
Gideon v. *Wainwright* (1963)
grand jury
Gregg v. *Georgia* (1976)
incorporation doctrine
Lemon v. *Kurtzman* (1971)
libel
Mapp v. *Ohio* (1961)
McDonald v. *City of Chicago* (2010)
Miranda rights
Miranda v. *Arizona* (1966)
New Jersey v. *T.L.O.* (1985)
New York Times Co. v. *U.S.* (1971)
Ninth Amendment
Oregon Employment Division
    v. *Smith* (1990)
prior restraint

Reno v. *ACLU* (1997)
Reynolds v. *United States* (1878)
right to privacy
Roe v. *Wade* (1973)
Santa Fe Independent School District
    v. *Doe* (2000)
Schenck v. *U.S.* (1919)
sedition laws
selective incorporation
Sixth Amendment
slander
strict scrutiny
substantive due process
symbolic speech
Terry v. *Ohio* (1968)
undue burden test
Warren Court
Wisconsin v. *Yoder* (1972)

LEARN THE NAMES

Warren E. Burger

Bettmann/Getty Images

WHO CONDUCTED THE UNDERGROUND RAILROAD?

Harriet Tubman was one of many brave individuals who conducted the Underground Railroad, a network of safe houses, barns, and warehouses leading from the South and Maryland north to Canada—to freedom. She ran multiple missions to help enslaved Black people in the South find freedom in the North. This photograph shows Tubman, far left, with a group of people she helped to escape to freedom.

CRITICAL THINKING QUESTION: *What vestiges of slavery remain today?*

CIVIL RIGHTS

LEARNING OBJECTIVES

5.1 Trace the roots of movements to guarantee rights to Black people and women.

5.2 Outline developments in Black people's and women's push for equality from 1890 to 1954.

5.3 Analyze the legal protections enacted for Black people's and women's civil rights since 1955.

5.4 Summarize the struggles of other group-differentiated minorities for civil rights.

5.5 Evaluate the standards by which civil rights are protected today.

Slavery first made its ugly appearance at the Jamestown Colony in Virginia in 1619 when settlers purchased "twenty and odd" enslaved people from Angola, Africa, who had been kidnapped by Portuguese traders. They were immediately put to work as much-needed field laborers, but most were treated as indentured servants who could work to buy their freedom.

Slavery was made legal in the Virginia Colony in 1661; other colonies soon followed, from Puritan Massachusetts to Quaker Pennsylvania. However, as their industrial economies evolved, the mid-Atlantic and northeastern colonies did not need many enslaved people. Moreover, most non-southern colonies had ways by which enslaved people could gain their freedom. That was not the case in the South, where its increasingly agrarian economy needed bodies to plant and harvest crops.

By the time of the Constitutional Convention, slavery was an issue that divided delegates from the northern and southern states; many of the Framers, including George Washington and Thomas Jefferson, were enslavers. Two major compromises regarding slavery were made as the Constitution was drafted; the consideration of five enslaved people to be counted as three persons for purposes of counting individuals to allocate seats by state in the House of Representatives (called the Three-Fifths Compromise), and the banning of the importation of enslaved people into the United States after 1808.

The invention of the cotton gin in 1793 made it easier to process raw cotton, a highly profitable crop, and dramatically raised the demand for more labor by enslaved people. Enslavers subjected enslaved people to a host of abuses, including beatings and sexual assault. Families were routinely separated when members were sold to other enslavers. As enslaved people desperate for freedom began escaping to free states in the North where slavery was illegal, the U.S. Congress enacted the Fugitive Slave Act in 1793, requiring the return of any fugitives from slavery to their enslavers.

The act did not deter the efforts of those united against slavery to create a series of safe houses and secret routes to help enslaved people escape to freedom in the North. This Underground Railroad is perhaps best embodied by the actions of **Harriet Tubman**.

Tubman was born into slavery on the Eastern Shore of Maryland in the early 1820s. In 1849, she escaped from the Maryland coast. Upon reaching freedom in Philadelphia in 1849, she immediately returned to Maryland and, in a series of thirteen daring escapes, led more than seventy relatives and friends to freedom—never losing a single man, woman, or child. Her actions are all the more noteworthy because Congress had passed an even more stringent Fugitive Slave Act in 1850. The act barred freedom seekers from becoming free anywhere in the United States or its territories. Flyers went up all over the nation offering huge rewards for the capture of the five-foot-tall "conductor"

Harriet Tubman

Born as an enslaved person in Maryland in the early 1820s, Tubman escaped to freedom and became a conductor on the Underground Railroad. She led more than seventy people to freedom in the North, served in the Union during the Civil War, and championed women's suffrage.

WHAT WERE SLAVE AUCTIONS?

Once in the Americas, enslaved people were auctioned to the highest bidder. Families were often split up, when the bidder did not want the whole family, only the strongest or healthiest members. This image shows the auctioning of a baby, from an enslaved person's narrative published in 1849.

Pictorial Press Ltd/Alamy Stock Photo

of the Underground Railroad. Noted **abolitionist** William Lloyd Garrison, a White New Englander, began referring to Tubman as "Moses."[1]

After the Civil War, Tubman continued her activism. She worked with noted suffragist Susan B. Anthony, traveling to suffrage conventions in New York City, Boston, and Washington, D.C. Her efforts brought her many accolades from women's rights organizations for her lifetime service to the cause of humanity. It was thus fitting that her image was to take the place of former president **Andrew Jackson**, a staunch supporter of slavery and foe of women's rights, on the front of the twenty-dollar bill. Although the Obama administration announced that Tubman was to be the first woman and African American on the twenty-dollar bill in 2016, the Trump administration put the brakes on the proposal in 2018, saying that the issue was being put on the back burner for at least six years. President Trump was a fan of President Jackson—a portrait of the seventh president hung in the Oval Office. In sharp contrast, the Biden administration is exploring ways to fast track the image of Tubman onto the twenty dollar bill.

. . .

Since the founding era, concepts of *civil rights*—the government-protected rights of individuals against arbitrary or discriminatory treatment by governments or individuals based on categories such as race, sex, national origin, age, religion, or sexual orientation—have changed dramatically. As we will discuss in this chapter, the Fourteenth Amendment, one of three Civil War Amendments ratified from 1865 to 1870, was the first provision to introduce the notion of equality into the Constitution by specifying that a state could not deny "any person within its jurisdiction equal protection of the laws." Throughout history, this **equal protection clause**, which guarantees that no citizen shall be denied rights or privileges given to any other citizen by constitution or law, has been the linchpin of efforts to protect a variety of groups from discrimination. As a result, the Fourteenth Amendment has generated more litigation to determine and specify its meaning than any other provision of the constitution. Within a few years of its ratification, women—and later, Black people and other minorities and disadvantaged groups—began to seek expanded civil rights and freedom from discrimination in all walks of life. Throughout this chapter, we will explore how litigation, lobbying, and social protest efforts have changed notions of equality and civil rights in the United States.

WHAT ARE THE ROOTS OF AMERICAN CIVIL RIGHTS?

5.1 Trace the roots of movements to guarantee rights to Black people and women.

The U.S. Declaration of Independence states that "all men are created equal." This simple language articulates a closely held American ideal: that of equality of opportunity. Though all people may not have the same skills, talents, or abilities, from the beginning, the United States has been built on the assumption that all citizens—"men"—should have the same chance to work hard and build a successful life for themselves and their families. Importantly, citizens are not guaranteed equality of result. In other words, there is no assumption that they will be guaranteed the same income, possessions, or outcomes, only that they will be able to pursue their goals equally, without interference on the basis of arbitrary personal characteristics.

Of course, the definition of "men" has broadened tremendously since the nation's inception. When the Framers wrote the Declaration, their language referred most directly to property-owning White men. Over time, that definition has grown to accommodate White men who do not own property, Black men, women, those over eighteen, and citizens of a wide variety of races, creeds, colors, and ethnicities. Today, we expect that all American citizens, regardless of their economic, political, or social status, should have equal opportunity to pursue their goals and dreams, although we are still far short of that goal.

abolitionist
A supporter, especially in the early nineteenth century, of ending the institution of slavery.

Andrew Jackson
Seventh president of the United States serving from 1829 to 1837 as a Democratic Republican. He became a national hero for leading American troops to victory over the British in the War of 1812's Battle of New Orleans. He depended on the labor of enslaved people for his plantation and was responsible for removing American Indians across the South to Oklahoma.

equal protection clause
Section of the Fourteenth Amendment that guarantees that all citizens receive "equal protection of the laws."

Voting rights—or suffrage—of women and Black people is considered a given in modern U.S. society, but that was not the case at the Founding. The period from 1800 to 1890 was one of tremendous change and upheaval in America. Despite the Civil War and the freeing of enslaved people, the promise of equality guaranteed to Black people by the Civil War Amendments failed to become a reality. Women's rights activists also began to make claims for equality, often using the arguments enunciated for the abolition of slavery, but they, too, fell far short of their goals.

Slavery and Congress

Congress banned the trading of enslaved people in 1808, after expiration of the twenty-year period specified by the Constitution. In 1820, Black people made up 25 percent of the U.S. population and formed majorities or near majorities in states including South Carolina, Mississippi, and Florida. By 1840, that figure had fallen to 20 percent of the total U.S. population. The South became increasingly dependent on agriculture, such as cotton, tobacco, and rice, with labor from enslaved people as its economic base. At the same time, technological advances were turning the northern states into an increasingly industrialized, more populated region that deepened cultural and political differences as well as the animosity between North and South.

As the nation grew westward in the early 1800s, conflicts between northern and southern states intensified over the slavery status of new states admitted to the union. The first major crisis occurred in 1820, when Missouri applied for admission as a state in which slavery would be legal. Missouri's admission would have weighted the Senate in favor of slavery and therefore was opposed by northern senators. To resolve this conflict, Congress passed the Missouri Compromise of 1820. The Compromise prohibited slavery north of the geographical boundary at 36 degrees latitude. This act allowed the union to admit Missouri as a state where slavery was legal. To maintain the balance of slave and free states, Maine was carved out of a portion of Massachusetts.

The First Civil Rights Movements: Abolition and Women's Rights

The Missouri Compromise solidified the South in its determination to keep slavery legal, but it also fueled the fervor of those opposing it. William Lloyd Garrison galvanized the abolitionist movement in the early 1830s with publication of the weekly antislavery newspaper *The Liberator*, which later was to publish many pro-woman suffrage tracts. Garrison cofounded the American Anti-Slavery Society in 1833; by 1838, it had more than 250,000 members.

Slavery was not the only practice that people began to question in the decades following the Missouri Compromise. In 1840, for example, Garrison and **Frederick Douglass**, a self-liberated person and a well-known Black abolitionist writer, left the Anti-Slavery Society when it refused to accept demands that women be allowed to participate equally in all its activities. Custom dictated that women not speak out in public, and most laws explicitly made women second-class citizens. In most states, for example, women could not divorce their husbands or keep their own wages and inheritances. And of course, they could not vote.

Bettmann/Getty Images

WHO WAS SOJOURNER TRUTH?
Sojourner Truth was an abolitionist and women's rights activist. She was born as an enslaved person but escaped around her thirtieth birthday. For more than fifty years after her escape, she travelled the country, speaking passionately for civil rights for all. Her most notable speech, "Ain't I a Woman?" played an important role in highlighting the underrepresentation of Black American women in the women's rights movement that began in the late 1840s.

Frederick Douglass
A formerly enslaved person born in the early 1800s who became a leading abolitionist, writer, and suffragist.

Elizabeth Cady Stanton and **Lucretia Mott**, founders of the first women's rights movement, attended the 1840 meeting of the World Anti-Slavery Society in London with their husbands, along with Douglass, Garrison, and others. In spite of their long journey, and the fact that Mott, along with several other women, was an officially elected delegate to the meeting, no women were permitted to participate in the convention solely because they were women. As they sat in a mandated area apart from the male delegates, they compared their status to that of the enslaved people they sought to free. They concluded that women were not much better off than enslaved people, and they resolved to address this issue. In 1848, they finally sent out a call for the first women's rights convention. Three hundred women and men, including Frederick Douglass, attended the first meeting for women's rights, held in Seneca Falls, New York.

The **Seneca Falls Convention** passed resolutions demanding the abolition of legal, economic, and social discrimination against women. All of the resolutions reflected the attendees' dissatisfaction with contemporary moral codes, divorce and criminal laws, and the limited opportunities for women in education, the church, medicine, law, and politics. Ironically, only the call for "woman suffrage"—a call to give women the right to vote—failed to win unanimous approval. Similar conventions took place later across the Northeast and Midwest. At an 1851 meeting in Akron, Ohio, for example, Sojourner Truth delivered her famous "Ain't I a Woman?" speech, calling on women to recognize the plight of their Black sisters. For the most part, however, White women's rights activists were quite racist.

The 1850s: The Calm Before the Storm

By 1850, much had changed in America. The Gold Rush that began in 1848 in California spurred westward migration, cities grew as people were lured from their farms, the westward expansion of railroads and the telegraph increased mobility and communication, and immigrants flooded into the United States. The women's movement gained momentum, and slavery continued to tear the nation apart. Harriet Beecher Stowe's *Uncle Tom's Cabin*, a widely circulated novel that depicted the evils of slavery, further inflamed the country.

The tremendous national reaction to *Uncle Tom's Cabin*, which later prompted President *Abraham Lincoln* to call Stowe "the little woman who started the big war," had not yet faded when a new controversy over the Missouri Compromise became the lightning rod for the first major civil rights case addressed by the U.S. Supreme Court. In *Dred Scott* v. *Sandford* (1857), the Court ruled that the Missouri Compromise, which prohibited slavery north of a set geographical boundary, was unconstitutional. Furthermore, the Court added that enslaved people were not U.S. citizens, and as a consequence, could not bring suits in federal court.[2]

The Civil War and Its Aftermath: Civil Rights Laws and Constitutional Amendments

The Civil War had many causes, but slavery was clearly a key issue. During the war, which lasted from 1861 to 1865, abolitionists continued to press for an end to slavery. They were partially rewarded when President Abraham Lincoln issued the **Emancipation Proclamation**, which provided that all enslaved people in states still in active rebellion against the United States would be freed automatically on January 1, 1863. Designed as a measure to gain favor for the war in the North, the Emancipation Proclamation did not free all enslaved people—it freed only those who lived in the Confederacy. Complete abolition of slavery did not occur until congressional passage and ultimate ratification of the Thirteenth Amendment in 1865. Juneteenth, which celebrates the announcement of the end of slavery in Texas on June 15, 1865, became a national day of recognition in 2020 marked by peaceful protests around the nation.

Elizabeth Cady Stanton

Leading nineteenth-century feminist, suffragist, and abolitionist who, along with Lucretia Mott, organized the Seneca Falls Convention. Stanton later founded the National Woman Suffrage Association (NWSA) with Susan B. Anthony.

Lucretia Mott

Leading nineteenth-century feminist, suffragist, and abolitionist who, along with Elizabeth Cady Stanton, organized the Seneca Falls Convention.

Seneca Falls Convention

The first major feminist meeting, held in New York state in 1848, which produced the historic "Declaration of Sentiments," calling for equal rights for women.

Emancipation Proclamation

President Abraham Lincoln issued this proclamation on January 1, 1863, in the third year of the Civil War. It freed all enslaved people in states that were in active rebellion against the United States.

Thirteenth Amendment

One of three major amendments ratified after the Civil War; specifically bans slavery in the United States.

The **Thirteenth Amendment** was the first of the three Civil War Amendments. It banned all forms of "slavery [and] involuntary servitude." Although the federal government required the southern states to ratify the Thirteenth Amendment as a condition of readmission to the Union after the war, most former Confederate states passed laws designed to restrict opportunities for formerly enslaved people. These *Black Codes* denied most legal rights to formerly enslaved people by prohibiting Black people from voting, sitting on juries, or even appearing in public places. The Black Codes laid the groundwork for *Jim Crow laws*, which later would institute segregation in all walks of life in the South.

An outraged Congress enacted the Civil Rights Act of 1866 to invalidate some state Black Codes. President *Andrew Johnson* vetoed the legislation, but—for the first time in history—Congress overrode a presidential veto. The Civil Rights Act formally made Black people citizens of the United States and gave Congress and the federal courts the power to intervene when states attempted to restrict the citizenship rights of Black males in matters such as voting. Congress reasoned that Black people were unlikely to succeed if they had to file discrimination complaints in state courts, where most judges were elected. Passage of a federal law allowed Black people to challenge discriminatory state practices in federal courts, where the president appointed judges for life.

Because controversy remained over the constitutionality of the act (since the Constitution gives states the right to determine qualifications of voters in Article I), Congress proposed the *Fourteenth Amendment* simultaneously with the Civil Rights Act to guarantee, among other things, citizenship to all formerly enslaved people. Other key provisions of the Fourteenth Amendment barred states from abridging *"the privileges or immunities of citizenship"* or depriving *"any person of life, liberty, or property, without due process of law."* As previously discussed, the Fourteenth Amendment also includes the equal protection clause, which prohibits states from denying *"any person within its jurisdiction the equal protection of the laws."*

Unlike the Thirteenth Amendment, which had near-unanimous support in the North, the Fourteenth Amendment faced opposition from many women because it failed to guarantee them suffrage. During the Civil War, women's rights activists put aside their claims for expanded rights for women, most notably the right to vote, and threw their energies into the war effort. They were convinced that once the government freed enslaved people and gave them the right to vote, women would receive this same right. They were wrong.

Fifteenth Amendment

One of three major amendments ratified after the Civil War; specifically enfranchised newly freed men who had been enslaved.

Susan B. Anthony

Nineteenth-century feminist, suffragist, and founder of the National Woman Suffrage Association with Elizabeth Cady Stanton. Anthony later formed the National American Woman Suffrage Association (NAWSA), which along with the National Woman's Party (NWP) helped to ensure ratification of the Nineteenth Amendment.

In early 1869, after ratification of the Fourteenth Amendment (which specifically added the word "male" to the Constitution for the first time), women's rights activists met in Washington, D.C., to oppose any new amendment that would extend suffrage to Black males and not to women. Many of the women used horribly racist arguments to state their case. Ending slavery was one thing, in their opinion, but extending voting rights to African American males and not White women was another. Nevertheless, Congress passed the **Fifteenth Amendment** in early 1869. It guaranteed the "right of citizens" to vote regardless of their "race, color or previous condition of servitude." Sex was not mentioned.

Women's rights activists were shocked. Abolitionists' continued support of the Fifteenth Amendment prompted many women's rights supporters to leave the abolition movement and to work solely for the cause of women's rights. Twice burned, **Susan B. Anthony** (who had joined the women's movement in 1851) and Elizabeth Cady Stanton decided to form their own group, the National Woman Suffrage Association (NWSA) in 1869, to achieve that goal and other women's rights. Another more conservative group, the American Woman Suffrage Association, was founded at the same time to pursue the sole goal of suffrage. In spite of the NWSA's opposition, however, the states ratified the Fifteenth Amendment in 1870.

Civil Rights, Congress, and the Supreme Court

Continued southern resistance to African American equality led Congress to pass the Civil Rights Act of 1875, designed to grant equal access to public accommodations such as theaters, restaurants, and transportation. The act also prohibited the exclusion of Black people from jury service. By 1877, however, national interest in the legal condition of Black people waned. Most White Southerners and even some Northerners never had believed in true equality for "freedmen," as formerly enslaved people were called. Any rights that freedmen received had been contingent on federal enforcement. And federal occupation of the South (known as Reconstruction) ended in 1877. National troops were no longer available to guard polling places and to prevent Whites from excluding Black voters, and southern states quickly moved to limit Black peoples' access to the ballot. Other forms of discrimination also came about as state judicial decisions upheld **Jim Crow laws**, which required segregation in public schools and facilities, including railroads, restaurants, and theaters. Some Jim Crow laws, specifically known as miscegenation laws, barred interracial marriage.

All these laws, at first glance, appeared to conflict with the Civil Rights Act of 1875. In 1883, however, a series of cases decided by the Supreme Court severely damaged the vitality of the 1875 act. The *Civil Rights Cases* (1883) were five separate cases involving convictions of private individuals found to have violated the Civil Rights Act by refusing to extend accommodations to Black people in theaters, a hotel, and a railroad.[3] In deciding these cases, the Supreme Court ruled that Congress could prohibit state or governmental action but not private acts of discrimination. The Court thus concluded that Congress had no authority to outlaw private discrimination in public accommodations. The Court's opinion in the *Civil Rights Cases* provided a moral reinforcement for the Jim Crow system. Southern states viewed the Court's ruling as an invitation to gut the reach and intent of the Thirteenth, Fourteenth, and Fifteenth Amendments.

In devising ways to make certain that Black people did not vote, southern states had to sidestep the intent of the Fifteenth Amendment. This amendment did not guarantee suffrage; it simply said that states could not deny anyone the right to vote on the basis of race or color. To exclude Black people in a way that seemed

Jim Crow laws

Laws enacted by southern states that required segregation in public schools, theaters, hotels, and other public accommodations.

WHAT DID JIM CROW LAWS DO?

Throughout the South, examples of Jim Crow laws abounded. There were Jim Crow schools, restaurants, hotels, and businesses. Some buildings even had separate "White" and "Colored" facilities, such as the bus station waiting room shown here. The Supreme Court would later rule that the creation of such distinctions relegated Black people to a form of second-class citizenship that was injurious to their "hearts and minds" and, as such, unconstitutional.

Everett Collection Historical/Alamy Stock Photo

poll tax

Taxes levied in many southern states and localities that had to be paid before an eligible voter could cast a ballot.

racially neutral, southern states used three devices before the 1890s: (1) **poll tax**, small taxes on the right to vote that often came due when poor African American share-croppers had the least amount of money on hand; (2) some form of property-owning qualifications; and, (3) "literacy" or "understanding" tests, which allowed local voter registration officials to administer difficult reading-comprehension tests to potential voters whom they did not know. For example, some potential voters were asked to rewrite entire sections of the Constitution by hand as the registrar dictated its text. Misspellings or faulty punctuation were grounds for denial.

These voting restrictions had an immediate impact. By the late 1890s, Black voting fell by 62 percent from the Reconstruction period, while White voting fell by only 26 percent. To make certain these laws did not further reduce the numbers of poor or uneducated White voters, many southern states added a **grandfather clause** to their voting qualification provisions, granting voting privileges to those men who failed to pass a wealth or literacy test only if their grandfathers had voted before Reconstruction. Grandfather clauses effectively denied the descendants of enslaved people the right to vote.

grandfather clause

Voter qualification provision in many southern states that allowed only those men whose grandfathers had voted before Reconstruction to vote unless they passed a wealth or literacy test.

WHAT WAS THE PUSH FOR EQUALITY, 1890–1954?

5.2 Outline developments in Black peoples' and women's push for equality from 1890 to 1954.

Progressive Era (1890–1920)

A period of widespread activism to re-form political, economic, and social ills in the United States.

The **Progressive Era (1890–1920)** was characterized by a concerted effort to reform political, economic, and social affairs. Evils such as child labor, the concentration of economic power in the hands of a few industrialists, limited suffrage, political cor-ruption, business monopolies, and prejudice against Black people all were targets of progressive reform. Distress over the inferior legal status of Black people increased with the U.S. Supreme Court's decision in *Plessy* v. *Ferguson* (1896), a case that some commentators point to as the Court's worst hour.[4]

Plessy **v.** *Ferguson* **(1896)**

Supreme Court case that challenged a Louisiana statute requiring that railroads provide separate accommodations for Blacks and Whites; the Court found that separate-but-equal accommoda-tions did not violate the equal protection clause of the Fourteenth Amendment.

In 1892, a group of Black people in Louisiana decided to test the constitutional-ity of a Louisiana law mandating racial segregation on all public trains. This meant that certain undesirable cars at the rear of the train were reserved for Black people. They convinced Homer Plessy, a man who was one-eighth Black and who easily "passed" for White, to board a train in New Orleans and proceed to the "Whites only" car. The authorities were alerted, and Plessy was arrested when he refused to take a seat in the car reserved for Black people, as required by state law. Plessy's lawyers challenged the law, arguing that the Fourteenth Amendment prohibited racial segregation.

The Supreme Court disagreed. After analyzing the history of Black people in the United States, the majority concluded that the Louisiana law was constitutional. The justices based the decision on their belief that separate facilities for Black and White people provided equal protection of the laws. After all, they reasoned, the Louisiana statute did not prevent Plessy from riding the train; it required only that the races travel separately. Justice John Marshall Harlan was the lone dissenter. He argued that "the Constitution is colorblind" and that it was senseless to hold constitutional a law "which, practically, puts the badge of servitude and degradation upon a large class of our fellow citizens."[5]

separate-but-equal doctrine

The central tenet of the *Plessy* v. *Ferguson* decision that claimed that separate accommodations for Blacks and Whites did not violate the Constitution. This doctrine was used by southern states to pass widespread discriminatory legislation at the end of the nineteenth century.

National Association for the Advancement of Colored People (NAACP)

An important rights organization founded in 1909 to oppose segrega-tion, racism, and voting rights violations targeted against Black people.

Not surprisingly, the **separate-but-equal doctrine** enunciated in *Plessy* v. *Ferguson* soon came to mean only separate, as new legal avenues to discriminate against Black people made their way into law. The Jim Crow system soon expanded and became a way of life and a rigid social code throughout the American South. By 1900, equality for Black people was far from the promise first offered by the Civil War Amendments. Again and again, the Supreme Court nullified the intent of the amendments and sanc-tioned racial segregation; southern states avidly followed its lead.[6]

It was not only segregation and Jim Crow laws that affected Black people, particularly in the South. Lynchings of Black men were common. Mobs of angry White men regularly took custody of Black men accused of looking at a White woman or failing to nod in deference to a White person. Without an arrest or trial, Black men were hoisted on trees, noosed, and hung for all to see.

The Founding of the National Association for the Advancement of Colored People

In 1909, a handful of individuals active in a variety of progressive causes, including women's suffrage and the fight for better working conditions for women and children, met to discuss the idea of a group devoted to addressing the problems of the "Negro." Major race riots had occurred in several American cities, and progressive reformers were concerned about these outbreaks of violence and the possibility of others. Oswald Garrison Villard, the influential publisher of the *New York Evening Post*—and the grandson of William Lloyd Garrison—called a conference to discuss the matter. This group soon evolved into the **National Association for the Advancement of Colored People (NAACP)**. Along with Villard, its first leaders included W.E.B. Du Bois, a founder in 1905 of the Niagara Movement, a group of African American intellectuals who took their name from their first meeting place in Niagara Falls, Ontario, Canada, the only place they could be assured that they could meet free from segregationist practices that were in force all over the country, not just in the South.

Library of Congress

WHY WAS THE NIAGARA MOVEMENT FOUNDED?

W.E.B. Du Bois (third from left in the second row, facing left) is pictured with the other male original leaders of the Niagara Movement in this 1905 photo. The meeting produced a detailed list of injustices suffered by Black people and, like the women of Seneca Falls, attendees issued a "Declaration of Principles" demanding political, social, and economic equality. It held its second meeting in Harpers Ferry, West Virginia. Women quickly came into leadership positions and many went on to form NAACP chapters in their home cities.

The Suffrage Movement

The struggle for women's rights was revitalized in 1890, when the National and American Woman Suffrage Associations merged. The new organization, the National American Woman Suffrage Association (NAWSA), was headed by Susan B. Anthony. Unlike NWSA, which had sought a wide variety of expanded rights for women, this new association largely devoted itself to securing women's suffrage. The proliferation of women's groups during the Progressive Era greatly facilitated its task. In addition to the rapidly growing temperance movement, whose members pressed to ban the sale of alcohol that many women blamed for a variety of social ills, women's groups sprang up to seek goals such as maximum hour or minimum wage laws for women and improved sanitation, public morals, and education.

NAWSA based its claim to the right to vote largely on the fact that women, as mothers, should be enfranchised. The new women's movement—called the **suffrage movement** because of its focus on voting rights—soon took on racist and nativist overtones. Suffragists argued that if undereducated Black men and immigrants could vote, why couldn't women?

By 1917, the new women's movement had more than 2 million members. Its growth was aided by the formation of the more radical National Woman's Party (NWP) in 1915. Members of the National Woman's Party gained publicity for the cause of women's suffrage through daily arrests in front of the White House as well as the force-feeding in prison of members staging a hunger strike. In 1920, a coalition

suffrage movement

The drive for voting rights for women that took place in the United States in the nineteenth and early twentieth centuries until ratification of the Nineteenth Amendment in 1920.

Nineteenth Amendment

Amendment to the Constitution passed in 1920 that guaranteed women the right to vote.

of women's groups, led by NAWSA and the more-militant NWP, was able to secure ratification of the **Nineteenth Amendment** to the Constitution through rallies, protest marches, and the eventual support of President Woodrow Wilson. The Nineteenth Amendment guaranteed all women the right to vote—fifty years after the Fifteenth Amendment had enfranchised African American males.

After passage of the suffrage amendment, also called the Susan B. Anthony Amendment, in 1920, the fragile alliance of diverse women's groups that had come together to fight for the vote quickly disintegrated. Women returned to their home groups to pursue their individualized goals. In fact, after the tumult of the suffrage movement, organized activity on behalf of women's rights did not reemerge in national politics until the 1960s. In the meantime, the NAACP continued to fight racism and racial segregation. Its activities and those of others in the civil rights movement would later give impetus to a new women's movement.

Litigating for Equality

During the 1930s, leaders of the NAACP began to sense that the time was right to launch a full-scale challenge to the constitutionality of *Plessy's* separate-but-equal doctrine. Traditional legislative channels were unlikely to work, given Black peoples' limited political power. Thus, the federal courts and a litigation strategy were the NAACP's only hopes. The NAACP mapped out a long-range plan that would first target segregation in professional and graduate education.

TEST CASES   The NAACP opted first to challenge the constitutionality of Jim Crow laws in higher education test cases. In 1935, all southern states maintained fully segregated elementary and secondary schools. Colleges and universities also were segregated, and most states did not provide for post-high school education for Black people. NAACP lawyers chose to target law schools because they were institutions that judges could well understand, and integration at the graduate level would prove less threatening to most White people.

Lloyd Gaines, a graduate of Missouri's all-Black Lincoln University, sought admission to the all-White University of Missouri Law School in 1936. The school immediately rejected him. In the separate-but-equal spirit, the state offered to build a law school at Lincoln (although no funds were allocated for the project), or if he did not want to wait, to pay his tuition at an out-of-state law school. Gaines rejected the offer, sued, lost in the lower courts, and appealed to the U.S. Supreme Court.

MR. PRESIDENT, HOW LONG MUST WOMEN WAIT FOR LIBERTY?

Members of the National Woman's Party (NWP) and other women's rights organizations used marches, protests, and rallies to mobilize for political change. Here, NWP members are shown protesting in front of the White House. Women engaging in these activities were routinely arrested, jailed, and even force-fed in an attempt to end their activism on behalf of women's suffrage.

Library of Congress

The attorneys filed Gaines's case at a promising time. A constitutional revolution of sorts occurred in Supreme Court decision-making in 1937. Prior to this, the Court was most receptive to, and interested in, the protection of economic liberties. In 1937, however, the Court began to regard the protection of individual freedoms and personal liberties as important issues. Thus, in 1938, Gaines's lawyers pleaded his appeal to a far more sympathetic Supreme Court. NAACP attorneys argued that the creation of a separate law school of a laughably lesser caliber than that of the University of Missouri would not and could not afford Gaines an equal education. The justices agreed and ruled that Missouri had failed to meet the separate-but-equal requirements of *Plessy*. The Court ordered Missouri either to admit Gaines to the school or to set up a law school for him.[7]

Recognizing the importance of the Court's ruling, the NAACP, in 1939, created a separate, tax-exempt legal defense fund to devise a strategy that would build on the Missouri case and bring about equal educational opportunities for all African American children. The first head of the **NAACP Legal Defense and Educational Fund (LDF)**, was **Thurgood Marshall**, who later became the first African American to serve on the U.S. Supreme Court. Sensing that the Court would be more amenable to the NAACP's broader goals if it were first forced to address a variety of less-threatening claims to educational opportunity, Marshall and the LDF brought a series of carefully crafted test cases to the Court. These cases attracted attention across the United States and helped to raise the visibility of civil rights issues.

The first case involved H. M. Sweatt, a forty-six-year-old African American mail carrier who applied for admission to the all-White University of Texas Law School in 1946. Rejected on racial grounds, Sweatt sued. The judge gave the state six months to establish a law school or to admit Sweatt to the university. The state legislature then authorized $3 million for the creation of the Texas State University for Negroes. One hundred thousand dollars of that money was allotted for a new law school in Austin across the street from the state capitol. It consisted of three small basement rooms, a library of 10,000 books, access to the state law library, and three part-time first-year instructors as the faculty. Sweatt declined the opportunity to attend the substandard university and instead chose to continue his legal challenge.

While working on the Texas case in the late 1940s, the LDF also decided to pursue a case involving George McLaurin, a retired university professor who had been denied admission to the doctoral program in education at the University of Oklahoma. Marshall reasoned that McLaurin, at age sixty-eight, would be immune from the charges that Black people wanted integration so they could intermarry with White people, an act that was illegal in most southern states. After a lower court ordered McLaurin's admission, the university reserved a dingy alcove in the cafeteria for him to eat in during off-hours, gave him his own table in the library behind a shelf of newspapers, and created a separate bathroom for him. In what surely "was Oklahoma's most inventive contribution to legalized bigotry since the adoption of the 'grandfather clause,'" McLaurin was forced to sit outside classrooms while lectures and seminars were conducted inside.[8]

The Supreme Court handled these two cases together.[9] The eleven southern states filed an *amicus curiae* (friend of the court) brief, in which they argued that *Plessy* should govern both cases. The LDF received assistance, however, from an unexpected source—the U.S. government. In a dramatic departure from the past, President **Harry S Truman** directed his Department of Justice to file an *amicus* brief urging the Court to overrule *Plessy*. Earlier, Truman had issued an executive order desegregating the military. President Truman believed that because so many Black people had fought and died for their country in World War II, these kinds of executive actions were not only proper but honorable as well.

Although the Court did not overrule *Plessy*, the justices found that measures taken by the states in each case failed to live up to the strictures of the separate-but-equal doctrine. The Court unanimously ruled that the remedies to each situation were

NAACP Legal Defense and Educational Fund (LDF)
The legal arm of the NAACP that successfully litigated the landmark case of *Brown* v. *Board of Education* and a host of other key civil rights cases.

Thurgood Marshall
A leading civil rights lawyer and the first head of the NAACP's Legal Defense and Educational Fund. Marshall was the first African American appointed to the Supreme Court and served on the Court from 1967 until 1991.

Harry S Truman
The thirty-third president, a Democrat, who served from 1945 until 1953. Truman became president when Franklin D. Roosevelt died in office; he led the United States through the end of World War II and into the start of the Cold War.

Bettmann/Getty Images

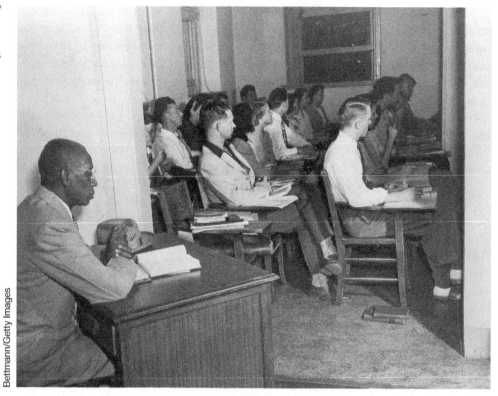

WHAT DID "SEPARATE BUT EQUAL" LOOK LIKE?

Here, George McLaurin, the plaintiff in one of the NAACP LDF's challenges to the separate-but-equal-doctrine, is shown outside his classroom. This was the university's accommodation when a federal district court ordered his admission into the University of Oklahoma's doctoral program.

inadequate to afford a sound education. In the *Sweatt* case, for example, the Court declared that the intangible characteristics of a law school—including such things as faculty reputation and alumni networks—made it impossible for the state to provide an equal education in a segregated setting.[10]

In 1950, after the Court had handed down these decisions, the LDF concluded that the time had come to launch a full-scale attack on the separate-but-equal doctrine. The Court's decisions were encouraging, and the position of the U.S. government and the population in general (especially outside the South) appeared more receptive to an outright overruling of *Plessy*.

Brown v. Board of Education (1954)

U.S. Supreme Court decision holding that school segregation is inherently unconstitutional because it violates the Fourteenth Amendment's guarantee of equal protection of the law.

BROWN v. BOARD OF EDUCATION *Brown v. Board of Education* (1954) actually was five cases brought from different areas of the South and border states involving public elementary or high school systems that mandated separate schools for Black and White students.[11] In *Brown*, LDF lawyers, again led by Thurgood Marshall, argued that the equal protection clause of the Fourteenth Amendment made *Plessy's* separate-but-equal doctrine unconstitutional, and that if the Court was still reluctant to overrule *Plessy*, the only way to equalize the schools was to integrate them. A major component of the LDF's strategy was to prove that the intellectual, psychological, and financial damage done to Black people as a result of segregation and violence prevented any court from finding that the separate-but-equal policy was consistent with the intent of the Fourteenth Amendment's equal protection clause.

In *Brown*, the LDF presented the Supreme Court with evidence of the harmful consequences of state-imposed racial discrimination. To buttress its claims, the LDF introduced the now-famous doll study, conducted by Kenneth and Mamie Clark, two prominent African American sociologists at the University of Chicago who had long studied the negative effects of segregation on African American children. Their research revealed that Black children not only preferred White dolls when shown Black dolls and White dolls but that many added that the Black doll looked "bad." The LDF attorneys used this information to illustrate the negative impact of racial segregation and bias on an African American child's self-image.

The LDF supported its legal arguments with important *amicus curiae* briefs submitted by the U.S. government, major civil rights groups, labor unions, and religious groups decrying racial segregation. On May 17, 1954, Chief Justice Earl Warren delivered the fourth opinion of the day, *Brown* v. *Board of Education*. Writing for the unanimous Court, Warren stated:

> To separate [some school children] from others . . . solely because of their race generates a feeling of inferiority as to their status in the community that may affect their hearts and minds in a way very unlikely ever to be undone. We conclude, unanimously, that in the field of public education the doctrine of "separate but equal" has no place.[12]

Brown was, without doubt, the most important civil rights case decided in the twentieth century. It immediately evoked an uproar that shook the nation. Some segregationists gave the name Black Monday to the day the decision was handed down. The governor of South Carolina denounced the decision, saying, "Ending segregation would mark the beginning of the end of civilization in the South as we know it."[13] The LDF lawyers who had argued these cases, as well as the cases leading to *Brown*, however, were jubilant.

WHAT STATUTORY PROTECTIONS FOR CIVIL RIGHTS WERE AND CONTINUE TO BE ENACTED, 1955–PRESENT?

5.3 Analyze the legal protections enacted for Black people's and women's civil rights since 1955.

Although it did not create immediate legal change, *Brown* served as a catalyst for a civil rights movement across the United States, and especially in the South. The decision emboldened activists and gave them faith that the government might one day change its segregationist policies in all areas of the law.[14] Subsequent successes in the civil rights movement also inspired a 1960s women's rights movement. This movement focused much of its effort on establishing protections for women in employment and education and attempting to enact an Equal Rights Amendment to the Constitution.

School Desegregation After *Brown*

One year after *Brown*, in a case referred to as *Brown* v. *Board of Education II* (1955), the Court ruled that racially segregated systems must be dismantled "with all deliberate speed."[15] To facilitate implementation, the Court placed enforcement of *Brown* in the hands of appointed federal district court judges, whom it considered more immune to local political pressures than elected state court judges.

The NAACP and its LDF continued looking to the courts for implementation of *Brown*, while the South entered into a near conspiracy to avoid the mandates of *Brown II*. In Arkansas, for example, Governor Orval Faubus, who was facing a reelection bid, announced that he would not "be a party to any attempt to force acceptance of change to which people are overwhelmingly opposed."[16] The day before school was to begin, he declared that National Guardsmen would surround Little Rock's Central High School to prevent African American students from entering. While the federal courts in Arkansas continued to order desegregation, the governor remained adamant. Finally, President Dwight D. Eisenhower sent federal troops to Little Rock to protect the rights of the nine African American students attending Central High as they walked with the students into school.

In reaction to the governor's illegal conduct, the Court broke with tradition and issued a unanimous decision in *Cooper* v. *Aaron* (1958), which was filed by the Little Rock School Board and asked the federal district court for a delay of two and one-half years in implementing desegregation plans. Each justice signed the opinion individually, underscoring his own support for the notion that "no state legislator or executive or judicial officer can war against the Constitution without violating his undertaking to support it."[17] The state's actions thus were ruled unconstitutional and its "evasive schemes" illegal.

A New Movement for African American Rights

In 1955, soon after *Brown II*, the civil rights movement took another step forward—this time in Montgomery, Alabama. **Rosa Parks**, the local NAACP's Youth Council adviser, decided to challenge the constitutionality of the segregated bus system. First, Parks and other NAACP officials began to raise money for litigation and made speeches around town to garner public support. Then, on December 1, 1955, Rosa Parks made history when she refused to leave her seat in the front of the colored section of the bus to make room for a White male passenger without a seat. Police arrested her for violating an Alabama law banning integration of public facilities, including buses. After being freed on bond, Parks and the NAACP decided to enlist city clergy to help her cause. At the same time, they distributed 35,000 handbills calling for Black people to boycott the Montgomery bus system on the day of Parks's trial. Black ministers used Sunday services to urge their members to support the boycott. On Monday morning, Black people walked, carpooled, or used Black-owned taxicabs. That night, local ministers decided the boycott should continue. A new twenty-six-year-old Southern Baptist minister, the Reverend **Martin Luther King Jr.**, was selected to lead the newly formed Montgomery Improvement Association.

As the boycott dragged on, Montgomery officials and local business owners, who were suffering negative economic consequences, began to harass the city's African American citizens. The Black residents held out, despite suffering personal hardship for their actions, ranging from threats to job loss to bankruptcy. In 1956, a federal court ruled that the segregated bus system violated the equal protection clause of the Fourteenth Amendment. After a year-long boycott, African American Montgomery residents ended their protest when city officials ordered the public transit system to integrate. The first effort at nonviolent protest had been successful. Organized boycotts and other forms of nonviolent protest were to follow.

Rosa Parks

A leading civil rights activist of the twentieth century. Parks was most notably involved with the Montgomery bus boycott.

Martin Luther King Jr.

A Southern Baptist minister, proponent of nonviolence, and the most prominent leader of the civil rights movement of the 1950s and 1960s. He was assassinated on April 4, 1968.

WHAT ROLE DID CIVIL DISOBEDIENCE PLAY IN THE CIVIL RIGHTS MOVEMENT?

Here, Rosa Parks is fingerprinted by a Montgomery, Alabama, police officer after her arrest for violating a city law requiring segregation on public buses. Parks refused to give up her seat to accommodate a White man, starting a city-wide bus boycott. Parks is just one of many citizens who engaged in these nonviolent acts of resistance and civil disobedience to unjust laws.

Pictorial Press Ltd/Alamy Stock Photo

Formation of New Groups

The recognition and respect earned by the Reverend Martin Luther King Jr. within the African American community helped him launch the Southern Christian Leadership Conference (SCLC) in 1957, soon after the end of the Montgomery bus boycott. Unlike the NAACP, which had northern origins and had come to rely largely on litigation as a means of achieving expanded equality, the SCLC had a southern base and was rooted more closely in Black religious culture. The SCLC's philosophy reflected King's growing belief in the importance of nonviolent protest and civil disobedience.

On February 1, 1960, a few students from the all-Black North Carolina Agricultural and Technical College in Greensboro, North Carolina, participated in the first sit-in for civil rights. The students went to a local lunch counter, sat down, and ordered cups of coffee. They were not served but stayed until closing. After the national wire services picked up the story, over the next several days, the students were joined by hundreds of others from the Greensboro area. When the students refused to leave, the police arrested and jailed them, rather than their White tormentors. Soon thereafter, African American college students around the South did the same. The national media extensively covered their actions at a time when most American households were beginning to own television sets and could witness police violence firsthand.

Over spring break 1960, with the assistance of an $800 grant from the SCLC, 200 student delegates—Black and White—met at the historically Black Shaw University in Raleigh, North Carolina, to consider recent sit-in actions and to plan for the future. Later that year, the Student Nonviolent Coordinating Committee (SNCC) was formed. Whereas the SCLC generally worked with church leaders in a community, SNCC was much more of a grassroots organization. Always perceived as more radical than the SCLC, SNCC tended to focus its organizing activities on the young, both Black and White, a strategy followed by the Black Lives Matter movement of today.

In addition to joining the sit-in bandwagon, SNCC also came to lead what were called freedom rides, designed to shine the spotlight on segregated public accommodations. Bands of college students and other civil rights activists traveled by bus throughout the South in an effort to force bus stations to desegregate. Often these protesters faced angry mobs of segregationists and brutal violence, as local police chose not to defend the protesters' basic constitutional rights to free speech and peaceful assembly. Black people were not the only ones to participate in freedom rides; increasingly, White college students from the North began to play an important role in SNCC.

While SNCC continued to sponsor sit-ins and freedom rides, in 1963 King launched a series of massive nonviolent demonstrations in Birmingham, Alabama, long considered a major stronghold of segregation. Thousands of Black and White people marched to Birmingham in a show of solidarity. Peaceful marchers were met there by the Birmingham police commissioner, who ordered his officers to use dogs, clubs, and fire hoses on the marchers. Americans across the nation were horrified as they witnessed on television the brutality and abuse heaped on the protesters. Reverend King was even thrown into the Birmingham jail for his defiance of the court order preventing the march. While he was in jail, he was shown a newspaper article calling the demonstrations wrong and "unwise." In response, he penned **"Letter from a Birmingham Jail,"** which is considered by many to be the single most important account of the long road to freedom and the duty of his supporters to fight for justice. In it, he set forth the four steps he believed key to nonviolent protest: (1) fact finding; (2) negotiation; (3) self-purification; and, (4) direct action. This letter, and the horrible abuses perpetrated by Birmingham police, helped convince President **John F. Kennedy** to propose important civil rights legislation. A copy of the letter can be found in Appendix C.

"Letter from a Birmingham Jail"

Document written by the Reverend Martin Luther King Jr., carefully setting out four key steps to nonviolent protest: (1) fact finding; (2) negotiation; (3) self-purification; and, (4) direct action.

John F. Kennedy

The thirty-fifth president, a Democrat, who served from 1961 to 1963 and marked a generational shift in U.S. politics at the height of the Cold War. He was assassinated on November 22, 1963.

The Civil Rights Act of 1964

In 1963, President John F. Kennedy requested that Congress pass a law banning discrimination in public accommodations. Seizing the moment, the Reverend Martin Luther King Jr. called for a monumental march on Washington, D.C., in August 1963 to demonstrate widespread support for far-ranging anti-discrimination legislation. It was clear that national legislation outlawing discrimination was the only answer: Southern legislators would never vote to repeal Jim Crow laws. At the March on Washington for Jobs and Freedom, more than 250,000 people heard King deliver his famous "I Have a Dream" speech from the Lincoln Memorial. Before Congress had the opportunity to vote on any legislation, however, President Kennedy was assassinated on November 22, 1963, in Dallas, Texas.

When Vice President Lyndon B. Johnson, a southern-born, former Senate majority leader, succeeded Kennedy as president, he put civil rights reform at the top of his legislative priority list, and civil rights activists gained a critical ally. Changes in public opinion also helped the push for civil rights legislation in the halls of Congress. Between 1959 and 1965, southern attitudes toward integrated schools changed enormously. The proportion of Southerners who responded that they would not mind their child's attendance at a racially balanced school doubled.

Civil Rights Act of 1964
Wide-ranging legislation passed by Congress to outlaw segregation in public facilities and discrimination in employment, education, and voting; created the Equal Employment Opportunity Commission.

In spite of strong presidential support and the sway of public opinion, the **Civil Rights Act of 1964** did not sail through Congress. Southern senators, led by South Carolina's Strom Thurmond, a Democrat who later switched to the Republican Party, conducted the longest filibuster in the history of the Senate. For eight weeks, Thurmond led the effort to hold up voting on the civil rights bill. Once passed, the act achieved the following:

- Outlawed arbitrary discrimination in voter registration and expedited voting rights lawsuits.
- Barred discrimination in public accommodations engaged in interstate commerce.
- Authorized the Department of Justice to initiate lawsuits to desegregate public facilities and schools.
- Provided for the withholding of federal funds from discriminatory state and local programs.
- Prohibited discrimination in employment on grounds of race, creed, color, religion, national origin, or sex.
- Created the Equal Employment Opportunity Commission to monitor and enforce the bans on employment discrimination.

Many Southerners adamantly believed that the Civil Rights Act of 1964 was unconstitutional because it went beyond the scope of Congress's authority to legislate under the Constitution, and they quickly brought lawsuits to challenge its scope. In 1964, on expedited review, the Supreme Court upheld its constitutionality, finding that Congress had operated within the legitimate scope of its commerce power as outlined in Article I.[18]

Still, tensions continued to grow in the aftermath of the new law. Black people in the North, who believed their brothers and sisters in the South were making progress against discrimination, found themselves frustrated. Black Northerners, too, were experiencing high unemployment, poverty, and discrimination, and had little political clout. Some, including African American leader Malcolm X, even argued that to survive, Black people must separate themselves from White culture in every way. These increased frustrations resulted in violent race riots in many major cities from 1964 to 1968, when many Black people in the North took to the streets, burning and looting to vent their rage. The assassination of the Reverend Martin Luther King Jr. in 1968 triggered a new epidemic of race riots. The full implementation of "equality" as defined under the Civil Rights Act of 1964 continues to lag today, as we discuss later in this chapter.

A New Movement for Women's Rights

As in the abolition movement of the 1800s, women from all walks of life participated in the civil rights movement. Women were important members of groups such as SNCC and the SCLC, as well as more traditional groups such as the NAACP, yet they often found themselves treated as second-class citizens. At one point during a SNCC national meeting, its male chair proclaimed: "The only position for women in SNCC is prone."[19] Statements and attitudes such as these led some women to found early women's liberation groups that generally were quite radical but small in membership. Others established more traditional groups, such as the **National Organization for Women (NOW)**. Modeled closely after the NAACP, the founders of NOW sought to work within the political system to prevent discrimination.

Three key events helped to forge a new movement for women's rights in the early 1960s. In 1961, soon after his election, President John F. Kennedy created the President's Commission on the Status of Women, headed by former First Lady **Eleanor Roosevelt**. The commission's report, *American Women*, released in 1963, documented pervasive discrimination against women in all areas of life. In addition, the civil rights movement, the passage in 1963 of the Equal Pay Act guaranteeing women equal pay for equal work, and the publication of Betty Friedan's *The Feminine Mystique* (1963), which led some women to question their lives and status in society, prompted many women to action.[20] Soon after, the Civil Rights Act of 1964 prohibited discrimination based not only on race but also on sex. Ironically, southern Democrats had added that provision to Title VII of the act. These lawmakers saw a prohibition against sex discrimination in employment as a joke and viewed its addition as a means to discredit the entire act and ensure its defeat. Thus, it was added at the last minute, and female members of Congress seized the opportunity to garner additional support for the measure.

Key victories for women's rights under Title VII of the Civil Rights Act of 1964 include the following:

- Consideration of sexual harassment as sex discrimination.[21]
- Inclusion of law firms, which many argued were private partnerships, in the coverage of the act.[22]
- Allowance of voluntary programs to redress historical discrimination against women.[23]
- A broad definition of what can be considered sexual harassment, including same-sex harassment.[24]

The issue of sexual harassment really came to the forefront in 2016. In the aftermath of an *Entertainment Tonight* audio tape that revealed then-candidate Donald J. Trump bragging in vulgar language about grabbing women's body parts, many women were outraged. On the day after his inauguration, over 1 million women marched in Washington to protest Trump's presidency and his treatment of women. Furthermore, men and women gathered in every major city of the United States (and on all seven continents) in the largest single-day demonstration ever to occur in the United States.

At around the same time, women began to speak out against sexual harassment and assault. In April 2017 it was revealed that FOX News had settled over $13 million in sexual harassment lawsuits against Bill O'Reilly, its most popular news host, in part because nearly 100 advertisers said they were pulling their ads from his popular show. Companies like Uber and Google also faced widespread criticism for work cultures that invited and/or ignored sexual harassment, which is illegal under Title VII of the Civil Rights Act of 1964. By October 2017, the news was filled with charges of sexual assault, including criticisms of many universities' failures to treat women students' claims seriously as required by Title IX (discussed later). The *New*

National Organization for Women (NOW)

The leading activist group of the women's rights movement, especially in the 1960s and 1970s.

Eleanor Roosevelt

First Lady of the United States from 1933 to 1945. Roosevelt championed human rights throughout her life and served as the U.S.'s first delegate to the United Nations (UN) General Assembly and later chaired the UN's Commission on Human Rights and JFK's Commission on the Status of Women.

York Times and *The New Yorker* published chilling accounts about movie mogul Harvey Weinstein, who was said to have sexually coerced or sexually assaulted female actors who met with him to discuss movie roles, for which he was tried and convicted in 2020.

In October 2017, actress Alyssa Milano popularized the #MeToo movement on Facebook and Twitter, a campaign originally begun by Black social activist Tarana Burke in 2006 against sexual harassment and assault. Hundreds of thousands of women posted their own stories. Together, Milano and Burke, along with other Hollywood actors including Reese Witherspoon, Ashley Judd, and Nicole Kidman, used their star power to highlight the problem while at the same time creating #TimesUp, which became the legal arm of the movement housed within the National Women's Law Center.

The fallout of these actions has been significant. Democratic Senator Al Franken resigned from office after photos appeared of him pretending to touch a woman in military fatigues while she was sleeping. Soon, other politicians were resigning. News anchors Matt Lauer and Charlie Rose were fired. And *TIME* Magazine named the "Silence Breakers" as its Person of the Year.

Other Statutory Remedies for Sex Discrimination

The Civil Rights Act of 1964—and a 1978 amendment that prohibited discrimination on the basis of pregnancy—is not the only piece of legislation that provides statutory protection for women. The **Equal Pay Act of 1963**, for example, requires employers to pay women and men equal pay for equal work. Although women have won important victories under the act, and subsequent legislation such as the Lilly Ledbetter Fair Pay Act of 2009 has been passed, a large wage gap between women and men continues to exist. Young male college graduates earn an average hourly rate of $20.94 compared to $16.58 for women.

Another important piece of legislation is **Title IX** of the Education Amendments of 1972. This act bars educational institutions that receive federal funds from discriminating against female students, faculty, or staff. Title IX greatly expanded the opportunities for women in elementary, secondary, and postsecondary institutions. Most of today's college students do not go through school being excluded from home economics or technology education classes because of their sex. Nor, probably, do many attend schools that have no team sports for females. Yet, this was commonly the case

Equal Pay Act of 1963

Legislation that requires employers to pay men and women equal pay for equal work.

Title IX

Provision of the Education Amendments of 1972 that bars educational institutions that receive federal funds from discriminating against female students.

WHO WERE "THE SILENCE BREAKERS"?

In 2017, *Time* magazine assigned this label to the women behind the #MeToo movement, declaring them "Person of the Year." Here, some of these women speak out about Harvey Weinstein's sexual misconduct during a news conference outside Los Angeles City Hall in 2020.

REUTERS/Alamy Stock Photo

in the United States prior to passage of Title IX. Major rulings by the U.S. Supreme Court that uphold the provisions of Title IX include the following:

* Holding school boards or districts responsible for both student-on-student harassment and harassment of students by teachers.[25]
* Allowing retaliatory lawsuits by coaches on behalf of their sports teams denied equal treatment by school boards.[26]

Work remains before equality under Title IX is achieved, however. One study found a huge difference in money spent on men's athletics in comparison to women's athletics in Division I colleges and universities.[27] Protection from sexual harassment and sexual violence is another key provision of Title IX. In the wake of highly publicized cases of sexual assault on college campuses and reports of discriminatory treatment of assault victims, the Department of Education during the Obama administration stepped up Title IX enforcement efforts. Colleges and universities are required to report allegations of sexual assault to the Department of Education and to investigate all charges fully. While Trump administration rules cut back on protections for victims of abuse, the Biden administration was quick to step up enforcement efforts.

The Equal Rights Amendment

Having achieved success in broadening statutory protections for women's civil rights, activists turned their efforts to lobbying Congress and the state legislatures to enact an **Equal Rights Amendment (ERA)**. The amendment, which was proposed in every Congress since 1923, read:

* Equality of rights under the law shall not be denied or abridged by the United States or by any state on account of sex.
* The Congress shall have the power to enforce, by appropriate legislation, the provisions of this article.

In 1972, in response to pressure from NOW, the National Women's Political Caucus, and a wide variety of other feminist groups, Congress voted in favor of the ERA by overwhelming majorities (84–8 in the Senate; 354–24 in the House). Within a year, twenty-two states ratified the amendment, most by overwhelming margins, but the tide soon turned. In *Roe* v. *Wade* (1973), the Supreme Court decided that women had a constitutionally protected right to privacy that included the right to terminate a pregnancy. Almost overnight, *Roe* provided the ERA's opponents with political fuel. Although privacy rights and the ERA have nothing to do with each other, opponents effectively persuaded many people in states that had yet to ratify the amendment that the two were linked. They also claimed that the ERA and feminists were anti-family and that the ERA would force women out of their homes and into the workforce because husbands would no longer be responsible for supporting their wives financially.

These arguments and the amendment's potential to make women eligible for the unpopular military draft brought the ratification effort to a near standstill. In 1974 and 1975, the amendment only squeaked through the Montana and North Dakota legislatures, and two states—Nebraska and Tennessee—voted to rescind their earlier ratifications. By 1978, one year before the expiration deadline for ratification, thirty-five states had voted for the amendment—three short of the three-fourths necessary for ratification. Efforts in key states such as Illinois and Florida failed as opposition to the ERA intensified. Faced with the prospect of defeat, ERA supporters heavily lobbied Congress to extend the deadline for ratification. Congress extended the ratification period by three years, but to no avail. No additional states ratified the amendment, and three more rescinded their votes. The proposed amendment died without ratification on June 30, 1982. Still, supporters continue to introduce it in every session of Congress.

As part of their involvement in #MeToo, Alyssa Milano and fellow actor America Ferrara have joined a group of women activists to lobby the states that

Equal Rights Amendment (ERA)

Proposed amendment to the Constitution that states, "Equality of rights under the law shall not be denied or abridged by the United States or any state on account of sex."

had not ratified the ERA. Nevada ratified it in 2017, and Illinois followed suit in 2018, becoming the thirty-seventh state to do so. In 2020, Virginia became the thirty-eighth state to ratify it in a largely symbolic move. A 2013 report by the Congressional Research Service concluded that Congress could vote to change the deadline or pass another ERA, which, however, in turn would have to go back to the states. Ratification of the ERA by Virginia is largely symbolic since the time to ratify has lapsed. However, the Democratic majority in the House with a host of newly-elected women could press to see the amendment passed and sent to the Senate. There, it would be likely to die, but it would force Republican members to go on record as for or against equal rights for women.

Ratification efforts to add the ERA to the Constitution are likely to see renewed fervor. With the U.S. Supreme Court controlled by six conservative members who all have objected to granting women a wide range of rights, a constitutional amendment may be the only way for gains made through stature and constitutional interpretation to be maintained.

WHAT OTHER GROUPS HAVE MOBILIZED FOR RIGHTS?

5.4 Summarize the struggles of other group-differentiated minorities for civil rights.

Black people and women are not the only groups that have suffered unequal treatment under the law. Denial of civil rights has led other disadvantaged groups to mobilize. Their efforts parallel in many ways the efforts made by Black people and women. Many groups recognized that litigation and the use of test-case strategies would be key to further civil rights gains. Others have opted for more direct, traditional forms of activism.

Hispanic Americans

Hispanics are the largest minority group in the United States. But Hispanic population growth in the United States is not a new phenomenon. In 1910, the Mexican Revolution forced Mexicans seeking safety and employment into the United States. And in 1916, New Mexico entered the union officially as a bilingual state—the only one in the United States.

League of United Latin American Citizens (LULAC)

An activist group founded in 1929 to combat discrimination against, and promote assimilation among, Americans of Hispanic origin.

Early Hispanic immigrants, many of whom were from families who had owned land when parts of the Southwest were still under Mexico's control, formed the **League of United Latin American Citizens (LULAC)** in 1929. LULAC continues to be the largest Hispanic organization in the United States, with local councils in every state and Puerto Rico. Hispanics returning home from fighting in World War II also formed the American G.I. Forum in Texas to fight discrimination and improve their legal status.

As large numbers of immigrants from Mexico and Puerto Rico entered the United States, they quickly became a source of cheap labor, with Mexicans initially tending to settle in the Southwest, where they most frequently found employment as migratory farm workers, and Puerto Ricans mainly moving to New York City. Both groups gravitated to their own neighborhoods, where life revolved around the Roman Catholic Church and the customs of their homeland, and both groups largely lived in poverty. Still, in 1954, the same year as *Brown*, Hispanics won a major victory when, in *Hernandez* v. *Texas*, the Supreme Court struck down discrimination based on race and ethnicity.[28] In *Hernandez*, the Court ruled unanimously that Mexican Americans had the right to a jury that included other Mexican Americans.

Cesar Chavez

Labor organizer who, with Dolores Huerta, founded the United Farm Workers Union (UFW) in the 1960s.

A push for greater Hispanic rights began in the 1960s. In 1962, **Cesar Chavez**, after rising through the ranks of the grassroots Community Service Organization (CSO), a group dedicated to organizing and local action, became frustrated when it refused to focus on the plight of immigrant farmworkers. Chavez, who was brought up in a very poor family of farmworkers, left to start the National Farm Workers Association. By 1965, Chavez and **Dolores Huerta**, who was in charge of farmworker relations for the CSO, were able to organize migrant farm workers into the United Farm Workers Union, which would become the largest such union in the United States. Together, they led those workers in a strike against produce growers in California.

Dolores Huerta

Labor organizer who, with Cesar Chavez, founded the United Farm Workers Union (UFW) in the 1960s.

They eventually coupled this strike with a national boycott of various farm products, including, most notably, lettuce and grapes. Declining sales eventually led producers to give in to some of the workers' demands.

Their efforts, in which they embraced the term "Chicano," were part of a larger push for Hispanic rights that began in the mid-1960s. This era marked the founding of the National Council of LaRaza, now called UnidosUS, which was to become the largest Hispanic organization in the United States. Referred to as the Chicano Movement, or El Movimiento, its leaders employed tactics used by Black people and women, such as sit-ins, boycotts, marches, and other actions designed to draw attention and support to their cause: expanded rights for Chicanos.

Many believe that there is a "renaissance" of sorts going on within the Chicano movement. The name "Chicano/a" is being embraced by a new generation of Hispanics who are or who know immigrants, Dreamers, and undocumented immigrants, and who believe that activism is key "as the nation wrestles over issues of race, rhetoric, and identity."[29] In California, for example, Hispanics make up the largest ethnic or racial group (15.5 million), followed by White people (14.5 million), Asians (5.7 million), and Black people (2.1 million).[30]

In addition to activism and organization, Hispanics also have relied heavily on litigation to secure legal change. The **Mexican American Legal Defense and Educational Fund (MALDEF)** began its life in 1968 after members of LULAC met with NAACP LDF leaders and with their assistance secured a $2.2 million startup grant from the Ford Foundation. The founders of MALDEF originally created it to bring test cases before the Supreme Court with the intent to force school districts to allocate more funds to schools with predominantly low-income minority populations, to implement bilingual education programs, to require employers to hire Hispanics, and to challenge election rules and apportionment plans that undercount or dilute Hispanic voting power.

MALDEF has been successful in expanding voting rights and electoral opportunities to Hispanic Americans. In 1973, for example, it won a major victory when the Supreme Court ruled that multimember electoral districts (in which more than one person represents a single district) in Texas discriminated against Black and Hispanic people.[31] In multimember systems, legislatures generally add members to larger districts instead of drawing smaller districts in which a minority candidate could garner a majority of the votes necessary to win. Since 2010, however, many southern states have passed laws or implemented practices that have the effect of suppressing African American and Hispanic voting. These include implementing stringent voter identification requirements, closing polling places in minority neighborhoods, limiting the availability of Spanish ballots, and even changing the citizenship status of naturalized citizens. These practices, said Thomas Saenez, the president and general counsel of MALDEF, "in places like Texas have been particularly hard for voters who immigrated to the US," largely affecting Hispanic voters. MALDEF continues to challenge these practices in the federal courts.[32]

The organization's success in educational equity cases came more slowly. In *San Antonio Independent School District* v. *Rodriguez*, the Supreme Court refused to find that a Texas law under which the state appropriated a set dollar amount to each school district per pupil, while allowing wealthier districts to enrich educational programs from other funds, violated the

Mexican American Legal Defense and Educational Fund (MALDEF)

An organization modeled on the NAACP Legal Defense and Educational Fund that works to protect the civil rights of Americans of Mexican and other Hispanic heritage.

HOW HAS VOTING BEEN SUPPRESSED FOR HISPANICS AND LATINOS?

Texas has a long history of disenfranchising voters, including barring people from voting based on whether they speak English, intimidation, and closing voting locations in minority areas.

In a state where nearly 40 percent of the population is Hispanic or Latino, prior to the 2020 election Governor Abbott refused to expand mail-in voting to accommodate people concerned about being exposed to the virus when they went to the polls. On the first day of voting, these voters in Austin waited hours in line to cast their votes.

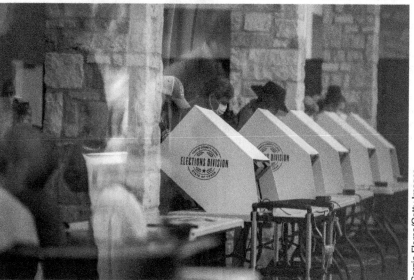
Sergio Flores/Getty Images

equal protection clause of the Fourteenth Amendment.[33] In 1989, however, MALDEF won a case in which a state district judge elected by the voters of only a single county declared the state's entire method of financing public schools to be unconstitutional under the state constitution.[34] And, in 2004, it entered into a settlement with the state of California in a case brought four years earlier to address, in MALDEF's words, "the shocking inequities facing public school children across the state."[35]

MALDEF continues to litigate and lobby in a wide range of areas of concern to Hispanics. High on its agenda today are equal access to education, affirmative action, health care for undocumented immigrants, workers' rights, and challenges to restrictive driver's license and voter ID laws. To ensure that Hispanics are adequately represented, it also continues to challenge state redistricting plans that dilute Hispanic voting impact.

The National Hispanic Leadership Agenda (NHLA), meanwhile, is a coalition of six major Hispanic groups. Established in 1991, its broad agenda includes enacting immigration reform, ensuring access to health care, raising the minimum wage, and protecting voting rights and educational opportunity. NHLA also works closely with members of the Congressional Hispanic Caucus.

Today, nearly all Hispanic groups are fighting immigration restrictions and policies aimed at restricting new immigration and returning undocumented immigrants to their home countries. Unequal treatment and racial profiling of Hispanics by law enforcement are also high on groups' lists of priorities.

Interestingly, after Puerto Rico was devastated by Hurricane Maria, many Americans did not know that residents of the island are American citizens. And, unlike other areas of the United States, aid to Puerto Rico has been painfully slow. More than a year after the disaster, large sections of the island still had no power. Two earthquakes in 2020 made the situation there worse. Many critics believe that had Puerto Rico not had a majority Hispanic population, assistance would have been quicker and ongoing.

In 2012, President Barack Obama directed the Department of Homeland Security to announce a new program of immigrant relief known as the Deferred Action for Childhood Arrivals, known as DACA. It allowed children and young adults who were brought to the U.S. illegally by their parents the opportunity to apply for a two-year extension of their removal from the U.S. to their native countries—many of which the recipients

HOW ARE HISPANIC AMERICANS FIGHTING IMMIGRATION RESTRICTIONS?

The Trump administration's "zero-tolerance policy" toward undocumented immigrants, involved separating children, some of whom were still nursing babies, from their parents, many of whom had come to the United States to seek legal asylum. Here a grandfather hugs his grandchild through a "Door of Hope" at the U.S.–Mexico border. Although since discontinued, the program allowed loved ones living on opposite sides of the border to reunite for a few minutes.

ZUMA Press, Inc./Alamy Stock Photo

had neither ties to nor spoke the language. DACA designees were made eligible to work legally and to receive Social Security and other benefits. In 2014, DACA eligibility was expanded and another program was created. The Deferred Action for Parents of Americans and Lawful Residents, called DAPA, was to cover 4.3 million parents of U.S. citizens and extend the eligibility for DACA. Texas and twenty-five additional states sued and won a national preliminary injunction barring implementation of DACA expansion and DAPA. After a circuitous route of several cases challenging DACA and DAPA, several cases arrived at the Supreme Court and were consolidated for review.

In January 2017, President Donald J. Trump ordered his acting secretary of DHS to rescind the DAPA memorandum and to bar any new DACA applications and allow only a few DACA recipients to stay beyond year two. In a stunning blow to the president's anti-immigration policies, writing for the five-justice majority, Chief Justice John G. Roberts, Jr. concluded that the abrupt reversal of policy was "arbitrary and capricious," and thus violated the requirements of the Administrative Procedures Act. This gave new hope to DACA recipients, of whom nearly 80 percent are Hispanic.[36]

In the summer of 2018, many people across the United States joined the Hispanic community in protest to the Trump administration's policy of separating parents from their children at the U.S. border. Even those who were attempting to gain access to the United States legally via asylum were detained in large warehouses, often in cages, while their children—including babies—were taken elsewhere. Videos and photos of crying children being separated from their parents led to widespread outcry, culminating in marches in D.C. and every state in the nation. In a highly unusual move, the Trump administration vowed to end family separations but despite this, hundreds of children remain separated from their parents. These practices continued throughout 2020. Poor record keeping contributed to children not being reunited with their parents. DHS's awful record keeping led to the "loss" of nearly 1,500 children. Compounding the problem, children and their parents were often taken to different states, complicating reunification efforts and posing problems for the Biden administration.[37]

American Indians

American Indians are the first true Americans, and their status under U.S. law is unique. The Constitution of the United States considers Indian tribes distinct governments, a situation that has affected the treatment of these Americans by Congress and the Supreme Court.

For years, Congress and the courts manipulated the law to promote westward expansion of the United States. The Northwest Ordinance of 1787, passed by the Continental Congress, specified that "good faith should always be observed toward the Indians; their lands and property shall never be taken from them without their consent, and their property rights, and liberty, they shall never be invaded or disturbed, unless in just and lawful wars authorized by Congress." The federal government did not follow this pledge. During the eighteenth and nineteenth centuries, it isolated American Indians on reservations as it confiscated their lands and denied them basic political rights. The U.S. government administered Indian reservations, and American Indians often lived in squalid conditions.

With passage of the Dawes Act in 1887, however, the government switched policies, promoting assimilation over separation. This act gave each American Indian family land within their reservation; the rest was sold to White people, thus reducing American Indian lands from about 140 million acres to about 47 million. Moreover, to encourage American Indians to assimilate, the act mandated sending American Indian children to boarding schools off the 112 reservations. It also banned their native languages and rituals. American Indians did not become U.S. citizens, nor were they given the right to vote, until 1924.

At least in part because tribes were small and scattered (and the number of members declining), American Indians did not begin to mobilize until the 1960s.[38]

The American Indian Movement (AIM) was founded in 1968 in Minneapolis, Minnesota. Working at the grassroots level in urban areas, its "aim" was to bring attention to the systematic poverty of and police brutality against American Indians. From late 1969 to mid-1971, its leaders, along with several other American Indian groups and tribes, participated in the occupation of Alcatraz, a well-known abandoned federal prison.

In 1973, AIM leaders took over the town of Wounded Knee in South Dakota on the Pine Ridge Indian Reservation. Rioting eventually broke out as protesters sought guarantees that negotiations concerning fair treatment of Indians would commence.[39] The town was inundated with FBI agents and the National Guard. Two Indian activists were killed. Many AIM members escaped, and all who were arrested were acquitted of all charges.[40]

Taking more conventional actions during this time, American Indian activists, many trained by the American Indian Law Center at the University of New Mexico, began to file hundreds of test cases in the federal courts involving tribal fishing rights, tribal land claims, and taxation of tribal profits. The Native American Rights Fund (NARF), founded in 1970, became the NAACP LDF of the American Indian rights movement.

WHEN DID AMERICAN INDIANS GAIN THE RIGHT TO VOTE?

American Indians were not given the right to vote in federal elections until 1924. However, some state constitutions prevented American Indians from voting for even longer. New Mexico, where these citizens are seen registering to vote for the first time in 1948, was one such state.

Charles O. Cecil/Alamy Stock Photo

American Indians have won some very important victories concerning hunting, fishing, and use of their lands. Tribal sovereignty allows American Indians to host gambling casinos across the country, frequently on lands abutting cities and in states where gambling is illegal. This phenomenon has resulted in billions of dollars of revenue for Indian tribes.

The 2018 midterm elections saw a well-focused effort to suppress American Indian voting in North Dakota, a state where a few thousand votes can change the outcome of a statewide election. Republicans in the state legislature enacted a law requiring voters to have an actual street address. American Indians living on reservations generally have post-office box numbers because few streets on reservations have names. Four Directions, which works to energize Indian voters, succeeded in getting more voters to the polls in record numbers in spite of the new law.

In 2020, the Supreme Court shocked the nation when it issued its decision in *McGirt* v. *Oklahoma*.[41] Writing for the Court's 5–4 majority, Justice Neil Gorsuch found that much of Tulsa and eastern Oklahoma was, in fact, still owned by the Muscogee Nation. The case came to the Court as McGirt challenged the authority of the state to prosecute him in a criminal matter. His lawyers argued that Oklahoma could not prosecute him because McGirt's offense occurred on Indian land because Congress never actually dissolved the boundaries of the Muscogee Reservation when Oklahoma became a state in 1907. The Court agreed. Jimcy McGirt, a member of the Seminole Nation, was tried in a state court and found guilty of committing serious sex crimes that took place on the Creek Reservation. The Court found that prosecution of crimes taking place on Indians lands by tribal members could not be prosecuted in state courts.

The significance of this case puts it in the echelons of *Brown* v. *Board of Education* (1954). *Brown* finally overruled *Plessey* v. *Ferguson* and paved the way for school integration in the South and found that racially segregated schools violated the equal protection clause of the Fourteenth Amendment. *McGirt* forcibly stated that treaty after treaty and agreement after agreement entered into by the U.S. government and hundreds of Indian tribes have been broken or ignored. Thus, in affirming McGirt's claims, the Court also opened up numerous new avenues for Indian rights litigation in issues from sovereignty to criminal law. "It's so momentous and it's immense," said Joy Harjo, the U.S. poet laureate and member of the tribe.[42]

McGirt v. Oklahoma (2020)
A 5–4 decision of the Supreme Court recognizing that broken treaties did not allow Oklahoma to prosecute individuals who commit serious criminal offenses on tribal lands. The Court found that nearly one-half of Oklahoma is legally owned by several Indian tribes.

Asian and Pacific Island Americans

Today, Asians and Pacific Islanders are the fastest-growing minority group in the United States. But one of the most significant difficulties for Asians and Pacific Islanders has been finding a Pan-Asian identity. Originally, Asians and Pacific Islanders were far more likely to identify with their individual Japanese, Chinese, Korean, or Filipino heritage.[43] Not until 1977 did the U.S. government decide to use "Asian and Pacific Islander" for all of those with these origins. Some subgroups have even challenged this identity; in the 1990s, native Hawai`ian people, the largest ethnic group of Pacific Islanders, unsuccessfully requested to be categorized with American Indians, with whom they felt greater affinity.

Discrimination against Asian and Pacific Island immigrants developed over time in the United States. In 1868, Congress passed a law allowing free migration from China because workers were needed to complete building the western extension of the transcontinental railroad. But in 1882, Congress passed the Chinese Exclusion Act, which was the first act to restrict the immigration of any identifiable nationality. This legislation implicitly invited more discriminatory laws against the Chinese, which closely paralleled the Jim Crow laws affecting Black people.

Several Supreme Court cases also slowed the progress of Asians and Pacific Islanders. This began to change in 1886, when the Court decided the case of *Yick Wo* v. *Hopkins*. A number of events precipitated this decision. Discriminatory provisions in

HOW WERE JAPANESE AMERICANS TREATED DURING WORLD WAR II?

The internment of Japanese Americans during World War II was a low point in American history. In *Korematsu* v. *U.S.* (1944), the U.S. Supreme Court upheld the constitutionality of this action. Here, children wait to be relocated from their homes to an internment camp.

Everett Collection Historical/Getty Images

Korematsu v. U.S. **(1944)**
Supreme Court ruling that upheld the authority of the U.S. government to require mass internment of people of Japanese ancestry in the United States during World War II.

the California Constitution prevented Chinese people from practicing many professions. However, the Chinese in California were allowed to open laundries, and many immigrants did. In response to this growing trend, the city of San Francisco passed a ban on laundries operating in wooden buildings, two-thirds of which were owned by persons of Chinese ancestry. The Court in *Yick Wo* found that the law violated the Constitution because one ethnic group was being targeted.[44]

In 1922, the Court took a step backward, ruling that Asians and Pacific Islanders were not White and therefore not entitled to full citizenship rights.[45] Conditions became even worse, especially for those of Japanese descent, after the Japanese attack on Pearl Harbor in 1941. In response to the attack, President Franklin D. Roosevelt issued Executive Order 9066, which led to the internment of over 130,000 Japanese Americans, Italian Americans, and German Americans, some of whom were Jewish refugees. More than two-thirds of those confined to internment camps were U.S. citizens. The Supreme Court upheld the constitutionality of these camps in ***Korematsu v. U.S.* (1944)**. In sharp contrast, as a goodwill gesture to an ally, the U.S. government offered Chinese immigrants the opportunity to apply for U.S. citizenship. At the end of the war, President Harry S Truman extended the same privilege to Filipino immigrants, many of whom had aided in the war effort. In 2018, in a case upholding an executive order often referred to as "the Muslim ban," Chief Justice John Roberts claimed that the decision finally overruled *Korematsu*.[46]

Partly in reaction to the Court's 1922 decision denying Asian and Pacific Islanders full citizen rights, the Japanese American Citizens League (JACL) was founded in 1922. It continues to be the largest organization dedicated to obtaining full civil rights for Japanese and other Asian and Pacific Islanders.

During the 1960s and 1970s, many new groups of Asians and Pacific Islanders were formed to be more political than the JACL. Filipino farm workers, for example, joined with Mexican immigrants to form the United Farm Workers Union. In 1973, the Movement for a Free Philippines emerged to oppose the government of Ferdinand Marcos, the president of the Philippines. Soon, it joined forces with the Friends of Filipino People, also founded in 1973. These groups worked with the Free Legal Assistance Group (FLAG) to openly oppose the Vietnam War and, with the aid of the Roman Catholic Church, established relief organizations for Filipinos in the United States and around the world.

In the 1970s and 1980s, Japanese Americans also mobilized, lobbying the courts and Congress for reparations for their treatment during World War II. In 1988, Congress passed the Civil Liberties Act, which apologized to the interned and their descendants and offered reparations to them and their families.

JACL was quick to criticize President Trump's characterization of COVID-19 as the "Kung Flu" and other names associating it with China.[47] In the wake of such connections, Asian Americans report a surge in acts of discrimination and verbal attacks blaming them for the virus.[48] Even Asian American doctors and nurses experienced verbal and physical attacks.[49] JACL has criticized these actions as blatant racism and is supporting passage of the George Floyd Justice in Policing Act of 2021 as a way of highlighting the fact that Black people are not the only minority group affected by discriminatory police practices.

The Lesbian, Gay, Bisexual, Transgender, and Queer (LGBTQ) Community

Until very recently, members of the **LGBTQ community** have experienced many challenges in achieving anything approximating equal rights.[50] However, gays and lesbians have, on average, far higher household incomes and educational levels than other minority groups, and they are converting these advantages into political clout. Like Black people and women, members of the LGBTQ community have worked through the courts to achieve incremental legal change. In the late 1970s, gay and lesbian activists dedicated to ending legal restrictions on the civil rights of homosexuals founded Lambda Legal, the National Center for Lesbian Rights, and Gay and Lesbian Advocates and Defenders (GLAAD).[51] These groups won important legal victories concerning HIV/AIDS discrimination, insurance policy survivor benefits, and even some employment issues. However, progress in other areas has relied on changing voters' and policy makers' hearts and minds.[52]

In 1993, for example, President Bill Clinton tried to ban discrimination against homosexuals in the armed services. Eventually, Clinton compromised with congressional and military leaders on what was called the "Don't Ask, Don't Tell" (DADT) policy. The military would no longer ask gays and lesbians if they were homosexual, but it barred them from revealing their sexual orientation under threat of discharge. Despite the compromise, the armed services discharged thousands on the basis of their sexual orientation. Government officials called the policy into question as the wars in Iraq and Afghanistan increased America's need for active-duty military personnel. In 2010, Congress passed and President Barack Obama signed into law a formal repeal of DADT. In September 2011, the policy officially ended, paving the way for many military members to openly acknowledge their homosexuality. In June 2016, Defense Secretary Ashton Carter announced an end to a longstanding ban on transgender people serving in the military. Just three years later, however, the Trump administration totally reversed course. Via Twitter, the president announced that the Pentagon, although caught off-guard by the tweet, would essentially be required to reinstate the ban.[53] In 2021, the Biden Administration removed the ban.

Changes in public opinion have also opened the door for greater legal and constitutional protection for LGBTQ rights.[54] These changes were reflected in the Court's decision in *Lawrence v. Texas* **(2003)**, in which the Court reversed an earlier ruling, finding a Texas statute banning sodomy to be unconstitutional.[55] Following the Court's ruling in *Lawrence*, many Americans were quick to call for additional rights for homosexuals. A good number of corporations responded to this amplified call. For example, Walmart announced it would ban job discrimination based on sexual orientation. In addition, editorial pages across the country praised the Court's ruling, arguing that the national view toward homosexuality had changed.[56] In *U.S. v. Windsor* (2013), the Supreme Court declared the 1996 Defense of Marriage Act (DOMA), a federal law

LGBTQ community

A minority group based on sexual orientation and gender identity that includes lesbian, gay, bisexual, transgender, and queer (LGBTQ) people.

Lawrence v. Texas **(2003)**

Supreme Court ruling that antisodomy laws violated the constitutional right to privacy.

WHY IS SAME-SEX MARRIAGE CONTROVERSIAL?

The legalization of same-sex marriage in California in 2008 allowed gay couples committed to one another for decades to tie the knot. Here, lesbian activists Del Martin (age 87) and Phyllis Lyon (age 83)—partners for more than fifty years—are married by then-mayor of San Francisco Mayor Gavin Newsom (now governor). Unions such as this face opposition by many religious conservatives, who believe homosexuality is a sin and support only the rights of heterosexual couples to marry. Martin died in August 2008, only a few months after her wedding. Lyon died in 2020.

Obergefell v. Hodges **(2015)**

Supreme Court ruling that held that same-sex couples have a fundamental right to marry under the Constitution.

Americans with Disabilities Act (ADA)

A law enacted by Congress in 1990 designed to guarantee accommodation and access for people with a wide range of disabilities.

defining marriage as between one man and one woman, unconstitutional.[57] This decision paved the way for same-sex marriages in all fifty states, which was mandated by the 2015 Supreme Court ruling in *Obergefell v. Hodges*.[58] President Trump vowed to appoint a justice to the Court to override this decision and appointed three conservative justices to the Court, hoping to accomplish this 2016 campaign pledge.

Thus, many Court watchers were stunned by the Court's decision in June 2020 that concluded that lesbians, gays, and transgender persons were protected from discrimination by their employers. The conservative Chief Justice Roberts and Trump-appointee Associate Justice Neil Gorsuch joined with four liberal justices to find that the Civil Rights Act of 1964's prohibition of discrimination "because of sex" included gay and transgender employees.[59]

In spite of decisions guaranteeing some civil rights to members of the LGBTQ community, discrimination toward the LGBTQ community continues. Recent state-level legislation banning transgender people from using the bathroom of their self-identified gender and "religious freedom" laws allowing individuals to choose not to provide goods and services to gay couples based on the religious beliefs of the individuals have been characterized as a backlash by rights advocates.

Americans with Disabilities

Americans with disabilities have lobbied hard for anti-discrimination legislation as well as equal protection under the Constitution. In the aftermath of World War II, many veterans returned to a nation unequipped to handle their disabilities. The Korean and Vietnam wars made the problems of veterans with disabilities all the more clear. These veterans saw the successes of Black people, women, and other minorities, and they too began to lobby for greater protection against discrimination.[60] In 1990, in coalition with other people with disabilities, veterans finally convinced Congress to pass the **Americans with Disabilities Act (ADA)**. The statute defines a person with a disability as someone with a physical or mental impairment that limits one or more "life activities," or who has a record of such impairment. It thus extends the protections of the Civil Rights Act of 1964 to all citizens with physical or mental disabilities. It guarantees access to public facilities, employment, and communication services. Furthermore, it requires employers to acquire or modify work equipment, adjust work schedules, and make existing facilities accessible to those with disabilities. For example, people in wheelchairs must have ready access to buildings, and deaf employees must have telecommunication devices made available to them.

The largest national nonprofit organization lobbying for expanded civil rights for people with disabilities is the American Association of People with Disabilities (AAPD). Acting on behalf of more than 56 million Americans who live with some form of disability, it works in coalition with other disability organizations to make certain that the ADA is implemented fully. The activists who founded AAPD lobbied for the ADA and recognized that "beyond national unity for ADA and our civil rights, people with disabilities did not have a venue or vehicle for working together for common goals."[61]

Jason R. Davis/AP Images

POLITICAL REFORM AND REALITIES: HOW ARE CIVIL RIGHTS PROTECTED?

5.5 Evaluate the standards by which civil rights are protected today.

The definition of equality, as well as conceptions of who deserves equal protection of the laws, has changed dramatically over the course of American history. No provision has done more to change Americans' conceptions of equality than the Fourteenth Amendment. However, as we will discuss below, different types of discrimination are subject to different standards of review under the Amendment's equal protection clause. We also need to note that discrimination has roots far deeper than in the law. Personal and institutional biases that have led to the shootings of unarmed Black men and teenagers, the stopping of motorists guilty of only what is often called "driving while Black," and other daily acts of discrimination affecting individuals in all the groups were brought to the political fore after the killing of George Floyd. His murder and that of others unleashed protests around the nation highlighting racial disparities in policing and in all walks of life.

WHOM DOES THE AMERICANS WITH DISABILITIES ACT PROTECT?

George Lane was the appellant in *Tennessee* v. *Lane* (2004), concerning the scope of the Americans with Disabilities Act, which guarantees people with disabilities access to public buildings, among other protections. Lane was forced to crawl up two flights of stairs to attend a state court hearing on a misdemeanor charge. Had he not, he could have been jailed.

The Equal Protection Clause and Constitutional Standards of Review

The Fourteenth Amendment protects all U.S. citizens from state action that violates "equal protection of the laws." The question of what constitutes equal protection has been the subject of much litigation; to make judgments on this issue more straightforward, the Supreme Court has applied three **standards of review**, or the level of deference the Court gives other governments in crafting policies that make distinctions on the basis of personal characteristics such as race, gender, or sexual orientation. As shown in Table 5.1, most laws are subject to what is called the rational basis or minimum rationality test. This lowest level of scrutiny means that governments must show a rational foundation for any distinctions they make. As early as 1937, however, the Supreme Court recognized that certain freedoms were so fundamental that a very heavy burden would fall on any government seeking to restrict those rights. When fundamental

standards of review

The levels of deference the Court gives governments to craft policies that make distinctions on the basis of personal characteristics. These standards stem from the Court's need to ensure that laws do not undermine the Fourteenth Amendment's equal protection clause.

TABLE 5.1 WHAT ARE THE STANDARDS OF REVIEW FASHIONED BY THE COURT UNDER THE EQUAL PROTECTION CLAUSE?

Type of Classification: *What kind of statutory classification is at issue?*	Standard of Review: *What standard of review will be used?*	Test: *What does the Court ask?*	Example: *How does the Court apply the test?*
Fundamental freedoms (including religion, speech, assembly, press, marriage): suspect classifications (including race, alienage, and national origin)	Strict scrutiny or heightened standard	Is the classification justified by a compelling governmental interest? Is it narrowly tailored to meet that interest? Is it the least restrictive means possible?	*Brown* v. *Board of Education* (1954): Racial segregation was not necessary to accomplish the state's goal of education its students.
Gender	Intermediate standard	Does the classification serve an important governmental objective, and is it substantially related to those ends?	*Craig* v. *Boren* (1976): Allowing 18- to 21-year-old women to drink alcohol while prohibiting men of the same age from doing the same is not substantially related to the goal of preventing drunk driving.
Other (including age, wealth, and mental capacity)	Minimum rationality standard	Are the government's actions "rationally" related to a "legitimate" government interest?	*Nebbia* v. *New York* (1934): It was rational for the state to set prices of milk for dairy farmers, dealers, and retailers.

suspect classifications

Category or class, such as race or a fundamental freedom, that triggers the highest standard of scrutiny from the Supreme Court.

freedoms such as those guaranteed by the First Amendment or **suspect classifications** such as race are involved, the Court uses a heightened standard of review called *strict scrutiny* to determine the constitutional validity of the challenged practices. In legal terms, this means that if a statute or governmental practice makes a classification based on one of these suspect classifications, the statute is presumed to be unconstitutional unless the state can provide "compelling affirmative justifications"—that is: (1) unless the state can prove that the law in question is necessary to accomplish a permissible goal, and, (2) that it is the least restrictive means of accomplishing that goal.

This strict scrutiny standard was most clearly articulated in *Korematsu* v. *U.S.* (1944), which involved a constitutional challenge to the internment of Japanese Americans as security risks during World War II. In the Court's opinion, Justice Hugo Black noted that "all legal restrictions which curtail the civil rights of a single racial group are immediately suspect" and should be given "the most rigid scrutiny."[62] Despite this, in *Korematsu*, the Court ruled that these internments served a compelling governmental objective and were not discriminatory on their face. In other words, the national security risks posed by Japanese Americans in a time of war were sufficient to justify their internment. During the 2016 presidential primary campaign, Donald J. Trump announced he would ban Muslim immigrants from entering the United States, relying on *Korematsu*. Upon taking office, he immediately tried to impose bans on Muslim people traveling into the United States, but his first two executive orders were ruled unconstitutional by several courts. In 2018, however, the Court, in a 5–4 decision, found that the third executive order, which added two non-Muslim majority countries to the list of nations from whom the U.S. will not accept immigrants, constitutional. As in *Korematsu*, the majority weighed on the side of presidential power in national security matters, ignoring strict scrutiny.[63]

affirmative action

Policies designed to give special attention or compensatory treatment to members of a previously disadvantaged group.

Since the 1970s, the Court has applied the strict scrutiny standard in cases involving **affirmative action**, or policies designed to give special attention or compensatory treatment to members of a previously disadvantaged group. In a series of cases involving admissions policies at the University of Michigan, the Court allowed universities to give preference to minority applicants.[64] However, the Court struck down Michigan's undergraduate point system, which gave minority applicants twenty automatic points simply because they were minorities.[65]

In 2016, the Court upheld a University of Texas affirmative action plan, noting that courts must give substantial leeway to colleges to design their admissions programs. Many hailed this decision, *Fisher* v. *University of Texas*, as the most important education discrimination case since *Brown*.[66] In 2018, Harvard and Yale Universities were sued by Asian American students who claimed that the universities affirmatively used measures to restrict the number of Asians accepted every year. Given the three Trump appointees to the Supreme Court, these kinds of challenges could very well become the next famous affirmation action cases with nationwide ramifications.

Treatment of gender under the equal protection clause came under scrutiny in a case argued in 1971 by Ruth Bader Ginsburg (later an associate justice of the Supreme Court) as director of the Women's Rights Project of the ACLU. In this case, the Supreme Court ruled that an Idaho law granting a male parent automatic preference over a female parent as the administrator of their deceased child's estate violated the equal protection clause of the Fourteenth Amendment. *Reed v. Reed* (1971), the Idaho case, turned the tide in terms of constitutional litigation. Although the Court did not rule that sex was a suspect classification, for the first time it concluded that the equal protection clause of the Fourteenth Amendment prohibited unreasonable classifications based on sex.[67]

In 1976, the Court ruled that sex discrimination complaints would be judged according to a new, judicially created intermediate standard of review, a step below strict scrutiny. In *Craig v. Boren* (1976), the Court carved out a new test for examining claims of sex discrimination alleged to violate the Constitution of the United States: "to withstand constitutional challenge, . . . classifications by gender must serve important governmental objectives and must be substantially related to achievement of those objectives."[68] According to the Court, it created an **intermediate standard of review** within what previously was a two-tier distinction—strict scrutiny and rational basis.

The level of review used by the Court has a crucial impact on the status of civil rights in the United States. Clearly, a statute excluding Black people from draft registration would be unconstitutional. But because gender is not subject to the same higher standard of review used in racial discrimination cases, the Court has ruled the exclusion of women from requirements of the Military Selective Service Act permissible because the policy serves "important governmental objectives."[69] Still, because women now can be placed in all military positions, including combat roles, in 2016 Congress began deliberating a requirement for women to register for the draft, and in 2021 military leaders supported it.

Standards for review of statutes involving sexual orientation remain undecided in some areas but not all. The Court has long held that marriage is a fundamental right but its decision in *Windsor* left commentators unsure of the standard of review used by the Court for same-sex marriage. In *Obergefell v. Hodges* (2015), the Court narrowly ruled that marriage is a fundamental freedom. Thus, restrictions on same-sex marriage are to be treated with strict scrutiny.

The **rational basis standard of review**, which the Court first clearly enunciated in *Nebbia v. New York* (1934), is fairly clear cut.[70] Basically, if the Court finds no fundamental liberty interest or a suspect classification, the Court will allow the law to stand as constitutional as long as it is rationally related to a legitimate government interest. Thus, in *Nebbia*, New York's desire to set prices on milk was deemed within its constitutional authority to regulate for the health and welfare of its citizens. Categories dealing with wealth and age still fall under this standard of review. Many decisions giving heightened scrutiny to some groups, such as members of the LGBTQ community, were decided by 5–4 or 5–3 decisions. Thus, the makeup of the Court is critical to the outcome of future civil rights cases.

intermediate standard of review

A standard of review in which the Court determines whether classifications serve an important governmental objective and are substantially related to serving that objective. Gender-related legislation is automatically accorded this level of review.

rational basis standard of review

A standard of review in which the Court determines whether any rational foundation for the discrimination exists. Legislation affecting individuals based on age, wealth, or mental capacity is generally given this level of review.

CONCLUSION AND REVIEW

What Are the Roots of American Civil Rights?

5.1 Trace the roots of movements to guarantee rights to Black people and women.

When the Framers tried to compromise on the issue of slavery, they only postponed dealing with a volatile question that eventually would rip the nation apart. Southern states with large populations of enslaved people feared the loss of their labor that made their agricultural economy so profitable. Ultimately, the Civil War brought an end to slavery. Among its results were the triumph of the abolitionist position and the adoption of the Thirteenth, Fourteenth, and Fifteenth Amendments. During this period, women also sought expanded rights, especially the right to vote, to no avail.

What Was the Push for Equality, 1890–1954?

5.2 Outline developments in Black people's and women's push for equality from 1890 to 1954.

Although the Civil War Amendments became part of the Constitution, the Supreme Court limited their application. As legislatures throughout the South passed Jim Crow laws, the NAACP was founded in the early 1900s to press for equal rights for Black people. Women's groups also were active during this period, successfully lobbying for passage of the Nineteenth Amendment, which ensured them the right to vote.

What Statutory Protections for Civil Rights Were and Continue to Be Enacted, 1955–Present?

5.3 Analyze the legal protections enacted for Black people's and women's civil rights since 1955.

Black people used bus boycotts, sit-ins, freedom rides, pressure for voting rights enforcement, and massive nonviolent demonstrations to win greater protection for their civil rights. These efforts culminated in passage of the Civil Rights Act of 1964. Women's rights activists won passage of the Equal Pay Act of 1963 and the Civil Rights Act of 1964. However, the new women's rights movement was unsuccessful in achieving passage of the Equal Rights Amendment.

What Other Groups Have Mobilized for Rights?

5.4 Summarize the struggles of other group-differentiated minorities for civil rights.

Building on the successes of Black people and women, other groups, including Hispanics, American Indians, Asians and Pacific Islanders, the LGBTQ community, and those with disabilities, organized to litigate for expanded civil rights and to lobby for anti-discrimination laws.

Political Reform and Realities: How Are Civil Rights Protected?

5.5 Evaluate the standards by which civil rights are protected today.

No provision has done more to change Americans' conceptions of equality than the Fourteenth Amendment's equal protection clause. Claims brought under this clause are evaluated using three standards of review. In general, strict scrutiny, the most stringent standard, is applied to race-based claims and cases involving fundamental freedoms. The Court developed an intermediate standard of review to assess the constitutionality of sex discrimination claims. All other claims are subject to the rational basis test.

LEARN THE TERMS

abolitionist
affirmative action
Americans with Disabilities Act (ADA)
Brown v. *Board of Education* (1954)
Civil Rights Act of 1964
Emancipation Proclamation
Equal Pay Act of 1963
equal protection clause
Equal Rights Amendment (ERA)
Fifteenth Amendment

Fourteenth Amendment
grandfather clause
intermediate standard of review
Jim Crow laws
Korematsu v. *U.S.* (1944)
Lawrence v. *Texas* (2003)
League of United Latin American Citizens (LULAC)
"Letter from a Birmingham Jail"
LGBTQ community

McGirt v. *Oklahoma* (2020)
Mexican American Legal Defense and Educational Fund (MALDEF)
NAACP Legal Defense and Educational Fund (LDF)
National Association for the Advancement of Colored People (NAACP)
National Organization for Women (NOW)

Nineteenth Amendment
Obergefell v. *Hodges* (2015)
Plessy v. *Ferguson* (1896)
poll tax
Progressive Era (1890–1920)

rational basis standard of review
Seneca Falls Convention
separate-but-equal doctrine
standards of review
suffrage movement

suspect classifications
Thirteenth Amendment
Title IX

LEARN THE NAMES

Andrew Jackson
Cesar Chavez
Dolores Huerta
Eleanor Roosevelt
Elizabeth Cady Stanton

Frederick Douglass
Harriet Tubman
Harry S Truman
John F. Kennedy
Lucretia Mott

Martin Luther King Jr.
Rosa Parks
Susan B. Anthony
Thurgood Marshall

Chronicle/Alamy Stock Photo

IS PARTISANSHIP IN CONGRESS NEW?

Partisanship is not new. As depicted in this cartoon, in 1798, Federalist Roger Griswold of Connecticut got into an argument on the Senate floor with Matthew Lyon, a Democratic-Republican from Vermont. Griswold called Lyon a "scoundrel"; Lyon then spit in his face. Tensions escalated. A few weeks later, Lyon (left) then came at Griswold with fire tongs and Griswold answered by going after him with a cane.

On January 6, 2021, the nation collectively gasped in horror as hordes of rioters charged the Capitol while Congress was in session to count Electoral College ballots and confirm the elections of Joe Biden and Kamala Harris. This was violence from the outside—not between members.

CRITICAL THINKING QUESTION: *How does congressional partisanship compare to that of yesteryear?*

CONGRESS

LEARNING OBJECTIVES

6.1 Describe the roots and the structure of the Constitution.

6.2 Analyze the ability of members of Congress to represent their constituents.

6.3 Describe how incumbency and redistricting help members of Congress to stay in office.

6.4 Assess the roles of leaders, political parties, and committees in Congress.

6.5 Describe the powers of Congress.

6.6 Describe the factors that influence how members of Congress make decisions.

6.7 Evaluate the strategic interactions between Congress, the president, the courts, and the people.

1798 was not the last time that there was violence on the floors of Congress. In the 1830s through the 1850s, heated arguments about slavery often led to such scenes. In a fight on the floor of the House in 1836, members were observed with pistols brandished. Later that year, a House committee meeting was dissolved when a member, distraught by the testimony of a witness, drew his pistol. The meeting was canceled, and the member was charged with contempt of Congress.

In 1856, emotions came to a peak when Representative Preston Brooks (D–SC) went to the Senate floor and beat Senator Charles Sumner (R–MA), an ardent abolitionist, with a gold-headed cane in retaliation for a speech Sumner had made against slavery two days earlier. Sumner was so badly injured that he had to be carried off the floor and was unable to resume his duties for three years due to the grievous nature of his injuries. Brooks was declared a hero by the South, and Sumner was declared a martyr by the North—further inflaming tensions over slavery. These examples of the lack of civility evident in the halls of Congress are far from a complete record. Reporters often did not report these types of incidents because they also were subject to similar threats or violence for their writings.

● ● ●

The Framers' original conception of Congress's authority, although considered at the time to be the most powerful branch, was much narrower than it is today. Those in attendance at the Constitutional Convention wished to create a legislative body that would be able to make laws as well as raise and spend revenues. Over time, Congress has attempted to maintain these roles, but changes in demands made on the national government have allowed the executive and judicial branches to gain powers at the expense of the legislative branch. Moreover, the power and the importance of individual members have grown.

Today, members of Congress must combine and balance the roles of lawmaker, budgeter, and policy maker with acting as a representative of their district, state, party, and sometimes race, ethnicity, or gender. Not surprisingly, this balancing act often results in role conflict. Members also have to deal with presidents and even the federal courts, which have the power to rule laws passed by Congress and signed by the president as unconstitutional. In particular, if a member is of the president's political party, he or she must decide how much they want to agree or disagree with his policies. Often this depends on how the president, as a candidate, performed in their state or congressional district.

In this chapter, we analyze the powers of Congress and the competing roles members play as they represent the interests of their constituents, make laws, and oversee actions of the other two branches of government. We also show that as these functions have changed throughout U.S. history, so has Congress itself.

WHAT ARE THE ROOTS AND STRUCTURE OF THE U.S. CONGRESS?

6.1 Describe the roots and the structure of the Constitution.

Beginning with the formation of the Virginia House of Burgesses in 1619 and the drafting of the Mayflower Compact in 1620, early colonial settlers understood the need for a document setting out rules of behavior for residents. They also recognized the need to have some sort of governmental structure to guide the actions of settlers and outline the role of government. Thus, when colonists representing their respective governments met in Philadelphia in the First Continental Congress, they understood the need to consider how the thirteen colonies could work together as war against Great Britain ultimately commenced. The first form of government adopted by the colonists mirrored the confederation style of government that many American Indian tribes operated within. The government created by the Articles of Confederation and Perpetual Union was "a loose league of friendship" of limited powers drawn from the states. In fact, a guiding principle of the Articles was to preserve the independence and sovereignty of each of the former colonies. Thus, under the Articles, the new national government of limited powers was to conduct the Revolutionary War and diplomacy with foreign nations and Indian tribes. The Continental Congress was renamed the Congress of the Confederation, but most Americans still referred to it as the Continental Congress. Eventually, after the war, the delegates, as described in Chapter 2, recognized that the Articles no longer provided a workable framework for governing a growing union. After much deliberation, the Framers turned to creating a new form of government in the Constitution of the United States of America. The "loose league of friendship" was abandoned to create a new, federal form of government in which the power of the national government drew its powers directly from the people, not the states. The first branch of government it created was Congress.

Constitutional Provisions That Define the Organization and Powers of Congress

Article I of the Constitution describes the structure of the legislative branch of government. The Great Compromise at the Constitutional Convention resulted in the creation of a lower house, the House of Representatives, and an upper house, the Senate. Any two-house legislature, such as the one created by the Framers, is called a **bicameral legislature**. The population of each state determines the number of representatives that each state sends to the House of Representatives. In contrast, two senators represent each state in the Senate, regardless of the state's population. The Congress of the Confederation, as created by the Articles of the Confederation, was a unicameral body and lacked key powers.

Article I of the Constitution of the United States sets forth the formal, or legal, requirements for membership in the House and Senate. As agreed to at the Constitutional Convention, House members must be at least twenty-five years of age; senators, thirty. Members of the House must be citizens of the United States for at least seven years; those elected to the Senate, at least nine years. Both representatives and senators must be legal residents of the states from which they are elected.

Today, many members of Congress find the job exciting and fulfilling in spite of public criticism of the institution. But it wasn't always so. Until Washington, D.C., got air conditioning and drained its swamps, it was a miserable town. Most representatives spent as little time there as possible, viewing Congress, especially the House, as a stepping stone to other political positions back home. Only after World War I did most House members become congressional careerists who viewed their work in Washington as long term.[1]

The eligible electorate in each congressional district votes to elect members of the House of Representatives to two-year terms. The Framers expected that House members would be more responsible to the people, both because they were elected directly by them and because they were up for reelection every two years. The Constitution of the United States requires that a census, which entails the counting of all Americans, be conducted every ten years. Until the first census could be taken, the Constitution fixed the number of representatives in the House of Representatives at sixty-five. In 1790, one member represented about 30,000 people. But, as the population of the new nation grew and states were added to the union, the House became larger and larger. In 1910, it expanded to 435 members, and in 1929, its size was fixed at that number by statute. When Alaska and Hawai'i became states in the 1950s, however, the number of seats increased to 437. The number reverted to 435 in 1963.

Each state is granted its share of these 435 representatives on the basis of its population. After each U.S. Census, a constitutionally mandated process called **apportionment** adjusts the number of seats allotted to each state. After seats are reapportioned with

bicameral legislature
A two-house legislature.

apportionment
The process of allotting congressional seats to each state according to its proportion of the population, following the decennial census.

some states gaining and others losing their number of representatives in the House, state legislatures must redraw congressional districts to reflect population shifts, thereby ensuring that each member in Congress represents approximately the same number of residents. This process of redrawing congressional districts to reflect increases or decreases in the number of seats allotted to a state, as well as population shifts within a state, is called redistricting. It is discussed in greater detail later in this chapter.

Senators are elected to six-year terms, and originally state legislatures chose them because the Framers intended senators to represent their states' interests in the Senate. State legislators lost this influence over the Senate with the ratification of the Seventeenth Amendment in 1913, which provides for the direct election of senators by voters. Then, as now, one-third of all senators are up for reelection every two years. Some states may have two open Senate races, such as when a senator dies or resigns from office. In those situations, the candidates run to fill the remainder of that particular senator's term.

The Constitution specifically gives Congress its most important powers: the authorities to make laws and raise and spend revenues. No **bill**, or proposed law, can become law without the consent of both houses. Examples of other powers shared by both houses include the power to declare war, raise an army and navy, coin money, regulate commerce, establish the federal courts and their jurisdiction, set forth rules of immigration and naturalization, and "make all Laws which shall be necessary and proper for carrying into Execution the foregoing Powers." As interpreted by the U.S. Supreme Court, the necessary and proper clause, found at the end of Article I, section 8, when coupled with one or more of the specific powers enumerated in Article I, section 8, has allowed Congress to increase the scope of its authority, often at the expense of the states and into areas not necessarily envisioned by the Framers (see Table 6.1 on the next page).

bill
A proposed law.

The Constitution gives formal law-making powers to Congress alone. But it is important to remember that presidents issue proclamations, executive orders, and executive agreements with the force of law; bureaucrats issue quasi-legislative rules and are charged with enforcing laws, rules, and regulations; and, the Supreme Court and lower federal courts render opinions that generate principles also having the force of law.

Reflecting the different constituencies and size of each house of Congress (as well as the Framers' intentions), Article I gives special, exclusive powers to each house in addition to their shared role in law-making. For example, as noted in Table 6.2 on the next page, the Constitution specifies that all revenue bills must originate in the House of Representatives.

Sue Ogrocki/Associated Press

WHO ARE THE NONVOTING MEMBERS OF THE HOUSE OF REPRESENTATIVES?

Called delegates, or resident commissioner in the case of Puerto Rico, seven representatives have floor privileges but no voting rights. Six hail from Puerto Rico, Washington, D.C., American Samoa, Guam, the Northern Mariana Islands, and the U.S. Virgin Islands. In late 2019, Congress made good on a 184-year-old promise to the Cherokee Nation in the Treaty of New Echota, which began the evacuation of members of the nation in what became known as the Trail of Tears, by allotting it a delegate. Shown here is Kimberly Teehee, the first person to serve in the House of Representatives representing the Cherokee Nation. Teehee was a senior policy adviser in the Obama administration.

TABLE 6.1 WHAT ARE THE POWERS OF CONGRESS?

The powers of Congress, found in Article I, section 8, of the Constitution, include the powers to:
Lay and collect taxes and duties
Borrow money
Regulate commerce with foreign nations and among the states and with Indian tribes
Establish rules for naturalization (the process of becoming a citizen) and bankruptcy
Coin money, set its value, and fix the standard of weights and measures
Punish counterfeiting
Establish a post office and post roads
Issue patents and copyrights
Define and punish piracies and felonies on the high seas and crimes against the law of nations
Create courts inferior to (below) the U.S. Supreme Court
Declare war
Raise and support an army and navy and make rules for their governance
Provide for a militia (reserving to the states the right to appoint militia officers and to train militias under congressional rules)
Exercise legislative powers over the seat of government (the District of Columbia) and over places purchased to be federal facilities (forts, arsenals, dockyards, and "other needful buildings")
"Make all Laws which shall be necessary and proper for carrying into Execution the foregoing Powers, and all other Power vested by this Constitution in the government of the United States"

TABLE 6.2 WHAT ARE THE KEY CONSTITUTIONAL DIFFERENCES BETWEEN THE HOUSE OF REPRESENTATIVES AND THE SENATE?

House	Senate
435 voting members (apportioned by population)	100 voting members (two from each state)
Two-year terms	Six-year terms (one-third up for reelection every two years)
Initiates all revenue bills	Offers "advice and consent" on many major presidential appointments
Initiates impeachment procedures and passes articles of impeachment	Tries impeached officials
	Approves treaties

Over the years, however, this mandate has become less clear, and it is not unusual to see budget bills being considered simultaneously in both houses. Ultimately, each house must approve all bills in their exact wording. The House also has the power of **impeachment**, that is, to charge the president, vice president, or other "civil officers," including federal judges, with "Treason, Bribery, or other high Crimes and Misdemeanors." But only the Senate has authority to conduct impeachment trials, with a two-thirds "yea" vote being necessary to remove a federal official, such as the president or a judge, from office.

The Senate also has the sole authority to approve major presidential appointments, including federal judges, ambassadors, and Cabinet- and sub-Cabinet-level positions, by a simple majority vote. The Senate, too, must approve all presidential treaties by a two-thirds vote.

HOW DO MEMBERS OF CONGRESS REPRESENT THE AMERICAN PEOPLE?

6.2 Analyze the workday of members of Congress.

Members must attempt to represent varied constituencies: party leaders, colleagues, and lobbyists in Washington, D.C., and voters at home.[2] In attempting to do so, members spend full days in their home districts as well as in D.C. (see Table 6.3). According to one study of House members, average representatives made about forty trips back home to their districts each year.[3] One member from a safe district, however, admitted

impeachment

The power delegated to the House of Representatives in the Constitution to charge the president, vice president, or other "civil officers," including federal judges, with "Treason, Bribery, or other high Crimes and Misdemeanors." This is the first step in the constitutional process of removing government officials from office.

TABLE 6.3   WHAT IS A TYPICAL DAY LIKE FOR A MEMBER OF CONGRESS?

5:00 a.m.	Arrive at office.
7:00 a.m.	Give a tour of the U.S. Capitol to high-donor constituents.
8:00 a.m.	Eat breakfast with the House Shipbuilding Caucus.
9:00 a.m.	Meet with Speaker of the House and other members of Congress.
10:00 a.m.	Attend House Armed Services Committee hearing.
11:00 a.m.	Prepare for afternoon press conference, return phone calls, and sign constituent mail.
12:00 p.m.	Meet with constituents who want the member to join a caucus that may benefit the district.
1:00 p.m.	Glance at several local and national newspapers to keep track of current events.
2:00 p.m.	Attend Homeland Security Subcommittee hearing.
3:00 p.m.	Attend floor vote.
3:30 p.m.	Meet with group of high school students on front steps of Capitol.
4:15 p.m.	Return to office to sign more constituent mail and to meet with representatives of the American Heart Association.
5:00 p.m.	Attend Sustainable Energy and Environment Caucus meeting.
6:00 p.m.	Fundraising Call Time—Party HQ.
7:00 p.m.	Attend fundraiser.
9:00 p.m.	Return to office to sign more constituent mail and read more newspapers.
11:00 p.m.	Leave office to go home.

SOURCE: Adapted from Bob Clark, "A Day in the Life of Eric Massa," *Evening Tribune* (October 9, 2009), www.eveningtribune.com.

spending no more than 180 days in his district—the minimum for legal residency in the state.[4] One journalist has aptly described a member's days as a

> ... kaleidoscopic jumble: breakfast with reporters, morning staff meetings, simultaneous committee hearings to juggle, back-to-back sessions with lobbyists and constituents, phone calls, briefings, constant buzzers interrupting office work to make quorum calls and votes on the run, afternoon speeches, evening meetings, receptions, fund-raisers, all crammed into four days so they can race home for a weekend gauntlet of campaigning. It's a rat race.[5]

One research report on Congress found that members worked an average of seventy hours per week while in Washington and fifty-nine hours per week when Congress was not in session.[6] While this report found that members' political and campaign work took up less than 20 percent of their time, another source revealed that a slide presentation for incoming Democratic freshmen assumed a nine- to ten-hour workday, with four hours per day set aside for "call time" (telephone fundraising conducted outside the members' office per federal election law) and an hour set aside for tasks such as meet-and-greets and media outreach.[7]

Congressional Demographics

One measure of the representativeness of Congress is how well members' demographic characteristics reflect those of the American public. A cursory examination of these characteristics reveals that members of Congress are better educated, richer, more often male, and more likely to be White Americans than the general population. Nearly three-quarters of the members of the House and Senate also hold advanced degrees.[8]

Many members of both houses have significant inherited wealth, but given their educational attainment, which is far higher than the average American's, it is not surprising to find so many members of Congress are wealthy. More than half of all members of Congress are millionaires. The Senate, in fact, is often called the Millionaire's Club. In 2020, it took a net worth of over 28 million dollars to be among its wealthiest members. Nearly 40 percent of the women in Congress are millionaires including Speaker of the House **Nancy Pelosi**, with an estimated net worth of $114 million.[9]

Nancy Pelosi

A California Democrat, Pelosi is the first woman Speaker of the House. She served from 2007 to 2011 when Democrats took control of Congress and again in the 116th and 117th Congresses when Democrats flipped the House. She served as House Minority Whip from 2002–2003.

The average age of members of Congress is far higher than that of the populace. House members average nearly 58 years of age; senators, 63. Since 2019, those ages are going down. Newly elected members of Congress in 2020 had an average of 49. In the 117th Senate, Jon Osoff (D-GA), who won in a January 2021 runoff against an incumbent, was the youngest senator elected at age 33. In the House, the youngest member was Madison Cawthorn (R-NC) at age 25, the minimum age the Framers set for members of the House of Representatives.

Members of Congress are significantly more religious than the general public, with 96 percent reporting some religious affiliation. The highest percentage of members identify as Protestant (54.5 percent) and are overrepresented in comparison to their percentage of the general population (48 percent), as are Roman Catholics (30.9 versus 21 percent) and Jews (5.8 versus 2 percent). In contrast, nonreligious Americans (23 percent versus 3 percent) are significantly underrepresented (see Figure 6.1).

The advantages of incumbency make turnover in Congress very low, but 2018 saw notable upsets by women of color in the midterm election. In Massachusetts, Ayanna Pressley defeated 10-term Representative Tom Capuano (D), and Alexandria Ocasio-Cortez beat eight-term Representative Joe Crowley (D–NY). At age 29, she became the youngest woman ever elected to Congress. Pressley was the first African American woman elected to Congress from that state. Pressley was among a host of firsts in the 116th Congress, including the first two Native American and Muslim women elected to the House. In 2020, Mark Kelly, a former astronaut, defeated the incumbent, Senator Martha McSally (R–AZ), becoming the first husband of a former congressperson to enter Congress. His wife, Gabrielle Giffords, represented Arizona in the House before she was permanently disabled in a mass shooting while she was conducting a town hall meeting in 2011.

Collectively, four of the new women of color elected to the House in 2018, Alexandria Ocasio-Cortez (D–NY), Ilhan Omar (D–MN), Ayanna Pressley (D–MA), and Rashida Tlaib (D–MI) were nicknamed the "Squad." All are young, with an average age of 39.3 years, and consider themselves Justice Democrats. They share interest in social justice reform, the Green New Deal, and climate change, among other issues. They are outspoken and are considered to be on the left of the Democratic Party. In 2021, they added two more members to their informal group including Cori Bush (D–MO), a Black Lives Matter activist.

They were not the only firsts in the 2018 and 2020 elections. A record number of new members were elected to Congress in 2018. In the House, a record number of new African American women (all Democrats) were elected in 2018 and 24 will serve in the 117th Congress, up from 22 in the 116th Congress. Their successes resulted in a record

WHAT MAKES MARK KELLY (D–AZ) UNIQUE?

Kelly, an identical twin, is the first husband ever elected to the Senate whose wife was a former congressperson. Kelly's wife, Gabby Giffords, was seriously injured in a mass shooting while she was conducting a town hall with her constituents. Kelly, a former astronaut (as was his twin), is often mentioned as a potential Democratic candidate for president.

Jacob Snow/Icon Sportswire/Associated Press

FIGURE 6.1 HOW WELL DOES THE HOUSE OF REPRESENTATIVES REFLECT THE AMERICAN PEOPLE?

Membership in the House of Representatives is more diverse than ever before, but ethnic and racial minorities and women remain significantly underrepresented relative to their proportions of the population. In 2020, non-Hispanic Whites were 76.3 percent of the American population, nearly mirroring their percentage in the House and Senate—75 percent men held roughly 75 percent of House and Senate seats. The following data for party, gender, and race reflect the demographics of the 435 members of the 117th House of Representatives excluding the non-voting delegates from American Samoa, the District of Columbia, Guam, the U.S. Virgin Islands, the Northern Mariana Islands, Puerto Rico, and the Cherokee Nation. Citizens in all these places, although American citizens, have no voting representation in Congress but do pay federal taxes.

SOURCE: "Membership of the 117th Congress: A Profile," *Congressional Research Service*, posted June 1, 2020, Center for American Women in Politics (CAWP) and updated by authors.

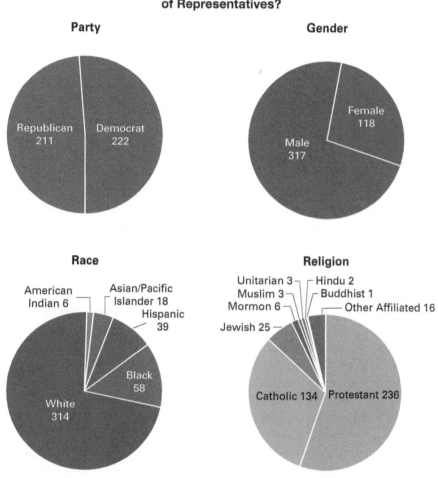

What are some key demographics of members of the House of Representatives?

number of Black members being elected, up four to 58 and up 25 since the 115th Congress. After shattering the glass ceiling in 2018 when 103 women were elected (up from 83 in the 115th Congress), 118 women (excluding five of the six nonvoting members) serve. 2018's elections also netted other firsts. Two new women were Muslim, and two were American Indians. Deb Haaland (D–NM) left the House in 2021 after her reelection to become the first Native American to serve as Secretary of the Interior, which oversees the Bureau of Indian Affairs.

The 2020 elections also saw a record number of new Republican women elected, more than doubling their previous numbers to 26. Only one of the forty-eight new women elected in 2018 was a Republican. Thus, many were motivated to run by the high number of Democratic women who had won in 2018. And, in most cases, Republican women ousted first term Democratic women in 2020.

New York added to the ranks of openly gay members with the election of two Black men, one who also identifies as Hispanic. Thus, the 117th Congress has a record of 11 openly LBGTQ members—nine in the House and two in the Senate.

The demographics of the Senate are fairly similar to that of the House. While the House is headed by a woman, Speaker Nancy Pelosi, the Senate is presided over by Vice President Kamala Harris. Given that the Senate is evenly divided between Democrats and Republicans, she is the deciding vote on many controversial issues.

Twenty-four women serve in the U.S. Senate (excluding the vice president). Sixteen are Democrats and eight are Republicans, the highest proportion of women ever to serve in the Senate. Two female senators, both initially appointed to their seats, lost in the general, or in the case of Georgia, the runoff election.

Only three senators are Black: Corey Booker (D–NJ), Tim Scott (R–SC), and Raphael Warnock (D–GA). Only ten Blacks have ever served in the Senate. Barack Obama and Kamala Harris both served in the Senate prior to winning national office. Two Asian/Pacific Islander women serve in the Senate. Five Hispanics serve in the Senate (one woman) and no American Indians serve in that body.

Representational Strategies

In addition to acting as physical representatives of their constituents, members of Congress must also represent their constituents' substantive policy interests. Over the years, political theorists have offered various ideas about how any legislative body can best achieve these goals. Are members of Congress, for example, bound to vote the way their constituents expect them to vote, even if they personally favor another policy? Your answer to these questions may depend on your view of the representative function of legislators.

Ireland-born and raised political philosopher **Edmund Burke** (1729–1797), who also served in the British Parliament, believed that although he was elected from Bristol, it was his duty to represent the interests of the entire nation. He reasoned that elected officials were obliged to vote as they personally thought best. According to Burke, a representative should be a **trustee** who listens to the opinions of constituents and then can be trusted to use his or her own best judgment to make final decisions.

A second theory of representation holds that a representative should be a **delegate**. True delegates are representatives who vote the way their constituents would want them to, regardless of their own opinions. Delegates, therefore, must be ready and willing to vote against their conscience or personal policy preferences if they know how their constituents feel about a particular issue.

Not surprisingly, members of Congress and other legislative bodies generally do not fall neatly into either category. It is often unclear how constituents regard a particular issue, or conflicting opinions may arise within a single constituency. With these difficulties in mind, a third theory of representation holds that a **politico** alternately dons the hat of a trustee or delegate, depending on the issue. On matters of great concern to their constituents, representatives most likely will vote as delegates; on other matters, representatives will act as trustees and use their own best judgment.[10] For senators, confirmation of Supreme Court nominees can be particularly thorny.

Edmund Burke

Irish-born political philosopher of the eighteenth century who, as an elected member of the House of Commons, articulated the view that elected representatives should act as "trustees" and use their own best judgement when voting.

trustee

A lawmaker who listens to their constituents, weighs their beliefs, and ultimately uses their own judgement as they vote.

delegate

Role played by a representative who votes the way his or her constituents would want, regardless of personal opinions; may refer to an elected representative to Congress or a representative to the party convention.

politico

An elected representative who acts as a trustee or as a delegate, depending on the issue.

HOW DO MEMBERS STAY IN CONGRESS?

6.3 Describe how incumbency and redistricting help members of Congress to stay in office.

Despite the long hours and hard work required of senators and representatives, thousands of people aspire to these jobs every year. Yet only 535 men and women (plus seven nonvoting members) actually serve in the U.S. Congress. Membership in one of the two major political parties is almost always a prerequisite for election because election laws in various states often discriminate against independents (those without party affiliation) and minor-party candidates. The ability to raise money often is key to any

TABLE 6.4   WHAT ARE THE ADVANTAGES OF INCUMBENCY?

Name recognition. Members' names have been on the ballot before, and voters may associate their names with programs or social services they have brought to the district.

Credit claiming. Members may claim to be responsible for federal money brought to the district.

Casework. Members and their staffs help constituents solve problems with the government, including navigating red tape and tracking down federal aid.

Franking privilege. Members may send mail or newsletters for free by using their signature in place of a stamp.

Access to media. Members and their staffs may have relationships with reporters and may find it easy to spin stories or give quotes.

Ease in fund-raising. Incumbents' high reelection rates make them a safe bet for individuals or groups wanting to give donations in exchange for access.

Experience in running a campaign. Members have already put together a campaign staff, made speeches, and come to understand constituent concerns.

Redistricting. In the House, member's district may be drawn to enhance electability.

member's victory, and many members spend much of their free time on the phone, dialing for dollars. In 2020, when congressional campaigns were conducted largely under pandemic restrictions, much fundraising took place over Zoom, and, ironically, broke all records. Incumbency and redistricting also affect members' chances at reelection.

Incumbency

Incumbency helps members stay in office once they are elected.[11] Traditionally, it is often very difficult for outsiders to win because they don't have the advantages enjoyed by incumbents, including name recognition, access to free media, an inside track on fund-raising, and a district often drawn to favor the incumbent (see Table 6.4). Still, recent trends point to a weakening of the incumbency effect.[12]

It is not surprising, then, that on average, about 90 percent of incumbents who seek reelection win their primary and general election races.[13] The majority of members who lose their reelection bids are affected by redistricting or changing demographics in their districts or strong primary challenges from the left or right. In 2018, only 3 incumbent representatives and 5 senators lost. In 2020, four senators lost, all Republicans. Eleven representatives lost. Four were women.

incumbency
Already holding an office.

Redistricting

The process of redrawing congressional districts to reflect increases or decreases in seats allotted to the states, as well as population shifts within a state, is called **redistricting**. Redistricting is a largely political process. In most states, partisan state legislatures draw district lines. As a result, the majority party in the state legislature uses the redistricting process as an opportunity to ensure formation of voting districts that protect their majority.

Until 1962, Tennessee had not redistricted since 1922. Over time, its urban population grew rapidly but the state districts woefully underrepresented city dwellers in the statehouse. *Baker* v. *Carr* **(1962)** became a landmark case when the Court ruled that the redistricting, although political, presents what the Constitution calls a *justiciable question*, because it did not qualify as a "political question." Prior cases had held redistricting cases were political questions over which the Court has no jurisdiction.

The process of drawing congressional districts is usually highly contentious. In recent years, redistricting battles in many states have become increasingly personal, with members of some state legislatures even walking out during the process. Hoping to avoid this sort of high political theater, some states, including Iowa and Arizona, appoint nonpartisan committees or use some other independent means of drawing district lines. Although the processes vary in detail, most states require legislative approval of redistricting plans.

The redistricting process often involves **gerrymandering**—the drawing of congressional districts to produce a particular electoral outcome without regard to the shape of the district (see Figure 6.2). Because of enormous population growth, the

redistricting
The process of redrawing congressional districts to reflect increases or decreases in seats allotted to the states, as well as population shifts within a state.

***Baker* v. *Carr* (1962)**
Supreme Court case ruling that issues presented by redistricting are within its jurisdiction to review.

gerrymandering
The drawing of congressional districts to produce a particular electoral outcome without regard to the shape of the district.

FIGURE 6.2   WHAT IS GERRYMANDERING?

This map of a Texas congressional district was created after the 2010 Census. It illustrates the bizarre geographical contortions that can result from gerrymandering. The term was coined by combining the last name of the Massachusetts governor first credited with politicizing the redistricting process, Elbridge Gerry, and the word "salamander," which looked like the oddly shaped district that Gerry created.

Texas 35th District, 2012

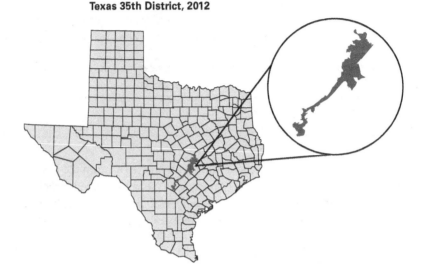

partisan implications of redistricting, and the requirement under the Voting Rights Act of 1965 for minorities to have an equal chance to elect candidates of their choice, legislators end up drawing oddly shaped districts to elect more members of their party.[14] Redistricting plans routinely meet with court challenges across the country.

For a long time, the U.S. Supreme Court considered redistricting based on partisan considerations to be a political question not within the scope of constitutional law but rather one worked out through the regular political process.[15] But in recent years, the Supreme Court has involved itself in some such cases and has ruled as follows:

- Congressional and state legislative districts may be apportioned on the basis of population.[16]
- District lines must be contiguous; one must be able to draw the boundaries of the district with a single unbroken line.[17]
- Purposeful gerrymandering of a congressional district to dilute minority strength is illegal under the Voting Rights Act of 1965.[18]
- Redrawing districts to enhance minority representation is constitutional if race is not the "predominant" factor.[19]
- States may redistrict more frequently than every ten years.[20]

Shaw v. *Reno* (1993)

Supreme Court case ruling that while race can be considered in drawing district lines, it cannot be the overriding reason.

Shaw v. *Reno* (1993), the North Carolina plan for reappointment after the 1990 Census, although racially neutral on its face, was actually an effort to separate voters, based on race, into separate districts. Thus, the Court held that a bizarrely drawn district is unconstitutional if race is the overriding reason for its shape.[21]

In 2018, the Supreme Court, in a 5–4 decision, ruled that the Texas legislature, where Republicans were in the majority, used race improperly when it drew a state house district to make it a heavily Hispanic district. The decision was narrowly written and left the rest of the districts intact. In 2019, however, the Court held that voters in Maryland and North Carolina lacked adequate standing to challenge their respective states' redrawing of congressional districts because they presented political questions beyond the Court's jurisdiction, harkening back to pre-*Baker* v. *Carr* days.[22]

Redistricting decisions may have significant consequences for members of Congress. The boundaries of a member's district determine the demographic and partisan makeup of their constituency. In districts that heavily favor members of one party over another, it may be hard to have competitive elections, and voters from the minority party may feel alienated from the political process. Some commentators suggest that increasingly partisan congressional redistricting is a major contributor to the high levels of partisanship exhibited in recent Congresses.

HOW IS CONGRESS ORGANIZED?

6.4 Assess the roles of leaders, political parties, and committees in Congress.

As demonstrated in Figure 6.3, Congress is a bicameral legislature. The organization of both houses of Congress is closely tied to political parties and their strength in each house. The basic division in Congress is between majority and minority parties. The majority party in each house is the party with the most members. The minority party in each house is the party with the second most members (see Figure 6.3). If the Senate is equally divided, as is the case in the 117th Congress, the vice president may cast the deciding vote.

At the beginning of each new Congress, the members of each party formally gather in their party caucus (or conference) (see Figure 6.4 for the partisan composition of Congress). Historically, these caucuses have enjoyed varied powers, but today the party caucuses have several roles, including nominating or electing party officers, reviewing committee assignments, discussing party policy, imposing party discipline, setting party themes, and coordinating media. Conference and caucus chairs are recognized party leaders who work with other leaders in the House or Senate.[23]

FIGURE 6.3 HOW ARE THE HOUSE OF REPRESENTATIVES AND THE SENATE ORGANIZED IN 2021?

Parties play a very important role in organizing both the House and Senate. The majority and minority leaders are chosen by the party caucus or conference, as are other key leaders in the party hierarchy. This structure helps to organize operations and avoid conflict in each of the institutions.

SOURCE: Adapted from Walter H. Davidson, et al., *Congress and Its Members*, 17th ed. (Washington, DC: CQ Press, 2019) and the authors.

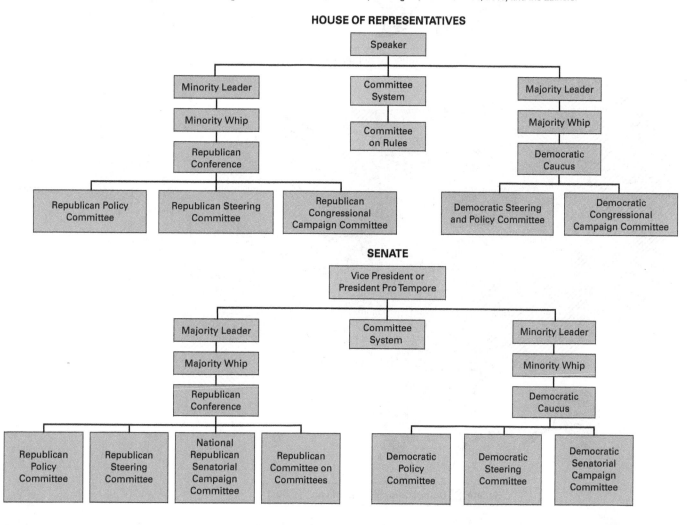

FIGURE 6.4A AND B WHAT IS THE PARTISAN COMPOSITION OF THE 117TH CONGRESS?

In the 2020 election, the Democrats retained their majority in the House of Representatives, but no party received a majority in the Senate. Thus, Democrats took a one vote lead because the Democratic Vice President presides over the Senate and casts votes in cases of a tie.

SOURCE: Data from Politico, www.politico.com, as of November 14, 2018.

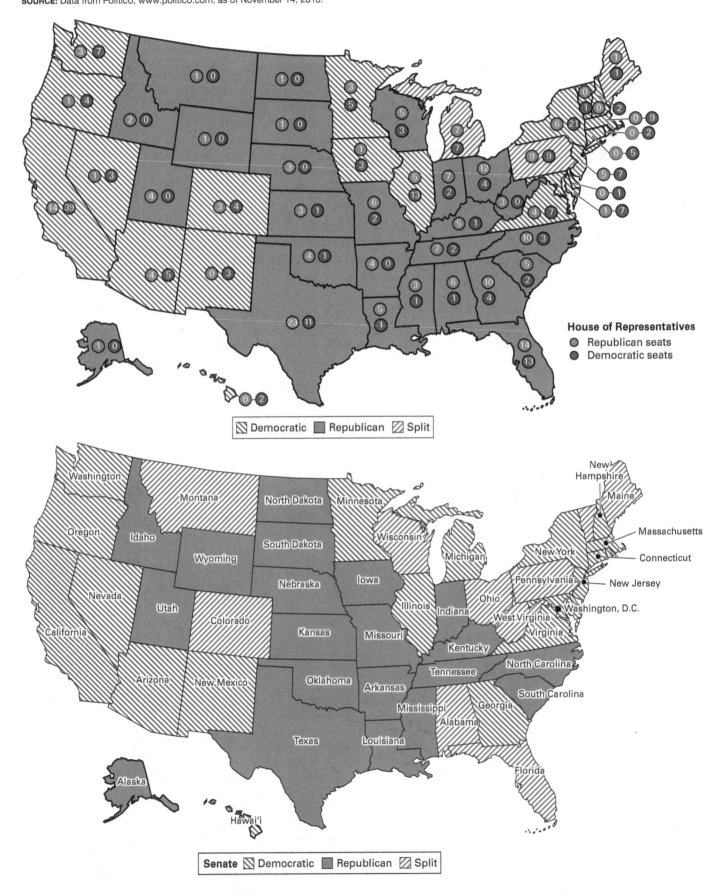

Each caucus or conference has specialized committees that fulfill certain tasks. House Republicans, for example, have a Committee on Committees that makes committee assignments. The Democrats' Steering Committee performs this function. Each party also has congressional campaign committees to assist members in their reelection bids.

Leadership in the House of Representatives

Even in the first Congress in 1789, the House of Representatives was almost three times larger than the Senate. It is not surprising, then, that from the beginning the House has shown tighter organization, more elaborate structure, and governance by stricter rules. Traditionally, loyalty to party leadership and voting along party lines have been more common in the House than in the Senate. House leaders also play a key role in moving the business of the House along. Historically, the Speaker of the House, the majority and minority leaders, and the Republican and Democratic House whips have made up the party leadership that runs the institution.

THE SPEAKER OF THE HOUSE The **Speaker of the House**, the chamber's most powerful position, is the only officer of the House of Representatives specifically mentioned in the Constitution. The office follows a model similar to the British Parliament—the Speaker was the one who spoke to the king and conveyed the wishes of the House of Commons to the monarch.[24]

> **Speaker of the House**
> The only officer of the House of Representatives specifically mentioned in the Constitution; the chamber's most powerful position; traditionally a member of the majority party.

The entire House of Representatives elects the Speaker at the beginning of each new Congress or, in the case of death or resignation of the Speaker, soon after the vacancy occurs. Traditionally, the Speaker is a member of the majority party. Although typically not the member with the longest service, the Speaker generally has served in the House for a long time and in other House leadership positions as an apprentice.

The Speaker presides over the House of Representatives, oversees House business, serves as the official spokesperson for the House, and is second in the line of presidential succession (after the vice president). The Speaker is also expected to smooth the passage of party-backed legislation through the House. To aid in this process, the Speaker generally has great political influence within the chamber and in policy negotiations with the president.

LEADERSHIP TEAMS After the Speaker, the next most powerful people in the House are the majority and minority leaders, who are elected in their individual party caucuses or conferences. The majority leader is the head of the party controlling the most seats in the House; his or her counterpart in the party with the second highest number of seats is the minority leader. The majority leader helps the Speaker schedule proposed legislation for debate on the House floor.

The Republican and Democratic whips, who are elected by party members in caucuses, assist the Speaker and majority and minority leaders in their leadership

Tom Williams/Associated Press

WHO IS THE FIRST FEMALE SPEAKER OF THE HOUSE?
Nancy Pelosi was the first woman Speaker and served in that role between January 2007 and January 2011, and again from 2019 to present. A strong Speaker, she is known for her ability to count votes before allowing any bill on the floor, resulting in the highest levels of party unity in recent history.

efforts. The position of whip originated in the British House of Commons, where it was named after the "whipper in," the rider who keeps the hounds together in a fox hunt. Party whips—first designated in the U.S. House of Representatives in 1899—do, as their name suggests, try to whip fellow Democrats or Republicans into line on partisan issues. They try to maintain close contact with all members on important votes, prepare summaries of content and implications of bills, take vote counts during debates and votes, and in general persuade members to toe the party line. Whips and their deputy whips also serve as communications links, distributing word of the party line from leaders to rank-and-file members and alerting leaders to concerns in the ranks. These tasks are more difficult today because both parties have dissension within their ranks.

Leadership in the Senate

Organization and formal rules never have played the same role in the Senate as in the House. Through the 1960s, the Senate was a gentlemen's club whose folkways— unwritten rules of behavior—governed its operation. One such folkway, for example, stipulated that political disagreements not become personal criticisms. A senator who disliked another referred to that senator as "the able, learned, and distinguished senator." A member who really could not stand another called that senator "my very able, learned, and distinguished colleague."

In the 1960s and 1970s, senators became increasingly active on a variety of issues on and off the Senate floor, and extended debates often occurred on the floor without the rigid rules of courtesy that had once prevailed. These changes have made the majority leader's role as coalition builder extraordinarily challenging, mirroring problems facing the Speaker.[25]

PRESIDING OFFICER   The Constitution specifies that the presiding officer of the Senate is the vice president of the United States. Because she is not a member of the Senate, Vice President Kamala Harris votes only in the case of a tie.

The official chair of the Senate is the president pro tempore, or pro tem, whom the majority party selects and who presides over the Senate in the absence of the vice president. The position of pro tem today is primarily an honorific office generally awarded to the most senior senator of the majority party. Once elected, the pro tem stays in that office until the majority party in the Senate changes. Since presiding over the Senate can be a rather perfunctory duty, neither the vice president nor the president pro tempore actually performs the task very often. Instead, this particular duty rotates among junior members of the majority party of the chamber, allowing more senior members to attend meetings of greater importance.

MAJORITY LEADER   The true leader of the Senate is the majority leader, elected to the position by the majority party. Because the Senate is a smaller and more collegial body, the majority leader is not nearly as powerful as the Speaker of the House.

LEADERSHIP TEAMS   The minority leader and the Republican and Democratic whips round out the leadership positions in the Senate and perform functions similar to those of their House counterparts. But leading and whipping in the Senate can be quite a challenge. Senate rules always have given tremendous power to individual senators; in most cases, senators can offer any kind of amendments to legislation on the floor, and an individual senator can bring all work on the floor to a halt indefinitely through a filibuster, unless three-fifths of the senators vote to cut him or her off.[26]

The Committee System

The saying "Congress in session is Congress on exhibition, whilst Congress in its committee rooms is Congress at work" may not be as true today as it was when Woodrow Wilson wrote it in 1885.[27] Still, "the work that takes place in the committee and subcommittee rooms of Capitol Hill is critical to the productivity and effectiveness of Congress."[28] Standing committees are the first and last places to which most bills go. Usually, committee members play key roles in floor debate about the merits of bills that have been introduced. When the House and Senate pass different versions of a bill, a conference committee with members of both houses meets to iron out the differences. Committee organization and specialization are especially important in the House of Representatives because of its size. The establishment of subcommittees allows for even greater specialization.

TYPES OF COMMITTEES   Congressional committees are of four types: (1) standing; (2) joint; (3) conference; and, (4) select (or special).[29]

1. **Standing committees** are those to which bills are referred for consideration; they are so called because they continue from one Congress to the next. They consider issues roughly parallel to those of the departments represented in the president's Cabinet. For example, there are standing committees on agriculture, education, the judiciary, veterans' affairs, transportation, and commerce.

2. **Joint committees** are standing committees that include members from both houses of Congress and are set up to conduct investigations or special studies. They focus public attention on major matters such as the economy, taxation, or scandals.

3. **Conference committees** are special joint committees created to reconcile differences in bills passed by the House and Senate. A conference committee comprises members from the House and Senate committees that originally considered the bill.

4. **Select (or special) committees** are temporary committees appointed for specific purposes, such as Speaker Pelosi's creation of the Select Committee on the Climate Crisis. These committees can be very partisan.

In the 117th Congress, the House had twenty *standing committees*, as shown in Table 6.5, each with an average of thirty-one members. Together, these standing committees had roughly ninety subcommittees that collectively acted as the eyes, ears, and hands of the House. The Senate had sixteen standing committees ranging in size from fifteen to twenty-nine members. It also had roughly seventy subcommittees, which allowed all majority party senators to chair at least one.

Although most committees in one house parallel those in the other, the House Committee on Rules, for which no counterpart in the Senate exists, plays a major role in the House's law-making process. As an indication of this committee's importance, the Speaker directly appoints its chair and majority party members. This committee reviews most bills after they come from a committee and before they go to the full chamber for consideration. Performing a traffic cop function, the Committee on Rules gives each bill what is called a rule, which contains the date the bill will come up for debate and the time that will be allotted for discussion, and often specifies what kinds of amendments can be offered. Bills considered under a closed rule cannot be amended.

Standing committees have considerable power. They can kill bills, amend them radically, or hurry them through the process. In the words of former President Woodrow Wilson, once a bill is referred to a committee, it "crosses a parliamentary bridge of sighs to dim dungeons of silence whence it never will return."[30] Committees report out to the full House or Senate only a small fraction of the bills assigned to them. A **discharge petition** signed by a majority (218) of the House membership can force bills out of a House committee.

In contrast to members of the House, who hold few committee assignments (an average of 1.8 standing and three subcommittees), senators each serve on an average of three to four committees and seven subcommittees. Whereas the committee system allows House members to become policy or issue specialists, Senate members often are generalists who must prioritize the importance of their committee work.

Senate committees have the same power over framing legislation as House committees, but the Senate, as an institution more open to individual input than the

standing committee
Committee to which proposed bills are referred; continues from one Congress to the next.

joint committee
Standing committee that includes members from both houses of Congress set up to conduct investigations or special studies.

conference committee
Special joint committee created to reconcile differences in bills passed by the House and Senate.

select (or special) committee
Temporary committee appointed for a specific purpose.

discharge petition
Petition that gives a majority of the House of Representatives the authority to bring an issue to the floor in the face of committee inaction.

TABLE 6.5 WHAT WERE THE COMMITTEES OF THE 117TH CONGRESS?

Standing Committees	
House	**Senate**
Agriculture	Agriculture, Nutrition, and Forestry
Appropriations	Appropriations
Armed Services	Armed Services
Budget	Banking, Housing, and Urban Affairs
Education and Labor	Budget, Commerce, Science, and Transportation
Energy and Commerce	Energy and Natural Resources
Ethics	Environment and Public Works
Financial Services	Finance
Foreign Affairs	Foreign Relations
Homeland Security	Health, Education, Labor, and Pensions
House Administration	Homeland Security and Governmental Affairs Housing, Urban Affairs Indian Affairs
Judiciary*	
Constitution and Civil Justice	Judiciary*
Courts, Intellectual Property, and the Internet	*Antitrust, Competition Policy, and Consumer Rights*
Crime, Terrorism, Homeland Security, and Investigations	*The Constitution*
Immigration and Border Security	*Crime and Terrorism*
Regulatory Reform, Commercial and Antitrust Law	*Immigration and the National Interest*
Natural Resources	*Oversight, Agency Action, Federal Rights and Federal Courts*
Oversight and Government Reform	*Privacy, Technology and the Law*
Rules	
Science, Space, and Technology	Rules and Administration
	Small Business and Entrepreneurship
Small Businesses	Veterans Affairs
Transportation and Infrastructure	
Veterans Affairs	
Ways and Means	

Select, Special, and Other Committees		
House	**Senate**	**Joint Committees**
Permanent Select Committee on Intelligence	Aging (special)	Economic
Select Committee on Economic Disparity and Fairness in Growth	Ethics	Library
Select Committee on the Climate Crisis	Indian Affairs	Printing
Select Committee on the Coronavirus Crisis	Intelligence	Taxation
Select Committee on the Modernization of Congress	International Narcotics Control	

*NOTE: The Subcommittees of the House and Senate Judiciary Committees during the 117th Congress are listed in italics.

House, gives less deference to the work done in committees. In the Senate, legislation is more likely to be rewritten on the floor, where all senators can generally participate and add amendments.

COMMITTEE CHAIRS Committee chairs enjoy tremendous power and prestige, with authorization to select all subcommittee chairs, call meetings, and recommend majority members to sit on conference committees. Committee chairs may even opt to kill a bill by refusing to schedule hearings on it. They also have a large committee staff at their disposal and are often recipients of favors from lobbyists, who recognize the chair's unique position of power. Interpersonal skills, influence, and expertise are a chair's best resources.

Historically, committee chairs were the majority party members with the longest continuous service on the committee. Committee chairs in the House, unlike the Senate, are no longer selected by **seniority**, or time of continuous service on the committee. Instead, to ensure that candidates demonstrate party loyalty, party leaders interview potential chairs. Six years of service on a particular committee is the limit on all committee chairs.

seniority
Time of continuous service on a committee.

COMMITTEE MEMBERSHIP Some committees, such as Energy and Commerce, facilitate reelection by giving House members influence over decisions that affect large campaign contributors. Other committees, such as Education and Labor or Judiciary, attract members eager to work on the policy responsibilities assigned to the committee even if the appointment does them little good at the ballot box. Another motivator for certain committee assignments is the desire to have power and influence within the chamber. The Appropriations and Budget Committees provide that kind of reward for some members, given the monetary impact on bills that come from other committees. Congress can approve programs, but unless money for them is appropriated in the budget, they are largely symbolic.

In both the House and the Senate, committee membership generally reflects party distribution within that chamber. On committees more critical to the operation of the House or to the setting of national policy, the majority often takes a disproportionate share of the slots. Since the Committee on Rules regulates access to the floor for legislation approved by other standing committees, control by the majority party is essential for it to manage the flow of legislation. For this reason, no matter how narrow its margin in the chamber, the majority party makes up more than two-thirds of the Committee on Rules's membership.

WHAT ARE THE POWERS OF CONGRESS?

6.5 Describe the powers of Congress.

The Framers wished to ensure that the national government had sufficient power to govern the states. Thus, Article I, section 7, of the Constitution details the procedures by which Congress can make laws and raise revenues. Article I, section 8, also details Congress's power to tax, spend, regulate commerce, coin money, and make "all Laws which shall be necessary and proper for carrying into Execution" of those powers.

Today, Congress not only makes laws dealing with substantive policy but also spends significant time negotiating and trying to pass the nation's budget. In addition, in accordance with the system of checks and balances, it has a key oversight role. Through the War Powers Resolution, congressional review, approval of nominations, and impeachment, Congress can check the power of the executive and judicial branches.

The Law-making Function

Congress's law-making power allows it to affect the day-to-day lives of all Americans and set policy for the future. Although proposals for legislation—be they about immigration, terrorism, Medicare, or tax policy—can come from the president, executive agencies, committee staffs, interest groups, or even private individuals, only members of the House or Senate can formally submit a bill for congressional consideration. Once a member of Congress introduces a bill, it usually reaches a dead end. In the case of the Republican House's initial efforts to reverse the Affordable Health Care Act, the bill was rushed by House leadership and presented for a vote before most members could read it—one of the reasons for its failure.

One or more standing committees and both chambers must approve each piece of legislation, and if House and Senate versions differ, each house must accept a conference report resolving those differences. Multiple stopping points provide many opportunities for legislation to die or members to revise the content of legislation and may lead representatives to alter their views on a particular piece of legislation several times over. Thus, it is much easier to defeat a bill than to pass one (see Figure 6.5). Of the 11,488 bills introduced during the 116th Congress only 283 were passed.

COMMITTEE REFERRAL The House and Senate have parallel processes, and often the same bill is introduced in each chamber at the same time. One member of

FIGURE 6.5 HOW DOES A BILL BECOME A LAW?

A bill must go through a carefully prescribed process in both the House of Representatives and the Senate to be enacted into law. After a bill has passed both houses, differences must be reconciled and the proposed legislation must meet with the president's approval. As a result, though many bills are introduced, few actually become law.

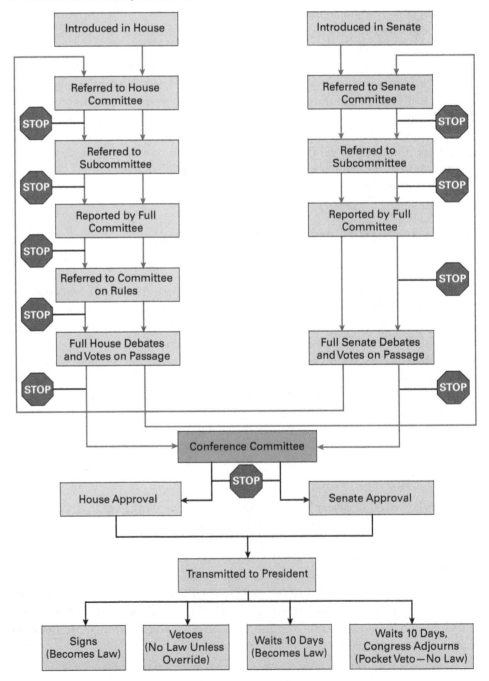

Congress must introduce a bill, but several other members (called co-sponsors) often sponsor a bill, in an attempt to show support for its aims. Once introduced, the bill is sent to the clerk of the chamber, who gives it a number (for example, HR 1 or S 1—indicating House or Senate bill number one, respectively). The bill is then printed, distributed, and sent to the appropriate committee or committees for consideration.

The committee usually refers the bill to one of its subcommittees, whose staff researches the proposed legislation, and then the chair decides whether or not to hold hearings on the bill. The subcommittee hearings provide an opportunity for those on both sides of the issue to voice their opinions. Since the 1970s, most hearings have been open to the public. After the hearings, the subcommittee revises the bill and then votes to approve or defeat it. If the subcommittee votes in favor of the bill, it is returned to the full committee. There, it goes through markup, a session during which committee members can offer changes to a bill before it goes to the floor. The full committee may also reject the bill before it goes to the floor in either house.

FLOOR DEBATE   The second stage of action takes place on the House or Senate floor. As previously discussed, in the House, before a bill may be debated on the floor, the Committee on Rules must approve it and give it a rule and a place on the calendar, or schedule. (House budget bills, however, do not go to the Committee on Rules.) In the House, the rule given to a bill determines limits on the floor debate and specifies what types of amendments, if any, may be attached to the bill. Once the Committee on Rules considers the bill, it is added to the calendar.

When the day arrives for floor debate, the House may choose to form a Committee of the Whole. This procedure allows the House to deliberate with only one hundred members present to expedite consideration of the bill. During this time, members may offer amendments, and the full House ultimately takes a vote. If the bill survives, it goes to the Senate for consideration if that body did not consider it simultaneously. In February 2018, Nancy Pelosi, then the House Minority Leader, took advantage of an arcane House rule that allows unlimited "magic minutes" to members of the House leadership. Breaking a record that had stood since 1909, Pelosi spoke for eight hours and fifteen minutes in four-inch high heels without a break, using her time to tell stories of Dreamers (young people brought illegally to the United States as children)

WHAT IS THE PRESIDENT'S ROLE IN LAW-MAKING?

After a bill has won the approval of both houses of Congress, the president has the final opportunity to approve the law or veto it, sending it back to Congress for a potential veto override. Here, President Barack Obama, surrounded by Vice President Joe Biden and legislative leaders, signs into law the Patient Protection and Affordable Care Act of 2010 (Obamacare), which reformed health care in the United States.

J. Scott Applewhite/Associated Press

because the budget put forth by the Republican majority did not deal with immigration issues.

Unlike the House, whose size necessarily limits debate, the Senate may hold up bills by a hold or a filibuster. A hold is a procedure by which a senator asks to be informed before a particular bill (or nomination) is brought to the floor. This request signals the Senate leadership and the sponsors of the bill that a colleague may have objections to the bill (or nomination) and should be consulted before further action is taken. A hold may be anonymous or public and can be placed for any reason—including reviewing, negotiating changes, or attempting to kill a bill. Holds can be lifted by a senator at any time or stand as permanent blocks to specific legislation or judicial and diplomatic nominations.

filibuster
A formal way of halting Senate action on a bill by means of long speeches or unlimited debate.

Filibusters, a formal way of halting Senate action on a bill by means of long speeches or unlimited debate, grew out of the absence of rules to restrict speech in the Senate. The content of a filibuster has no limits as long as a senator keeps talking. A senator may read from a phone book, recite poetry, or read cookbooks to delay a vote. Often, a team of senators takes turns speaking to continue the filibuster in the hope of tabling or killing a bill. The use of filibusters has increased in recent years. Moreover, simply the threat of a filibuster can be quite potent; in the modern Senate, it often takes the assured votes of sixty senators for a bill to come to a final vote because of the threat of a filibuster.

cloture
Mechanism requiring the vote of sixty senators to cut off debate.

Unless Senate rules are altered to require only a simple majority to end a filibuster—a step referred to as the nuclear option that was taken by Senate Democrats in 2013 to advance votes on President Obama's judicial nominees to the lower federal courts—senators may forcibly end a filibuster in only one way. Sixty of them must sign a motion for **cloture**. After a cloture motion passes the Senate floor, members may spend no more than thirty additional hours debating the legislation at issue. In 2017, Senate Majority Leader Mitch McConnell (R–KY) took the unprecedented move of using what is called the nuclear option to gain confirmation of President Trump's first nominee to the U.S. Supreme Court, Judge Neil Gorsuch. The nuclear option is a Senate rule that allows only fifty-one votes, instead of the usual sixty, required to amend Senate rules. Aware that they lacked the sixty votes required to end a filibuster, Senate Republicans used the option that Democrats had reserved for lower federal court appointments. In 2018, the same process was used to advance the confirmation of Brett Kavanaugh, and again in 2020 for Amy Coney Barrett.

FINAL APPROVAL   The third stage of action takes place when the two chambers of Congress approve different versions of the same bill. When this happens, they establish a conference committee to iron out the differences between the two versions. The conference committee, whose members are from the original House and Senate committees, hammers out a compromise, which is returned to each chamber for a final vote. Sometimes, the conference committee fails to agree and the bill dies there. No changes or amendments to the compromise version are allowed. If the bill does not pass in both houses, it dies. If the bill passes, it is sent to the president, who has ten days to consider a bill. He has four options:

veto
The formal, constitutional authority of the president to reject bills passed by both houses of Congress, thus preventing them from becoming law without further congressional action.

1. The president can sign the bill, at which point it becomes law.

2. The president can **veto** the bill, which is more likely to occur when the president is of a different party from the majority in Congress; Congress may override the president's veto with a two-thirds vote in each chamber, a very difficult task.

3. The president can wait the full ten days, at the end of which time the bill becomes law without his signature if Congress is still in session.

pocket veto
If Congress adjourns during the ten days the president has to consider a bill passed by both houses of Congress, the bill is considered vetoed without the president's signature.

4. If Congress adjourns before the ten days are up, the president can choose not to sign the bill, which is called a **pocket veto**. To become law, the bill then has only one path: to be reintroduced in the next session of Congress and put through the process all over again.

The Budgetary Function

Since the writing of the Constitution, Congress has enjoyed significant authority over the budgetary process. For much of American history, however, congressional budgets were piecemeal and made without an eye toward setting the course of public policy. By the 1920s, as a result of growing federal regulation and the bureaucracy, many policy makers sensed a need for greater centralization and order in the budgetary process. Thus, Congress passed the Budget and Accounting Act of 1921. This legislation required the president—for the first time—to submit a budget to Congress. To aid the executive branch in this role, the act also created the Bureau of the Budget. In 1970, the name of this agency was changed to the Office of Management and Budget.

This process continued relatively unfettered until the early 1970s, when tension between a Democratic-controlled Congress and a Republican president, **Richard M. Nixon**, exposed several shortcomings in the system. For example, although Congress authorized the expenditure of funds for many social problems, President Nixon refused to spend appropriated money for them. Angered and frustrated by Nixon's flagrant use of executive power, Congress solidified its role in the budgetary process by passing the Congressional Budget Act of 1974.

Richard M. Nixon
The thirty-seventh president, a Republican, who served from 1969 through 1974. Nixon advocated détente during the Cold War and resigned rather than face impeachment and likely removal from office due to the Watergate scandal.

CONGRESSIONAL BUDGET ACT OF 1974   The Congressional Budget Act of 1974 established the congressional budgetary process in use today. The act also created the Congressional Budget Office (CBO), a nonpartisan agency to help members make accurate estimations of revenues and expenditures and to lay out a plan for congressional action on the annual budget resolution, appropriations, reconciliation, and any other revenue bills. In general, these bills and resolutions establish levels of spending for the federal government and its agencies during the next fiscal year. (The federal government's fiscal year runs from October 1 of one year to September 30 of the next.) Although these levels rarely change dramatically from year to year, the programs and policies that receive increases and decreases in federal spending make a powerful statement about the goals of Congress and the president.

One special process detailed by the Congressional Budget Act of 1974 is reconciliation. The reconciliation procedure allows consideration of controversial issues affecting the budget by limiting debate to twenty hours, thereby ending the threat of a filibuster in the Senate. This process received a great deal of attention in 2010, when members of Congress used it to pass the health care reform bill.

The Congressional Budget Act of 1974 also includes a timetable intended to make sure that action on the budget occurs without unnecessary delay (see Table 6.6). Under this constraint, Congress must complete initial action on the budget resolution by

TABLE 6.6   WHAT IS THE TIMELINE FOR THE CONGRESSIONAL BUDGETARY PROCESS?

Date	Action
First Monday in February	**President submits budget to Congress**—President's budget is prepared by the Office of Management and Budget; includes requested levels of spending for the next fiscal year.
February 15	**Budget outlooks**—Congressional Budget Office submits economic projections to the House and Senate Budget Committees.
April 15	**Budget resolution**—Congress must complete action on the initial version of a budget resolution.
May 15	**Appropriation begins**—House begins to consider appropriations bills.
June 10	**Appropriations Committee**—House Appropriations Committee should conclude consideration of appropriations issues.
June 15	**Reconciliation ends**—Full House should conclude consideration of all appropriations bills.
October 1	**Fiscal year begins**—Government's fiscal year runs from October 1 to September 30.

April 15 of the preceding fiscal year. The budget resolution—or one or more continuing resolutions allowing the government to spend money at the same rates as the previous fiscal year—must receive approval by the start of the new fiscal year on October 1. When this does not occur, the federal government may shut down.

pork

Legislation that allows representatives to bring money and jobs to their districts in the form of public works programs, military bases, or other programs.

PORK AND PROGRAMMATIC REQUESTS Representatives often seek to win appropriations known as **pork**, legislation that allows representatives to bring money and jobs to their districts in the form of public works programs, military bases, or other programs. Many of these programs, called earmarks or programmatic requests, are funds that an appropriations bill designates for specific projects within a state or congressional district. Legislators who bring jobs and new public works programs back to their districts are hard to defeat when up for reelection. But ironically, these programs also attract much of the public criticism directed at the federal government in general and Congress in particular.

The Oversight Function

divided government

The political condition in which different political parties control the presidency and at least one house of Congress.

Historically, Congress has performed its oversight function by holding committee hearings in which members question bureaucrats to determine whether they are enforcing and interpreting the laws as intended by Congress. These hearings, now routinely televised, are among Congress's most visible and dramatic actions, especially in times of **divided government**, that is, when the executive and legislative branches are controlled by different parties. Congress uses hearings not only to gather information but also to focus on particular executive-branch actions. They often signal that Congress believes an agency needs to make changes in policy or performance before it next comes before the committee to justify its budget or actions. Congress also uses hearings to improve program administration. They also can be used for partisan reasons. Usually, congressional committees simply request witnesses to appear. When that fails, subpoenas can be issued, although Trump administration officials routinely ignored these subpoenas and ordered administration officials not to appear before House and Senate committees dealing with an array of issues from impeachment to COVID-19.

Congress may also exercise its oversight powers in a number of other ways. It may, for example, use its powers under the War Powers Resolution or the Congressional Review Act of 1996 to examine actions taken by the president. The Senate also has the authority to offer advice and consent on executive and judicial branch nominees or may refuse to consider them at all. Congress's ultimate oversight power, however, is the power to impeach other federal officials and remove them from office, as the Democratic-controlled House of Representatives did in 2019 when it passed Articles of Impeachment against President Donald J. Trump. The Republican-controlled Senate, not surprisingly, did not find the president's actions worthy of removal from office.

In 2021, the U.S. Capitol was invaded by domestic terrorists as the Congress was voting to certify the election of Joe Biden and Kamala Harris. Many believed that President Trump had stirred up protesters and condoned if not endorsed violence. On January 13, 2021, one Article of Impeachment charging him with "incitement of insurrection" passed on a vote of 232 to 197, making Trump the only president to be impeached twice. He was acquitted by the Senate by a vote of 57 to 43, falling short of the two-thirds vote required to convict.

War Powers Resolution

Passed by Congress in 1973; limits the president in the deployment of troops overseas to a sixty-day period in peacetime (which can be extended for an extra thirty days to permit withdrawal) unless Congress explicitly gives its approval for a longer period.

THE WAR POWERS RESOLUTION In a delayed response to Lyndon B. Johnson's conduct of the Vietnam War, in 1973 Congress passed the **War Powers Resolution** over President Nixon's veto. The resolution permits the president to send troops into action only with the authorization of Congress or if the United States, its territories, or the armed forces are attacked. It also requires the president to notify Congress within forty-eight hours of committing troops to foreign soil. In addition, the president must withdraw troops within sixty days unless Congress votes to declare war. The president also must consult with Congress, if at all possible, prior to committing troops.

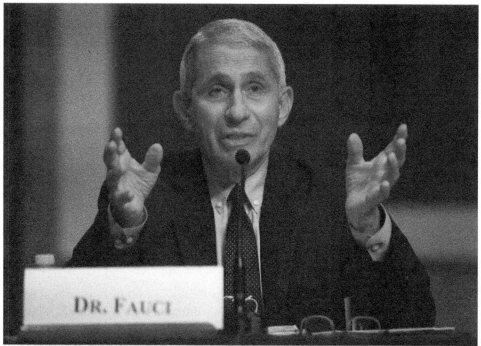

dpa picture alliance/
Alamy Stock Photo

The War Powers Resolution, however, has had limited effectiveness in claiming an oversight role for Congress in international crisis situations. Presidents Gerald R. Ford, Jimmy Carter, and Ronald Reagan never consulted Congress in advance of committing troops, citing the need for secrecy and swift movement, although each president did notify Congress shortly after the deployment of troops abroad. They contended that the War Powers Resolution was probably unconstitutional because it limits presidential prerogatives as commander in chief.

CONGRESSIONAL REVIEW The Congressional Review Act of 1996 allows Congress to exercise its oversight powers by nullifying agency regulations. Under the home rule charter of the District of Columbia, the House and Senate may also nullify actions of the Washington, D.C., City Council. This process is called **congressional review**.[31] If using this oversight power as originally intended, Congress has sixty days after the implementation of an administrative action—or, in the case of the District of Columbia, any laws, resolutions, or ballot measures—to pass a joint resolution of legislative disapproval. The president must also approve the resolution. If the president vetoes the resolution of disapproval, Congress needs a two-thirds majority to override the president's veto. Historically, congressional review was used only twice until President Trump found congressional review to be a way to undo nearly twenty Obama-era regulations.[32]

While in office, President Trump used this once "obscure law" many times. He used congressional review to specifically target environmental protection regulations as well as end a Securities and Exchange Commission rule designed to limit graft in elections. He also used it to loosen rules on the coal industry, allow the mentally ill to purchase guns, lessen the ability of the federal government to preserve lands for national parks, and repeal a mandate that required states to fund Planned Parenthood. In 2018, the Senate used it to get rid of Consumer Financial Protection Bureau rules related to ending racial discrimination in the financing of cars. Democrats tried to use congressional review to block the administration's efforts to end net neutrality, but failed—paving the way for Internet providers to employ content discrimination and enabling them to change the type of services offered preferentially to their advertisers, for example. Thus, the Internet will no longer be treated as a public utility, leaving carriers free of most government regulation.

CONFIRMATION OF PRESIDENTIAL APPOINTEES The Senate plays a special oversight function through its ability to confirm key members of the executive branch

congressional review

A process whereby Congress can nullify agency regulations within a sixty-day window by passing a joint resolution of legislative disapproval. The president's approval of the resolution or a two-thirds majority vote in both houses to overrule a presidential veto is also required.

senatorial courtesy
A process by which presidents generally allow senators from the state in which a judicial vacancy occurs to block a nomination by simply registering their objection.

as well as presidential nominations to the federal courts. Although the Senate generally confirms most presidential nominees, it does not always do so. A wise president considers senatorial reaction before nominating potentially controversial individuals to his administration or to the federal courts.

In the case of federal district court appointments, senators often have considerable say in the nomination of judges from their states through **senatorial courtesy**, a process by which presidents generally defer to the senators who represent the state where the vacancy occurs. Through the "blue slip" process, senators may submit a favorable or unfavorable review of a nominee; they may also choose not to comment. Despite this procedure, the judicial nominees of recent presidents have encountered particularly hostile Senates. "Appointments have always been the battleground for policy disputes," says one political scientist. But now, "what's new is the rawness of it—all of the veneer is off."[33] Senate Majority Leader Mitch McConnell's refusal to hold hearings or vote on President Barack Obama's Supreme Court nominee Merrick Garland, who was tapped to replace Justice Antonin Scalia after Scalia's death in office on February 13, 2016, is an obvious illustration of this approach.

IMPEACHMENT The impeachment process is Congress's ultimate oversight of the U.S. president and federal court judges. The Constitution of the United States is quite vague about the impeachment process, and much debate over it concerns what constitutes an impeachable offense. The Constitution specifies that Congress can impeach a president for treason, bribery, or other "high crimes and misdemeanors." Most commentators agree that the Framers intended this phrase to mean significant abuses of power.

House and Senate rules control how the impeachment process operates. Yet because Congress uses the process so rarely, and under such disparate circumstances, few hard and fast rules exist. The U.S. House of Representatives has voted to impeach only seventeen federal officials. Of those, seven were convicted and removed from office, and three resigned before the process was completed.

Although resolutions against only five presidents have resulted in further action, two of the last four presidents were impeached by the House: (1) Bill Clinton, who was charged with perjury and obstruction of justice in 1998; and, (2) Donald J. Trump, who was charged with abuse of power and obstruction of Congress in its investigation of the president's conduct regarding Ukraine. The other three were: (3) John Tyler, charged with corruption and misconduct in 1843; (4) Andrew Johnson, charged with serious misconduct in 1868; and (5) Richard M. Nixon, charged with obstruction of justice and abuse of power in 1974. The House rejected the charges against Tyler; the Senate acquitted Johnson by a one-vote margin; Nixon resigned before the full House voted on several articles of impeachment; and the Senate acquitted Clinton by a vote of 55–45 after the House voted for impeachment. President Trump's trial in the Republican-controlled Senate netted only one Republican vote for impeachment—Mitt Romney of Utah.

HOW DO MEMBERS OF CONGRESS MAKE DECISIONS?

6.6 Describe the factors that influence how members of Congress make decisions.

Members of Congress consider a number of factors when deciding how to vote on a piece of legislation. Among these are political parties; constituents; colleagues and caucuses; interest groups, lobbyists and political action committees; and staff and support agencies.

Political Parties

Political parties exercise considerable influence on members' votes. Congressional party unity is a measure of the solidarity of the members of a political party. In 2017, 76 percent of the total House votes were cast on party lines. This fell to 59 percent in 2018. The Senate experienced even more dramatic declines.[34] In 2019, however,

Speaker Nancy Pelosi ruled her party with an iron fist, recording the highest party unity score—95 percent—since 1956.[35] In the Senate, majority leader Mitch McConnell (R–KY) enjoyed similar unity. Senate Democrats, under the leadership of Majority Leader Chuck Schumer (D–NY), are expected to do the same. Members of both the Democratic and Republican parties in the House and Senate vote together on approximately 90 percent of all legislation considered by those bodies.

The incentives for members to vote with their party also rarely have been higher—or more creative. In addition to lending members campaign support through party organizations or member-to-member political action committees (PACs), leadership in both houses may also offer committee assignments or chairs as rewards to members who toe the party line.

The president may also act as chief of the party and attempt to coerce members to support his legislative package. This is particularly true in times of **unified government**, when the presidency and Congress are controlled by members of the same party and share a similar policy agenda. Divided government, however, often helps the party that controls Congress, to the frustration of presidents or the opposition party.

unified government

The political condition in which the same political party controls the presidency and Congress.

Constituents

When they are voting, members of Congress always have in mind their constituents—the people who live and vote in a representative's home district or state. Studies by political scientists show that members vote in conformity with prevailing opinion in their districts about two-thirds of the time. On average, Congress passes laws that reflect national public opinion at about the same rate.[36] It is rare for a legislator to vote against the wishes of his or her constituents regularly, particularly on issues of social welfare, domestic policy, or other highly publicized issues.

Gauging how voters regard any particular issue often is not easy. Because it is virtually impossible to know how the people back home feel on all matters, a representative's perception of his or her constituents' preferences is important. In 2017, House members in particular found themselves in new territory with their constituents. Traditionally respectful town hall meetings became loud and raucous over issues such as a member's support for (or opposition to) Obamacare, funding of Planned Parenthood, and dramatic decreases in funding for the arts, sciences, and studies of climate change. Even before COVID-19, many members refused to hold town meetings or see their constituents in venues other than small, monitored meetings, and the quarantines required to combat the novel coronavirus ended them all. Abortion is an issue about which many voters feel passionate, but a legislator whose district has roughly equal numbers of pro-choice and pro-life advocates can satisfy only a portion of his or her constituents.

In short, legislators tend to act on their own preferences as trustees when dealing with topics that have come through the committees on which they serve or with issues they know about as a result of experience in other contexts, such as their vocation.

HOW DO MEMBERS OF CONGRESS LEARN ABOUT THEIR CONSTITUENTS' OPINIONS ON POLITICAL ISSUES?

Members and their staffs spend a substantial portion of their time meeting with constituents in Washington, D.C., and in their home district offices. Here, Representative Tom MacArthur (R–NJ), who played a key role in helping the GOP-led House pass an Affordable Care Act replacement bill, faced angry voters at a town meeting in Willingboro, NJ. Failure to remain in touch with their constituents at home may decrease a member's likelihood of winning another term in Congress. MacArthur was defeated in 2018 by Democratic Asian-American Andy Kim in a tight race.

Tom Gralish/The Philadelphia Inquirer via AP

On items of little concern in their district or when they have limited firsthand knowl-edge, legislators tend to turn to other sources for voting cues. But members are always keenly aware of the consequences of voting against their constituents' views on "wedge issues"—topics such as insurance coverage for contraceptives, medical coverage for pre-existing conditions, immigration, and moving jobs abroad—that tend to divide voters.

Colleagues and Caucuses

logrolling
Vote trading; voting to support a col-league's bill in return for a promise of future support.

The range and complexity of issues confronting Congress means that no one can be up to speed on more than a few topics. When members must vote on bills concerning issues about which they know very little, they often turn for advice to colleagues who have served on the committee that handled the legislation. On issues that are of little interest to a legislator, **logrolling**, or vote trading, often occurs. Logrolling often takes place on specialized bills targeting money or projects to selected congressional dis-tricts. An unaffected member may exchange a yea vote now for the promise of a future yea vote on a similar piece of specialized legislation.

Members may also look to other representatives who share common interests. Special-interest caucuses created around issues, home states, regions, congressional class, or other commonalities facilitate this communication. Although all caucuses are informal in nature, some, such as the Black and Hispanic Caucuses, are far more organized than others. The House Congressional Caucus for Women's Issues, for example, has formal elections of its Republican and Democratic co-chairs and vice chairs, its members provide staff to work on issues of common concern to caucus members, and staffers meet regu-larly to facilitate support for legislation of interest to women. As the number of Repub-lican women in the House has spiked in 2021, as did the number of Black Democratic women, the Caucus may find it harder to work together across party lines.

Interest Groups, Lobbyists, and Political Action Committees

A primary function of most lobbyists, whether they work for interest groups, trade associations, or large corporations, is to provide information to supportive or poten-tially supportive legislators, committees, and their staffs. It is likely, for example, that a representative knows the National Rifle Association's (NRA) position on gun control legislation. What the legislator needs from the NRA is information and substantial research on the feasibility and impact of such legislation. How could the states imple-ment such legislation? Is it constitutional? Will it really have an impact on violent crime or crime in schools? Organized interests can persuade undecided legislators or confirm the support of their friends by providing information that legislators use to justify the position they have embraced. They also can supply direct campaign contri-butions, volunteers, and publicity to members seeking reelection.

The high cost of campaigning has made members of Congress, especially those without huge personal fortunes, attentive to those who help pay the tab for such expenses. Political action committees (PACs) organized by interest groups are an important source of most members' campaign funding. When an issue arises that is of little consequence to a member's constituents, that member, not surprisingly, tends to support the positions of those interests who helped pay for their last campaign. After all, who wants to bite the hand that feeds them?

Interest groups also use grassroots appeals to pressure legislators by urging their members in a particular state or district to call, write, fax, e-mail, text, or tweet their sen-ators or representatives. Lobbyists cannot vote, but constituents back home can and do.

Staff and Support Agencies

Members of Congress rely heavily on their staffs for information on pending legisla-tion.[37] House members have an average of fifteen staffers; senators, an average of thirty-five. Staff is divided between D.C. and district offices. When a bill is nonideological or one on which the member has no real position, staff members can be very influential. In many offices, they are the greatest influence on their boss's votes, and lobbyists are just as likely to contact key staffers as they are members. Congressional committees and sub-committees also have their own dedicated staff to assist committee members.

Additional help for members comes from support personnel at the Congressional Research Service (CRS) at the Library of Congress, the Government Accountability Office (GAO), and the Congressional Budget Office (CBO).

Created in 1914, the CRS is administered by the Library of Congress. It responds to thousands of congressional requests for information each year and thousands more from members of the public. Its staff conducts nonpartisan studies of public issues, as well as major research projects for committees at the request of members. The CRS also prepares summaries and tracks the progress of all bills introduced.

The GAO was established in 1921 as an independent regulatory agency for the purpose of auditing the financial expenditures of the executive branch and federal agencies. The GAO performs four additional functions: It sets government standards for accounting, it provides legal opinions, it settles claims against the government, and it conducts studies upon congressional request.

The CBO was created in 1974 to evaluate the economic effect of different spending programs and to provide information on the cost of proposed policies. It is responsible for analyzing the president's budget and economic projections. The CBO provides Congress and individual members with a valuable second opinion to use in budget debates.

POLITICAL REFORM AND REALITIES: HOW IS INSTITUTIONAL POWER BALANCED?

6.7 Evaluate the strategic interactions between Congress, the president, the courts, and the people.

The Framers envisioned that the Congress, the president, and the judiciary would have discrete powers, and that one branch would be able to hold the others in check. These checks and balances would also allow citizens to influence their government but temper the will of the people. Especially since the 1930s, the president often has held the upper hand in institutional power. In times of crisis or simply when it was unable to meet public demands for solutions, Congress has willingly handed over its authority to the chief executive. Even though the inherent powers of the chief executive give the president greater latitude, Congress does, of course, retain ultimate legislative authority to question executive actions and to halt administration activities by cutting off funds for programs a president wants. Similar checks and balances affect relations between Congress and the courts.

Congress and the Executive

The balance of power between Congress and the president has fluctuated over time. The post–Civil War Congress tried to regain control of the vast executive powers that the recently slain President Abraham Lincoln had assumed. Angered at the refusal of Lincoln's successor, Andrew Johnson, to go along with its radical Reconstruction of the South, Congress passed the Tenure of Office Act, which prevented the president, under threat of civil penalty, from removing any Cabinet-level appointees of the previous administration. Johnson accepted the challenge and fired Lincoln's secretary of war, who many believed was guilty of heinous war crimes. The House voted to impeach Johnson, but the desertion of a handful of Republican senators prevented him from being removed from office. (The effort fell short by one vote.) Nonetheless, this attempt to remove the president greatly weakened his power, and Congress again became the center of power and authority in the federal government.

Beginning in the early 1900s, however, a series of strong presidents acted at the expense of congressional power. Theodore Roosevelt, Franklin D. Roosevelt, and Lyndon B. Johnson viewed the presidency as carrying with it enormous powers.

Especially since the presidency of Franklin D. Roosevelt, Congress has ceded to the president a major role in the legislative process.

President Donald J. Trump took on a major role in the policy process, often ignoring the Democrats in the House and Senate. His refusal to allow members of his administration or executive branch to testify before Congress stymied congressional efforts to fully investigate charges of Russian interference in the 2016 presidential election as well as learn more about the executive branch actions concerning COVID-19, thereby denying Congress's oversight of the executive branch.

Congress and the Judiciary

As part of our system of checks and balances, the power of judicial review gives the Supreme Court of the United States the ability to review the constitutionality of acts of Congress. Historically, the Court has used this power very carefully. From 1787 to 2020, the Supreme Court struck down only 236 federal laws.

Congress also interacts with the judiciary in a number of other ways. It is ultimately up to Congress to determine the number of judges on each court, as well as the boundaries of judicial districts and circuits. Congress also sets the jurisdiction of the federal courts. During recent Congresses, for example, several members, unhappy with Supreme Court actions on abortion and LGBTQ rights, pushed for a bill to prevent federal courts from hearing challenges related to these civil liberties issues. When Congress threatens the Court's jurisdiction, it is signaling its belief that federal judges have gone too far. In 2019 and 2020, then Majority Leader McConnell largely devoted Senate time to filling every vacancy on the federal bench before President Trump left office.

Congress and the People

Congress, especially the House, is often considered the people's branch of government. Nevertheless, since 1990, but for an uptick in the public's approval of Congress in 1997 with 56 percent approving of the job Congress was doing, it has been on a decline. From 2000, approval of Congress has been on a relatively sharp decline, hovering in the 15 to 17 percent approval range in the last decade. Interestingly, most polls people approve of *their* member of Congress (as stated by nearly half of the respondents to a Gallup poll in 2020), just not the body as a whole.

On January 6, 2021, the nation collectively gasped as protestors stormed the Capitol, killing at least five and injuring hundreds more including nearly sixty police officers from the District of Columbia. Earlier that morning, supporters of President Trump heard him speak to the masses who had come to D.C. to try to prevent both chambers of Congress from counting state—and also several judicially-certified—Electoral

FIGURE 6.6 WHAT DO AMERICANS THINK ABOUT CONGRESS?

This graph shows the American public's views on Congress as an institution from October 1990 to August 2020, when it dropped to 17 percent favorable. Approval of Congress has been below 50 percent since late August 2000 and below 20 percent since August 2010.

SOURCE: "Congressional Approval," The Gallup Organization, https://news.gallup.com/poll/1600/congress-public.aspx

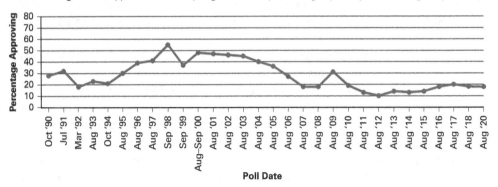

College votes. His son Donald Jr. and his lawyer, former New York City Mayor Rudy Giuliani, appeared to stoke the huge crowd who believed they needed to "Stop the Steal" as the president had been proclaiming that he actually won the election by millions of votes and that victory was stolen from him. The president even urged Vice President Mike Pence, who was to preside over the proceedings in Congress that afternoon, to somehow stop the certification process. Pence's announcement that he would not do so ultimately led some Trump supporters to hang a noose outside of the nation's Capitol and to chant "Hang Mike Pence." When it began to look as if the chamber might not be secure, mobs began to penetrate the poorly secured Capitol from numerous entrances. Pence, Speaker of House Nancy Pelosi, and Senate Pro Tem Chuck Grassley (R–IO), those next in line to the presidency, were rushed out of the chamber, and other members hid or fled.

Most Americans watched in horror as the events occurred in real time. Undaunted, the Congress went back into session, staying well into the middle of the night to certify the election of Joe Biden and Kamala Harris, both of whom served in the Senate with many of those who found themselves running for safety. Both Democratic and Republican leaders called for the resumption of the certification process to assure the people that democracy and order had prevailed in Congress. And, a week later, in a bipartisan effort, the House of Representatives voted to impeach President Trump for his role in the armed insurrection, making this the first time a departed president was impeached.

CONCLUSION AND REVIEW

What Are the Roots and Structure of the U.S. Congress?

6.1 Describe the roots of the Constitution.

The Constitution created a bicameral legislature with members of each body to be elected differently and thus to represent different constituencies. Article I of the Constitution sets forth qualifications for office, states age minimums, and specifies how legislators are to be distributed among the states. In addition, the Constitution also provides a vast array of enumerated and implied powers to Congress. Both houses of Congress share some, such as law-making and oversight, but not others, such as confirmation of presidential appointees.

How Do Members of Congress Represent the American People?

6.2 Analyze the workday of members of Congress.

Congress is the representative branch of the American national government. Representation can be measured in several ways. In general, members of Congress are better educated, richer, more likely to be male, more likely to be White, and more likely to be religious than the general population. How well members represent their constituents' beliefs also varies with how they view their representational role—as trustees, delegates, or politicos.

How Do Members Stay in Congress?

6.3 Describe how incumbency and redistricting help members of Congress to stay in office.

Members of Congress are elected by their constituents to two-year terms in the House of Representatives and to six-year terms in the Senate. Once elected, incumbency is a powerful advantage. Redistricting may also affect a member's ability to stay in Congress.

How Is Congress Organized?

6.4 Assess the roles of leaders, political parties, and committees in Congress.

Political parties play a major role in the way Congress is organized. The Speaker of the House is traditionally a member of the majority party, and the parties also control other leadership roles such as majority and minority leaders and whips. In addition to the party leaders, Congress has a labyrinth of committees and subcommittees that cover the entire range of government policies. In these environments, many policies take shape and members make their primary contributions to solving public problems.

What Are the Powers of Congress?

6.5 Describe the powers of Congress.

The three most significant powers of Congress are its law-making, budgetary, and oversight functions. The road to enacting a bill into law is long and strewn with obstacles, and only a small share of the proposals introduced become law. The Congressional Budget Act of 1974 solidified Congress's role in the budgetary process. Congress conducts oversight in a number of ways, including through hearings. Congress also offers advice and consent on executive and judicial branch nominees and has the power to impeach federal officials and remove them from office.

How Do Members of Congress Make Decisions?

6.6 Describe the factors that influence how members of Congress make decisions.

A number of factors, including political party; constituents; colleagues and caucuses; staff and support agencies; and interest groups, lobbyists, and political action committees, may influence a member's decisions. In modern Congresses, political party is a particularly influential factor.

Political Reform and Realities: How Is Institutional Power Balanced?

6.7 Evaluate the strategic interactions between Congress, the president, the courts, and the people.

The balance of power between Congress and the executive branch has fluctuated tremendously over time. Congress was most powerful in the early years of U.S. history, but since the New Deal, the president has played an important role in proposing legislation and spending. An ongoing power struggle also characterizes legislative–judicial relations. Although the judiciary can declare acts of Congress unconstitutional, Congress also exercises control over the judiciary in a variety of ways. The people also hold an important check on all political institutions.

LEARN THE TERMS

apportionment
Baker v. *Carr* (1962)
bicameral legislature
bill
cloture
conference committee
congressional review
delegate
discharge petition
divided government

filibuster
gerrymandering
impeachment
incumbency
joint committee
logrolling
pocket veto
politico
pork
redistricting

select (or special) committee
senatorial courtesy
seniority
Shaw v. *Reno* (1993)
Speaker of the House
standing committee
trustee
unified government
veto
War Powers Resolution

LEARN THE NAMES

Edmund Burke
Nancy Pelosi
Richard M. Nixon

Dennis Brack Photography

WHY ARE PRESIDENTIAL FUNERALS OCCASIONS FOR NATIONAL MOURNING?
Presidents are leaders who unite the American public—in life and in death. Former presidents and vice presidents and their spouses attend the funeral service for President Ronald Reagan in the National Cathedral in Washington, D.C., prior to his interment in California. In attendance (left to right) are Presidents George H. W. Bush with wife Barbara, Jimmy Carter (Roslyn), Gerald Ford (Betty), and Bill Clinton (Hillary). These are times when partisan differences are put aside.

CRITICAL THINKING QUESTION: *How did the Trump presidency differ from others?*

THE PRESIDENCY

LEARNING OBJECTIVES

7.1 Describe the constitutional provisions that provide the roots of the American presidency.

7.2 Identify the roles and responsibilities of the president under the Constitution.

7.3 Trace the expansion of presidential power.

7.4 Describe the organization and functions of the Executive Office of the President.

7.5 Analyze how presidents have led over time.

7.6 Describe the role that public opinion plays in presidential effectiveness.

7.7 Describe the relationship between Congress and the president and the tools available for the president to make policy.

When Ronald Reagan died on June 5, 2004, many Americans, first in California and then in Washington, D.C., lined up for hours to pay their respects to the man who had been the fortieth president of the United States. Many people could see, for the first time in recent memory, the grandeur of a presidential state funeral. The first president to lie in state in the Rotunda of the Capitol since Lyndon B. Johnson died in January 1973, Reagan was one of only nine American presidents to receive that honor. Presidential funerals underscore the esteem that most Americans accord the office of the president, regardless of its occupant. Just before the first president, George Washington, died, he made it known that he wanted his burial to be a quiet one, "without parade or funeral oration." He also requested a three-day delay of his burial—a common request at the time because of the fear of being buried alive. Despite these requests, Washington's funeral was a state occasion as hundreds of soldiers, with their rifles held backward, marched to Mount Vernon, Virginia, where he was interred. Across the nation, imitation funerals took place, and the military wore black armbands for six months.[1] When President Abraham Lincoln was assassinated in 1865, his funeral became a nationwide event. He lay in state in the East Room of the White House, where more than 25,000 mourners came to pay their respects. Black cloth draped the room, and two dozen Union soldiers formed an honor guard. Following the funeral, a parade to the Capitol was held in Washington, D.C. Thousands of free Black Americans escorted Lincoln to the Rotunda, where he lay in state for another day. The body of the deceased president then embarked on a national train tour to his burial site in Springfield, Illinois, allowing Americans across the country an opportunity to grieve.

Today, one of the first things a president does upon leaving office is to consider funeral plans. The military has a 138-page book devoted to the kind of ceremony and traditions so evident in the Reagan funeral: a horse-drawn caisson, a riderless horse with boots hung backward in the stirrups to indicate that the deceased will ride no more, a twenty-one-gun salute, and a flyover by military aircraft. Each president's family, however, has personalized their private, yet also public, opportunity to mourn. The Reagan family, for example, filed a 300-page plan for the funeral in 1989 and updated it regularly. President Gerald R. Ford filed a plan that was implemented after his death in 2006. So did George H. W. Bush before his death. President Jimmy Carter also filed formal plans. Bill Clinton and George W. Bush have filed preliminary plans, as have Presidents Barack Obama and Donald J. Trump.

The Reagan funeral also created a national timeout from the news of war, and even presidential campaigns halted in respect for the deceased president. One historian commented that the event gave Americans the opportunity to "rediscover . . . what holds us together instead of what pulls us apart."[2] This is often the role of presidents—in life or in death.

• • •

The authority granted to the **president** by the Constitution of the United States and through subsequent congressional legislation makes it a position with awesome power and responsibility. Not only did the Framers not envision such a powerful role for the president, but they also could not have foreseen the skepticism with which the modern media greet many presidential actions. The modern media, used by successful presidents to help advance their agendas, have brought us closer to our presidents and made them seem more human, a mixed blessing for those trying to lead. Only two photographs exist of President Franklin D. Roosevelt in a wheelchair, his paralysis kept a closely guarded secret. Seven decades later, unsuccessful Republican presidential candidate Mitt Romney was asked on national TV what he wore to bed.

Public opinion and confidence greatly affect a president's ability to get programs adopted and implemented. As one political scientist has noted, the president's power often rests on the power to persuade.[3] To persuade, a president must have the capacity to forge links with members of Congress as well as gain the support of the American

president
The chief executive officer of the United States, as established by Article II of the Constitution of the United States.

people and the respect of foreign leaders. The tension between public expectations about the presidency and the formal powers of the president permeates our discussion of how the office has evolved from its humble origins in Article II of the Constitution to its current stature. Much of this conventional wisdom has been turned on its head as President Donald J. Trump adopted a unique approach to foreign policy, often criticizing our allies while praising traditional foes, including Vladimir Putin of Russia and Kim Jong-un of North Korea. He also used tweets to connect directly with the public, sometimes even announcing major policy initiatives and staff firings, as well as often criticizing the media for reporting what he termed "fake news."

WHAT ARE THE ROOTS OF THE OFFICE OF PRESIDENT OF THE UNITED STATES?

7.1 Describe the constitutional provisions that provide the roots of the American presidency.

The earliest example of executive power in the colonies was the position of royal governor. The king of England appointed a royal governor to each British colony and normally entrusted them with the "powers of appointment, military command, expenditure, and—within limitations—pardon, as well as with large powers in connection with the powers of law making."[4] Royal governors often found themselves at odds with the colonists and especially with elected colonial legislatures. The people, many of whom had fled from Europe to escape royal domination, distrusted and disdained the governors as representatives of the British Crown. Other colonists, generations removed from England, no longer felt strong ties to the king and his power over them.

When the colonists declared their independence from Great Britain in 1776, their distrust of a strong chief executive remained. Most state constitutions reduced the once-powerful office of governor to a symbolic post elected annually by the legislature. However, some states did entrust wider powers to their chief executives. In New York, the people directly elected the governor. Perhaps because the people could then hold him accountable, they gave him the power to pardon, the duty to faithfully execute the laws, and the power to act as commander in chief of the state militia.

Under the Articles of Confederation, no executive branch of government existed; the eighteen different men who served as the president of the Continental Congress of the United States of America were president in name only—they held no actual authority or power in the new nation. When the delegates to the Constitutional Convention met in Philadelphia to fashion a new government, the need for an executive branch to implement the laws made by Congress created little dissent. Although some delegates suggested that multiple executives would be preferable, the Framers eventually agreed that executive authority should be vested in one person. This agreement was relatively easy because the Framers felt certain that George Washington—whom they had trusted with their lives during the Revolutionary War—would become the first president of the new nation.

The Framers also concurred on a title for the new office. Borrowing from the title used at several American colleges and universities, the Framers called the new chief executive "the president." And Article II of the Constitution says that "The executive Power shall be vested in a President of the United States of America." Also in Article I, section 1, is what is known as the Emoluments Clause. The purpose of this was to make certain that the president could not receive gifts or money from any "King, Prince, or foreign State." In 2017, the attorneys general of the District of Columbia and Maryland brought suit in federal court, arguing that President Trump's expansive real estate holdings, including hotels, golf courses, and private clubs, provided opportunities for foreign governments to spend money that directly benefitted the president. They argued, in particular, that the president's interest in D.C.'s Trump International Hotel was illegal under the Emoluments Clause. The meaning of the clause has never been before the Supreme Court, and Justice Department lawyers on behalf of the president argued that unless there is money paid with an expectation of some favor, foreign payments to the hotel are legal. In addition to this lawsuit, 200 Democrats in Congress went to court to force the president to obtain congressional approval before accepting any emoluments. These are just two of the cases in federal court. The appeal by the members of Congress was rejected by the U.S. Supreme Court in October 2020.[5]

How the president was to be chosen and by whom created a major stumbling block. James Wilson of Philadelphia suggested that the people should elect the president, who should remain "independent of the legislature." Wilson also suggested giving the executive an absolute veto over the acts of Congress. "Without such a defense," he wrote, "the legislature can at any moment sink it [the executive] into non-existence."[6]

The manner of the president's election troubled the Framers for some time. Their solution to the dilemma was the creation of the Electoral College. We leave the resolution of that issue aside for now and turn instead to details of the issues the Framers resolved quickly.

Presidential Qualifications and Terms of Office

The Constitution requires the president (and the **vice president**, whose major function is to succeed the president in the event of his death or disability) to be a natural-born citizen of the United States, at least thirty-five years old, and a resident of the United States for fourteen years or longer. In the 1700s, those engaged in international diplomacy often traveled out of the country for substantial periods of time, and the Framers wanted to make sure that prospective presidents spent significant time on this country's shores before running for its highest elective office.

Although three of the last six presidents failed to win a second term, at one time the length of a president's term created controversy. Various delegates to the Constitutional Convention suggested four-, seven-, and eleven-year terms with no eligibility for reelection. The Framers ultimately reached agreement on a four-year term with eligibility for reelection.

The first president, George Washington (1789–1797), sought reelection only once, and a two-term limit for presidents became traditional. Although Ulysses S. Grant unsuccessfully sought a third term, the two terms established by Washington remained the standard for 150 years, avoiding the Framers' much-feared "constitutional monarch," a perpetually reelected tyrant. In the 1930s and 1940s, however, Franklin D.

vice president

The position of chief executive officer created by Article II of the Constitution of the United States to preside over the U.S. Senate and to fill any vacancy in the office of president due to death, resignation, removal, or (since 1967) disability.

HOW FREQUENTLY DO FORMER PRESIDENTS MEET?

Presidents rarely meet, but generally do so at funerals or the openings of their presidential libraries. Here, four former presidents—George W. Bush, Bill Clinton, George H. W. Bush, and Jimmy Carter—join Barack Obama at the dedication of the George W. Bush Presidential Library on the campus of Southern Methodist University in Dallas, Texas.

Charles Dharapak/AP Images

Roosevelt ran successfully in four elections as Americans fought first the Great Depression and then World War II. Despite Roosevelt's popularity, negative reaction to his long tenure in office led to passage (and ratification in 1951) of the **Twenty-Second Amendment**. It limits presidents to two four-year terms. A vice president who succeeds a president due to death, resignation, or impeachment is eligible to serve a maximum of ten years in office: two years of a president's remaining term and two elected terms or more than two years of a president's term followed by one elected term.

The Framers paid little attention to the office of vice president beyond the need to have an immediate official stand-in for the president. Initially, for example, the vice president's only function was to assume the office of president in the case of the president's death or some other emergency. After further debate, the delegates made the vice president the presiding officer of the Senate (except in cases of presidential impeachment). The delegates gave the vice president authority to vote in that body only in the event of a tie, which happens very rarely. Still, Vice President Mike Pence was called on thirteen times to break a senatorial tie vote. And Vice President Kamala Harris cast three tie-breaking Senate votes during her first two months in office.

During the Constitutional Convention, Benjamin Franklin staunchly supported inclusion of a provision allowing for impeachment, the first step in a formal process to remove a specified official from office. Each house of Congress was given a role in the impeachment process to ensure that the chief executive could be removed only for "Treason, Bribery, or other high Crimes and Misdemeanors." The Framers empowered the House to impeach the president by a simple majority vote. The Senate then acts as a court of law and tries the president for the charged offenses, with the chief justice of the U.S. Supreme Court presiding. A two-thirds majority vote in the Senate on any count contained in the articles of impeachment is necessary to remove the president from office. The House of Representatives has impeached only three presidents: Andrew Johnson, Bill Clinton, and Donald J. Trump (twice). The Senate, however, did not vote to remove them from office.

In 1974, President Richard M. Nixon resigned from office rather than face the certainty of impeachment, trial, and removal from office for his role in covering up details about a break-in at the Democratic Party's national headquarters in the Watergate office complex. What came to be known simply as **Watergate**, which began after a White House-sanctioned burglary of the Democratic National Committee and included President Richard M. Nixon's firing of a special prosecutor when he did not like the direction the inquiry was taking, also produced a major decision from the Supreme Court on the scope of what is termed **executive privilege**. In *U.S. v. Nixon* **(1974)**, the Supreme Court ruled unanimously that no overriding executive privilege sanctioned the president's refusal to comply with a court order to produce information for use in the trial of the Watergate defendants. Since then, presidents have varied widely in their claim to executive privilege. President Bill Clinton asserted it several times, especially during the impeachment proceedings against him. President George W. Bush made such claims less frequently, instead often arguing that he and the vice president had what he called "constitutional prerogatives."[7]

Rules of Succession

Through 2021, eight presidents have died in office from illness or assassination. William H. Harrison was the first president to die in office—he caught a cold at his inauguration in 1841 and died one month later. John Tyler thus became the first vice president to succeed to the presidency. In 1865, Abraham Lincoln became the first assassinated president.

Knowing that a system of orderly transfer of power was necessary, the Framers created the office of the vice president. To further clarify presidential succession, in 1947, Congress passed the **Presidential Succession Act**, which lists—in order—those in line to succeed the president (see Table 7.1).

The Succession Act has never been used because a vice president has always been available to take over when a president died in office. To ensure this will continue to be the

TABLE 7.1 WHAT IS THE PRESIDENTIAL LINE OF SUCCESSION?

1. Vice President	10. Secretary of Commerce
2. Speaker of the House	11. Secretary of Labor
3. President Pro Tempore of the Senate	12. Secretary of Health and Human Services
4. Secretary of State	13. Secretary of Housing and Urban Development
5. Secretary of the Treasury	14. Secretary of Transportation
6. Secretary of Defense	15. Secretary of Energy
7. Attorney General	16. Secretary of Education
8. Secretary of the Interior	17. Secretary of Veterans Affairs
9. Secretary of Agriculture	18. Secretary of Homeland Security

case, the **Twenty-Fifth Amendment** became part of the Constitution in 1967 as a response to the assassination of President John F. Kennedy. Should a vacancy occur in the office of the vice president, the Twenty-Fifth Amendment directs the president to appoint a new vice president, subject to the approval (by a simple majority) of both houses of Congress.

The Twenty-Fifth Amendment also contains a section that allows the vice president and a majority of the Cabinet (or some other body determined by Congress) to deem a president unable to fulfill their duties. It sets up a procedure to permit the vice president to become acting president if the president is incapacitated. The president also can voluntarily relinquish his power for a specified and limited period of time, as in the case of undergoing surgery. President Trump did not make the vice president acting president when he was hospitalized for COVID-19.

Twenty-Fifth Amendment
Adopted in 1967; establishes procedures for filling vacancies in the office of president and vice president as well as providing procedures to deal with the disability of a president.

WHAT ARE THE CONSTITUTIONAL POWERS OF THE PRESIDENT?

7.2 Identify the roles and responsibilities of the president under the Constitution.

In contrast to Article I's laundry list of enumerated powers for the Congress, Article II details few specific presidential powers. Perhaps the most important section of Article II is its first sentence: "The executive Power shall be vested in a President of the United States of America." Nonetheless, presidents' combined powers, discussed below, make them major players in the policy process.

The Appointment Power

To help the president enforce laws passed by Congress, the Constitution authorizes him to appoint, with the advice and consent of the Senate, "Ambassadors, other public Ministers and Consuls, judges of the supreme Court, and all other Officers of the United States, whose Appointments are not herein otherwise provided for, and which shall be established by Law." Although this section of the Constitution deals only with appointments, behind that language lies a powerful policy-making tool. The president has the authority to make nearly 3,500 appointments to his administration (of which about 1,125 require Senate confirmation).[8] He also holds the power to remove many of his appointees at will. In addition, he technically appoints all military personnel subject to Senate approval, although often by voice vote. Many of these appointees are in positions to wield substantial authority over the course and direction of public policy. Especially in the context of a president's ability to make appointments to the federal courts, presidential influence can last far past terms in office. President Obama's policy initiatives suffered because so many of his nominations stalled in the Republican-controlled Senate during his last two years in office. In contrast, through 2020, President Donald J. Trump failed to nominate hundreds of individuals to positions requiring Senate confirmation where Republicans presided. Although all his Cabinet-level appointees were confirmed, the president effectively had no bench leaving career civil servants to run their respective departments, agencies and bureaus.

Tim Sloan/AFP/Getty Images

UNDER WHAT CIRCUMSTANCES DOES A PRESIDENT REMOVE AN APPOINTEE?

Presidents have a large number of aides who help them craft policy. These aides are often held accountable for a president's policy-making failures. Here, President George W. Bush, quite literally, shows Secretary of Defense Donald Rumsfeld the door following Republican losses in the 2006 midterm elections. These defeats were at least in part attributable to Rumsfeld's failures in the conduct of wars in Afghanistan and Iraq. President Trump removed a record number of his appointees, some even via Twitter.

President Trump was quick to oust those whom he distrusted. The secretary of state, Rex Tillerson, was fired by tweet, as was James Comey, the director of the Federal Bureau of Investigation. He also announced via Twitter his plans to replace his secretary of veterans affairs, which he did. President Trump faced greater turnover in appointees than any other president. The turnover in just the White House broke all records.[9] In fact, 489 appointees willingly left top spots in his first three years in office.[10] Some, however, were fired.

In the past, when a president forwarded nominations to the Senate for its approval, the Senate traditionally gave his selections great respect—especially those for the **Cabinet**, an advisory group chosen by the president to help him make decisions and execute laws. In fact, until the 1990s, the Senate confirmed the vast majority of all presidential nominations.[11] This is no longer the case, as investigations into nominees' pasts and political wrangling in the Senate can delay the approval of nominees for months. Many appointees end up withdrawing from consideration, as hearings often are not held within 18 months or more of a nomination. On the other hand, the Senate under the leadership of Mitch McConnell (R–KY), strove to confirm all of the president's nominees, especially vacancies on the federal bench.

Delay or rejection of nominees can have a major impact on the course of an administration. Rejections leave a president without first choices, affect a president's relationship with the Senate, and influence how the public perceives the president. The Republican-controlled Senate moved fairly quickly to approve Trump's Cabinet nominees, but the process was slowed because so many of his appointees had complicated financial situations that needed vetting before the Senate could vote. Many subcabinet-level positions remained unfilled through the end of his term.

The Power to Convene Congress

The Constitution requires the president to inform the Congress periodically of "the State of the Union" and authorizes the president to convene either one or both houses of Congress on "extraordinary Occasions." The power to convene Congress had more importance when Congress did not sit in nearly year-round sessions, although it may still be significant in times of national crisis.

The Power to Make Treaties

The president's power to make treaties with foreign nations is checked by the Constitution's stipulation that at least two-thirds of the members of the Senate must approve

Cabinet
The formal body of presidential advisers who head the fifteen executive departments. Presidents often add others to this body of formal advisers.

HOW DO PRESIDENTS REPORT TO CONGRESS ON "THE STATE OF THE UNION"?
Here, President Trump delivers his last State of the Union speech. Directly behind him are Vice President Mike Pence, who presided over the Senate, and the Speaker of the House, Nancy Pelosi.

all treaties. The chief executive can also "receive ambassadors," wording that has been interpreted to allow the president to recognize the existence of other nations.

Historically, the Senate ratifies about 90 percent of the treaties submitted by the president.[12] Perhaps the most notable example of a rejected treaty was the Senate's defeat of the Treaty of Versailles submitted by President Woodrow Wilson in 1919. The treaty was an agreement among the major nations to end World War I. At Wilson's insistence, it also called for the creation of the League of Nations—a precursor of the United Nations—to foster continued peace and international disarmament. In struggling to gain international acceptance for the League, Wilson had taken American support for granted. This was a dramatic miscalculation. Isolationists, led by Senator Henry Cabot Lodge (R–MA), opposed U.S. participation in the League on the grounds that the League would place the United States in the center of every major international conflict. Proponents countered that, League or no League, the United States had emerged from World War I as a world power and that membership in the League of Nations would enhance its new role. The vote in the Senate for ratification was very close, but the isolationists prevailed—the United States stayed out of the League, and Wilson was devastated.

The Senate also may require substantial amendment of a treaty prior to its approval. When President Jimmy Carter proposed the controversial Panama Canal Treaty in 1977 to turn the canal back to Panama, for example, the Senate demanded settlement of several conditions before approving the canal's return. More recently, during Donald J. Trump's 2016 presidential campaign, Trump pledged to pull the United States out of the North American Free Trade Agreement (NAFTA), a 1994 agreement between the United States, Canada, and Mexico. In May 2017, President Trump notified Congress that he planned to renegotiate the agreement that he once labeled the "worst trade deal ever." Trade agreements, like treaties, require a two-thirds vote in the Senate. On January 28, 2020, President Trump fulfilled that promise by signing a new trade deal, now renamed the United States-Mexico-Canada Agreement. It updated NAFTA and contains stronger protection for workers, expanded markets for farmers, and a set of new rules to encourage automakers to return manufacturing to the United States.[13]

When presidents don't think they can obtain Senate approval for deals, they may try to use **executive agreements** to form secret and highly sensitive arrangements with foreign nations without Senate approval. Presidents have used these agreements since the days of George Washington, and the courts have upheld their use. Since 1900, many presidents have favored executive agreements over treaties. But they are not binding on subsequent administrations and can be undone immediately by successors. President Trump was thus able to pull the United States out of the Joint Comprehensive Plan of Action, an agreement made by President Barack Obama regarding loosening sanctions on Iran in return for it delaying its procurement of nuclear weapons. Trump also withdrew the United States from the Paris Agreement, believing that the climate change it sought to curb is fiction. He also withdrew from several other agreements President Obama made with other nations regarding trade and tariffs. His decision to withdraw the nation from the World Health Organization (WHO) during the COVID-19 pandemic was particularly jarring to public health officials worldwide. Scientists criticized the WHO for being too slow to label COVID-19 a global pandemic, and Trump used this criticism to justify withdrawal of financial support from an organization that the U.S. played a major part in creating.[14] These actions underscore just how much power a president has over public policy and international relations, circumstances never envisioned by the Framers. President Joe Biden is expected to lead the U.S. to rejoin the WHO and the Paris Agreement, among others.

executive agreements
Formal international agreements entered into by the president that do not require the advice and consent of the U.S. Senate.

The Veto Power

During the Constitutional Convention, proponents of a strong executive argued that the president should have an absolute and final *veto* over acts of Congress. Opponents of this idea, including Benjamin Franklin, countered that in their home states, the executive veto "was constantly made use of to extort money" from legislators. James Madison, however, argued that an executive veto was necessary to maintain the system of checks and balances.

Thus, the Framers gave the president veto power, but only as a "qualified negative." Although the president has the authority to veto any act of Congress (with the exception of joint resolutions that propose constitutional amendments), the Framers gave Congress the authority to override an executive veto by a two-thirds vote in each house. Congress, however, rarely can muster enough votes to override a veto. A notable exception occurred in late December 2020 when Congress overrode President Trump's veto of a massive defense bill, the National Defense Authorization Act, by a vote of 81–13. The act included pay raises for soldiers and weapons modernization. Of his seven vetos, this was the only one overridden by both houses of Congress.

Even the threat of a presidential veto has become a powerful way for a president to influence law-making. Such a threat often prompts members of Congress to fashion legislation they know will receive presidential acquiescence, if not support.[15] In situations where the Congress and president are of the same party, vetoes are rare.

The Power to Preside over the Military as Commander in Chief

One of the most important executive powers is that over the military. Article II states that the president is "Commander in Chief of the Army and Navy of the United States." While the Constitution specifically grants Congress the authority to declare war, presidents since Abraham Lincoln have used the commander in chief clause in conjunction with the chief executive's duty to "take Care that the Laws be faithfully executed" to wage war (and to broaden various presidential powers).

Modern presidents continually clash with Congress over the ability to declare war. The Vietnam War, in which 58,000 American soldiers were killed and 300,000 were wounded, was conducted (at a cost of $150 billion) without a congressional declaration of war.

During that highly controversial war, Presidents Lyndon B. Johnson and Richard M. Nixon routinely assured members of Congress that victory was near. In 1971, however, publication of what were called *The Pentagon Papers* revealed what many people had suspected all along: the Johnson administration had systematically altered casualty figures and distorted key facts to place the progress of the war in a more positive light. Angered that this misinformation had led Congress to defer to the executive in the conduct of the Vietnam War, in 1973, Congress passed the *War Powers Resolution* to limit the president's authority to introduce American troops into hostile foreign lands without congressional approval. President Nixon vetoed the resolution, but both houses of Congress overrode it by a two-thirds majority.

Presidents since Nixon have continued to insist that the War Powers Resolution is an unconstitutional infringement on their executive power. Still, in 2001, President George W. Bush complied with the resolution when he sought, and both houses of Congress approved, a joint resolution authorizing the use of force against "those responsible for the recent [September 11] attacks launched against the United States." In October 2002, after President Bush declared Iraq to be a "grave threat to peace," the House (296–133) and Senate (77–23) also voted overwhelmingly to allow the president to use force in Iraq "as he determines to be necessary and appropriate," thereby conferring tremendous authority on Bush and future presidents to wage war.

On February 12, 2020, in a surprising show of bipartisanship, both houses of Congress voted to implement the War Powers Resolution (also called the War Powers Act) by requiring that President Trump seek approval of both houses before he ordered the use of force against Iran. Nearly six weeks earlier, without congressional authorization, the president had ordered a targeted drone strike that killed a top Iranian general. It was more symbolic than practical, given that there was no way that the Senate could muster the 60 votes needed to override a presidential veto.

VIEW: PRESIDENTIAL ROLES

HOW HAVE PAST PRESIDENTS FULFILLED THE POWERS OF THE OFFICE?

The president of the United States is asked to wear many hats. A good number of these roles extend from the powers the Framers enumerated in Article II of the Constitution of the United States. Others have evolved out of necessity over time. Examine how presidents (below) have fulfilled these roles.

John Bryson/The LIFE Images Collection/Getty Images

CHIEF LAW ENFORCER:
Troops sent by President Dwight D. Eisenhower enforce a federal court decision ordering the integration of public schools in Little Rock, Arkansas.

Bettmann/Getty Images

LEADER OF THE PARTY:
President Ronald Reagan mobilizes conservatives at the Republican National Convention in 1980, conservatizing the nature of the party.

Charles Dharapak/AP Images

COMANDER IN CHIEF:
President Barack Obama meets with members of the armed forces.

MPI/Archive Photos/Getty Images

SHAPER OF PUBLIC POLICY:
President Richard M. Nixon cheers on the efforts of Apollo 11 astronauts in 1969 as he celebrates U.S. space policy.

Associated Press

KEY PLAYER IN THE LEGISLATIVE PROCESS:
Here, President Lyndon B. Johnson celebrates his signing of the Civil Rights Act of 1964 by giving the Reverend Martin Luther King Jr. a signing pen.

Bettmann/Getty Images

CHIEF OF STATE:
President John F. Kennedy and his wife, Jacqueline, pose for cameras with the president of France and his wife during the Kennedys' widely publicized 1961 trip to that nation, solidifying the friendship of the two nations.

The Pardoning Power

Presidents can exercise a check on judicial power through their constitutional authority to grant reprieves or pardons. A **pardon** is an executive grant releasing an individual from the punishment or legal consequences of a crime before or after conviction, and restores all rights and privileges of citizenship. Presidents exercise complete pardoning power for federal offenses except in cases of impeachment, which cannot be pardoned. President Gerald R. Ford gave the most famous presidential pardon of all to former President Richard M. Nixon—who had not been formally charged with

pardon

An executive grant providing restoration of all rights and privileges of citizenship to a specific individual charged with or convicted of a crime.

any crime—"for any offenses against the United States, which he, Richard Nixon, has committed or may have committed while in office." This unilateral, absolute pardon unleashed a torrent of public criticism against Ford and raised questions about whether Nixon had discussed the pardon with Ford before resigning. Many analysts attribute Ford's defeat in the 1976 election to that pardon.

Even though pardons generally apply to a specific individual, presidents have also used them to offer general amnesties. President Jimmy Carter, for example, incurred the wrath of many veterans groups when he made an offer of unconditional amnesty to approximately 10,000 men who had fled the United States or gone into hiding to avoid the draft for military service in the Vietnam War.

Presidents may also use their pardoning power to make a policy statement. During his presidency, Barack Obama used his clemency power to commute the sentences of hundreds in federal prison for nonviolent drug offenses, sending a clear message to Congress that it ought to vote on legislation to reduce incarceration levels for such offenses. Obama has said of his use of the pardoning power, "I believe that at its heart, America is a nation of second chances, and I believe these folks deserve their second chance."[16]

President Trump's use of pardons was unusual. Unlike Presidents Clinton, Bush, and Obama, who waited to use their pardoning power until after they had been in office more than two years, President Trump used his pardoning power to free conservatives who were charged in high-profile cases. Presidents may also commute prison sentences. After reality television star Kim Kardashian West personally lobbied the president, he commuted the life sentence of an African American woman serving for a first-time drug offense. President Trump also commuted the sentence of long-time ally Roger J. Stone Jr., who was convicted of seven felonies and was scheduled to report to prison to begin a 40-month stint. Trump's accompanying statement called the prosecution a "witch hunt," expressing his anger at Stone's conviction.[17] President Trump has also joked about his pardoning powers with reporters, noting that using the power "gave him a thrill." In his final hours in office, Trump pardoned dozens of people, including both supporters and defendants in criminal cases.

HOW HAS PRESIDENTIAL POWER DEVELOPED AND EXPANDED?

7.3 Trace the expansion of presidential power.

Every president brings to the position not only a vision of America but also expectations about how to use presidential authority. But most presidents find accomplishing their goals much more difficult than they envisioned. As he was leaving office, for example, President Harry S Truman mused about what surprises awaited his successor, Dwight D. Eisenhower, a former general: "He'll sit here and he'll say, 'Do this! Do that!' And nothing will happen. Poor Ike—it won't be a bit like the army. He'll find it very frustrating."[18]

The formal powers enumerated in Article II of the Constitution and the Supreme Court's interpretation of those constitutional provisions limit a president's authority. The times in which the president serves, his confidantes and advisers, and his personality and leadership abilities all affect how he wields these powers. Furthermore, not only do different times call for different kinds of leaders; they also often provide limits or, conversely, wide opportunities for whomever serves as president at the time. Historically, crises, in particular, trigger expansions of presidential power.

Establishing Presidential Authority: The First Presidents

When President George Washington was sworn in on a cold, blustery day in New York City on April 30, 1789, he took over an office and a government yet to be created.

Eventually, the government hired a few hundred postal workers and Washington appointed a small group of Cabinet advisers and clerks. George Washington set several important precedents for future presidents:

- He took every opportunity to establish the primacy of the national government. In 1794, for example, Washington used the militia of four states to put down the Whiskey Rebellion, an uprising of 3,000 western Pennsylvania farmers opposed to a federal excise tax on liquor. To emphasize the significance of the action, Washington, along with Secretary of the Treasury Alexander Hamilton, led the 15,000 troops into battle himself. Washington's action helped establish the idea of federal supremacy and the authority of the executive branch to collect taxes levied by Congress.

- He began the practice of regular meetings with his advisers, thus establishing the Cabinet system.

- He asserted the chief executive's prominent role in the conduct of foreign affairs. He sent envoys to negotiate the Jay Treaty to end continued hostilities with Great Britain. Then, over senatorial objection, he continued to wield his authority first to negotiate treaties and then simply to submit them to the Senate for approval. Washington made it clear that the Senate's function was limited to approval of treaties and did not include negotiation with foreign powers.

- He claimed the powers of the presidency as the basis for establishing a policy of strict neutrality when the British and French were at war. Although the Constitution is silent about a president's authority to declare neutrality, Washington's supporters argued that the Constitution granted the president *inherent powers*—that is, powers belonging to the president because they can be inferred from the Constitution, such as that authorizing him to conduct diplomatic relations.

Like Washington, the next two presidents, John Adams and Thomas Jefferson, acted in ways critical to the development of the presidency as well as to the president's role in the political system. Adams's poor leadership skills, for example, heightened the divisions between Federalists and Anti-Federalists and probably hastened the development of political parties. Jefferson took critical steps to expand the role of the president in the legislative process. Like Washington, he claimed that certain presidential powers were inherent and used such powers to justify nearly doubling the size of the nation through the Louisiana Purchase in 1803.

Incremental Expansion of Presidential Powers: 1809–1933

Although the first three presidents made enormous contributions to the office of the chief executive, the way government functioned in its formative years caused the balance of power to be heavily weighted in favor of a strong Congress. Americans routinely had close contacts with their representatives in Congress, while to most citizens the president seemed a remote figure. By the end of Jefferson's first term, it was clear that the Framers' initial fear of an all-powerful, monarchical president was unfounded. The strength of Congress and the relatively weak presidents who came after Jefferson allowed Congress quickly to assert itself as the most powerful branch of government.

President Andrew Jackson from Tennessee was the first strong national leader who represented more than just a landed elite. By the time Jackson ran for president in 1828, eleven new states had been added to the union, and the number of White males eligible to vote had increased dramatically, as nearly all states had removed property requirements for voting. The election of Jackson as the seventh president signaled the end of an era: He was the first president to be neither a Virginian nor an Adams. Jackson personified the western, frontier, egalitarian spirit, and his election launched the beginning of Jacksonian democracy. White masses loved him, and legends arose around his down-to-earth image. Jackson, for example, once was asked to give a position to a soldier who had lost his leg on the battlefield and needed the job to support his family. When told that the man hadn't voted for him, Jackson responded, "If he lost his leg fighting for his country, that is vote enough for me."[19] Still, because of—or in spite of—his popularity, he was a die-hard supporter of slavery and responsible for the killing of thousands of American Indians as he ordered their repatriation from the Southeast to Oklahoma in what is known as the Trail of Tears.

Jackson used his image and personal power to buttress the developing party system by rewarding loyal followers of his Democratic Party with presidential appointments. Frequently at odds with Congress, he made use of the veto power against twelve bills, surpassing the combined total of ten vetoes used by his six predecessors. Jackson also reasserted the supremacy of the national government (and the presidency) by facing down South Carolina's nullification of a federal tariff law.

Abraham Lincoln's approach to the presidency was similar to Jackson's. To combat the unprecedented emergency of the Civil War, Lincoln assumed powers that no president before him had claimed. Because Lincoln believed he needed to act quickly for the very survival of the nation, he frequently took action without first obtaining the approval of Congress. Among many of Lincoln's legally questionable acts were the following:

- He suspended the writ of *habeas corpus*, which allows those in prison to petition for release, citing the need to jail persons suspected of disloyal practices.
- He expanded the size of the U.S. Army above congressionally mandated ceilings.
- He ordered a blockade of southern ports without the approval of Congress.
- He closed the U.S. mail to treasonable correspondence and had newspaper editors critical of him jailed.

Lincoln argued that the inherent powers of his office allowed him to circumvent the Constitution in a time of war or national crisis. Since the Constitution confers on the president the duty to make sure that the laws of the United States are faithfully executed, reasoned Lincoln, these acts were constitutional. He simply refused to allow the nation to crumble because of what he viewed as technical requirements of the Constitution.

HOW DID ABRAHAM LINCOLN EXPAND PRESIDENTIAL POWER?

During the Civil War, Lincoln assumed inherent powers that no president before him had claimed. He argued that these actions were necessary for the preservation of the Union. After the war, the president's powers never returned to their previous levels. Here, Lincoln is shown meeting with military leaders following the battle of Antietam, fought in northwestern Maryland, which was one of the bloodiest battles of the Civil War.

Encyclopaedia Britannica/Universal Images Group/Getty Images

Creating the Modern Presidency

Since the 1930s, the general trend has been for presidential—as opposed to congressional—decision making to assume greater importance. The start of this trend can be traced to the four-term presidency of Franklin D. Roosevelt (FDR), who led the nation through several crises. Many now criticize this growth of presidential power as well as of the federal government and its programs. To understand the basis for a large number of today's calls for reform of the political system, it is critical to learn how the government and the role of the president grew.[20]

FDR took office in 1933 in the midst of the Great Depression, a major economic crisis in which a substantial portion of the U.S. workforce was unemployed. Noting the sorry state of the national economy in his inaugural address, FDR concluded: "This nation asks for action and action now." To jumpstart the American economy, FDR asked Congress for and was given "broad executive powers to wage a war against the emergency, as great as the power that would be given to me if we were in fact invaded by a foreign foe."[21]

Just as Abraham Lincoln had taken bold steps upon his inauguration, Roosevelt also acted quickly. He immediately fashioned a plan for national recovery called the New Deal, a package of bold and controversial programs designed to invigorate the failing American economy.

Roosevelt served an unprecedented twelve years in office; he was elected to four terms but died shortly after the beginning of the fourth. During his years in office, the nation went from the economic war of the Great Depression to the real international conflict of World War II. The institution of the presidency changed profoundly and permanently with the creation of new federal agencies to implement the New Deal.

FDR also personalized the presidency by establishing a new relationship between the president and the people. In his radio addresses, or fireside chats, as he called them, he spoke directly to the public in a relaxed and informal manner about serious issues.

To his successors, FDR left the modern presidency. This included a burgeoning federal bureaucracy, an active and usually leading role for the president in both domestic and foreign policy and legislation, and a nationalized executive office that used technology—first radio, then TV, and now the Internet and social media, especially by a tweeting president—to bring the president closer to the public than ever before.

WHAT IS THE PRESIDENTIAL ESTABLISHMENT?

7.4 Describe the organization and functions of the Executive Office of the President.

As the responsibilities and scope of presidential authority grew over the years, so did the executive branch, including the number of people working directly for the president in the White House. The presidential establishment includes the vice president and the vice president's staff, the Cabinet, the president's wife and her staff, the Executive Office of the President, and the White House staff. All help presidents fulfill their duties as chief executive.

The Vice President

For many years, political observers considered the vice presidency a sure place for a public official to disappear into obscurity. When John Adams wrote to his wife, Abigail, about his position as America's first vice president, he said it was "the most insignificant office that was the invention of man . . . or his imagination conceived."[22]

Historically, presidents have selected their vice presidents largely to balance—politically, geographically, or otherwise—the presidential ticket, with little thought given to the possibility that the vice president could become president. Vice President Dick Cheney was selected to assuage concerns that ex-governor George W. Bush lacked foreign relations experience. And, in 2020, Joe Biden's naming of

Kamala Harris was also done with a desire to reach out to a category of voters: women and especially, Black women and other women of color. During the primary, he promised to appoint a woman as his running mate, a vow he honored. A sitting U.S. Senator (like Pence, Biden, and Al Gore had been before), Harris had extensive experience as the District Attorney for San Francisco County and as California's Attorney General. As the first woman, first Black woman, and first woman of Indian descent to hold the office of vice president, it is expected that Biden will try to replicate the close working relationship he enjoyed when he was vice president to Barack Obama.

How much power a vice president has depends on how much the president is willing to give. Jimmy Carter was the first president to grant his vice president, Walter Mondale, more than ceremonial duties. In fact, Mondale was the first vice president to have an office in the White House. More recent vice presidents, including Joe Biden, attained significant powers and access to the president, elevating the office to new heights. President Trump sent mixed signals about his relationship with his vice president, Mike Pence. Pence, at times, seemed to soften the president's statements and often remained above the turmoil that was often reported in the White House. As an evangelical Christian, Pence also helped solidify Trump's support with that part of his base of voters. In 2020, President Trump made him head of the task force guiding the federal government's actions during the COVID-19 pandemic, although it was the president himself who gave daily press briefings.

The Cabinet

The Cabinet, which has no official basis in the Constitution but is implied by Article II, section 2, is an informal institution based on practice and precedent whose membership is determined by tradition and presidential discretion. By custom, this advisory group selected by the president includes the heads of major executive departments. Presidents today also include their vice presidents in Cabinet meetings as well as any other agency heads or officials to whom they would like to accord Cabinet-level status (see Chapter 8).

As a body, the Cabinet's major function is to assist the president in executing the laws and in making decisions. Although the Framers discussed the idea of some form of national executive council, they did not include a provision for one in the Constitution. They did recognize, however, the need for departments of government and departmental heads.

Over the years, the Cabinet has grown alongside the responsibilities of the national government. As interest groups, in particular, pressured Congress and the president to recognize their demands for services and governmental action, they often were rewarded by the creation of an executive department. Since a secretary heading an executive department automatically became a member of the president's Cabinet, powerful clientele groups, including farmers (Agriculture), business people (Commerce), workers (Labor), and teachers (Education), saw the creation of a department as a way to expand their access to the national government.

The size of the president's Cabinet has increased over the years, but the reliance of most presidents on their Cabinet secretaries has decreased. Biden's Cabinet and advisors contained a number of firsts as well as many who had served in the Obama administration. Biden announced his Cabinet appointees during the transition period, vowing to make his Cabinet representative of America. His chief of staff, Ron Klain, was the Obama administration's Ebola-response coordinator. Janet Yellen, the former head of the Federal Reserve, was the first woman to head the Treasury Department. Deb Haaland was the first woman and Native American to head the Department of the Interior. Cuban-born Alejandro Mayorkas was the first Hispanic to head the Department of Homeland Security. And Pete Buttigieg, as Secretary of Transportation, was the first openly LGBTQ person to be named to the Cabinet.

First Ladies

From the time of Martha Washington, the wives of U.S. presidents (formally called the first lady, a term coined in 1849) have assisted presidents as informal advisers while making other, more public, and significant contributions to American society. Abigail Adams, for example, was a constant sounding board for her husband, John. An early feminist, in 1776 she cautioned him "to Remember the Ladies" in any new code of laws.

Edith Bolling Galt Wilson was probably the most powerful first lady. When President Woodrow Wilson collapsed and was left partly paralyzed in 1919, she became his surrogate and decided who and what the stricken president saw. Her detractors dubbed her "Acting First Man."

Eleanor Roosevelt also played a powerful and much criticized role in national affairs. Not only did she write a nationally syndicated daily newspaper column, she also traveled and lectured widely, worked tirelessly on countless Democratic Party matters, and raised six children. After FDR's death, she shone in her own right as U.S. delegate to the United Nations, where she headed the commission that drafted the covenant on human rights. Later, she headed President John F. Kennedy's Commission on the Status of Women.

Michelle Obama not only led efforts to encourage healthy eating and to combat childhood obesity, but also took an active role in the 2016 and 2020 presidential campaigns. She spoke at the Democratic National Convention and served as a popular surrogate for Hillary Clinton. Melania Trump forged a different path. She often stayed in suburban Maryland during the week with her son and took on fewer projects. Her "Be Best" antibullying message received mixed reviews. At ceremonial events, she has acted much in the nature of former First Lady Jacqueline Kennedy, who was noted for her almost regal appearance when with foreign dignitaries.

Dr. Jill Biden has been at the president's side throughout most of his career as a wife, mother, educator, and campaigner in chief. When Eleanor Roosevelt's husband, FDR was elected, she was happy for him but bemoaned that she would have to give up her teaching job saying "I've liked teaching more than anything else I've done, but it's got to go."[23] Nearly a hundred years later, Biden is making a different choice. As the wife of the vice president, Biden carried a full load of courses at Northern Virginia Community College. Michelle Obama was often noted to say that every time she was with Biden, she had along a stack of papers for grading. She also was a keen multitasker, even bringing evening clothes to campus to change before formal events.[24]

Now, as First Lady, she intends to bring the "Office of the First Lady" into the twentieth century and has vowed to continue teaching. She also is committed to work to bring about free community college nationwide. She also plans to continue her work she began as Second Lady to support members of the military, and, in particular, military families. And, to round out her portfolio, she plans to continue her work to raise funds for cancer awareness, a cause she and the president took up after the cancer death of their son Beau.

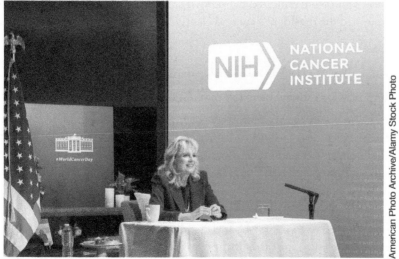

American Photo Archive/Alamy Stock Photo

WHAT DO FIRST LADIES DO?

The spouse of the president plays many roles. They act as informal advisers, champions of their own causes, and goodwill ambassadors for the United States. Here, First Lady Dr. Jill Biden participates in a virtual visit to the National Cancer Institute. Fighting cancer is one of Dr. Biden's principle causes, along with supporting education and military families.

Executive Office of the President (EOP)

A mini-bureaucracy created in 1939 to help the president oversee the executive branch bureaucracy.

The Executive Office of the President (EOP)

In 1939, FDR established the **Executive Office of the President (EOP)** to oversee his New Deal programs. Its purpose was to provide the president with a general staff to help him direct the diverse activities of the executive branch. In fact, it is a mini-bureaucracy of advisers, many of whom are located in the ornate Eisenhower Executive Office Building next to the White House on Pennsylvania Avenue as well as in the White House itself.

The EOP has expanded to include several advisory and policy-making agencies and task forces. Over time, the units of the EOP have become the prime policy makers in their fields of expertise, as they play key roles in advancing the president's policy preferences. Among the EOP's most important members in past as well as the current administrations were the heads of the Council of Economic Advisers, the Office of Management and Budget, the Vice President, the U.S. Trade Representative, and the National Security Council (NSC). The NSC is headed by a national security adviser and comprises the president; the vice president; and the secretaries of state, defense, and treasury. The chair of the Joint Chiefs of Staff and the director of the Central Intelligence Agency also participate.

The White House Staff

Often more directly responsible to the president are the members of the White House staff: the personal assistants to the president, including senior aides, their deputies, assistants with professional duties, and clerical and administrative aides. As personal assistants, these advisers are not subject to Senate confirmation, nor do they have divided loyalties. Their power derives from their personal relationship with the president, and they have no independent legal authority.

Although presidents organize the White House staff in different ways, they typically have a chief of staff whose job is to facilitate the smooth running of the executive branch of government. Successful chiefs of staff also have protected the president from mistakes and helped implement policies to obtain the maximum political advantage for the president. Other important White House aides include domestic, foreign, and economic policy strategists; the communications staff; the White House counsel; and the liaison between the president and Congress. President Trump had more turnover in White House staff and advisers than any president before him. He demanded loyalty and was quick to fire those he saw as problematic or not supporting him to the hilt.

New to the Executive Office of the President in the Trump administration were two members of President Trump's immediate family: his daughter, Ivanka Trump, as an unsalaried adviser, and her husband, Jared Kushner, who was given a larger issue-area portfolio than any other adviser. Kushner's responsibilities included reining in the federal government and advancing peace in the Middle East. Their joint appointments raised many eyebrows and were criticized by many legal ethics experts. But Ivanka Trump and Jared Kushner had the president's ear and clearly were among his most trusted advisers.

HOW DO PRESIDENTS LEAD?

7.5 Analyze how presidents have led over time.

A president's success in having preferred programs adopted or implemented depends on many factors, including individual leadership capabilities, personality and powers of persuasion, the president's ability to mobilize public opinion, the public's perception of the president's performance, and Congress's perception of the president's public support.

Presidential Leadership and Personality

Leadership is not easy to exercise, and it remains an elusive concept for scholars to identify and measure, but it is important to all presidents seeking support for their programs and policies. Frequently, the difference between great and medio-cre presidents centers on their ability to grasp the importance of leadership style. Truly great presidents, such as Lincoln and FDR, understood that the White House was a seat of power from which decisions could flow to shape the national destiny. They recognized that their day-to-day activities and how they went about them should be designed to bolster support for their policies and to secure congressional and popular backing that could translate their intuitive judgment into meaningful action. President Trump, while adopting a somewhat unusual leadership style, made good on many of his campaign promises concerning trade, immigration, climate change, Iran, America's relationship within the G-7, and the appointment of three conservative Supreme Court justices chosen for their likely agreement with his policies, including a promised eventual overturning of *Roe v. Wade* (1973). Mediocre presidents, on the other hand, have tended to regard the White House as "a stage for the presentation of performances to the public" or a fitting honor to cap a career.

Political scientist Richard E. Neustadt called the president's ability to influence members of Congress and the public "the power to persuade." Neustadt believed this power is crucial to presidential leadership because it enables presidents to get their policy goals enacted and win support for their policies in the electorate.[25] Persuasion may come from a variety of sources, including a president's natural charisma. President Trump took a somewhat combative style, frequently lashing out at members of the media, his administration, and celebrities—often in tweets, a style that he cultivated on the campaign trail.

Going Public

Even before radio, TV, and the Internet, presidents tried to reach out to the public to gain support for their programs through what President Theodore Roosevelt called the bully pulpit. The development of commercial air travel, radio, TV, computers, cell phones, and social media has made direct communication to larger numbers of voters much easier. Presidents, their spouses and family members, and other presidential advisers travel the world over to publicize their views and to build support on a personal level for administration programs.

Direct presidential appeals to the electorate, such as those often made by recent presidents, are referred to as "going public."[26] Going public means that a president bypasses the heads of members of Congress to gain support from the people, who can then place pressure on their elected officials in Washington. President Bill Clinton, for example, was keenly aware of the importance of maintaining his connection with the public. At a black-tie dinner honoring radio and TV correspondents, Clinton responded to criticisms leveled against him for not holding traditional press conferences by pointing out how clever he was to ignore the traditional press. "You know why I can stiff you on the press conferences? Because Larry King [then the host of a widely watched CNN evening interview program] liberated me from you by giving me to the American people directly."[27]

Donald Trump's public outreach via his Twitter account, @realDonaldTrump, was a new method of "going public"—as of 2020 he had 88 million followers. He opened his Twitter account in 2009 and regularly tweeted even more before he became president. As president, he sent more than 47 thousand tweets, some of them retweets. He has received nearly 100 million likes. Unlike President Obama, who often left staffers to tweet for him, President Trump did not rely on others to tweet for him. His use of Twitter came to an abrupt end on January 8, 2021, just two days after the January 6 riot at the Capitol. Twitter permanently suspended @realDonaldTrump because he was considered to have violated Twitter Rules by appearing to incite violence. Twitter listed several Trump tweets that violated its Glorification of Violence Policy.[28]

Modern presidents often excel at carefully scripted media events that allow them to reach out directly to supporters and place their critics on the hot seat. Here, President Barack Obama marks his final appearance at the White House Correspondents' Dinner in 2016 with a literal mic drop and the words "Obama Out." President Trump declined to attend any of these annual dinners, bucking a tradition running fifteen presidential administrations long.

Susan Walsh/AP Images

HOW DOES PUBLIC OPINION AFFECT PRESIDENTS?

7.6 Describe the role that public opinion plays in presidential effectiveness.

Since the 1970s in particular, presidents, in general, lose public support over time. Times of crisis, however, tend to produce short-lived rally-round-the flag upticks. Without public support, presidents often find themselves in trouble with voters.

Presidents and other public figures often use approval ratings as tacit measures of their political capital: their ability to enact public policy simply because of their name and their office.[29] People assume that presidents who have high approval ratings—as President George W. Bush did in the immediate aftermath of the September 11, 2001, terrorist attacks—are more powerful leaders with a mandate for action that comes largely by virtue of high levels of public support. These presidents are often able to use their clout to push controversial legislation, such as the USA PATRIOT Act, which restricted or limited several specific civil liberties, through Congress. A public appearance from a popular president can even deliver a hotly contested congressional seat or gubernatorial contest to the president's party.

In sharp contrast, low approval ratings often cripple presidents in the policy arena. Their low ratings can actually prevent favored policies from being enacted on Capitol Hill, even when their party controls the Congress, as many of their partisans locked in close elections shy away from being seen or affiliated with an unpopular president.

The 2018 midterm elections were unusual in that by Labor Day weekend, often viewed as the true start of the election cycle when voters return from summer vacations, President Trump's overall disapproval ratings stood at 60 percent and almost half of those polled thought he should be impeached. Even with high disapproval ratings, President Trump very effectively used his star power to campaign for candidates in red states in 2018, when several Democratic senators lost their seats in the states Trump carried in 2016.

Presidential popularity, though, generally follows a cyclical pattern. These cycles have been recorded since 1938, when pollsters first began to track presidential popularity. Typically, presidents enjoy their highest level of public approval at the beginning of their terms and try to take advantage of this honeymoon period to get their programs passed by Congress as soon as possible. Each action a president takes, however, is divisive—some people will approve, and others will disapprove. Disapproval tends to have a negative cumulative effect on a president's approval rating. Since Lyndon B. Johnson's presidency, only five presidents have left office with approval ratings of more than 50 percent.

President Donald J. Trump assumed the presidency with the lowest approval ratings ever for an incoming president, as well as strained relationships with House and Senate leaders. His popularity failed to rebound from numbers in the mid-40s to high-30s as his presidency proceeded past his first one hundred days. While he managed to place a new conservative justice on the Supreme Court, his initial rollout of an immigration ban and actions to overturn the Affordable Care Act failed, supporting conventional wisdom of the importance of high approval ratings for achieving legislative accomplishments in a president's first one hundred days. Throughout his presidency President Trump's approval ratings hovered in the low 40s, then ticked upward slightly as the novel coronavirus spread. In times of crisis, citizens often turn to their leaders for guidance. The 2020 presidential election results found that many voters were unhappy with President Trump's handling of the virus, and that it likely caused his loss.

POLITICAL REFORM AND REALITIES: WHAT IS THE PRESIDENT'S ROLE AS A POLICY MAKER?

7.7 Describe the relationship between Congress and the president and the tools available for the president to make public policy.

When President Franklin D. Roosevelt sent his first legislative package to Congress, he broke the traditional model of law-making.[30] As envisioned by the Framers, the responsibility of making laws fell to Congress. Now FDR was claiming a leadership role for the president in the legislative process. Said the president of this new relationship, "It is the duty of the President to propose and it is the privilege of the Congress to dispose."[31] With those words and the actions that followed, FDR shifted the presidency into a law- and policy-making role. Now the president and the executive branch not only executed the laws but generally suggested them and proposed budgets to Congress to fund those proposals.

The President's Role in Proposing and Facilitating Legislation

Modern presidents play a major role in setting the legislative agenda, especially in an era when the House and Senate are narrowly divided along partisan lines. Without working majorities, "merely placing a program before Congress is not enough," as President Lyndon B. Johnson once explained. "Without constant attention from the administration, most legislation moves through the congressional process at the speed of a glacier."[32]

Presidents often have a difficult time persuading Congress to pass their legislative packages. They are, however, more likely to get their policy objectives passed in their first one hundred days if the policy issues concern items at the top of their campaign promises, although—again—President Trump's experiences fly in the face of conventional political science wisdom. His first one hundred days weren't great, but by his second year, he saw many of his campaign pledges fulfilled, often working without Congress.[33]

Historically, because presidents generally experience declining support for policies they advocate throughout their terms, it was considered important for presidents to propose key plans early in their administrations. Even President Lyndon B. Johnson, who was able to push nearly 60 percent of his programs through Congress, noted: "You've got to give it all you can, that first year before they start worrying about themselves. You can't put anything through when half the Congress is thinking how to beat you."[34]

Presidents can also bolster support for legislative packages by calling on their political party. As the informal leader of their party, presidents should build coalitions in Congress, where party loyalty is very important. This strategy works best when the president has helped to carry party members into office as well as when the president's party has a majority in the legislature.

Once the House of Representatives flipped control to the Democrats under the leadership of Speaker Nancy Pelosi in 2019, the road to legislative victories became rocky as the two leaders appeared to butt heads at every meeting.

The Budgetary Process and Legislative Implementation

Closely associated with the presidential ability to have legislation passed is a president's capacity to secure funding for new and existing programs. A president sets national policy and priorities through budget proposals and continued insistence on their congressional passage. The budget proposal not only outlines the programs the president wants but also indicates the importance of each program by the amount of funding requested for each and for its associated agency or department.

Because the Framers gave Congress the power of the purse, Congress had primary responsibility for the budgetary process until 1930. The economic disaster set off by the stock market crash of 1929, however, gave FDR the opportunity to involve himself in the congressional budget process, just as he inserted himself into the legislative process. In 1939, the Bureau of the Budget, which had been created in 1921 to help the president inform Congress of the amount of money needed to run the executive branch of government, was made part of the newly created Executive Office of the President. In 1970, President Nixon changed its name to the Office of Management and Budget (OMB) to clarify its function in the executive branch.

The OMB works exclusively for the president and employs hundreds of budget and policy experts. Major OMB responsibilities include preparing the president's annual budget proposal, assessing the costs of the president's proposals, and reviewing the progress, budget, and program proposals of the executive department agencies. It also supplies economic forecasts to the president and conducts detailed analyses of proposed bills and agency rules. OMB reports allow presidents to attach price tags to their legislative proposals and defend their budgets. The Trump administration initially took a different approach by proposing legislation or supporting health care reform legislation without budgets from the OMB.

On February 10, 2020, just days before the WHO declared COVID-19 a pandemic, President Trump proposed a budget that included massive cuts in safety net programs, student loans, work requirements for many forms of federal assistance and a record $2.8 trillion spending plan. It called for cutting the Centers for Disease Control and Prevention's (CDC) budget by 9 percent, and gutting environmental protections. All of these were consistent with Trump's goals but they were met with resistance from House Democrats, in particular. As passed by Congress on December 21, 2020, a combined omnibus appropriations bill and a COVID-19 relief package were passed and eventually signed

HOW IMPORTANT IS A BALANCED BUDGET?

Many economists urge lawmakers to put forward balanced budgets. Pictured is, President Bill Clinton and Vice President Al Gore celebrate the first balanced budget in years. Since the 1990s, no president has presided over a balanced budget. In October 2020, the federal deficit was predicted to jump to 3.3 trillion dollars. The coronavirus and its extraordinary impact on the economy, as millions were left unemployed, resulted in a huge budget shortfall.

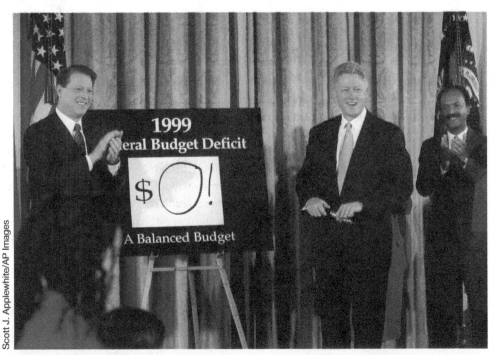

Scott J. Applewhite/AP Images

by the president late on December 27, with the president resolving to send Congress a request to remove funding for several social programs he viewed as wasteful.[35]

The resultant trillions plus budget was passed to shore up the worst economy since the Great Depression. COVID-19 and the resultant record unemployment rates and budget shortfalls in all likelihood doomed President Trump's bid for re-election. As a Democratic political pundit noted, "It's the economy, stupid," when commenting on Bill Clinton's win over incumbent George Bush. The same may have held true about Trump's defeat.[36]

Policy Making Through Executive Order

Proposing legislation and using the budget to advance policy priorities are not the only ways that presidents can affect the policy process, especially in times of highly divided government when the policies of the president and Congress may differ. Presidents may institute major policy changes by issuing an **executive order**, a rule or regulation set forth by the president that has the effect of law without congressional approval.

Presidents Franklin D. Roosevelt and Harry S Truman used executive orders to seize mills, mines, and factories whose production was crucial to World War II and Korean War efforts. Roosevelt and Truman argued that these actions were necessary to preserve national security. In *Youngstown Sheet & Tube* v. *Sawyer* (1952), the Supreme Court disagreed with Truman, stating that he had overstepped the boundaries of his office as provided by the Constitution.[37] Although Truman had seized the steel mills so as to prevent a strike, the Court found that presidential power, even during a time of war, was limited and definitely did not include the right to seize private property.

While many executive orders help clarify or implement legislation enacted by Congress, others have the effect of making new policy. President Truman also used an executive order to end segregation in the military, and affirmative action was institutionalized as national policy through Executive Order 11246, issued by Lyndon B. Johnson in 1966. These orders can be retracted by future presidents.

President Trump came into office without a cohesive, well-defined legislative agenda. Instead, among his 220 executive orders, many have simply overturned key Obama policy items. Other orders were used to limit programs not favored by President Trump. He used executive orders, for example, to cut away many provisions of the Affordable Care Act after he was unable to convince Congress to do so legislatively. Unlike presidents of the past, however, he often "floated" ideas about possible executive orders and appeared then to gauge their popularity with lawmakers or his supporters.

During his eight years in office, President Obama issued 276 executive orders, a number in line with his recent predecessors. During his first 100 days in office, President Trump issued thirty-two, using them as an attempt to fulfill many of his campaign pledges. Some of his orders included the establishment of the Presidential Advisory Commission on Election Integrity (he believed that up to 3 million voters cast their votes illegally), the implementation of the America-First Offshore Energy Strategy (to allow more drilling for oil in American waters), and the White House Initiative to Promote Excellence and Innovation at Historically Black Colleges and Universities. During the 2020 pandemic, while governors around the nation issued executive orders concerning a wide array of issues from wearing masks to quarantining travel, President Trump was noticeably quiet. He did, however, announce Executive Orders 13933 and 13934 to protect American monuments, memorials, and statues, making the removal or destruction of Confederate monuments a federal crime. President Trump justified sending troops into cities where protesters were targeting Confederate monuments as symbols of persistent racism to grasp power from local and state officials by these orders.

Presidents also issue proclamations, which are quite similar to executive orders, yet do not claim the same prestige. President Trump issued hundreds of these policy announcements throughout his first term. President Trump used them to bar funding

executive order
Rule or regulation issued by the president that has the effect of law. All executive orders must be published in the *Federal Register*.

Youngstown Sheet & Tube v.
Sawyer (1952)
After President Truman seized the nation's steel mills as part of his conduct of the Korean War, the Court ruled that without legislative approval, the president had no constitutional authority under his aggregated powers.

for organizations that perform abortions abroad using U.S. funding, withdraw from the Trans-Pacific Partnership, and approve construction of both the Dakota and Keystone XL pipelines. In general, presidents also use proclamations to announce holidays, days of national observance, or new appointees not requiring Senate approval. The most famous of these is perhaps the Emancipation Proclamation issued by President Abraham Lincoln, which freed enslaved people in all states at war with the Union. It is celebrated nationally as Juneteenth, the day on which enslaved people in Texas got notification that the Civil War had ended two months earlier, thus freeing them from bondage.

President Trump did issue proclamation 9994 on March 13, 2020, to declare the virus a national emergency, retroactively to March 1. He also suspended the entry of persons from some nations. And, on May 19, he issued an executive order to "combat the economic consequences of COVID-19." He ordered the director of the Office of Management and Budget to monitor its compliance.[38] President Trump used many proclamations to announce new trade initiatives, including the imposition of tariffs on many imported goods to the United States—an act that angered many traditional American allies, especially Canada.

signing statements
Occasional written comments attached to a bill signed by the president.

Presidents may also issue **signing statements**, occasional written comments attached to a bill, when signing legislation. Often, these written statements merely comment on the bill signed, but they sometimes include controversial claims by the president that some part of the legislation is unconstitutional and that the president intends to disregard it or to implement it in other ways. For example, President George W. Bush used signing statements to express his belief that portions of more than 1,200 laws were unconstitutional. "Among the laws Bush said he [could] ignore [were] military rules and regulations, affirmative action provisions, requirements that Congress be told about immigration services problems, 'whistle-blower' protections for nuclear regulator officials, and safeguards against political interference in federally funded research."[39]

Signing statements, thus, have become another way for presidents to use informal powers to make and influence public policy. These statements invite litigation and may delay policy implementation. Because signing statements happen at the end of the legislative process, they also represent a largely unchecked way for presidents to assert themselves in ongoing power struggles with Congress.

President Trump issued 58 signing statements through November 2020. By July 2020, he was "on course" to issue statements affecting 890 provisions of existing laws. That number was fourteen times more than President Barack Obama and 1.5 times that of President George W. Bush.[40] Key statements were issued after he signed several laws related to COVID-19, including the Paycheck Protection Program Flexibility Act, the Coronavirus Aid, Relief, and Economic Security Act, and the Families First Coronavirus Response Act.[41]

During his first twenty-four days in office, President Joe Biden signed 34 executive orders, some accompanied by signing statements. He noted his preference for keeping signing statements to a minimum preferring his executive orders to stand on their own without needing further commentary.

CONCLUSION AND REVIEW

What Are the Roots of the Office of President of the United States?

7.1 Describe the constitutional provisions that provide the roots of the American presidency.

To keep any one president from becoming too powerful, the Framers created an executive office with limited powers. They mandated that a president be at least thirty-five years old, a natural-born citizen, and a resident of the United States for fourteen years or more, and they opted not to limit the president's term of office. To further guard against tyranny, they made provisions for the removal of the president.

What Are the Constitutional Powers of the President?

7.2 Identify the roles and responsibilities of the president under the Constitution.

The Framers gave the president a variety of specific constitutional powers in Article II, including the powers to appoint, to convene Congress, and to make treaties. The Constitution also gives the president the capacity to grant pardons and to veto acts of Congress. In addition, the president derives considerable power from being commander in chief of the military.

How Has Presidential Power Developed and Expanded?

7.3 Trace the expansion of presidential power.

The development of presidential power has depended on the personal force of those who have held the office. George Washington, in particular, took several actions to establish the primacy of the president in national affairs and as chief executive of a strong national government. With only a few exceptions, subsequent presidents often let Congress dominate in national affairs. Franklin D. Roosevelt (FDR), however, took more power for the office of the president, and made more decisions in national and foreign affairs.

What Is the Presidential Establishment?

7.4 Describe the organization and functions of the Executive Office of the President.

As the responsibilities of the president have grown, so has the executive branch of government. Perhaps the most important policy advisers are those closest to the president: the vice president, the White House staff, some members of the Executive Office of the President, and the president's spouse.

How Do Presidents Lead?

7.5 Analyze how presidents have led over time.

To gain support for their programs or proposed budgets, presidents use a variety of skills, including personal leadership and direct appeals to the public. The leadership abilities and personal style of each president determine how they go about winning support.

How Does Public Opinion Affect Presidents?

7.6 Describe the role that public opinion plays in presidential effectiveness.

Since the 1970s in particular, presidents, in general, lose public support over time. Times of crisis, however, tend to produce short-lived rally-round-the-flag upticks. Without public support, presidents often find themselves in trouble with voters.

Political Reform and Realities: What Is the President's Role as a Policy Maker?

7.7 Describe the relationship between Congress and the president and the tools available for the president to make policy.

Since FDR, the public has looked to the president to propose legislation to Congress. Through proposing legislation, advancing budgets, being involved in the regulatory process, and issuing executive orders, proclamations and signing statements, presidents make policy.

LEARN THE TERMS

Cabinet
executive agreements
Executive Office of the President (EOP)
executive order
executive privilege

pardon
president
Presidential Succession Act
signing statements
Twenty-Fifth Amendment
Twenty-Second Amendment

U.S. v. *Nixon* (1974)
vice president
Watergate
Youngstown Sheet & Tube v. *Sawyer* (1952)

Science History Images/Alamy Stock Photo

WHAT IS THE ROLE OF THE PRESIDENT'S CABINET?

President George Washington stands with the first Cabinet in this undated lithograph by Currier and Ives. Shown from left to right: Henry Knox, secretary of war; Washington; Alexander Hamilton, secretary of the treasury; Thomas Jefferson, secretary of state; and Edmund Randolph, attorney general.

CRITICAL THINKING QUESTION: *Why has the executive branch of government grown so much over time?*

THE EXECUTIVE BRANCH AND THE FEDERAL BUREAUCRACY

LEARNING OBJECTIVES

8.1   Outline the development of the federal bureaucracy.

8.2   Describe how the federal bureaucracy is organized.

8.3   Describe how the federal bureaucracy is staffed.

8.4   Identify the roles and responsibilities of the federal bureaucracy.

8.5   Identify the means of making the federal bureaucracy accountable.

Whmen General George Washington took office as the first president of the United States, he vowed to hire only those "as shall be the best qualified." While Washington's first Cabinet appointee, Alexander Hamilton, the first secretary of the treasury, advocated for a strong national government, Washington's secretary of state, Thomas Jefferson, believed that the states should retain the lion's share of power in the new nation. Washington appointed Jefferson, knowing that he and Hamilton would clash on many fundamental ideas about the role and scope of government. Later, Jefferson recalled his term of service alongside Hamilton: "Hamilton and myself were daily pitted. Like two fighting cocks." Washington, however, relished this conflict, believing diverse political views could lead him to make the best decisions.

When Thomas Jefferson took office as the third president of the United States of America, he took a very different, highly partisan approach, immediately firing most of President John Adams's Federalist appointees. He replaced them with men who agreed with his philosophy of a more limited national government. So began the principle of political patronage, which was to reach its apex with the election of Andrew Jackson in 1828.

• • •

The federal **bureaucracy** consists of thousands of federal government agencies and institutions that implement and administer federal laws and programs. It was loosely created by Article II, which speaks of "all civil officers"—implying the need for presidential aides but nowhere specifically mentioning them. The federal bureaucracy is frequently called the "fourth branch of government." Critics often charge that the bureaucracy is too large, too powerful, and too unaccountable to the people or even to elected officials. Many politicians, elected officials, and voters complain that the federal bureaucracy is too wasteful. Only 31 percent of those polled approved of the federal government's response to handling COVID-19 in May 2020, dropping from 40 percent in April. Few critics of the federal government discuss the fact that state and local bureaucracies and bureaucrats, whose numbers are proportionately far larger, also implement laws and policies and are often far less accountable than those working for the federal government. But, in the era of the pandemic, state governments get higher marks for their actions to contain the virus—51 percent in May 2020, although that was down from 61 percent in April[1] (see Figure 8.1).

Harold D. Lasswell once defined political science as the "study of who gets what, when, and how."[2] Those questions of "what, when, and how" can perhaps best be answered by examining what the bureaucracy is, how it works, and how it is controlled—the topics in this chapter.

bureaucracy

The government agencies, institutions, and personnel that implement and administer laws and programs.

WHAT ARE THE ROOTS OF THE FEDERAL BUREAUCRACY?

8.1 Outline the development of the federal bureaucracy.

The term "bureaucracy" is French in origin taking the word bureau (a desk or office) and combining it with the Greek word *kratos*, meaning political power or rule. The word did not find its way into English usage until 1818, nearly thirty years after the new federal government began organizing into bureaus, or, more commonly, departments. German sociologist Max Weber defined bureaucracy as any system of administration conducted by trained professionals.

In 1789, the federal bureaucracy consisted of three departments: Foreign Affairs, War, and Treasury. President George Washington inherited these departments from the government under the Articles of Confederation. A secretary headed each department, and the Department of State almost immediately became the new name for what was called Foreign Affairs in the Articles. To provide the president with legal advice, Congress also created the office of attorney general, a part-time position, for

FIGURE 8.1 WHAT AGENCIES RATE WELL IN PUBLIC OPINION POLLS?

In 2020, public opinion toward several federal agencies was very positive, as revealed in Figure 8.1. In late March 2020, as the coronavirus was beginning its spread in some areas of the country, Americans rated the Centers for Disease Control and Protection (CDC) and the Department of Health and Human Services, as handling the pandemic very highly.

SOURCE: Pew Research Center, U.S. Politics and Policy, "Public Holds Broadly Favorable Views of Many Federal Agencies, Including CDC and HHS," PEW Research Center, April 9, 2020, https://www.pewresearch.org /politics/2020/04/09/public-holds-broadly-favorable-views-of-many-federal-agencies-including-cdc-and-hhs/.

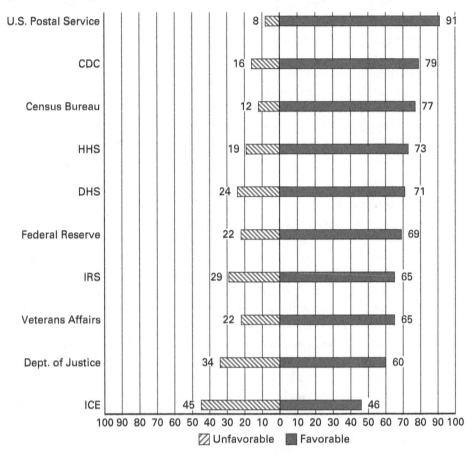

one "learned in the law" to represent the interests of the United States government before the Supreme Court and to provide legal advice to the president.

From the beginning, individuals appointed as Cabinet secretaries (as well as the attorney general) were subject to approval by the U.S. Senate, but the president alone could remove them from office. Even the first Congress realized how important it was for a president to be surrounded by those in whom he had complete confidence and trust.

From 1816 to 1861, the size of the federal executive branch and the bureaucracy grew as existing departments faced increased demands and new departments were created. The Post Office, for example, which Article I constitutionally authorized Congress to create, was enlarged to meet the needs of a growing and westward-expanding population. President Andrew Jackson removed the Post Office from the jurisdiction of the Department of the Treasury in 1829 and promoted the postmaster general to Cabinet rank. The Postal Service is now an independent government corporation. What was formerly the Post Office Department was reorganized in 1971 as a semi-independent agency and its name was changed to the United States Postal Service, and the postmaster was removed from the Cabinet.

The Post Office quickly became a major source of jobs President Jackson could fill by presidential appointment, as every small town and village in the United States had its own postmaster. In commenting on Jackson's wide use of political positions to reward friends and loyalists, one fellow Jacksonian Democrat commented: "To the victors belong the spoils." From that statement came the term **spoils system**, which describes an executive's ability to fire public-office holders of the defeated political party and replace them with party loyalists. The spoils system was a form of **patronage**—jobs, grants, or other special favors given as rewards to friends and political allies for their support.

The U.S. Civil War and the Growth of Government

The Civil War, fought from 1861 to 1865, permanently changed the nature of the federal bureaucracy. As the nation geared up for war, President Abraham Lincoln authorized the addition of thousands of new employees to existing departments. The Civil War also spawned the need for new government agencies in response to a series of poor harvests and distribution problems. President Lincoln, who understood that well-fed troops are necessary to conduct a war, created the Department of Agriculture in 1862, although it was not given full Cabinet-level status until more than twenty years later.

Congress also created the Pension Office in 1866 to pay benefits to the thousands of Union veterans who had fought in the war. More than 127,000 veterans initially were eligible for benefits. Overwhelmed with post–Civil War litigation and the high cost of outsourcing government litigation to private attorneys, in 1870 Congress also created the Department of Justice as a Cabinet department headed by the attorney general. Congress and the president added other departments through 1900. Agriculture became a full-fledged department in 1889 and began to play an important part in informing farmers about the latest developments in soil conservation, livestock breeding, and planting.

From the Spoils System to the Merit System

By the time James A. Garfield, a distinguished Civil War officer, was elected president in 1880, many reformers were calling for changes in the patronage system. Garfield's immediate predecessor, Rutherford B. Hayes, had favored the idea of replacing the spoils system with a **merit system**, a system of employment based on qualifications, test scores, and ability rather than loyalty. Congress, however, failed to pass the legislation he proposed. Possibly because potential job seekers wanted to secure positions before Congress had the opportunity to act on an overhauled civil service system, thousands pressed Garfield for positions. Garfield's life was cut short by the bullets of an assassin who was a frustrated job seeker.

Public reaction to Garfield's death and increasing criticism of the spoils system prompted Congress to pass the Civil Service Reform Act in 1883, more commonly known as the Pendleton Act. It established a merit system of federal employment on the basis of open, competitive exams and created a bipartisan three-member Civil Service Commission, which operated until 1978. Initially, the law covered only about 10 percent of positions in what was called the federal **civil service system**, but later laws and executive orders extended coverage of the act to more than 90 percent of all federal employees today.

spoils system
The practice that allows the firing of public-office holders of a defeated political party to be replaced by loyalists of the newly elected party.

patronage
Jobs, grants, or other special favors that are given as rewards to friends and political allies for their support.

merit system
A system of employment based on qualifications, test scores, and ability, rather than party loyalty.

civil service system
The merit system by which many federal bureaucrats are selected.

WHICH U.S. PRESIDENT POPULARIZED THE SPOILS SYSTEM?

Here, a political cartoonist depicts how President Andrew Jackson might have been immortalized for his use of the spoils system. Note that President Jackson is shown riding a pig, rather than a horse. Words written in the ground below the animal include "fraud," "bribery," and "plunder."

Bettmann/Getty Images

WHAT FRUSTRATED BUREAUCRAT TOOK THE LIFE OF PRESIDENT JAMES A. GARFIELD?

As depicted in this illustration, a frustrated federal job seeker, Charles J. Guiteau, shot the president at the D.C. railroad station. Garfield died 79 days later, just six months after taking office. Guiteau was convicted of the murder and hanged one year later.

Photo12/Alamy Stock Photo

Regulating Commerce

As the nation grew, so did the bureaucracy. In the wake of the tremendous growth of big business (especially railroads), widespread price fixing, and other unfair business practices that occurred after the Civil War, Congress created the Interstate Commerce Commission (ICC) in 1887. In doing so, Congress was reacting to public outcries over exorbitant rates charged by railroad companies for hauling freight. It became the first independent regulatory commission as an entity outside a major executive department. Congress creates independent regulatory commissions such as the ICC, which generally focus on particular aspects of the economy. Commission members are appointed by the president and hold their jobs for fixed terms, but the president cannot remove commissioners unless they fail to uphold their oaths of office. The creation of the ICC also marked a shift in the focus of the bureaucracy from service to regulation, giving the government—in the shape of the bureaucracy—vast powers over individual and property rights.

Theodore Roosevelt, a progressive Republican, became president in 1901. Immediately, he strengthened the movement toward governmental regulation of the economic sphere. When he asked Congress to establish and oversee employer–employee relations, Congress agreed—and the size of the bureaucracy grew further. At that time, many workers toiled long hours for low wages in substandard conditions. Many employers refused to recognize the rights of workers to join unions, and many businesses had grown so large and powerful they could force workers to accept awful conditions and wages. Progressives wanted new government regulations to cure some of the ills suffered by workers and to control the power of increasingly monopolistic corporations. Thus, the U.S. Department of Commerce and Labor was created in 1903.

In 1913, when it became clear that one agency could not represent the interests of both employers and employees, President Woodrow Wilson divided the Department of Commerce and Labor with the approval of Congress, creating two separate departments: Commerce and Labor. One year later, Congress created the Federal Trade Commission (FTC) to protect small businesses and the public from unfair competition, especially from big business.

The ratification of the *Sixteenth Amendment* to the Constitution in 1913 also affected the size and growth potential of government. It gave Congress the authority to implement a federal income tax to supplement the national treasury and provided a huge infusion of funds to support new federal agencies, services, and programs. See Figure 8.2 to get a sense of the demographic makeup of executive branch workers today.

FIGURE 8.2 WHO WORKS IN THE FEDERAL EXECUTIVE BRANCH?

The size of the federal executive branch has fluctuated with the needs of the nation. In 2020, there were over 2.1 million civilian workers in the executive branch. This bar graph shows that of these workers, the majority are male and White.

SOURCE: Congressional Research Service, "Federal Workforce Statistics Sources: OPM and OMB," ver. 11 (October 24, 2019), https://fas.org/sgp/crs/misc/R43590.pdf.

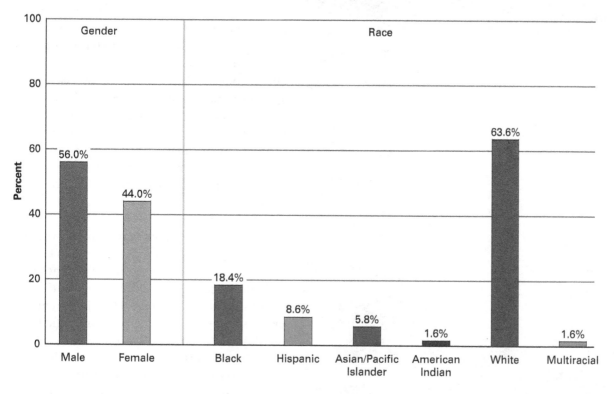

The World Wars and the Growth of Government

The economy appeared to boom as U.S. involvement in World War I, fought by the U.S. from 1917 to 1918, caused an increase in manufacturing, but ominous events loomed just over the horizon. Farmers were in trouble after a series of bad harvests, the nation experienced a severe slump in agricultural prices, the construction industry went into decline, and bank failures became common throughout the 1920s. After stock prices crashed in 1929, the nation plunged into the **Great Depression**. To combat the resultant high unemployment and weak financial markets, President Franklin D. Roosevelt (who was first elected in 1932) created hundreds of new government agencies to regulate business practices and various aspects of the national economy. Roosevelt believed that a national economic depression called for national intervention. Thus, the president proposed and the Congress enacted far-ranging economic legislation. The desperate mood of the nation supported these moves, as most Americans began to reconsider their ideas about the proper role of government and the provision of governmental services. Formerly, most Americans had believed in a hands-off approach; now they considered it the federal government's job to get the economy going and get Americans back to work.

Great Depression

A severe global economic downturn marked by mass unemployment and poverty that began in the United States in 1929 and persisted to some degree until the end of the 1930s.

As the nation struggled to recover from the Great Depression, the Japanese attack on U.S. ships at Pearl Harbor, Hawai'i, on December 7, 1941, forced the United States into World War II, which lasted until 1945. The war immediately affected the economy: healthy, eligible men went to war, and women went to work at factories or in other jobs to replace the men. Factories operated around the clock to produce the armaments, materials, and clothes necessary to equip, shelter, and clothe a vast army.

During World War II, the federal government also continued to grow tremendously to meet the needs of a nation at war. Tax rates were increased to support the

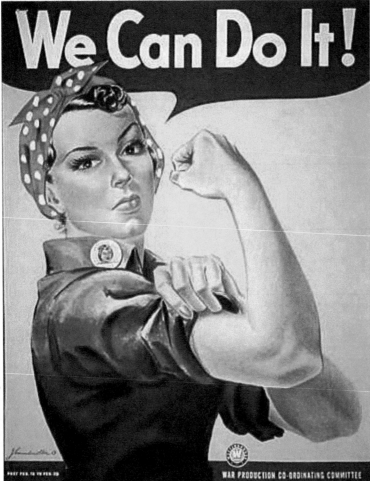

Pictorial Press Ltd/Alamy Stock Photo

HOW DID WORLD WAR II CHANGE GOVERNMENT?

During World War II, the size of the federal government grew dramatically. Men went off to war, and the government developed a comprehensive plan to encourage women to work outside the home to help the war effort, as exemplified by this famous poster of the fictional Rosie the Riveter. When the war ended, veterans returned to their jobs, forcing many women out of work and back into the home.

war, and they never again fell to prewar levels. After the war, this infusion of new monies and veterans' demands for services led to a variety of new programs and a much bigger federal government. The G.I. (Government Issue) Bill, for example, provided college loans for returning veterans and reduced mortgage rates to enable them to buy homes. For the first time in the nation's history, men of lower economic means were able to obtain college educations and purchase homes. The national government's involvement in these programs not only affected a large proportion of citizens, but also led to greater government involvement in a wide array of areas. With these new programs, Americans became increasingly accustomed to the national government's expanded role.

Within two decades after World War II, the national government's response to the civil rights movement and President Lyndon B. Johnson's Great Society program to combat poverty and discrimination produced additional growth in the bureaucracy. The Civil Rights Act of 1964 brought about the creation of the Equal Employment Opportunity Commission (EEOC) in 1965 to handle complaints of employment discrimination based on race, color, religion, sex, or national origin. Congress also created the Departments of Housing and Urban Development (HUD) and Transportation in 1965 and 1966, respectively. These expansions of the bureaucracy corresponded to increases in the president's power and his ability to persuade Congress that new commissions and departments would prove an effective way to solve pressing social problems at the national level.

HOW IS THE FEDERAL BUREAUCRACY FORMALLY ORGANIZED?

8.2 Describe how the federal bureaucracy is organized.

The modern federal bureaucracy is comprised of fifteen Cabinet departments and countless other agencies. These agencies are so varied and diverse that even experts cannot agree on the exact number of separate governmental agencies, commissions, and departments that make up the federal bureaucracy.[3] The bureaucracy has grown so large and politically significant that many observers refer to it as the "fourth branch" of government.

Formal Organization

Federal agencies are classified based on their area of specialization, method of appointing officials, and accountability to the president and Congress. For example, the Occupational Safety and Health Administration, a non-Cabinet-level office, handles occupational safety, while the Department of State specializes in foreign affairs. It is normal, however, for more than one agency to be involved in a particular issue or for one agency to be involved in many issues. The largest and newest department, the Department of Homeland Security, created after the September 11, 2001, terrorist attacks to coordinate domestic security efforts, is probably the best example of this phenomenon. In fact, numerous agencies often have authority in the same issue areas, making administration even more difficult.

Agencies fall into four general categories: (1) Cabinet departments; (2) government corporations; (3) independent executive agencies; and, (4) independent regulatory commissions.

CABINET DEPARTMENTS The fifteen **Cabinet departments** are major administrative units that have responsibility for conducting broad areas of government operations (see Figure 8.3). Cabinet departments account for about 60 percent of the federal workforce. The vice president, the heads of all the departments, and, depending on the president, additional appointees and staff make up the formal Cabinet. Joe Biden's Cabinet is the largest to date with over thirty members. Along with his chief of staff and the secretaries of each department, he has included a Special Envoy for Climate and a Climate Czar. Reflecting his desire to make a huge shift in the federal response to COVID-19, he has included the Surgeon General, a Coordinator of COVID-19 Response and Counselor to the President, and Dr. Anthony Fauci as the Chief Medical Adviser on COVID-19. These appointments and several others immediately underscored the president's committments to finding solutions to climate change and COVID-19.

Cabinet members, called secretaries, head the executive branch departments (except the Department of Justice, which the attorney general leads). Cabinet secretaries

Cabinet departments

Major administrative units with responsibility for a broad area of government operations. Departmental status usually indicates a permanent national interest in a particular governmental function such as defense, commerce, or agriculture.

FIGURE 8.3 WHAT ARE THE CABINET DEPARTMENTS?

Cabinet departments reflect the government's permanent interest in a particular issue area much in the same way as congressional committees do. The modern Cabinet includes the heads of the fifteen executive departments focusing on issues ranging from commerce and foreign affairs to education and health as well as the vice president and the heads of several other major agencies and offices.

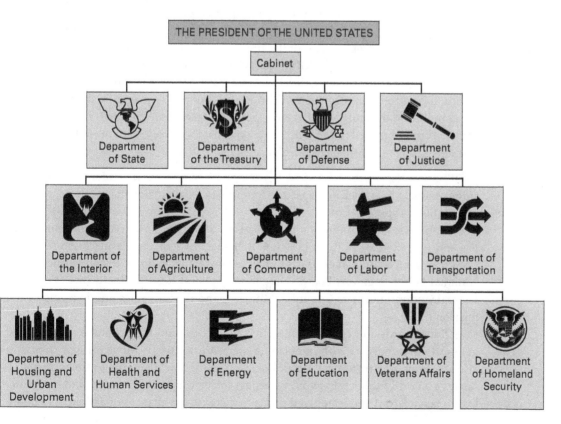

are responsible for establishing their department's general policies and overseeing operations. They are directly responsible to the president but are often viewed as having two bosses—the president and citizens affected by the business of their departments.[4] Cabinet secretaries also are tied to Congress through the appropriations, or budgetary, process and their role in implementing legislation and making rules and policy. They serve at the pleasure of the president.

Usually three to four undersecretaries or deputies assist the secretary by taking part of the administrative burden off their shoulders, and several assistant secretaries lend support by directing major programs within the department. In addition, each secretary has numerous assistants who help with planning, budgeting, personnel, legal services, public relations, and key staff functions. Some of these individuals are political appointees, while others are career civil servants.

Most departments are subdivided into bureaus, divisions, sections, or other smaller units, and the real work of each agency is done at this level. Subdivision usually takes place along functional lines, but the basis for division may be geography, work processes (for example, the Transportation Security Administration is housed in the Department of Homeland Security), or clientele (such as the Bureau of Indian Affairs in the Department of the Interior, now headed for the first time by an American Indian woman, Deb Haaland.) Clientele agencies representing clearly defined interests, such as labor, large corporations, banks, or defense contractors, are particularly subject to outside lobbying. These organized interests are also active at the regional level, where the agencies conduct most of their program implementation.

independent executive agencies

Governmental units that closely resemble a Cabinet department but have narrower areas of responsibility and perform services rather than regulatory functions.

INDEPENDENT EXECUTIVE AGENCIES   **Independent executive agencies** closely resemble Cabinet departments but have narrower areas of responsibility. Generally speaking, independent agencies perform services rather than regulatory functions. The president appoints the heads of these agencies.

Independent agencies exist apart from executive departments for practical or symbolic reasons. The National Aeronautics and Space Administration (NASA), for example, could have been placed within the Department of Defense. Such positioning, however, might have conjured up thoughts of a space program dedicated solely to military purposes, rather than to civilian satellite communication or scientific exploration. Similarly, the Department of the Interior could have been home to the Environmental Protection Agency (EPA); instead, Congress created the EPA as an independent agency in 1970 to administer federal programs aimed at controlling pollution and protecting the nation's environment. Although an independent agency, the EPA was targeted by President Trump for cuts in scope and personnel. President Biden selected a seasoned pro-climate activist with deep experience to work with other Biden climate specialists to completely reenergize the agency.

independent regulatory commission

An entity created by Congress outside a major executive department that regulates a specified interest or economic activity.

INDEPENDENT   REGULATORY   COMMISSIONS   **Independent regulatory commissions** are agencies created by Congress to exist outside the major departments and regulate a specific economic activity or interest. Because of the complexity of modern economic issues, Congress sought to create commissions that could develop expertise and provide continuity of policy with respect to economic issues because neither Congress nor the courts have the time or specific talents to do so. Examples include the National Labor Relations Board (NLRB), the Federal Reserve Board (the "Fed"), the Federal Communications Commission (FCC), and the Securities and Exchange Commission (SEC).

Older boards and commissions, such as the SEC and the Federal Reserve Board, generally are charged with overseeing a certain industry. Most were created specifically to be free from partisan political pressure. Each has five to seven members (always an odd number, to avoid tie votes) selected by the president, and confirmed by the Senate, for fixed, staggered terms to increase the chances of a bipartisan board.

Unlike the case of executive department heads, the president cannot easily remove them. In 1935, the U.S. Supreme Court ruled that in creating independent commissions, Congress had intended them to be independent panels of experts sequestered, as far as possible, from immediate political pressures.[5]

Regulatory boards established since the 1960s largely concern themselves with how the business sector relates to public health and safety. The Occupational Safety and Health Administration (OSHA), for example, promotes job safety. These boards and commissions often lack autonomy and freedom from political pressures; a single administrator who is subject to removal by the president generally heads them. Thus, they are far more susceptible to the political wishes of the president who appoints them.[6]

GOVERNMENT CORPORATIONS   **Government corporations** date from the early 1930s. They are businesses established by Congress to perform functions that private businesses could provide. Some of the better-known government corporations include the U.S. Postal Service, Amtrak, and the Federal Deposit Insurance Corporation (FDIC). Unlike other governmental agencies, government corporations charge a fee for their services. The Tennessee Valley Authority (TVA), for example, provides electricity at reduced rates to millions of Americans in Appalachia.

The government often forms corporations when the financial incentives for private industry to provide services are minimal. The area served by the TVA demonstrates this point; it was a poor region of Appalachia that had failed to attract private electric companies. In other cases, Congress intervenes to salvage valuable public assets. For example, when passenger rail service in the United States became unprofitable, Congress stepped in to create Amtrak, nationalizing the passenger-train industry to keep passenger trains running, especially along the Northeast Corridor.

government corporations
Businesses established by Congress to perform functions that private businesses could provide, such as the U.S. Postal Service and Amtrak. Often established when the financial incentives for private industry to provide services are minimal.

WHAT DO GOVERNMENT CORPORATIONS DO?

Amtrak provides train service across the United States. Its most profitable line runs through the Northeast Corridor from Boston to Washington, D.C. Thousands of travelers use these train lines to navigate the important business centers and congested airspace of the Northeast. Vice President Joe Biden was among these commuters; he frequently took the train from the nation's Capital to his home in Wilmington, Delaware.

Reuters/Alamy Stock Photo

Government Workers and Political Involvement

As the number of federal employees and agencies grew during the 1930s, many Americans began to fear that members of the civil service would play major roles not only in implementing public policy but also in electing members of Congress and even the president. Consequently, Congress enacted the Political Activities Act of 1939, commonly known as the **Hatch Act**. It prohibited federal employees from becoming directly involved in working for political candidates. Although this act allayed many critics' fears, other people argued that the Hatch Act was too extreme.

In 1993, the Hatch Act was liberalized to allow employees to run for public office in nonpartisan elections, contribute money to political organizations, and campaign for or against candidates in partisan elections. Federal employees still, however, are prohibited from engaging in political activity while on duty, soliciting contributions from the general public, and running for office in partisan elections (see Table 8.1).[7]

Hatch Act

The 1939 act to prohibit civil servants from taking activist roles in partisan campaigns. This act prohibited federal employees from making political contributions, working for a particular party, or campaigning for a particular candidate.

WHO ARE BUREAUCRATS?

8.3   Describe how the federal bureaucracy is staffed.

The national government differs from private business in numerous ways. Governments exist for the public good, not to make money. Businesses are driven by a profit motive; many government leaders are driven by reelection concerns. Businesses earn their money from customers; the national government raises revenue from taxpayers and users of many public services. Your cell phone, for example, includes a federal surcharge or tax. Bureaucracies also differ from businesses because it is difficult to determine to whom bureaucracies are responsible. Is it the president? Congress? The people?

TABLE 8.1   WHAT DOES THE LIBERALIZED HATCH ACT STIPULATE?

Federal Employees May	Federal Employees May Not
Be candidates for public office in nonpartisan elections	Use their official authority or influence to interfere with an election
Assist in voter registration drives	Collect political contributions unless both individuals are members of the same federal labor organization or employee organization and the one solicited is not a subordinate employee
Express opinions about candidates and issues	Knowingly solicit or discourage the political activity of any person who has business before the agency
Contribute money to political organizations	Engage in political activity while on duty
Attend political fund-raising functions	Engage in political activity in any government office
Attend and be active at political rallies and meetings	Engage in political activity while wearing an official uniform
Join and be active members of a political party or club	Engage in political activity while using a government vehicle
Sign nominating petitions	Solicit political contributions from the general public
Campaign for or against referendum questions, constitutional amendments, and municipal ordinances	Be candidates for public office in partisan elections
Campaign for or against candidates in partisan elections	
Make campaign speeches for candidates in partisan elections	
Distribute campaign literature in partisan elections	
Hold office in political clubs or parties	

SOURCE: U.S. Office of Special Counsel, https://osc.gov/Services/Pages/HatchAct.aspx.

The different natures of government and business have a tremendous impact on the way the bureaucracy operates. Because all of the incentive in government "is in the direction of not making mistakes," public employees view risks and rewards very differently from their private-sector counterparts.[8] Government employees have little reason to take risks or go beyond their assigned job tasks. In contrast, private employers are far more likely to reward ambition. One key to understanding the modern bureaucracy is to learn who bureaucrats are, how the bureaucracy is organized, how organization and personnel affect each other, and how bureaucrats act within the political process. It also is important to recognize that government cannot be run entirely like a business, much as President Trump, a businessperson, quickly found upon entering the White House. An understanding of these facts and factors can help in the search for ways to motivate positive change in the bureaucracy.[9]

Profiling Bureaucrats

Most federal bureaucrats are career government employees who work in the Cabinet-level departments and independent agencies that comprise more than 2,000 bureaus, divisions, branches, offices, services, and other subunits of the federal government. In 2020, civilian federal employees numbered slightly more than 2.1 million, slightly more than recent years. There are an additional 1.3 million men and women on active duty in the military. The U.S. Postal Service employs approximately 497,000 persons, making it the nation's second-largest employer behind Walmart. Small percentages work as legislative and judicial staff. The remaining federal civilian workers are spread out among the various executive departments and agencies throughout the United States. Most of these federal employees are paid according to what is called the "General Schedule" (GS). They advance within fifteen GS grades (as well as steps within those grades), moving into higher GS levels and salaries as their careers progress.

At the lower levels of the U.S. Civil Service, competitive examinations are used to fill most positions. These usually involve a written test. Veterans automatically get points added to their scores. Mid-level to upper ranges of federal positions do not normally require tests; instead, applicants submit resumes online. Personnel departments then evaluate potential candidates and rank them according to how well they fit a particular job opening. The personnel department then forwards to the agency filling the vacancy only the names of those deemed "qualified." This can be a time-consuming process; it often takes six to nine months to fill a position in this manner. Positions requiring extensive background checks for security clearances can take up to two years.

Persons not covered by the civil service system make up the remaining 10 percent of the federal workforce. Their positions generally fall into three categories:

1. *Appointive policy-making positions.* Nearly 4,000 civilian presidential appointees along with 65,000 military nominations are sent to the Senate each two-year session. About fifteen hundred of these, including Cabinet secretaries and under- and assistant secretaries, are subject to Senate confirmation.[10] These appointees, in turn, are responsible for appointing high-level policy-making assistants who form the top of the bureaucratic hierarchy and who are not subject to Senate confirmation. These are called "Schedule C" political appointees.[11]

2. *Independent regulatory commissioners.* Although each president has the authority to appoint as many as one hundred commissioners, they become independent of the president's direct political influence as soon as they take office.

3. *Low-level, nonpolicy patronage positions.* These types of positions generally concern administrative assistants to policy makers.

More than 15,000 job skills are represented in the federal government. Government employees, whose average age is approximately forty-six years old, have a length of service averaging between fifteen and twenty years. They include forest rangers, FBI agents, foreign service officers, computer programmers, security guards, librarians, administrators, engineers, plumbers, lawyers, doctors, postal carriers, and zoologists, among others. The diversity of jobs in the government mirrors that in the private sector. The federal workforce, itself, is also diverse. Black people make up 18.1 percent of the workforce, Hispanics 8.4 percent, Asians 6 percent, and American Indians 1.2 percent.[12] The overall employment of women at 43.2 percent lags behind that of men at 56.8 percent (see Figure 8.4).[13]

About 15 to 20 percent of all federal workers are found in or around the nation's Capital; the rest are located in regional, state, and local offices scattered throughout the country. To enhance the efficiency of the bureaucracy, the United States is divided into ten regions, with most agencies having regional offices in at least one city in that region (see Figure 8.5). The decentralization of the bureaucracy facilitates accessibility to the public. The Social Security Administration, for example, has numerous offices so that its clients can have a place nearby to take their paperwork, questions, and problems. Decentralization also helps distribute jobs and incomes across the country.

A major concern about the federal workforce is the high rate of turnover in many of the most important positions. During the Obama administration, for example, at the Department of State, which once boasted many of the most highly coveted jobs in the federal bureaucracy, the dangers associated with postings throughout parts of the Middle East and Africa made it harder to find well-qualified people to staff critical positions.[14]

FIGURE 8.4 WHO ARE FEDERAL WORKERS?

The federal government employs people in a diverse range of jobs, from administrative assistant to scientist. But bureaucrats do not necessarily match the demographics of America. Men are overrepresented at the highest levels of the federal workforce, while women notably hold far fewer of the highest paying GS 12–15 positions.[15]

SOURCE: U.S. Equal Opportunity Commission Annual Report on the Federal Workforce and Federalpay.org (for 2020 salaries), Fiscal Year 2015, Part II, Workforce Statistics, https://www.eeoc.gov/federal-sector/reports/annual-report-federal -workforcefiscal-year-2015#_bookmark36; and FederalPay.org (2020 salaries), https://www.federalpay.org/gs/2020. This figure is based on New York – Newark, NY-NJ-CT-PA G5 Locality Area, which is one of fifty-three areas for 2020.

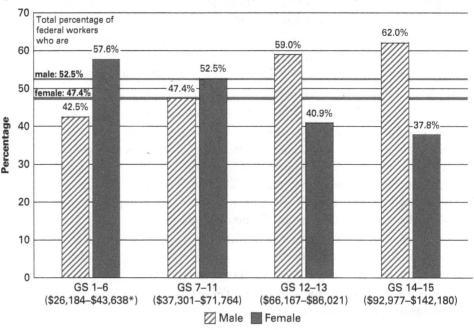

FIGURE 8.5 WHAT ARE THE FEDERAL AGENCY REGIONS AND WHERE ARE THEIR HEADQUARTERS?

To bring the federal bureaucracy closer to citizens and increase the efficiency of providing government services, the federal agencies maintain an office in Washington, D.C., and in ten other regional locations across the country. These cities are shown on the map below. Departments and agencies also often have offices in large cities in addition to regional headquarter locations.

SOURCE: U.S. Department of Health and Human Services, www.hhs.gov.

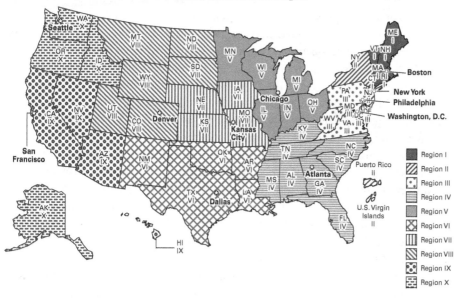

The Trump administration confronted problems with finding individuals from the start. As of November 2, 2020, nearly 250 of the approximately 700 most key jobs requiring Senate confirmation were unfilled. Sixty-five percent of the top jobs at the Department of Homeland Security went unfilled by the day before the 2020 national election. Consequently, private contractors fill many bureaucratic positions in these potentially dangerous sites. Many of these private contractors are former government employees who can make almost twice the amount of money working for private companies.

The graying of the federal workforce is another concern. More than 15 percent are eligible for retirement, and by 2023, it will be 30 percent.[16] Many in government hope that the Presidential Management Fellows Program, which began in 1977 to hire and train future managers and executives, will be enhanced to make up for the shortfall in experienced managers that the federal government now faces. Agencies even are contemplating ways to pay the college loans of prospective recruits, while at the same time trying to improve benefits to attract older workers.[17]

HOW DOES THE BUREAUCRACY WORK?

8.4 Identify the roles and responsibilities of the federal bureaucracy.

Max Weber believed bureaucracies were a rational way for complex societies to organize themselves. Model bureaucracies, said Weber, exhibit certain features, including the following:

- A chain of command in which authority flows from top to bottom.
- A division of labor whereby work is apportioned among specialized workers to increase productivity.
- Clear lines of authority among workers and their superiors.
- A goal orientation that determines structure, authority, and rules.

- Impersonality, whereby all employees are treated fairly based on merit and all clients are served equally, without discrimination, according to established rules.
- Productivity, whereby all work and actions are evaluated according to established rules.[18]

Clearly, this Weberian idea is somewhat idealistic, and even the best run government agencies do not always work this way, but most try.

When Congress creates any kind of department, agency, or commission, it is actually delegating some of its powers listed in Article I, section 8, of the U.S. Constitution. Therefore, the laws creating departments, agencies, corporations, or commissions carefully describe their purpose and give them the authority to make numerous policy decisions, which have the effect of law. Congress recognizes that it does not have the time, expertise, or ability to involve itself in every detail of every program; therefore, it sets general guidelines for agency action and then allows the agency to work out the details. How agencies execute congressional wishes is called implementation, the process by which a law or policy is put into operation.

Historically, in attempting to study how the bureaucracy made policy, political scientists investigated what they termed **iron triangles**, the relatively ironclad relationships and patterns of interaction that occur among federal workers in agencies or departments, interest groups, and relevant congressional committees and subcommittees. Today, iron triangles no longer dominate most policy processes. Some do persist, however, such as the relationships between career employees at the Department of Veterans Affairs, staffers and members of the House and Senate Committees on Veterans Affairs, and members and lobbyists for what are called the "Big Six": the American Legion, Veterans of Foreign Wars, Paralyzed Veterans of America, Amvets, Disabled American Veterans, and Vietnam Veterans of America (see Figure 8.6).[19]

Many political scientists who examine external influences on the modern bureaucracy prefer to study **issue networks**. In general, issue networks, like iron triangles, include agency officials, members of Congress (and committee staffers), and interest

iron triangles
The relatively ironclad relationships and patterns of interaction that occur among agencies, interest groups, and congressional committees or subcommittees.

issue networks
The loose and informal relationships that exist among a large number of actors who work in broad policy areas.

FIGURE 8.6 WHAT CONSTITUTES AN IRON TRIANGLE?

Iron triangles are the relatively stable relationships formed among bureaucratic agencies, congressional committees, and interest groups. Cooperation between these three policy actors may make policy making in some issue areas, such as veterans affairs, an insular process confined to a small clientele.

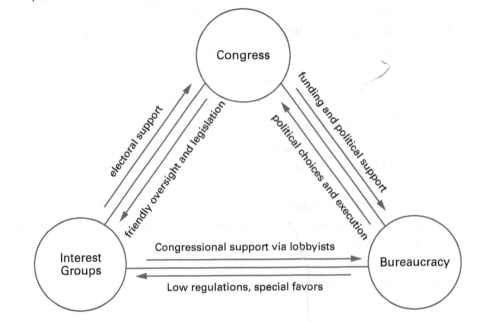

group lobbyists. But they also include lawyers, consultants, academics, public relations specialists, and sometimes even the courts. Unlike iron triangles, issue networks constantly are changing as members with technical expertise or newly interested parties become involved in issue areas and others phase out. Examples include environmental, drug, and gun ownership networks.

As a result of the increasing complexity of many policy domains, a number of alliances have also arisen within the bureaucracy. One such example are **interagency councils**, working groups established to facilitate the coordination of policy making and implementation across a host of agencies. Depending on the amount of funding these councils receive, they can be the prime movers of administration policy in any area where an interagency council exists. President George W. Bush formed an interagency council to address the economic crisis resulting from the September 11, 2001, terrorist attacks.

In areas marked by extraordinarily complex policy problems, recent presidential administrations have set up **policy coordinating committees (PCCs)** to facilitate interaction among agencies and departments at the sub-Cabinet level to deal with complex policies. For example, the Homeland Security Council PCC (the HSC-PCC) is composed of representatives from various executive departments as well as the FBI, CIA, Federal Emergency Management Agency, and the vice president's office, among others. It oversees multiple agencies and executive departments to ensure the creation and implementation of consistent, effective homeland security policies.

interagency councils
Working groups created to facilitate coordination of policy making and implementation across a host of governmental agencies.

policy coordinating committees (PCCs)
Committees created at the sub-Cabinet level to facilitate interactions between agencies and departments to handle complex policy problems.

Making Policy

The main purpose of all of these decision-making bodies is policy making. Policy making and implementation take place on both informal and formal levels. From a practical standpoint, many decisions are left to individual government employees on a day-to-day basis. Department of Justice lawyers, for example, make daily decisions about whether to prosecute suspects or launch special investigations such as the one created by Attorney General Jeff Sessions to investigate possible unlawful Russian interference in the 2016 presidential election. Because Sessions worked with the Trump campaign and transition team, he recused himself from the investigation. This provoked a Twitter storm of criticism from President Trump, who frequently bemoaned selecting Sessions as his attorney general. On a different scale, street-level Internal Revenue Service agents make many decisions during personal audits. These street-level bureaucrats make policy on two levels. First, they exercise broad judgment in decisions concerning citizens with whom they interact. Second, taken together, their individual actions add up to agency behavior.[20] Thus, how bureaucrats interpret and how they apply (or choose not to apply) various policies are equally important parts of the policy-making process.

Administrative discretion, the ability of bureaucrats to make choices concerning the best way to implement congressional or executive intentions, also allows decision makers (whether they are in a Cabinet-level position or at the lowest GS levels) a tremendous amount of leeway. In contrast, bureaucrats also exercise administrative discretion through two formal procedures: rule making and administrative adjudication.

RULE MAKING   **Rule making** is a quasi-legislative process resulting in regulations that have the characteristics of a legislative act. **Regulations** are the rules that govern the operation of all government programs and have the force of law. In essence, then, bureaucratic rule makers often act as lawmakers as well as law enforcers when they make rules or draft regulations to implement various congressional statutes. Some political scientists say that rule making "is the single most important function performed by agencies of government" (see Figure 8.7).[21]

rule making
A quasi-legislative process resulting in regulations that have the characteristics of a legislative act.

regulations
Rules governing the operation of all government programs that have the force of law.

FIGURE 8.7 HOW IS A REGULATION MADE?

The 1946 Administrative Procedures Act spells out a specific process for rule making in the federal bureaucracy. Similar to the process of making legislation, a proposed rule has many opportunities to fail to be implemented. Affected citizens also have a number of opportunities to offer their opinions of a proposed rule. The flow chart indicates the procedure for forming regulations.

Federal Register

The official journal of the U.S. government, including all federal rules and public notices so that citizens and organization can follow proposed changes and comply with rule changes.

Because regulations often involve political conflict, the 1946 Administrative Procedures Act established rule-making procedures to give everyone the chance to participate in the process. The act requires that: (1) public notice of the time, place, and nature of the rule-making proceedings be provided in the *Federal Register*; (2) interested parties be given the opportunity to submit written arguments and facts relevant to the rule; and, (3) the statutory purpose and basis of the rule be stated. After rules are published, thirty days generally must elapse before they take effect.

Sometimes the law requires an agency to conduct a formal hearing before issuing rules. Staffers collect evidence and call interested parties and interest groups to testify on the issue. The process can take weeks, months, or even years, at the end of which agency administrators must review the entire record and then justify the new rules. Although cumbersome, the process has reduced criticism of some rules and bolstered the deference given by the courts to agency decisions.

Many Americans are unaware of their opportunity to influence government through the rule-making process. All private citizens with interest in potential rules have the right to submit comments. Recent presidents have taken efforts to make commenting easier for citizens by using the government's regulations.gov portal. As a result, the average rule receives about eighty comments, but some rules may receive thousands of comments from citizens.

ADMINISTRATIVE ADJUDICATION Agencies regularly find that persons or businesses are not in compliance with the federal laws the agencies are charged with enforcing or that they are in violation of an agency rule or regulation. To force compliance, some agencies resort to administrative adjudication, a quasi-judicial process in which a bureaucratic agency settles disputes between two parties in a manner similar to the way courts resolve disputes. Administrative adjudication is referred to as quasi-judicial because adjudication by any body other than the judiciary would be a violation of the constitutional principle of separation of powers.

Several agencies and boards employ administrative law judges to conduct hearings. Although employed by the agencies, these judges are strictly independent and cannot be removed except for gross misconduct. Their actions, however, are reviewable in the federal courts, as are the findings of judges in agencies such as the Equal Employment Opportunity Commission and the Social Security Administration.

POLITICAL REFORM AND REALITIES: HOW CAN THE BUREAUCRACY BE MADE ACCOUNTABLE?

8.5 Identify the means of controlling the federal bureaucracy.

Although many critics of the bureaucracy argue that federal employees should be responsive to the public interest, the public interest is difficult to define. As it turns out, several factors control the power of the bureaucracy, and to some degree, the same kinds of checks and balances that operate among the three branches of government serve to rein in the bureaucracy (see Table 8.2).

Many political scientists argue that presidents should take charge of the bureaucracy because it is their responsibility to see that popular ideas and expectations are translated into administrative action. But under our constitutional system, the president is not the only actor in the policy process. Congress creates the agencies, funds them, and establishes the broad rules of their operation. Moreover, Congress continually reviews the various agencies through oversight committee investigations, hearings, and its power of the purse. The federal judiciary, as in most other matters, has the ultimate authority to review administrative actions, although the judiciary generally

TABLE 8.2 HOW ARE AGENCIES MADE ACCOUNTABLE?

The President Has the Authority to	The Congress Has the Authority to	The Judiciary Has the Authority to
Appoint and remove agency heads and other top bureaucrats	Pass legislation that alters the bureaucracy's activities	Rule on whether bureaucrats have acted within the law and require policy changes to comply with the law
Reorganize the bureaucracy (with congressional approval)	Abolish or create programs and agencies	Force agencies to respect the right of individuals through hearings and other proceedings
Make changes in an agency's annual budget proposals	Refuse to appropriate funds for certain programs	Rule on the constitutionality of all challenged rules and regulations
Ignore legislative initiatives originating within the bureaucracy	Investigate agency activities and compel bureaucrats to testify about them	
Initiate or adjust policies that would, if enacted by Congress, alter the bureaucracy's activities	Accept or reject presidential appointments of agency heads and other top bureaucratic officials	
Issue executive orders and memoranda	Write legislation to limit bureaucratic discretion	

defers to the judgments of the federal administrative agencies and administrative courts. However, in 2019, it appeared that the Supreme Court might be ready to strip federal agencies' ability to interpret ambiguous regulations without challenge. Deference "is sometimes appropriate and sometimes not," wrote Associate Justice Elena Kagan on behalf of a unanimous Court.[22]

Executive Control

As the size and scope of the American national government, in general, and of the executive branch and bureaucracy, in particular, have grown, presidents have delegated more and more power to bureaucrats. But most presidents have continued to try to exercise some control over the bureaucracy. They have often found that task more difficult than first envisioned. President John F. Kennedy, for example, once lamented that to give anyone at the Department of State an instruction was comparable to putting your request in a dead-letter box.[23] No response would ever be forthcoming.

Recognizing these potential problems, presidents try to appoint the best possible people to carry out their wishes and policy preferences. Presidents make hundreds of appointments to the executive branch; in doing so, they have the opportunity to appoint individuals who share their views on a range of policies. Although presidential appointments account for a very small proportion of all federal jobs, presidents or the Cabinet secretaries usually appoint most top policy-making positions. Executive control over these positions can be severely hampered when Congress refuses to approve nominees. Challenges also are presented when a president, such as Donald J. Trump, suffers massive attrition in the ranks of Cabinet secretaries and operates with many top jobs headed by "acting," that is, non-Senate-approved, personnel. Moreover, during the Trump administration, the Republican-controlled Senate was criticized for basically stalling the confirmation process of sub-Cabinet positions while it filled federal judgeships at record speed.[24]

With the approval of Congress, presidents can reorganize the bureaucracy. They also can make changes in an agency's annual budget requests and ignore legislative initiatives originating within the bureaucracy. Several presidents have made a

HOW DOES THE FEDERAL GOVERNMENT RESPOND TO A PANDEMIC DISASTER?

Shown here is a federal health professional administering a nasal swab test for COVID-19. The federal government also relied heavily on its scientists for advice and safety protocols during the pandemic.

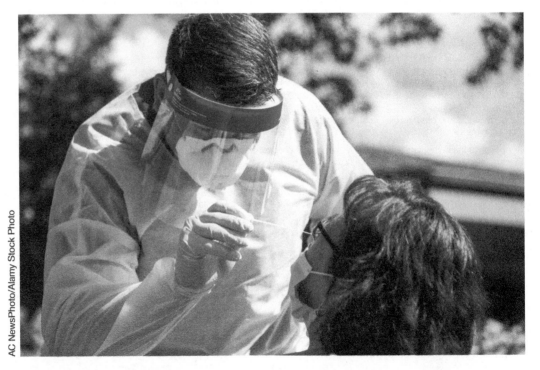

AC NewsPhoto/Alamy Stock Photo

priority of trying to tame the bureaucracy to increase its accountability. Thomas Jefferson, the first president to address the issue of accountability, attempted to cut waste and bring about a "wise and frugal government."

Presidents also can shape policy and provide direction to bureaucrats by issuing executive orders, as discussed in Chapter 7.[25] Executive orders are rules or regulations issued by the president that have the effect of law; the *Federal Register* must publish all executive orders. A president can direct an agency to act, but it may take some time to carry out the order. Few presidents can ensure that the government will implement all their orders or will like all the rules that have been made. For example, even before Congress acted to protect women from discrimination by the federal government, the National Organization for Women convinced President Lyndon B. Johnson to sign a executive order preventing federal contracts to any employers who discriminated against workers based on race, creed, color, national origin, or sex. Although he signed the order in 1967, actual guidelines for implementation were not drafted until several years later.[26] In contrast, at times President Trump issued directives and even fired of top advisers via Twitter. His initial ban on Muslims from entering the Unites States, for example, was issued by tweet and later by an executive order that ultimately was upheld as constitutional by the Supreme Court.[27]

Republican candidates for president often promise to reduce the size or authority of the bureaucracy. President Donald J. Trump, a climate change skeptic, appointed to the directorship of the Environmental Protection Agency ex-Texas Governor Rick Perry, who did not believe in the concept of climate change. For the Department of Education, he appointed a secretary who favored charter schools over public schools. He also proposed drastic cuts for many programs headed by Cabinet secretaries, such as Medicaid (Department of Health and Human Services) and foreign assistance, and called for a 32 percent decrease in the Department of State's 2018 budget. Trump's Cabinet clearly reflected his views, and its members acted to facilitate his policy wishes. Perhaps the biggest problem he encountered is the record number of resignations from career employees. At the same time, his administration failed to act quickly to fill key positions at the assistant secretary level and below, making some policy decisions more difficult to enforce. The Executive Office of the President has also had the highest level of turnover of any administration in modern history, which often

HOW DID PRESIDENT TRUMP SHAPE CORONAVIRUS POLICY?

President Trump appointed a Coronavirus Task Force, whose mission was to monitor and contain the spread of the virus. But Trump did not always listen to the experts, and shifted the team's focus to suit his agenda of re-opening the country. Under the Biden administration, the task force was succeeded by the White House COVID-19 Response Team.

White House Photo/Alamy Stock Photo

interfered with the day-to-day running of the executive branch. The Brooking Institution, in fact, found that among the president's "A Team" of advisers, turnover was an unprecedented 82 percent by March 2020.[28]

Congressional Control

The Senate can confirm (or reject) nominees to top bureaucratic positions. Both the House and the Senate play important roles in checking the power of the bureaucracy. Constitutionally, Congress possesses the authority to create or abolish departments and agencies. It may also transfer agency functions and expand or contract bureaucratic discretion.

Congress can also use its investigatory powers to conduct program evaluations or hold oversight hearings. It can also call sitting and even former government officials to testify, as was the case when several Trump advisers from both before and during his presidency were called before House and Senate committees investigating Russia's possible interference with the 2016 presidential election. Several Trump advisers were also called to answer questions put forward by a special (independent) counsel appointed by the number two ranking official at the Justice Department after the attorney general recused himself. The Democratic House of Representatives opened scores of investigations into the actions of Cabinet secretaries, their subordinates, and the president and his aides as well ending in two presidential impeachments.

Political scientists distinguish between two different forms of congressional oversight. One is proactive and allows Congress to set its own agenda for programs or agencies to review. For example, bureaucrats appear before congressional committees on a regular basis to inform members about agency activities, ongoing investigations, and budget requests. A second kind of oversight is reactive and generally involves a congressional response to a complaint filed by a constituent, a politically significant actor, or the media. It is not at all unusual for a congressional committee or subcommittee to conduct hearings on a particular problem and then direct the relevant agency to study the problem or find ways to remedy it. For example, when the Aliso Canyon natural gas storage facility owned by the Southern California Gas Company began leaking gas in late 2015, residents of the affected Porter Ranch neighborhood as well as local and state officials called for a response. Congressman Brad Sherman (D–CA) wrote a letter to the Environmental Protection Agency requesting an investigation into the leak, which the agency began almost immediately.

A third kind of hearing often becomes political theater. Both the Senate and House were quick to hold hearings about the coronavirus. Medical experts from universities around the nation were called to testify as were the directors of the CDC, the National Institute of Allergy and Infectious Diseases (NIAID), and the coordinator for the White House Coronavirus Task Force. The White House, however, refused to allow some members of the White House Task Force to appear before any House committees. Oversight is difficult when key actors are not allowed to testify.

Attorney General William Barr went before the House Judiciary Committee in late July 2020 and was peppered with hostile questions by House Democrats. Instead of gleaning information about the decision-making process in several areas from the prosecution of associates of President Trump's, his actions to remove protesters from Lafayette Square to facilitate a photo opportunity for the president, and his removal of a U.S. attorney and even his response to COVID-19, representatives used their time not to make policy or exercise oversight but simply to put Barr in the hot seat for several hours.[29]

In one notable exchange, after the attorney general said he did not believe that institutional racism existed in police departments, Representative Sheila Jackson Lee (D–TX) urged him and the Department of Justice to "focus on systemic institutional racism," showing the chasm that exists that exists between Democrats and Republicans on policing.[30]

Congress also has the power of the purse. To control the bureaucracy, it can use its abilities to authorize spending and appropriate funds for an agency's activities. Money can be a powerful tool to coerce bureaucrats into making particular policies. President Trump's alleged failure to release congressionally authorized military aid to Ukraine without promises that then former Vice President Joe Biden and his son, Hunter, would be investigated is an extreme example of executive branch action.

Judicial Control

Where the president and Congress have direct ongoing control over the actions of the bureaucracy, the judiciary's oversight is less apparent but equally important because ultimately, the Supreme Court has the final word on the constitutionality of government acts. Federal judges can issue injunctions or orders to an executive agency even before a rule is publicized, giving them a potent check on the bureaucracy and the president. Such was the case when several federal district court judges found the president's executive order banning immigrants violated the freedom of religion clause in the First Amendment of the Constitution, only to be reversed by the Supreme Court.

The courts also have ruled that agencies must give all affected individuals their due process rights guaranteed by the U.S. Constitution. The Social Security Administration cannot stop a recipient's checks, for example, unless that individual receives reasonable notice and an opportunity for a hearing. These types of cases make up the largest proportion of cases filed in federal district courts.

On a more informal, indirect level, litigation, or even the threat of litigation, often exerts a strong influence on bureaucrats. Injured parties can bring suit against agencies for their failure to enforce a law and can challenge agency interpretations of any law. In general, however, the courts give great weight to the opinions of bureaucrats and usually defer to their expertise.[31]

CONCLUSION AND REVIEW

What Are the Roots of the Federal Bureaucracy?

8.1 Outline the development of the federal bureaucracy.

The federal bureaucracy has changed dramatically since President George Washington's time, when the executive branch had only three departments—State, War, and Treasury. The size of the federal bureaucracy increased significantly following the Civil War. As employment opportunities within the federal government expanded, a civil service system was created to ensure that more and more jobs were filled according to merit and not by patronage. By the late 1800s, reform efforts led to further growth of the bureaucracy, as independent regulatory commissions came into existence. In the wake of the Great Depression, President Franklin D. Roosevelt's New Deal created many new agencies to get the national economy back on course.

How Is the Federal Bureaucracy Formally Organized?

8.2 Describe how the federal bureaucracy is organized.

The federal bureaucracy is comprised of fifteen Cabinet departments and countless other agencies. Federal agencies are classified based on their area of specialization, method of appointing officials, and accountability to the president and Congress. In general, bureaucratic agencies fall into four categories: departments, independent agencies, independent regulatory commissions, and government corporations. The Hatch Act regulates the political activity of employees in the federal government.

Who Are Bureaucrats?

8.3 Describe how the federal bureaucracy is staffed.

The modern bureaucracy has approximately 2.6 million civilian workers from all walks of life. Most of these federal employees are paid according to what is called the "General Schedule" (GS). They advance within fifteen GS grades (as well as steps within those grades), moving into higher GS levels and salaries as their careers progress.

How Does the Bureaucracy Work?

8.4 Identify the roles and responsibilities of the federal bureaucracy.

The bureaucracy is responsible for implementing many laws passed by Congress. A variety of formal and informal mechanisms, such as rule making and administrative adjudication, help bureaucrats make policy.

Political Reform and Realities: How Can the Bureaucracy Be Made Accountable

8.5 Identify the means of controlling the federal bureaucracy.

Agencies enjoy considerable discretion, but they are also subject to many formal controls that help make them more accountable. The president, Congress, and the judiciary all exercise various degrees of control over the bureaucracy through oversight, funding, or litigation.

LEARN THE TERMS

bureaucracy
Cabinet departments
civil service system
Federal Register
government corporations
Great Depression
Hatch Act

independent executive agencies
independent regulatory commissions
interagency councils
iron triangles
issue networks
merit system
patronage

policy coordinating committees
    (PCCs)
regulations
rule making
spoils system

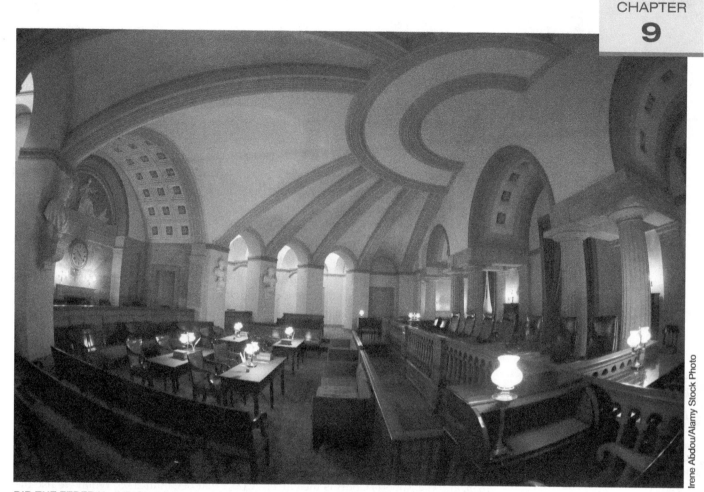

DID THE FEDERAL JUDICIARY, WHICH FRAMER ALEXANDER HAMILTON THOUGHT TO BE "THE LEAST DANGEROUS BRANCH OF GOVERNMENT," ACTUALLY TURN OUT TO BE SO?

When the Framers created the Supreme Court in 1787, they thought it was little more than a theoretical necessity. They even failed to include a building to house the Court and the justices. However, over time, the Court has gained significant powers, both as an institution and as a policy maker. The Supreme Court chamber pictured above is in the Capitol and was the Court's home from 1800 until the present building housing the Court was completed in 1935, located directly across the street from the Capitol Building. This chamber served as a storeroom from 1960 until 1972, when Congress voted to restore it to its nineteenth-century appearance in time for the 1976 Bicentennial celebrations.

CRITICAL THINKING QUESTION: *What role does the Supreme Court play in times of crisis? How can justice and the rule of law be upheld in times of crisis?*

THE JUDICIARY

LEARNING OBJECTIVES

9.1 Describe the constitutional foundations of the federal judiciary and judicial review.

9.2 Describe the structure of the federal judiciary.

9.3 Outline the criteria for nominating and the process of approving federal judges and Supreme Court justices.

9.4 Outline the process by which the Supreme Court makes decisions and the factors that influence judicial decision making.

9.5 Evaluate the role of the Supreme Court in national policy making.

The judicial branch of the national government seemed so inconsequential that when the young government made its move to the District of Columbia in 1800 from New York City, Congress actually forgot to include any space to house the justices of the Supreme Court. Last-minute conferences with Capitol architects led to the allocation of a small area in the basement of the Senate wing of the Capitol Building for a courtroom. Noted one commentator, "A stranger might traverse the dark avenues of the Capitol for a week, without finding the remote corner in which justice is administered to the American Republic."[1]

Historically, Americans have remained unaware of the political power held by the courts. As part of their upbringing, they learned to regard the federal courts as above the fray of politics. That, however, has never been the case. Elected presidents nominate judges to the federal courts and justices to the Supreme Court, and elected senators ultimately confirm (or decline to confirm or even vote on) presidential nominees to the federal bench. The process by which cases ultimately get heard—if they are heard at all—by the Supreme Court often is political as well. Interest groups routinely seek out good test cases to advance their policy positions. Even the U.S. government, generally through the Department of Justice and the U.S. solicitor general (a political appointee in that department), seeks to advance its position in court. Interest groups then often line up on opposing sides to advance their positions, much in the same way lobbyists do in Congress. Today, the role of the courts, particularly the Supreme Court of the United States, differs significantly from what the Framers envisioned.

We offer a note on terminology: In referring to the "Supreme Court," the "Court," or the "high Court" here, we always mean the U.S. Supreme Court, which sits at the pinnacle of the federal and state court systems. The Supreme Court is referred to by the name of the chief justice who presided over it during a particular period. For example, the Marshall Court is the Court presided over by John Marshall from 1801 to 1835, and the Roberts Court is the current Court that began in 2005. When we use the term "courts," we refer to all federal or state courts unless otherwise noted.

Federalist No. 10

A *Federalist Papers* essay authored by James Madison that rejects the principles of direct democracy, arguing that a representative republic is more effective against partisanship and factionalism.

THE

FEDERALIST:

A COLLECTION

OF

E S S A Y S,

WRITTEN IN FAVOUR OF THE

NEW CONSTITUTION,

AS AGREED UPON BY THE FEDERAL CONVENTION,
SEPTEMBER 17, 1787.

IN TWO VOLUMES.

VOL. I.

NEW-YORK:

PRINTED AND SOLD BY J. AND A. M'LEAN,
No. 41, HANOVER-SQUARE.
M,DCC,LXXXVIII.

Fotosearch/Getty Images

WHAT DID THE FEDERALIST PAPERS LOOK LIKE?

Here is one of Thomas Jefferson's editions of Volume I of *The Federalist: A Collection of Essays Written in Favor of the New Constitution*. It was gifted by Elizabeth Hamilton, Alexander Hamilton's wife, to her sister, Angelica Church, who was a friend of Jefferson's.

WHAT ARE THE ROOTS OF THE FEDERAL JUDICIARY?

9.1 Describe the constitutional foundations of the federal judiciary and judicial review.

Under the Articles of Confederation, which governed the united colonies as they fought the Revolutionary War, there was no judicial branch of government. The Continental Congress had no way of enforcing its laws. Thus, it was not surprising that those attending the Constitutional Convention argued for the inclusion of a judicial branch of government. Not all were in agreement, but in 1787, in *Federalist No. 10*, Alexander Hamilton argued that it would be "the least dangerous branch of government." (See Appendix III.) So, as adopted by the Framers, a judicial branch of government was created, setting out its jurisdiction and powers quite vaguely. Article III, which establishes the judicial branch, left it to Congress to create a judicial system and determine the size of the Supreme Court, the only court specifically mentioned there.

Nevertheless, the detailed notes James Madison took at the Constitutional Convention in Philadelphia make it clear that the Framers devoted little time to writing Article III. One scholar has suggested that, for at least some delegates to the Constitutional Convention, "provision for a national judiciary was... more in deference to the maxim of separation [of powers] than in response to clearly formulated ideas about the role of a national judicial system and its indispensability."[2]

The Framers also debated the need for any federal courts below the Supreme Court. Some argued in favor of deciding all cases in state courts, with only appeals going before the Supreme Court. Others argued for a system of federal courts. A compromise left the final choice to Congress, and Article III, section 1, begins simply by vesting "The judicial Power of the United States... in one supreme Court, and in such inferior Courts as the Congress may from time to time ordain and establish."

TABLE 9.1 WHAT KINDS OF CASES DOES THE U.S. SUPREME COURT HEAR?

The following are the types of cases the Supreme Court was given the jurisdiction to hear as initially specified in Article III, section 2, of the Constitution:

All cases arising under the Constitution and laws or treaties of the United States

All cases of admiralty or maritime jurisdiction

Cases in which the United States is a party

Controversies between a state and citizens of another state (later modified by the Eleventh Amendment)

Controversies between two or more states

Controversies between citizens of different states

Controversies between citizens of the same state claiming lands under grants in different states

Controversies between a state, or the citizens thereof, and foreign states or citizens thereof

All cases affecting ambassadors or other public ministers

Article III, section 2, specifies the judicial power of the Supreme Court. It also discusses the types of cases the Court can hear, or its **jurisdiction** (see Table 9.1). Courts have two types of jurisdiction: original and appellate. Original jurisdiction refers to a court's authority to hear disputes as a trial court; these courts determine the facts of a case. The Supreme Court has original jurisdiction in cases involving a conflict between two or more state governments or public officials. Appellate jurisdiction refers to a court's ability to review and/or revise cases already decided by a trial court. The Supreme Court has appellate jurisdiction in all other cases. Article III, section 2, also specifies that all federal crimes, except those involving impeachment, shall be tried by jury in the state in which the crime was committed. The third section of the article defines treason and mandates that at least two witnesses appear in such cases.

Had the Framers envisioned the Supreme Court as the potential policy maker it is today, they most likely would not have provided for life tenure with "good behavior" for all federal judges in Article III. The Framers agreed on this feature because they did not want the justices (or any federal judges) subject to the whims of politics, the public, or politicians. Moreover, Alexander Hamilton argued in *Federalist No. 78* that the "independence of judges" was needed "to guard the Constitution and the rights of individuals." (See Appendix III.)

The Constitution nonetheless did include some checks on the power of the judiciary. One such check gives Congress the authority to alter the Court's ability to hear certain kinds of cases. Congress can also propose constitutional amendments that, if ratified, can effectively reverse judicial decisions. Congress also can impeach and remove federal judges. In one further check, it is the president who, with the "advice and consent" of the Senate, appoints all federal judges.

The Court can, in turn, check the presidency by presiding over presidential impeachment as laid out in Article I, section 3. It says about the process: "When the President of the United States is tried, the Chief Justice shall preside." The Court also can review the constitutionality of executive orders, agreements, and other actions. Such was the case in June 2018 when the Supreme Court upheld the constitutionality of President Donald J. Trump's executive order banning immigrants from seven nations believed by the administration to harbor individuals who jeopardized national security.[3] National security, it should be noted, is an area in which the Court often gives great leeway to presidential powers.

jurisdiction

Authority vested in a particular court to hear and decide the issues in a particular case. Original jurisdiction is the jurisdiction of courts that hear a case first, usually in a trial. These courts determine the facts of a case. Appellate jurisdiction is the power vested in particular courts to review and/or revise the decision of a lower court.

Federalist No. 78

A *Federalist Papers* essay authored by Alexander Hamilton that covers the role of the federal judiciary, including the power of judicial review.

Drew Angerer/Getty Images

WHAT ROLE DOES THE COURT HAVE IN PRESIDENTIAL IMPEACHMENTS?

The Constitution requires the Supreme Court chief to preside in presidential impeachments, as did Chief Justice John Roberts in President Trump's first impeachment trial in 2019. Here, Fiona Hill, the National Security Council's former senior director for Europe and Russia, and David Holmes, an official from the American embassy in Ukraine, are sworn in before testifying to the House Intelligence Committee.

The Judiciary's Acts of 1789 and 1801 and the Creation of the Federal Judicial System

In spite of the Framers' intentions, the pervasive role of politics in the judicial branch quickly became evident with the passage of the Judiciary Act of 1789. Congress spent nearly the entire second half of its first session deliberating the various provisions of the act to give form and substance to the federal judiciary. As one early observer noted, "The convention has only crayoned in the outlines. It left it to Congress to fill up and colour the canvas."[4]

Judiciary Act of 1789

Legislative act that established the basic three-tiered structure of the federal court system.

The **Judiciary Act of 1789** established the basic three-tiered structure of the federal court system. At the bottom were the federal district courts—at least one in each state. If people participating in a lawsuit (called litigants) are unhappy with a district court's verdict, they can appeal their case to circuit courts (see Figures 9.1 and 9.2),

FIGURE 9.1 HOW IS THE AMERICAN JUDICIAL SYSTEM STRUCTURED?

The American judicial system is a dual system consisting of the federal court system and the judicial systems of the fifty states. In both the federal court system and the judiciaries of most states, there are both trial and appellate courts. The U.S. Supreme Court sits at the top of both court systems and has the power to hear appeals from both federal and state courts.

FEDERAL COURT SYSTEM

Original Jurisdiction   *Appellate Jurisdiction*

U.S. Supreme Court
(2019–2020 term: heard 74 cases; decided 63)

The Supreme Court rarely exercises its original jurisdiction (1–3 percent of cases heard). Cases are heard by the Supreme Court first when they involve:
- Two or more states
- The United States and a state
- Foreign ambassadors and other diplomats
- A state and a citizen of another state (if the action is begun by the state)

Most cases heard by the Supreme Court are under its appellate jurisdiction (97–99 percent of cases heard). The Supreme Court can agree to hear cases involving appeals from:
- U.S. courts of appeals
- Highest state courts (only in cases involving federal questions)
- Court of Military Appeals

U.S. Courts of Appeals
(13 courts handling about 50,000 cases per year)

No original jurisdiction

Hear appeals of cases from:
- Lower federal courts
- U.S. regulatory commissions
- Legislative courts, including the U.S. Court of Federal Claims and U.S. Court of Veterans Claims

U.S. District Courts
(94 courts handling about 426,000 cases per year)

Cases are heard in U.S. district courts when they involve:
- The federal government as a party
- Civil suits under federal law
- Civil suits between citizens of different states if the amount at issue is more than $75,000
- Admiralty or maritime disputes
- Bankruptcy
- Other matters assigned to them by Congress

No appellate jurisdiction

STATE COURT SYSTEM

Highest State Courts
(52 courts handling 95,000 cases per year)

State Intermediate Appellate Courts
(found in 39 states; handling 240,000 cases per year)

State Trial Courts
(83 million filings per year)

constituting the second tier. As discussed later in the chapter, district courts function as trial courts. Circuit courts were initially created to function as trial courts for important cases. Originally, they were made up of one district court judge and two Supreme Court justices who met as a circuit court twice a year to hear appeals from district courts. Not until 1891 did circuit courts (or, as we know them today, courts of appeals) take on their exclusively appellate function and begin to focus solely on reviewing the findings of lower courts. The third tier of the federal judicial system as specified in Article III is the Supreme Court of the United States. Although the Constitution mentions "the supreme Court," it did not designate its size. In the Judiciary Act of 1789, Congress set the size of the Supreme Court at six—the chief justice plus five associate justices. After being reduced to five members by the Judiciary Act of 1801, Congress expanded and contracted the Court's size until it was fixed at nine in 1869.

Article III, section 1, guarantees that the salaries of all federal judges will not be reduced during their service on the bench. At the Constitutional Convention, considerable debate raged over how to treat the payment of federal judges. Some believed Congress should have an extra check on the judiciary by being able to reduce their salaries. This provision was a compromise after James Madison suggested that Congress have the authority to bar increases and decreases in the salaries of these unelected jurists. The delegates recognized that decreases—as well as no opportunity for raises—could negatively affect the perks associated with life tenure.

John Jay was appointed chief justice of the Supreme Court of the United States by President George Washington. From this time onward, Courts were known by the name of the chief justice. Thus, the first Supreme Court was known as the *Jay Court*. When the justices met in their first public session in New York City in 1790, they were garbed magnificently in black and scarlet robes in the English fashion. The elegance of their attire, however, could not compensate for the relative ineffectiveness of the Court. Its first session had to be adjourned when fewer than half the justices attended. Later, once a sufficient number of justices assembled, the Court decided only one major case. Moreover, as an indication of its lowly status, one associate justice left the Court to become chief justice of the South Carolina Supreme Court. Although today we might consider such a move as a step down, keep in mind that in the early years of the United States, many people viewed the states, and thus their courts, as more important than the national government.

Hampered by frequent changes in personnel, limited space for its operations, no clerical support, and no system of reporting its decisions, the early Court did not impress many people. From the beginning, the circuit court duties of the Supreme Court justices presented problems for the prestige of the Court. Few good lawyers were willing to accept nominations to the Court because circuit court duties entailed a substantial amount of travel—most of it on horseback over poorly maintained roads. Southern justices often rode as many as 10,000 miles a year on horseback. President George Washington tried to prevail on several friends and supporters to fill vacancies on the Court, but most refused the "honor." John Adams, the second president of the United States, ran into similar problems. When Adams asked John Jay to resume the position of chief justice after Jay resigned to become governor of New York, Jay declined the offer.

In spite of these problems, in its first decade, the Court took several actions to mold the new nation. First, by declining to give George Washington advice on the legality of some of his actions, the justices attempted to establish the Supreme Court as an independent, nonpolitical branch of government. Although John Jay frequently gave the president private advice, the Court refused to answer questions President George Washington posed to it concerning the construction of international laws and treaties.

The early Court also tried to advance Federalist principles of nationalism and to maintain the national government's supremacy over the states. As circuit court jurists, the justices rendered numerous decisions on such matters as the legality of national suppression of the Whiskey Rebellion, which occurred in 1794 after imposition of a national excise tax on whiskey, and the unconstitutionality of the Alien and Sedition Acts, which made it a crime to criticize national governmental officials or their actions.

During the ratification debates, Anti-Federalists warned that Article III extended federal judicial power to controversies "between a State and Citizens of another State"—meaning that a citizen of one state could sue any other state in federal court, a prospect unthinkable to defenders of state sovereignty. Although Federalists, including Alexander Hamilton and James Madison, had scoffed at the idea, the nationalist Supreme Court quickly proved them wrong in *Chisholm* v. *Georgia* (1793). In *Chisholm*, the justices interpreted the Court's jurisdiction under Article III, section 2, to include the right to hear suits brought by a citizen against a state in which he did not reside. Writing in *Chisholm*, Associate Justice James Wilson denounced the "haughty notions of state independence, state sovereignty, and state supremacy."[5] The states' reaction to this perceived attack on their authority led to passage and ratification in 1798 of the **Eleventh Amendment** to the Constitution, which specifically limited judicial power by stipulating that the authority of the federal courts could not "extend to any suit commenced or prosecuted against one of the United States by citizens of another State."

The debate between Federalists and Anti-Federalists that had fueled many of the conflicts surrounding ratification of the Constitution found new life as the Federalist-dominated Sixth Congress passed the **Judiciary Act of 1801**, which gave Federalists the opportunity to pack the courts with Federalist judges with lifetime appointments. Thomas Jefferson, a Democratic-Republican, defeated John Adams, a Federalist, in Adams's failed bid for a second term in office. The election was decided on February 17, 1801. However, President-elect Jefferson had to wait until March 4, 1801, to assume office. Adams surprised and angered Democratic-Republicans by convincing the outgoing Federalist Congress to pass the Judiciary Act of 1801.

While the Judiciary Act of 1789 set out the general framework of the federal judiciary, the 1801 act went further. It reduced the size of the Supreme Court from six to five and created sixteen additional federal judgeships. It also created new circuit courts to relieve Supreme Court justices from dreaded circuit court duties, which required considerable travel and personal inconvenience. By March 3, 1801, the Senate had confirmed all fifty-eight nominations made by Adams to fill judicial positions created by the new act. Once Adams received notice of the confirmations, he stayed on the job until midnight on March 3, his last day in office, to execute the official commissions of the fifty-eight nominees. All were Federalists. Adams's Federalist secretary of state sealed all of the commissions and gave them to his brother to deliver. When Jefferson heard the news the next day before his inauguration, he was livid. All of those who had commissions in hand were duly sworn in, guaranteeing a Federalist Supreme Court for years to come. Some commissions, however, remained undelivered and eventually culminated in one of the Supreme Court's most seminal decisions, *Marbury* v. *Madison* (1803). William Marbury was among the judicial nominees who did not receive his commission to be a justice of the peace for the District of Columbia.

The Marshall Court: *Marbury* v. *Madison* (1803) and Judicial Review

The actions of *John Marshall*, who headed the Court from 1801 to 1835, brought much needed respect and prestige to the Court. President John Adams appointed Marshall as chief justice in 1800, three years after he declined to accept a nomination as associate justice. An ardent Federalist, Marshall is considered the most important justice to serve on the Court. Part of his reputation results from the duration of his service and the historical significance of this period in our nation's history.

As chief justice, Marshall helped to establish the role and power of the Court. The Marshall Court discontinued the practice of *seriatim* (Latin for "in a series") opinions, which was the custom of the King's Bench in Great Britain. Prior to the Marshall Court, the justices delivered their individual opinions in order of seniority. For the Court to take its place as an equal branch of government, Marshall believed the justices needed to speak as a Court

---

Eleventh Amendment

An amendment adopted in 1789 protecting states from being sued in federal court by a citizen of a different state or country.

Judiciary Act of 1801

A partisian effort by Federalists to pack the federal courts with Federalist judges. It also reduced the size of the Supreme Court from six to five to limit incoming President Thomas Jefferson's ability to appoint state's rights minded Democratic-Federalists.

and not as six individuals. In fact, during Marshall's first four years in office, the Court routinely spoke as one, and the chief justice wrote twenty-four of its twenty-six opinions.

The Marshall Court also established the authority of the Supreme Court over the judiciaries of the various states.[6] In addition, the Court established the supremacy of the federal government and Congress over state governments through a broad interpretation of the necessary and proper clause in *McCulloch* v. *Maryland* (1819).[7]

Finally, and most importantly, the Marshall Court claimed the right of **judicial review**, the power of the courts to review acts of other branches of government and of the states. The Supreme Court derives much of its day-to-day power and impact on the policy process from this right. This claim established the Court as the final arbiter of constitutional questions, with the right to declare congressional acts void.[8]

Alexander Hamilton first publicly endorsed the idea of judicial review in *Federalist No. 78*, noting, "Whenever a particular statute contravenes the Constitution, it will be the duty of the judicial tribunals to adhere to the latter and disregard the former." Nonetheless, because the Constitution of the United States does not mention judicial review, the actual authority of the Supreme Court to review the constitutionality of acts of Congress was an unsettled question. But, in ***Marbury* v. *Madison* (1803)**, Chief Justice John Marshall claimed this sweeping authority for the Court by asserting that the Constitution's supremacy clause implies the right of judicial review.[9]

Marbury v. *Madison* arose amid a sea of political controversy. In the final hours of his administration, John Adams appointed William Marbury as a justice of the peace for the District of Columbia. But, in the confusion of winding up matters, when Adams's secretary of state failed to deliver Marbury's commission, Marbury then asked James Madison, Thomas Jefferson's secretary of state, for the commission. Under direct orders from Jefferson, who was irate over the Adams administration's last-minute appointment of Federalist judges, often referred to as "Midnight Judges," Madison refused to turn over the commission. Marbury and three other Adams appointees who were in the same situation then filed a writ of *mandamus* (a legal motion) asking the Supreme Court to order Madison to deliver their commissions.

Political tensions ran high as the Court met to hear the case. Jefferson distrusted and detested Marshall, who was his distant cousin, and threatened to ignore any order of the Court. Marshall realized that a refusal of the executive branch to comply with the decision could devastate both him and the prestige of the Court. Marshall responded to this challenge, in a brilliant opinion that reads more like a lecture to Jefferson than a discussion of the merits of Marbury's claim. Marshall concluded that although Marbury and the others were entitled to their commissions, the Court lacked the power to issue the writ sought by Marbury. In *Marbury* v. *Madison*, Marshall further ruled that those parts of the Judiciary Act of 1789 that extended the original jurisdiction of the Court to allow it to issue writs of *mandamus* were inconsistent with the Constitution and therefore unconstitutional.

Although the immediate effect of the decision was to deny power to the Court, its long-term effect was to establish the implied power of judicial review. Said Marshall, writing for the Court, "it is emphatically the province and duty of the judicial department to say what the law is." Since *Marbury*, the Court has routinely exercised the power of judicial review to determine the constitutionality of acts of Congress, the executive branch, and the states.

judicial review
Power of the courts to review acts of other branches of government and the states.

***Marbury* v. *Madison* (1803)**
Case in which the Supreme Court first asserted the power of judicial review by finding that part of the congressional statute extending the Court's original jurisdiction was unconstitutional.

Stock Montage/Getty Images

WHY IS JOHN MARSHALL IMPORTANT TO THE DEVELOPMENT OF JUDICIAL AUTHORITY?

A single person can make a major difference in the development of an institution. Such was the case with John Marshall (1755–1835), who served thirty-four years as chief justice. More of a politician than a lawyer, Marshall served as a delegate to the Virginia legislature and played an instrumental role in Virginia's ratification of the Constitution in 1787. When Oliver Ellsworth resigned as chief justice of the United States in 1800, Adams nominated Marshall. Marshall served on the Court until the day he died, participating in more than 1,000 decisions and authoring more than 500 opinions.

WHAT IS THE STRUCTURE OF THE FEDERAL COURT SYSTEM?

9.2 Describe the structure of the federal judiciary.

The judicial system in the United States can best be described as a dual system consisting of the federal court system and the judicial systems of the fifty states. Cases may arise in either system. Both systems are basically three-tiered. At the bottom of the system are **trial courts**, where litigation begins. In the middle are **appellate courts**; these courts generally review only findings of law made by trial courts. At the top of both the federal and state court systems sits a court of last resort (see Figure 9.1). In the federal court system, trial courts are called district courts, appellate courts are termed courts of appeals, and the Supreme Court is the court of last resort. Various states have different names for their courts but all follow a basic, three-tiered system. State courts actually handle 95 percent of all cases filed.

The federal district courts, courts of appeals, and the Supreme Court are called **constitutional (or Article III) courts** because Article III of the Constitution either established them or authorized Congress to establish them. The president nominates (with the advice and consent of the Senate) judges who preside over these courts, and they serve lifetime terms, as long as they engage in "good behavior."

In addition to constitutional courts, six **legislative courts** were set up by Congress, under its implied powers, generally for special purposes. Examples of legislative courts are the U.S. Tax Court and the U.S. Bankruptcy Court, which some call Article I courts. The president appoints (subject to Senate confirmation) the judges who preside over these federal courts; they serve fixed, fifteen-year renewable terms.

The District Courts

As we have seen, Congress created U.S. district courts when it enacted the Judiciary Act of 1789. District courts are federal trial courts. Currently, the federal district courts number ninety-four. Only one district court cuts across state lines (see Figure 9.2). Every state has at least one federal district court, and California, Texas, and New York each have four (see Figure 9.2).[10]

Federal district courts, in which the bulk of the judicial work takes place in the federal system, have original jurisdiction over only specific types of cases. Rules governing district court jurisdiction can be complex. Cases, which are heard in federal district courts by a single judge (with or without a jury), generally fall into one of three categories:

1. They involve the federal government as a party.
2. They present a federal question based on a claim under the Constitution, a treaty with another nation, or a federal statute. This is called federal question jurisdiction, and it can involve criminal or civil law.
3. They involve civil suits in which citizens are from different states, and the amount of money exceeds the sum or value of $75,000. Claims of $75,000 or lower will not be heard. Cases involving citizens from different states can be filed in state or federal court.

Each federal judicial district has a U.S. attorney, nominated by the president and confirmed by the Senate. The U.S. attorney in each district is that district's chief law enforcement officer. U.S. attorneys serve at the pleasure of the president but require Senate confirmation. President Trump accepted the resignation of or fired every U.S. attorney after he came into office, leaving all ninety-four districts without a political appointee. U.S. attorneys have a considerable amount of discretion regarding whether they pursue criminal or civil investigations or file charges against individuals or corporations. They also have several staff lawyers to help them in their work. The number of assistant U.S. attorneys in each district depends on the amount of litigation each handles. Some cases are conducted with a jury; others are not.

trial court
Court of original jurisdiction where cases begin.

appellate court
Court that generally reviews only findings of law made by lower courts.

constitutional (or Article III) courts
Federal courts specifically created by the Constitution of the United States or by Congress pursuant to its authority in Article III.

legislative courts
Courts established by Congress for specialized purposes, such as the Court of Appeals for Veterans Claims.

The Courts of Appeals

Established in 1789, the federal courts of appeals (known as the circuit courts of appeals prior to 1948) hear cases from the district courts and are the intermediate courts in the federal system. The losing party in a case heard and decided in a federal district court can appeal the decision to the appropriate court of appeals. There are thirteen courts; eleven are numbered. The twelfth is the U.S. Court of Appeals for the D.C. Circuit, which handles most appeals involving federal regulatory commissions and agencies, including the National Labor Relations Board and the Securities and Exchange Commission. The thirteenth federal appeals court is the U.S. Court of Appeals for the Federal Circuit, which has nationwide authority over cases dealing with patents and from the U.S. Court of International Trade and the U.S. Court of Federal Claims.

There are 179 court of appeals judgeships in total. The number of judges within each court of appeals varies—depending on the workload and the complexity of the cases—and ranges from eleven to nearly thirty. Supervising each court is a chief judge, the most senior judge in terms of service below the age of sixty-five, who can serve no more than seven years as the chief. In deciding cases, judges are divided into rotating three-judge panels, made up of the active judges within the court of appeals, visiting judges (primarily district judges from the same court), and judges on "senior service." In rare cases, all the judges in a court of appeals may choose to sit together (*en banc*) to decide a case of special importance by majority vote.

The courts of appeals have no original jurisdiction. Rather, Congress has granted these courts appellate jurisdiction over two general categories of cases: (1) appeals from criminal and civil cases from the district courts, and, (2) appeals from administrative agencies. Criminal and civil case appeals constitute about 90 percent of the workload of the courts of appeals; those from administrative agencies constitute about 10 percent.

Once a federal court of appeals makes a decision, a litigant no longer has an automatic right to an appeal. The losing party may submit a petition to the U.S. Supreme Court to hear the case, but the Court grants few of these requests. The courts of appeals, then, are the courts of last resort for almost all federal litigation. Keep in mind, however, that most cases, if they actually go to trial, go no further than the district court level where most cases are actually solved by pleas (criminal cases) or settlements (civil cases).

In general, courts of appeals try to correct errors of law and procedure that have occurred in lower courts or administrative agencies. Courts of appeals hear no new testimony; instead, lawyers submit written arguments in what is called a **brief** (also submitted in trial courts), and lawyers then appear to present and argue the case orally to the three-judge court. Decisions of any court of appeals are binding on only the district courts within its geographic confines (see Figure 9.2).

brief
A document containing the legal written arguments in a case filed with a court by a party prior to a hearing or trial.

The Supreme Court

The U.S. Supreme Court is often at the center of highly controversial issues that the political process has yet to resolve successfully. It reviews cases from the U.S. courts of appeals and state supreme courts (as well as other courts of last resort) and acts as the final interpreter of the Constitution.

Since 1869, the U.S. Supreme Court has consisted of eight associate justices and one chief justice, whom the president nominates specifically for that position. The number nine holds no special significance, and the Constitution does not specify the size of the Court. Between 1789 and 1869, Congress periodically altered the size of the Court. The lowest number of justices on the Court was five; the most, ten. Through March 2021, only seventeen chief justices and 115 justices had served on the Court.

Compared with the president or Congress, the Supreme Court operates with few support staff. Along with the four clerks each justice employs, the Supreme Court has only about 400 staff members.

FIGURE 9.2 WHAT ARE THE BOUNDARIES OF FEDERAL DISTRICT COURTS AND COURTS OF APPEALS?

This map shows the location of each U.S. court of appeals and the boundaries of the federal district courts in states with more than one district. Note that there are eleven numbered and two unnumbered courts of appeals. There are also ninety-four district courts. States are divided into between one and four districts; no district court crosses state lines, with the exception of the Tenth Circuit, which includes those portions of the Yellowstone National Park extending into Montana and Idaho (but not shown on this map).

SOURCE: Data from United States Courts, http://www.uscourts.gov/.

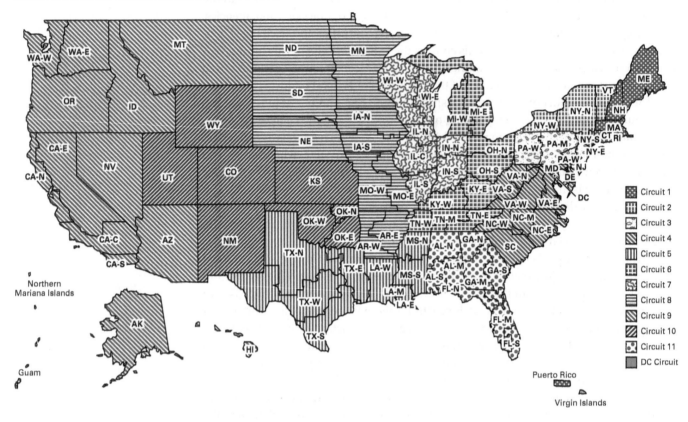

Decisions of the U.S. Supreme Court, however, are binding throughout the nation and establish national **precedents**. Precedents are rules for settling subsequent cases of similar nature. This reliance on past decisions or precedents to formulate decisions in new cases is called *stare decisis* (a Latin phrase meaning "let the decision stand"). The principle of *stare decisis* allows for continuity and predictability in our judicial system. Although *stare decisis* can be helpful in predicting decisions, at times judges carve out new ground and ignore, decline to follow, or even overrule precedents to reach a different conclusion in a case involving similar circumstances. This is a major reason why so much litigation exists in America today. Parties to a suit know that the outcome of a case is not always predictable; if such prediction were possible, there would be little reason to go to court.

precedent

A prior judicial decision that serves as a rule for settling subsequent cases of a similar nature.

stare decisis

In court rulings, a reliance on past decisions or precedents to formulate decisions in new cases.

HOW ARE FEDERAL COURT JUDGES SELECTED?

9.3 Outline the criteria for nominating and the process of approving federal judges and Supreme Court justices.

The selection of federal judges is often a highly political process with important political ramifications. The president must nominate judges and the U.S. Senate must confirm them. Presidents, in general, try to select well-qualified individuals for the bench. But these appointments also provide presidents with opportunities to shape the federal courts philosophically (see Figure 9.3).

FIGURE 9.3 WHO ARE FEDERAL JUDGES?

Judicial appointments provide presidents with an opportunity to make a lasting impact on public policy. Recent presidents have also used them as an opportunity to increase the gender and racial diversity of the federal branch and to gain favor with traditionally underrepresented groups. In the first years of the Trump presidency, this trend did not continue. By the end of his term, President Trump had appointed Hispanic judges and the same number of Black judges to the Court of Appeals. One quarter of all federal judges were appointed by President Trump before the November 2020 election—a record percentage.

SOURCE: Federal Judicial Center, *Biographical Directory of Federal Judges* and Pew Research Center, "Trump Trails Recent Predecessors in Appointing Non-White Federal Judges." Posted July 14, 2020.

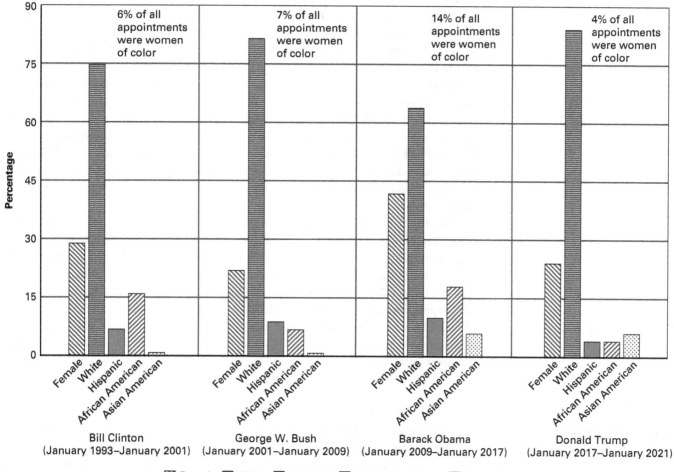

In selecting nominees, the president may look for guidance from members of Congress, advisers, confidantes, or other high-ranking party officials.[11] The Constitution mandates that presidents receive advice and consent from the Senate. Historically, presidents have screened their lower court nominees through a process known as *senatorial courtesy*. This is the process by which presidents generally allow senators from the state in which a judicial vacancy occurs to block a nomination by simply registering their objection if they belong to the president's political party. One way senators may voice their opposition is through an informal process known as the "blue slip." When a judicial nomination is forwarded to the Senate Judiciary Committee, senators from the state in which a vacancy occurs are sent a letter, usually printed on light blue paper, asking them to register their support or opposition to a nominee. How seriously senators take the blue slips varies from one Congress to the next.[12] Senators not of the president's party frequently object to nominations on party principles.

Who Are Federal Judges?

Justice Oliver Wendell Holmes once remarked that a justice should be a "combination of Justinian, Jesus Christ and John Marshall."[13] Individuals who serve on judicial tribunals gain this knowledge through a number of common experiences. Most judges have held other political offices, such as a lower federal or state court judge or prosecutor. Many have been involved in politics, which is what usually brings them into consideration for a position on the federal bench. White males continue to dominate as federal judges, but since the 1970s, with the exception of President Donald J. Trump, presidents have pledged (with varying degrees of success) to do their best to appoint more Black Americans, Hispanic Americans, women, and other underrepresented groups to the federal bench. President Barack Obama's appointees to the district courts set new records—41.7 percent of his appointees were from underrepresented groups, more than double that of George W. Bush. Seventy percent of President Obama's nominees were women and minorities, but many of them were not confirmed. When President Obama left office in January 2017, a record-high number of judicial vacancies (107) had not been filled, more than two times the number left by President George W. Bush. Senate Republicans stalled all of his nominees, including to the Supreme Court, in anticipation of a Republican presidential victory and an opportunity to reshape the federal courts for decades in a more conservative direction.

President Donald J. Trump's nominees were approved by the Republican-controlled Senate without the challenges Obama faced. Trump had more court of appeals judges confirmed in his first year than any other president, not including the appointment of a Supreme Court justice, as vacancies continued to occur at record rates.[14] His appointments led to a "Whitening" of the federal courts. In fact, 84 percent of his appointments through July 2020 were White people. On the Fifth Circuit Court of Appeals, for example, which includes Texas—where 40 percent of the population is Hispanic—there are no active Hispanic judges on the Court, although President Trump appointed six of its seventeen members."

Nomination Criteria

Sandra Day O'Connor

An associate justice of the Supreme Court from 1981 to 2005 who was appointed by President Ronald Reagan as the first woman to serve on the Court.

Justice **Sandra Day O'Connor** once remarked that "You have to be lucky" to be appointed to the judiciary.[15] Although luck certainly factors in, over the years a variety of reasons have accounted for nominations to the bench. Depending on the timing of a vacancy, a president may or may not have a list of possible candidates or even a specific individual in mind. Until recently, presidents often looked within their circle of friends or their administration to fill a vacancy. Nevertheless, whether the nominee is a friend or someone known to the president only by reputation, at least five criteria are especially important: experience; ideology or policy preferences; pursuit of political support; religion; and race, ethnicity, and gender.

EXPERIENCE Most nominees have had at least some judicial, legal, or governmental experience. For example, John Jay, the first chief justice, was one of the authors of *The Federalist Papers* and was active in New York politics.

Elena Kagan

An associate justice of the Supreme Court, appointed by President Barack Obama in 2009 while she was serving as solicitor general in his administration.

Service on a lower federal court has become almost a de facto requirement for nomination to the Supreme Court.[16] All nine sitting Supreme Court justices but one—former U.S. Solicitor General **Elena Kagan**—have prior judicial experience (see Table 9.2). Many of the sitting justices also served as law professors; notably, Justice Kagan was past dean of the Harvard Law School. Coincidentally, both of President Trump's picks for the Court, Neil Gorsuch and Brett Kavanaugh, clerked for the same justice: Anthony Kennedy. Gorsuch served alongside Justice Kennedy, and Kavanaugh filled his vacancy when he retired. His third appointee, Amy Coney Berrett, clerked for Justice Antonin Scalia.

TABLE 9.2 WHO ARE THE JUSTICES OF THE SUPREME COURT IN DECEMBER 2020?

Name of Justice	Year of Birth	Year Appointed	Political Party	Law School	Appointing President	Religion	Prior Judicial Experience	Prior Government Experience
John G. Roberts, Jr.	1955	2005	R	Harvard	G. W. Bush	Roman Catholic	U.S. Court of Appeals	Dept. of Justice, associate White House counsel
Clarence Thomas	1948	1991	R	Yale	G. H. W. Bush	Roman Catholic	U.S. Court of Appeals	Chair, Equal Employment Opportunity Commission
Stephen A. Breyer	1938	1994	D	Harvard	Clinton	Jewish	U.S. Court of Appeals	Chief counsel, Senate Judiciary Committee
Samuel A. Alito	1950	2006	R	Yale	G. W. Bush	Roman Catholic	U.S. Court of Appeals	Dept. of Justice, U.S. attorney
Sonia Sotomayor	1954	2009	D	Yale	Obama	Roman Catholic	U.S. Court of Appeals	Assistant attorney general, City of New York
Elena Kagan	1960	2010	D	Harvard	Obama	Jewish	None	U.S. solicitor general, associate White House counsel
Neil Gorsuch	1967	2017	R	Harvard	Trump	Roman Catholic or Episcopalian	U.S. Court of Appeals.	Principal deputy to the associate attorney general
Brett Kavanaugh	1965	2018	R	Yale	Trump	Roman Catholic	U.S. Court of Appeals	White House staff secretary
Amy Coney Barrett	1972	2020	R	Notre Dame	Trump	Roman Catholic	U.S. Court of Appeals	None

IDEOLOGY OR POLICY PREFERENCES   Most presidents also seek to appoint individuals who share their policy preferences, and almost all have political goals in mind when they appoint a judge or justice. The previous political experience of judges if often an indicator of some of the ideological beliefs about the role of courts or their stands on policy issues. Chief Justice John G. Roberts, Jr. and Justice Samuel A. Alito, for example, both Republicans, worked in the Department of Justice during the Reagan and George Bush administrations. More recently, Justice Kagan worked in the Obama administration, and Justice Gorsuch for George W. Bush.

Presidents, however, often have erred in their assumptions about their appointees' ideological or policy preferences. President Dwight D. Eisenhower, a moderate conservative, for example, was appalled by the liberal opinions written by his appointee to Chief Justice, Earl Warren, concerning criminal defendants' rights. Most legal commentators were stunned when Neil Gorsuch, a Trump appointee, authored the 6–3 opinion, joined by the Chief Justice and the four liberals on the Court—Justices Stephen Breyer, Ruth Bader Ginsburg, Sonia Sotomayor, and Elena Kagan—ruling that the Civil Rights Act of 1964 protects lesbian, gay, and transgender employees from employment discrimination. President Trump's Justice Department argued that members of the LGBT community were *not* protected by the act.

PURSUIT OF POLITICAL SUPPORT   During Ronald Reagan's successful campaign for the presidency in 1980, some of his advisers feared the gender gap would hurt him. Polls repeatedly showed that he was far less popular with female voters than with men. To gain support from women, Reagan announced during his campaign that should he win, he would appoint a woman to fill the first vacancy on the Supreme Court. When Justice Potter Stewart, a moderate, announced his retirement from the bench, President Reagan, under pressure from women's rights groups, nominated Sandra Day O'Connor of the Arizona Court of Appeals to fill the vacancy. During the 2020 presidential campaign, Joe Biden promised he would appoint an African American woman to the next vacancy on the Supreme Court.

In 2016, with a Supreme Court vacancy on the line, then-candidate Trump often rallied his supporters on the need to have him, and not Hillary Clinton, appoint the next Supreme Court justice. After his win, not only did Trump pick a highly regarded, very conservative justice in Neil Gorsuch, but Gorsuch became the second-youngest justice on the Court at the time of his appointment, ensuring a conservative voice on the Court long after the president's departure. With Justice Anthony Kennedy's retirement in 2018, the addition of a second appointment, Brett Kavanaugh, allowed Trump to further reward his supporters by creating a majority on the Court of justices who oppose any federal abortion rights—something no other Republican president had been able to do. Nevertheless, as discussed in Chapter 4, when the newly constituted Court decided its first case dealing with the constitutionality of a state law that required physicians performing abortions to have hospital privileges, Chief Justice Roberts, an appointee of Republican President George W. Bush, side with the four liberals to find the law unconstitutional. But in 2021, he flipped, joining the other conservative justices including Amy Coney Barrett, in reinstating a state law requiring women seeking medication to produce an abortion must visit a physician in person to get the pill.

RELIGION   Through fall 2020, of the 114 justices who have served or are serving on the Court, almost all were members of traditional Protestant faiths. Fewer than fifteen have been Roman Catholic, and only eight have been Jewish.[17] Today, more Catholics—John Roberts, Clarence Thomas, Samuel Alito, Sonia Sotomayor, Neil Gorsuch, Brett Kavanaugh, and Amy Coney Barrett—serve on the Court than at any other point in history. Neil Gorsuch attended Roman Catholic schools from kindergarten through high school, but now attends church services with his wife, an Episcopalian. Two Jewish justices—Stephen Breyer and Elena Kagan—round out the Court. At one time, no one could have imagined that Catholics would someday make up a majority of the Court or that but one Protestant, Neil Gorsuch, who was raised a Catholic and attended Catholic high school, would serve on the Court.

RACE, ETHNICITY, AND GENDER   Through December 2020, only two Black Americans and five women have served on the Court. Race was undoubtedly a critical issue in the appointment of Clarence Thomas to replace Thurgood Marshall, the first Black American justice.

As the ethnic diversity of the United States increased, presidents also faced greater pressure to nominate a Hispanic justice to the Supreme Court. Early in his presidency, President Barack Obama fulfilled these expectations by nominating Sonia Sotomayor. A Puerto Rican woman and self-proclaimed "wise Latina woman" who grew up in the Bronx, New York, Sotomayor became the first Hispanic Supreme Court justice at the height of a fierce immigration debate.

Today, more women—three—serve on the Supreme Court than at any other time in history. Significant numbers of female judges serve in the lower federal courts, but their numbers are far from representative in comparison to the overall percentage of women in the legal profession.

The Confirmation Process

The Constitution gives the Senate the authority to approve all nominees to the federal bench. Ordinarily, nominations are referred to the Senate Judiciary Committee. This committee investigates the nominees, holds hearings, and votes on its recommendation for Senate action. At this stage, the committee may reject a nominee or send the nomination to the full Senate for a vote. The full Senate then deliberates on the nominee before voting. A simple majority vote is required for confirmation. During the 2016 presidential campaign, Donald J. Trump took the unprecedented action of releasing two lists of potential Supreme Court nominees. Both lists were put together for hm by the highly respected conservative Federalist Society, made up of law students, professors, and lawyers, and the also conservative Heritage Society.[18]

INVESTIGATION   As a president proceeds to narrow the list of possible nominees for a judicial vacancy, White House staff begin an investigation into their personal and professional backgrounds. The Federal Bureau of Investigation also receives names of potential nominees for background checks. In addition, traditionally, the names are forwarded to the American Bar Association (ABA), the politically powerful organization that represents the interests of the legal profession. After its own investigation, the ABA rates each nominee, based on his or her qualifications, as Well Qualified (previously "Highly Qualified"), Qualified, or Not Qualified.

After a formal nomination is made and sent to the Senate, the Senate Judiciary Committee embarks on its own investigation. To start, the Senate Judiciary Committee asks each nominee to complete a lengthy questionnaire detailing previous work (dating as far back as high school summer jobs), judicial opinions written, judicial philosophy, speeches, and even all interviews ever given to members of the press. Committee staffers also contact potential witnesses who might offer testimony concerning the nominee's fitness for office.

LOBBYING BY INTEREST GROUPS   Many organized interests show keen interest in the nomination process. Interest groups are particularly active in Supreme Court nominations. For example, in 1987, the nomination of Judge Robert H. Bork to the Supreme Court led liberal groups to launch an extensive radio, TV, and print media campaign against the nominee. These interest groups decried Bork's actions as U.S. solicitor general, especially his firing of the Watergate special prosecutor at the request of President Richard M. Nixon, as well as his political beliefs. As a result of this outcry, the Senate rejected Bork's nomination by a 42–58 vote. The role of the Federalist Society, of which Justices Roberts, Thomas, Alito, Gorsuch, Kavanaugh and Barrett have been members, is stunning. Basically, it drew up lists of acceptable judicial nominees for all federal courts, taking over the selection process from the President Trump.

More and more, interest groups are also involving themselves in district court and court of appeals nominations. They recognize that these appointments increasingly pave the way for future nominees to the Supreme Court. In

Andrew Harnik/AP Images

WHAT ROLE DOES THE SENATE JUDICIARY COMMITTEE PLAY IN THE JUDICIAL NOMINATION PROCESS?

The Senate Judiciary Committee must hold hearings concerning the nominations of all federal judges. Its recommendation of approval is then sent to the full Senate for a vote. It holds public hearings, usually televised gavel to gavel, grilling nominees on their judicial philosophies, decisions they've written, and even personal questions. Trump's last Supreme Court appointee, Amy Coney Barrett, was confirmed by a vote of 52-48 on October 26, 2020. Confirmation hearings for Trump's second Supreme Court nominee, Brett Kavanaugh, began September 4, 2018, and lasted four days. Controversy followed the nominee throughout the process. On the first day of hearings, Kavanaugh refused to shake the hand of Fred Guttenberg, the father of a Parkland shooting victim, and later, when Dr. Christine Blasey Ford testified that Kavanaugh had sexually assaulted her, he responded with anger and tears. Observers, including former Justice John Paul Stevens, concluded that he lacked the temperament to serve on the high Court. The Senate Judiciary Committee's vote was along straight party lines: 11–10. He was confirmed by a vote of 50–48 by the full Senate on October 6, 2018.

addition to the Federalist Society, scores of other conservative groups were influential in President Trump's efforts to reshape the entire federal judiciary into one that is highly conservative.

THE SENATE COMMITTEE HEARINGS AND SENATE VOTE   Not all nominees inspire the kind of intense reaction that kept Bork from the Court. Until 1929, all but one Senate Judiciary Committee hearing on a Supreme Court nominee were conducted in executive session. The 1916 hearings on Louis Brandeis, the first Jewish justice, took place in public and lasted nineteen days, although Brandeis himself never was called to testify. In 1925, Harlan Fiske Stone became the first nominee to testify before the committee.

Since the 1980s, it has become standard for senators on the Judiciary Committee to ask the nominees probing questions. Most nominees have declined to answer many of these questions on the grounds that the issues raised ultimately might come before the courts.

After the conclusion of hearings, the Senate Judiciary Committee usually makes a recommendation to the full Senate. Any rejections of presidential nominees to the Supreme Court generally occur only after the Senate Judiciary Committee has recommended against a nominee's appointment. It is now increasingly common for appointees to be confirmed on relatively close votes on straight party lines.

HOW DOES THE SUPREME COURT MAKE DECISIONS?

9.4   Outline the process by which the Supreme Court makes decisions and the factors that influence judicial decision making.

Given the judicial system's vast size and substantial, although often indirect, power over so many aspects of our lives, it is surprising that so many Americans know very little about the judicial system in general and the U.S. Supreme Court in particular. While the American public's lack of interest can take the blame for much of this ignorance, the Court has also taken great pains to ensure its privacy and sense of decorum. The Court's rites and rituals contribute to its mystique. Consider, for example, the way the Supreme Court conducts its proceedings. Oral arguments are not televised, and utmost secrecy surrounds deliberations concerning the outcome of cases. Unlike Congress or many state courts, the Supreme Court remains adamant in its refusal to televise its proceedings, including public oral arguments.[19]

The COVID-19 pandemic essentially forced the Supreme Court to go public. After postponing March and April hearings, the nine justices heard their first of ten live stream cases from May 4 to May 13. As the justices participated by conference call, the public was able to listen as the Court, for the first time in history, heard oral arguments by phone. Justice Ginsburg even participated from her hospital room.[20, 21] She died months later on September 18, 2020.

Deciding to Hear a Case

As many as 8,000 cases are filed at the Supreme Court each term; traditionally the Roberts Court accepted about seventy-six per term. In its 2019–2020 term, although approximately 8,000 petitions were filed asking for review, only sixty-three cases were decided and several cases were decided that summarily reversed eleven lower court decisions without written opinions, making it the least productive Court in several decades. In contrast, from 1790 to 1801, the Court received only 87 cases total under its appellate jurisdiction. In the Court's early years, most of the justices' workload involved their circuit-riding duties.[22] As recently as the 1940s, fewer than 1,000 cases were filed annually. Filings increased at a dramatic rate until the mid-1980s, yet cases have since decreased to such a low number that many Court observers are shocked by the Court's paltry workload. Because so many cases are decided by 5–4 opinions, some believe that the Court is opting to avoid cases that could affect its collegiality.

The content of the Court's docket is every bit as significant as its size. During the 1930s, cases requiring the interpretation of constitutional law began to account for a growing portion of the Court's workload, leading the Court to assume a more important role in the policy-making process. At that time, only 5 percent of the Court's cases involved questions concerning the Bill of Rights. By the late 1950s, one-third of filed cases involved such questions; by the 1960s, half did.[23]

WRITS OF *CERTIORARI* **AND THE RULE OF FOUR** Since 1988, nearly all appellate cases that have gone to the Supreme Court arrived there on a petition for a **writ of** *certiorari* (from the Latin "to be informed"), which is a request for the Supreme Court—at its discretion—to order up the records of the lower courts for purposes of review (see Figure 9.4).

writ of *certiorari*
A request for the Supreme Court to order up the records from a lower court to review the case.

FIGURE 9.4 HOW DOES A CASE GET TO THE SUPREME COURT?

This figure illustrates both how cases get on the Court's docket and what happens after a case is accepted for review. A case may take several years to wind its way through the judicial system and another year or two to be heard and decided by the Supreme Court, if the justices decide to grant *certiorari*.

The Supreme Court controls its own caseload through the *certiorari* process, deciding which cases it wants to hear and rejecting most cases that come to it. All petitions, or writs of *certiorari*, must meet two criteria:

1. The case must come from a U.S. court of appeals, a court of military appeals, a district court, or a state court of last resort.

2. The case must involve a federal question. Thus, the case must present questions of federal constitutional law or involve a federal statute, action, or treaty. The reasons that the Court should accept the case for review and legal argument supporting that position are set out in the petitioner's writ of *certiorari*.

The clerk of the Court transmits petitions for writs of *certiorari* first to the chief justice's office, where his clerks review the petitions, and then to the individual justices' offices. On the Roberts Court, all of the justices except Justice Samuel A. Alito and Neil Gorsuch (who allow their clerks great individual authority in selecting the cases for them to review) participate in what is called the *cert* pool. Pool participants review their assigned fraction of petitions and share their notes with each other. Those cases deemed noteworthy by the justices then make it onto the "discuss list" prepared by the chief justice's clerks and are circulated to the chambers of the other justices. All other petitions are dead listed and go no further. Only about 30 percent of submitted petitions make it to the discuss list. During one of their weekly conference meetings, the justices review the cases on the discuss list. The chief justice speaks first, then the rest of the justices, according to seniority. The decision process ends when the justices vote, and by custom, *certiorari* is granted according to the **Rule of Four**—when at least four justices vote to hear a case.

The cases the Court chooses to hear—or not to hear—make a powerful statement about the justices' policy priorities. Cases the Court decides to hear may establish new national policy standards or clarify the decisions of lower courts. When the Court chooses not to hear a case, it allows the decision of the lower court to stand, effectively making another type of statement on public policy.

Rule of Four

At least four justices of the Supreme Court must vote to consider a case before it can be heard.

WHY ARE SUPREME COURT CLERKSHIPS IMPORTANT?

Supreme Court clerkships are awarded to a small number of elite law school graduates each year. In addition to providing valuable experience at the Court, clerkships can open doors to opportunities in government and private practice. Justice Elena Kagan (right, seated with former Justice Sandra Day O'Connor) served as a law clerk to Justice Thurgood Marshall. She later went on to serve as White House counsel, Harvard Law School dean, solicitor general, and, ultimately, Supreme Court justice. Chief Justice Roberts and Associate Justices Breyer, Gorsuch, Kavanaugh and Barrett also served as clerks.

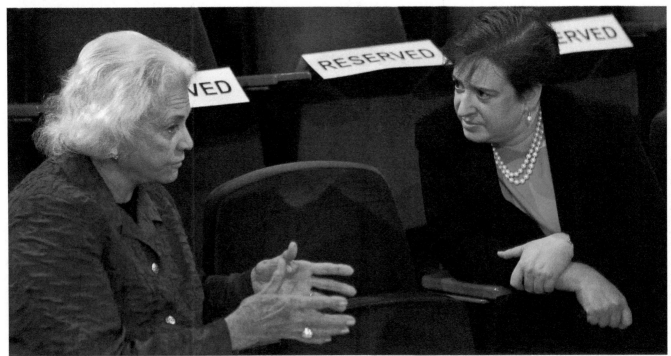

Chip Somodevilla/Getty Images News/Getty Images

THE ROLE OF CLERKS   As early as 1850, the justices of the Supreme Court beseeched Congress to approve the hiring of a clerk to assist each justice. Congress denied the request, so when Justice Horace Gray hired the first law clerk in 1882, he paid the clerk himself. Justice Gray's clerk was a top graduate of Harvard Law School whose duties included cutting Justice Gray's hair and running personal errands. Finally, in 1886, Congress authorized each justice to hire a stenographer clerk for $1,600 a year.

Clerks typically are selected from candidates at the top of the graduating classes of prestigious law schools like the justices themselves, who all, but Justice Barrett, attended Harvard or Yale Law Schools. They perform a variety of tasks, ranging from researching arcane facts to playing tennis or taking walks with the justices. Clerks spend most of their time researching material, reading and summarizing cases, and helping justices write opinions. Clerks also make the first pass through the petitions that come to the Court, undoubtedly influencing which cases get a second look. They often help draft opinions and serve as informal conduits for communication between the justices' chambers. Just how much assistance they provide in the writing of opinions is unknown.[24] However, it is noteworthy that as the number of clerks has grown, so has the length of the Court's written opinions.[25]

How Does a Case Survive the Process?

It can be difficult to determine why the Court decides to hear a particular case. The Court does not offer reasons, and "the standards by which the justices decide to grant or deny review are highly personalized and necessarily discretionary," noted former Chief Justice Earl Warren.[26] Political scientists nonetheless have attempted to determine the characteristics of the cases the Court accepts. Among the cues increasing the odds of the Court hearing a case are the following:

- The federal government is the party asking for review.
- The case involves conflict among the courts of appeals.
- The case presents a civil rights or civil liberties question.
- The case involves the ideological or policy preferences of the justices.
- The case has significant social or political interest, as evidenced by the presence of interest group *amicus curiae* briefs.

THE FEDERAL GOVERNMENT   One of the most important cues for predicting whether the Court will hear a case is the U.S. solicitor general's position. The **solicitor general**, appointed by the president, is the fourth-ranking member of the Department of Justice. The solicitor general is responsible for handling nearly all appeals on behalf of the U.S. government to the Supreme Court. The solicitor's staff resembles a small, specialized law firm within the Department of Justice. But because this office has such a special relationship with the Supreme Court, even having a suite of offices within the Supreme Court building, the solicitor general often is called the Court's tenth member. Moreover, the office of the solicitor general, on behalf of the U.S. government, appears as a party or as an *amicus curiae*, or friend of the court, in more than 50 percent of the cases heard by the Court each term.

This special relationship helps to explain the overwhelming success the solicitor general's office enjoys before the Supreme Court. The Court generally accepts 70 to 80 percent of cases in which the U.S. government is the petitioning party, compared with about 5 percent of all others.[27] But because of this special relationship, the solicitor general often ends up playing two conflicting roles: representing in Court both the president's policy interests and the broader interests of the United States. At times, solicitors may find these two roles difficult to reconcile.

solicitor general
The fourth-ranking member of the Department of Justice; responsible for handling nearly all appeals on behalf of the U.S. government to the Supreme Court.

amicus curiae
"Friend of the court"; *amici* may file briefs or even appear to argue their interests orally before the court.

CONFLICT AMONG THE COURTS OF APPEALS Conflict among the lower courts is another reason justices take cases. When interpretations of constitutional or federal law are involved, justices seem to want consistency throughout the federal court system. Often these conflicts occur when important civil rights or civil liberties questions arise. Political scientists have noted that justices' ideological leanings play a role.[28] It is not uncommon to see conservative justices voting to hear cases to overrule liberal lower court decisions, or vice versa. Justices also take cases when several circuit courts disagree over a main issue.

INTEREST GROUP PARTICIPATION A quick way for justices to gauge the ideological ramifications of a particular civil rights or liberties case is by the nature and amount of interest group participation. Political scientist Richard C. Cortner has noted that "Cases do not arrive on the doorstep of the Supreme Court like orphans in the night."[29] Instead, most cases heard by the Supreme Court involve interest group participation. This participation may come in a number of forms.

Liberal groups, such as the American Civil Liberties Union, People for the American Way, or the NAACP Legal Defense and Educational Fund, and conservative groups, including Americans United for Life, Concerned Women for America, and the American Center for Law and Justice, routinely sponsor cases before the Supreme Court. Sponsorship implies that a group has helped to devise the legal strategy, pay the costs of litigation, and shepherd the case through the court system. It can be very costly and time consuming.

Other groups participate as *amicus curiae*, or a friend of the Court. *Amicus* participation has increased dramatically since the 1970s. Because litigation is so expensive, few individuals have the money, time, or interest to sponsor a case all the way to the U.S. Supreme Court. All sorts of interest groups, then, find that joining ongoing cases through *amicus* briefs is a useful way to advance their policy preferences. Major cases addressing issues of great national importance, such as campaign finance, health care, reproductive rights, or affirmative action attract large numbers of *amicus* briefs as part of interest groups' efforts to lobby the judiciary and bring about desired political objectives.[30] In the Court's 2015–2016 term, a new record number of *amicus* briefs were filed in *Obergefell* v. *Hodges*, a case involving the constitutionality of same-sex marriage.[31] A total of 148 briefs were submitted, most by multiple groups filing one brief. Seventy-six briefs were filed arguing against the federal ban on gay marriage; fifty-eight defended it and five were neutral.[32]

The *amicus curiae* briefs filed by interested parties, especially interest groups or other parties potentially affected by the outcome of the case, often echo or expand the positions of both parties in a case and often provide justices with additional information about the potential consequences of a case. They can be filed urging the Court to accept or reject a case or after the Court has accepted a case for review. Research by political scientists has found that "not only does [an *amicus*] brief in favor of *certiorari* significantly improve the chances of a case being accepted, but two, three, and four briefs improve the chances even more."[33]

Finally, interest groups also support litigants' efforts by holding practice oral arguments during mock court sessions. In these sessions, the lawyer who will argue the case before the justices participates in several complete rehearsals, with prominent lawyers and law professors from various law firms and law schools around Washington, D.C., role-playing the nine justices.

Hearing and Deciding the Case

Once the Court accepts a case for review, a flurry of activity begins. Lawyers on both sides of the case prepare their written arguments for submission to the Court. In these briefs, lawyers cite prior case law and make arguments regarding why the Court should find in favor of their client.

WHY ARE ORAL ARGUMENTS IMPORTANT?

The Supreme Court hears oral argument in most cases in which it reaches a final decision. Scholars have found that oral argument serves a number of important functions. For example, it provides an opportunity for the justices to highlight important case themes and to ask questions about the impact of a case that go beyond what is detailed in the party or *amicus curiae* briefs. Here, an artist's rendering of oral arguments during one of the 2012 cases that decided the constitutionality of the health care reform bill (Obamacare). No cameras are allowed in the courtroom.

ORAL ARGUMENTS After the Court accepts a case and each side has submitted briefs and *amicus* briefs, oral arguments take place. The Supreme Court's annual term begins the first Monday in October, as it has since the late 1800s, and generally runs through June, although COVID-19 led to an extended session with opinions coming from the Court through mid-July 2020, and some cases were postponed until its 2020–2021 term. Justices hear oral arguments from the beginning of the term until early April. Special cases, such as *U.S. v. Nixon* (1974)—which involved President Richard M. Nixon's refusal to turn over tapes of Oval Office conversations to a special prosecutor investigating a break-in at the Democratic Party headquarters in the Watergate complex—have been heard even later in the year.[34] During the term, "sittings," periods of about two weeks in which cases are heard, alternate with "recesses," also about two weeks long, to allow the justices to begin to write opinions. Justices usually hear oral arguments Monday through Wednesday.

Generally, only the immediate parties in the case take part in oral argument, although it is not uncommon for the U.S. solicitor general or one of their deputies to make an appearance to argue orally as an *amicus curiae*. Oral argument at the Court is fraught with time-honored tradition and ceremony. At precisely ten o'clock every morning when the Court is in session, the Court marshal, dressed in a formal morning coat, emerges to intone "Oyez! Oyez! Oyez!" as the justices emerge from behind a reddish-purple velvet curtain to take their places on the raised and slightly angled bench. The chief justice sits in the middle. The remaining justices sit to the left and right, alternating in seniority.

Almost all attorneys are allotted one half-hour to present their cases, including the time required to answer questions from the bench. As a lawyer approaches the mahogany lectern, a green light goes on, indicating that the attorney's time has begun. A white light flashes when five minutes remain. When a red light goes on, Court practice mandates that counsel stop immediately. One famous piece of Court lore told to all attorneys concerns a lawyer who continued talking and reading from his prepared argument after the red light went on. When he looked up, he found an empty bench—the justices had risen quietly and departed while he continued to talk.

Although many Court watchers have tried to figure out how a particular justice will vote based on the questioning at oral argument, most researchers find that the nature and number of questions asked do not help much in predicting the outcome of a case. Nevertheless, an oral argument has several important functions:

- Pre-COVID-19, it was the only opportunity for even a small portion of the public (who may attend the hearings) and the press to observe the workings of the Court.
- It assures lawyers that the justices have heard the parties' arguments, and it forces lawyers to focus on arguments believed important by the justices.
- It provides the Court with additional information, especially concerning the Court's broader political role, an issue not usually addressed in written briefs.
- As Justice Stephen Breyer notes, oral arguments are a good way for the justices to try to highlight certain issues for other justices.
- COVID-19 changes allow the people to hear oral arguments conducted via phone contemporaneously.

THE CONFERENCE AND THE VOTE   The justices meet in closed conference twice a week when the Court is hearing oral arguments. Since the ascendancy of Chief Justice Roger B. Taney to the Court in 1836, the justices have begun each conference session with a round of handshaking. Once the door to the conference room closes, no others are allowed to enter. The justice with the least seniority acts as the doorkeeper for the other eight, communicating with those waiting outside to fill requests for documents, water, and any other necessities.

Conferences highlight the importance and power of the chief justice, who presides over them and makes the initial presentation of each case. Each individual justice then discusses the case in order of his or her seniority on the Court, with the most senior justice speaking next. Most accounts of the decision-making process reveal that at this point some justices try to change the minds of others, but that most enter the conference room with a clear idea of how they will vote on each case.

The Roberts Court is much more informal than past courts, especially since the court moved to allowing justices, several of whom are over age sixty-five, to teleconference on account of the coronavirus. The justices' regular conferences now last longer and, unlike some past courts, Roberts encourages discussion.[35]

WRITING OPINIONS   After the Court has reached a decision in conference, the justices must formulate a formal opinion of the Court. If the chief justice is in the majority, he selects the justice who will write the opinion. This privilege enables him to wield tremendous power and is a very important strategic decision; the author of the decision may determine the tone and content of the Court's opinion. If the chief justice is in the minority, the assignment falls to the most senior justice in the majority.

The opinion of the Court can take several different forms. Most decisions are reached by a majority opinion written by one member of the Court to reflect the views of at least five justices. This opinion usually sets out the legal reasoning justifying the decision, and this legal reasoning becomes a precedent for deciding future cases. The reasoning behind any decision is often as important as the outcome. Under the system of *stare decisis*, both are likely to be relied on as precedent later by lower courts confronted with cases involving similar issues.

In the process of creating the final opinion of the Court, informal caucusing and negotiation often take place, as justices may hold out for word changes or other modifications as a condition of their continued support of the majority opinion. This negotiation process can lead to divisions in the Court's majority. When this occurs, the Court may be forced to decide cases by a **plurality opinion**, which attracts the support of three or four justices. While these decisions do not have the precedential value of majority opinions, they nonetheless have been used by the Court to decide many major cases. Justices who agree with the outcome of the case, but not with the legal rationale for the decision, may file **concurring opinions** to express their differing approach.

Justices who do not agree with the outcome of a case may file a **dissenting opinion**. Although these opinions have little direct legal value, they can be an important indicator of legal thought on the Court and are an excellent platform for justices to note their personal and legal disagreements with other members of the Court. Traditionally, Justice Ginsburg signaled she was about to file a dissenting opinion by wearing what the media called her "dissent collar." Her collars regularly changed from ones made up of colorful fabrics to large, ornate lace ones, but her "go to" collar was from Banana Republic.

Factors Influencing Judicial Decisions

Justices do not make decisions in a vacuum. Principles of *stare decisis* dictate that the justices follow the law of previous cases in deciding cases at hand. But a variety of legal and extra-legal factors have also been found to affect Supreme Court decision making. These include a judge's view on the role of the courts, their ideology, and public opinion.

JUDICIAL PHILOSOPHY AND IDEOLOGY One of the primary issues concerning judicial decision making focuses on judicial philosophy, particularly on what is called the activism/restraint debate. Those advocating that the Constitution should be read as the Framers intended are self-called "originalists." These advocates of **judicial restraint** argue that courts should allow the decisions of other branches to stand, even when they offend a judge's own principles. Originalists defend their position by asserting that unelected judges make up the federal courts, which renders the judicial branch the least democratic branch of government. Consequently, the courts should defer policy making to other branches of government as much as possible.

Jurists believing in judicial restraint refer to *Roe* v. *Wade* (1973), the case that liberalized abortion laws, as a classic example of **judicial activism** run amok. They maintain that the Court should have deferred policy making on this sensitive issue to the states or to the elected branches of the federal government, especially because the Court's decision invalidated the abortion laws of forty-seven states.

Originalists generally agree that judges should be **strict constructionists**; that is, they should interpret the Constitution as the Framers wrote and originally intended it as narrowly as possible. They argue that in determining the constitutionality of a statute or policy, the Court should rely on the explicit meanings of the clauses in the document, which can be clarified by looking at founding documents. Six justices on the Court, all Republican appointees, call themselves originalists.

Advocates of what is called judicial activism contend that judges should use their power broadly to further justice. Activists argue that it is appropriate for courts to correct injustices committed by other branches of government. Implicit in this

Mark Wilson/Getty Images

WHAT WILL BE JUSTICE RUTH BADER GINSBURG'S LEGACY?
Serving twenty-seven years, Ruth Bader Ginsburg was the second female ever to be appointed to the U.S. Supreme Court. A legal trailblazer, she was a tireless advocate for gender equality, women's interests, citizenship rights, and civil rights and liberties.

plurality opinion
A type of judicial opinion, the reasoning of which is agreed to by fewer than a majority of judges on a court; although it resolves the particular case, the opinion does not establish a binding precedent.

concurring opinion
A type of judicial opinion issued by a minority of judges on a court who agree with the outcome of a case but wish to express different legal reasoning.

dissenting opinion
A type of judicial opinion issued by a minority of judges on a court who disagree with the outcome of a case and wish to explain their legal reasoning.

judicial restraint
A philosophy of judicial decision making that posits courts should allow the decisions of other branches of government to stand, even when they offend a judge's own principles.

judicial activism
A philosophy of judicial decision making that posits judges should use their power broadly to further justice.

strict constructionist
An approach to constitutional interpretation that emphasizes interpreting the Constitution as it was originally written and intended by the Framers.

argument is the notion that courts need to protect oppressed minorities, especially since the Constitution, as originally adopted, legitimized slavery and contained no rights for women.[36]

Although judicial activists are often considered politically liberal and originalists politically conservative, in recent years a new brand of conservative judicial activism has become prevalent. Liberal activist decisions often expanded the rights of political and legal minorities. But conservative activist judges view their positions as an opportunity to issue broad rulings that impose their own political beliefs and policies, such as expanding the rights of corporations, which were not likely envisioned by the Framers as having rights.

PUBLIC OPINION   Whether or not public opinion directly influences justices, it can act as a check on the power of the courts. To maintain its institutional prestige, the Court must be wary not to make too many decisions that call its authority into question.[37] The Court must also rely on the support of leaders in the other, popularly elected, branches of government to implement its decisions. Thus, many judicial decisions are strategic ones, balancing constitutional and legal interpretation against the court of public opinion. For example, between 1933 and 1936, the Court resisted upholding the constitutionality of President Franklin D. Roosevelt's New Deal programs, viewing them as outside the national powers prescribed by the Constitution. However, the justices eventually capitulated to political pressures and public opinion, and after 1936, they reversed many of their earlier decisions. These decisions led to the growth and expansion of many federal programs regulating economic activity, including minimum wage laws. Many claim, however, that the New Deal era cases were an exception to the rule that the Court follows public opinion generally. Thus, with the exception of the very liberal Warren Court (1953–1969), whose decisions often seemed to track liberal public opinion on myriad civil liberties and civil rights decisions, the Court has turned a deaf ear on public opinion. Many times in the last fifty years, the Court has gone its own way, much to the chagrin of the president, Congress, or interested parties. This is not to say that the Court ignores or is oblivious to public opinion especially in very high-profile cases such as abortion.

The courts, especially the Supreme Court, also can be the direct target of public opinion. When *Webster* v. *Reproductive Health Services* (1989) was about to come before the Supreme Court, unprecedented lobbying of the Court took place as groups and individuals on both sides of the abortion issue marched and sent appeals to the Court. Mail at the Court, which usually averaged about 1,000 pieces a day, rose to an astronomical 46,000 pieces per day. This virtually paralyzed normal lines of communication.

The Supreme Court also appears to affect public opinion. Political scientists have found that the Court's initial rulings on controversial issues such as abortion or capital punishment positively influence public opinion in the direction of the Court's opinion. However, this research also finds that subsequent decisions have little effect.[38]

Public confidence in the Court, as with other institutions of government, has ebbed and flowed. Public support for the Court was highest after the Court issued *U.S.* v. *Nixon* (1974).[39] At a time when Americans lost faith in the presidency because of the Watergate scandal, they could at least look to the Supreme Court to do the right thing. Although the percentage of Americans with confidence in the courts has fluctuated over time, more recently, polls have shown some confidence in the Court—albeit with caveats. According to three well-respected polls, the public has far more trust in the Court than the other two branches of government. (See Figure 1.6 in Chapter 1.) One poll found that 68 percent of those polled trust the Court to act in the best interest of the country. Across all polls, trust in or confidence in the Court was highly dependent on political ideology. While 52 percent of the "very conservative" respondents had high confidence in the Court, only 36 percent of self-identifying "very liberal" respondents felt the same way. Fifty-seven percent of those polled thought that the Court "gets too mixed up in politics." Intriguingly, 72 percent of those asked said that they thought that term limits for federal judges was a good idea. Remember, when the Constitution was written, it was rare for an average man to live until his 50s. The Framers, in all likelihood, would be astonished to learn that many justices serve well into their 80s.[40]

Overall public support for the Supreme Court as an institution began to decline in the 1990s. Researchers have found that a possible source of those feelings is the way that the media covers the Court. Decisions are reported in terms of winners and losers, using sports- or war-affiliated language such as "attack," bombshell," and "won" or "lost" "the battle." Those who watched network and cable coverage of the Court were more likely to have negative impressions of it than those who did not.

POLITICAL REFORM AND REALITIES: HOW MUCH POWER DOES THE COURT HAVE IN POLICY MAKING?

9.5 Evaluate the role of the Supreme Court in national policy making.

All judges, whether they recognize it or not, make policy. The decisions of the Supreme Court, in particular, have a tremendous impact on American politics and policy. Over the past 250 years, the justices have helped to codify many of the major rights and liberties guaranteed to the citizens of the United States. Although justices need the cooperation of the executive and legislative branches of the federal and state governments to implement and enforce a good number of their decisions, it is safe to say that many policies we take for granted in the United States would not have come to fruition without support of the Supreme Court.[41] These include the right to privacy and equal rights for Black Americans, women, Hispanic Americans, the LGBT community, and other minority groups.

Several Courts have played particularly notable roles in the development of the judiciary's policy-making role. As discussed earlier in the chapter, the Marshall Court played an important role in establishing the role and power of the Supreme Court, including the power of judicial review in *Marbury v. Madison* (1803). The Warren Court decided a number of civil rights cases that broadly expanded civil and political rights. These decisions drew a great deal of criticism but played a major role in broadening public understanding of the Court as a policy maker. The Rehnquist Court made numerous decisions related to federalism, which caused observers to take note of the Court's ability to referee conflicts between the federal government and the states. The Roberts Court reversed the general trend of the Court's agreement with executive actions during times of war by finding in 2008 that the Bush administration's denial of *habeas corpus* rights to prisoners being held at Guantanamo Bay was an unconstitutional exercise of presidential power.[42]

One measure of the power of the courts and their ability to make policy is that 182 federal laws have been declared unconstitutional through the end of the Court's 2019–2020 term. Although many of these laws have not been particularly significant, others have. The Court also reviews the constitutionality of laws passed by the states; the justices have overruled nearly 1,000 such laws over the years. In 2012, for example, the Roberts Court struck down portions of an Arizona state law regulating immigration on the grounds that it violated the Constitution's supremacy clause.[43]

DO UNPOPULAR SUPREME COURT RULINGS THREATEN THE NATION?
The Warren Court's broad expansions of civil and political rights led to a great deal of criticism, including a movement to impeach the chief justice. Here, two California billboards present contrasting views of Warren's performance.

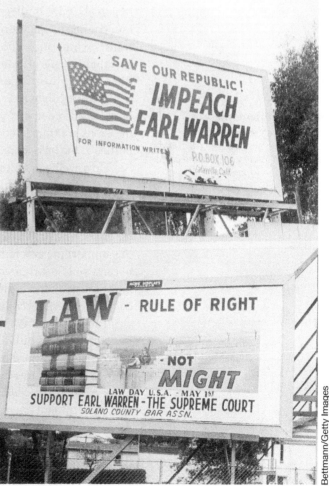

Bettmann/Getty Images

Another measure of the policy-making power of the Supreme Court is its ability to overrule itself. Although the Court generally abides by the informal rule of *stare decisis*, by one count, it has overruled itself in 236 cases.[44] *Brown* v. *Board of Education* (1954), for example, overruled *Plessy* v. *Ferguson* (1896), thereby reversing years of constitutional interpretation concluding that racial segregation was not a violation of the Constitution. In the past few years, the Court repeatedly has reversed earlier decisions in the areas of criminal defendants' rights, reproductive rights, and free speech, revealing its powerful role in determining national policy—and in 2018, specifically overruling *Korematsu*, which had upheld the constitutionality of the internment of Japanese-American citizens during World War II.[45] A measure of the growing power of the federal courts in the degree to which they now handle issues that had been considered political questions more appropriately settled by other branches of government. Prior to 1962, for example, the Court refused to hear cases questioning the size (and population) of congressional districts, no matter how unequal they were.[46] The boundary of a legislative district was considered a political question. Then, in *Baker* v. *Carr* (1962), Justice William Brennan, writing for the Court, concluded that simply because a case involved a political issue, it did not necessarily involve a political question. This opened the floodgates to cases involving a variety of issues that the Court formerly had declined to address.[47] In particular, over the last decade at least one voting rights case has appeared on the Courts docket each term. In 2018, the Court, when faced with the challenge to election districts drawn to favor one political party over the other, acknowledged the politically partisan nature at issue in several states' redistricting plans, sending challenges back to the trial courts for more fact-finding.

Implementing Court Decisions

President Andrew Jackson, annoyed about a particular decision handed down by the Marshall Court, is alleged to have said, "John Marshall has made his decision; now let him enforce it." Jackson's statement raises a question: how do Supreme Court rulings translate into public policy? In fact, although judicial decisions carry legal and even moral authority, all courts must rely on other units of government to carry out their directives. If the president or members of Congress do not like a particular Supreme Court ruling, they can underfund programs needed to implement a decision or seek only lax enforcement. **Judicial implementation** refers to how and whether judicial decisions are translated into actual public policies affecting more than the immediate parties to the lawsuit.

judicial implementation

How and whether judicial decisions are translated into actual public policies affecting more than the immediate parties to a lawsuit.

How well a decision is implemented often depends on how well crafted or popular it is. Hostile reaction in the South to *Brown* v. *Board of Education* (1954) and the absence of precise guidelines to implement the decision, which found state and local school segregation unconstitutional, meant that the ruling went largely unenforced for years. The *Brown* experience also highlights how much the Supreme Court needs the support of both federal and state courts as well as other governmental agencies to carry out its judgments. For example, in 1992 the Supreme Court ruled that public middle school and high school graduations could not include a prayer, yet your own commencement ceremony may have included one.[48]

The implementation of judicial decisions involves what political scientists call an implementing population and a consumer population.[49] The implementing population consists of those people responsible for carrying out a decision. Depending on the policy and issues in question, the implementing population can include lawyers, judges, public officials, police officers and police departments, hospital administrators, government agencies, and corporations. In the case of school prayer, the implementing population could include teachers, school administrators, or school boards. The consumer population consists of those people who might be directly affected by a decision—in this case, students and parents.

For effective implementation of a judicial decision, the first requirement is for members of the implementing population to show they understand the original decision. For example, the Supreme Court ruled in *Reynolds* v. *Sims* (1964) that every person should have an equally weighted vote in electing governmental representatives.[50] This "one person, one vote" rule might seem simple enough at first glance, but in practice it can be very difficult to understand. The implementing population in this case consists chiefly of state legislatures and local governments, which determine voting districts for federal, state, and local offices. If a state legislature draws districts in such a way that African American or Hispanic voters are spread thinly across a number of separate constituencies, the chances are slim that any particular district will elect a representative who is especially sensitive to minority concerns. Does that violate "equal representation"? That is often a question for the Court to address, given the particular facts of the situation.

The second requirement is that the implementing population actually must follow Court policy. Thus, when the Court ruled that men could not be denied admission to a state-sponsored nursing school, the implementing population—in this case, university administrators and the state board of regents governing the nursing school—had to enroll qualified male students.[51]

Implementation of judicial decisions is most likely to be smooth if a few highly visible public officials, such as the president or a governor, shoulder the responsibility of seeing to the task. By the same token, these officials also can thwart or impede judicial intentions. Recall the effect of Governor Orval Faubus's initial refusal to allow Black children to attend all-White public schools in Little Rock, Arkansas after the *Brown* decision.

The third requirement for implementation is for the consumer population to be aware of the rights that a decision grants or denies them. Teenagers seeking an abortion, for example, are consumers of the Supreme Court's decisions on abortion and contraception. They need to know that most states require them to inform their parents of their intention to have an abortion or to get parental permission to do so. Similarly, criminal defendants and their lawyers are consumers of Court decisions and need to know the implications of recent Court decisions regarding evidence presented at trial, sentencing guidelines, and prison reform.

The Roberts Court

The judicial philosophy of the person who occupies the position of chief justice of the Supreme Court of the United States has significant impact on public policy. Chief Justice John Marshall carved out powers for the Court not necessarily envisioned by the Framers; Chief Justice Earl Warren carved out important protections for criminal defendants and presided over the Court that ruled that the doctrine of "separate but equal" was no longer constitutional dramatically changing race relations in the nation. Chief Justice John G. Roberts Jr. was hailed by some as a "formidable counterpart to President Trump and the Congress."[52]

Of the Court's 2019–2020 term, former solicitor general Gregory G. Garre, said: "This is one of the most consequential terms for a chief justice in modern history, given his role as the decisive vote in the most important cases and the landmark opinions he wrote."[53] A Harvard constitutional law scholar went so far as to say "Roberts is the most powerful chief justice since John Marshall."[54] While this may be a bit of hyperbole, consider the role that the Chief Justice played in the following decisions in these divisive issues.

Abortion. The Court ruled that Louisiana's law that required abortion providers have admitting privileges in nearby hospitals was an undue burden on women seeking abortions and therefore unconstitutional, but later upheld a state law requiring an in-person physician's visit during COVID-19 to obtain prescription medications to end a pregnancy in a 6-3 decision;

Immigration. The Court rejected the efforts of the Trump administration to end protection for about 650,000 undocumented illegal aliens known as "Dreamers" under the provisions of the Deferred Action for Childhood Arrivals (DACA);

LBGT Rights. Roberts joined with four liberals and Neil Gorsuch to find that the Civil Rights Act of 1964's prohibition against discrimination on account of sex prohibited discrimination against lesbians, gays, and transgender persons. This was after he dissented in a 2014 case that established the right of individuals to marry regardless of their gender;

Presidential Power. In two cases, the Court ruled that the president was subject to a subpoena for his taxes issued in New York state while Congress was not. Both cases were returned to the lower courts so that the president did not have to release his taxes before the 2020 election. In discussing the New York prosecution of Trump, he lectured the president saying As Marshall explained, a king is born to power and can do no wrong. The president, by contrast, is 'of the people' and subject to the law;[55]

Religion. Roberts wrote that the First Amendment's establishment clause did not prohibit Montana from public funding of scholarships for students in religious schools.

There was something for everyone in the decisions made by the Court in its 2019–2020 term. The Chief led from the center, initially the first Chief Justice to be the "swing" vote in decades. In the 2019–2020 term, as well as in those that preceded it, Roberts consistently appeared to have the reputation of the Court at the heart of many of his decisions that also appeared to reflect public opinion.[56] They may also reflect his desire to "play the long game," knowing that two of the Court's most liberal members are in their 80s and may present the president with additional opportunities to put new, younger justices on the Court as evidenced by the replacement of the late, liberal Justice Ruth Badar Ginsburg with the far-right conservative Amy Coney Barrett.[57] A relatively young man, himself, he is poised to lead the Court into a new era. Should any vacancies arise, it is very likely that President Joe Biden will fulfill his campaign promise and nominate a young, liberal Black woman to the High Court.

CONCLUSION AND REVIEW

What Are the Roots of the Federal Judiciary?

9.1 Describe the constitutional foundations of the federal judiciary and judicial review.

Many Framers viewed the judicial branch of government as little more than a minor check on the other two branches, ignoring Anti-Federalist concerns about an unelected judiciary and its potential for tyranny. The Judiciary Act of 1789 established the basic federal court system we have today. It was the Marshall Court (1801–1835), however, that interpreted the Constitution to include the Court's major power, that of judicial review.

What Is the Structure of the Federal Court System?

9.2 Describe the structure of the federal judiciary.

The federal court system is made up of constitutional and legislative courts. Federal district courts, courts of appeals, and the Supreme Court are constitutional courts.

How Are Federal Court Judges Selected?

9.3 Outline the criteria for nominating and the process of approving federal judges and Supreme Court justices.

District court, court of appeals, and Supreme Court justices are nominated by the president and must also win Senate confirmation. Important criteria for selection include experience, ideology, pursuit of political support, religion, race, ethnicity, and gender.

How Does the Supreme Court Make Decisions?

9.4 Outline the process by which the Supreme Court makes decisions and the factors that influence judicial decision making.

Several factors influence the Court's decision to hear a case. Not only must the Court have jurisdiction, but at least four justices must vote to hear the case. Cases with certain characteristics are most likely to be heard. Once a case is set for review, briefs and *amicus curiae* briefs are filed and oral argument is scheduled. The justices meet in conference after oral argument to discuss the case; votes are taken; and opinions are written, circulated, and then announced.

Judges' decisions are influenced by a number of factors, including the law of previous cases, personal philosophy and ideology, and public opinion.

Political Reforms and Realities: How Much Power Does the Court Have in Policy Making?

9.5 Evaluate the role of the Supreme Court in national policy making.

The Supreme Court is an important participant in the policy-making process. The power to interpret laws gives the Court a tremendous policy-making power never envisioned by the Framers. However, if the president or members of Congress oppose a particular Supreme Court ruling, they can underfund programs needed to implement a decision or seek only lax enforcement. Chief Justice John G. Roberts, Jr. is playing a critical role in the direction of the Court as the powerful swing justice in many cases.

LEARN THE TERMS

amicus curiae
appellate court
brief
concurring opinion
constitutional (or Article III) courts
dissenting opinion
Eleventh Amendment
Federalist No. 10
Federalist No. 78

Jay Court
judicial activism
judicial implementation
judicial restraint
judicial review
Judiciary Act of 1789
Judiciary Act of 1801
jurisdiction
legislative courts

Marbury v. Madison (1803)
plurality opinion
precedent
Rule of Four
solicitor general
stare decisis
strict constructionist
trial court
writ of *certiorari*

LEARN THE NAMES

Elena Kagen
Sandra Day O'Connor

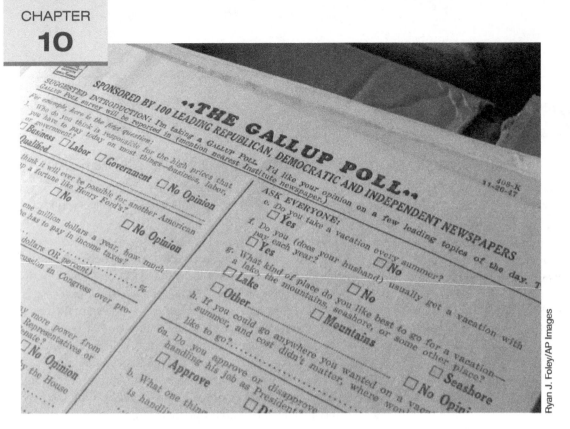

Ryan J. Foley/AP Images

WHY WERE THE FRAMERS SO CONCERNED ABOUT PUBLIC OPINION?

It is crucial for representative governments to account for citizens' viewpoints. The Framers believed that any government that derives its powers from the consent of the governed must have ways to gauge public opinion. Pictured is the Gallup Poll used collectively by 100 leading newspapers to gauge support for a variety of programs and issues in 1947. Note that this is an in-person poll at a time before most print news organizations conducted their own polls.

CRITICAL THINKING: *Has the development of technologies affected attempts to gauge public opinion?*

PUBLIC OPINION AND POLITICAL SOCIALIZATION

LEARNING OBJECTIVES

10.1   Describe the beginnings of public opinion research.

10.2   Describe the methods for conducting and analyzing different types of public opinion polls.

10.3   Define and assess the influence of political ideology on political attitudes and behaviors.

10.4   Explain how the agents of socialization influence the development of political attitudes.

10.5   Evaluate the effects of public opinion on policy making.

ree, honest, and open communication from citizens to their governments on matters of public concern has been considered the bedrock of a legitimate government by political philosophers for centuries.[1] Hans Spier Political theorists during the Age of Reason such as John Locke stressed the importance of public opinion in how effective politics works.

The Framers of the United States agreed with this line of argument and addressed it in their writings. The Declaration of Independence, for example, implies that public opinion must be considered and acknowledged by the government since government expressly functions on "the consent of the governed." And James Madison argued that democratic governments must have knowledgeable citizens with educated opinions to sharpen important political debate. The Federalist Papers express the general belief that Americans had more in common than not, which supports its arguments that the Constitution of the United States would succeed as author's governing document. In *Federalist No. 2*, John Jay wrote that we are "one united people—a people descended from the same ancestors, speaking the same language, professing the same religion, attached to the same principles of government, very similar in manners and customs." Many of those who could vote in Jay's time were of European heritage; almost all were Christian. Moreover, most believed that certain rights—such as freedom of speech, association, and religion—were rights that could not be revoked. Jay also wrote about the importance of shared public opinion and of the need for a national government that reflected American ideals.

In 1863, during another perilous time for the United States, Abraham Lincoln proudly summarized American government as one "of the people, by the people, and for the people." Though this sentiment has always been true to some degree, our modern political landscape has given this old idea new perspective in the midst of a much more diverse population.

* * *

Political scientists define **public opinion** as the aggregate of public attitudes or beliefs about government and politics.[2] Today, in an increasingly diverse nation, the growth of modern public opinion research has helped us to better understand Americans' views on political issues and how our varying experiences, values, and heritage shape them. In part, this is attributable to the pervasiveness of polls. Not a day goes by that major cable news networks, newspapers, foundations, or colleges and universities do not poll Americans on something—from views on political issues, such as the environment, race, and health care, to their emotions, including happiness and stress, especially during the COVID-19 pandemic. Polling is so common now that the public needs the ability to interpret often-conflicting poll results. This is especially true when some issues aren't front and center on the public agenda. As shown in Figure 10.1, polling about the **Green New Deal** advanced by many liberal activists is difficult since so many know "nothing at all" about it. In this chapter, we explore how polls are conducted and analyzed as well as how Americans' beliefs and demographic and cultural experiences shape public opinion.

FIGURE 10.1   HOW MANY AMERICANS ARE FAMILIAR WITH THE GREEN NEW DEAL?

With very few Americans being aware of the Green New Deal, it will be difficult to convince voters of its importance as it requires major rethinking of climate change.

SOURCE: Abel Gustafson, et al., "The Green New Deal has Strong Bipartisan Support," Yale Program on Climate Change Communication, December 14, 2018, https://climatecommunication.yale.edu/publications/the-green-new-deal-has-strong-bipartisan-support/.

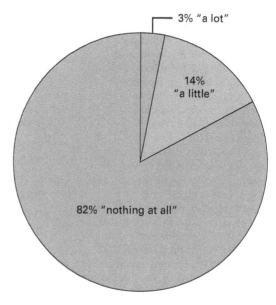

3% "a lot"

14% "a little"

82% "nothing at all"

public opinion

What the public thinks about a particular issue or set of issues at any point in time.

Green New Deal

A program to accelerate the transition from fossil fuels to clean, renewable energy with the goal of generating 100 percent of the nation's electricity from these sources within ten years.

public opinion polls

Interviews or surveys with samples of citizens that are used to estimate the feelings and beliefs of the entire population.

George Gallup

One of the earliest developers of scientific methods for public opinion polling and a proponent for a strong role for the voice of the public in politics and government.

WHAT ARE THE ROOTS OF PUBLIC OPINION RESEARCH?

10.1   Describe the beginnings of public opinion research.

Since the 1930s, governmental decision makers have relied heavily on **public opinion polls**—interviews with samples of citizens that estimate the outlook and preferences of larger populations—to gauge the feelings and beliefs of the American public. According to **George Gallup** (1901–1983), considered the founder of modern-day polling, polls have played a key role in defining issues of concern to the public, shaping administrative decisions, and helping "speed up the process of democracy" in the United States.[3]

WHAT IS ONE OF THE FIRST TOOLS USED BY POLLSTERS?

Pictured is a map of Philadelphia's 7th Ward. Noted Black academic and theorist W.E.B. Du Bois's *The Philadelphia Negro* is considered to be a groundbreaking study that was the first to combine sociological theory buttressed by hard data. The illustration shows where Black people lived in the city's 7th Ward. From 1896–1897, Du Bois and his wife, Nina, went door to door in the Ward asking Census-like questions while also mapping homes, places of worship, and social services. They conducted over 5,000 personal interviews in an effort to identify social and political problems in what became the first ever statistically based study of Black Americans, and his complete findings were published by the University of Pennsylvania Press in 1899 at the height of the Progressive movement.

Source: Du Bois, W.E.B. (William Edward Burghardt). "The Seventh Ward of Philadelphia." Map. 1899. Norman B. Leventhal Map & Education Center, https:// collections.leventhalmap.org/search/ commonwealth:gb19h9947 (accessed April 21, 2021).

straw poll

Unscientific survey used to gauge public opinion on a variety of issues and policies.

sample

A subset of the whole population selected to be questioned for the purposes of prediction or gauging opinion.

The Earliest Public Opinion Research

At first glance, public opinion seems to be a straightforward concept: it is what the public thinks about a particular issue or set of issues at any point in time. As early as 1824, one Pennsylvania newspaper tried to predict the winner of that year's presidential contest, showing Andrew Jackson leading over John Quincy Adams. In 1883, the *Boston Globe* sent reporters to selected election precincts to poll voters as they exited voting booths, in an effort to predict the results of key contests. In 1896–1897, prominent Black rights activist W.E.B. Du Bois surveyed 5,000 persons, culminating in his classic systemic, data-based study of race in *The Philadelphia Negro*.[4]

Public opinion polling as we know it today really began to develop in the 1930s, however. Walter Lippmann's seminal work, *Public Opinion* (1922), prompted much of this growth.[5] Lippmann observed that research on public opinion was far too limited, especially in light of its importance. Researchers in a variety of disciplines, including political science, heeded Lippmann's call to learn more about public opinion. Some tried to use scientific methods to measure political thought through the use of surveys or polls. As methods for gathering and interpreting data improved, survey data began to play an increasingly significant role in all walks of life, from politics to retailing.

Literary Digest, a popular magazine that first began national presidential polling in 1916, was a pioneer in the use of the **straw poll**, an unscientific survey used to gauge public opinion, to predict the popular vote, which it did, for Woodrow Wilson. Its polling methods were hailed widely as "amazingly right" and "uncannily accurate."[6] In 1936, however, its luck ran out. *Literary Digest* predicted that Republican Alfred M. Landon would beat incumbent President Franklin D. Roosevelt by a margin of 57 percent to 43 percent of the popular vote. Roosevelt, however, won in a landslide election, receiving 62.5 percent of the popular vote and carrying all but two states.[7]

Literary Digest's 1936 straw poll had three fatal errors. First, it drew its **sample**, a subset of the whole population selected to be questioned for the purposes of prediction or gauging opinion, from telephone directories and lists of automobile owners. This technique oversampled the upper-middle class and the wealthy, groups heavily Republican in political orientation. Moreover, in 1936, voting polarized along class lines. Thus, the oversampling of wealthy Republicans was particularly problematic because it severely underestimated working-class Democratic voters, who had neither cars nor telephones.

Literary Digest's second problem was timing. The magazine mailed its questionnaires in early September. This did not allow *Literary Digest* to measure the changes in public sentiment that occurred as the election drew closer.

Its third error occurred because of a problem we now call self-selection. Only highly motivated individuals sent back the cards—a mere 22 percent of those surveyed responded. Those who answer mail surveys (or today, online surveys) are quite different from the general electorate; they often care more fervently about the candidate or issues being asked about in the poll. *Literary Digest*, then, failed to observe one of the now well-known cardinal rules of survey sampling: "One cannot allow the respondents to select themselves into the sample."[8] In 2020, most pollsters correctly predicted the outcome of the vote, which was won handily by the Biden/Harris ticket.

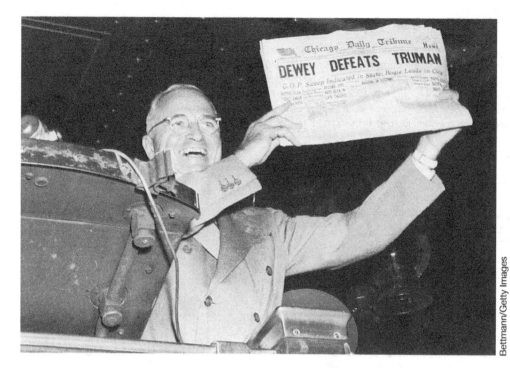

IS POLLING DATA ALWAYS ACCURATE?

Polls often can provide inaccurate predictions. Not only did advance polls in 1948 predict that Republican nominee Thomas E. Dewey would defeat Democratic incumbent President Harry S Truman, but on the basis of early and incomplete vote tallies, some newspapers' early editions published the day after the election declared Dewey the winner. Here, a triumphant Truman holds aloft the *Chicago Daily Tribune*.

The Gallup Organization

At least one pollster, however, correctly predicted the results of the 1936 election: George Gallup. Gallup had written his dissertation in psychology at the University of Iowa on how to measure the readership of newspapers. He then expanded his research to study public opinion about politics. He was so confident about his methods that he gave all of his newspaper clients a money-back guarantee: If his poll predictions weren't closer to the actual election outcome than those of *Literary Digest*, he would refund their money. Although Gallup underpredicted Roosevelt's victory by nearly 7 percent, the fact that he got the winner right was what everyone remembered, especially given *Literary Digest's* dramatic miscalculation.

Through the late 1940s, polling techniques increased in sophistication. The number of private polling firms also dramatically rose, as businesses and politicians began to rely on polling information to market products and candidates. But in 1948, the polling industry suffered a severe, although fleeting, setback when Gallup and many other pollsters incorrectly predicted that Thomas E. Dewey would defeat President Harry S Truman.

Nevertheless, as revealed in Figure 10.2, polling organizations continue to predict most presidential popular vote winners successfully. In 2016, however, polling organizations incorrectly called the presidential election for Hillary Clinton. Their miscalculations included assuming Clinton had a lead of 1 to 7 percent nationally, and forecasters generally gave Clinton a better than 70 percent chance of winning the Electoral College and popular vote. Donald J. Trump's Electoral College victory in light of these predictions was a major surprise, and political scientists and polling organizations began analyzing their methods and assumptions to prevent similar errors in future elections. Other individuals don't trust pollsters, so they refuse to participate or supply misleading answers.

The American National Election Studies

In 1952, researchers at the University of Michigan—later joined by Stanford University researchers—began to conduct the American National Election Studies (ANES), funded in large part by the National Science Foundation. Focusing on the political attitudes and behavior of the electorate, ANES surveys include questions about how respondents voted, their party affiliation, and their opinions of major political parties and candidates. In addition, ANES surveys contain questions about interest in politics and political participation. ANES data are no longer as widely used by academics, as

FIGURE 10.2 HOW SUCCESSFUL ARE PRESIDENTIAL ELECTION POLLS?

As seen in this graph, prominent polling organizations such as Gallup have been able to produce solid, if not perfectly exact, estimations of the popular vote in presidential elections dating back to the 1930s. Until 2016, years with significant discrepancies between polling predictions and election outcomes were influenced by third-party candidates. In 1948, Strom Thurmond ran on the Dixiecrat ticket; in 1980, John Anderson ran as the American Independent Party candidate; and, in 1992, Ross Perot ran as an Independent. But in 2016, polling organizations got it wrong when Donald J. Trump had a winning majority in the Electoral College, although he lost the popular vote by 3 million votes. In 2020, predictions were more successful, pointing to a Biden win.

SOURCES: Data from Gallup (Years 1936–2012) and Real Clear Politics (Years 2016–2020).

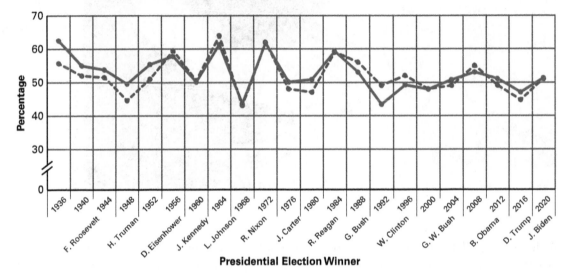

was once the case. Additional scientific studies are available now, and as a result election research no longer relies almost exclusively on ANES.

Pew Research Center

The nonprofit Pew Research Center conducts hundreds of polls on a variety of issues every year. Its American Trends Panel (ATP) is a nationally representative panel of randomly selected adults. ATP participants regularly take online, Web-based surveys. The original panelists who did not have Internet access were provided a tablet and a wireless connection. To construct its most recent panel, 7,855 persons were contacted with an astonishing 81 percent response rate. Because of its ability to survey so many persons, the sampling error of Trends polls is 1.59 percent, making it the most reliable of all polls. As revealed in Table 10.1, since Pew began to use panels of adults using a Web-based platform, its researchers have amassed a total of 15,454 active panelists by late 2019.

TABLE 10.1 WHAT DO THE AMERICAN TRENDS PANEL RECRUITMENT SURVEYS SHOW?

American Trends Panel Recruitment Surveys				
Recruitment dates	Mode	Invited	Joined	Active panelists remaining
Jan. 23 to March 16, 2014	Landline/cell RDD	9,809	5,338	2,315
Aug. 27 to Oct. 4, 2015	Landline/cell RDD	6,004	2,976	1,337
April 25 to June 4, 2017	Landline/cell RDD	3,905	1,628	685
Aug. 8 to Oct. 31, 2018	ABS/Web	9,396	8,778	6,417
Aug. 19 to Nov. 30, 2019	ABS/Web	5,900	4,720	4,700
	Total	**35,014**	**23,440**	**15,454**

SOURCE: Pew Research Center, "Methodology," March 5, 2020, www.pewresearch.org/politics/2020/03/05/methodology-229/.

NOTE: Approximately once per year, panelists who have not participated in multiple consecutive waves or who did not complete an annual profiling survey are removed from the panel. Panelists also become inactive if they ask to be removed from the panel.

HOW ARE PUBLIC OPINION POLLS CONDUCTED AND ANALYZED?

10.2 Describe the methods for conducting and analyzing different types of public opinion polls.

The polling process most often begins when someone says, "Let's find out about X and Y." Potential candidates for local office may want to know how many people have heard of them. (The device used to find out is called a "name recognition survey.") Better-known candidates contemplating a run for higher office might wish to discover how they might fare against an incumbent. Polls also can help gauge the effectiveness of particular ads or how well (or negatively) the public perceives a candidate. Political scientists have found that public opinion polls are critical to successful presidents and their staffs, who use poll results to "create favorable legislative environment(s) to pass the presidential agenda, to win reelection, and to be judged favorably by history."[9]

Designing the Survey

When deciding to conduct a poll, candidates, political groups, or news organizations must first consider what questions they want answered. Polls may ask, for example, about job performance, demographics, and specific issue areas. Determining the content of a survey is critical to obtaining the desired results; for this reason, candidates, companies, and news organizations generally rely on pollsters. Public opinion polls were used by the Democratic National Committee during the 2020 presidential primary as part of its calculus to determine which candidates were allowed to participate in televised debates, requiring candidates to make threshold percentages in multiple polls.

Special care must be taken in constructing the questions. For example, if your professor asked you, "Do you think my grading procedures are fair?" rather than asking, "In general, how fair do you think the grading is in your American Politics course?" you might give a slightly different answer. The wording of the first question tends to put you on the spot and personalize the grading style; the second question is more neutral. Even more obvious differences appear in the real world of polling. Responses to highly emotional issues, such as immigration and abortion, often are skewed, depending on the phrasing of a particular question. Even in unbiased polls, how a question is worded can unintentionally skew results.

During a political campaign, strategists will often ask questions that help candidates judge their own strengths and weaknesses as well as those of their opponents. However, sometimes these questions go too far. Questions that cross the line are called **push polls** and often result from ulterior motives.[10] The intent of push polls is to give respondents some negative or even untruthful information about a candidate's opponent so that they will move away from that candidate and toward the one paying for the poll. A typical push poll might ask a question such as, "If you knew Candidate X beat his wife, would you vote for him?" Push poll takers do not even bother to record the responses because they are irrelevant; the questions are meant to push away as many voters from a candidate as possible. Although campaign organizations generally deny conducting push polls, research shows that this type of polling has targeted more than three-quarters of political candidates.

push polls

Polls taken for the purpose of providing information on an opponent that would lead respondents to vote against that candidate.

Selecting the Sample

After deciding to conduct a poll, pollsters must determine the **population**, or the entire group of people whose attitudes a researcher wishes to measure. This universe could be all Americans, all voters, all city residents, all Hispanics, or all Republicans. In a perfect world, the poll would ask every individual to give an opinion, but such comprehensive polling is not practical. Consequently, pollsters take a sample of the population

population

The entire group of people whose attitudes a researcher wishes to measure.

random sampling

A method of poll selection that gives each person in a group the same chance of being selected.

stratified sampling

A variation of random sampling; the population is divided into subgroups and weighted based on demographic characteristics of the national population.

that interests them. One way to obtain this sample is by **random sampling**. This method of selection gives each potential voter or adult approximately the same chance of being selected.

Simple random samples, however, are not very useful for predicting voting because they may undersample or oversample key populations not likely to vote. To avoid such problems, reputable polling organizations use **stratified sampling** (the most rigorous sampling technique) based on U.S. Census data that provide the number of residences in an area and their location. Researchers divide the population into several sampling regions. In each primary sampling unit, pollsters then use demographic characteristics to select a set number of respondents to be interviewed. Both landlines and cell phones may be called, since 96 percent of Americans own a cell phone.[11] The typical sample formerly totaled 600 to 1,000 respondents, but in 2020 many pollsters made do with smaller numbers. These selected primary sampling units often are used for many years because it is cheaper for polling companies to train interviewers to work in fixed areas.

Contacting Respondents

Most modern polls are conducted using telephone interviews. The most common form of telephone polls is the random-digit dialing survey, in which a computer randomly selects telephone numbers for dialing. More than half of Americans use cell phones only; most polls done for newspapers and news magazines target those with landlines. In 2016, the Pew Research Center announced that 75 percent of the polling calls it made would be to cell phones.[12] Response votes for phone surveys are on life support. Pew reports that only 6 percent of those contacted by phone by pollsters were willing to participate. Thus, thousands have to be contacted to get a viable sample.[13] And pollsters compete with others using phone banks, including candidates, political parties, and special interests. Pollsters are exempt from federal and state do-not-call lists because poll taking is a form of constitutionally protected speech.

tracking polls

Continuous surveys that enable a campaign or news organization to chart a candidate's daily or weekly rise or fall in support.

During the 1992 presidential election, the introduction of **tracking polls**, which were taken on a daily basis via phone by some news organizations, allowed presidential candidates to monitor short-term campaign developments and the effects of their campaign strategies. In 2016, presidential tracking polls involved small samples (usually of registered voters contacted at certain times of the day) and took place over three- to five-day periods (see Figure 10.3). In 2020, almost all polls overestimated support for Biden.

Some polls, such as the American National Election Studies (ANES), continue to perform individual, in-person interviews, which allow surveyors to monitor respondents' body language and to interact on a more personal basis; thus, its surveys may

WHAT DO PHONE BANKS LOOK LIKE?

The most common method of conducting a public opinion poll is via telephone. These polls are often administered by survey researchers working at large phone banks. Phone banks can also be used to call potential voters to identify supporters, raise funds, get them to attend events, or persuade them to vote for a candidate or cause.

vm/Getty Images

FIGURE 10.3   WHAT DOES A TRACKING POLL LOOK LIKE?

Short-term fluctuations in public opinion during election contests are often shown by tracking polls. This tracking poll figure shows the ups and downs of the 2020 presidential election.

SOURCE: Data from Real Clear Politics, www.realclearpolitics.com/epolls/2020/president/us/general_election_trump_vs_biden-6247.html.

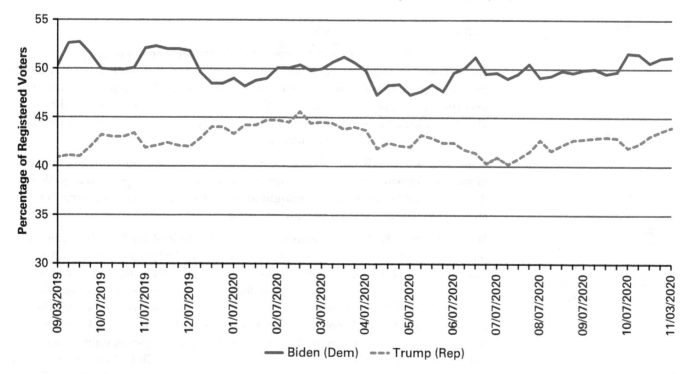

yield higher rates of completion. However, the unintended influence of the questioner or pollster may lead to interviewer bias. How the pollster dresses, relates to the person being interviewed, and asks the questions can affect responses.

Exit polls, a special form of in-person poll, are conducted as voters leave selected polling places on Election Day. Generally, large news organizations send pollsters to selected precincts to sample every tenth voter as they emerge from the polling site. The results of these polls help the media predict the outcome of key races, often just a few minutes after the polls close in a particular state and generally before voters in other areas—sometimes in a later time zone—have cast their ballots. By asking a series of demographic and issue questions, these polls also provide an independent assessment of why voters supported particular candidates.

exit polls

Polls conducted as voters leave selected polling places on Election Day.

Finally, survey researchers are increasingly using Internet surveys to predict election outcomes and gauge opinions on numerous issues of importance to the American public. Political scientists, too, use online polling to collect survey research data. The biannual Cooperative Congressional Election Study conducted by political scientists at a consortium of universities is one example of this kind of research.

Contrasting sharply with scientific Internet surveys are unscientific Web polls that allow anyone to weigh in on a topic. Such polls are common on many Web sites, such as CNN.com and ESPN.com. These polls resemble a straw poll in terms of sampling and thus produce results that are largely inconclusive and of interest only to a limited number of people.

Analyzing the Data

Analyzing the collected data is a critical step in the polling process. Analysis reveals the implications of the data for public policy and political campaigns. Data are entered into a computer program, which can be as basic as an Excel spreadsheet or more complex such as SPSS and STATA, common tools of political scientists. Answers to questions are recorded and analyzed. Often, analysts pay special attention to subgroups within the data, such as Democrats versus Republicans, men versus women, age groups, or political ideology, among others. Reporting the results of this analysis can happen in a variety of ways, such as by news organizations, university research centers, or campaigns.

Shortcomings of Polling

Information derived from public opinion polls has become an important part of governance. When the results of a poll are accurate, they express the attitudes of the electorate and help guide policy makers. However, when the results of a poll are inaccurate, disastrous consequences can result. Polls may be inaccurate for a number of reasons. These include survey error, limited respondent options, lack of information, difficulty measuring intensity, and lack of interest.

SURVEY ERROR All polls contain errors. They may come about from natural errors in statistical measurement that arise from using a sample to extrapolate the opinions of the general public, known as the **margin of error**. They may also result from drawing an improper sample, known as **sampling error**.

margin of error

A measure of the accuracy of a public opinion poll within statistical parameters.

sampling error

Errors resulting from the size or the quality of a survey sample.

Margin of Error: Typically, the margin of error in a sample of 1,000 will be about 4 percent. If you ask 1,000 people, "Do you like ice cream?" and 52 percent say yes and 48 percent say no, the results are too close to tell whether more people like ice cream than not. Why? Because the margin of error implies that somewhere between 56 percent (52 + 4) and 48 percent (52 − 4) of the people like ice cream, while between 52 percent (48 + 4) and 44 percent (48 − 4) do not. The margin of error in a close election makes predictions very difficult, especially when smaller samples with higher margins of error are used. For example, the margin of error for 2016 presidential primary polls that used fewer than a thousand respondents was around 3 percent. Some pollsters opted to take their polls over a five- or six-day period. This method usually netted as many as 2,100 to 3,600 respondents with a 2.3 to 4.5 percent margin of error. Thus, while 2016 polling results were off, they nearly always fell within the margin of error. In 2020, the margin of error reported by many pollsters was sufficiently off to prod some to argue that their methods need to be reevaluated. Some even argue that changes need to be made as to how results are reported.[14]

Sampling Error: Errors may also result from the size or quality of the sample. Small samples, if properly drawn, can be very accurate if each unit in the potential sample universe has an equal opportunity to be sampled. If a pollster fails to sample certain populations, however, the results may reflect that shortcoming. Often, polls underrepresent the opinions of the poor people and homeless people because pollsters give insufficient attention to representatively sampling these groups.

LIMITED RESPONDENT OPTIONS Famed political scientist V. O. Key Jr. was among the first social scientists to note the problem of limited respondent options. He cautioned students of public opinion to be certain their questions adequately allowed respondents the appropriate range in which they could register their opinions. Simple yes/no (or approve/disapprove) questions may not be sufficient to "take the temperature" of the public. For example, if someone asks you, "How do you like this class?" and then gives only like or dislike options, your full sentiments may not be tapped if you like the class very much or feel only so-so about it. Thus, most polling agencies ask citizens to rank their opinion on five- or seven-point scales that can better gauge variations in public opinion. Other surveys use "feeling thermometer" questions, wherein respondents provide a response from 0 to 100 measuring how they "feel" about a particular issue.

LACK OF INFORMATION Public opinion polls may also be inaccurate when they attempt to gauge attitudes toward issues about which the public has little information, as in the case concerning the Green New Deal (see Figure 10.1). Most academic public opinion research organizations use some kind of filter question that first asks respondents whether or not they have thought about the question. These screening procedures generally allow survey researchers to exclude as many as 20 percent of their respondents, especially on complex issues such as the federal budget. Questions on more personal issues, such as moral values, drugs, crime, race, women's role in society, and wearing masks, receive far fewer "no opinion" or "don't know" responses.

DIFFICULTY MEASURING INTENSITY   Another shortcoming of polls concerns their inability to measure intensity of feeling about particular issues. Whereas a respondent might answer affirmatively to any question, it is likely that his or her feelings about issues such as the death penalty, support for mask wearing, or a particular candidate are much more intense than questions about the Electoral College. In 2020, Donald J. Trump had the highest intensity negatives of any presidential candidates in recent history.

One sign of voter intensity is voter turnout. In the 2018 midterm elections, many more individuals reported that they intended to vote than in past pre-midterm surveys. We do know that the surge in the number of Democratic women running across the nation was largely a reaction to the presidency of Donald J. Trump and his views on women. We also know that turnout was the highest for any midterm since 1970 and that college-age students turned out in record numbers. Young people continued to exceed prior turnout in 2020, and 66.3 percent of all voters turned out—a new record.

LACK OF INTEREST IN POLITICAL ISSUES   When we face policies that do not affect us personally and do not involve moral issues, we often have difficulty forming an opinion. This phenomenon is especially true with regard to foreign policy. Most Americans often know little of the world around them. Unless major issues of national importance take center stage, American public opinion on foreign affairs is likely to be volatile in the wake of any new information. In contrast, most Americans are more interested in domestic policy issues, such as COVID-19 Stimulus Relief Checks, which have a greater impact on their daily lives. Obviously, no issue has affected the political landscape as has the novel coronavirus.

WHAT IS POLITICAL IDEOLOGY?

10.3 Define and assess the influence of political ideology on political attitudes and behaviors.

Many citizens' opinions on political issues are determined by their **political ideology**, or the coherent set of values and beliefs people hold about the purpose and scope of government.[15] Ideologies shape the thinking of individuals and how they view the world, especially in regard to issues of "race, nationality, the role and function of government, the relations between men and women, human responsibility for the natural environment, and many other matters."[16] Observers increasingly have recognized these beliefs as a potent political force. Some argue that two factors above all others shaped human history in the twentieth century: "One is science and technology; the other is ideological battles—totalitarian tyrannies of both right and left and the explosions of nationalism, racism, and religious bigotry that the most perceptive social thinkers of the nineteenth century failed to predict."[17]

It is easier to understand how ideology affects public opinion when we examine the four functions political scientists attribute to ideologies:

1. *Explanation.* Ideologies can offer reasons why social and political conditions are the way they are, especially in time of crisis.
2. *Evaluation.* Ideologies can provide standards for evaluating social conditions and political institutions and events.
3. *Orientation.* Much like a compass, ideologies provide individuals with an orientation toward issues and a position within the world on them.
4. *Political Program.* Ideologies help people make political choices and guide their political actions from doing nothing to voting to protesting.

political ideology
The coherent set of values and beliefs about the purpose and scope of government held by groups and individuals.

CAN POLLS MEASURE INTENSITY OF OPINION?

One of the greatest shortcomings of most public opinion polls is that they measure direction of public opinion, but not intensity. Here, members of the ultraconservative Westboro Baptist Church, well known for showing up at the funerals of the LGBTQ community around the nation, demonstrate their intense opposition to homosexuality by protesting outside the Supreme Court.

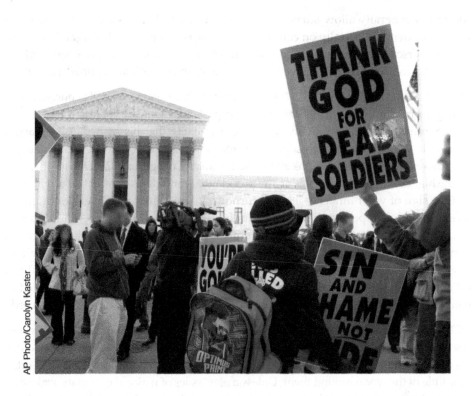

AP Photo/Carolyn Kaster

Types of Political Ideologies

The four functions of ideology discussed previously clearly have real-world implications. Political ideologies create natural groups within society and can lead to political conflict. In America, we often hear about conservative, liberal (or progressive), and moderate political ideologies (see Table 10.2). Americans' political ideologies have been relatively constant for most of the last twenty years. Since 1992, when Gallup began studying political ideology, conservatives have trended higher than liberals, but did decline from February to June 2020; in 2020, conservatives measured 34 percent vs. 26 percent liberal, with moderates at 40 percent.

CONSERVATIVES According to William Safire's *New Political Dictionary*, a **conservative** "is a defender of the status quo who, when change becomes necessary in tested institutions or practices, prefers that it come slowly, and in moderation."[18] Conservatives tend to believe that limited government is best, especially in terms of regulating the economy. Conservatives favor local and state action over federal

conservative

One who favors limited government intervention, particularly in economic affairs.

TABLE 10.2   DO MEN AND WOMEN THINK DIFFERENTLY ABOUT POLITICAL ISSUES?

As seen in this table, men and women differ in issue priorities, such as the need to address race and climate change. The largest gender gap is in support for online education.

	Men Agreeing (%)	Women Agreeing (%)
Addressing issues around race*	41	56
Reducing health care costs*	52	63
Women get fewer opportunities than men for good jobs.**	45	52
Is global climate change a problem?**	66	83
Would you choose an online learning option during COVID-19?***	33	48

*Pew Research Center, 2021
**Pew Research Center, 2016
***Lindsay McKensie, "COVID-19 and Online Education Decision." *Inside Higher Education*. Posted July 30, 2020.

intervention, and they emphasize fiscal responsibility. Conservatives are also likely to believe that the private sector is better equipped than the government to address domestic problems such as homelessness, poverty, and discrimination.

Since the 1970s, a growing number of **social conservative** voters (many with ties to the evangelical or Religious Right) increasingly have affected politics and policies in the United States. Social conservatives believe that moral decay must be stemmed and that government should support and further traditional moral teachings. These voters favor government intervention to regulate sexual and social behavior and have led efforts to restrict contraceptives, abortion, and same-sex marriage. While a majority of social conservatives are evangelical Christians, Mormons, and Roman Catholics, some Jews and many Muslims are also social conservatives. Others are not affiliated with a traditional religion.

social conservative
One who believes that the government should support and further traditional moral teachings.

LIBERALS   A **liberal** is one who seeks to use the government to change the political, economic, and social status quo and foster the development of equality and the well-being of individuals.[19] The meaning of the word "liberal" has changed over time, but in the modern United States, liberals (who may also refer to themselves as progressives) generally support well-funded government social welfare programs that seek to protect individuals from economic disadvantages or to correct past injustices. In contrast, they generally oppose government efforts to regulate private behavior or infringe on civil rights and liberties.

liberal
One who favors greater government intervention, particularly in economic affairs and in the provision of social services.

MODERATES   In general, a **moderate** takes a relatively centrist view on most political issues. Most political philosophers from ancient Greece favored moderate politics, believing a balanced viewpoint was best when it came to managing issues of wealth, poverty, or the role of government.

moderate
A person who takes a relatively centrist or middle-of-the-road view on most political issues.

Problems with Ideological Labels

In a perfect world, liberals would be liberal and conservatives would be conservative. Studies reveal, however, that many people who call themselves conservative actually take fairly liberal positions on many policy issues. In fact, anywhere from 20 percent to 60 percent of people will hold a traditionally conservative view on one issue and a traditionally liberal view on another.[20] People who take conservative stances against "big government," for example, often support increases in spending for the elderly, education, or health care. It is also not unusual to encounter a person who could be considered a liberal on social issues such as abortion and civil rights but a conservative on economic or pocketbook issues. Views on particular persons or issues can change quickly. During the COVID-19 pandemic, for example, President Trump's job approval went from a high of 49 percent in February 2020 to 38 percent in June 2020 as the pandemic continued unabated, the economy fell to the worst in recorded history, and racial unrest over policing continued in cities across the nation.[21]

Some critics also charge that a simple left-to-right continuum cannot capture the full complexity of most citizens' political ideologies (see Figure 10.5). They suggest that the ideologies of most people are better represented by a spectrum measuring individuals' viewpoints on government interference in both economic and personal liberties. This spectrum includes not only liberal, conservative, and moderate ideologies but also **statist** (pro-governmental interference) and **libertarian** (anti-governmental interference) perspectives. Recently, some theorists have added feminism as an additional ideology. Globally, this ideology is considered to advance the emancipation of women and to guarantee their equality. It is also an approach to politics advocating for equal rights for women in all spheres of politics, law, and society.

statist
One who believes in extensive government control of personal and economic liberties.

libertarian
One who believes in limited government interference in personal and economic liberties.

FIGURE 10.4 HOW CAN YOU CLASSIFY IDEOLOGY?

The Nolan Chart, created by Libertarian Party leader David Nolan, is a political ideology chart that helps to classify citizens' political beliefs on two key dimensions—economic and personal freedoms. The chart identifies five key political ideologies: left (liberal), centrist or moderate, right (conservative), libertarian, and statist. Where do you believe you fall on this chart? Take the test and find out.

SOURCE: Advocates for Self-Government. Take the test at nolanchart.com.

HOW ARE POLITICAL OPINIONS FORMED?

10.4 Explain how the agents of socialization influence the development of political attitudes.

Political scientists believe that many of our attitudes about issues are grounded in our political values. The process through which individuals acquire their beliefs is known as **political socialization**.[22] Demographic characteristics, many noted in Figure 10.4, also include family, school, peers, the mass media, and political leaders that often act as important influences or agents of political socialization.

Demographic Characteristics

Individuals have little control over most demographic characteristics. But, from birth, these characteristics begin to affect you and your political values. Some of the major demographic characteristics that pollsters routinely expect will affect political opinions include gender, race and ethnicity, age, and religion.

political socialization

The process through which individuals acquire their political beliefs and values.

FIGURE 10.5 WHAT ARE AMERICANS' POLITICAL IDEOLOGIES AND HOW ARE THEY AFFECTED BY KEY VARIABLES?

Americans' political ideologies differ considerably based on a number of key factors, including gender*, age, education, race/ethnicity, and party identification.

	% Conservative	% Moderate	% Liberal
Gender			
Men	38	36	22
Women	31	35	30
Age			
18 to 34	25	36	35
35 to 54	34	38	25
55 and older	41	34	21
Education			
College graduate	25	40	34
Not college graduate	40	34	22
Race/Ethnicity			
Non-Hispanic White Americans	38	34	25
Non-Hispanic Black Americans	22	47	28
Hispanic Americans	31	35	30
Type of Community			
Big/Small city	33	36	28
Suburb	28	40	31
Town/Rural area	43	33	22
Party ID			
Republicans	73	20	5
Independents	28	49	20
Democrats	11	35	53

SOURCE: Gallup, May–June 2020

*Gallup does not offer a transgender catagory.

GENDER From the time of the earliest public opinion polls, women have held more liberal attitudes than men about social issues such as education, poverty, capital punishment, and the environment. Public opinion polls have also found that women's views about war and military intervention are more negative than men's. Some analysts suggest that women's more nurturing nature and their role as mothers influence their more liberal attitudes on issues affecting the family or children. Research by political scientists, however, finds no support for a maternal explanation (see Table 10.2).[23] Still, as reflected in Table 10.2, as of 2020, women are much more likely to prefer online-distance learning over men in 2020.

RACE AND ETHNICITY Race and ethnicity are exceptionally important factors in the study of public opinion. The direction and intensity of Black Americans' and Hispanic Americans' opinions on a variety of issues often are quite different from those of White Americans. These differences generally appear at a very young age. For example, young Black children generally show very positive feelings about American society and political processes, but this attachment lessens considerably over time. Racially motivated shootings and movements such as Black Lives Matter are keeping public opinion on race at the fore of the public agenda as revealed in Table 10.2.

Differences of opinion also appear on political issues. Minorities, for example, are more likely to favor government-sponsored health insurance. And, Hispanics are more likely than other groups to support liberalized immigration policies.[24]

AGE Age seems to have a decided effect on political socialization. Our view of the proper role of government, for example, often depends on the era in which we were born and our individual experiences with a variety of social, political, and economic forces. The oldest Americans, for example, continue to be affected by having lived through the hard economic times of the Great Depression and World War II. Millennials overwhelmingly favor same-sex marriage. The attention to the killing of George Floyd, a Black man, which came after several police shootings of unarmed Blacks, drew national attention to issues of racial profiling and attacks by the police. Not only were reports coming out that found dramatic differences in the way COVID-19 was affecting minority communities, killings appeared to be going on unabated. Huge numbers of Americans polled—69 percent—believed that Floyd's killing represented a much more systemic problem. Six years earlier when an unarmed Black man was killed in Ferguson, Missouri, only 43 percent thought it was an example of larger policing issues.[25] Seventy-five percent of non-Whites said that Floyd's death was evidence of deeper anti-minority views held by police. For Whites, it was 68 percent.[26]

Age also affects how citizens view government programs.[27] Young people are disproportionately likely to be concerned about student loan debt and gun violence, while the elderly prioritize the protection of Medicare and Social Security. In states such as Florida, where many northern retirees have flocked to seek relief from cold winters and high taxes, the elderly have voted as a bloc to defeat school tax increases and to pass tax breaks for themselves.

RELIGION   Political scientists have found significant evidence that religion affects the political beliefs and behaviors of the American citizenry. Many American ideals, including hard work and personal responsibility, are widely considered to be rooted in our nation's Protestant heritage. These ideals have affected the public policies adopted by government; they may be one reason why the United States has a less developed welfare state than many other industrialized democracies.

Religious beliefs also shape individual attitudes toward political issues. Evangelical Christians and Roman Catholics, for example, may support programs that provide aid to parochial schools, even if it comes at the expense of lowering the wall of separation between church and state. Similarly, Jewish Americans are more likely to favor aid to Israel—a policy at odds with Muslim Americans' support for a Palestinian state. Some Americans have chosen to openly criticize followers of Islam. In 2016, presidential candidate Donald J. Trump openly called for a ban on allowing Muslims into the United States during his campaign rallies.

How strictly we practice and follow religious doctrine may also affect political beliefs. For example, strict Roman Catholics, Orthodox Jews, Mormons, and evangelical Christians believe that abortion should be illegal in all cases; they also believe in more traditional roles for women.

Family, Peers, and Education

The influence of the family on political socialization can be traced to two factors: communication and receptivity. Children, especially during their preschool years, spend tremendous amounts of time with their parents; early on, they learn their parents' political values, even though these concepts may be vague. One study of first graders, for example, found that they already had developed political orientations consistent with those of their parents.[28]

A child's peers—that is, children about the same age—also seem to have an important effect on the socialization process. While parental influences are greatest from birth to age five, beyond that point a child's peer group becomes increasingly important, especially as they enter middle school or high school. Groups such as the Girl Scouts of the USA recognize the effect of peer pressure and are trying to influence more young women to participate in, and have a positive view of, politics. Numerous other local, state, and national women's groups work to engage girls to become leaders in the political process.

School-age children are also clearly influenced by their daily education. In elementary school, children are taught respect for their nation and its symbols. In many schools, the day begins with the Pledge of Allegiance, and patriotism and respect for country are important components of most school curricula. Support for flag and country creates a foundation for national allegiance that prevails despite the negative views about politicians and government institutions that many Americans develop later in life. Middle and high schools continue the elementary school tradition of building good citizens and often reinforce textbook learning with trips to Washington, D.C., or state capitals. High schools also offer courses on current U.S. affairs and Advanced Placement United States Government and Politics. Many high schools impose a compulsory service-learning requirement, which some studies report positively affects later political participation.[29]

At the college level, teaching style often changes. Many college courses and texts like this one are designed in part to provide the information necessary for thinking critically about issues of major political consequence. It is common in college for students to be called on to question the appropriateness of certain political actions or to discuss underlying reasons for certain political or policy decisions that were avoided in high school. Therefore, most researchers believe that college has a liberalizing effect on students. Since the 1920s, studies have shown that students become more liberal each year that they are in college.

The Mass Media

Over the years, more and more Americans have turned away from traditional news sources, such as nightly news broadcasts on the major networks and daily newspapers, in favor of different outlets. TV talk shows, talk radio, online magazines, Instagram, Twitter, Facebook, and blogs are important sources of political news for many people. Cable news, the Internet, and social media are almost omnipresent in the lives of modern Americans. American teenagers, for example, consume almost eleven hours of media content each day.[30]

Cable and Internet news sources are often skewed. President Trump charged that major networks and newspapers report what he calls "fake news." Facebook and Twitter now try to exclude some types of news they find false or misleading, and both actually first deleted material posted by the president and then suspended his account permanently, robbing him of important mechanisms to reach his supporters. Consuming slanted views may affect the way citizens process political information, form opinions on public policy, obtain political knowledge, and receive new ideas. One recent study, for example, revealed that Americans who get most of their news from cable news outlets such as Fox News and MSNBC are even less knowledgeable about political issues than citizens who consume no political news. Individuals who rely on alternative sources, such as Sunday morning talk shows and National Public Radio, are generally more knowledgeable.[31]

Cues from Leaders or Opinion Makers

Political leaders, members of the news media, and a host of other experts have regular opportunities to affect public opinion because of the lack of deep conviction with which most Americans hold many of their political beliefs. The president, especially, is often in a position to mold public opinion through effective use of the bully pulpit. The president derives this power from the majesty of his office and his singular position as head of state. Thus, presidents often take to TV and social media in an effort to drum up support for their programs.[33] During the first few months of the novel coronavirus,

WHAT HAPPENS WHEN POLITICS AND SCIENCE COLLIDE?

Anthony Fauci quickly became a calm, scientific voice of reason about how to respond to the new coronavirus. The director of the National Institute of Allergy and Infectious Diseases gathered with the Coronavirus Task Force daily in the Situation Room. He then usually flanked President Trump addressing the media. Afterward, he spoke "science" to reporters and fell out of the president's favor.[32]

AC NewsPhoto/Alamy Stock Photo

President Trump held a daily press briefing that was followed by statements and a question-and-answer corrections session by Dr. Anthony Fauci, the director of the National Institute of Allergy and Infectious Diseases. To the dismay of many, these daily events were halted by the president as the virus spread.

President Donald J. Trump is the first president to use tweets to signal his support for new programs or to criticize the media and to complain about other developments. Trump released tweets when he disagreed with judicial decisions that delayed implementation of his immigration plan and when Congress failed to appropriate money to build a wall between Mexico and the United States, and he even used tweets to call out individuals who he believed were hostile to him. For example, he has been very critical of Alec Baldwin's portrayal of him on *Saturday Night Live* as well as of the show itself. The president's tweets resonate well with his base of support, which is critical to shoring up public opinion for many of his domestic, trade, and tariff programs. He often used tweets to sway public opinion, particularly on issues surrounding the removal of Confederate monuments and Black Lives Matter protests, flaming racial divisions in the electorate and among his most ardent supporters, many of whom invaded the Capitol. He was impeached for his inflammatory speech but was acquitted by the Senate.

Political Knowledge

Political knowledge and political participation have a reciprocal effect on one another—an increase in one will increase the other. Knowledge about the political system is essential to successful political involvement, which, in turn, teaches citizens about politics and expands their interest in public affairs.[34] And, although few citizens know everything about all of the candidates and issues in a particular election, they can, and often do, know enough to impose their views and values on the general direction the nation should take.

This observation is true despite the fact that most Americans' level of knowledge about history and politics has gaps. According to the U.S. Department of Education, today's college graduates have less civic knowledge than high school graduates did fifty years ago. Americans also do not appear to know much about foreign policy; some critics even argue that many Americans are geographically illiterate.[35]

Significant gaps exist when we look deeper into demographics. While 71 percent of the males sampled could identify that the Speaker of the House was Nancy Pelosi, only 53 percent of the women could do so. However, on issues of concern to women, such as representation in the legislature, women do as well or better than their male counterparts.[36] Those with a high school education could identify Speaker Pelosi only 50 percent of the time. Eighty-five percent of those with postgraduate degrees identified her correctly. The gender gap in political knowledge also appears to be affected by education, age, number of children, and marital status.[37]

POLITICAL REFORM AND REALITIES: WHAT ARE THE EFFECTS OF PUBLIC OPINION ON POLITICS?

10.5 Evaluate the effects of public opinion on policy making.

Public opinion inevitably influences the actions of politicians and public officials. Today, we know more about what "the people" want from their government than ever before. Much of this knowledge comes from our increasing ability to collect representative data on aggregate public opinion. The tools available to pollsters, including the Internet and social media, statistical software, and computerized robocall technology, make data collection, analysis, and dissemination easier than ever, with phone call surveys being the exception.

However, there can be dangerous consequences to having so much data. Just about anything can be proven—or disproven—with a public opinion poll. Moreover, the

"NICE WORK, — SHAKE!"

PUBLIC OPINION

RECIPROCAL TRADE BILL

PASSED

CONGRESS

HOW DO PUBLIC OPINION POLLS AFFECT POLITICS?

The emergence of a growing number of public opinion research firms means that citizens, the media, and political leaders know more than ever before about how voters perceive political issues and candidates. This information may be useful for promoting a more democratic and representative government. But it may also be notoriously mercurial, marked by dramatic fluctuations from week to week or even day to day. And public opinion inevitably influences the actions of politicians and public officials, as illustrated in this historical cartoon.

volume of polls conducted and information available about these studies makes them an attractive topic for news coverage. This phenomenon is especially prevalent during election season. And while on one hand, it may be interesting to examine the relationship between events and citizens' evaluations of political leaders, on the other hand, constant reports of the results of the latest poll only serve to intensify the horse-race atmosphere of every campaign. More critically, it may also distract from the true issues of the election and obscure citizens' understanding of the political process.

Andrew Kohut, the late president of the Pew Research Center, argued that the public has become more of a critical player in national and international politics in the past three decades in large part because of the rise in the number of polls regularly conducted and reported.

According to Kohut, it is impossible to find any major policy proposal for which polling has not "played a significant, even critical, role."[38] Another observer of public opinion polls says, "Polls have become more important and necessary in news writing and presentation, to the point that their significance overwhelms the phenomena they are supposed to be measuring or supplementing."[39] Policy makers thus respond intently to the often-mercurial changes in citizens' opinions. These opinions also influence the way that political campaigns are run.

CONCLUSION AND REVIEW

What Are the Roots of Public Opinion Research?

10.1 Describe the beginnings of public opinion research.

Public opinion is what the public thinks about an issue or a particular set of issues. Polls are used to estimate public opinion. Almost since the beginning of the United States, various attempts have been made to influence public opinion about particular issues or to sway elections. *Literary Digest* first began national presidential polling in 1916, using unscientific straw polls. Modern-day polling did not begin until the 1930s. George Gallup was the first to use scientific polling methods to determine public opinion.

How Are Public Opinion Polls Conducted and Analyzed?

10.2 Describe the methods for conducting and analyzing different types of public opinion polls.

Those who conduct polls must follow a careful process: first determining questions, identifying the sample, and selecting the method for contacting respondents. The different types of polls include telephone polls, in-person interviews, and Internet polls. Once the poll results are in, they must be analyzed. Polls, however, may have several shortcomings that create inaccuracies. These include survey errors, limited respondent options, lack of knowledge, inability to measure the intensity of public opinion on an issue, and a lack of interest in political issues.

What Is Political Ideology?

10.3 Define and assess the influence of political ideology on political attitudes and behaviors.

Ideologies, the belief systems that shape the thinking of individuals and how they view the world, affect public opinion. The major categories of political ideology in America are conservative, liberal, and moderate. Critics of this approach believe that statist (pro-governmental interference) and libertarian (anti-governmental interference) perspectives should also be considered when discussing ideology.

How Are Political Opinions Formed?

10.4 Explain how the agents of socialization influence the development of political attitudes.

The first step in forming opinions occurs through a process known as political socialization. Demographic characteristics—including gender, race, ethnicity, age, and religion—as well as family, school, and peers all affect how we view political events and issues. The views of leaders and opinion makers as well as the news media also influence our opinions about political matters.

Political Reforms and Realities: What Are the Effects of Public Opinion on Politics?

10.5 Evaluate the effects of public opinion on policy making.

The prevalence of opinion polling in American culture has a significant impact on media coverage and how individuals view government. Politicians often use knowledge of the public's views on issues to tailor campaigns or to drive policy decisions.

LEARN THE TERMS

conservative
exit polls
Green New Deal
liberal
libertarian
margin of error
moderate

political ideology
political socialization
population
public opinion
public opinion polls
push polls
random sampling

sample
sampling error
social conservative
statist
stratified sampling
straw poll
tracking polls

Steve Sanchez Photos/Shutterstock.com

WHAT DIVIDES THE POLITICAL PARTIES?

Stark divisions by race, age, education, and gender have come to define American politics and the political parties. Key issues in the 2020 presidential election were the COVID-19 pandemic, the economy and jobs, racial justice, climate change, and the Supreme Court, but voters identifying with each of the political parties were divided over which issues were a priority. Furthermore, the trend of voters casting a ballot in opposition to, rather than for, a candidate of a party continued.

CRITICAL THINKING QUESTION: *Why is the country divided and how are divisions the reflected in the coalitions of the political parties?*

POLITICAL PARTIES

LEARNING OBJECTIVES

11.1 Trace the evolution of political parties.

11.2 Describe the structure of political parties at the national, state, and local levels.

11.3 Identify the functions of political parties.

11.4 Describe the forces that create and shape party identification.

11.5 Evaluate the role of minor parties in the U.S. electoral system.

11.6 Assess the reasons for the persistence of the two-party system in American politics.

partisanship

Prejudice in favor of a particular cause; bias.

Partisanship and partisan tribalism are driving much of American politics today. The permanent campaigning by political leaders encourages political attitudes that make compromise in governing more difficult. As "historic" or unique as this period of time may seem, the nation has experienced similar periods of hyperpartisanship and partisan polarization throughout our history. Like our own time, historical periods of partisan polarization featured the rise of populist and anti-establishment movements; high levels of social, political, and economic inequality; fierce party competition to persuade and mobilize different segments of the population; shifts in coalitional alignments; and a great deal of negativity in political rhetoric.

Many analyses of the parties and the electorate suggest that one result of partisan polarization is that Democrats and Republicans live in separate worlds. The parties tend to speak in their own terms to very different constituencies, and even through different media. The parties and the candidates offer completely divergent messages and views of the country, and each camp offers its own set of facts to back these positions. On many issues, Democratic and Republican voters differ on which are most important to them. At the same time, the political parties are quite weak in many respects, especially as a growing number of people describe themselves as Independents and many tune out politics altogether. While they may still vote, the same motivations driving a growing number of people to identify as Independent are also diminishing their willingness to engage in political action (like volunteering for campaigns), thereby diminishing grassroots support and further saturating elections with the voices that are loudest and most extreme.

Furthermore, partisan polarization should not mask the high degree of factionalism within the parties, which has concomitantly risen with the growth of interest groups and money in politics. Even as there is growing disdain for political parties, they continue to play an important role in organizing coalitions of political leaders, interest groups, and voters around ideas and issues about the direction the country should take. With the increasingly negative feelings Americans hold toward members of the opposite party, their candidates in elections, and their policy positions, what is perhaps most needed is the opportunity for people of differing worldviews to listen to one another in order to rehumanize the other side.

Without mutual respect, it will be difficult to reach compromises and solve the most pressing challenges the nation faces. Even as there are discussions about potential reforms to the parties and the electoral process, we can bridge our partisan divides by working together to revive civic engagement, volunteerism, and community engagement—the pillars of our shared democratic tradition and experiment.

• • •

political party

An organized group that may include office holders, candidates, activists, and voters who pursue their common interests by gaining and exercising power through the electoral process.

At the most basic level, a **political party** is an organized effort by office holders, candidates, activists, and voters to pursue their common interests by gaining and exercising power through the electoral process. The goal, of course, is to win office in order to influence public policy. Nominating candidates to run under the party label is, notably, the key differentiating factor between political parties and interest groups. However, as we will discuss later in this text, political parties and interest groups now work together so closely that it may be difficult to tell where one stops and the other begins.

Political scientists sometimes describe political parties as consisting of three separate but related entities: (1) the office holders who organize themselves and pursue policy objectives under a party label (the governmental party), (2) the workers and activists who make up the party's formal organization structure (the organizational party), and (3) the voters who consider themselves allied or associated with the party (the party in the electorate).[1]

In this chapter, we will address contemporary party politics from each of these vantage points. We will trace parties from their roots in the late 1700s to today and will cover reforms to party politics that have been pursued throughout American history. A discussion of the increasing polarization of American political parties will conclude the chapter.

WHAT ARE THE ROOTS OF THE TWO-PARTY SYSTEM?

11.1 Trace the evolution of political parties.

By tracing the history and development of political parties, we will see that even as dramatic shifts in party coalitions and reforms have taken place to democratize the electoral process, the competitive two-party system has always featured prominently in the United States.

The Development of Political Parties, 1800–1824

Though the Framers warned against a government ruled by permanent political alliances, these alliances actually had their roots in the creation of the Constitution. Those who supported the stronger central government fashioned in the new Constitution identified with what eventually became the Federalist Party, while the future Democratic-Republicans favored a system of greater state authority similar to that created by the Articles of Confederation. These alliances, however, did not codify into permanent groups until President George Washington stepped off the national stage. To win the presidency in 1796, Washington's vice president, John Adams, narrowly defeated archrival *Thomas Jefferson*. According to the Constitution, Jefferson became vice president. Over the course of Adams's single term, the Federalists and Democratic-Republicans became increasingly organized around these clashing men and their principles. The Federalists were mainly organized around mercantile groups in New England who supported protective tariffs to encourage manufacturing, the assumption of states' Revolutionary War debts, the creation of a national bank, and the resumption of commercial ties to England. On the other hand, the Democratic-Republicans supported free trade, the promotion of agrarian interests, and stronger ties to France. In the presidential election of 1800, the Federalists supported Adams's bid for a second term, but this time the Democratic-Republicans prevailed with their nominee, Jefferson, who became the first U.S. president elected as the nominee of a political party.

Jefferson was deeply committed to the ideas of his party but not nearly as devoted to the idea of a party system. He regarded his party as a temporary measure necessary to defeat Adams, not a long-term political tool or an essential element of democracy. As a result, Jefferson's party never achieved widespread loyalty among the nation; rather, it drew most of its support from the agrarian South. The Federalists, too, remained a

Keith Lance/Getty Images

WHAT ROLE DID BLACK AMERICANS PLAY IN THE NEW REPUBLICAN PARTY?

In its early years, the Republican party differed greatly from what it is today, advocating a strong central government and certain entitlements for the underprivileged. It also received broad support from Black voters. The three men depicted, all Republicans, are regarded as heroes of the era. From left to right: Blanche Kelso Bruce, second Black U.S. Senator and first to be elected to a full term; Frederick Douglass, abolitionist, orator, writer, and first Black U.S. marshal; Hiram Rhodes Revels, first Black U.S. Senator.

regional party, drawing their support from the commercial New England states. No broad-based national party organizations existed to mobilize popular support.[2] Just as the nation was in its infancy, so too was the party system. Nominations of candidates were informal and usually led by local party leaders in meetings called caucuses. Each of the parties organized political clubs and newsletters designed to mobilize elites in society and bring along their followers.

Jacksonian Democracy, 1824–1860

After the spirited confrontations of the republic's early years, political parties faded somewhat in importance for a quarter of a century. By 1820, the Federalist Party dissolved, leaving the nation with only one political party, the Democratic-Republicans, until the 1830s. James Monroe's presidency from 1817 to 1825 produced the so-called Era of Good Feelings, when party competition was nearly nonexistent at the national level. However, there was intense factional fighting within the Democratic-Republican Party during this period, particularly among supporters and opponents of General Andrew Jackson, the military hero of the War of 1812.

Party organizations continued to develop at the state level, fueled in part by the enormous growth in the electorate that took place between 1820 and 1840. During this twenty-year period, the United States expanded westward and most states abolished property requirements as a condition of White male suffrage. The number of votes cast in presidential contests rose from 300,000 to more than 2 million.

Party membership broadened along with the electorate. Formed around President Andrew Jackson's popularity, the Democratic Party, which succeeded the old Jeffersonian Democratic-Republicans, attracted most of the newly enfranchised voters, who were drawn to Jackson's charismatic style. Martin van Buren, Jackson's vice president, was the political organizer behind the movement who established a central party committee, state party organizations, and party newspapers. Jacksonians also established state and national party conventions as the forum for nominating presidential candidates, thus opening the process for greater mass mobilization.

Jackson's strong personality polarized many people, and opposition to the president coalesced into the Whig Party. Among the Whig Party's early leaders was Henry Clay, speaker of the House from 1811 to 1820. The incumbent Jackson, having won a first term as president in 1828, defeated Clay in the 1832 presidential contest. This election was the first in which the party's nominee was chosen at a large party convention rather than the small undemocratic caucuses popular until that time. Thus, Jackson was the first chief executive to win the White House as the nominee of a truly national, popularly based political party.

The Whigs and the Democrats continued to strengthen after 1832. Their competition usually proved fierce and closely matched, and they brought the United States the first broadly supported two-party system in the Western world.[3] Unfortunately for the Whigs, the issue of slavery sharpened the many divisive tensions within the party, which led to its gradual dissolution and replacement by the new Republican Party. Formed in 1854 by anti-slavery and "free soil" activists, the Republican Party set its sights on the abolition (or at least containment) of chattel slavery. After John C. Frémont's losing presidential effort in 1856, the party was able to assemble enough support primarily from former Whigs and anti-slavery northern Democrats to win the presidency for Abraham Lincoln in a fragmented 1860 vote. From the presidential election of 1860 to this day, the same two major parties, the Republicans and the Democrats, have dominated elections in the United States, and control of an electoral majority has seesawed between them.

The Golden Age, 1860–1932

Party stability, the dominance of party organizations in local and state governments, and the impact of those organizations on the lives of millions of voters were the central traits of the era called the "Golden Age" of political parties. This era, from the end of post-Civil War Reconstruction until the reforms of the Progressive Era, featured remarkable stability in the identity of both the Republican and Democratic parties. Such stability has been exceptionally rare in democratic republics around the world.

Political machines, organizations that use tangible incentives such as jobs and favors to win loyalty among voters, were a central element of life for millions of people in the United States during the Golden Age. In fact, for city-dwellers, and particularly immigrants from European countries such as Ireland, Italy, and Germany, party and government were virtually interchangeable during this time. In addition to providing housing, employment, and even food to many voters, parties in most major cities offered entertainment by organizing torchlight parades, weekend picnics, socials, and other community events. Many citizens—even those who were not particularly "political"—attended, thereby forming some allegiance to one party or the other.

The parties also gave individuals the opportunity for upward social mobility as they rose in the organization. As a result, parties generated intense loyalty and devotion among their supporters and office holders, which contributed to relatively high levels of voter turnout among the electorate at the time—75 percent or better in all presidential elections from 1876 to 1900.[4]

The Modern Era

As a result of one of the great reform movements in American history, the so-called Progressive Era, between 1900 and the 1930s, the government gradually took over a number of important functions previously performed by the parties, such as printing ballots, conducting elections, and providing social welfare services. These changes had a major impact on party loyalty and strength. Beginning in the 1930s with Franklin D. Roosevelt's New Deal, social services began to be regarded as a right of citizenship rather than as a privilege extended in exchange for a person's support of a party. The flow of immigrants also slowed dramatically in the 1920s, causing party machines to lose even greater power in many places.

In the post–World War II era, extensive social changes continued to contribute to the move away from strong parties. A weakening of the party system gave rise to **candidate-centered politics**, which focus on candidates, their particular issues, and character rather than party affiliation. Parties' diminished control over issues and campaigns also gives candidates considerable power in how they conduct themselves during election season and how they seek resources. Interest groups and lobbyists stepped into the void that weaker parties left behind. Candidates today compete for endorsements and contributions from a variety of multi- and single-issue organizations.

Population migration and demographic shifts also contribute to both weakening and greater sorting of the parties. For example, during the post–World War II era, millions of people moved from the cities to the suburbs, where a sense of privacy and detachment can deter even the most energetic party organizers. In addition, population growth in the last half-century has created legislative districts with far more people, making it less feasible to knock on every door or shake every hand.

political machine

A party organization that recruits voter loyalty with tangible incentives and is characterized by a high degree of control over member activity.

candidate-centered politics

Politics that focus on the candidates, their particular issues, and their character, rather than party affiliation.

HOW DID POLITICAL MACHINES AFFECT POLITICS?

During the Golden Age of political parties, political machines performed the functions of government and used tangible incentives to recruit voters, especially for city dwellers and immigrants. This satirical cartoon depicts presidential candidate General Ulysses S. Grant as a common minstrel in league with notoriously corrupt New York City politicians, like Boss Tweed, during the election of 1872.

Everett Collection Historical/Alamy Stock Photo

HOW DID THE WEAKENING OF THE PARTY SYSTEM INFLUENCE PRESIDENTIAL ELECTIONS?

A weakening of the party system in the post–World War II era contributed to the rise of candidate-centered politics under the modern presidency. President Dwight D. Eisenhower, a former military general and World War II hero, exemplifies candidate-centered politics, as he was personally popular and appealed to both Democratic and Republican voters. In turn, Eisenhower's moderate agenda and unwillingness to work with party leaders translated into little support for the Republican Party.

Bettmann/Getty Images

party realignment

Dramatic shifts in partisan preferences that drastically alter the political landscape.

critical election

An election that signals a party realignment through voter polarization around new issues and personalities.

secular realignment

The gradual rearrangement of party coalitions, based more on demographic shifts than on shocks to the political system.

Citizen Support and Party Realignment

Periodically, voters make dramatic shifts in partisan preference that drastically alter the political landscape. During these **party realignments**, existing party affiliations are subject to upheaval: many voters may change parties, and the youngest age group of voters may permanently adopt the label of the newly dominant party.[5]

Preceding a major realignment are one or more **critical elections**, which may polarize voters around new issues and personalities in reaction to crucial developments, such as a war or an economic depression. Historically, three tumultuous eras in particular have produced significant critical elections. First, Thomas Jefferson, in reaction to the Federalist Party's agenda of a strong, centralized federal government, formed the Democratic-Republican Party, which won the presidency and Congress in 1800. Second, in reaction to the growing crisis over slavery, the Whig Party gradually dissolved and the Republican Party gained strength and ultimately won the presidency in 1860. Third, the Great Depression caused large numbers of voters to repudiate Republican Party policies and embrace the Democratic Party in 1932. Each of these cases resulted in fundamental and enduring alterations in the party's base of supporters. During the New Deal realignment, for example, blue-collar workers, labor union members, White Southerners, and poor people gravitated toward the Democratic Party.

A critical election is not the only occasion when changes in partisan affiliation are accommodated. More gradual shifts in party coalitions, called **secular realignments**, may also change voters' loyalties.[6] This piecemeal process depends not on convulsive shocks to the political system but on slow, barely discernible demographic shifts— the shrinking of one party's base of support and the enlargement of the other's, for example—or simple generational replacement (that is, the dying off of the older generation and the maturing of the younger generation).

The most significant recent examples of this phenomenon began with Richard Nixon's "southern strategy" of appealing to disaffected White Southerners and was extended with Ronald Reagan's outreach to religious conservatives. By the late 1980s and early 1990s, the southern states, traditionally Democratic stalwarts since the Civil War, shifted dramatically toward the Republican Party. More recently, responses to Trump's tumultuous presidency have created a stark demographic separation between the Republican and Democratic parties, with minorities, millennials, and college-educated White Americans consolidating around Democrats, and blue-collar workers and White evangelicals consolidating around Republicans (see Figure 11.1). Furthermore, geographical sorting has led to an urban–rural divide, with major metropolitan areas largely skeptical of Republicans led by President Trump, and the rural and exurban areas where the president remains strong.[7]

FIGURE 11.1   ARE URBAN–RURAL POLITICAL DIFFERENCES ROOTED IN GEOGRAPHY?

Research shows that partisan affiliation gets shaped by proximity to an urban area, driving the political divide. Here, the probability of identifying as a Democrat is higher when closer to or in a more densely populated urban area.

SOURCE: https://source.wustl.edu/2020/02/the-divide-between-us-urban-rural-political-differences-rooted-in-geography/

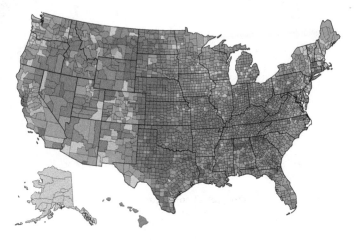

HOW ARE AMERICAN POLITICAL PARTIES ORGANIZED?

11.2 Describe the structure of political parties at the national, state, and local levels.

Despite significant changes in their structure and functions, the two major parties remain fairly well organized. Parties organize conflict and represent citizens' interests in Washington, D.C., state capitals, and local governments throughout the nation (see Figure 11.2). They also engage in many of the fund-raising activities necessary to run candidates for political office and provide manpower and electoral expertise to deliver voters on Election Day. However, examining the national, state, and local parties separately should not lead us to overlook the increasing integration of these party units.

The National Party

The national party organization sits at the pinnacle of the party system in the United States. Its primary function is to establish a cohesive vision for partisan identifiers nationwide and to disseminate that vision to party members and voters. A chairperson, who serves as the head of the national committee, leads the national party. Every four years, the national committee organizes a convention designed to reevaluate policies and nominate a candidate for the presidency.

THE NATIONAL CONVENTION   Every four years, each party holds a **national convention** to nominate its presidential and vice presidential candidates. Because the party's chosen candidate is now usually known before the event, organizers of modern party conventions can heavily script the event to present an inclusive and positive image of the party. Modern party conventions, therefore, serve an important role as pep rallies to mobilize supporters and engage more casual observers. The convention also fulfills its function as the ultimate governing body for the party. The rules adopted and the party platform serve as durable guidelines to steer the party until the next convention. In addition, party rules play a role in determining the relative influence of factions within the party and can increase or decrease the party's chances for electoral success.

Delegates, or representatives to the party conventions, do much of the work at the conventions. Delegates are no longer selected by party leaders but by citizens participating in primary elections and grassroots caucuses. The apportionment of delegates to presidential candidates varies by party. A Democratic Party rule decrees that a state's delegates be apportioned in proportion to the votes cast in support of

national convention

A party meeting held in the presidential election year for the purposes of nominating a presidential and vice presidential ticket and adopting a platform.

FIGURE 11.2   HOW ARE POLITICAL PARTIES ORGANIZED?

American political parties are national in scope, but their real roots—and power—lie in state and local party organizations. Thus, the organization of political parties in America is often presented as a pyramid, with identifiers and voters as the "base" and the national chair as the "pinnacle."

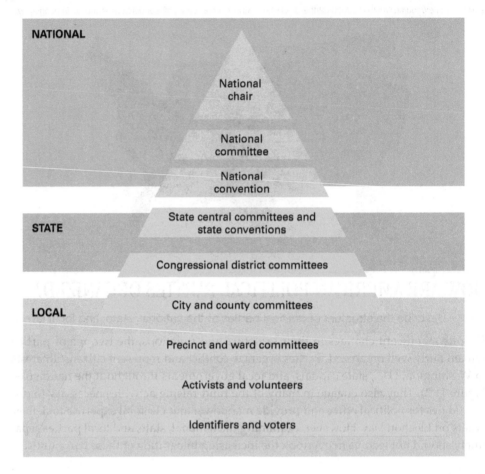

each candidate in the state primary or caucus (so that, for example, a candidate who receives 30 percent of the vote gains about 30 percent of the convention delegates). A candidate is typically only eligible to receive a share of the pledged delegates at stake if they win at least 15 percent of votes cast in a primary or caucus.

The Republican Party uses three primary methods to allocate delegates. Most Republican delegate allocation rules are set by state parties and state laws, though the Republican National Committee sets some rules that states must comply with. Some states use a proportional system to allocate delegates based on the statewide vote, or they allocate at-large delegates proportionally based on the statewide vote and congressional district delegates proportionally based on the vote at the district level. Other states use a winner-take-all system to allocate all their delegates to the candidate who receives a plurality of votes in the primary election or caucus. Finally, some states use a hybrid method such as awarding at-large delegates on a winner-take-all basis according to the statewide vote and congressional district delegates on a winner-take-all basis according to the vote within the districts. Other states directly elect delegates, who are usually bound to a particular candidate on the ballot.[8]

Who the delegates are, a topic of less importance today than when delegates enjoyed more power in the selection process, still reveals interesting differences between political parties. Both parties draw their delegates from an elite group whose income and educational levels are far above the average American's. About 50 percent of delegates at the 2016 Democratic convention were minorities, and 60 percent were women. Only 6 percent of the delegates to the 2016 Republican convention were racial and ethnic minorities. Just eighteen delegates were Black Americans, which, according to one analysis, is the lowest percentage of Black delegates at a GOP convention since 1912. Because of the COVID-19 pandemic, the 2020 conventions were held virtually and broadcast widely, preventing delegates from convening in person.

Both parties also use **superdelegates**—delegates who are not pledged to a candidate and may support whichever candidate they choose at the convention—in some way during their presidential nominating process. However, in the wake of the 2016 presidential election and calls for the parties to be more responsive to their constituents, the Democratic National Committee dramatically reduced in 2018 the power and influence of superdelegates in selecting the party's presidential nominee. Under new rules, it is up to delegates selected in party's primaries and caucuses to select the party's presidential nominee, and superdelegates only play a role if the process becomes deadlocked.

superdelegate
Delegate to each party's national convention that is reserved for a party official and whose vote at the convention is unpledged to a candidate.

THE NATIONAL COMMITTEE   The first national party committees were skeletal and formed some years after the first presidential nominating conventions in the 1830s. First the Democrats in 1848 and then the Republicans in 1856 established national governing bodies—the Democratic National Committee, or DNC, and the Republican National Committee, or RNC—to make arrangements for the national conventions and to coordinate the subsequent presidential campaigns. Since 1972, the size of staff and the amount of money raised by the national committees has increased substantially. In addition to engaging in general party-building activities and aiding presidential campaigns, the committees raise campaign funds primarily for the presidential race, mitigate factional disputes within the parties, and liaise with the media in order to enhance the party's image.

THE NATIONAL CHAIRPERSON   A chairperson serves as the key national party official. The chair is usually selected by the sitting president or newly nominated presidential candidate, who is accorded the right to name the individual for at least the duration of his or her campaign. The national committee may also choose the chair when the election has ended and the party has been defeated. The chair is the primary spokesperson and arbitrator for the party during the four years between elections. He or she has the responsibility of damping down factionalism, negotiating candidate disputes, and preparing the machinery for the next presidential election. Perhaps most critically, the chair is called on to raise funds and keep the party financially strong. Balancing the interests of all potential party candidates is a particularly difficult job, and strict neutrality is normally expected from the chair.

Each party has also party committees in both chambers of Congress that are loosely allied with the DNC and RNC. The Democratic committees are called the Democratic Congressional Campaign Committee and the Democratic Senatorial Campaign Committee. The Republican committees are called the National Republican Campaign Committee and the National Republican Senatorial Committee. These organizations raise and distribute campaign funds for House and Senate seats, develop campaign strategies, recruit candidates, and conduct on-the-ground campaigns. In the past two decades, all six national committees have become major players in American campaigns and elections.[9] The congressional committees and the national committees can sometimes be rivals as they seek funds from the same pools of donors but for different candidates.

State and Local Parties

Although national committee activities attract most of the media attention, the roots of the party lie not in Washington, D.C., but in the states and localities. Both of the two major parties have a central committee in each state, and virtually all government regulation of political parties falls to the states. Most important, the vast majority of party leadership positions are filled at subnational levels.

The arrangement of party committees provides for a broad base of support. The smallest voting unit, the precinct, usually takes in a few adjacent neighborhoods and is the fundamental building block of the party. The United States has more than 100,000 precincts. The precinct committee members are the foot soldiers of any

WHAT ROLE DOES THE NATIONAL PARTY CHAIRPERSON PLAY?

The chairperson serves as the key national party official. Among other things, the chairperson is responsible for fund-raising, unifying the party, and preparing for the next elections. Former labor secretary Thomas Perez (left) was selected as the first Hispanic chair of the Democratic National Committee in 2017, and has since been replaced by Jaime Harrison in 2021. Ronna Romney McDaniel (right), a third-generation politician from Michigan, was President Trump's pick to serve as chair of the Republican National Committee, becoming the second woman to hold the post in RNC history.

party, and their efforts are supplemented by party committees above them in the wards, cities, counties, towns, villages, and congressional districts.

The state governing body supervising this collection of local party organizations is usually called the state central (or executive) committee. Its members come from all major geographic units, as determined by and selected under state law. Generally, state parties are free to act within the limits set by their state legislatures without interference from the national party. One key exception is the selection and seating of presidential convention delegates. Here, the national committee may establish quotas or mandates regarding the type, number, or manner of electing delegates.

Since the 1980s, the national party organizations have become the dominant political players, controlling more money and messaging. While state and local parties recruit candidates, conduct voter registration drives, and provide funds to candidates, their funds are limited compared to the national party organizations that have enormous fund-raising abilities. Furthermore, while the national parties are limited by law in the amount of money they can spend on candidates, federal election laws permit state and local parties to spend unlimited amounts of money on party-building activities such as voter registration drives and get-out-the-vote efforts. Thus, the national organizations transfer millions of dollars each year to the state and local organizations to promote national, state, and local candidates. As a result, the parties have become more integrated and nationalized than ever before. In addition, increased fund-raising, campaign events, registration drives, publicity, and distribution of campaign literature have also enabled the national parties to become more effective political actors over the past three decades.[10] Meanwhile, state and local parties have been reduced to little more than clearinghouses for voter rolls and pass-through vehicles for national parties' fund-raising efforts. There is also not much variation between state and national party platforms.

As local parties have become stand-ins for the national Republican or Democratic Party, the candidates themselves matter less. As political scientist Daniel Hopkins observed, these trends mean voters are faced with similar choices irrespective of where they live, but these standardized brands could come at a cost for democratic accountability.[11] If local candidates aren't evaluated by much more than an R or a D after their name, politicians can't build a reputation separate from that of their party, leaving their electoral fate dependent almost entirely on national tides.

Informal Groups

Numerous official and semi-official groups also attempt to affect the formal party organizations. Both the DNC and RNC have affiliated organizations of state and local party women (the National Federation of Democratic Women and the National Federation of Republican Women) as well as numerous college campus organizations, including the College Democrats of America and the College Republican National Committee. The youth divisions (the Young Democrats of America and the Young Republican National Federation) have a generous definition of "young," up to and including age thirty-five. State governors in each party have their own party associations, too (the Democratic Governors Association and the Republican Governors Association). Each of these organizations provides loyal and energetic foot soldiers for campaigns and voter mobilization.

Just outside the party orbit are the supportive interest groups and associations that often provide money, labor, or other forms of assistance to the parties. Labor unions, progressive groups, teachers, African American and women's groups, and Americans for Democratic Action are some of the Democratic Party's most important supporters. Businesses, the U.S. Chamber of Commerce, evangelical Christian organizations, and some pro-life groups work closely with the Republicans.

Each party also has several institutionalized sources of policy ideas. Though unconnected to the parties in any official sense, these think tanks—or institutional collections of policy-oriented researchers and academics who are sources of policy ideas—influence party positions and platforms. Republicans have dominated the world of think tanks with prominent conservative groups, including the Hudson Institute, American Enterprise Institute, and Heritage Foundation. And the libertarian Cato Institute is closely aligned with the Republican Party. While generally fewer in number, prominent think tanks that generally align with the Democratic Party include the Center for American Progress, Center for National Policy, and Open Society Foundations.

WHAT ARE THE ACTIVITIES OF AMERICAN POLITICAL PARTIES?

11.3   Identify the functions of political parties.

For more than 200 years, the two-party system has served as the mechanism American society uses to organize and resolve social and political conflict. Political parties often are the chief agents of change in our political system. They are mainly involved in running candidates for office, getting out the vote, facilitating electoral choice, providing leadership in policy formulation, and organizing institutions of government such as congressional committees.

Running Candidates for Office

Recruiting candidates for local, state, and national office is one of the most important tasks the parties conduct. Party leaders identify strong candidates and interest them in running for the thousands of open or vulnerable state, local, and congressional seats each year.[12] However, it has become increasingly difficult to find and persuade attractive candidates to run for office, particularly in an era when candidates know they will be intensely scrutinized by the press and public.

RAISING MONEY   The average cost of winning a seat in Congress has increased some 555 percent since 1984. In 2016, a winning U.S. Senate candidate spent an average of $10.4 million and a winning House of Representatives candidate spent $1.3 million (through October 19, 2016), and these figures do not factor in outside spending. The Center for Responsive Politics found that a record-breaking $5.7 billion was spent on the 2018 congressional races, surpassing the amount spent in the 2008 presidential election and smashing the previous midterm spending record of $3.8 billion in 2014. And spending only rose in 2020, with eight of the ten most expensive Senate races ever. Four Senate races in 2020—in North Carolina, Iowa, South Carolina, and Arizona—exceeded the $200 million spending mark.

Although candidates must raise substantial funds on their own, political parties, particularly during mid-term and presidential election years, spend a great deal of time raising and disseminating money for candidates. Historically, Republicans enjoyed

FIGURE 11.3 HOW MUCH MONEY DO PARTIES RAISE?

Changes in political campaigns and campaign finance laws have allowed both political parties to raise increasing amounts of money over the past twenty years, though fund-raising was lower in 2016 than recent presidential elections. Historically, the Republican Party's fund-raising dwarfed that of their Democratic counterparts. From 2008 to 2016, the Democratic Party out-raised the Republican Party. In 2018 and 2020, the Republican Party once again led in fund-raising.

SOURCES: 2003–2020 from Center for Responsive Politics, www.opensecrets.org, and earlier years from Harold W. Stanley and Richard Niemi, *Vital Statistics on American Politics, 2003–2004* (Washington, DC: CQ Press, 2004). 2019–2020 data as of December 14, 2020.

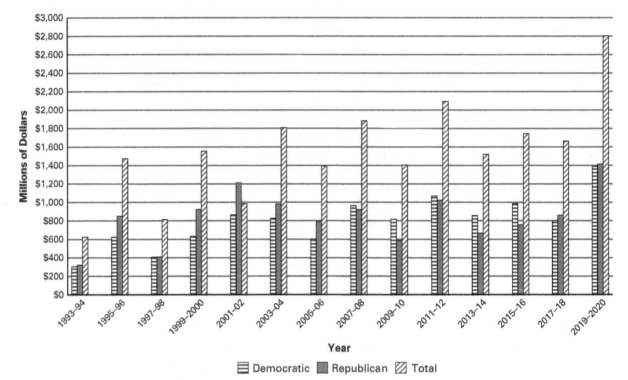

greater fund-raising success than Democrats, due in large part to a significant number of wealthy identifiers and donors. However, in recent years, Democrats caught up, even out-raising Republicans since the 2008 presidential election (see Figure 11.3).

The parties can raise so much money because they have developed networks of donors accessed by a variety of methods. The Republican effort to reach donors through the mail dates back to the early 1960s and accelerated in the mid-1970s when postage and production costs were relatively low. Nowadays, both parties have highly successful mail, phone, and e-mail solicitation lists. Members of Congress, for example, are pressured to raise some $18,000 a day by dialing for dollars at call centers organized by both parties, hours spent away from the jobs they were elected to do. The parties also use digital platforms and advertising, and social media such as Facebook and Twitter, to help reach supporters and raise money for their candidates' electoral pursuits.

MOBILIZING SUPPORT AND GETTING OUT THE VOTE The parties take a number of steps to broaden citizens' knowledge of candidates and campaigns in the days leading up to the election. Parties, for example, spend millions of dollars for national, state, and local public opinion surveys. In important contests, the parties also commission tracking polls to chart the daily rise or fall of public support for a candidate. The information provided in these polls is invaluable to developing campaign strategy in the tense concluding days of an election.

Both parties also operate sophisticated media divisions that specialize in the design and production of TV and digital advertisements for party nominees at all levels. And both parties train the armies of political volunteers and paid operatives who run the candidates' campaigns. Early in each election cycle, the national parties also help prepare voluminous research reports on opponents, analyzing their public statements, votes, and attendance records.

In addition, the parties, along with civic organizations, register and mobilize large numbers of people to vote. Both parties greatly emphasize their duty to "get out the vote" on Election Day. One tactic used by modern parties is "micro-targeting," a practice derived from the field of consumer behavior. With data obtained from a growing volume of government census records and marketing firms, parties use advanced computer models to identify potential voters based on consumer preferences, personal habits, and past voting behavior. Once identified, these voters' names are stored in a database and shared with individual campaigns, whose volunteers contact voters by phone, text, e-mail, and personal visits. The detailed information accessed from these databases allows campaigns to carefully tailor their messages to individual voters. The parties also capitalize on what is called a "relational voter turnout" model that exploits people's friendships and social attachments by having volunteers try to turn out people close to them, like friends and family.

Formulating and Promoting Policy

The **national party platform** is the most visible instrument parties use to formulate, convey, and promote public policy. Every four years, each party writes a lengthy platform explaining its positions on key issues. In a two-party system, a party's platform argues why its preferences are superior to those of the rival party. This is particularly true for contentious social issues, such as abortion and same-sex marriage, which leave little room for compromise and divide the electorate.

Scholarship suggests that about two-thirds of the promises in the victorious party's presidential platform are completely or mostly implemented. Moreover, about one-half or more of the pledges of the losing party also tend to find their way into public policy, a trend no doubt reflecting the effort of both parties to support broad policy positions that enjoy widespread support in the general public.[13] For example, in 2020, both party platforms supported prioritizing military readiness and taking care of military veterans; auditing the Pentagon for waste, fraud, and abuse; and ending previous cuts to defense spending enacted by Congress as part of sequestration (see Table 11.1).

national party platform

A statement of the general and specific philosophy and policy goals of a political party, usually promulgated at the national convention.

Organizing Government

Political parties are able to implement their policy agendas in part because they play such a significant role in organizing the operations of government and providing structure for

TABLE 11.1   WHAT DO PARTY PLATFORMS SAY?

Issue	2020 Democratic Platform	2016 & 2020 Republican Platform
Abortion	Every woman should have access to quality reproductive health care services, including safe and legal abortion	Upholds the "sanctity of human life"; affirms that unborn children have "individual right to life" protected under the 14th Amendment to the Constitution
Defense	Will ensure that military has no peer; would spend defense dollars more wisely and strategically and revitalize American diplomacy	Supports lifting the budget cap for defense; would audit the Pentagon
Health Care	Health care is fundamental human right; Americans should be able to access public coverage through a public option; secure universal health care	Would repeal Obamacare
Education	Universal preschool; new investments by the federal government in higher education; relief from student debt	Calls for choice in K–12 education; restoring private-sector participation in financing college loans
Same-Sex Marriage	Applauds 2015 Supreme Court decision; will fight for comprehensive federal non-discrimination protections for all LGBT Americans to guarantee equal rights	Doesn't accept 2015 Supreme Court decision and urges reversal; laws and government's regulations should recognize marriage as the union of one man and one woman

SOURCES: 2020 Democratic National Platform, www.demconvention.com/wp-content/uploads/2020/08/2020-07-31-Democratic-Party-Platform-For-Distribution.pdf; Republican National Platform, www.gop.com/the-2016-republican-party-platform/.

political conflict within and between the branches. Here, we consider the role of parties in the legislative, executive, and judicial branches at the federal and state levels.

PARTIES IN CONGRESS Nowhere is the party more visible or vital than in the Congress. In this century, political parties have dramatically increased the sophistication and impact of their internal congressional organizations. Prior to the beginning of every session, the parties in both houses of Congress gather (or "caucus") separately to select party leaders and to arrange for the assignment of members to each chamber's committees. In effect, the parties organize and operate Congress.

Congressional party leaders enforce discipline among party members in various ways. These leaders can, for example, award committee assignments and chairs to the loyal or withhold them from the rebellious, regardless of seniority. **Pork-barrel** projects—government projects yielding rich patronage benefits that sustain many legislators' electoral survival—may be included or deleted during the appropriations process. Small favors and perquisites (such as the allocation of desirable office space or the scheduling of floor votes for the convenience of a member) can also be useful levers.

Perhaps as a response to these increased incentives, party labels have become the most powerful predictor of congressional voting. In the past few years, party-line voting has increased noticeably. Although not invariably predictive, a member's party affiliation has proven to be the best indicator of how he or she will vote. In 2016, Republican and Democratic members of the House both had a **party unity** score of 96 percent, the highest ever, but what united the parties was opposition to the other party and its policies.[14]

THE PRESIDENTIAL PARTY The president carries the mantle of leader of his or her party, and he or she is often the public face of his party's agenda. Some presidents have taken their party responsibilities more seriously than others.[15] Democrats Woodrow Wilson and Franklin D. Roosevelt dedicated themselves to building their party in both the electorate and in government. Republicans Ronald Reagan and George W. Bush also exemplified the "pro-party" presidency.

With few exceptions, presidents appoint fellow members of their party to key executive departments and other positions. The president and White House also work closely with congressional party leaders to pass legislation. Because presidents cannot introduce legislation on their own, they nearly always rely on party members in

pork barrel

Legislation that allows representatives to bring money and jobs to their districts in the form of public works programs, military bases, or other programs.

party unity

When a major political party is in agreement about their politics, policies, and/or leadership.

WHAT DOES A PARTISAN PRESIDENT LOOK LIKE?

President Franklin D. Roosevelt dedicated himself to building the Democratic Party both in the electorate and in government. His rise to the presidency and spirited campaigns contributed to the New Deal realignment that drew blue-collar workers, labor union members, White Southerners, and poor people to the Democratic Party. Here, he is greeted by Georgia farmers while en route to Warm Springs, Georgia, just before the 1932 election.

Associated Press

Congress to propose their legislative initiatives. Furthermore, presidents work with party leaders in Congress to construct a majority to pass White House-backed legislation. Presidents reciprocate the support they receive from members of Congress by appointing many activists to office, recruiting candidates, raising money for the party treasury, and campaigning extensively for party nominees during election seasons. The electoral fortunes of the parties also rise and fall with the success of the president. Even when the president is not on the ballot during mid-term elections, voters will still hold the president's party accountable for current problems.

PARTIES IN THE FEDERAL COURTS Although federal judges do not run for office under a party label, judges are creatures of the political process, and their posts are considered patronage plums. Judges are often chosen not only for their abilities but also as representatives of a certain philosophy or approach to government. Most recent presidents have appointed judges overwhelmingly from their own party. Democratic executives tend to select more liberal judges who are friendly to social programs or labor interests. Republican executives generally lean toward conservatives, hoping they will be tough on criminal defendants, opposed to abortion, and supportive of business interests. These opposing ideals may lead to conflict between the president and the Senate. President *Barack Obama*, for example, saw many of his judicial appointments blocked by Senate Republicans, who refused to allow a vote on the nominations. This tactic is an attempt to forestall ideological changes that can last far beyond the next election cycle.

PARTIES IN STATE GOVERNMENT Most of the conclusions discussed about the parties' relationships to the national legislative, executive, and judicial branches also apply to those branches at the state level. State legislators, however, depend on their state and local parties for election assistance much more than their congressional counterparts. Whereas members of Congress have significant support from interest groups and large government-provided staffs to assist (directly or indirectly) their reelection efforts, state legislative candidates need party workers and, increasingly, the party's financial support and technological resources at election time.

Governors in many states hold greater influence over their parties' organizations and legislators than do presidents. Many governors have more patronage positions at their command than the president, and these material rewards and incentives give governors added clout with party activists and office holders. In addition, tradition in some states permits the governor to play a part in selecting the legislature's committee chairs and party floor leaders, and some state executives even attend and help direct the party legislative caucuses, activities no president would ever undertake.

The influence of party organizations in state judiciaries varies tremendously. Some states have taken dramatic actions to ensure that their Supreme Court judges can make independent decisions. Many of these states use a selection system called the Missouri Plan, which relies on a nonpartisan judicial nominating commission, to choose appointed state court judges. But in other states (and in many local judicial elections), Supreme Court judges run as party candidates. These partisan elections have received a great deal of criticism in recent years, as they have become more costly and personal. Many commentators argue that they are contrary to the ideal of blind justice.

Furthering Unity, Linkage, and Accountability

Parties, finally, are the glue that holds together the disparate elements of the U.S. governmental and political apparatus. The Framers designed a system that divides and subdivides power, making it possible to preserve individual liberty but difficult to coordinate and initiate action in a timely fashion. Parties help compensate for this drawback by linking the branches of government. Although rivalry between the branches is inevitable, the partisan and ideological affiliations of the leaders of each branch constitute a common basis for cooperation, as the president and his fellow party members in Congress usually demonstrate daily. Not surprisingly, presidential candidates and presidents are also inclined to push policies similar to those advocated by their party's congressional leaders.

Even within each branch, party affiliation helps bring together members of the House of Representatives and the Senate or the president and the department heads in the bureaucracy. Similarly, the division of national, state, and local governments, while always an invitation to struggle, is made more workable by the intersecting party relationships that exist among office holders at all levels. Party affiliation, in other words, provides a basis for mediation and negotiation laterally among the branches of government and vertically among national, state, and local layers.

The party's linkage function does not end there. Party identification and organization foster communication between the voter and the candidate as well as between the voter and the office holder. The party connection represents one means of increasing accountability in election campaigns and in government. Candidates on the campaign trail and elected party leaders are required from time to time to account for their performance at party-sponsored forums, nominating primaries, and on Election Day.

WHAT DETERMINES PARTY IDENTIFICATION?

11.4   Describe the forces that create and shape party identification.

The party in the electorate—the mass of potential voters who identify with a party label—is a crucial element of the political party. But in some respects, it is the weakest component of the U.S. political party system. Although **party identification**, or a citizen's attachment to a political party based on issues, ideology, past experience, or upbringing, tends to be a reliable indicator of likely voting choices, the trend is for fewer voters to declare loyalty to a party; 38 percent of voters called themselves Independents in 2019, according to surveys conducted by the Pew Research Center, but fewer than 10 percent have no partisan leaning.

party identification

A citizen's attachment to a political party based on issues, ideology, past experience, or upbringing, which tends to be a reliable indicator of likely voting choices.

FIGURE 11.4   HOW MUCH HAS PUBLIC TRUST IN GOVERNMENT DECLINED?

When asked in surveys about their level of trust in the government, Americans are guided by partisanship—Democrats and Republicans each think government runs better when their party is in charge. With public trust in government at historic lows and substantial general dissatisfaction with both major parties, many Americans believe that a third-party option is needed in the United States.

SOURCE: Data from Pew Research Center, www.pewresearch.org/politics/2019/04/11/public-trust-in-government-1958-2019/.

For those Americans who do firmly adopt a party label, their attachment is likely to persist and become a central political reference symbol and perceptual screen. Strong party identifiers are more likely than other Americans to turn out on Election Day. Party activists who not only vote but also contribute time, energy, efforts, and financial support to the party are drawn from the ranks of the strong identifiers.

Political Socialization

Not surprisingly, parents are the single greatest influence in establishing a person's first party identification. Parents who are politically active and share the same party identification raise children who will be strong party identifiers, whereas parents without party affiliations or with mixed affiliations produce offspring more likely to be Independents. However, early socialization is hardly the last step in an individual's acquisition and maintenance of a party identity; marriage, economic status, and other aspects of adult life can change one's loyalty. Charismatic political personalities, particularly at the national level (such as Franklin D. Roosevelt, Ronald Reagan, and Barack Obama), can influence party identification, as can cataclysmic events (the Civil War, the Great Depression, or the rise of school shootings are the best examples). Hot-button social issues (for instance, abortion and same-sex marriage), sectionalism, and candidate-oriented politics may also influence party ties.

Group Identity

Pluralists view political parties as coalitions of many organized groups. Groups try to influence what government does and can offer resources to the parties, such as campaign workers, contributions, and votes, in exchange for party support for policies. In the same vein, party leaders build coalitions of groups to win elections and find electoral support for their policies. The challenge for parties is to build winning coalitions that do not create too many conflicting policy demands.

Just as individuals vary in the strength of their partisan choice, so do groups vary in the degree to which they identify with the Democratic Party or the Republican Party. Variations in party identification are particularly noticeable when geography, gender, race and ethnicity, age, social and economic status, and religion are examined (see Figure 11.5). It is important to note, however, that all of the general party

FIGURE 11.5A   HOW DOES GENDER RELATE TO PARTY IDENTIFICATION?

SOURCE: Data from Pew Research Center, www.pewresearch.org/politics/2020/06/02/the-changing-compositionof-the-electorate-and-partisan-coalitions/pp_2020-06-02_party-id_2-02/.

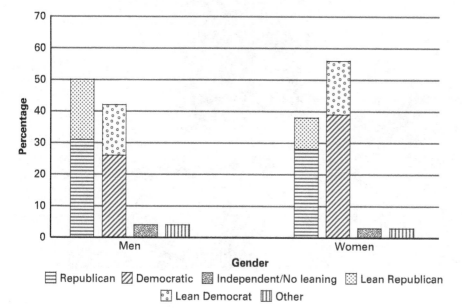

identifications discussed below are broad tendencies that reflect and reinforce the issue and policy positions the two parties take.

GEOGRAPHY While the map has been fairly rigid since 2000, with fewer states changing political sides from one election to the next, there were more competitive states in the 2016 election than in recent previous elections. The 2020 election highlighted deep divisions between urban and rural communities. While **Joe Biden** won almost 90 percent of urban cores, *Donald Trump* won the vast majority—between 75 and 90 percent—of suburbs, small cities, and rural areas.[16]

GENDER Some political scientists argue that the difference in the way men and women vote first emerged in 1920, when newly enfranchised women registered overwhelmingly as Republicans. Not until the 1980 presidential election, however, did scholars observe a noticeable and possibly significant gender gap—that is, the difference between women's aggregate preferences compared to men's—in party identification. This pattern continues to play an important role in politics. Today, about 54 percent of women identify as Democrat or lean Democrat, and 44 percent as Republican or lean Republican.

Most researchers, however, now explain the gender gap by focusing not on the Republican Party's difficulties in attracting female voters, but rather on the Democratic Party's inability to attract the votes of men, especially White men. As one study notes, the gender gap exists because of the lack of support for the Democratic Party among men and the corresponding male preference for the Republican Party. These differences stem largely from differences in the how the sexes see the size and role of government and divergences of opinions about social welfare and military issues.[17] Race also plays an important role in widening the gender gap. While small gender gaps exist among both White and Black people, the most remarkable difference of opinions on all issues is between Black women and White men.

RACE AND ETHNICITY Race is a significant indicator of party identification. For example, Republicans hold the advantage among White voters, and the party's base of supporters is roughly 90 percent White people. Meanwhile, Democrats hold the advantage among minoritized groups, and people of color are becoming a larger share of the electorate across the country. Non-Whites now make up four in ten Democratic

Joe Biden

Elected 46th president of the United States, a Democrat, who ran against President Donald J. Trump in 2020. Vice President from 2009 to 2016; Delaware senator from 1973 to 2009.

WHICH POLITICAL PARTY DO BLACK AMERICANS SUPPORT?

Since the Democratic Party championed key civil rights measures in the twentieth century, Black Americans increasingly identified with the party and became a crucial voting bloc. However, Democrats were criticized in recent elections for failing to treat Black women as viable political candidates and for failing to center the issues of Black women voters. In the 2018 elections, at least 468 Black women ran for political office and more than 20 Black women were elected to serve in Congress. In 2020, Democratic presidential candidate Joe Biden selected Kamala Harris as his running mate, making her the first Black and multiracial woman to be a major party's vice presidential nominee. Democrats included racial equity and justice in their 2020 platform.

Maverick Pictures/Shutterstock

FIGURE 11.5B   HOW DOES RACE RELATE TO PARTY IDENTIFICATION?

SOURCE: Data from Pew Research Center, www.pewresearch.org/politics/2020/06/02/the-changing-composition-of-the-electorate-and-partisan-coalitions/pp_2020-06-02_party-id_2-02/.

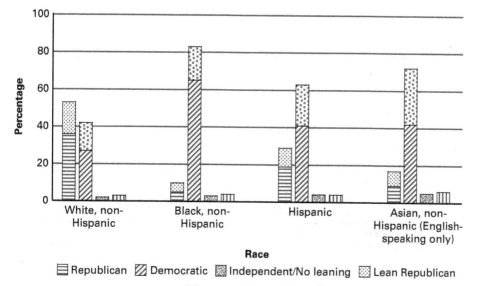

Republican   Democratic   Independent/No leaning   Lean Republican   Lean Democrat   Other

voters, but fewer than one-fifth of Republican voters. Black Americans are over-whelmingly Democratic in their partisan identification, with some 80 percent describing themselves as Democrats. Black Americans provide approximately 25 percent of the Democratic Party's support in presidential elections. The advantage they offer the Democrats in party affiliation dwarfs the edge given to either party by any other significant segment of the electorate, and their proportion of strong Democrats is three times that of White Americans. Hispanic Americans supplement Black Americans as Democratic stalwarts; by about two-thirds, Hispanic Americans tend to vote Democrat. Some divisions do exist by country of origin. Mexican Americans, Puerto Rican Americans, and Central Americans have historically aligned with the Democratic Party, while Cuban Americans have historically identified as Republican. Asian Americans also tend to be divided based on country of origin, but higher-income Asian Americans tend to identify as Republican.

AGE   Political socialization creates a strong relationship between age and party identification. Individuals in the same age range are likely to have experienced similar events during the period in which they formed their party loyalties. Today, middle-aged voters tend to favor the Republican Party. These voters, often at the height of their career and, consequently, their earning potential, tend to favor the low taxes championed by Republicans.[18] In contrast, the Democratic Party's more liberal positions on social issues tend to resonate with today's moderate but socially progressive young adults. The nation's oldest voters, who were alive during the Great Depression, tend to favor the Republican Party.

SOCIAL AND ECONOMIC FACTORS   Occupation, income, and education are closely related, so many of the same partisan patterns appear in all three classifications. While higher-income Americans are more likely to affiliate with Republicans, middle-class and lower-income Americans are more likely to identify with Democrats. Those with higher levels of education, a college or post-graduate degree, are more likely to identify as Democrat, while those who have some college or less are more likely to identify as Republican.

FIGURE 11.5C   HOW DOES AGE RELATE TO PARTY IDENTIFICATION?

SOURCE: Data from Pew Research Center, www.pewresearch.org/politics/2020/06/02/the-changing-composition-of-the-electorate-and-partisan-coalitions/pp_2020-06-02_party-id_2-01-2/.

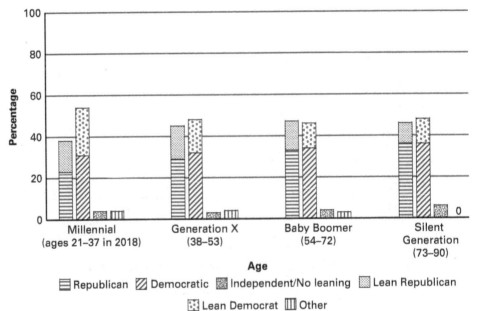

RELIGION   Religion can be evaluated based on both denomination and religiosity, or how frequently an individual engages in activities such as prayer and church attendance. With respect to religious denomination, Jewish and Black Protestant voters tend to favor the Democratic Party, while Mormons and White Protestants—especially Methodists, Presbyterians, and Episcopalians—align with the Republicans. Religiously unaffiliated voters align primarily with the Democratic Party by a more-than-40-point gap. The Republican Party has also made gains among the most religious identifiers of all sects; and these increases may reflect the party's visible support for socially conservative viewpoints, including opposition to abortion and contraception.[19]

FIGURE 11.5D   HOW DOES INCOME RELATE TO PARTY IDENTIFICATION?

SOURCE: Data from Pew Research Center, www.people-press.org/2016/09/13/2-party-affiliation-among-voters-1992-2016/.

FIGURE 11.5E HOW DOES RELIGION RELATE TO PARTY IDENTIFICATION?

SOURCE: Data from Pew Research Center, www.pewresearch.org/politics/2020/06/02/the-changing-composition-of-the-electorate-and-partisan-coalitions/pp_2020-06-02_party-id_2-05/.

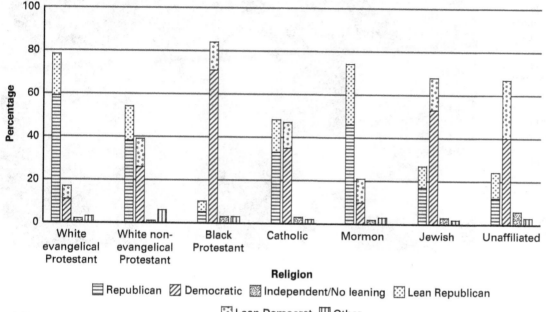

HOW DO MINOR PARTIES AFFECT THE AMERICAN TWO-PARTY SYSTEM?

11.5 Evaluate the role of minor parties in the U.S. electoral system.

To this point, our discussion has focused largely on the activities of the two major political parties, the Democrats and the Republicans. This is not an entirely complete picture of the political system. Although minor parties face a challenge in surviving and thriving in the American political system, these parties continue to make important contributions to the political process, revealing sectional and political divides and bringing to light new issues and ideas.

FIGURE 11.5F HOW DOES EDUCATION RELATE TO PARTY IDENTIFICATION?

SOURCE: Data from Pew Research Center, www.pewresearch.org/politics/2020/06/02/the-changing-composition-of-the-electorate-and-partisan-coalitions/pp_2020-06-02_party-id_2-03/.

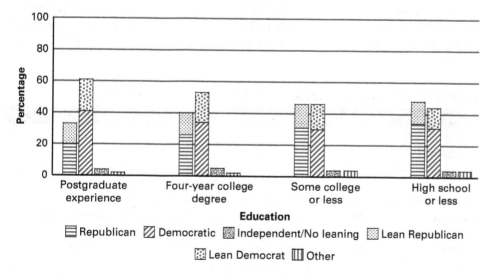

WHAT ROLE DO MINOR PARTIES PLAY IN THE ELECTORAL PROCESS?

Since President Donald J. Trump was elected, the Democratic Socialists of America (DSA) has gained more traction responding to what they view as an extreme right-wing and pro-corporate agenda in power. DSA membership has grown from 7,000 to 50,000 individuals. At least 46 Democratic Socialist candidates and two DSA-backed ballot measures won their primaries in 2018. Most significantly, DSA member Alexandria Ocasio-Cortez in New York (pictured here) and Rashida Tlaib in Michigan were officially elected as members of Congress. DSA candidates can push the ideological trajectory of the Democratic Party to the left by emphasizing social justice issues.

Paul Sancya/AP Images

The Formation and Role of Minor Parties

The decision to form a political party can be a difficult one. Most parties are rooted in social movements made up of activists and groups whose primary goal is to influence public policy. Parties aim to accomplish the same goal, but they also run candidates for elective office. Making this transition requires a substantial investment of financial and human resources as well as a broad base of political support to compete in elections. Throughout history, therefore, very few social movements have evolved into parties. Those that have succeeded in this mission have had the support of political elites and uninhibited access to the ballot.

For example, during the 1840s and 1850s, the Liberty and Free Soil Parties formed around the abolition of slavery issue. The parties' leaders were well-educated Northerners who accounted for a significant proportion of the electorate. In contrast, when civil rights issues emerged on the agenda again in the early twentieth century, it was through a social movement led by activists in groups such as the National Association for the Advancement of Colored People. One reason why this social movement did not become a party was the fact that Black voters in areas where segregation had the most significant impact were largely denied the franchise and thus could not have voted for potential party candidates.

Minor parties based on causes neglected by the major parties have significantly affected American politics (see Table 11.2). These parties find their roots in sectionalism (as did the southern states' rights Dixiecrats, who broke away from the Democrats

TABLE 11.2   WHAT ARE SOME OF AMERICA'S MINOR PARTIES?

Minor Party	Year Founded	Primary Purpose
Liberty/Free Soil	1840	Abolition of slavery
Prohibition	1880	Prohibition of alcohol sale and consumption
Progressive/Bull Moose	1912	Factionalism in Republican Party; gave Theodore Roosevelt the platform to run for the presidency
American Independent	1968	States' rights; opposition to desegregation
Libertarian	1971	Opposition to governmental intervention in economic and social policy
Reform	1996	Economic issues: tax reform, national debt, federal deficit
Green	2000	Environmentalism and social justice

in 1948), in economic protest (such as the agrarian revolt that fueled the Populists, an 1892 prairie-states party), in specific issues (such as the Green Party's support of the environment), in ideology (the Socialist, Communist, and Libertarian Parties are examples), and in appealing, charismatic personalities (Theodore Roosevelt's affiliation with the Bull Moose Party in 1912 is perhaps the best example).

Minor parties achieve their greatest successes when they incorporate new ideas or alienated groups or nominate attractive candidates as their standard-bearers. They also thrive when declining trust in the two major political parties plagues the electorate.

Barriers to Minor-Party Success

The ability of the two major parties to evolve and co-opt the ideas and issues of minor parties is one explanation for the short duration of minor parties. The major parties are eager to take the politically popular issue that gave rise to the minor party and make it their own to secure the allegiance of the minor party's supporters. For example, the Republicans of the 1970s absorbed many of the states' rights planks of George Wallace's 1968 presidential bid. Both major parties also more recently attempted to attract Independent voters by sponsoring reforms of the governmental process.

Scholars point out that third parties are hampered by the single-member-district plurality election system in the United States. Many other countries use **proportional representation**, a voting system that apportions legislative seats according to the percentage of votes a political party receives, giving the candidates of weaker parties a better chance of winning at least some seats. In the American **winner-take-all system**, the party that receives at least one more vote than any other party wins the election. To paraphrase the legendary football coach Vince Lombardi, finishing first is not everything, it is the *only* thing in U.S. politics; placing second, even by one vote, doesn't count. The winner-take-all system encourages the grouping of interests into as few parties as possible (the democratic minimum being two).

The Electoral College system and the rules of public financing for American presidential elections also make it difficult for minor parties to seriously compete. Not only must a candidate win popular votes, but the candidate also must win majorities in states that allow him or her to gain a total of 270 electoral votes.

proportional representation
A voting system that apportions legislative seats according to the percentage of the vote won by a particular political party.

winner-take-all system
An electoral system in which the party that receives at least one more vote than any other party wins the election.

POLITICAL REFORM AND REALITIES: UNITED OR DIVIDED?

11.6 Assess the reasons for the persistence of the two-party system in American politics.

In recent years, the existence, consequences, and causes of **partisan polarization**, or the increasingly conflicting and divided viewpoints of the Democratic and Republican parties, has incited much debate. In this section, we detail each of these factors, making a careful distinction between elite polarization, or divergence among members of the party in government and the most engaged citizens, and mass polarization, or division among members of the general public.[20]

partisan polarization
The presence of increasingly conflicting and divided viewpoints between the Democratic and Republican parties.

Causes of Polarization

Scholars have noted increasing partisan divisions between members of Congress over the past two decades. As northern liberal Republicans and, particularly, southern conservative Democrats have become increasingly rare, the parties have retreated in two separate directions, with the Republican caucus appearing to move rightward and their Democratic counterparts appearing to shift to the left. These changes have created a Congress with a bimodal distribution of members' ideologies—and fewer members in the center. While Congress is now more polarized than at any time since the end of Reconstruction, it is also worth noting that hyperpartisanship is not just a current phenomenon. Some scholars argue that every major transformation in American politics, beginning with the contest between Hamilton's Federalists and Jefferson's Republicans, has included intense partisanship.

Recent scholarship also suggests that the American public is becoming more polarized. Scholars have documented a fundamental change in the nature of partisan affect in the American electorate—the rise of negative partisanship, in which voters have formed strong loyalties based more on loathing for the opposing party.[21] Some scholars assert that bipartisanship remains elusive, not because of politicians in the capitol, but because of the American public and their fixation on party membership and loyalty.[22] Other scholars argue that the complex realignment of parties along different demographic and issue dimensions, the decline of civic responsibility and civic life, and the segregation of individuals into "lifestyle enclaves" where they no longer live around people who share differing views are sources of polarization. But other scholars have attempted to show that the electorate only appears polarized because of the choices they are given in elections. That is, polarization of electoral choices is a result of movement by the candidates.[23] They also question the empirics of geographical sorting in the electorate and argue that even if this type of sorting were proved to occur, the effects would be minimal.[24] Still others take a more middle-of-the-road approach, asserting that polarization has electoral roots, but also that the reactions to members of Congress have amplified the effect of polarization in the electoral environment.[25]

While most Americans still identify overwhelming as politically moderate, that number has shrunk considerably in the last two decades (from 49 percent in 1994 to 33 percent in 2017). Furthermore, the positions of the most politically active citizens seem to suggest a growing division among these members of the electorate. Recent research and polls have found that the level of antipathy that members of each party feel toward the opposing party has surged since 1994.[26] Not only do more partisans have negative views of the other party, it is also more intense. In 1994, just 23 percent of consistent liberals expressed a very unfavorable view of the Republican Party. And just 28 percent of consistent conservatives saw the Democratic Party in equally negative terms. According to a 2018 Pew Research Center survey, 71 percent of Republicans and 62 percent of Democrats cite the harm of the other party's policies as a major reason for identifying as partisans. Perhaps not surprisingly, those who are more politically active are more likely to have a more unfavorable view of the opposing party. For example, 54 percent of Republicans and 46 percent of Democrats who have made campaign donations in the past two years describe the other political party as a threat to the nation (see Figure 11.6).

Changing patterns in news and information production and consumption have also contributed to partisan polarization (see Chapter 13). The perception of deep division not only in Congress but in the mass electorate also has its roots in changing political campaigns. As parties have increasingly used microtargeting to identify, mobilize, and demobilize partisans, they have created stereotypes of party identifiers in our heads. Finally, research also points to individual and group psychological forces empowering polarization, such as in-grouping, out-grouping, and tribalism by which we sort ourselves into groups that compete against each other in a zero-sum game where negotiation and compromise are perceived as betrayal, whether those groups are political, racial, economic, religious, gender, or generational.

Finally, partisan rancor may also be rooted in the clearer articulation of party positions on a range of issues, from national defense and foreign policy to economic affairs to so-called cultural "wedge issues." These cultural issues—summarized by some commentators as "guns, God, and gays"—include such matters as religious freedom, same-sex marriage, and abortion and contraception, on which the parties have

FIGURE 11.6   HOW POLARIZED ARE AMERICAN POLITICAL PARTIES?

Over the last two decades, American political parties have become increasingly polarized. In the 2020 election, stark contrasts between voters who supported Trump and those who supported Biden appeared across a range of political values—around race, gender and family, immigration, and religion. These differences may have consequences for how Americans view the political parties, the political process, and institutions of government. Even more striking, Biden and Trump supporters say they fundamentally disagree with each other not just on political priorities, but on core American values.

SOURCE: Data from Pew Research Center, www.pewresearch.org/politics/2020/09/10/voters-attitudes-about-race-and-gender-are-even-more-divided-than-in-2016/pp_2020-09-10_voter-attitudes-race-gender_0-01/.

Top issues for Trump supporters are economy, crime; Biden supporters prioritize health care, coronavirus

% of registered voters saying each is "very important" to their vote in the 2020 presidential election

	Biden supporters	Trump supporters	Total
Economy	72	88	79
Health care	48	84	68
Supreme Court appointments	61	66	64
The coronavirus outbreak	39	82	62
Violent crime	46	74	59
Foreign policy	57	57	57
Gun policy	50	60	55
Racial and ethnic inequality	24	76	52
Immigration	46	61	52
Economic inequality	28	65	49
Climate change	11	68	42
Abortion	35	46	40

Note: Based on registered voters.
Source: Survey of U.S. adults conducted July 27–Aug 2, 2020.

PEW RESEARCH CENTER

taken increasingly opposing viewpoints in recent years. Today, for example, being pro-choice on abortion is a litmus test for Democratic candidates in most areas of the country. Some scholars contend that this is not polarization—a term carrying a negative connotation—but, rather, party sorting, which means that parties develop clear issue positions that more efficiently and effectively cue the electorate to identify with a particular label.

Consequences of Polarization

Perhaps just as critical as understanding the sources of partisan rancor are its implications for democratic governance. The consequences of the growing division between the two parties in government have been on clear display in recent Congresses. These Congresses have been among the least productive in history in terms of the number of bills passed. The lack of moderate members, lower incentives to compromise and cross party lines, and the close margins by which the parties have held both the House and the Senate have made it nearly impossible to enact important policy proposals. Furthermore, as some scholars noted, hyperpartisanship might also subordinate the integrity of governmental institutions and contribute to a decline in unbiased information.

Some scholars suggest that forcing the American people to choose between two clearly divided political parties has led to increased political apathy, less trust in government, and lower rates of participation and engagement in politics and government. Other scholars charge that polarization has had positive outcomes, including more meaningful choices for the electorate between the parties, parties that are more attentive to their bases, higher voter turnout in elections, and greater engagement in campaign activism.

Other consequences of partisan antagonism for Americans are myriad and complex. Research shows that polarization is affecting families, workplaces, schools, neighborhoods, and religious organizations, stressing the social fabric of our society. Antagonism is necessary in conditions of injustice, but partisan antagonism may come with costs, including undermining relationships with friends and family, making us less likely to help each other out, pressuring individuals to conform to groups, and elevating levels of stress and other physiological responses that, over time, can wear down our muscles and damage our immune systems.

CONCLUSION AND REVIEW

What Are the Roots of the Two-Party System?

11.1 Trace the evolution of political parties.

Political parties have been a presence in American politics since the nation's infancy. The Federalists and the Democratic-Republicans were the first two parties to emerge in the late 1700s. In 1832, the Democratic Party (which succeeded the Democratic-Republicans) held the first national presidential nomination convention, and the Whig Party formed around opposition to President Andrew Jackson. The Democratic and Whig Parties strengthened for several years until the issue of slavery led to the Whig Party's gradual dissolution and replacement by the Republican Party (formed by anti-slavery activists to push for the containment of slavery). From 1860 to this day, the same two political parties—Democratic and Republican—have dominated elections in the United States.

How Are American Political Parties Organized?

11.2 Describe the structure of political parties at the national, state, and local levels.

The national party organization sits at the top of the party system. A chairperson leads the national party, and every four years the national committee of each party organizes a national convention to nominate a candidate for the presidency. The state and local parties are the heart of party activism, as virtually all government regulation of political parties falls to the states. The state governing body, generally called the state central or executive committee, supervises the collection of local party organizations.

What Are the Activities of American Political Parties?

11.3 Identify the functions of political parties.

For more than 200 years, the two-party system has served as the mechanism by which American society organizes and resolves social and political conflict. The two major parties provide vital services to society, including running candidates for office, proposing and formulating policy, organizing government, and furthering unity, linkage, and accountability.

What Determines Party Identification?

11.4 Describe the forces that create and shape party identification.

Most American voters have a personal affinity for a political party, which summarizes their political views and preferences and is expressed by a tendency to vote for the candidates of that party. This party identification begins with political socialization; parents are the single greatest influence on a person's political leanings. However, different group affiliations, including geographic region, gender, race and ethnicity, age, social and economic factors, and religion, also affect individuals' loyalties to political parties, and these may change over the course of a lifetime.

How Do Minor Parties Affect the American Two-Party System?

11.5 Evaluate the role of minor parties in the U.S. electoral system.

Minor parties have often significantly affected American politics. Ideas of minor parties that become popular with the electorate are often co-opted by one of the two major parties eager to secure supporters. Minor parties make progress when the two major parties fail to incorporate new ideas or alienated groups or if they do not nominate attractive candidates for office. However, many of the institutional features of American politics, including the winner-take-all system and the Electoral College, encourage the grouping of interests into as few parties as possible.

Political Reform and Realities: United or Divided?

11.6 Assess the reasons for the persistence of the two-party system in American politics.

In recent years, scholars have debated the presence and origins of growing polarization between the two political parties. Though the cause of these growing divisions can in part be attributed to our own perceptions of polarization and the changing patterns in news and information consumption, clear differences also exist between the parties' positions both in government and in the most active segments of the electorate. The divide between the two parties can make it difficult to create policy in American political institutions and is undermining the social fabric of political and civic life.

LEARN THE TERMS

candidate-centered politics
critical election
national convention
national party platform
partisan polarization
partisanship

party identification
party realignment
party unity
political machine
political party
pork barrel

proportional representation
secular realignment
superdelegate
winner-take-all system

Nicole Glass Photography/Shutterstock

HOW DO CAMPAIGNS MOBILIZE VOTERS?

A record number of more than 159 million voters participated in the 2020 presidential elections. At an estimated 66.7 percent of the voter-eligible population, the voter turnout rate was the highest in more than a century. Voter turnout increased in every state and in 98 percent of the nation's counties. One of the biggest stories was the role of young people (defined as ages 18–29) who made a difference in key battleground states. The Center for Information and Research on Civic Learning and Engagement at Tufts University estimates that 52–55 percent of voting-eligible young people cast a ballot in the 2020 presidential election.

CRITICAL THINKING QUESTION: *Are reforms needed for the electoral system? If so, how should they be enacted?*

CAMPAIGNS, ELECTIONS, AND VOTING

LEARNING OBJECTIVES

12.1 Compare and contrast presidential and congressional elections, and explain the incumbency advantage.

12.2 Outline how campaigns are organized, and evaluate methods for reaching voters.

12.3 Evaluate the influence of money in elections and the main approaches to campaign finance reform.

12.4 Analyze the factors that influence voter turnout and voter choice.

12.5 Evaluate concerns with the electoral process and proposed reforms to address them.

The 2020 presidential elections were historic for many reasons, including record levels of fund-raising and spending. But the other crucial factor was high turnout even amidst a global pandemic. In 2020, a record number of more than 159 million voters cast a ballot in the elections, according to the U.S. Elections Project, which is equivalent to 66.7 percent of the nation's voting-eligible population and the largest turnout for a presidential election since 1900.

With the COVID-19 pandemic, the ability of every eligible individual to cast a free and fair ballot, and especially without risking their health, came into question in the 2020 elections. When the COVID-19 pandemic forced many states to lock down in Spring 2020, many voters were caught in the middle of state partisan political struggles. In Wisconsin's primary elections, voters were unable to vote by mail and forced to risk infection by waiting in lines, without proper distancing, to vote at crowded polling stations that had been consolidated to fewer sites.

The pandemic brought to the fore the critical role that states play in determining who can vote, when they can vote, and by what means. States adapted for the general election by increasing ballot access through expanded early voting and mail-in voting. State election officials and lawmakers in thirty-seven states made changes to voting laws in 2020. Five states for the first time sent mail-in ballots to all eligible voters, eleven states sent mail-in ballot applications to all eligible voters, and twelve states expanded eligibility for mail-in voting. As a result, 101,453,111 Americans voted early, including more than 65 million who voted by mail—higher than the number of people who voted in person on Election Day.

Following a presidential election with the highest turnout rate since 1900, state election officials are now working to codify many of the pandemic-specific changes that broadened ballot access. Since Election Day 2020, Democratic and Republican lawmakers in at least seven states have introduced legislation to expand ballot access by improving mail-in and early voting systems, and legislators in at least eight other states have said they plan to introduce similar bills.

Even as ballot access increased in 2020, there were also more legal challenges, with over 260 lawsuits about who could vote, when ballots could be cast, and by when they must be counted. In addition, legal challenges made by President Donald Trump's campaign post-Election Day to contest results in key states, combined with the spread of false information and unfounded claims of fraud by Trump supporters and the president himself, led to concerns about the further erosion of legitimacy and trust in the election administration process.

In addition to ballot access laws, states also play an often overlooked but critical role in nonpartisan election administration. The story of Brad Raffensperger, a Republican and the secretary of state in Georgia, demonstrates how state election officials upheld potential threats to election integrity during a highly contested campaign in a state that went narrowly for Joe Biden. As Georgia's top election official, Raffensperger was attacked by higher-ranking members of his own party, including prominent Republican political figures who demanded he resign for no apparent reason other than his failure to prevent Biden from winning the state. Raffensperger, Georgia Governor Brian Kemp, and the overwhelming majority of state elections officials around the country didn't cave to partisan political pressure and refused to "discover" voting fraud without good evidence of it.

How can we think critically about how to understand election outcomes? First, there are rules and procedures that structure and govern the electoral system. From the nomination process to the regulation of campaign finance to ballot access, rules structure the strategies of political candidates, how campaigns are carried out and financed, and who gets to vote and when. Second, the political, historical, and economic context of the time (for example, whether the economy is doing well or the president's approval rating)—what political scientists often refer to as fundamentals—can affect public opinion. Third, candidates, political parties, interest groups, and the media have different interests and agendas that they pursue in the electoral process in attempts to influence public opinion and election outcomes. Finally, individuals make choices about whether and how to vote based on their political identities, the political and economic environment, issues that matter to them, and information from campaigns.

There are many criticisms about the state of the electoral system, including archaic rules governing nomination and election processes, excessively expensive campaigns that distract and have the potential to corrupt politicians, negative campaigning, too much influence from outside and special interest groups, and restrictions on ballot access that might temper participation, especially for low-income and minoritized populations. It is important to think analytically about these criticisms, but also to think creatively about what reforms might create more ideal democratic practices and processes.

• • •

In the United States, frequent and regular elections are the means by which the majority of the electorate can hold politicians accountable and keep them attentive to public preferences. Every year, on the Tuesday following the first Monday in November, a plurality of voters, simply by casting ballots peacefully across a continent-sized nation, reelects or replaces politicians at all levels of government—from the president of the United States to members of the U.S. Congress to governors to state legislators to local mayors, councilors, and commissioners, and in some states, judges. While many Americans tend to take this process for granted, in truth it is a marvel. Many countries do not enjoy the benefit of competitive elections and the peaceful transition of political power made possible through the electoral process.

By choosing who will govern—not what they should do or what laws should be passed—voters elect politicians to act on their behalf. This chapter focuses on presidential and congressional contests in the United States and examines the range of factors that affect voter choice and voter turnout. We will examine how campaigns try to mobilize supporters and persuade voters. We will also assess the shortcomings of the democratic process in the United States, including low rates of participation in American elections.

WHAT ARE THE ROOTS OF AMERICAN ELECTIONS?

12.1 Compare and contrast presidential and congressional elections, and explain the incumbency advantage.

Elections are responsible for most political changes in the United States. At fixed intervals, the **electorate**—individuals who are eligible to vote—is called on to judge those in power. Elections confirm the concept of popular sovereignty, the idea that legitimate political power derives from the consent of the governed, and they serve as the bedrock for democratic governance. Regular free elections guarantee mass political action, enable voters to influence the actions of their government, and confer legitimacy on that government. Societies that cannot vote their leaders out of office are left with little choice other than to force them out by means of strikes, riots, or *coups d'état*. Elections are also the primary means to fill public offices and to organize and staff the government. Because candidates and parties advocate and take positions on certain policies, elections also provide a choice of direction on a wide range of issues, from the economy to abortion to racial justice to national defense to the environment, and the winners sometimes claim a **mandate** (a command) from the people to carry out a party platform or policy agenda.

Types of Elections

The United States is almost unrivaled in the variety and number of elections it holds. Under the Constitution, the states hold much of the administrative power over elections, even when national office holders are being elected. Thus, as we will see, states

electorate
Individuals who are eligible to vote.

mandate
A command, indicated by an electorate's votes, for the elected officials to carry out a party platform or policy agenda.

have great latitude to set the date and type of elections, determine the eligibility requirements for candidates and voters, and tabulate the results.

The electoral process has two stages: primary or caucus and general elections. In most jurisdictions, candidates for state and national office must compete in both of these races. Some states (but not the national government) also use the electoral process to make public policy and remove office holders. These processes are known as the initiative, referendum, and recall.

PRIMARY ELECTIONS   In **primary elections**, voters decide which candidates within a party will represent the party in the general elections. Primary elections take on a number of different forms, depending on who is allowed to participate. **Closed primaries** allow only a party's registered voters to cast a ballot. In **open primaries**, however, independents and sometimes members of the other party are allowed to participate. Closed primaries are considered healthier for the two-party system because they prevent members of one party from influencing the primaries of the opposition party. Studies of open primaries indicate that **crossover voting**—participation in the primary of a party with which the voter is not affiliated—occurs frequently, though little evidence exists for organized attempts by voters of one party to influence the primary results of the other party.[1]

In eleven states, when none of the candidates in the initial primary secures a majority of the votes, there is a **runoff primary**, a contest between the two candidates with the greatest number of votes.[2]

GENERAL ELECTIONS   Once the parties have selected their candidates for various offices, each state holds its general election. In the **general election**, voters decide which candidates will actually fill elective public offices. These elections take place at many levels, including municipal, county, state, and national. Whereas primaries are contests between the candidates within each party, general elections are contests between the candidates of opposing parties.

INITIATIVE AND REFERENDUM   Taken together, the initiative and referendum processes are collectively known as ballot measures; both allow voters to enact public policy. They are used by some state and local governments, but not by the national government. Twenty-six states and the District of Columbia have initiative and/or veto referendum processes at the state level.

primary election
Election in which voters decide which of the candidates within a party will represent the party in the general election.

closed primary
A primary election in which only a party's registered voters are eligible to cast a ballot.

open primary
A primary election in which party members, independents, and sometimes members of the other party are allowed to participate.

crossover voting
Participation in the primary election of a party with which the voter is not affiliated.

runoff primary
A second primary election between the two candidates receiving the greatest number of votes in the first primary.

general election
Election in which voters decide which candidates will actually fill elective public offices.

WHAT IS A PRIMARY?

In a primary election, registered voters may participate in choosing the candidate to represent the party in a general election by casting a secret ballot. Primary elections were a Progressive-era reform intended to reduce the potential for mischief in a nomination system controlled by the parties. States hold considerable power in determining the rules for primary (and general) elections. In 2020, more than forty candidates ran for the Democratic Party's nomination for president, including a record number of women and non-White candidates. By March 2020, the field had narrowed to former Vice President Joe Biden and Vermont Senator Bernie Sanders. But 2020 was also remarkable because the COVID-19 pandemic forced sixteen states to delay their primaries and to adopt measures to protect public health. The full effects of the pandemic on voter turnout and vote choice are still being studied.

Win McNamee/Getty Images

An **initiative** is a process that allows *citizens* to propose legislation or state constitutional amendments by submitting them to the electorate for popular vote, provided the initiative supporters receive a certain number of signatures on petitions supporting the placement of the proposal on the ballot. There are two primary types of referenda. In a legislative **referendum**, the *state legislature* submits proposed legislation or state constitutional amendments to the voters for approval. A popular referendum is a measure to approve or repeal an act of the legislature that appears on the ballot as a result of a voter petition drive.

Ballot measures have been the subject of heated debate in the past decades. Critics charge that ballot measures—intended to give citizens more direct control over policy making—are now unduly influenced by interest groups and "the initiative industry—law firms that draft legislation, petition management firms that guarantee ballot access, direct-mail firms, and campaign consultants who specialize in initiative contests."[3] Critics also question the ability of voters to deal with the numerous complex issues that appear on a ballot. In addition, the wording of a ballot measure can have an enormous impact on the outcome. In some cases, a "yes" vote will bring about a policy change; in other cases, a "no" vote will cause a change.[4] Moreover, ballot initiatives are not subject to the same campaign contribution limits applied to donations in candidate campaigns. Consequently, a single wealthy individual can bankroll a ballot measure and influence public policy in a manner that is not available to the individual through the normal policy process.

Supporters of ballot measures argue that critics have overstated their case and that the process has historically been used to champion popular issues that were resisted at the state level by entrenched political interests. Individuals have used initiatives, for example, in popular progressive causes such as banning child labor, expanding suffrage to women, promoting environmental laws, establishing same-sex marriage, and passing campaign finance reform. The process has also been instrumental in passing popular conservative proposals such as enacting tax relief and banning gay marriages.[5] Furthermore, supporters point out that ballot measures can heighten public interest in elections and can increase voter participation.

RECALL **Recall** elections—or deelections—allow voters to remove an incumbent from office prior to the next scheduled election. Recall elections are historically very rare, and sometimes they are thwarted by an official's resignation or impeachment prior to the vote. In recent years, however, recall has become a more popular technique to challenge officials at the state and local levels. In fact, 65 percent of all recalls of state legislators have taken place in the past thirty years, and nearly half have occurred just since 2010.[6] In the first recall election in Colorado's history, voters successfully recalled in 2013 two Democratic state senators who provided crucial support for a package of stricter gun laws. In 2016, there were multiple efforts to recall Governor Rick Snyder in Michigan over the Flint water crisis. Other efforts in 2016 included proposed recalls of seven state legislators, two governors (Bill Walker of Alaska in addition to Rick Snyder of Michigan), twenty-six special districts, six sheriffs, twenty-one school board members, fifty-seven mayors, eight county officials, sixteen county commissioners, ten city officials, and sixty-six city council members. In 2018, there were some 206 recalls against 299 elected officials. Of the 123 elected officials who faced recall elections, seventy-seven officials were recalled.

Observers attribute this growing use of recall to the fact that the majority of state legislatures are ruled by a single party and are more politically polarized than ever before. The recall provides a solution for minority-party legislators and voters to slow down or stop legislation they don't like. In addition, the development of new technologies, such as online petitions and digital and social media, makes fund-raising and signature gathering easier. Digital news sources, too, may turn local recall elections into national news.[7]

initiative

An election that allows citizens to propose legislation or state constitutional amendments by submitting them to the electorate for popular vote.

referendum

An election whereby the state legislature submits proposed legislation or state constitutional amendments to the voters for approval.

recall

An election in which voters can remove an incumbent from office prior to the next scheduled election.

Presidential Elections

No U.S. election can compare to the presidential contest. This quadrennial spectacle brings together all the elements of politics and attracts the most ambitious and energetic politicians to the national stage. Voters in a series of state contests that run through the winter and spring of the election year select delegates who will attend each party's national convention. Following the national convention for each party, a final set of fifty separate state elections to select the president are held on the first Tuesday after the first Monday in November. This lengthy process exhausts candidates and voters alike, but it allows the diversity of the United States to be displayed in ways a shorter, more homogeneous presidential election process could not.

THE NOMINATION PROCESS   The state party organizations use several types of methods to elect the national convention delegates who will ultimately select the candidates running against each other in the general election:

1. *Winner-take-all primary.* Under this system, the candidate who wins the most votes in a state secures all of that state's delegates. While Democrats no longer permit its use because they view it as less representative than a proportional system, Republicans generally prefer this process, as it enables a candidate to amass a majority of delegates quickly and shortens the divisive primary season.

2. *Proportional representation primary.* Under this system, candidates who secure a threshold percentage of votes are awarded delegates in proportion to the number of popular votes won. Democrats now use this system in many state primaries, where they award delegates to anyone who wins more than 15 percent of the vote in any congressional district. Although proportional representation is probably the fairest way of allocating delegates to candidates, its downside is that it renders majorities of delegates more difficult to accumulate and thus can lengthen the presidential nomination contest.

3. *Caucus.* The caucus is the oldest, most party-oriented method of choosing delegates to the national conventions. Traditionally, the caucus was a closed meeting of party activists in each state who selected the party's choice for presidential candidate. Today, caucuses (in Iowa, for example) are more open and attract a wider range of the party's membership. Indeed, new participatory caucuses more closely resemble primary elections than they do the old, exclusive party caucuses.[8] At a

WHEN DO CITIZENS RECALL THEIR LEADERS?

Although historically rare, recall has become a more popular method to challenge officials at the state and local levels. Public furor over state and local officials' actions in handling the water crisis in Flint, Michigan, led to several recall efforts, including of Flint Mayor Karen Weaver (center). Nineteen states and the District of Columbia allow recalls of state and local officials.

Jake May/The Flint Journal-MLive.com/AP Images

caucus, participants spend several hours learning about politics and the party. They listen to speeches by candidates or their representatives and receive advice from party leaders and elected officials, then cast a well-informed vote. The downside to this type of caucus is that it is not as accessible to or inclusive of all populations and can be confusing.

The mix of preconvention contests has changed over the years, with the most pronounced trend being the shift from caucuses to primary elections. Only seventeen states held presidential primaries in 1968; in 2016, thirty-eight states chose this method. Many people support the increase in number of primaries because they believe that primaries are more democratic than caucuses because they are accessible to most registered voters. Although both primaries and caucuses attract the most ideologically extreme voters in each party, primaries tend to nominate more moderate and appealing candidates—those whom primary voters believe can win in the general election. Primaries are also more similar to the general election and thus constitute a rigorous test for the candidates and a chance to display, under pressure, some of the skills needed to be a successful president.

Critics contend that the qualities tested by the primary system, such as skill at handling national and local media, are by no means a complete list of those needed by a successful president. In addition, primaries may attract more participants than do caucuses, but this quantity does not substitute for the quality of information held by caucus participants.

SELECTING A PRESIDENT: THE ELECTORAL COLLEGE Given the enormous amount of energy, money, and time expended to nominate two major-party presidential contenders, it is difficult to believe that the general election could be more arduous than the nominating contests, but it usually is. The object of campaigning for the presidency is clear: winning a majority of the **Electoral College**. This uniquely American institution consists of representatives of each state who cast the final ballots that actually elect a president. The total number of **electors**—the members of the Electoral College—for each state is equivalent to the number of senators and representatives that state has in the U.S. Congress. The District of Columbia is accorded three electoral votes, making 538 the total number of votes cast in the Electoral College. Thus, the magic number for winning the presidency is 270 votes.

Through **reapportionment**, representation in the House of Representatives and consequently in the Electoral College is altered every ten years to reflect population shifts. Reapportionment is simply the reallocation of the number of seats in the House of Representatives that takes place after each decennial **census**. After the 2010 Census, for example, the Electoral College map was redrawn to reflect a sizeable population shift from the Midwest and the Democratic-dominated Northeast to the South and West, where Republicans are much stronger (see Figure 12.1). Texas, for example, gained four congressional districts, and therefore four additional seats in the House of Representatives and four additional votes in the Electoral College. Florida gained two seats and two votes, while six other states gained one. New York and Ohio both lost two seats and two votes, and eight states lost a single seat and electoral vote.

The Electoral College resulted from a compromise among those Framers who argued for selection of the president by the Congress and those who favored selection by direct popular election. Three points are essential to understanding the Framers' design of the Electoral College. The system was constructed to (1) work without political parties, (2) cover both the nominating and electing phases of presidential selection, and (3) produce a nonpartisan president.

For example, because the Framers expected partisanship to have little influence, they originally designed the Electoral College to elect the president and vice president from the same pool of candidates; the one who received the most votes would become president and the runner-up would become vice president. To accommodate

Electoral College

The system established by the Constitution through which the president is chosen by electors from each state, which has as many electoral votes as it has members of Congress.

elector

Member of the Electoral College.

reapportionment

The reallocation of the number of seats in the House of Representatives after each decennial census.

census

Mandated under Article 1, Section 2, of the Constitution, the census provides data necessary to appoint representatives among the states for the House of Representatives and to redistrict legislative districts.

Donald Trump was a top factor in the 2020 election, turning out record numbers of voters both for and against him. Joe Biden received 306 Electoral College votes compared to Donald Trump, who received 232. A closer look at the map of how all 3,141 counties or county equivalents in the fifty states, plus Washington, D.C., shifted—or didn't—from 2016 to 2020, reveals the United States as a very divided country. The overwhelming majority of counties didn't change which party won the majority of votes. In 2020, just seventy-seven counties total have flipped so far, and Joe Biden won fifty-nine of them. However, voters in many parts of the highly populated Northeast; in cities in key Midwestern states, the West, and the West Coast; and in many suburban areas went for Joe Biden by wider margins in 2020 than they did for Hillary Clinton in 2016.

NOTE: Data available as of December 21, 2020.

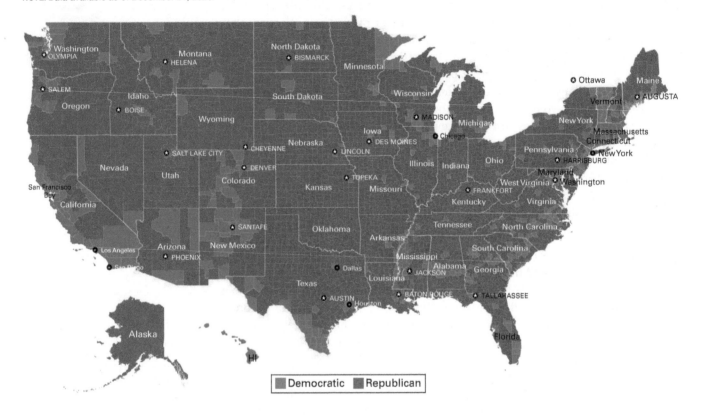

Thomas Jefferson

Principal drafter of the Declaration of Independence; second vice president of the United States; third president of the United States from 1801 to 1809. Co-founder of the Democratic-Republican Party created to oppose Federalists.

this system, each elector was given two votes. Following the development of the first party system, the republic's fourth presidential election soon revealed a flaw in this plan. Since there was no way under the constitutional arrangements for electors to earmark their votes separately for president and vice president, the presidential election of 1800 resulted in a tie between **Thomas Jefferson** and Aaron Burr, the presidential and vice presidential candidates advanced by the Democratic-Republican Party. Even though most understood Jefferson to be the actual choice for president, the Constitution mandated that a tie be decided by the House of Representatives, which the Federalists controlled. The controversy was settled in Jefferson's favor, but only after much energy was expended to persuade Federalists not to give Burr the presidency.

The Twelfth Amendment, ratified in 1804 and still the constitutional foundation for presidential elections today, attempted to remedy the confusion between the selection of vice presidents and presidents that beset the election of 1800 by providing for separate elections for each office. In the event of a tie or when no candidate received a majority of the total number of electors, the election still went to the House of Representatives; now, however, each state delegation would have one vote to cast for one of the three candidates who had received the greatest number of electoral votes. Although the Electoral College modified by the Twelfth Amendment has fared better than the College as originally designed, it has not been problem free. On five occasions—the elections of 1824, 1876, 1888, 2000, and 2016—the electoral process resulted in the selection of a president who received fewer popular votes than his opponent.

Most of the challenges faced by the Electoral College today are the result of the democratization of the Constitution, development of the two-party system, and changes in presidential elections that have occurred over time. Proponents of reform argue that the Electoral College has created political inequality by valuing the voice of some individuals over others, depending solely upon the state in which voters cast their ballots in the presidential selection process.

Congressional Elections

Although congressional elections do not receive as much media attention as presidential elections, the way journalists cover Congress can shape the public's perception and understanding of critical issues that matter to voters. Recent studies find that members of Congress with the most extreme political views receive more attention from print and broadcast media than political moderates.[9] Studies have also found that House leaders and committee chairmen are more likely to be mentioned than other members of Congress. Differences in coverage by race and by gender also persist. Studies show female House members are included less often in news articles than male House members. One of the most consistent—and persistent—findings to emerge from studies is that women candidates receive more attention to appearance, personality, and family than do male candidates, and that the press is more likely to distort the messages of female candidates.[10] Studies have also shown that media produce stereotyped coverage of minorities and are less favorable in their coverage of minorities than of White candidates.[11]

Media coverage of candidates can have implications for representation and for democracy. Research shows that voters living in areas with less coverage of their U.S. House representative are less likely to recall their representative's name, and less able to describe and rate them. And members of Congress who are less covered by the local press work less for their constituencies and are less likely to stand witness before congressional hearings, to serve on constituency-oriented committees, and to vote against the party line.[12]

THE INCUMBENCY ADVANTAGE The current system enhances the advantages of **incumbency**, or already holding an office. Those people in office tend to remain in office. In 2020, 95 percent of House members and 91 percent of senators who sought reelection were successful (with two races still pending as of publication). To the political novice, these reelection rates might seem surprising, as public trust in government and satisfaction with Congress has remained remarkably low during the very period that reelection rates have been on the rise. To understand the nature of the incumbency advantage, it is necessary to explore its primary causes: staff support, visibility, and the "scare off" effect.

Members of the U.S. House of Representatives are permitted to hire eighteen permanent and four nonpermanent aides to work in their Washington and district offices. Senators typically enjoy far larger staffs, with the actual size determined by the number of people in the state they represent. Both House and Senate members also enjoy the additional benefits provided by the scores of unpaid interns who assist with office duties. Many activities of staff members directly or indirectly promote the legislator through constituency services—the wide array of assistance provided by members of Congress to voters in need. Constituent service may include tracking a lost Social Security check, helping a veteran receive disputed benefits, or finding a summer internship for a college student. Research has shown that if a House incumbent's staff helped to solve a problem for a constituent, that constituent rated the incumbent more favorably than constituents who were not assisted by the incumbent,[13] therefore providing the incumbent an advantage over any challenger.

Most incumbents are highly visible in their districts, and they tend to enjoy an enormous financial advantage. They have easy access to local media, cut ribbons galore,

incumbency
Already holding an office.

attend important local funerals, and speak frequently at meetings and community events. Moreover, convenient schedules and generous travel allowances increase the local availability of incumbents. Nearly a fourth of the people in an average congressional district claim to have met their representative, and about half recognize their legislator's name without prompting. This visibility has an electoral payoff, as research shows district attentiveness is at least partly responsible for incumbents' electoral safety.[14]

Research also identifies an indirect advantage of incumbency: the ability of the office holder to fend off challenges from quality challengers, something scholars refer to as the "scare off" effect.[15] Incumbents have the ability to scare off these opponents because of the institutional advantages of office such as high name recognition, large war chests, free constituent mailings, staffs attached to legislative offices, and overall experience in running a successful campaign. Potential strong challengers facing this initial uphill battle will often wait until the incumbent retires rather than challenge him or her (see Figure 12.2).[16]

WHY INCUMBENTS LOSE While most incumbents win reelection, in every election cycle some members of Congress lose their positions to challengers. Members lose their reelection bids for four major reasons: redistricting, scandals, presidential coattails, and midterm elections.

At least every ten years, state legislators redraw congressional district lines to reflect population shifts, both in the state and in the nation at large. This political process may be used to secure incumbency advantage by creating "safe" seats for members of the majority party in the state legislature. But it can also be used to punish incumbents in the out-of-power party. Some incumbents can be put in the same districts as other incumbents, or other representatives' base of political support can be weakened by adding territory favorable to the opposition party. The number of incumbents who actually lose their reelection bids because of redistricting is lessened

FIGURE 12.2 WHAT ARE REELECTION RATES OVER THE YEARS?

With wide name recognition, and usually an insurmountable advantage in campaign cash, House incumbents typically have little trouble holding onto their seats. While incumbency still benefits senators, it's not as reliable a margin as House races. Big swings in national mood can sometimes topple long-time office holders, as happened with the Reagan Revolution in 1980.

SOURCE: Data from the Center for Responsive Politics, www.opensecrets.org.

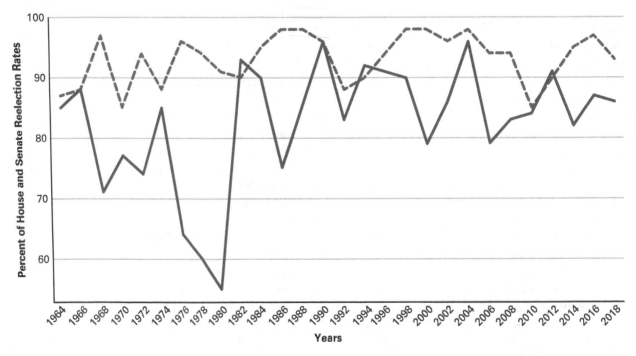

by the strategic behavior of redistricted members—who often choose to retire rather than wage an expensive reelection battle.[17]

Modern scandals come in many varieties. Incumbents implicated in financial impropriety or by other forms of career-ending incidents typically do not lose reelections—because they simply choose to retire rather than face defeat.[18] In 2020, Republican Senators Richard Burr of North Carolina and Kelly Loeffler of Georgia came under fire for suspiciously timed stock market trades that came right as the market tumbled in February amid the deepening coronavirus crisis. In North Carolina, the race was close, but a sexting scandal by the Democratic challenger who had run on character helped Senator Burr win reelection. The results of the Georgia race led to a runoff election that produced wins for Democrats Jon Ossoff and Raphael Warnock.

The defeat of a congressional incumbent can also occur as a result of **presidential coattails**. Successful presidential candidates usually carry into office congressional candidates of the same party in the year of their election. The strength of the coattail effect has, however, declined in modern times, as party identification has weakened and the powers and perks of incumbency have grown. Whereas Harry S Truman's party gained seventy-six House seats and nine additional Senate seats in 1948, **Barack Obama's** party gained only twenty-one House members and eight senators in 2008. The gains can be minimal, even in presidential landslide reelection years such as 1972 (Nixon) and 1984 (Reagan) (see Table 12.1).

Elections in the middle of presidential terms, called **midterm elections**, present a threat to incumbents of the president's party. Just as the presidential party usually gains seats in presidential election years, it usually loses seats in off years. The problems and tribulations of governing normally cost a president some popularity, alienate

presidential coattails
When successful presidential candidates carry into office congressional candidates of the same party in the year of their election.

Barack Obama
The first Black president of the United States, a Democrat, who served as forty-fourth president from 2009 to 2017. Senator from Illinois from 2005 to 2008; member of the Illinois Senate from 1997 to 2004.

midterm election
An election that takes place in the middle of a presidential term.

TABLE 12.1 HOW DOES THE PRESIDENT AFFECT CONGRESSIONAL ELECTIONS?

Gain (1) or Loss (2) for President's Party					
Presidential Election Years			Midterm Election Years		
President/Year	House	Senate	Year	House	Senate
Truman (D): 1948	+76	+9	1950	−28	−5
Eisenhower (R): 1952	+24	+2	1954	−18	−1
Eisenhower (R): 1956	−2	0	1958	−47	−13
Kennedy (D): 1960	−20	−2	1962	−2	+4
L. Johnson (D): 1964	+38	+2	1966	−47	−3
Nixon (R): 1968	+7	+5	1970	−12	+1
Nixon (R): 1972	+13	−2	Ford (R): 1974	−48	−3
Carter (D): 1976	+2	0	1978	−15	−3
Reagan (R): 1980	+33	+12	1982	−26	−1
Reagan (R): 1984	+15	−2	1986	−5	−8
Bush (R): 1988	−3	−1	1990	−10	−1
Clinton (D): 1992	−10	0	1994	−52	−9[a]
Clinton (D): 1996	+10	−2	1998	+3	0
G. W. Bush (R): 2000	−2	−4	2002	+8	+2
G. W. Bush (R): 2004	+3	+4	2006	−30	−6
Obama (D): 2008	+21	+8	2010	−63	−6
Obama (D): 2012	+5	+2	2014	−9	−13
Trump (R): 2016	−6	−2	2018	−35	+2
Biden (D): 2020	−9	+3			

[a]Includes the switch from Democrat to Republican of Alabama U.S. Senator Richard Shelby one day after the election.

SOURCE: *Congressional Quarterly Guide to U.S. Elections*, 6th ed. Washington, DC: CQ Press: 2010. Updated by the authors since 2010.

key groups, or cause the public to want to send the president a message of one sort or another. An economic downturn or presidential scandal can underscore and expand this circumstance.

In 2018, opposition to President Trump galvanized support for Democratic candidates, allowing them to gain control of the House of Representatives. Gains were especially made by Democratic women candidates, with thirty-five women comprising the rising Democrat freshman class out of sixty-one (compared to only one woman in the rising Republican freshman class out of thirty-one).

Voters also tend to punish the president's party much more severely in the sixth year of an eight-year presidency. After six years, voters are often restless for change. For example, in what many saw as a repudiation of President Obama's policies, the Republican Party increased its majority in the House of Representatives in the 2014 midterm election to its highest total since the one it held after the 1928 election, netting at least a dozen additional House seats. Senate elections are less inclined than House elections to follow these off-year patterns. The idiosyncratic nature of Senate contests is due to their intermittent scheduling (only one-third of the seats come up for election every two years) and the existence of well-funded, well-known candidates who can sometimes swim against whatever political tide is rising. When you consider all the sixth-year midterm elections of two-term presidencies since World War II, the president's party has lost an average of five seats. However, in the 2018 midterm election, President Trump's party lost more than the average, making the election look a lot like the sixth year of Ronald Reagan and George W. Bush.

HOW DO CANDIDATES RUN FOR OFFICE AND REACH VOTERS?

12.2 Outline how campaigns are organized, and evaluate methods for reaching voters.

Candidates are the center of political campaigns. While a candidate may not make all of the decisions, or even have the expertise or knowledge to handle the wide variety of issues and concerns that affect the campaign, it is ultimately the candidate's name that appears on the ballot. And on Election Day, voters hold only the candidate truly accountable.

Candidates employ a wide variety of people to help them run an effective campaign. Most candidates for higher offices hire a campaign manager, finance chair, and communications staff. They may also contract the assistance of a variety of political consultants. In addition, candidates rely on networks of grassroots volunteers to spread the campaign's message and to get out the vote.

The Candidate

Candidates run for office for any number of reasons, including personal ambition, the desire to promote ideological objectives or pursue specific public policies, or simply because they think they can do a better job than their opponents.[19] In any case, to be successful, candidates must spend a considerable amount of time and energy in pursuit of their desired office, and all candidates must be prepared to expose themselves and often their families to public scrutiny and the chance of rejection by the voters.

A novel survey of candidates by Run for Something after the 2018 midterms elections revealed insights into the experience of running for office from the perspectives of candidates.[20] Although determination was cited by 52 percent of respondents and was the leading emotion when deciding to run for office, women experienced significantly higher levels of anxiety and fear, while men experienced more excitement and hope. The data suggest these feelings are justified—woman report more challenges with discrimination, community support, home-life tension, and recruitment of experienced staff. There were also significant differences between the motivations, experiences, and emotions of White candidates and candidates of color. Candidates of color cited significantly more challenges with fund-raising and support from the establishment, as well as racism. Candidates of color were more motivated by positive impact and positive role models, and were more likely to define success in terms of resonating, inspiring, and connecting with voters.

Finally, there are also differences between candidates who have experience campaigning and those who don't. First-time candidates, many of whom are young and female, are more likely to cite a desire to make a difference, to fight against something, or to step into a need in making their decision to run. First-time candidates cite experiencing high levels of discrimination and are more likely to cite being challenged by not having their party's support. Paradoxically, they also tend to be more influenced by party support. When referencing their greatest challenge, first-time candidates are more likely to cite early campaign activities like getting started, organizing volunteers, and running a primary.

Candidates' personal attributes—such as race, ethnicity, religion, gender, or social background—can influence voters' decisions. As Peter Hamby wrote in his review of Halperin and Heilemann's best-selling journalistic account of the 2012 campaign, "Candidates matter. Voters tell pollsters that they make their choices based on issues such as education, health care, taxes and the economy—and they do. But they also care about temperament, empathy, strength, reason, trust and the human side of these strange and wily people who think they're up to the task of running the country."[21] Scholars have shown how presidents have used polls to devise methods to focus on personality features, such as strong leadership and competence.[22] While some voters also care about candidates' personality characteristics such as competence, honesty, and vigor, research has shown that that the electorate's focus on candidate attributes has declined substantially in recent presidential elections.[23]

In an effort to show voters they are hardworking, thoughtful, and worthy of the office they seek, candidates try to meet as many citizens as possible in the course of a campaign. To some degree, such efforts are symbolic, especially for presidential candidates, since it is possible to have direct contact with only a small fraction of the millions of people who are likely to vote in a presidential contest. But one should not discount the value of visiting numerous localities both to increase media coverage and to motivate local activists who are working for the candidate's campaign.

UPI/Alamy
Stock Photo

HOW DO CANDIDATES REACH OUT TO VOTERS FOR SUPPORT?

In typical election years, candidates hold large rallies and events in an attempt to energize potential supporters. As the COVID-19 pandemic and public safety measures limited many campaigns, some candidates pivoted to more digital outreach or smaller events with proper physical distancing and mask protocols. President Trump's campaign was criticized for holding rallies during the COVID-19 pandemic, and in 2020, TikTok users and K-pop fans mobilized in protest and registered hundreds of thousands of fans for one of President Trump's events as a prank.

The Campaign

Paid staff, political consultants, and dedicated volunteers work behind the scenes to support the candidate. Collectively, they plan general strategy, conduct polls, write speeches, craft the campaign's message, and design a communications plan to disseminate that message in the form of TV and digital advertisements, social media posts, radio spots, Web sites, and direct-mail pieces. Others are responsible for organizing fund-raising events, campaign rallies, and direct voter contacts.

It is important to note that the campaign staff varies significantly in size and nature, depending on the type of race. Presidential, senatorial, and gubernatorial races employ large professional staffs and a number of different consultants and pollsters (see Table 12-2). In contrast, races for state legislatures will likely have only a paid campaign manager and rely heavily on volunteer workers.

campaign manager

The individual who travels with the candidate and coordinates the campaign.

A **campaign manager** runs nearly every campaign at the state and national levels. The campaign manager travels with the candidate and coordinates the campaign. He or she is the person closest to the candidate who makes the essential day-to-day decisions, such as whom to hire and when to air TV, social media, and radio advertisements. The campaign manager also helps to determine the campaign's overall strategy and works to keep the campaign on message throughout the race. Campaign

TABLE 12-2   HOW IS A CAMPAIGN STAFF ORGANIZED?

Presidential candidates have large staffs that help them run the day-to-day operations of their lengthy campaigns to be the chief executive of the United States. Among these officers are the campaign manager, finance chair, communications director, and a large number of professional political consultants.

Staff	Position	Prior Experience	Twitter handle
Jennifer O'Malley Dillon	Campaign manager	Campaign manager, Beto O'Rourke for President of the United States, 2020	@jomalleydillon
Kate Bedingfield	Deputy campaign manager and communications director	Vice president of communications, Monumental Sports & Entertainment	@KBeds
Pete Kavanaugh	Deputy campaign manager	President of Revolution Field Strategies	@petekavanaugh
Rufus Gifford	Deputy campaign manager	Finance director, Barack Obama for President of the United States, 2012	@rufusgifford
Natalie Quillian	Deputy campaign manager	Partner and principal, Boston Consulting Group	N/A
Zeppa Kreager	Chief of staff	Director, Creative Allliance at Civic Nation	@ZeppaKreager
Anita Dunn	Senior advisor	Managing director, SKDKnickerbocker	N/A
Greg Schultz	General election strategist and senior advisor	Executive director, American Possibilities PAC	@schultzohio
Symone Sanders	Senior advisor	Strategist and CNN political commentator	@SymoneDSanders
Cristóbal Alex	Senior advisor	President, Latino Victory Project	@CristobalJAlex
Brandon English	Senior advisor	Senior advisor, GPS IMPACT	@brandonenglish
Julie Chavez Rodriguez	Senior advisor	Co-national political director, Kamala Harris for the People	N/A
Karine Jean-Pierre	Senior advisor	Political analyst, MSNBC; chief public affairs officer, MoveOn	@K_JeanPierre
Erin Wilson	Political director	State director, Sen. Bob Casey	N/A
Kurt Bagley	National organizing director	National field director, Democratic Congressional Campaign Committee	@kurt_bagley
Jamal Brown	National press secretary	Consultant, Civic Advisors	@JTOBrown
TJ Ducklo	National press secretary	Senior communications director, NBC News	@TDucklo
Yamamoto	Traveling national press secretary	Communications director, Fred Hubbell for Governor of Iowa, 2018	@RemiMYamamoto
	Chief financial officer	Venture partner, Congruent Ventures	N/A
	Senior advisor for financial operations	Treasurer, Kamala Harris for the People	N/A
	National finance director	Director of development, Biden Foundation	N/A
	Digital director		

managers can usually run only one campaign during a given election cycle, and he or she may be the only full-time employee of the campaign.

The major role of the **finance chair** is to coordinate the financial efforts of the campaign. This job includes raising money, keeping records of funds received and spent, and filing the required paperwork with the Federal Election Commission, the bureaucratic agency in charge of monitoring campaign activity. As the cost of campaigns has risen and fund-raising has become more important, the finance chair has also grown in prestige and significance. Although a volunteer accountant may fill the role of finance chair in state and local elections, candidates for most federal offices hire someone to fill this position.

A **communications director**, who develops the overall media strategy for the campaign, heads the communications staff. It is the communications director's job to stay apprised of newspaper, TV, radio, and digital coverage as well as supervise media consultants who craft campaign advertisements.

In many campaigns, the communications director works closely with the **press secretary**, who interacts and communicates with journalists on a daily basis and acts as the spokesperson for the campaign. It is the press secretary's job to be quoted in news coverage, to explain the candidate's issue positions, and to react to the actions of opposing candidates. He or she also has the job of delivering bad news and responding to attacks from opponents or interest groups.

A significant part of the campaign's communications staff is the digital team, which manages the campaign's online communications, outreach, and fund-raising. Members of the digital team are responsible for the candidates' social media presence, which plays a central role in educating and mobilizing voters, especially, for example, during the COVID-19 pandemic. They also generate content for supporters to share on social media. However, sometimes this content includes misinformation, disinformation, or propaganda aimed at suppressing turnout of supporters of the opposing party or mobilizing their own supporters. Campaign staff may organize online town hall forums or real-world meet-ups and grassroots events. They also act as important liaisons with the campaign's volunteers.

Campaign consultants are the private-sector professionals and firms that sell the technologies, services, and strategies many candidates need to get elected. The number of consultants has grown exponentially since they first appeared in the 1930s, and their specialties and responsibilities have increased accordingly.[24] Candidates generally hire specialized consultants who focus on only one or two areas, such as fund-raising, polling, media relations, Internet outreach, and speech writing. Media consultants, for example, design advertisements for distribution on TV, on social media, and across the Internet, radio, billboards, and flyers.

Pollsters are campaign consultants who conduct public opinion surveys from a candidate's potential constituents. They are useful because they can tell a candidate where he or she stands relative to opponents or provide useful information about the issues and positions important to voters. Pollsters may also work with the media staff to gauge the potential impact of proposed social media, radio, or TV advertisements.

Volunteers are the lifeblood of every national, state, and local campaign. Volunteers answer phone calls, staff candidate booths at festivals and county fairs, copy and distribute campaign literature, and serve as the public face of the campaign. Armed with apps that tell them which voters to target, they go door to door to solicit votes or use computerized telephone banks to call or text targeted voters with scripted messages, two basic methods of **voter canvass**. Most canvassing, or direct solicitation of support, takes place in the month before the election, when voters are most likely to be paying attention. Closer to Election Day, volunteers begin vital **get-out-the-vote (GOTV)** efforts, contacting supporters to encourage them to vote and arranging for their transportation to the polls if necessary. In recent years, digital apps and social networking sites such as Facebook, Snapchat, Instagram, TikTok, and Twitter have been important tools used by volunteers and supporters.

finance chair
The individual who coordinates the financial business of the campaign.

communications director
The person who develops the overall media strategy for the candidate.

press secretary
The individual charged with interacting and communicating with journalists on a daily basis.

campaign consultant
A private-sector professional who sells to a candidate the technologies, services, and strategies required to get that candidate elected.

pollster
A campaign consultant who conducts public opinion surveys.

voter canvass
The process by which a campaign reaches individual voters, either by door-to-door solicitation or by telephone.

get-out-the-vote (GOTV)
A push at the end of a political campaign to encourage supporters to the polls.

The Role of Conventions and Debates

With the rise of primaries as the means for nominating candidates, the national party conventions are not as important as they were before reforms to the nominating process post-1968. Today, conventions serve primarily as coronation events to formally nominate the parties' candidates for president and vice president of the United States. The gatherings are also designed to engage the party faithful and energize them for the general election campaign.

Conventions also attempt to increase voters' interest in the upcoming contest, especially through media coverage of the presidential candidate's acceptance speech on the last night of the convention. The acceptance speech is particularly important because it is the first opportunity for the presidential candidate to address voters in the general electorate and showcase presidential qualities. The speech also outlines policies the candidate will focus on in the general election campaign. Candidates hope the speech will provide a boost, called a "bounce," in their opinion poll ratings. Recent scholarship has shown that it is around convention time when voter preferences are the most volatile, and the party conventions play a major role in shuffling the electorate's vote choices. Thus, they do a good job of getting voters' attention sufficiently enough to change minds. But preferences harden nearly every year following the party conventions, with fewer voters changing their minds in the fall general campaign season.[25]

The basic format of conventions hasn't changed since they began in 1831. Due to the COVID-19 pandemic, the 2020 party conventions were held virtually and gave journalists more opportunities than usual to highlight substantive issues facing the country and fewer opportunities to highlight in-party clashes or controversies that have traditionally arisen with in-person proceedings. National polls in the aftermath of the Republican National Convention collectively showed no major shifts in the race between Donald Trump and Joe Biden, though President Trump may have enjoyed a very slight convention bounce. There was a marked contrast in their technical approach. Democrats produced television programming that served as a convention, while Republicans produced a traditional convention that was televised with the feel of a theatrical production. While the 2020 conventions were considered successful, fewer viewers tuned into the conventions, and prime-time viewership for the Republican National Convention was consistently below figures for the Democratic Party's virtual convention, according to figures released by Nielsen.

WHAT ROLE DO CAMPAIGN CONSULTANTS PLAY?

Campaign consultants are hired to help candidates focus on areas such as fund-raising, polling, media relations, Internet outreach, and speech writing. Pictured here are Clem Whitaker and Leone Baxter, a husband-and-wife team who together founded Campaigns, Inc., the nation's first public relations agency for political campaigns.

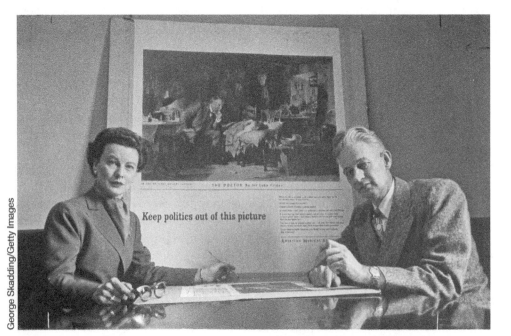

Keep politics out of this picture

George Skadding/Getty Images

The first face-to-face presidential debate in U.S. history did not occur until 1960, and debates did not become a regular part of presidential campaigns until the 1980s. The last few elections have seen a rise in debates during the nominating process, with a staggering thirteen sanctioned debates among the Republican Party candidates seeking the 2016 nomination and twelve sanctioned debates among Democratic Party candidates seeking the 2020 nomination. The frequency not only matches a prime-time series, it also shares some of the same elements of a scripted show, including distinct personalities, drama, and in some cases, a dose of vitriol.

Candidates and their staffs recognize the importance of debates as a tool not only for consolidating their voter base but also for correcting misperceptions about the candidate's suitability for office. However, while candidates have complete control over what they say in debates, they cannot control what the news media will highlight and focus on after the debates. Media coverage during the nominating contest debates can benefit some candidates more than others, as it did for Donald Trump in 2016 and Joe Biden in the Democratic Party nomination for president in 2020. And even though candidates prepare themselves by rehearsing their responses, they cannot avoid the perils of spontaneity. For example, President Gerald R. Ford's erroneous insistence during an October 1976 debate with Jimmy Carter that Poland was not under Soviet domination (when, in fact, it was) may have cost him in a close election. In most cases, however, debates do not alter the results of an election, but rather increase knowledge about the candidates and their respective personalities and issue positions, especially among voters who had not previously paid attention to the campaign. Scholars have also shown that presidential debates can further polarize partisan attitudes by reinforcing their existing beliefs. As with everything else in 2020, the presidential debates were also different and were held as tens of millions of voters were casting their ballots earlier than usual. One debate between Donald Trump and Joe Biden devolved into chaos. President Trump contracted coronavirus before the second debate and then refused to participate in a virtual debate.

The Role of Media

Both traditional news media, including newspapers, magazines, radio and television, and digital native media, including content on the Web, podcasts, apps, blogs, and social media, are central intermediaries between candidates and the public. The media play a large role in determining what voters actually see and hear about the candidates. Both traditional and digital media can be very difficult for a campaign to control. Campaigns, however, have a great deal of control over the content they disseminate directly to followers on social media and include in their campaign advertisements and messaging.

HOW DO PRESIDENTIAL DEBATES MATTER?

We know from extant research and from polling that debates have a limited effect on vote choice and on voting intention. Most people who watch the debates have already made up their mind about the candidates. However, debates do play an important role in providing information on candidates and in rousing citizens to vote. Debates can also have a polarizing effect by reinforcing the existing beliefs of viewers. Pictured left, Richard M. Nixon and John F. Kennedy debate in the first televised debate. Pictured right, Donald J. Trump and Joe Biden debate in 2020.

Bettmann/Getty Images

JIM WATSON/AFP/Getty Images

In the modern campaign, innovation is the name of the game and candidates are always experimenting with new ways of communicating with the public. The rise of radio advertising in the 1920s replaced handbills and door-to-door canvassing. In the 1960s, television replaced radio. Cable television and new marketing strategies in the 1980s and 1990s (especially the rise of robo-calling and focus groups) allowed candidates to use media to target specific constituencies and demographics. The great innovation of President Obama's campaigns was combining digital tools with old-style grassroots organizing, which resulted in a massive communications and fund-raising network, in what came to be termed a "netroots campaign."

Contemporary campaigns have an impressive new array of communications weapons at their disposal to gather and disseminate information more quickly and effectively than ever: text messaging tools, faster printing technologies, reliable databases, instantaneous digital publishing and mass e-mail, social media sites, autodialed pre-recorded messages, and enhanced videotelephony (for example, Zoom). Social media provides constant public access to candidates in a way that dwarfs all previous communications forms between candidates and the public.

In an age dominated by social media and greater media fragmentation, reporters have less control over setting the agenda of what they report than in previous eras. Reporters are frequently in the position of reacting to what the candidates and campaigns do and say (at all hours of the day). Coverage of modern political campaigns has been less reflective of the issues that matter to voters and instead dominated by negativity. This negativity bias tells us what's wrong with politics without telling us what is right. This kind of reporting from mainstream press creates a sense of false equivalency about the candidates and makes it difficult for voters to make distinctions between candidates portrayed as "equally" deeply flawed. Such coverage can contribute to lack of trust in the political system and has been shown to especially turn off young voters and other demographics from participating in elections.

Instead of covering substantive issues facing the nation, the media has focused primarily on campaign tactics and strategy. Even "positive press" coverage tends to be of the horse race, who is ahead, who is behind, and who is gaining.[26] This horse-race coverage can have an effect on how the public views and evaluates the candidates. Using poll data, journalists often predict the margins by which they expect contenders to win or lose. A projected margin of victory of 5 percentage points can be judged a setback if the candidate had been expected to win by Twelve or fifteen points. The tone of the media coverage, that a candidate is either gaining or losing support in polls, can also affect whether people decide to give money and other types of support to a candidate.[27] Decades of studies find that horse-race reporting is linked to distrust in politicians and news outlets, an uninformed electorate, and inaccurate reporting opinion poll data. Horse-race coverage is also detrimental to female political candidates, who tend to focus on policy issues to build credibility. And, while horse-race coverage gives an advantage to novel and unusual candidates, it shortchanges third-party candidates, who often are overlooked or ignored because their chances of winning are slim compared to Republican and Democratic candidates.[28]

Candidates and their media consultants use various strategies in an effort to obtain favorable press coverage. These strategies include seeking to isolate the candidate from the press, staging media events, putting forward the most favorable interpretation for the candidate (and the most negative for their opponent), and circumventing traditional media by appearing on talk shows such as *The Tonight Show with Jimmy Fallon*, *The Daily Show with Trevor Noah*, and *The Late Show with Stephen Colbert*.

As a result of the rise of digital media, candidates both have a greater ability to influence the news cycle and can employ "rapid response" techniques, such as formulating prompt responses to changing events on the campaign trail. In response to breaking news of a scandal or issue, for example, candidates can conduct background research, implement an opinion poll and tabulate the results, devise a containment strategy or simply spin the story, and deliver a reply. This capability contrasts strongly with techniques used in earlier campaigns, which took much longer to prepare and had little of the flexibility enjoyed by the contemporary digital campaign.[29]

Campaigns also use social media, including Facebook, Twitter, Instagram, TikTok, and Snapchat, as well as a range of popular apps, including Spotify, to target specific demographics who might be sympathetic or engaged constituencies and provide them with messages and advertisements in the hopes that they might be mobilized to vote.[30] Although these sites have been effective in reaching the politically engaged, how effective they will be in inspiring new demographic groups to become engaged in electoral politics remains to be seen.[31]

CAMPAIGN ADVERTISEMENTS   Campaign ads may take a number of different forms and appear in a range of communications platforms, from television to direct mail to digital platforms. While the bulk of advertising is spent in local broadcast, there is a clear shift to digital advertising since Americans now spend an average of 5.5 hours per day on digital media. In the 2019–2020 election cycle, total political advertising spending reached $8.5 billion across TV, radio, and digital media, 108 percent more than spending in 2017–2018, which was a record at that time. In the 2019–2020 cycle, 80 percent of paid advertising still went to broadcast and cable TV, and there were 9.3 million TV ads alone in more than 4,300 federal, state, and local elections. $1.6 billion was spent on digital ads, which ran most often on Facebook and Google, with a lot of experimentation for what kind of ads work where. Seventy-five percent of Facebook spending was focused on soliciting campaign contributions or merchandise purchasing. A far smaller percentage was aimed at voter persuasion, which is still the focus of most TV ads.

Positive ads tend to stress the candidate's qualifications, family, and issue positions with no direct reference to the opponent. **Negative ads** attack the opponent's character or platform. And with the exception of the candidate's brief, legally required statement that he or she approved the ad, a negative ad may not even mention the candidate who is paying for the airing. **Contrast ads** compare the records and proposals of the candidates, with a bias toward the candidate sponsoring the ad.

Although the number of negative advertisements has increased dramatically during the past two decades, negative advertisements have been a part of American campaigns almost since the nation's founding. In 1796, Federalists portrayed losing presidential candidate Thomas Jefferson as an atheist and a coward. In Jefferson's second bid for the presidency in 1800, Federalists again attacked him, this time spreading a rumor that he was dead. The effects of negative advertising are well documented. Rather than voting

positive ad

Advertising on behalf of a candidate that stresses the candidate's qualifications, family, and issue positions, with no direct reference to the opponent.

negative ad

Advertising on behalf of a candidate that attacks the opponent's character or platform.

contrast ad

Ad that compares the records and proposals of the candidates, with a bias toward the candidate sponsoring the ad.

HOW DO NEGATIVE ADS AFFECT CAMPAIGNS?

Negative attack ads are an important part of the rough and tumble of the democratic election process. Recent scholarship has shown that negative ads can stimulate voter interest and enrich the information environment available for voters.

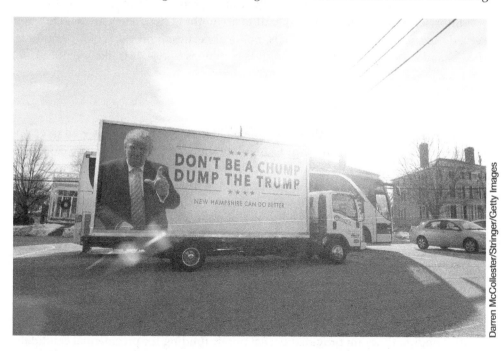

Darren McCollester/Stringer/Getty Images

for a candidate, voters frequently vote *against* a candidate by voting for the opponent, and negative ads can provide the critical justification for such a decision.

Before the 1980s, well-known incumbents usually ignored negative attacks from their challengers, believing that the proper stance was to rise above the fray. But, after some well-publicized defeats of incumbents in the early 1980s in which negative TV advertising played a prominent role,[32] incumbents began attacking their challengers in earnest. The new rule of politics became "An attack unanswered is an attack agreed to." Studies show a sharp rise in negative ads, especially since the 2012 presidential election, with a full 86 percent of President Obama's television advertising and 79 percent of Mitt Romney's ads being negative, and more than three-quarters of ads appealing to anger. In 2016, just over 60 percent of Hillary Clinton's ads attacked President Trump, while 31 percent were positive, focusing on Clinton. President Trump, on the other hand, largely used contrast ads, which both promoted himself and attacked Clinton. He aired no positive ads.[33]

In a further attempt to stave off criticisms from challengers, incumbents began anticipating the substance of their opponents' attacks and airing **inoculation ads** early in the campaign to protect themselves in advance from the other side's spots. Inoculation advertising attempts to counteract an anticipated attack from the opposition before such an attack is launched. For example, a senator who fears a broadside about her voting record on veterans' issues might air advertisements that feature veterans or their families in praise of her support.

inoculation ad

Advertising that attempts to counteract an anticipated attack from the opposition before the attack is launched.

HOW ARE ELECTIONS INFLUENCED BY CAMPAIGN FINANCE AND REFORM?

12.3 Evaluate the influence of money in elections and the main approaches to campaign finance reform.

Successful campaigns require a great deal of money and election costs have been soaring. The Center for Responsive Politics projects that the 2020 elections cost more than $13.8 billion, making it the most expensive election in history and twice as expensive as the previous presidential election cycle. Moreover, outside spending hit an all-time high of $3.2 billion in 2020. Even spending in midterm elections has been rising, with $5.2 billion spent in the 2018 election cycle, making it the most expensive midterm election ever by a wide margin and rivaling presidential election-year spending.[34] But the increase in spending comes even as there are historically fewer undecided voters.

Efforts to regulate campaign spending are nothing new. They are also far from settled. As spending from individuals, political parties, political action committees (PACs) and super PACs, and other sources continues to rise, it is likely that calls for reform will also continue.

Regulating Campaign Finance

The United States has struggled to regulate campaign spending for well over one hundred years. One early attempt to regulate the way candidates raise campaign resources was enacted in 1883, when Congress passed civil service reform legislation that prohibited solicitation of political funds from federal workers, attempting to halt a corrupt and long-held practice. In 1907, the Tillman Act prohibited corporations from making direct contributions to candidates for federal office. The Corrupt Practices Acts (1910, 1911, and 1925), Hatch Act (1939), and Taft-Hartley Act (1947) all attempted to regulate the manner in which federal candidates finance their campaigns and, to some extent, limit the corrupting influence of campaign spending.

Congress did not enact serious, broad campaign finance regulation, however, until the 1970s, in the wake of the Watergate scandal. The **Federal Election Campaign Act (FECA)** and its amendments established disclosure requirements; the Presidential Public Funding Program provided partial public funding for presidential candidates

ection Campaign Act

's the primary law
npaign spend-
riginally
of con-

who meet certain criteria; and the **Federal Election Commission (FEC)**, an independent federal agency, was created to enforce the nation's election laws. Although these provisions altered the campaign landscape, by 2002, it became clear that they were insufficient to regulate ever-increasing campaign expenditures in the United States. Under the leadership of Senators John McCain (R–AZ) and Russell Feingold (D–WI), Congress enacted and President George W. Bush signed into law a new set of campaign finance regulations known as the **Bipartisan Campaign Reform Act (BCRA)** (see Table 12.2).

BCRA regulates political advertising and funding. The act, as it was originally passed, limited the broadcast of issue advocacy ads within thirty days of a primary election and sixty days of a general election, and set hard limits on campaign contributions from a number of sources, including individuals, political parties, political action committees, and members of Congress. Opponents of BCRA, including Senator Mitch McConnell (R–KY) and the National Rifle Association, wasted little time in challenging its limits as an infringement on their right to free speech. In a 2003 decision, the Supreme Court maintained that the government's interest in preventing corruption overrides the free speech rights and upheld restrictions on individual expenditures.[35]

The Supreme Court has, however, declared other sections of BCRA unconstitutional. In 2007, for example, the Court held that the thirty- and sixty-day limits placed on issue advocacy ads were unconstitutional, thus opening the door to these electioneering communications throughout the election cycle.[36] And, in 2008, the Court overturned another provision of the act that had attempted to limit the amount of a candidate's own money that could be spent on running for office.[37] More recently, in 2010, the Court handed down a decision in *Citizens United v. FEC* that declared unconstitutional BCRA's ban on electioneering communications made by corporations and unions.[38] This decision struck a significant blow to BCRA's provisions and has had a dramatic effect on the power of interest groups and corporations in campaigns and elections. As a result of these rulings, subsequent campaign spending surpassed all recent records, with spending exceeding $13.8 billion on the 2020 election. In *McCutcheon v. FEC* (2014), the Supreme Court struck down the aggregate limits on the amount of money individuals may contribute to all federal candidates, parties, and political action committees combined. Although the ruling maintained the federal campaign limits that restrict how much a donor can give to any one candidate or to any one party committee, it paved the way for increased influence of individual donors in campaigns and elections. It has also allowed candidates and parties to create huge joint fund-raising committees.

The cumulative result of these decisions—and the Supreme Court's willingness to equate money with speech—has been to effectively gut campaign finance law in

Federal Election Commission (FEC)

An independent regulatory agency founded in 1975 by the U.S. Congress to regulate the campaign finance legislation in the United States.

Bipartisan Campaign Reform Act (BCRA)

Passed in 2002, this act amended the Federal Election Campaign Act of 1971 with several provisions designed to end the use of nonfederal, or "soft money" (money raised outside the limits and prohibitions of federal campaign finance law) for activity affecting federal elections.

Citizens United v. FEC

2010 Supreme Court ruling that enabled corporations and unions have the same political speech rights as individuals under the First Amendment. As part of this ruling, the Supreme Court found that the government may not prohibit corporations or unions from using their general treasury funds to support or denounce political candidates in elections.

McCutcheon v. FEC

2014 Supreme Court ruling that declared Section 441 of the Federal Election Campaign Act (FECA) unconstitutional. Section 441 imposed limits on any individual's total political contributions (to federal candidates, parties, or political action committees) in a two-year period.

TABLE 12.3 WHAT ARE THE CONTRIBUTION LIMITS FOR THE 2019–2020 FEDERAL ELECTIONS?

	To each candidate or candidate committee per election	To each PAC	To state, district, and local party committee per calendar year	To national party committee per calendar year	Additional national party committee accounts
Individual may give	$2,800*	$5,000	$10,000 (combined limit)	$35,500* per year	$106,500* per account per year
Authorized campaign committee may give	$2,000	$5,000	No limit	No limit	
PAC (multicandidate) may give	$5,000	$5,000	$5,000 (combined limit)	$15,000 per year	$45,000 per account per year
PAC (not multicandidate) may give	$2,800	$5,000	$10,000 (combined limit)	$35,500* per year	$106,500* per account per year
State, district, and local party committee may give	$5,000	$5,000	No limit	No limit	
National party committee may give	$5,000 †	$5,000	No limit	No limit	

SOURCE: Federal Election Commission, www.fec.gov.
*Indexed for inflation in odd-numbered years.
†Additionally, a national party committee and its Senatorial campaign committee may contribute up to $49,600 combined per campaign to each Senate candidate.

the United States. Though limits still exist on individuals' expenditures to parties and candidates, independent expenditures, or funds spent to advocate for the election of a candidate without coordinating with that candidate's campaign committee, are virtually unlimited. To date, efforts to advance further campaign finance reforms have met with little success in Congress (see Figure 12.3).

Sources of Campaign Funding

As mentioned previously, the Bipartisan Campaign Reform Act regulates campaign contributions from a number of sources, including individuals, political parties, members of Congress, personal savings, and political action committees. The Federal Election Commission regulates, records, and discloses these expenditures. The FEC also monitors infractions of campaign finance rules and acts as a quasi-judicial arbiter of conflicts.

BCRA and more recent judicial interpretations of the law also opened the door to a number of other actors in political campaigns. Immediately following enactment of the law, 527 political committees became active in the campaign process. Following the Supreme Court's 2007 actions to lift the limits on issue advocacy ads, 501(c) groups increased their role in electoral politics. Since the *Citizens United* decision, super PACs have become important players in elections, and joint individual-party fund-raising committees played a greater role in 2016 following the *McCutcheon* v. *FEC* decision.

INDIVIDUALS Individual contributions are donations from independent citizens. The maximum allowable contribution under federal law for congressional and

---

FIGURE 12.3   HOW HAS CAMPAIGN FINANCING CHANGED OVER TIME?

Campaign financing has changed dramatically in the last ten years. Following the passage of the Bipartisan Campaign Reform Act (BCRA) in 2002, some expenditures traditionally used in political campaigns were outlawed. But subsequent interpretations of BCRA by the Supreme Court opened the door for other forms of money to play increasingly large roles in the political process. The rise of super PACs has been one such change. These political action committees have come under a great deal of fire in the last three presidential elections because of the unlimited sums of money they raised and spent from wealthy donors, potentially silencing the voices of average citizens.

SOURCE: Data from the Center of Responsive Politics, www.opensecrets.org.

NOTE: 2020 527 dollars not available as of April 15, 2021

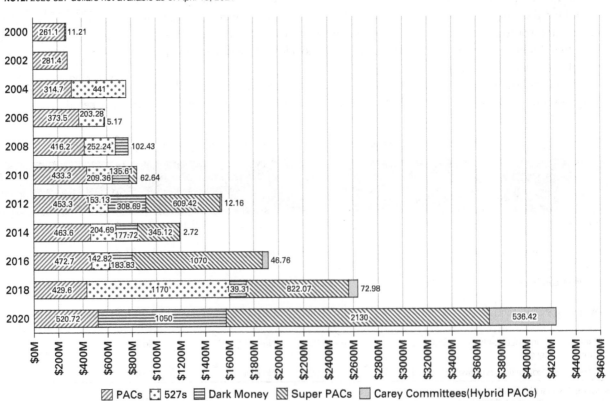

presidential elections was $2,800 per election to each candidate in 2019–2020, with primary and general elections considered separately. As previously noted, following the 2014 Supreme Court decision in *McCutcheon* v. *FEC*, individuals were no longer limited in the total amount they could donate to all candidates, political action committees, and parties combined per two-year election cycle. However, individuals still may not write unlimited checks to their favorite candidate. Most candidates receive a majority of all funds directly from individuals. In one recent election, researchers found that individual donors accounted for 60 percent of contributions to candidates for the House of Representatives, 75 percent of contributions to candidates for the Senate, and 85 percent of contributions to presidential candidates.[39] According to the Center for Responsive Politics, just 1.38 percent of the U.S. population contributed more than $200 to federal candidates, PACs, parties and outside groups in the 2019–2020 election cycle. These 4,503,416 donors gave a hefty 76.21 percent of all contributions.[40]

POLITICAL PARTIES   As a result of the 2014 *McCutcheon* v. *FEC* decision and an expansion of party fund-raising slipped into an appropriations bill later that year, the parties have been able to vastly increase their top donor levels by pooling numerous accounts and affiliates together into joint fund-raising committees. For example, in 2020 President Trump had two partnerships with the Republican National Committee, one called the Make America Great Again Fund and one called the Trump Victory Fund that took donations that were split among the Trump campaign, the Republican National Committee (RNC), and thirty-eight state party committees. A similar partnership was established among Joe Biden's campaign, a forty-eight-state joint fund-raising committee, and the Democratic National Committee. The joint fund-raising committees have allowed the parties that were previously struggling with spending caps to raise funds in excess of the $2,800 limit for a campaign committee. It is also increasingly common for members of Congress to have their own joint fund-raising committees.

In 2020, the Republican and Democratic Parties raised over $3.5 billion. In addition, candidates receive substantial donations from the national and state committees of the Democratic and Republican Parties. Under the current rules, national parties can give up to $5,000 per election to a House candidate and $46,800 to a Senate candidate. In competitive races, the parties may provide almost 20 percent of their candidates' total campaign funds.

PERSONAL SAVINGS   The U.S. Supreme Court ruled in *Buckley* v. *Valeo* (1976) that no limit could be placed on the amount of money candidates can spend from their own families' resources, since such spending is considered a First Amendment right of free speech.[41] For wealthy politicians, this allowance may mean personal spending in the millions. In the 2020 presidential race, former New York Mayor Michael Bloomberg provided more than $1 billion to his campaign for the Democratic nomination, and Tom Steyer provided more than $340 million in funding to his own campaign. Both candidates lost in the primary process. In 2020, eleven senate candidates self-funded a primary or general election campaign, though none were successful. All of the candidates spent more than $1 million of their personal savings. Kelly Loeffler (R–GA) spent more than $23 million in a campaign that went to a run-off that she lost. Twenty-two candidates for the House of Representatives self-funded their campaigns, including Kathaleen Wall (R–TX) who spent more than $9 million in personal funds in a primary contest she lost. David Trone (D–MD) self-funded a campaign for a second time and won (he lost in a primary contest in 2016). All of the House candidates who self-funded in 2020 spent more than $1 million of personal savings.

POLITICAL ACTION COMMITTEES (PACS)   **Political action committees (PACs)** are officially recognized fund-raising organizations allowed by federal law to make contributions directly to candidates' campaigns. A wide variety of groups, including labor unions, corporations, trade unions, ideological issue groups, and even members

political action committee (PAC)

Officially recognized fund-raising organization that represents interest groups and is allowed by federal law to make contributions directly to candidates' campaigns.

WHAT ROLE DO INDIVIDUAL DONORS PLAY IN CAMPAIGN FINANCING?

Although private money has long played a big role in American elections, thanks to *McCutcheon* v. *FEC* (2014), there are no longer aggregate limits on the amount of money that individuals may contribute to all federal candidates, parties, and political action committees combined. One of President Biden's top financial backers was former New York Mayor Michael Bloomberg. Bloomberg gave over $113 million to Democrats in the 2019–2020 election cycle and also self-funded his own bid for the Democratic presidential nomination.

Mark Ralston/Getty Images

of Congress seeking to build their party's membership in Congress, may create them. Under current rules, a multicandidate PAC can give no more than $5,000 per candidate per election, and $15,000 each year to each of the national party committees.

Although a good number of PACs of all persuasions existed prior to the 1970s, it was during the 1970s—the decade of campaign finance reform—that the modern PAC era began. PACs grew in number from 113 in 1972 to a peak of 4,268 in 1988. Today, approximately 5,800 PACs are registered with the FEC. Since Watergate-era campaign reforms, the number of corporate PACs has increased from eighty-nine in 1974 to 1,624 in July 2020, but union PACs only grew from 201 to 271 in the same time period. These political committees have historically played a major role, particularly in congressional elections. In 2019–2020, a record $5 billion was raised by PACs as of September 2020. In 2020, PACs spent $454.43 million on candidates, with $223.32 million spent on Republican candidates and $231.11 million on Democratic candidates.[42]

PACs remain one of the most controversial parts of the campaign financing process. Some observers claim that PACs are the embodiment of corrupt special interests that use campaign donations to buy the votes of legislators. Studies, in fact, have confirmed this suspicion. PACs effectively use contributions to punish legislators and affect policy, at least in the short run.[43] Legislators who vote contrary to the wishes of a PAC see their donations withheld, but those who are successful in legislating as the PAC wishes gain the reward of even greater donations.[44]

527 political committee

Organization created with the primary purpose of influencing electoral outcomes; the term is typically applied only to freestanding interest groups that do not explicitly advocate for the election of a candidate.

527 POLITICAL COMMITTEES   Named for the section of the tax code from which they draw their name, **527 political committees** are organizations created with the primary purpose of influencing electoral outcomes. Although 527s technically include candidate campaign committees and party committees, the term is typically applied only to freestanding interest groups that do not explicitly advocate for the election of a candidate. Many unions and partisan organizations, such as the College Republican National Committee, have formed 527s.

527s are subject to very limited government regulation. The FEC monitors the contributions given to these groups. However, no limits are set on how much an individual or other organization may contribute or on how much a group may spend on electoral activities. During the 2018 elections, 527 groups spent record amounts summing over $1.2 billion and favoring Democratic candidates nearly two to one.[45]

501(C) GROUPS **501(c) groups** are interest groups whose primary purpose is not electoral politics. Federal rules, in fact, mandate that no more than half of a 501(c) group's budget be spent on campaign politics. Like 527s, they take their name from the section of the tax code under which they are established. These groups first became significantly involved in electoral politics after the Supreme Court lifted BCRA's ban on issue advocacy. Thus, most of their electoral activity focuses on raising awareness of candidates' positions on issues of interest to the group.

In 2020, 501(c)(4) and 501(c)(6) groups reported just $89 million in political spending to the Federal Elections Commission.

SUPER PACS The fastest-growing and arguably most significant external actor in elections, **super PACs** are a special kind of political action committee funded by some of the nation's richest people and established to make **independent expenditures**, or spending for campaign activity that is not coordinated with a candidate's campaign. Unlike traditional PACs, they may not give money directly to candidates or party committees. However, they may advocate on behalf of candidates.

Though super PACs must disclose the sources of their contributions to the FEC, they may take money from any person or organization interested in influencing the political process. Since the 2010 *Citizens United* v. *FEC* decision, super PACs and "dark money" groups have spent over $1 billion almost each election cycle, but 2020 marked an all-time high of about $3.2 billion in spending. Super PACs account for 63 percent of all outside spending, while spending by groups that don't disclose their donors is down to just 4 percent. Still, the 2020 elections included at least $100 million in the spending of dark money, which doesn't disclose the source of funding. Dark money can be routed through opaque nonprofits, including 501(c)(4) social welfare organizations and 501(c)(6) trade associations.

Super PACs are not subject to contribution or expenditure limits, which was abundantly clear in the 2020 elections. Some 2,259 groups organized as super PACs reported expenditures of over $2 billion for the 2020 election cycle (see Figure 12.4).

501(c) group
Interest group whose primary purpose is not electoral politics.

super PAC
Political action committee established to make independent expenditures.

independent expenditures
Spending for campaign activity that is not coordinated with a candidate's campaign.

FIGURE 12.4   HOW DO SUPER PACS ALLOCATE THEIR CAMPAIGN CONTRIBUTIONS?

The rise of super PACs followed the July 2010 federal court decision known as *SpeechNow.org* v. *Federal Election Commission*. Super PACs may raise unlimited sums of money from corporations, unions, associations, and individuals. They can also spend unlimited sums to overtly advocate for or against political candidates, though they may not directly donate to candidates and they are not supposed to coordinate efforts with the candidates they support.

SOURCE: Data from the Center for Responsive Politics, www.opensecrets.org/pacs.

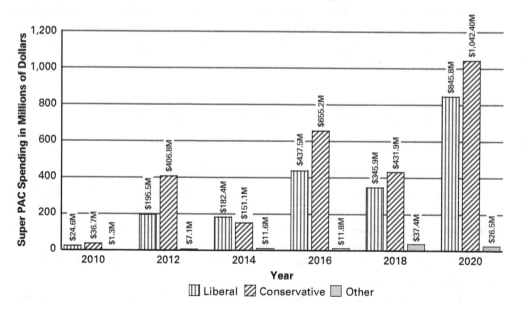

Groups with a conservative view spent 55 percent of that funding, while groups with a liberal view spent some 43.6 percent.

In addition to super PACs, hybrid PACs known as Carey Committees maintain one account for making contributions to candidates, like regular PACs, and a separate account for making independent expenditures, like super PACs. In 2020, Carey Committees spent $540 million, with almost 92 percent going to liberal candidates and independent expenditures and just 8 percent going to conservative ones.

Public Funds

public funds

Donations from general tax revenues to the campaigns of qualifying presidential candidates.

Public funds are donations from general tax revenues to the campaigns of qualifying candidates. On the federal level, only presidential candidates are eligible to receive public funds, although in recent years, few candidates have chosen to accept them. Some states also offer public funds to qualifying individuals running for particular offices, especially within the judiciary.

matching funds

Donations to presidential campaigns whereby every dollar raised from individuals in amounts less than $251 is matched by the federal treasury.

A candidate for president can become eligible to receive public funds during the nomination campaign by raising at least $5,000 in individual contributions of $250 or less in each of twenty states. The candidate can then apply for federal **matching funds**, whereby every dollar raised from individuals in amounts less than $251 is matched by the federal treasury on a dollar-for-dollar basis. Of course, this assumes the Presidential Election Campaign Fund has enough money to do so. Taxpayers who designate $3 of their taxes for this purpose each year when they send in their federal tax returns provide the money for the fund. (Only about 20 percent of taxpayers check off the appropriate box, even though participation does not increase their tax burden.)

During the general election campaign, the presidential nominee of each major party may become eligible for a public grant of $20 million (plus a cost-of-living adjustment) for campaigning in the general election. To be eligible to receive the public funds, the candidate must limit spending to the amount of the grant and may not accept private contributions for the campaign.[46] A candidate may refuse the money and be free from the spending cap the government attaches to it. In 2008, Barack Obama was the first presidential candidate to opt out of the public financing system. Now, nearly all major-party candidates choose not to accept the public funding in favor of raising unrestricted amounts of private donations. This trend will likely continue into the future.

Minor-party candidates are also eligible for public financing in the general election. The amount of public funding to which a minor-party candidate is entitled is based on the ratio of the party's popular vote in the preceding presidential election to the average popular vote of the two major-party candidates in that election. A new party candidate receives partial public funding after the election if he or she receives 5 percent or more of the vote.

WHAT ARE THE PATTERNS IN VOTER TURNOUT AND CHOICE?

12.4 Analyze the factors that influence voter turnout and voter choice.

political participation

Activism that attempts to influence the political process through commonly accepted forms of persuasion, such as voting or contacting elected officials.

political activism

Activism that attempts to influence the political process through protests, boycotts, buycotts, and picketing.

turnout

The proportion of the voting-age public that casts a ballot.

The act of voting is the most common form of **political participation**, or activism that attempts to influence the political process through commonly accepted forms of persuasion. Other examples of political participation include contacting elected officials, submitting public comments, and making campaign contributions. Citizens may also engage in **political activism** to influence the political process by participating in protests, boycotts, and picketing.

Turnout refers to the proportion of the voting-age public that casts a ballot. Generally, voter turnout is much higher in years of presidential elections, around 50 or

Chuck Nacke/Alamy Stock Photo

CAN A SOCIAL MOVEMENT AFFECT ELECTIONS?
The Black Lives Matter movement has attempted to shift public discourse on systemic racism regarding police brutality toward the Black community. Although primarily a social movement and not directly linked to a political campaign, the protests did influence voter turnout and decisions at the ballot box.

60 percent, than for midterm elections, around 40 to 45 percent of the eligible electorate. We care about turnout because it's considered a measure for the health of democracy. However, there are different socioeconomic indicators associated with turnout. If different groups of people turnout at lower rates, it may be a sign that some individuals are being excluded from the process.

A number of factors influence citizens' choices about which candidate to support and whether or not they will turn out on Election Day. A person's reported level of interest in government and public affairs is the single most important individual factor affecting whether a person participates in the electoral process. Individuals also vary substantially in how much they know about politics, and political knowledge is a powerful predictor of voting, on par with formal education. Party affiliation stands at the forefront of predictors for vote choice, but issues and policy preferences and the candidates' personal attributes also influence voters' decisions. Who turns out is important because politicians listen to those who vote. There are some demographic characteristics that are strong predictors of voter turnout, the most important of which are age, income, residential mobility, and education. To a lesser extent, race, ethnicity, gender, civic engagement, and interest in politics matter.

Party Identification and Ideology

Party identification remains the most powerful predictor of vote choice. Stated simply, self-described Democrats tend to vote for Democratic candidates and self-described Republicans tend to vote for Republican candidates. This trend is particularly obvious in less-visible elections, where voters may not know anything about the candidates and need a cue to help them cast their ballot. However, even in presidential elections, a high correlation exists between voter choice and party affiliation. In 2020, for example, 94 percent of self-identified Democrats voted for Joe Biden, and 94 percent of self-identified Republicans voted for Donald Trump, according to Edison Research.

There are different views about what party identification means, though these different understandings are not necessarily exclusive of each other. One view of party identification can be understood as a psychological attachment to a party. In this view, individuals learn about politics from parents, other adults, and peers, and they develop an attachment to a party as part of that socialization process. A second view of party identification is that individuals have a running tally of experience with political leaders and representatives, especially the presidents of each party. As a result of how a president and other members of his party in office performed on issues like the economy or foreign affairs, individuals raise or lower their assessment of the president's party's ability to govern. Individuals update their beliefs about whether that party can run the government competently or has the right approach to achieve outcomes desired by the public.

A third view of party attachment emphasizes voters' underlying ideologies and policy positions. Ideology represents one of the most significant divisions in contemporary American politics. Liberals, generally speaking, favor government involvement in social programs and are committed to the ideals of tolerance and social justice. Conservatives, on the other hand, are dedicated to the ideals of individualism and market-based competition, and they tend to view government as a necessary evil rather than an agent of social improvement. So-called "moderates" lie somewhere else on the ideological spectrum; they may favor conservative positions, including extreme positions, on some issues and liberal positions, including extreme positions, on others.

The ideological alignment of voters and parties has shifted over the last two decades. Not surprisingly, ideology is very closely related to vote choice. Liberals tend to vote for Democrats, and conservatives tend to vote for Republicans. In 2020, 89 percent of self-described liberals voted for Joe Biden, whereas only 10 percent voted for Trump. Conservatives, on the other hand, voted for Trump over Biden at a rate of 85 to 14 percent.[47]

Income and Education

Scholars have found that citizens who vote tend to have higher incomes than nonvoters. According to political science research, those with a family income of less than $50,000 turn out at an average rate of 50 percent, while those families with an income of more than $50,000 turn out to vote at an average rate of 69 percent. Recent analysis has also shown that the correlation between income and voting is different among liberal and conservative states. In richer, liberal states such as New York and California, there is essentially no correlation between income and voting—rich and poor people vote the same way—while in conservative states such as Texas, the rich people are much more Republican than poor people. Scholars have also linked higher income inequality within states to lower voter turnout and also to a stronger Democratic vote. Those who are more affluent typically have more education and a professional career in which they have developed skills that are also useful in politics. The more affluent also have social networks that encourage participation and they can be more easily reached by those seeking to mobilize them.

All other things being equal, college graduates are much more likely to vote than those with less education, and people with advanced degrees are the most likely to vote. People with more education tend to learn more about politics, are less hindered by registration requirements, and are more self-confident about their ability to affect public life.[48] Those without a high school degree tend to vote at an average rate of 4 percent, while those with more than a high school education turn out at an average rate of 77 percent.

Although we do not have exact turnout rates by demographics, there is some exit polling data about vote choice among groups. In 2020, those making *less* than $50,000 per year voted for Biden by a margin of 55 percent to 44 percent for Donald Trump, while those making *more* than $50,000 per year voted for Biden by a margin of 51 percent to 47 percent for Trump. Those making $100,000 or more, however, voted for Trump by a margin of 54 percent to 42 percent for Biden, according to Edison Research. Education was one of the best predictors of vote choice in the presidential election based on current available data. Counties with high percentages of college graduates voted for Joe Biden with some of his biggest margins of victory. Among the nation's fifty counties with the most college graduates, Biden won forty-five.

Race and Ethnicity

Historically, Black Americans and other minorities have faced voting barriers in the United States, especially in areas of the Deep South. For example, in the wake of Reconstruction, the southern states made voter registration extremely difficult for Black Americans even after the Fifteenth Amendment to the Constitution, ratified in 1870, articulated that the right to vote could not be denied on account of race, color, or previous condition of servitude. Until the 1960s, only a small percentage of the eligible Black American population was registered throughout the South. The Voting Rights Act (VRA) of 1965 helped change this situation by targeting states that once used literacy or morality tests or poll taxes to exclude minorities from the polls. As a result of the VRA and other civil rights reforms, turnout among Black Americans has increased dramatically (see Figure 12.5). Since 2004, White and Black people have turned out at virtually the same rates. However, Hispanic people and other minority groups have turned out at lower rates—by about 20 percentage points lower.

For minoritized groups, there are still many barriers to voting. For example, one recent survey found Black and Hispanic people were three times as likely as White people to not have requisite identification and to have difficulty finding the correct polling place. They were also more than three times as likely as White people to not receive a requested absentee ballot, and roughly twice as likely to be out of town on Election Day or to have to wait in long lines. They were also substantially more likely than White people to report transportation problems and bad time and location as reasons for not getting to the polls. Pathbreaking research by political scientist Bernard Fraga has also shown that the racial gaps in voting persist not because of socioeconomics or voter suppression, but because minority voters have limited influence in shaping election outcomes. Voters turn out at higher rates when their votes matter. Although there have been significant demographic changes in the United States, in most elections and most places, minorities are less electorally relevant than White people. However, when politicians engage the minority electorate, they are more likely to turn out.[49]

FIGURE 12.5 HOW HAS THE RACIAL AND ETHNIC COMPOSITION OF VOTERS CHANGED?

The U.S. Census Bureau projects that people of color will become a majority of the population by 2043. However, the shift in the electorate is occurring at different rates. For example, Hispanic Americans account for a larger share of the total U.S. population (17 percent) than they do the total U.S. electorate (10.7 percent). Although people of color are becoming a larger share of the eligible electorate across the United States, voter turnout among different races and ethnicities varies.

SOURCE: Data from Pew Research Center and CNN.com.

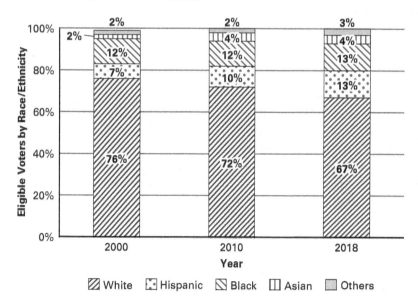

While White people have shown an increasing tendency to vote Republican, Black American voters remain overwhelmingly Democratic in their voting decisions. Despite the best efforts of the Republican Party to garner Black voter support, this pattern shows no signs of waning. In 2020, 87 percent of Black voters cast a ballot for Joe Biden, while Donald Trump made gains over 2016 and received 12 percent of the Black vote.[50]

The Hispanic community in the United States is now slightly larger than the Black American community; thus, Hispanic people have the potential to wield enormous political power. In California, Texas, Florida, Illinois, and New York, five key electoral states, Hispanic voters have emerged as powerful allies for candidates seeking office. Moreover, their increasing presence in New Mexico, Arizona, Colorado, and Nevada has forced candidates of both parties to place more emphasis on issues that affect the Hispanic communities. Hispanic people also are likely to identify with and vote for Democrats, although not as monolithically as Black people.

Asian and Pacific Islander Americans are more variable in their voting than either the Hispanic or the Black communities. The considerable political diversity within this group is worth noting: Chinese Americans tend to prefer Democratic candidates, but older Vietnamese Americans, with strong anti-communist leanings, tend to support Republicans. A typical voting split for the Asian and Pacific Islander American community runs about 65 percent Democratic and 35 percent Republican, though it can reach the extreme of a 50–50 split, depending on the election.[51]

Gender and Age

With passage of the Nineteenth Amendment in 1920, White women gained the right to vote in the United States. While early polling numbers are not reliable enough to shed light on the voting rate among women in the period immediately following ratification of the Nineteenth Amendment, it is generally accepted that women voted at a lower rate than men. Recent polls suggest that today women vote at a slightly higher rate than their male counterparts. Since women constitute slightly more than 50 percent of the U.S. population, they now account for a majority of the American electorate.

Since 1980, the gender gap—the difference between the voting choices of men and women—has become a staple of American politics. The gender gap (discussed further in Chapter 11) varies considerably from election to election, though normally women support the average Democrat 5 to 7 percent more than men. Based on exit poll data, Joe Biden won 57 percent of the female vote, but only 45 percent of the male vote.[52] According to national exit poll data in the 2018 midterm elections, 59 percent of women voted for Democrats and 40 percent voted for Republicans, which adds up to a record margin of 19 percentage points—nearly double the margin by which they voted for Democrats in 2016.

A strong correlation also exists between age and voter turnout. The Twenty-Sixth Amendment to the Constitution, ratified in 1971, lowered the voting age to eighteen. While this amendment obviously increased the number of eligible voters, this age group has been least likely to vote. A much higher percentage of citizens age thirty and older vote than citizens younger than thirty, although voter turnout decreases over the age of seventy, primarily due to the difficulties some older voters experience in getting to their polling locations.

Youth turnout hit record levels in the 2018 midterm elections, but only one out of every three eligible young voters cast a ballot that year. According to new research by political scientists John Holbein and Sunshine Hillygus, the hidden driver of low youth turnout isn't a lack of political interest or motivation; it's that the act of voting is "costly." Individuals have to expend time and effort familiarizing themselves with candidates and policies, decide which they prefer, and then overcome distractions long enough to find the right polling station on the right day (assuming they met the registration deadline, of course). Voting may sound simple to some, but for tens of millions of Americans, the abstract duties of democratic participation can only be considered after work, homework, or grocery shopping.

Studies also find that systems and key civic institutions are not doing enough to reach young people with accessible information to register and vote, and this was especially problematic during the COVID-19 pandemic. Only about 50 percent of eligible eighteen- to twenty-nine-year-olds are even registered to vote. [53] The Center for Information and Research on Civic Learning and Engagement found that more than one-third of young people said they did not know whether their state has online voter registration. Just 25 percent had voted by mail before, and more than a quarter said they wouldn't know where to get information about mail-in voting.[54] Furthermore, young people with no college experience are less likely to be contacted by campaigns and parties and less likely to have information on casting an absentee ballot or to know where to get it, which both reflects and potentially perpetuates inequalities in political participation.

In the 2020 election, age was also a dividing line, with Democrats widening their advantage from 2016 in counties with a younger population. In the 2020 presidential elections, young voters aged eighteen to twenty-nine turned out at a record rate of 52–55 percent, according to preliminary estimates by the Center for Information and Research on Civic Learning and Engagement. Data suggest that this group voted for Joe Biden and Democratic candidates by a margin of two to one.

Religious Groups and Civic Organizations

People who frequently attend church or other religious services and individuals who are members of civic organizations, trade and professional organizations, and labor unions are more likely to vote and participate in politics than those who are not members of these or similar types of groups. Many of these organizations emphasize community involvement, which often encourages voting and exposes members to requests for support from political parties and candidates. These groups also encourage participation by providing opportunities for members to develop organizational and communication skills relevant to political activity. Religious groups have tended to vote in distinct patterns, but some of these patterns have changed in recent years as parties have sorted and polarized (see Chapter 11).

Candidate Traits and Issues

Individual issues can have important effects in any given election year. Voters have preferences for the types of policies or outcomes they would like the government to pursue, and they choose the candidates and parties that they think will produce the best results. Candidates seek to make salient certain issues in any given election and to define those issues in ways that will serve their interests. Different issues matter in any given election, and voters differ in how they weigh the issues. While the economy tends to be identified by voters as the most important issue, social issues, foreign affairs, and national security are also important.

Voters tend to reward the party in government, usually the president's party, during good economic times and punish that party during periods of economic downturn. When this occurs, the electorate is exercising **retrospective judgment**; that is, voters are rendering judgment on the party in power based on past performance on particular issues. At other times, voters might use **prospective judgment**; that is, they vote based on what a candidate pledges to do about an issue if elected. The 2020 election provides an example of how both retrospective and prospective judgments helped voters reach their ballot decisions. Voters who were relatively satisfied with how the Trump administration handled the economy and the pandemic, for example, used retrospective judgment to bolster their support for his reelection, while voters who expressed concern about the pandemic used prospective judgment to bolster their support for Joe Biden.

The candidates' personal attributes and characteristics also affect voters' decisions. In general, voters prefer candidates who are closer to them on characteristics

retrospective judgment
A voter's evaluation of a candidate based on past performance on a particular issue.

prospective judgment
A voter's evaluation of a candidate based on what he or she pledges to do about an issue if elected.

The gender gap is one of the most powerful and consistent patterns in American elections. In 2020, the year women celebrated the centennial of the Nineteenth Amendment guaranteeing their right to vote, many had expected—and some polls suggested—a dramatic repudiation of Donald Trump with a widened gender gap. While Joe Biden held an advantage in support among women overall, Trump held a modest advantage among White women. The gender gap was also not as wide as expected, in part because Biden received more support from male voters, although Kamala Harris reinforced Biden's appeal with Black and suburban women, and those who wished to see themselves reflected in the country's leadership.

Julia Hansen/Alamy Stock Photo

such as race, ethnicity, religion, gender, and social background. Research has commonly found that voters employ gender- or race-based trait stereotypes when evaluating female and minority candidates and a persistent racial bias against minority candidates of almost all racial and political stripes. Despite a purported willingness to support minority candidates, Whites are not voting for their minority candidates at the same rate as their White counterparts.[55]

The candidates' personality and leadership traits also matter, though not as much in an era of partisan polarization. In one Gallup study, the leadership strengths most highly correlated with likely voters were ability to inspire, care for individuals, vision, and courage.

POLITICAL REFORM AND REALITIES: MENDING THE ELECTORAL PROCESS

12.5 Evaluate concerns with the electoral process and proposed reforms to address them.

Political observers and the public alike have expressed numerous concerns with the electoral process—from the excessive length of campaigns, to the growing costs and ways in which campaigns are financed, to the almost irrational methods we employ to choose presidential nominees and the archaic way in which the Electoral College functions. Inspiring individuals to turn out to vote in this winner-take-all electoral system is particularly challenging. The following sections discuss the concerns with, and potential reforms to, the electoral process.

Front-loading

One of the concerns with the way in which we nominate presidential candidates is the incoherent organization of primaries and caucuses that requires candidates to make mad-dash attempts to move around the country. The system leaves little time between primaries for midcourse corrections in the selection of nominees. The nominations process has been altered even more in recent times by **front-loading**, the tendency of states to choose an early date on the nomination calendar (see Figure 12.6). This trend is hardly surprising, given the added press emphasis on the first contests and the voters' desire to cast their ballots before the competition is decided. Front-loading

front-loading

The tendency of states to choose an early date on the nomination calendar.

FIGURE 12.6   WHEN DO STATES CHOOSE THEIR NOMINEE FOR PRESIDENT?

These maps show when Republican Party caucuses and primary elections were held in 1976 and 2020. The trend toward front-loading is evident. In 2020, for example, most states held their primaries and caucuses in March; in comparison, in 1976, most states held their nominating contests in May. In 2020, sixteen states moved their primaries to later dates because of the coronavirus pandemic.

SOURCE: Joshua T. Putnam, frontloading.blogspot.com.

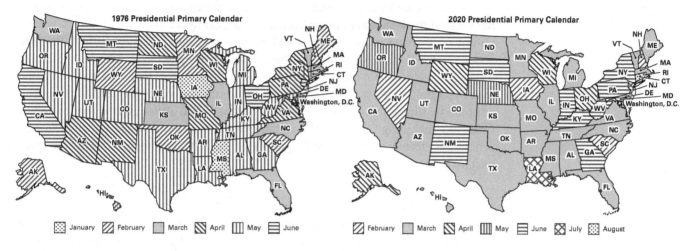

has contributed to the elongation of the presidential campaign, and a front-loaded schedule generally benefits the front-runner, since opponents have little time to turn the contest around once they fall behind. Furthermore, although online fund-raising has emerged as a means to soften the advantage of a large campaign fund going into a primary battle, front-loading advantages the candidate who wins the "invisible primary," that is, the one who can raise the bulk of the money (as well as also garner party endorsements and respect from various gatekeepers) *before* the nomination season begins, though this was not the case for Republicans in 2016. Once primaries and caucuses begin, fewer opportunities are available to raise money to finance campaign efforts simultaneously in many states.

Electoral College

While there hasn't been an Electoral College crisis since 1888, following the 2016 presidential election, many political observers suggested that the system of electing a president be reformed. Similarly, throughout the 2000 presidential campaign, many analysts foresaw that the election would likely be the closest since the 1960 race between John F. Kennedy and Richard M. Nixon. The election was so close that George W. Bush, who lost the popular vote, was not officially declared the Electoral College winner for more than five weeks after Election Day following the Supreme Court's controversial decision in *Bush* v. *Gore* (2000) that stopped a recount of votes cast in Florida.

Some observers have suggested using a national popular vote to choose the president. While this is the most democratic reform, it is least likely to be enacted, given that the Constitution would have to be amended to abolish the Electoral College. It is unlikely that the Senate, which serves as the bastion of equal representation for all states, regardless of population, would ever pass such an amendment. Another proposed reform is known as the congressional district plan. This plan would retain the Electoral College but give each candidate one electoral vote for each congressional district that he or she wins in a state, and the winner of the overall popular vote in each state would receive two bonus votes (one for each senator) for that state. Maine and Nebraska currently use the congressional district plan.

Although this reform could be adopted without a constitutional amendment, under the congressional district plan, the winner of the popular vote might still lose the presidency. In addition, this reform might further politicize the congressional redistricting process, as parties would seek to maximize the number of safe electoral districts for their presidential nominee while minimizing the number of competitive districts. Finally, although candidates might not ignore entire states, they would quickly learn to focus their campaigning on competitive districts while ignoring secure districts, thereby eliminating some of the democratizing effects of such a reform.

To circumvent the Electoral College, some states and the District of Columbia have joined the National Popular Vote Interstate Compact to award all their electoral votes to whichever presidential candidate wins the overall popular vote in the fifty states and the District of Columbia. The compact is designed to ensure that the candidate who receives the most votes nationwide is elected president, and it would come into effect only when it would guarantee that outcome. As of July 2020, it has been adopted by fifteen states and the District of Columbia, although it is suspended in Colorado. Including Colorado, these states have 196 electoral votes, which is 36 percent of the Electoral College and 73 percent of the 270 votes needed to give the compact legal force.

Improving Voter Access and Participation

Inspiring citizens to turn out is particularly important because of the winner-take-all electoral system, yet voter turnout is quite low in the United States. Nonparticipation may be rooted in something as complicated as an individual's political philosophy or something as simple as the weather—voter turnout tends to be lower on rainy Election Days. Some voters are alienated, and others are just plain apathetic, possibly because of satisfaction with the status quo, or noncompetitive elections. Furthermore, many citizens may be turned off by the quality of campaigns in a time when petty issues and personal mudslinging are more prevalent than ever.

Reformers have proposed many ideas to increase voter turnout in the United States. Always on the list is raising the political awareness of young people, a reform that inevitably must involve our nation's schools. The rise in formal education levels among Americans has had a significant effect on voter turnout.[56] No less important, and perhaps simpler to achieve, are institutional reforms such as making Election Day a national holiday, easing constraints on voter registration, allowing vote-by-mail and online voting, modernizing the ballot, and strengthening political parties.

REGISTRATION A major reason for lack of participation in the United States remains the relatively low percentage of the adult population that is registered to vote. Requiring citizens to take the initiative to register is an American invention; nearly every other democratic country places the burden of registration on the government rather than on the individual. Thus, the cost (in terms of time and effort) of registering to vote is higher in the United States than in other industrialized democracies.

Registration laws vary by state, but in most states, people must register prior to Election Day. Forty states plus the District of Columbia now allow voters to register online. Although some critics have expressed concerns about the security of this process, it has proved an effective way to increase registration. In Arizona, the first state to implement the online option in 2003, voter registration increased by almost 10 percent as a result of the law.[57] Another way to increase registration would be to allow voters to register on the same day as the election. Among the twenty-one states that permit Election Day registration, turnout is generally higher.[58] Better yet, all U.S. citizens could be registered automatically at the age of eighteen. Critics, however, argue that such automatic registration could breed even greater voter apathy and complacency.

VOTING Stringent ballot access laws are another factor affecting voter turnout in the United States. Voters in thirty-five states, for example, must provide some form of identification to cast a ballot (see Table 12.4). In six of these states, that identification must include a photo. Though supporters charge that voter identification laws are simply intended to prevent voter fraud, opponents argue that this legislation may disproportionately limit

TABLE 12.4   HOW DO STATES REGULATE VOTER ELIGIBILITY?

Restrict felons' ability to vote after completion of their sentence; require action to restore rights	11 states
Allow incarcerated felons to vote from prison	2 states
Require all voters to show some form of identification to vote	35 states
Strict requirement that all voters show photo identification to vote	6 states
Require no voter registration	North Dakota
Allow same-day registration	21 states and DC
Require voters to register to vote at least 28 days prior to an election	15 states and DC
Allow no-excuse absentee balloting	44 states and DC
Allow early voting	40 states and DC
Can vote by mail and automatically send ballot	WA, OR, CO, CA, NV, UT, VT, NJ, DC

SOURCE: Pew Center on the States, www.pewcenteronthestates.org; National Council on State Legislatures, www.ncsl.org; and CIRCLE, www.civicyouth.org.

the ballot access of a number of groups, including women, racial and ethnic minorities, poor people, elderly people, and people with disabilities.[59] As a result of concerns about their constitutionality, courts continue to review these laws in many states.

Citizens who plan to be out of state on Election Day or who are physically unable to go to the polls may also face challenges in casting an absentee ballot. Many states, for instance, require citizens to apply in person for absentee ballots, a burdensome requirement given that a person's inability to be present in his or her home state is often the reason for absentee balloting in the first place. Recent literature in political science links liberalized absentee voting rules and higher turnout.[60]

With public health and safety at the forefront of concerns in 2020, over 190 million Americans who were eligible to vote lived in states where they could cast a ballot by mail. Five states, including California and Colorado, for the first time sent mail-in ballots to all eligible voters, eleven states sent mail-in ballot applications to all eligible voters, and twelve states expanded eligibility for mail-in voting. Thirty-four states and the District of Columbia already allowed anyone to vote absentee. As a result, 101,453,111 Americans voted early, including more than 65 million who voted by mail—higher than the number of people who voted in person on Election Day. But many of these places made the process easier. With concerns about precinct closures and public health and safety during the COVID-19 pandemic, more than a dozen professional sports teams allowed their arenas to be voting centers during the 2020 elections to accommodate physical distancing measures.

There are a number of institutional ways by which the barriers to voting might be reduced. Some reformers have proposed that Election Day should be a national holiday to eliminate the busy workday as an obstacle to voting. Early voting is another attempt to make voting more convenient for citizens who may have other commitments on Election Day. Forty states (largely in the West, Midwest, and South) and the District of Columbia currently allow voters to engage in the practice, and several additional states allow voters with a valid excuse to cast a ballot early. Early voting allows citizens to cast their ballot up to a month before the election—the time frame varies by state—either by mail or at a designated polling location. Many citizens have found early voting to be a preferable way to cast their ballot. During the 2020 election, approximately 64 percent of all voters took advantage of early voting, equivalent to more than twice the early vote in 2016.

Critics of early voting, however, charge that the method decreases the importance of the campaign. They also fear that voters who cast early ballots may not be fully informed or later come to regret their choices. It is possible, for example, that a voter could change his or her mind after hearing new information about candidates just prior to Election Day, or that a voter could cast a ballot for a candidate who subsequently withdraws from the race.

Reformers have also proposed several ways that citizens could vote from their own homes. For example, citizens of Colorado, Oregon, Washington, and California vote almost entirely by mail-in ballots. These systems have been credited with increasing voter turnout rates in those states. Opponents to vote-by-mail express concerns about social pressure, decreased ballot security, and increased potential for fraud with mail-in elections. Another problem is that it may delay election results as the Board of Elections waits to receive all ballots.

Although the right to vote is a fundamental right, it is not absolute. States regulate the right to vote and establish criteria that voters must meet before they can participate in elections. Such criteria include residence, age, citizenship, and nonfelon status. They also may be able to establish other participation criteria.

Internet voting may be a more instantaneous way to tally votes. Some states, including Arizona and Michigan, have already experimented with using this method to cast ballots in primary elections. In addition, military members and their families from thirty-two states and Washington, D.C., used Internet voting to cast absentee ballots in the 2016 elections.[61] However, online voting is not yet secure, especially given Russian interference in U.S. elections and the highly decentralized nature of the American election infrastructure, according to researchers at MIT and Stanford. Furthermore, many voters are wary of the security of this method and worry about online hackers and an inability to prevent voter fraud. Other observers fear that an all-online system could unintentionally disenfranchise poor voters, who may be less likely to have access to an Internet connection.

Help America Vote Act (HAVA)
A federal law passed in 2002 that addresses issues of voting systems and voter access that were identified following the 2000 election. It established minimum election administration standards for states and units of local government with responsibility for the administration of federal elections and for other purposes related to the Act.

As a result of the **Help America Vote Act (HAVA)**, which the federal government enacted in the wake of the 2000 election when the outcome of the presidential election in Florida, and by extension the nation, hinged on "hanging chads," states and localities have made significant upgrades to the types of ballots they use. Traditional, hand-counted, paper ballots are now used in fewer than 10 percent of jurisdictions. Sixty-five percent of registered voters live in jurisdictions that use hand-marked paper ballots for most voters that create a tangible, tamper-evident, and auditable record of voter selections. In addition, 20.5 percent of registered voters live in jurisdictions that use ballot-marking devices for all voters, which allows for the electronic presentation of a ballot, electronic selection of valid contest options, and the production of a human-readable paper ballot, but does not make any other lasting record of the voter's selections. The remaining 13.5 percent of registered voters live in jurisdictions using Direct Recording Electronic (DRE) systems for all voters (see Table 12.5). A DRE is a vote-capture device that allows for the electronic presentation of a ballot, electronic selection of valid contest options, and the electronic storage of voter selections as individual records. Some DREs can be equipped with voter-verified paper audit trail (VVPAT) printers that allow the voter to confirm their selections on an independent paper record before recording their votes into computer memory. This paper record is preserved and, depending on state election codes, counted in the event of a

TABLE 12.5   WHAT BALLOTS DO STATES USE?

States that require paper ballots	Colorado, Florida, Georgia, Iowa, Michigan, Minnesota, Montana, New Hampshire, New Mexico, Oregon, Rhode Island, South Dakota, Vermont, and Washington
States that require a voter-verifiable paper record for voting machines	Alaska, Arizona, Arkansas, California, Connecticut, District of Columbia, Hawaii, Idaho, Maine, Maryland, Nevada, New Jersey, New York, North Carolina, Ohio, Utah, West Virginia, and Wisconsin
States that require voting machines to have a permanent paper record	Alabama, Illinois, Indiana (voter-verified paper trails will be required by 2029), Kansas, Mississippi, and Pennsylvania
States that do not have a statutory requirement for voting machines to have a paper trail	• Nine states (Delaware, Massachusetts, Missouri, Nebraska, North Dakota, Oklahoma, South Carolina, Virginia, and Wyoming) use paper ballots or machines with a paper trail statewide, even though there is no statutory requirement. • Three states (Kentucky, Tennessee, and Texas) have some jurisdictions with a paper trail and others without.

SOURCE: National Conference of State Legislatures, https://www.ncsl.org/research/elections-and-campaigns/voting-system-paper-trail-requirements.aspx; and Verified Voting, https://verifiedvoting.org/verifier/#mode/navigate/map/ppEquip/mapType/normal/year/2020.

post-election audit or recount. States have also experimented with other new technologies for casting ballots. In Oregon, for example, residents with disabilities were able to vote with iPads; several other states are exploring expanded use of this technology.[62]

Supporters of electronic voting believe that training poll workers, administrators, and voters on how to effectively use the new equipment is vital. Critics maintain that lack of a paper trail leaves electronic machines vulnerable to fraud and worry that the machines could crash during an election. Still other critics cite the expense of the machines. All, however, agree that updating election equipment and ensuring fair elections across the country should be a legislative priority.

Reformers have also suggested ranked-choice voting (RCV), which allows voters to rank candidates in order of preference and then uses those rankings to elect candidates who best represent their constituents.[63] Coined by Fair Vote, the term *ranked-choice voting* has come to also encompass instant-runoff voting, preferential voting, and alternative voting. RCV differs from the traditional method of selecting only one of the available choices (generally a plurality vote decides the winner) and guarantees that the victor is truly representative of the majority of the voters. Proponents argue that RCV discourages negative/toxic campaigning by creating an incentive to acquire second-ranked votes from an opponent's supporters. It also allows people to vote their conscience rather than strategically casting ballots, thereby eliminating the feeling of a "wasted vote" or "lesser of two evils" situation. RCV is currently used or scheduled to be used in twenty-six U.S. states.

STRENGTHEN POLITICAL PARTIES   Political parties today are not as effective as they once were in mobilizing voters, ensuring they are registered, and getting them to the polls. The parties at one time were grassroots organizations that forged strong party–group links with their supporters. Today, candidate- and issue-centered campaigns and the growth of expansive party bureaucracies have resulted in more nationalized and distant parties with which fewer people identify very strongly. While efforts have been made in recent elections to bolster the influence of parties—in particular, through sophisticated get-out-the-vote efforts—the parties' modern grassroots activities still pale in comparison to their earlier efforts.

Reformers have long argued that strengthening political parties would increase voter turnout, because parties have historically been the most successful at mobilizing citizens to vote in the United States. During the late 1800s and early 1900s, the country's "Golden Age" of powerful political parties, one of their primary activities was getting out the vote on Election Day. Even today, the parties' Election Day get-out-the-vote drives increase voter turnout by several million people in national contests. The challenge is how to go about enacting reforms that strengthen parties. One way would be to allow political parties to raise and spend greater sums of money during the campaign process. Such a reform, however, raises ethical questions about the role and influence of money in politics. Another potential change would be to enact broader systemic reforms that allow for a multiparty system and facilitate greater party competition. But the current two-party system makes such reforms very difficult to pass into law.

Ultimately, the solution to ensuring greater voter turnout may lie in encouraging the parties to enhance their get-out-the-vote efforts beyond their existing partisan bases. Additional voter education programs, too, may show voters what is at stake in elections and thereby inspire higher turnout in future elections.

CONCLUSION AND REVIEW

What Are the Roots of American Elections?

12.1 Compare and contrast presidential and congressional elections, and explain the incumbency advantage.

Elections in the United States are of four major types: primary elections, general elections, initiatives and referenda, and recall elections. The parties select presidential candidates through either primary elections or caucuses, with the primary process culminating in each party's national convention, after which the general election campaign begins. The American political system uses indirect electoral representation in the form of the Electoral College. In congressional elections, incumbents have a strong advantage over their challengers because of staff support, the visibility they get from being in office, and the "scare-off" effect. Redistricting, scandals, presidential coattails, and midterm elections serve as countervailing forces to the incumbency advantage and are the main sources of turnover in Congress.

How Do Candidates Run for Office and Reach Voters?

12.2 Outline how campaigns are organized, and evaluate methods for reaching voters.

Candidates rely on a campaign manager, professional staff, and political consultants to coordinate the strategy and message of his or her campaign. Volunteer support is also particularly important for mobilizing citizens and getting out the vote. Candidates and campaigns rely on traditional media coverage, news media coverage, and paid campaign advertisements for reaching voters. The national party convention and presidential debates also serve as forums for reaching voters.

How Are Elections Influenced by Campaign Finance and Reform?

12.3 Evaluate the influence of money in elections and the main approaches to campaign finance reform.

Since the 1970s, campaign financing has been governed by the terms of the Federal Election Campaign Act (FECA). This act was amended in 2002 by the Bipartisan Campaign Reform Act (BCRA). BCRA regulates political advertising and funding from a number of sources from which campaigns raise money. In 2010, the Supreme Court, in *Citizens United* v. *FEC*, declared unconstitutional BCRA's ban on electioneering communications made by corporations and unions, opening the way for an increase in the power of interest groups and corporations in campaigns and elections. Sources of campaign funding include political parties, individuals, personal savings, political action committees (PACs), 527 political committees, 501(c) groups, super PACs, and public funds.

What Are the Patterns in Voter Turnout and Choice?

12.4 Analyze the factors that influence voter turnout and voter choice.

A number of factors influence citizens' choices about which candidate to support and whether or not they will turn out on Election Day. Party affiliation, issues, and the candidates' characteristics and traits all influence voter choice. Factors that influence voter turnout include age, education, race and ethnicity, gender, civic engagement, and interest in politics.

Political Reform and Realities: Mending the Electoral Process

12.5 Evaluate concerns with the electoral process and proposed reforms to address them.

Political observers and citizens alike have expressed numerous concerns with the electoral process. The incoherent organization of primaries and caucuses is compounded by front-loading. Furthermore, the archaic way in which the Electoral College functions might be updated by instituting a national popular vote or a congressional district plan. Inspiring voters is also challenging when they face difficulty registering to vote, difficulty voting, and a weakened connection to the political parties. Suggestions for improving voter turnout include making Election Day a holiday, enabling early voting, allowing for mail-in and online voting, making the registration process easier, modernizing the ballot, ranked choice voting, and strengthening political parties. Each of these suggested reforms has both pros and cons.

LEARN THE TERMS

501(c) group
527 political committees
Bipartisan Campaign Reform Act
    (BCRA)
campaign consultant
campaign manager
census
Citizens United v. *FEC*
closed primary
communications director
contrast ad
crossover voting
elector
electorate
Electoral College
Federal Election Campaign Act
    (FECA)

Federal Election Commission (FEC)
finance chair
front-loading
general election
get-out-the-vote (GOTV)
Help America Vote Act (HAVA)
incumbency
independent expenditures
initiative
inoculation ad
mandate
matching funds
McCutcheon v. *FEC*
midterm election
negative ad
open primary
political action committee (PAC)

political activism
political participation
pollster
positive ad
presidential coattails
press secretary
primary election
prospective judgment
public funds
reapportionment
recall
referendum
retrospective judgment
runoff primary
super PAC
turnout
voter canvass

LEARN THE NAMES

Barack Obama
Thomas Jefferson

Bloomberg/Getty Images

WHAT KIND OF MEDIA DOES THE PUBLIC NEED AND SHOULD THEY DEMAND TO ENSURE DEMOCRATIC ACCOUNTABILITY AND SELF-GOVERNANCE?

An unfettered press has been upheld as essential for democratic self-governance, given the media's role in influencing and relaying public opinion, and providing and conveying information on issues of public importance. While digital, social, and online media pose challenges for democratic practices and institutions and for the civic function of the media, they are also transforming the ways communities communicate and share information. Pictured here, Facebook bolsters its efforts to combat election misinformation and the use of its platform to undermine democratic institutions.

CRITICAL THINKING QUESTION: *What role should the media have in the political process?*

THE NEWS MEDIA

LEARNING OBJECTIVES

13.1 Describe the structure and the functions of the media, past and present.

13.2 Assess the influence of the media on American politics.

13.3 Analyze the impact of the media on public opinion and political behavior.

13.4 Summarize the ethical standards and federal regulations that govern the news media.

13.5 Describe the effect of recent trends in the news media on political outcomes.

The American public has a complicated relationship with the news media, often expressing negative views toward and distrust of journalists and news organizations even as those organizations provide vital information on major stories—a contentious election, a global pandemic, or nationwide protests over racial injustice.

As a result of dramatic changes in news media production and consumption over the last decade, many Americans see exaggeration, conspiracy theories, and partisanship, making it difficult to know what is true about many facets of American social, economic, and political life. Today, political news is happening—and being reported—almost instantaneously. No longer do newspaper publishers have to typeset every individual letter, as they did in the earliest days of the republic. No longer do journalists file daily reports to be aired on the nightly news, well after a political event has occurred. Instead, reporters, and any member of the public, can post live Facebook, Twitter, Snapchat, and Instagram updates, complete with photos and video, as events are occurring.

The way citizens consume their news has changed. In addition to using social media, news outlets employ many options for reaching their consumers, including apps, newsletters, podcasts, and aggregation platforms like Apple News or Flipboard. The newspaper, once the lifeblood of American democracy, was supplanted by TV news in the 1960s. Today, TV is still a popular news source for all Americans, but the majority of Americans across generations now combine a mix of sources and technologies to get their news. Social media is an important tool for people from all generations to get news, but it is not the only one, even for younger generations. Furthermore, social media seems to be adding to, rather than replacing, other ways that people get their news.[1] As sources of news have diversified and catered to individual and group preferences, it has become more challenging for individual consumers to evaluate the information broadcast through digital and social media, including distinguishing between credible sources and those propagating misinformation and disinformation.

During the 2020 Elections, the Pew Research Center found that while Americans were getting information about key storylines, their knowledge and opinions about election-related issues—as well as the candidates themselves—differed strikingly based on their party affiliation and news sources. For example, about six in ten (61 percent) of the Republicans whose only major sources of election news (among the eight asked about) are those with right-leaning audiences—talk radio and/or Fox News—said mail-in voter fraud was a major problem. That the primary source of false information was the president of United States also presented major challenges for democracy. Even after the Electoral College met on December 14, 2020, to confirm Joe Biden as the 46th president of the United States, President Donald J. Trump and members of his administration and his campaign continued to spread misinformation about voter fraud and conspiracies of a stolen election.

While some changes in the information ecosystem may result in many positives for American democracy and may serve to engage traditionally underserved populations, they also can have negative consequences. The growth of media sources and platforms that cater to partisan audiences may polarize the segment of the population tuning in, contributing to more extreme attitudes among those most engaged in politics. Furthermore, challenges to traditional revenue models and the COVID-19 global public health pandemic are creating a crisis that has left millions of Americans without a vital source of local news and deprived communities of an institution essential for ensuring accountability, exposing corruption, and encouraging civic engagement. Meanwhile, the growth of choices has allowed broad swaths of the public to avoid political conversations altogether and find something more agreeable, like sports or entertainment. And moving from professional journalists publishing on clear deadlines to a free-for-all world of nearly constant updates may weaken the media's traditional watchdog role and adherence to journalistic standards.

. . .

The Framers agreed that a free press was necessary to monitor government and ensure the continuation of a democratic society, a tenet they codified in the First Amendment to the Constitution. Throughout history, the press has fulfilled this watchdog role, acting as an intermediary between citizens and their government. The news media inform the public, giving citizens the information they need to choose their leaders and influence the direction of public policy. As this chapter will discuss, the way the media interact with and report on these political leaders can also significantly influence individuals' views of political issues.

The news media's impact on American politics is so important that it has often been called the "fourth estate," a term harkening back to the British Parliament and implying an integral role for the press in government. This so-called fourth estate comprises a variety of entities, from traditional local news outlets to media corporations, to digital-native news outlets (like BuzzFeed and Breitbart), social media, and average citizens. It is evident in all facets of American life, from morning newspapers to nightly comedy news shows to tweets, Snapchats, and Facebook posts.

Though media forms have changed significantly since our nation's founding, the potential for media's informational and watchdog roles remain. This chapter traces the development of media in the United States, explores recent developments affecting the media, and considers how these changes influence politics and government.

WHAT ARE THE ROOTS OF THE NEWS MEDIA IN THE UNITED STATES?

13.1 Describe the structure and the functions of the media, past and present.

The **mass media**—the entire array of organizations through which information is collected and disseminated to the general public—have become a colossal enterprise in the United States. The mass media include print sources, movies, TV, radio, and **digital-native** news outlets. Collectively, the mass media use broadcast, cable, satellite, newsletters, podcasts, aggregation platforms, and other technologies to distribute information that reaches every corner of the United States and the world. A powerful tool for both entertaining and educating the public, they reflect American society but are also the primary lens through which citizens view American culture and politics. The **news media**, one component of the larger mass media, provide new information about subjects of public interest and play a vital role in the political process.[2] Although often referred to as a large, impersonal whole, the media are made up of diverse personalities and institutions, and they form a spectrum of opinion. Through the various outlets composing the news media—from so-called "legacy" news organizations (those that originated in print or broadcast) to digital-native news outlets to social media sites—journalists inform the public, influence public opinion, and affect the direction of public policy in our democratic society.

Throughout American history, technological advances have had a major impact on the way in which Americans receive their news. High-speed presses and more cheaply produced paper made mass-circulation daily newspapers possible. The telegraph and then the telephone enabled easier and much faster newsgathering. When radio became widely available in the 1920s, millions of Americans could hear national politicians instead of merely reading about them. With TV—first introduced in the late 1940s, and nearly a universal fixture in U.S. homes by the early 1960s—citizens could see and hear political candidates and presidents. Now, with the rise of the Internet and mobile digital platforms, access to information has once again changed form. Never before has information been more widely available, and never have the lines between news producer and consumer been less clear.

mass media

The entire array of organizations through which information is collected and disseminated to the general public.

digital-native

News publishers originally founded on the Web.

news media

Media providing the public with new information about subjects of public interest.

Print Media

The first example of news media in America took the form of newspapers, which were published in the colonies as early as 1690. The number of newspapers grew throughout the 1700s, as colonists began to realize the value of a press free from government oversight and censorship. The battle between Federalists and Anti-Federalists over ratification of the Constitution played out in various partisan newspapers in the late eighteenth century. Thus, it came as no surprise that one of the Anti-Federalists' demands was a constitutional amendment guaranteeing freedom of the press.

The partisan press eventually gave way to the penny press. In 1833, Benjamin Day founded the *New York Sun*, which cost a penny at the newsstand. Beyond its low price, the *Sun* sought to expand its audience by freeing itself from the grip of a single political party. Inexpensive and politically independent, the *Sun* was the forerunner of modern newspapers; it relied on mass circulation and commercial advertising to produce profit. By 1861, the penny press had so supplanted partisan papers that President Abraham Lincoln announced his administration would have no favored or sponsored newspaper.

Although the print media were becoming less partisan, they were not necessarily gaining in respectability. Mass-circulation dailies sought wide readership, attracting customers with the sensational and the scandalous. The sordid side of politics became the entertainment of the times. One of the best-known examples occurred in the presidential campaign of 1884, when the *Buffalo Evening Telegraph* headlined "A Terrible Tale" about Grover Cleveland, the Democratic nominee.[3] The story alleged that Cleveland, an unmarried man, had fathered a child in 1871, while sheriff of Buffalo, New York. Even though paternity was indeterminate because the child's mother had been seeing other men, Cleveland willingly accepted responsibility, since all the other men were married, and he dutifully paid child support for years. The strict Victorian moral code that dominated American values at the time made the story even more shocking than it would be today. Fortunately for Cleveland, another newspaper, the *Democratic Sentinel*, broke a story that helped offset this scandal: the first child of Republican presidential nominee James G. Blaine and his wife had been born just three months after their wedding.

Throughout the nineteenth century, payoffs to the press were common. Andrew Jackson, for instance, gave one in ten of his early appointments to loyal reporters.[4] During the 1872 presidential campaign, the Republicans slipped cash to about 300 newsmen.[5] Wealthy industrialists also sometimes purchased investigative cease-fires for tens of thousands of dollars.

UNCLE SAM DETERMINED TO RID THE COUNTRY OF THIS DOUBLE-HEADED MONSTER.

LIBRARY OF CONGRESS

DID THE PRACTICE OF YELLOW JOURNALISM CONTRIBUTE TO THE RISE OF OBJECTIVE JOURNALISM?

In the late nineteenth century, with competition for newspaper readership fiercer than ever, certain newspapers begin publishing exaggerated and sensational content to attract readers. In the wake of President McKinley's assassination, the yellow press was accused of inciting anarchy through its reporting. In this 1901 cartoon, Uncle Sam uses his sword, labeled "JUSTICE," to attack the double-headed serpent, labeled "YELLOW JOURNALISM – ANARCHY."

yellow journalism

A form of newspaper publishing, in vogue in the late nineteenth century, that featured pictures, comics, color, and sensationalized news coverage.

muckraking

A form of journalism, in vogue in the early twentieth century, devoted to exposing misconduct by government, business, and individual politicians.

In the late 1800s and early 1900s, prominent publishers such as William Randolph Hearst and Joseph Pulitzer expanded the reach of newspapers in their control by practicing what became pejoratively known as **yellow journalism**, perhaps because both Hearst and Pulitzer published a popular cartoon of the era called "The Yellow Kid." Yellow journalism featured pictures, comics, color, and sensationalized news coverage. These innovations were designed to increase readership and capture a share of the burgeoning immigrant population.

The Progressive movement gave rise to a new type of journalism in the early 1900s. **Muckraking** journalists—so named by President Theodore Roosevelt after a special rake designed to collect manure—devoted themselves to exposing misconduct by government, business, and individual politicians.[6] For Roosevelt, muckraking was a derogatory term used to describe reporters who focused on the carnal underbelly of politics rather than its more lofty pursuits. Nevertheless, much good came from these efforts. Muckrakers stimulated demands for anti-trust regulations—laws that prohibit companies, such as large steel companies, from controlling an entire industry—and exposed deplorable working conditions in factories, as well as outright exploitation of workers by business owners. An unfortunate side effect of this emphasis on crusades and investigations, however, was the frequent publication of gossip and rumor without sufficient proof.

As the news business grew, so did the focus on increasing its profitability. Newspapers became more careful and less adversarial in their reporting, to avoid alienating the advertisers and readers who produced their revenues. Clearer standards were applied in evaluating the behavior of people in power. Journalism also changed during this period as the industry became more professionalized. Reporters learned to adhere to principles of objectivity and balance and to be motivated by a never-ending quest for the "truth."[7]

More recently, faced by an onslaught of competing forms of media, including radio, TV, and digital media, newspapers have struggled to maintain their circulation. According to a Brookings Institution report, there were 1,749 American newspapers in 1945, but only 1,331 by the end of 2014. Over that same period, circulation per capita declined from 35 percent in the mid-1940s to under 15 percent. Though some print dailies have moved to digital–print hybrids or have created digital versions with pay plans to monetize their content, other papers have failed to adapt to the changing news environment. More than 65 million Americans live in counties with only one local newspaper—or none at all. Furthermore, driven primarily by declines in the

HOW DID THE PROGRESSIVE MOVEMENT AFFECT JOURNALISM?

Reform-minded investigative journalists in the Progressive Era devoted themselves to exposing misconduct by governments, businesses, and individual politicians. In a speech in 1906, President Roosevelt called it muckraking journalism, drawing from a character in John Bunyan's 1678 classic, *Pilgrim's Progress*. President Roosevelt tried to steer stories his way by giving journalists, such as Lincoln Steffans, interviews and access to the White House.

WINDN/Associated Press

A NAUSEATING JOB, BUT IT MUST BE DONE

newspaper industry, overall newsroom employment—including employees working full time in the newspaper, broadcasting, and Internet publishing industries—dropped by a quarter between 2008 and 2018.[8]

The full consequences of these changes for citizens' knowledge of politics and public affairs remain to be seen, but preliminary scholarly research of newspaper closures and the declining capacity of newsrooms to investigate stories has revealed falling political participation, increased ideological polarization, and the elimination of a check on government corruption.[9] Without adequate local coverage, people living in a community do not have all the information they need to participate in the political process and hold government and powerful private actors accountable. As Americans have paid less attention to local and community-based information and more attention to national news, studies also show turnout in state and local elections has declined and communities that have lost reporters have seen fewer candidates run for local office.[10] Whatever the full impact, the laws governing political communication in this country will likely need to be revisited.

Radio News

The advent of radio in the early twentieth century was a media revolution and a revelation to the average American, who rarely, if ever, had heard the voice of a president, governor, or senator. The radio became the center of most homes in the evening, when national networks broadcast the news as well as entertainment shows. Calvin Coolidge was the first president to speak on radio on a regular basis, but President Franklin D. Roosevelt made the radio broadcast a must-listen by presenting "fireside chats" to promote his New Deal.

News radio, which had begun to take a back seat to TV by the mid-1950s, regained popularity with the advent of AM talk radio in the mid-1980s. Controversial radio host Rush Limbaugh began the trend with his unabashedly conservative views, opening the door for other conservative commentators such as Laura Ingraham, Sean Hannity, and Glenn Beck. Studies show that these conservative radio hosts resurrected the radio as a news medium by giving a strong ideological bent to the information they broadcast. However, most truly liberal political talk radio has struggled. Many liberals turn to National Public Radio (NPR), which receives government funding as well as private donations, and does not air solely political content. It also covers a variety of cultural and socially important issues. Studies of the overall political coverage of NPR, moreover, have failed to find any overt liberal bias.[11]

Radio reaches hundreds of million listeners each week, with all Americans spending nearly 15 billion hours listening to radio each month. Local radio is a vital resource especially to rural communities, home to one-fifth of the U.S. population, providing them with entertainment and important news and emergency information they rely on each day. Religious broadcast station owners are a growing presence among broadcasters, with thirty-four owners operating 119 full-power broadcast television stations across the U.S. in small markets that include rural areas.

TV News

TV was first demonstrated in the United States at the 1939 World's Fair in New York, but it did not take off as a news source until after World War II. While most homes had TVs by the early 1960s, it took several years more for TV to replace print and radio as the nation's chief news provider. In 1963, most networks provided just fifteen minutes of news per day; only two major networks devoted thirty minutes to news coverage. During this period, a substantial majority of Americans still received most of their news from newspapers. Today, while most Americans get their news from many sources, television is the most common, and it even experienced a surge in viewership as a result of the COVID-19 pandemic.[12]

Television provides a platform for a range of news outlets, including commercial broadcast network news and cable news. The commercial broadcast networks—ABC, CBS, and NBC—have maintained stable audiences over the last decade, with a viewership of over 23 million for evening news. As the nation adjusted to increasing restrictions intended to slow the spread of the coronavirus, Sunday morning political talk shows saw surges in viewership in 2020. The three networks' online presences remain among the top domestic news destinations.[13] Among cable news outlets that provide twenty-four-hour news channels, Fox News is the most prominent, drawing an average of 2.4 million viewers during evening primetime and 1.5 million viewers during the day in 2017 (its best year on record), followed by MSNBC with 1.6 million primetime viewers, which outpaced CNN with just over 1 million viewers.[14] There are some demographic differences that stand out among respondents to surveys about political news sources. For example, women are much more likely than men to favor network TV, and while those who name Fox News as their main news source are predominantly White, nearly half of those who rely on CNN identify as some other race or ethnicity.

Cable and satellite providers also give consumers access to a less glitzy and more unfiltered source of news. For example, C-SPAN is a basic cable channel that offers gavel-to-gavel coverage of congressional proceedings, as well as major political events when Congress is not in session. It also produces some of its own programming, such as *Washington Journal*, which invites scholars and journalists to speak about topics pertaining to their areas of expertise. Because the content of C-SPAN can be erudite, technical, and sometimes downright tedious (such as the fixed camera shot of the Senate during a roll-call vote), audiences tend to be very small, but they are loyal and give C-SPAN its place as a truly content-driven news source (see Figure 13.1).

FIGURE 13.1   WHERE DO AMERICANS GET THEIR POLITICAL NEWS?

Fox News and CNN are named by the largest segments of U.S. adults as their main political news source—16 percent and 12 percent, respectively. Six other news outlets—NPR, NBC News, ABC News, MSNBC, CBS News, and the *New York Times*—are named by at least 2 percent of adults. The sources named by the remaining 51 percent of U.S. adults result in a long tail of more than fifty other individual brands. In general, Americans tend to seek information that reinforces their politics. For instance, Fox News's conservative approach attracts more Republicans, while Democrats are more likely to get their news from the *New York Times* and National Public Radio.

SOURCE: Data from the Pew Research Center.

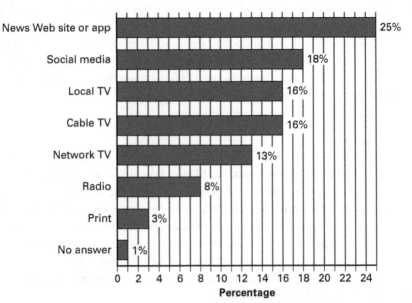

Digital Media

Digital media, including news outlets born on the Web, podcasts, social networking sites, and blogs, are transforming the relationship between the media and the public, even challenging our perceptions of what is defined as "news media" (See Figure 13.2). They remove many of the traditional filters, such as editors and journalistic standards, which previously were a source of credibility to professional news outlets. Moreover, digital media has reduced the cost to consumers for information and made information more widely accessible than before, especially with consumers embracing on-demand formats.

The rise of digital media has challenged the revenue models for the news industry. With digital platforms embracing a subscription model, half (50 percent) in the United States now come across one or more barriers each week when trying to read online news. But despite the efforts of the news industry, only about 16 percent of Americans say they pay for any online news—whether by subscription, membership, or donation.

As a result, journalists are expected to do more with less. Whereas in the past, journalists were responsible solely for gathering information, typing out a story, and submitting it to section editors, today most are expected to write a story for the physical newspaper, post the story online, blog about the story, post about it on various social network platforms, and—in the case of TV news—some must even record a segment on their story to be aired. Digital media has also enabled individuals to become directly involved in creating and interpreting the news, and in organizing around shared political beliefs.

Trends in digital media have brought into question the sustainability of quality journalism. Toxic hyperpartisanship and political polarization (discussed in Chapter 11) have encouraged the growth of partisan agendas in digital media outlets. Clickbait and other forms of misinformation also contribute to undermining trust in news media, posing challenges for news organizations about how to deliver balanced and fair reporting in the digital age.

SOCIAL MEDIA Social media sites are fundamentally changing both the media and politics. A majority of U.S. adults—62 percent—get news on social media, and 18 percent do so often, according to the Pew Research Center. One in five Americans tend to say they rely primarily on social media for news. Compared to other news consumers, those who rely primarily on social media are less likely to closely follow major news stories; tend to be less knowledgeable about major news; are less likely to get the facts right about COVID-19, elections, and politics; and are more likely to see unproven claims.[15]

FIGURE 13.2 WHERE DO AMERICANS GET THEIR NEWS IN THE DIGITAL ERA?

Americans get their news from a range of sources and platforms. Many news providers also produce content on a range of platforms. This table shows consumption patterns.

	7%	6%	5%	4%	3%	2%	1%	0%
Platforms								
TV	78	8	6	2	2	1	2	*
Radio	41	6	25	5	7	10	5	2
Print publications	61	11	5	3	6	4	6	3
Digital Platforms								
News websites or apps	62	7	11	6	5	3	2	3
Social Media	65	6	14	3	5	*	1	5
Internet Search	52	5	13	8	10	6	3	2

NOTE: Among U.S. adults who get news **often** from each source, % who have done so _____ days per week.
SOURCE: Data from the Pew Research Center, www.journalism.org/2020/12/08/news-consumption-detailed-tables/.

Although not their primary purpose, social media sites, such as Facebook, Reddit, YouTube, and Twitter, serve as a resource for hearing political news, obtaining information, and finding others who share the same political views. Politicians and candidates also use these sites to reach citizens and engage them in the political process, for example, by conducting town hall forums or responding to questions from citizens. Political leaders also use social media sites to broadcast live events, to organize supporters, to raise money, and to attack their opponents. As Americans have increasingly relied on technology companies for both communication and social connection, there is also heightened concern about how such companies censor information. According to a Pew Research Center survey, majorities of both major parties believe censorship is likely occurring, but this belief is especially common—and growing—among Republicans.[16] Furthermore, even before the 2020 election concluded, many social media users in the United States reported being "exhausted" by how much political content they see on social media platforms. In addition, seven in ten users say it's "stressful" to talk politics on social media with people they disagree with.[17]

Twitter plays a prominent role in how politicians, media outlets, and advocacy organizations promote their agendas and engage with political issues. Local and national leaders, and their digital media staff working on their behalf, use Twitter to make announcements, send messages, and respond to breaking political events so their words can be spread even more widely than they would be from a videotaped news conference or written statement. Politicians are also using Twitter to reach out to supporters and to raise money for political campaigns. Average citizens, too, have used Twitter to spread political news. Users have tweeted from political rallies, offered commentary on presidential debates and the president's State of the Union Address, and used hashtags to mark political issues such as health care during the pandemic, jobs, and the economy as trending topics.

As CNN political reporter Peter Hamby commented, Twitter has replaced the campaign bus as the place where political reporters swap information and where media narratives develop.[18] The proportion of journalists on Twitter is roughly three times that of Internet-using adults.[19] Meanwhile, politicians can interact directly with citizens, without using reporters and editors as intermediaries. Though this may seem more democratic, critics worry that a growing reliance on social networking sites will weaken the media's role as a filter, educator, and watchdog. They also express increasing concerns that politicians may not engage in deliberative democracy, but may instead make policy decisions designed to placate the mobs of citizens that James Madison and the Framers feared would trouble their republican form of government. One commentator, for example, asked whether there would have even been a Constitution if the Framers had tweeted the proceedings of the famously secret Philadelphia Convention.[20]

PODCASTS The growth of the use of smartphones, better content, and increased distribution have increased the popularity of podcasts, especially for those under 35. More than one-third of Americans report consuming a podcast about news, politics, or international news in the last month, according to a Reuters International report. News outlets such as the *Washington Post*, the *Economist*, and the *Financial Times* are among dozens of publishers that have launched daily podcasts following the success of "The Daily" from the *New York Times*, which has around 5 million daily listeners. Users say that ease of use, the ability to listen while doing something else, more authentic voices, and the control and choice make podcasts appealing.

BLOGS Blogs provide an editorial and news outlet for individuals. They also provide an opportunity for news organizations to offer original analysis and updates on emerging news stories. The ESPN-owned blog "FiveThirtyEight," the *New York Times* blog "The Upshot," and the *Washington Post* blog "The Monkey Cage" all focus on politics and government. Though blogs often offer more commentary than traditional news sources, they are also important informational tools, linking people with common ideological or issue-specific interests. Most political blogs, for example, are targeted to a sophisticated political elite that is already interested in and knowledgeable about public affairs.

While blogs and their user-generated content seem to offer people a more democratic means of engaging in public discussion, concern is growing that the blogosphere has become dominated by a small elite. Although more than 173 million blogs can be found on the Web, only a very small number of sites have a sizeable audience and thus attract most of the advertising dollars available.[21] Moreover, most of the best-known political bloggers are graduates of the nation's top colleges, and many have postgraduate degrees. And the linking practices common on many blogs and Web sites mean that content produced by the top political bloggers often rises to the top, homogenizing the message received by political sophisticates and policy makers.[22]

HOW DO THE NEWS MEDIA COVER POLITICS?

13.2 Assess the influence of the media on American politics.

The news media focus an extraordinary amount of attention on politicians and the day-to-day operations of government. With more than 3,600 members, the Radio and Television Correspondents Association, the major organization of reporters covering Congress, in theory outnumber members of Congress nearly six to one.[23] The media have a visible presence at the White House as well; these reporters come from traditional and online media outlets and hail from across the country and, increasingly, around the world. Consequently, the media report, then intensively scrutinize and interpret, a politician's every public utterance.

How the Press and Public Figures Interact

Communication between elected officials or public figures and the media takes a number of different forms. A **press release**, also called a news release, is a written document offering an official comment or position on an issue or news event; it is usually faxed, e-mailed, or handed directly to reporters. A **press briefing** is a relatively restricted live engagement with the press, with the range of questions limited to one or two specific topics. In a press briefing, a press secretary or aide represents the elected official or public figure, who does not appear in person. In a full-blown **press conference**, an elected official appears in person to talk with the press at great length about an unrestricted range of topics. Press conferences provide a field on which reporters struggle to obtain the answers they need and public figures attempt to retain control of their message and spin the news and issues in ways favorable to them. Recent presidents have also pursued a strategy of giving exclusive access to news outlets deemed sympathetic to the president's message on a particular topic, in a dramatic setting that showcases and reinforces that message.

Another way officials and public figures interact with the media is by leaking news. News leaks, also called "unauthorized disclosures," early in the administration of Donald J. Trump forced the resignation of Michael T. Flynn as national security adviser. Although **news leaks**, or the intentional disclosure of confidential information often made by an anonymous source whose goal is to make the information public, have been salient in conflicts between President Trump and the media, they have long been an important source of information for journalists, with thousands of leaks from whistleblowers and government officials each year. Proponents argue that they are an

press conference
An unrestricted session between an elected official and the press.

press briefing
A relatively restricted session between a press secretary or aide and the press.

press release
A document offering an official comment or position.

news leaks
The intentional disclosure of confidential information often made by an anonymous source whose goal is to make the information public.

WHAT IS THE PRESIDENT'S RELATIONSHIP WITH THE NEWS MEDIA?

President Joe Biden stated that he intends to restore credibility to government and to the White House briefing room. Announcing the historic appointment of his communications team comprised of four highly qualified women, President Biden's advisers said the team will endeavor for a return to pre-Trump "normalcy" and transparency.

important source of information for public debate and democratic self-government, though it is not uncommon for leakers to have personal motives. Leaks often come from low- or mid-level employees or contractors who are typically dissatisfied with the current state of affairs, but they can also come from people in the highest ranks of government. While leaking government secrets is generally not illegal, unauthorized disclosures related to national security can be prosecuted under the Espionage Act of 1917. Usually, it is the leakers who are prosecuted and not the journalists who publish the information.

Starting with the George W. Bush administration and intensifying with the Barack Obama administration, leak-related prosecutions have become more common, largely because digital footprints can now help identify leakers. President Obama presided over roughly ten leak-related cases—more than all previous presidents combined.

Politicians and media interact in a variety of other ways as well. Politicians hire campaign consultants who use focus groups and polling in an attempt to gauge how to present the candidate to the media and to the public. In addition, politicians can attempt to bypass the national news media through social media, paid advertising, and appearances on talk shows and local news programs. Politicians also use the media to attempt to retain a high level of name recognition and to build support for their ideological and policy ideas.

Covering the Presidency

The three branches of the U.S. government—the executive, the legislative, and the judicial—are roughly equal in power and authority. But in the world of media coverage, the president stands first among equals. The White House beat is one of the most prestigious posts a political reporter can hold. The careers of many of the most famous network news journalists, including CBS's John Dickerson, were launched by covering the presidency.

The attention of the press to the White House enables a president to appear even on very short notice and to televise live, interrupting regular programming. Previously, the White House's press briefing room was a familiar sight on the evening news, not just because presidents used it fairly often but also because the presidential press secretary had almost daily question-and-answer sessions there. According to reporters who cover the White House, there have been far fewer press briefings under the Trump administration and they have been shorter in duration than under previous administrations.

The post of press secretary to the president has existed only since Herbert Hoover's administration (1929–1933). The power of this position, however, has grown tremendously over time. Presidents increasingly resist facing the media on their own and leave this task to their press secretary. As a result, press secretaries have a difficult job; they must convince the media of the importance of the president's policy decisions as well as defend any actions taken by the executive branch. In many ways, the prestige and power of the presidency depend on the "spin" of the press secretary and his or her ability to win over the media. Thus, many presidents choose close aides with whom they have worked previously and who are familiar with their thinking.

Covering Congress

With 535 voting members representing distinct geographic areas, covering Congress poses a difficult challenge for the media. Most news organizations solve the size and decentralization problems by concentrating coverage on three groups of individuals. First, the leaders of both parties in both chambers receive the lion's share of attention because only they can speak for a majority of their party's members. Usually, the majority and minority leaders in each house and the Speaker of the House are the preferred spokespersons, but the whips also receive a substantial share of airtime and column inches. Second, key committee chairs command center stage when subjects in their domain are newsworthy. Heads of the most prominent committees (such as Appropriations or Judiciary) are guaranteed frequent coverage, but even the chairs and members of minor committees or subcommittees can achieve fame when the time and issue are right. For example, a sensational scandal may lead to congressional committee hearings that receive extensive media coverage. Third, local newspapers and broadcast stations normally devote some resources to covering local senators and representatives, even when these legislators are junior and relatively lacking in influence.

As with coverage of the president, media coverage of Congress is disproportionately negative. A significant segment of media attention given to the House and Senate focuses on conflict among members. Some political scientists believe that such reporting is at least partially responsible for the public's negative perceptions of Congress.[24]

Covering the Supreme Court

Numerous studies question whether citizens are able to learn what they need to know about the Supreme Court and find that lack of knowledge is a product of two related factors: court communication and adequate media coverage. While members of Congress and presidents are often characterized by their publicity-seeking behavior, this is not true of the judicial branch. However, media coverage is important for the U.S. Supreme Court because it doesn't have the same public affairs mechanisms of the other two branches of government and it is dependent on media dissemination of information about its decisions. However, stories involving complex legal issues are always as easy to sell as well-illustrated stories dealing with the Congress or president.[25]

TV cameras have never been permitted to record Supreme Court proceedings. However, recent research suggests the U.S. Supreme Court has lost public support in recent decades partly because TV news coverage has often framed its decisions as political or insincere.[26] Print and broadcast reporters, however, are granted access to the Court. Still, fewer than a dozen full-time reporters cover the Supreme Court. A recent study of the 2014 Supreme Court term found that variation in media coverage

HOW DOES THE MEDIA COVER THE SUPREME COURT?

TV cameras have traditionally not been allowed inside the Supreme Court. As a result of the COVID-19 pandemic, the Supreme Court pivoted and announced it would hold arguments remotely and, in an unprecedented move, make the live audio of those arguments available to the public. Here, Supreme Court Justice nominee Judge Amy Coney Barrett is sworn in before the Senate.

Pool/Getty Images

of the Supreme Court is the product of legal factors, the size of the majority coalition in a case, the news outlet producing content, and the case being discussed.[27]

As longtime Court reporter Tony Mauro noted, "Of course we don't want the Supreme Court playing to the crowd, ruling to please the majority. But that does not mean the [C]ourt should be invisible and unaccountable. Clarence Thomas on *Face the Nation*? John Roberts taking questions posted on YouTube? Sam Alito blogging? Why not? Really, why not?"[28]

HOW DO NEWS MEDIA INFLUENCE AND NEWS MEDIA BIAS AFFECT PUBLIC CONFIDENCE?

13.3 Analyze the impact of the media on public opinion and political behavior.

Many important questions pertain to the news media's relationship with the public. For instance, how much influence do the media actually have on the public's understanding of political issues? Do the media have a discernible ideological bent or bias, as some people suggest? Are people able to resist information that is inconsistent with their preexisting beliefs? And how much confidence does the public have in the news media?

News Media Influence

Some political scientists argue that the content of news coverage accounts for a large portion of the volatility and changes in public opinion and voting preferences of Americans, when measured over relatively short periods of time.[29] These changes are called **media effects**. These effects may be visible in a number of ways.

First, the media can influence the list of issues to be addressed by government through a process known as **agenda setting**. Significant media attention to an issue often increases the salience of that issue with average citizens. These citizens then pressure the government to take action. For example, media coverage of immigrant children separated from their families after crossing the border made immigration

media effects

The influence of news sources on public opinion.

agenda setting

The process of forming the list of issues to be addressed by government.

policy a hot topic in many 2018 congressional campaigns. The media's agenda-setting role was particularly critical in the 2020 presidential election, and the news media played a positive and important role in communicating how long it would take to count ballots given the increase in early voting and vote-by-mail as a result of the pandemic and differences in state laws and procedures.

Second, the media influence public opinion through **framing**—the process by which a news organization defines a political issue and consequently affects opinion about the issue. For example, an experiment conducted by one group of scholars found that if a news story about a Ku Klux Klan rally was framed as a civil rights story (that is, a story about the right of a group to express its ideas, even if they are unpopular), viewers were generally tolerant of the rally. However, if the story was framed as a law and order issue (that is, a story about how the actions of one group disrupted a community and threatened public safety), public tolerance for the rally decreased. In either case, the media exert subtle influence over the way people respond to the same information.[30]

framing
The process by which a news organization defines a political issue and consequently affects opinion about the issue.

Third, the media have the power to indirectly influence the way the public views politicians and government. For example, voters' choices in presidential elections often relate to their assessments of the economy. In general, a healthy economy motivates voters to reelect the incumbent president or members of their party, whereas a weak economy impels them to choose the challenger. Hence, if the media paint a consistently dismal picture of the economy, that picture may well hurt the incumbent president or the incumbent party seeking reelection.

Fourth, reporting can sway the public opinion and votes of people who lack strong political beliefs. So, for example, the media have a greater influence on political independents than on strong partisans.[31] That said, the sort of politically unmotivated individual who is subject to media effects may be less likely to engage in political affairs, in which case the media's influence may be more limited.

Finally, the media likely have a greater impact on topics far removed from the lives and experiences of readers and viewers. News reports can probably shape public opinion about events in foreign countries somewhat easily. Yet what the media say about domestic issues, such as rising food or gas prices, neighborhood crime, or child rearing, may have relatively little effect, because most citizens have personal experience of, and well-formed ideas about, these subjects.

News Media Bias

Are journalists biased? The answer is simple and unavoidable. Of course they are. Journalists, like all human beings, have values, preferences, and attitudes—some conscious, others subconscious, but all reflected at one time or another in the subjects covered or the portrayal of events or content communicated. Given that the press is biased, in what ways is it biased, and when and how are the biases shown?

Much of the debate over media bias in contemporary politics has centered on the ideological bias of the people who report the news. Surveys conducted by the Pew Center for Excellence and the Knight Foundation have found that about twice as many journalists self-identify as liberal or Democratic than as conservative or Republican.[32] However, several studies have shown that there is little evidence of political favoritism or bias in coverage.[33]

One of the ways in which bias does appear in news stories is in the language journalists use to describe politicians. In a 2005 study, Timothy Groseclose and Jeffrey Milyo found that reporters used ideological terms to describe some politicians, but not others. For example, journalists might editorialize by referring to a politician as a *radical* or *extreme conservative*. When taking into account this more subtle measure of bias, they found that the reporting of most media organizations slanted to the left, with the exception of the *Wall Street Journal* and Fox News, which slanted to the right. PBS was the only outlet that presented a balanced and evenhanded reporting of government and politics.[34]

Editorial endorsements of newspapers may also serve as a measure of journalistic bias. According to *Editor and Publisher*, a trade journal of the media business that tracks endorsements of newspapers, a majority of American newspapers who endorse political candidates for president have preferred the Republican candidate in sixteen of the last twenty-one elections. Democrats typically lose the endorsement race, though in 2016, Hillary Clinton received more than 200 endorsements, while Donald Trump received a mere six.[35] In addition, the partisan differences in support of incumbent reelection campaigns are striking. While Democratic incumbents are supported by 30 percent of all newspapers that take a position on the race, Republican incumbents have been supported by 70 percent of newspapers.[36] Other scholars have shown that the partisan tilt that appears in newspapers is a result of the markets that they're catering to.[37]

Scholars also examine whether media consolidation has produced a news environment biased toward corporations and conservative politics. These scholars point to the elite background of the typical journalist, who tends to be White, male, highly educated, and relatively affluent. As a result, many of these journalists, in their reporting, may unconsciously ignore issues important to racial and ethnic minorities, poor people, and others who might be critical of government and big business.[38] They may also look to different sources for expertise to enrich their reporting. One study of the 2012 election, for example, revealed that, even on issues of concern to women, male pundits were four to seven times more likely to be quoted by the news media than their female counterparts.[39]

Perhaps the deepest bias among political journalists is the desire to grab a good story. News people know that if they report news with spice and drama, they will increase their audience. The fear of missing a good story shapes how media outlets develop headlines and frame their stories.

In the absence of an intriguing story, news people may attempt to create a horse race where none exists. While the horse-race components of elections are intrinsically interesting, the limited time that TV devotes to politics is disproportionately given to electoral competition, leaving less time for adequate discussion of public policy.[40] One study of media coverage of the 2016 national party conventions found that policies and issues comprised only 8 percent of media coverage and that tone of coverage was overwhelmingly negative for both candidates.[41]

One other source of bias, or at least of nonobjectivity, is the increasing celebrity status of many people who report the news. In an age of media stardom and blurred boundaries between entertainment and news, journalists in prominent media positions have unprecedented opportunities to attain fame and fortune. And especially in the case of journalists with highly ideological perspectives, close involvement with wealthy or powerful special-interest groups can blur the line between reporting on policy issues and influencing them. Some journalists find work as political consultants or members of government—which seems reasonable, given their prominence, abilities, and expertise, but which can become problematic when they attempt to straddle both spheres. A good example of this phenomenon is Donna Brazile, who served both as interim chair of the Democratic National Committee and as a political contributor on CNN. When hacked e-mails revealed that she had passed along questions to the Clinton campaign in advance of CNN debates during the Democratic primary, she resigned from her network role.

An interactive tool from the *Wall Street Journal* allows you to "See Liberal Facebook and Conservative Facebook, Side by Side." Some sites like "All Sides" show ratings of "bias" of major news sources. Other sources, like the Pew Research Center, show how respondents report levels of trust in major news organizations from partisan audiences. However, these ratings may be impacted by the *hostile media effect*, wherein "partisans perceive media coverage as unfairly biased against their side."[42]

Public Confidence

Surveys allow us to measure public confidence in the press and compare it to that in other institutions. Americans' general assessment of the news media is considerably unfavorable and has trended downward since the 1980s. According to recent Gallup polls, American trust in media is at an historic low; 13 percent trust the media "a great deal," while 28 percent express only "a fair amount" of trust and confidence in the mass media to report the news fully, accurately, and fairly.[43] The Pew Research Center also found that only two in ten Americans trust the information they get from news organizations and only 4 percent of Web-using adults have a lot of trust in the information they find on social media. Furthermore, 74 percent believe that news organizations tend to favor one side, with conservative Republicans most likely to think this.[44]

While overall, seven in ten Americans continue to value the watchdog role of the media, attitudes about the role of the press are sharply divided along partisan lines. The biggest shift has occurred among Republicans, whose support for the watchdog role dropped 35 points from 2016 to 2017 (see Figure 13.3). With public confidence in the media on the decline, the press will have to grapple with reforms. As press critic Jay Rosen asserted, one of the problems at the center of declining trust in news media is that it has become disconnected from the public. For example, during the 2016 presidential election, the media's focus was more on asking pundits to define and present the candidates, policies, and issues, and to interpret what was going on in particular constituencies rather than listening to those constituencies. The broader news media might follow the example of the *Texas Tribune*, which recognized this

FIGURE 13.3 HOW DOES PARTISANSHIP RELATE TO SOURCES OF POLITICAL AND ELECTION NEWS?

	All U.S adults	Democrat/Lean Democrat	Republican/Lean Republican
Fox News	39	23	60
CNN	39	53	24
NBC News	34	40	28
ABC News	33	37	30
CBS News	30	33	26
MSNBC	24	33	14
NPR	20	30	11
New York Times	20	31	9
Washington Post	17	26	8
PBS	16	22	11
BBC	16	22	10
Wall Street Journal	13	15	11
USA Today	11	13	10
Politico	9	14	5
Hannity (radio)	9	1	19
HuffPost	8	12	3
Limbaugh (radio)	8	1	17

SOURCE: Pew Research Center; survey of U.S. adults conducted Oct. 29–Nov. 11, 2019.

Greg Nash/AFP/Getty Images

disconnect and, in the aftermath of the election, created a new community reporter position whose job it is to talk and listen to Texans in order to make sure that the issues it reports on speak to the troubles Texans experience in their lives.

WHAT RULES GOVERN THE NEWS MEDIA?

13.4 Summarize the ethical standards and federal regulations that govern the news media.

Professional journalists may obtain and publish information in a number of ways. They are, however, subject to boundaries in this pursuit. Journalists are primarily limited by the ethical standards of their profession. In some cases, additional governmental regulations may apply.

Journalistic Standards

The heaviest restrictions placed on reporters come from the industry's own professional norms and each journalist's level of integrity, as well as from oversight by editors who are ultimately responsible for the accuracy of the news they produce. To guide the ethical behavior of journalists, the Society of Professional Journalists publishes a detailed "Code of Ethics" that includes principles and standards governing issues such as avoiding conflicts of interest and verifying the information being reported.

One dilemma faced by reporters is how to deal ethically with sources. Informants may speak to reporters in a number of ways. If a session is **on the record**, as in a formal press conference, every word an official utters can be printed. In contrast, a journalist may obtain information **off the record**, which means that nothing the official says may be printed. Reporters may also obtain information **on background**, meaning that none of the information can be attributed to the source by name. Whereas background talks can be euphemistically attributed to sources, such as "unnamed senior officials," information on **deep background** must be completely unsourced, with the reporter giving the reader no hint about the origin. When reporters obtain information in any of these ways, they must take care to

on the record
Information provided to a journalist that can be released and attributed by name to the source.

off the record
Information provided to a journalist that will not be released to the public.

on background
Information provided to a journalist that will not be attributed to a named source.

deep background
Information provided to a journalist that will not be attributed to any source.

respect their source's wishes. Otherwise, not only might that person refuse to talk to them in the future, but other potential sources may do the same.

Journalists also grapple with the competitive nature of the news business. The pressure to get the story right is often weighed against the pressure to get the story first, or at the very least to get it finished before the next deadline. The twenty-four-hour news cycle, brought to life by cable news stations and nourished by the expansion of digital media, has heightened the pressure to produce interesting copy in a timely manner.

To ensure professional integrity, several major newspapers and magazines, including the *Washington Post* and the *New York Times*, have hired internal media critics, or ombudsmen, who assess how well their newspaper and its reporters are performing their duties. Some nonprofits, such as Media Matters and the Project for Excellence in Journalism at the Pew Research Center in Washington, D.C., conduct scientific studies of the news and entertainment media. Other groups, including the conservative watchdog group Accuracy in Media and its liberal counterpart Fairness and Accuracy in Reporting, critique news stories and attempt to set the record straight on important issues they believe have received biased coverage. All of these organizations have a role in making sure the media treat topics important to citizens in a fair and objective manner.

Government Regulations

The U.S. government regulates media in a number of ways. Some regulations apply to all forms of media. Libel and slander, for example, are illegal in all cases. Beginning with the landmark case in 1931 of *Near* v. *Minnesota*, the Supreme Court has upheld that, except under the most extraordinary circumstances, the Constitution places a limit on **prior restraint**—that is, the government may not limit any speech or publications before they actually occur. This principle was clearly affirmed in *New York Times Co.* v. *U.S.* (1971).[45] In this case, the Supreme Court ruled that the government could not prevent publication by the *New York Times* of the Pentagon Papers, classified government documents about the Vietnam War that had been photocopied and sent to the *Times* and the *Washington Post* by Daniel Ellsberg, a government employee. "Only a free and unrestrained press can effectively expose deception in the government," Justice Hugo Black wrote in a concurring opinion for the Court. "To find that the President has 'inherent power' to halt the publication of news by resort to the courts would wipe out the First Amendment."

prior restraint
Constitutional doctrine that prevents the government from prohibiting speech or publication before the fact; generally held to be in violation of the First Amendment.

Government can, however, regulate electronic media such as radio or TV more heavily than print content. Two reasons account for this unequal treatment. First, the airwaves used by the electronic media are considered public property and are leased by the federal government to private broadcasters. Second, those airwaves are in limited supply; without some regulation, the nation's many radio and TV stations would interfere with one another's frequency signals. The scope of government regulation of the Internet remains unclear and has been debated hotly in recent years. Government regulations of electronic media apply in two major areas: ownership and content.

MEDIA OWNERSHIP   In 1996, Congress passed the sweeping Telecommunications Act, deregulating whole segments of the electronic media. The Telecommunications Act sought to provide an optimal balance of competing corporate interests, technological innovations, and consumer needs. It appeared to offer limitless opportunities for entrepreneurial companies to give consumers enhanced services. This deregulation, however, resulted in the sudden merger of previously distinct kinds of media in order to create a more "multimedia" approach to communicating information and entertainment. This merger paved the way for the formation of multimedia corporations such as Viacom, Warner Media, and Comcast, and the media consolidation discussed later in this chapter.

Since the initial passage of this act, the Federal Communications Commission (FCC) has continued to relax ownership standards, leading to even greater media consolidation. Today, a single company may own up to 45 percent of media in a given market. Whether a media conglomerate may own both a newspaper and a TV station in a single market, however, continues to be fiercely debated.

content regulations
Limitations on the substance of the mass media.

equal time rule
The rule that requires broadcast stations to sell airtime equally to all candidates in a political campaign if they choose to sell it to any.

right of rebuttal
The rule that requires broadcast stations to give individuals the right to have the opportunity to respond to personal attacks made on a radio or TV broadcast.

CONTENT   The government also subjects the electronic media to substantial **content regulations**, or limitations on the substance of the mass media. To ensure that the airwaves "serve the public interest, convenience, and necessity," the FCC has attempted to promote equity in broadcasting. For example, the **equal time rule** requires that broadcast stations sell airtime equally to all candidates in a political campaign if they choose to sell it to any, which they are under no obligation to do. An exception to this rule is a political debate: stations may exclude from this event less well-known and minor-party candidates. Another regulation is the **right of rebuttal**, which requires that individuals be given the opportunity to respond to personal attacks made on a radio or television broadcast.

The emergence of the Internet has posed new regulatory challenges. One of the foremost concerns has centered on protecting intellectual property and making the Internet a profitable means for distributing content. Preventing free distribution of copyrighted content, especially music and movies, has been the locus of concern. In *A&M Records* v. *Napster* (2001), the Ninth Circuit court ruled against the file-sharing service, arguing that it had infringed the copyrights of the record companies.

Internet service providers (ISPs) have also attempted to limit users' access to pirated movies and music, slowing the network connections of those suspected of using illegal file-sharing programs. But following more than a decade of controversy, the FCC approved along partisan lines the Open Internet Order in 2015, which bans ISPs, like Comcast, AT&T, and Verizon, from blocking, throttling, and paid-prioritization fast lanes. The so-called "net neutrality" rule was a victory for Web-based companies such as Google and Yahoo, which argued that any other ruling would infringe on users' First Amendment rights. President Trump's FCC issued an order, which took effect in June 2018, rolling back the "net neutrality" rule, a ruling that was reaffirmed by the Republican-controlled FCC in October 2020. Critics argue that broadband companies will raise prices, stifle online competition, and selectively control the speed of access to certain content as a result of the repeal of net neutrality

HOW DOES THE GOVERNMENT REGULATE THE INTERNET?

The Internet poses a regulatory challenge for the U.S. government. On the one hand, there is a need to protect intellectual property and ensure the Internet can profitably distribute content. On the other hand, consumers and businesses alike are concerned that Internet service providers and the government should treat all data on the Internet equally. When the Federal Communications Commission repealed the laws that protected consumers from companies themselves determining Internet speeds—net neutrality rules—fears arose that the Internet will come to resemble cable TV, in which a handful of big companies dominate broadcasting and charge customers more for faster service.

Jaap Arriens/Associated Press

rules. Some states, like Washington, are setting up their own net neutrality requirements as a result of the FCC's repeal. California passed a net neutrality law in 2018, but the federal government is seeking to block the law before the state is able to enforce it.

Congress has attempted to take actions to limit online piracy. In early 2012, controversy arose over two similar pieces of legislation—the Stop Online Piracy Act (SOPA) and the PROTECT IP Act (PIPA). These acts, which were supported by content producers such as the Recording Industry Association of America and the Motion Picture Association of America, would have given officials the power to shutter entire Internet domains if federal law enforcement officers suspected they were infringing on copyright laws. Opponents of the law, concerned that the government could potentially have the power to shut down any Web site at will, feared the consequences of such a mandate. An Internet "blackout" led by online content providers such as Wikipedia and Google raised citizens' awareness of these bills. During early January 2012, Google estimates that more than 7 million people petitioned Congress, asking members to vote against SOPA and PIPA, ultimately leading to the defeat of both pieces of legislation.[46]

With the rise in use of social media, major questions have emerged about how technology companies should be regulated and how they themselves should flag content on social media sites. Facebook, YouTube, Twitter, and other social media companies are grappling with how to take down and fact-check rampant misinformation about topics like COVID-19 and the 2020 election that spread on their platforms. Major social media platforms don't share much data or insights about what kind of content people see on the platform, or why they do or don't see certain content. These practices feed public perceptions that social media companies engage in political censorship. However, the vast majority of what people see on social media is controlled by a set of algorithms, tailored to show content that will keep users engaged and interested in sharing that content with other people.

POLITICAL REFORM AND REALITIES: CURRENT NEWS MEDIA TRENDS

13.5 Describe the effect of recent trends in the news media on political outcomes.

A number of ongoing transformations define the news media today. Among these are the growth in corporate ownership and media consolidation; the targeting of programming at specific populations, known as narrowcasting; and infotainment. The people who deliver the news, too, have changed. Media news coverage today increasingly relies both on subject-matter experts and on average citizens.

Taken together, these changes create a news environment in which the boundaries between producers and consumers of news are increasingly blurred. Without the traditional lines of demarcation between news owners and objects of the news, and consumers and producers, the media's informational and watchdog roles are at risk of compromise.

Corporate Ownership and Media Consolidation

Private ownership of the media in the United States has proved to be a mixed blessing. While private ownership ensures media independence, something that cannot be said about state-controlled media in countries such as China, it also brings market pressures to journalism that do not exist in state-run systems. The news media in the United States are multibillion-dollar, for-profit businesses that ultimately are driven by the bottom line. As with all free market enterprises, the pressure in privately owned media is to increasingly consolidate media ownership, to reap the benefits that come from larger market shares and fewer large-scale competitors.

Consequently, the top six media chains—Viacom, News Corporation, Comcast, CBS, Warner Media, and Disney—account for more than 90 percent of news media content. Large media conglomerates such as Gannett, Media News Group, and News Corporation own most daily newspapers; fewer than 300 of the approximately 1,400 daily newspapers are independently owned. AT&T's acquisition of Time Warner set off alarm bells regarding consolidation over control of both the pipes of distribution and much of content that travels through the pipes. In addition, media companies are also seeking to commodify and privatize the Internet, which some view as the next great media battle. In raw numbers, 80 percent of the top twenty online news sites are owned by the one hundred largest media companies. Time Warner owns two of the most visited sites, CNN.com and AOL News, while Gannett, which is the twelfth largest media company, owns USAToday.com along with many local online newspapers.

Unlike traditional industries, in which the primary concern associated with consolidation is price manipulation, consolidation of the media poses far greater potential risks. As the media have increasingly become dominated by a few mega-corporations, observers have grown fearful that these groups could limit the flow of information and ideas that define the essence of a free society and that make democracy possible. These profit-driven media chains, aimed at expanding market shares and pleasing advertisers, may overwhelmingly focus on sensational issues and avoid those that could alienate their audiences, anger executives, or compromise relationships with government regulators. Former *CBS Evening News* anchor Dan Rather, for example, summarizes media consolidation's threat to democracy by saying, to put it bluntly, "Very big business is in bed with very big government in Washington, and has more to do with what the average person sees, hears, and reads than most people know."[47]

Narrowcasting

narrowcasting
Targeting media programming at specific populations within society.

In recent years, fierce competition to attract viewers and the availability of additional TV channels made possible by cable and satellite TV have led media outlets to move toward **narrowcasting**—targeting media programming at specific populations within society. Within the realm of cable news, MSNBC and Fox News are most notable for engaging in this form of niche journalism. The two stations divide audiences by ideology. Fox News emphasizes a conservative viewpoint, and MSNBC stresses a more liberal perspective.

Audiences also divide along partisan lines over other news sources. Republicans, for example, are more likely than Democrats and Independents to listen to AM talk radio.[48] And while only a small disparity in newspaper reading exists between Republicans and Democrats, newspapers can be categorized by ideology; for instance, the *Washington Times* offers more conservative fare than its rival, the *Washington Post* (see Figure 13.4). As a result, political scientists have found that simply knowing where someone gets his or her news can predict party affiliation.[49]

Other narrowcasting targets specific racial, ethnic, or religious groups. Examples include Spanish-language news programs on stations such as Univision and Telemundo, as well as news programming geared toward Black viewers on cable's Black Entertainment Television (BET). For evangelical Christians, Pat Robertson's Christian Broadcasting Network (CBN), with its flagship *700 Club*, has been narrowcasting news for over forty years. The rising use of smartphones and mobile apps has helped narrowcasting to grow.

While narrowcasting can promote the interests specific to segments of the population, especially racial and ethnic minorities who may ordinarily be left out of mainstream media coverage, it comes with a social cost. Narrowcasting increases the chance that group members will rely on news that appeals to their preexisting views. By limiting one's exposure to a broad range of information or competing views, narrowcasting could result in further polarization of public opinion. The polarization made possible by narrowcasting is particularly problematic when it comes to programs that are narrowcasted in a specific ideological direction.[50] These broadcasts may result in what has been

FIGURE 13.4 WHERE DO NEWS AUDIENCES FIT ON THE POLITICAL SPECTRUM?

When it comes to getting news about government and politics, there are stark ideological differences in the sources that online Americans use. Those with consistently conservative political values are oriented around a single outlet—Fox News—to a much greater degree than those in any other ideological group. On the left of the political spectrum, no single outlet predominates. Among consistent liberals, CNN (15 percent), NPR (13 percent), MSNBC (12 percent), and the *New York Times* (10 percent) all rank near the top of the list.

SOURCE: Data from the Pew Research Center.

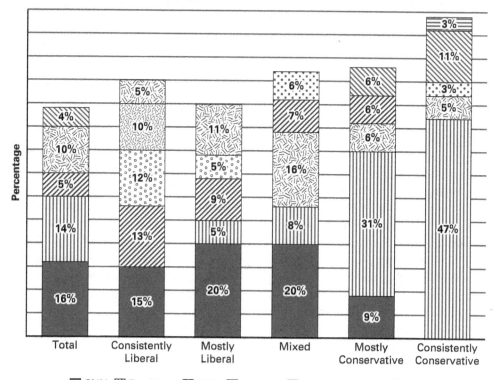

called the "Fox effect" or the "CNN effect." These effects result when a network chooses an ideologically favorable storyline—true or untrue—to cover almost *ad nauseam*. In so doing, the network sets the agenda both for partisans, who adopt the storyline being sold, and for other news networks, who feel compelled to address the issue.[51]

Narrowcasting also enables political leaders to exercise extraordinary levels of message control, as they can choose on which shows to appear and custom tailor a message for that audience. In addition, recent trends toward "hyperpersonalization" afforded by digital networked media may also have important political and social consequences. As companies like Google, Microsoft, Apple, and Facebook have begun directing personalized searches and news feeds, users have been categorized into neatly defined clusters that may create "walls" between them and may contribute to social fragmentation.[52]

Infotainment

Infotainment—or TV programming that blends political news and information with entertainment—has exploded as a way for citizens to engage with the political process. Different forms of infotainment exist, including late-night comedy shows, daytime talk shows, and comedy news shows.

Late-night comedy shows, such as *Saturday Night Live* and those hosted by Jimmy Fallon and Stephen Colbert, have mocked politicians and the news for years. What is new, however, is that political leaders have embraced these programs as a way to connect with citizens, both on the campaign trail and while in office. During the 2020 presidential campaign, for example, *Saturday Night Live* sketches spoofed a wide variety of political themes, including the presidential debates. During the 2020 presidential election campaigns, Joe Biden appeared on *The Daily Show with Trevor Noah* and Kamala Harris appeared on *The Late Show* and *Jimmy Kimmel Live.*

Daytime talk shows are also central to the political game. Daytime talk shows, like *The View*, have also been an important venue for presidents and their surrogates to promote policy initiatives. Even cable news channels have attempted to create shows that follow the talk show format; Fox News's *The Five* is an example of this phenomenon.

Political leaders see many advantages to appearing on late night and talk shows. These soft news programs give politicians an opportunity to reach much larger and more diverse audiences than do Sunday morning talk shows or cable news channels. In addition, the questions asked by hosts of *Live! With Kelly* or *The Today Show* are often less technical and hard-hitting than those asked by the traditional news media. And infotainment programs may also provide a venue to humanize the politician and make viewers connect with him or her on a more personal level.

In addition, the emergence of comedy news shows such as *Last Week Tonight with John Oliver*, *Real Time with Bill Maher*, or *The Daily Show with Trevor Noah* has also changed the way Americans receive their political news. These shows present news "freed from the media's preoccupation with balance, the fixation with fairness. They have no obligation to deliver the day's most important news, if that news is too depressing, too complicated or too boring. Their sole allegiance is to comedy."[53] As a result, many viewers find news presented by comedy shows to be more palatable, and more entertaining, than what they might view on a nightly network news show. The shows are especially popular news sources among younger Americans, who are often jaded by the conventions of traditional journalism and politics.

Infotainment, overall, makes political news and events more accessible to Americans. But research has shown that the effects of infotainment may be clearest for those who are highly attentive to politics. Watching soft news about politics makes sophisticates' political behavior more consistent. In essence, for these people, infotainment acts as an information shortcut that helps them to better remember facts and figures about the governmental process.[54] The effects of infotainment on less sophisticated audiences, however, are not as clear. Those who are less politically engaged may also fail to find humor in shows like *Saturday Night Live*'s political

HOW HAS INFOTAINMENT AFFECTED POLITICAL NEWS?

Political leaders see many advantages to appearing on infotainment programs, including connecting with citizens. Infotainment makes political news and events more accessible to Americans. However, research has shown that the effects of infotainment may be clearest for those citizens who are already the most politically knowledgeable.

CBS Photo Archive/Getty Images

coverage or *Last Week Tonight* because they lack the context in which to process the information provided by the programming; however, such individuals may connect with a show like *The View*.

Experts and Pundits

Most journalists know a little bit about many subjects but do not specialize in any one area and certainly do not possess enough knowledge to fill the hours of airtime made possible by cable TV's twenty-four-hour news cycle. Therefore, especially on cable stations, the news media employ expert consultants from a number of different disciplines, ranging from medical ethics to political campaigning. These experts, also referred to as pundits, or the more derogatory term "talking heads," are hired to discuss the dominant issues of the day. For example, during the 2016 presidential campaign, one could not turn on the TV or read a newspaper without encountering a stable full of government officials, campaign consultants, former candidates, academics, and other experts giving their thoughts about the election.

Experts have a significant impact on how we view political news stories. One study, for example, finds that "news from experts or research studies is estimated to have almost as great an impact" as anchorpersons, reporters in the field, or special commentators. These "strong effects by commentators and experts are compatible with a picture of a public that engages in collective deliberation and takes expertise seriously."[55]

However, two main concerns arise about the increasing use of experts in news reporting. First, it is unclear how objective these experts are. Many of the pundits on the air during presidential campaigns, for example, had ties to one of the two major candidates. Others were political operatives closely connected to the Democratic and Republican Parties and to members of Congress. Second, so-called experts may weaken democratic deliberation, even though they are not particularly accurate in their predictions. But because many pundits have official-sounding titles such as "strategist" or "former administration official," viewers assign privilege to experts' beliefs and do not take time to form their own political opinions. In many cases, the educated evaluations of members of the public would be as accurate as the "expert" opinions they hear on TV or read in newspapers.[56]

Citizen Journalists

In the past, only professionals whose occupation was to cover current events filed news reports. Today, however, much of what we call "news" content is written and filmed by amateur **citizen journalists**, ordinary individuals who collect, report, and analyze news content.

citizen journalists
Ordinary individuals who collect, report, and analyze news content.

Many citizen journalists use social and other forms of digital media as a way to reach an interested news audience. Some sites cover a broad range of issues. Other sites, such as local news and politics blogs, focus on niche issues and local events, such as town meetings, school closings, and recycling initiatives, that often are left out of larger publications. Uploading videos to Twitter, Snapchat, and YouTube may also allow citizens to showcase content not covered by traditional news outlets or provide a location to share common experiences, such as natural disasters. Citizens may also use social media to highlight narratives or opinions about newsworthy occurrences.

Many traditional news organizations have embraced the value of citizen journalism. In addition to bringing new perspectives—and perhaps new readers and viewers—into the fold, citizen journalists may reach the scene of important events before news crews. Citizen journalism also has financial benefits for traditional news outlets: using citizen coverage and footage is far cheaper than hiring reporters. This can be a way for news outlets to continue offering coverage of a broad range of issues in an era of decreasing budgets.

Media scholars have hotly debated the value of citizen journalism. On one hand, citizen journalism can act as a democratizing force, allowing more people to

HOW HAVE CITIZEN JOURNALISTS CHANGED JOURNALISM?

Ahmaud Arbery. Sean Reed. Breonna Taylor. Tony McDade. George Floyd. These are only the newest of painful stories and images of Black people targeted, harassed, arrested, and killed by police and racist vigilantes that have sparked renewal of a mass movement calling for the reformation of policing and racial justice in America. Citizen journalism has harnessed a broad set of tools, from podcasts to social media, to show the disconnect between mass media coverage (or the lack thereof) of racism and the reality of the lived experiences of Black, Indigenous, Latino/a/x Hispanic people and other people of color.

Samuel Corum/AFP/Getty Images

participate in setting agendas and framing issues. It can also give more instantaneous coverage than traditional media. On the other hand, citizen journalists are often not trained in the rules and standards of journalism. They may not treat their sources with the same respect or fact-check as thoroughly as professional reporters. Perhaps as a result, research has shown that consumers of citizen journalism score lower on political knowledge than those who rely on professional news organizations.[57] Finally, and perhaps most importantly, citizen journalists once again blur the line between producers and consumers of news, compromising the objectivity of news coverage.

CONCLUSION AND REVIEW

What Are the Roots of the News Media in the United States?

13.1 Describe the structure and the functions of the media, past and present.

News media, a component of the larger mass media, provide the public with key information about subjects of public interest and play a crucial role in the political process. The news media consist of print, broadcast, and new media. The nation's first newspaper was published in 1690. Until the mid- to late 1800s, when independent papers first appeared, newspapers were partisan; that is, they openly supported a particular party. In the twentieth century, first radio in the late 1920s and then TV in the late 1940s revolutionized the transmission of political information. The growth of digital media, such as the Internet, blogs, and social media sites, continues to transform the relationship between media and citizens.

How Do the News Media Cover Politics?

13.2 Assess the influence of the media on American politics.

The news media cover every aspect of the political process, including the executive, legislative, and judicial branches of government, though the bulk of attention focuses on the president. Congress, with its 535 members and complex committee system, poses a challenge to the modern media, as does the Supreme Court, with its legal rulings and aversion to media attention. Politicians have developed a symbiotic relationship with the media, both feeding the media a steady supply of news and occasionally being devoured by the latest media feeding frenzy.

How Do News Media Influence and News Media Bias Affect Public Confidence?

13.3 Analyze the impact of the media on public opinion and political behavior.

By controlling the flow of information, framing issues in a particular manner, and setting the agenda, the media have the potential to exert influence over the public, though generally they have far less effect than people believe. While the media do possess biases, a wide variety of news options is available in the United States, providing news consumers with an unprecedented amount of information from which to choose. Public opinion regarding the media is largely critical, although Americans continue to value the news media's watchdog role.

What Rules Govern the News Media?

13.4 Summarize the ethical standards and federal regulations that govern the news media.

Journalists are guided in ethical behavior by a detailed "Code of Ethics" published by the Society of Professional Journalists, which includes principles and standards concerning issues such as avoiding conflicts of interest, verifying the information being reported, and dealing ethically with sources. In addition, the U.S. government regulates both media ownership and content. The Telecommunications Act of 1996 deregulated whole segments of the electronic media, paving the way for greater media consolidation. Content regulation such as network neutrality has also been a subject of significant government attention.

Political Reform and Realities: Current News Media Trends

13.5 Describe the effect of recent trends in the news media on political outcomes.

Five trends affecting the modern media are (1) corporate ownership and increasing consolidation of media outlets; (2) narrowcasting in order to capture particular segments of the population; (3) the growth of infotainment; (4) the increasing use of experts; and (5) the rise of citizen journalists—ordinary individuals who collect, report, and analyze news content. These trends have all altered the news content citizens receive.

LEARN THE TERMS

agenda setting
citizen journalists
content regulations
deep background
digital-native
equal time rule
framing
mass media

media effects
muckraking
narrowcasting
news leaks
news media
off the record
on background
on the record

press briefing
press conference
press release
prior restraint
right of rebuttal
yellow journalism

Craig Jack Photographic/Alamy Stock Photo

WHY IS IT SO DIFFICULT TO GET MALE LAWMAKERS TO SUPPORT THE EFFORTS OF WOMEN'S RIGHTS GROUPS?

This portrait monument of White leaders of the suffragist movement (left to right: Elizabeth Cady Stanton, Susan B. Anthony, and Lucretia Mott) was commissioned by the National Woman's Party. It was displayed in the Capitol six months after the passage of the Nineteenth Amendment guaranteeing women the right to vote, with women in attendance from more than seventy women's organizations. Its inscription read: "Women first denied a soul, then called mindless, now arisen, declaring herself an entity to be reckoned." The statue was moved to a closet the next day, and its inscription was scraped off. After several women members of Congress tried to get it out of storage, they were told by the then Speaker of the House that no money would be allotted for the move, forcing women around the United States alone and within women's interest groups to raise the money to have the statue moved and put on permanent display in the Capitol Rotunda in 1997.

The uncarved portion of the slab initially was to represent all of the women who continue to toil for women's rights. Others have urged that either Sojourner Truth or Harriet Tubman be added to recognize one of these former slaves for their work on behalf of women's suffrage.

CRITICAL THINKING QUESTION: *What are some of the myriad ways that interest groups make their presence known in the political process?*

INTEREST GROUPS

LEARNING OBJECTIVES

14.1   Explain the origins of interest groups in America.

14.2   Describe the beginnings of modern American interest groups.

14.3   Describe how interest groups form.

14.4   Identify the different types of political interest groups.

14.5   Analyze the methods and activities that interest groups use to influence political outcomes.

14.6   Evaluate the factors that affect the relative success of interest groups.

14.7   Assess the effectiveness of regulations designed to control interest groups.

nterest groups are organized collections of people or organizations that try to influence public policy; they have various modern names: special interests, pressure groups, organized interests, nongovernmental organizations, political groups, lobby groups, and public interest groups. Interest groups are differentiated from political parties largely by the fact that interest groups do not run candidates for office, although they may be a source of candidates or support.

The face of interest group politics in the United States is constantly changing. In the wake of Supreme Court decisions that equate money with speech, a protected right under the First Amendment, big business and trade groups are increasing their activities and engagement in the political system. At the same time, evidence concerning whether ordinary citizens join political groups is conflicting. Political scientist Robert Putnam, for example, has argued that fewer Americans are joining groups of all kinds, a phenomenon he labeled "bowling alone."[1] Other observers disagree, concluding that America is in the midst of an "explosion of voluntary groups, activities and charitable donations [that] is transforming our towns and cities."[2] The number of groups, especially at the local level, that were founded around partisan divides certainly supports this notion. Ironically, it is Putnam's daughter, Lara, a historian, who is setting his thesis on end. In particular, she finds that women, mobilized by the election of Donald J. Trump, are joining politicized interest groups at the local level, and grassroots efforts are working at recreating civil society. For many, social life now revolves being around likeminded people in partisan groups, and in the wake of the COVID-19 pandemic and protests for racial justice led by Black Lives Matter organizers on the local, state, and national levels, America saw daily protests throughout spring and summer of 2020, with a huge uptick in grassroots mobilization.

interest group
A collection of people or organizations that tries to influence public policy.

WHAT ARE THE ROOTS OF AMERICAN INTEREST GROUPS?

14.1 Explain the origins of interest groups in America.

It is ironic that James Madison in *Federalist No. 10* (See Appendix III) cautioned about the mischief of factions, or what today we call interest groups. He feared that one individual or a collection of individuals of great wealth could wrest power from the people. Indeed, placating existing factions was key to the ratification of the Constitution of the United States. Before and during the Revolutionary War (1775–1783), Federalists and Anti-Federalists argued passionately over whether or not the new nation required a strong national government. Anti-Federalists, those favoring a decentralized political structure in which states (the former colonies) largely were free to act as independent nations, won this initial round of the debate with ratification of the Articles of Confederation. While the government created under the Articles successfully managed to conduct and win the war with Great Britain, problems soon arose as a weak national government attempted to repay its war-created debts without any means of raising funds other than appealing to the thirteen member states.

The heated disagreements among Federalists, arguing for a stronger national government, and Anti-Federalists, arguing that a strong national government could lead to tyranny of the kind practiced by the British, ultimately led to the ratification of the Constitution and the Bill of Rights. This outcome suggests that interest groups (factions, in eighteenth-century parlance) have placed an indelible stamp on our nation from the beginning.

• • •

Their experiences under British rule led the Framers to tailor a governmental system of multiple pressure points to check and balance political factions. It was their belief that the division of power between national and state governments and across the three branches would prevent any one individual or group of individuals from becoming too influential. They also believed that decentralizing power would neutralize the effect of special interests, who would find it impossible to spread their efforts with any effectiveness throughout so many different levels of government. But as farsighted as they were, the Framers could not have envisioned the vast sums of money and political influence interest groups would wield as the nature of these groups evolved over time.

National Groups Emerge (1830–1889)

The Constitution, or more specifically, the Bill of Rights, directly aided the development of interest groups. The First Amendment not only secures the right to peaceable assembly but also the rights to free speech and to petition the government directly. It was almost as though those in the First Congress foresaw the eventual development of interest groups of all kinds.

Although myriad local groups proliferated throughout the colonies and in the new states, the first national groups did not emerge until the 1830s when communication networks improved. Many were single-issue groups deeply rooted in the Christian religious revivalism sweeping the nation. Concern with humanitarian causes such as temperance, peace, education, abolition of slavery, and women's rights led to the founding of numerous associations dedicated to addressing these issues. Among the first of these groups was the American Anti-Slavery Society, founded in 1833 by William Lloyd Garrison. By 1838, it had about 250,000 members.

After the Civil War, more groups were founded. For example, the Women's Christian Temperance Union (WCTU) was created in 1874 with the goal of outlawing the sale of liquor. Its members, many of them quite religious, believed that alcohol consumption was an evil injurious to family life because many men drank away their paychecks, leaving no money to feed or clothe their families. The WCTU's activities took conventional and unconventional forms, which included organizing prayer groups, lobbying for prohibition legislation, conducting peaceful marches, and engaging in more violent protests, such as the destruction of saloons.[3]

The Grange also was formed during the period after the Civil War. Created with help from the federal government as an educational society for farmers, it taught them about the latest agricultural developments. Although its charter formally stated that the Grange was not to involve itself in politics, in 1876 it formulated a detailed plan to pressure Congress into enacting legislation favorable to farmers.

Business interests also began to figure even more prominently in both state and national politics during the late 1800s. In fact, a popular saying of the day noted that the Standard Oil Company did everything to the Pennsylvania legislature except refine it. Increasingly large trusts, monopolies, business partnerships, and corporate conglomerations in the oil, steel, and sugar industries became sufficiently powerful to control the votes of many representatives in state and the national legislatures.

Perhaps the most effective organized interest of the day was the railroad industry. In a move that could not take place today because of its clear impropriety,

WHAT WAS AMONG THE FIRST NATIONAL GROUPS TO EMERGE FOLLOWING THE CIVIL WAR?

One of the first truly national groups was the National Grange of the Order of Patrons of Husbandry, or more simply, The Grange. Established in 1867 to educate and disseminate knowledge to farmers, the group also lobbied for farmers' interests.

Fine Art/Corbis Historical/Getty Images

the Central Pacific Railroad sent its own **lobbyist** to Washington, D.C., in 1861, where he eventually became the clerk (staff administrator) of the committees of both houses of Congress that were charged with overseeing regulation of the railroad industry. Subsequently, Congress awarded the Central Pacific Railroad (later called the Southern Pacific) vast grants of lands along its route and large subsidized loans.

The Progressive Era (1890–1920)

By the 1890s, a profound change had occurred in the nation's political and social outlook. A host of problems, including crime, poverty, squalid and unsafe working conditions, and widespread political corruption were created by rapid industrialization, an influx of immigrants, and monopolistic business practices. Many Americans began to believe that new measures would be necessary to impose order on this growing chaos and to curb some of the more glaring problems in society. The political and social movement that grew out of these concerns was called the **Progressive movement**.

Progressive-era groups ranged from those rallying for public libraries and kindergartens to those seeking better labor conditions for workers—especially for White women and children. Other groups, including the National Urban League, were dedicated to ending racial discrimination. Groups such as the National American Woman Suffrage Association and the National Woman's Party seeking women's suffrage also were active during this time.

Not even Progressives could agree on what the term "progressive" actually meant, but their desire for reform led to an explosion of all types of interest groups, including single-issue, trade, labor, and the first **public interest groups**. Politically, the movement took the form of the Progressive Party, which sought on many fronts to limit or end the power of the industrialists' near-total control of the steel, oil, railroad, and other key industries. The Progressive Party was founded in 1912 by former President Theodore Roosevelt. A progressive at heart, he was stung by the Republican Party's refusal to back his nomination for a third term. Its platform endorsed most progressive goals, including more regulation of business, safer food and drugs, and the preservation of the vast natural resources that existed at that time.

In response to the pressure applied by Progressive era groups, the national government began to regulate business. Because businesses had a vested interest in keeping wages low and costs down, more business groups organized to consolidate their strength and to counter Progressive moves. Not only did governments have to mediate Progressive and business demands, but they also had to accommodate the role of organized labor, which often allied itself with Progressive groups against big business.

ORGANIZED LABOR   Until creation of the American Federation of Labor (AFL) in 1886, no real national union activity had taken place. The AFL brought skilled workers from several trades together into one stronger national organization for the first time in American history. As the AFL grew in power, many business owners began to press individually or collectively to quash the unions. As business interests pushed states for what are called open shop laws to outlaw unions from organizing workers in their factories, the AFL became increasingly political. It also was forced to react to the success of big businesses' use of legal injunctions to prohibit union organization. In 1914, massive lobbying by the AFL and its members led to passage of the Clayton Act, which labor leader Samuel Gompers hailed as the Magna Carta of the labor movement. This law allowed unions to organize free from prosecution and guaranteed their members' right to strike—a powerful weapon against employers.

BUSINESS GROUPS AND TRADE ASSOCIATIONS   The National Association of Manufacturers (NAM) was founded in 1895 by manufacturers who had suffered business losses in the economic panic of 1893 and who believed they were being affected adversely by the growth of organized labor. NAM first became active politically in

lobbyist
Interest group representative who seeks to influence legislation that will benefit their organization or client through political and/or financial persuasion.

Progressive movement
A broad group of political and social activists from the 1890s to the 1920s who opposed corruption in government, supported regulation of monopolies, and sought improvement of socioeconomic conditions.

public interest group
An organization that seeks a collective good that if achieved will not selectively and materially benefit group members.

1913, when a major tariff bill was under congressional consideration. NAM's tactics were "so insistent and abrasive" and its expenditures so lavish that President Woodrow Wilson was forced to denounce its lobbying tactics as an "unbearable situation."[4] Congress immediately called for an investigation of NAM's activities but found no member of Congress willing to testify that he had ever even encountered a member of NAM (probably because many members of Congress had received illegal contributions and gifts).

The second major business organization, the U.S. Chamber of Commerce, came into being in 1912, with the assistance of the federal government. NAM, the Chamber of Commerce, and other **trade associations**, groups representing specific industries, were effective spokespersons for their member companies. They planned elaborate and successful litigation campaigns to overturn key regulations affecting business.[5]

trade association
A group that represents a specific industry.

HOW DID THE MODERN INTEREST GROUP STATE DEVELOP?

14.2 Describe the beginnings of modern American interest groups.

Whether you realize it or not, you have probably encountered many interest groups in your daily life. For example, the American Civil Liberties Union lobbies for the protection of individuals' rights and liberties as citizens. The National Association for the Advancement of Colored People (NAACP) Legal Defense and Educational Fund, now called the LDF, litigates for equality for African Americans and other minorities. Labor unions work to assure workplace safety and fair compensation for employees in a variety of fields, including manufacturing, education, and service industries. Modern interest groups are more numerous and just as ideologically divided as they were at the Founding, and have changed dramatically with the growth of social media. Americans United for Life provides draft pro-life legislation for states and litigates to protect that legislation. Somewhat similarly, the Campaign for Working Families, which calls itself a "nonpartisan political action committee dedicated to electing pro-family, pro-life, and pro-free enterprise candidates to state and federal office," endorses hundreds of candidates each election cycle.[6] The Proud Boys and related groups, including QAnon, along with White nationalist groups, support myriad conspiracy theories including "Stop the Steal" as justification for their use of unlawful force at the U.S. Capitol building on January 6, 2021.

The Rise of Public Interest Groups

During the 1960s and 1970s, the Progressive spirit reappeared in the rise of public interest groups. Generally, these groups devoted themselves to representing the interests of African Americans, women, the elderly, the poor, and consumers, or to working on behalf of the environment. Many of their leaders and members had been active in the civil rights and anti-Vietnam War movements of the 1960s. Other groups formed during the Progressive era, such as the American Civil Liberties Union (ACLU) and the NAACP, gained renewed vigor. Many of them had as their patron the liberal Ford Foundation, which helped to bankroll numerous groups, including the Women's Rights Project of the ACLU, the Mexican American Legal Defense and Educational Fund, the Puerto Rican Legal Defense and Education Fund (now called Latino Justice PRLDEF), and the Native American Rights Fund.[7] The American Association of Retired Persons, now simply called AARP, also came to prominence in this era.

The civil rights and anti-war struggles left many Americans feeling cynical about a government that, in their eyes, failed to respond to the will of the majority. They

Keystone Press/Alamy Stock Photo

also believed that if citizens banded together, they could make a difference. Thus, two major new public interest groups—Common Cause and Public Citizen—were founded during this time. Common Cause, a good-government group that acts as a watchdog over the federal government, is similar to some of the early Progressive movement's public interest groups and advocates for what it believes are the core values of American democracy. Public Citizen is a group that advocates for consumer safety and awareness.

CONSERVATIVE RESPONSE: RELIGIOUS AND IDEOLOGICAL GROUPS
Conservatives, concerned by the activities of these liberal public interest groups, responded by forming religious and ideological groups that became a potent force in U.S. politics in the late 1970s and early 1980s. In 1979, the Reverend **Jerry Falwell** co-founded the first major new religious interest group, the **Moral Majority**. The Moral Majority was widely credited with assisting in the election of Ronald Reagan as president in 1980.[8] However, the group dissolved in the late 1980s. To fill this void, **Pat Robertson**, a televangelist, formed the **Christian Coalition** in 1989. Since then, it has grown in power and influence. Each election cycle, the group distributes tens of millions of voter guides in evangelical churches throughout the United States. Although these guides do not explicitly advocate for the selection of a particular candidate, they do highlight party nominees' stances on a number of key issues—ranging from abortion to taxation to health care—and it is not unusual for candidates to be endorsed from the pulpit.

In fact, federal law prohibits nonprofit public interest groups and religious organizations, called C-3 groups (after their designation in the U.S. Tax Code), from supporting candidates if they want to keep their tax-exempt status. President Donald J. Trump, however, signed an executive order allowing churches and religious associations to become more engaged politically by instructing the Internal Revenue Service not to take "adverse actions" against said groups.

Jerry Falwell
An American Southern Baptist pastor, televangelist, and conservative activist. He co-founded the Moral Majority in 1979.

Moral Majority
A prominent American political organization associated with the Christian right and Republican Party. It was founded in 1979 by Baptist minister Jerry Falwell and dissolved in the late 1980s.

Pat Robertson
An American media mogul, televangelist, political commentator, former Republican presidential candidate, and former Southern Baptist minister.

Christian Coalition
A U.S. Christian advocacy group created in 1987 by religious broadcaster and former presidential candidate Pat Robertson.

The Roman Catholic Church is also active politically in a wide array of issues, including its opposition to contraceptives, abortion, the death penalty, and same-sex marriages. It often coordinates with evangelical Christians on these issues. In 2015, Pope Francis, the spiritual leader of the global Roman Catholic Church, took a public stand at odds with the Republican Party's view on climate change, declaring that it is a man-made problem. During recent campaigns, Catholic candidates have found themselves in a quandary given the Pope's views. Top Democrats, including President Joe Biden and House Speaker Nancy Pelosi, are Roman Catholics who regularly vote or have voted on issues such as abortion contrary to Church teachings. Consequently, both individuals have been denied Holy Communion by various priests.[9] The pandemic, however, led to the live-streaming of most church services, so pro-choice candidates weren't confronted with embarrassing moments.

Religious-based groups are not the only conservatives to play an important role in the policy process as well as in elections at the state and national level. The **National Rifle Association (NRA)**, an opponent of gun control legislation, remains a major player in the political process, although it filed for bankruptcy in 2021. And groups such as the Young America's Foundation have made special efforts to reach conservative high school and college students through its Young Americans for Freedom program.

At odds with these groups are the students who staged the March for Our Lives protest in Washington, D.C., after the Parkland, Florida, high school shooting. With no national office or network, this group sprang up spontaneously on Facebook and Instagram urging changes in gun laws. This group, like many others, shows the power of the media, which first gave voice to the eloquent students at Parkland, and then the thousands who felt the need to express their support via social media. You might even have been among the hundreds of thousands of students who staged walkouts at their high schools in "Stand for the Second" on the one-month anniversary of the shootings.

BUSINESS GROUPS, CORPORATIONS, AND ASSOCIATIONS Business leaders, unsatisfied with the work of the National Association of Manufacturers and the U.S. Chamber of Commerce, decided during the 1970s to start new organizations to advance their political and financial interests in Washington, D.C. The Business Roundtable, for example, was created in 1972. The Roundtable is "an association of chief executive officers of leading U.S. companies working to promote sound public policy and a thriving U.S. economy."[10] It urges its members to engage in direct lobbying to influence the course of policy formation.

Most large corporations, in addition to having their own governmental affairs departments, employ D.C.-based lobbyists to keep them informed of legislation that may affect them, or to lobby bureaucrats for government contracts. Large corporations also channel significant sums of money to favored politicians or political candidates.

ORGANIZED LABOR Membership in labor unions held steady throughout the early twentieth century and then skyrocketed toward the end of the Depression. Labor became a stronger force in U.S. politics when the American Federation of Labor (AFL) merged with the Congress of Industrial Organizations (CIO) in 1955. Concentrating its efforts largely on the national level, the new AFL-CIO immediately channeled its energies into pressuring the government to protect concessions won from employers at the bargaining table and to other issues of concern to its members, including minimum-wage laws, workplace safety, civil rights, medical insurance, and health care. Organized labor began to wield potent political power, as it was able to turn out its members in support of particular political candidates, many of whom were Democrats.

More recently, the political clout of organized labor has waned at the national level (see Figure 14.1). Membership peaked at about 30 percent of the workforce in the late 1940s. Since that time, union membership has plummeted as the nation changed from a land of manufacturing workers and farmers to a nation of white-collar professionals

National Rifle Association (NRA)

The major gun-rights lobbying group in the United States, which opposes gun control and advances an expansive interpretation of the Second Amendment.

FIGURE 14.1   WHERE IS UNION MEMBERSHIP HIGHEST?

During the peak of union membership in the 1950s, nearly 30 percent of working Americans were members of a union. However, union membership, especially among private-sector employees, has declined in recent years. It also varies dramatically by region, with southern states having much lower rates of union membership than other parts of the country. New York leads the nation in the percentage of union members.

SOURCE: Data from Bureau of Labor Statistics.

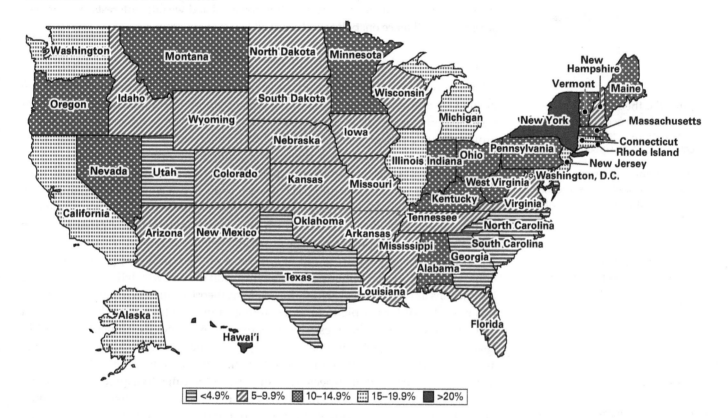

<4.9%   5–9.9%   10–14.9%   15–19.9%   >20%

and service workers. In recent years, unions have tried to stop the hemorrhaging of their members. Membership in unions stayed around 10 percent of the workforce for several years. Men and African Americans have higher rates of participation than women or White, Asian, or Hispanic workers.

Public-sector membership in unions (33.6 percent in 2020) greatly outpaces that of those employed in the private sector (6.2 percent). Public-sector union membership took a huge hit in June 2018 when a divided Supreme Court ruled that government workers no longer could be forced to pay union dues. The Court ruled that state laws that required all employees to join unions even if they disagree with union's political positions are unconstitutional; employees have a First Amendment right to freedom of association that includes not joining a union. The forced union fees affected about 5 million individuals in 23 states. This decision was detrimental to the union movement in the United States and also hurt the Democratic Party, which relies heavily on union support.

WHY DO INTEREST GROUPS FORM?

14.3   Describe how interest groups form.

Interest group formation, development, and maintenance have many significant implications for the American political system. Political scientists believe that involvement in community groups and activities with others of like interests enhances the level of **social capital**, "the web of cooperative relationships between citizens that facilitates resolution of collective action problems."[11] The more social capital that exists in a given community, the more citizens are engaged in its governance and well-being, and the more likely they

social capital

Cooperative relationships that facilitate the resolution of collective problems.

civic virtue

The tendency to form small-scale associations for the public good.

pluralist theory

The theory that political power is distributed among a wide array of diverse and competing interest groups.

disturbance theory

The theory that interest groups form as a result of changes in the political system.

transactions theory

The theory that public policies are the result of narrowly defined exchanges or transactions among political actors.

collective good

Something of value that cannot be withheld from a nonmember of a group, for example, a tax write-off or a better environment.

are to work for the collective good.[12] This tendency to form small-scale associations for the public good, or **civic virtue**, creates fertile ground within communities for improved political and economic development.[13] Interest groups may give the unrepresented or underrepresented an opportunity to have their voices heard, thereby making the government and its policy-making process more representative of diverse populations and perspectives. In addition, interest groups offer powerful and wealthy interests even greater access to, or influence on, policy makers at all levels of government.

Theories of Interest Group Formation

Interest groups may form in society for a variety of reasons. Political scientists have posited several theories to explain this phenomenon. **Pluralist theory** argues that political power is distributed among a wide range of diverse and competing interest groups. Pluralist theorists such as David B. Truman explain the formation of interest groups through **disturbance theory**. According to this approach, groups form as a result of changes in the political system. Moreover, one wave of groups will give way to another wave representing a contrary perspective (a countermovement). Thus, Truman argues, all salient issues will be represented in government. The government, in turn, should provide a forum in which the competing demands of groups and the majority of the U.S. population can be heard and balanced.[14]

Transactions theory arose out of criticisms of the pluralist approach. Transactions theory argues that public policies are the result of narrowly defined exchanges or transactions among political actors. Transactions theorists offer two main contentions: It is not rational for people to mobilize into groups, and therefore, the groups that do mobilize will represent elites. This idea arises from economist Mancur Olson's *The Logic of Collective Action*.[15] In this work, Olson assumes that individuals are rational and have perfect information on which to make informed decisions. He uses these assumptions to argue that, especially in the case of the **collective good**, or something of value that may not be withheld from nonmembers, such as a better environment, it makes little sense for individuals to join a group if they can gain the benefits secured by others at no cost and become "free riders." (The problem of free riders is discussed later in this chapter.)

The elite bias that transactionists expect in the interest group system is the result of differences in the relative cost of mobilization for elite and nonelite citizens.

HOW DID THE WOMEN'S MARCH ON D.C. PRESENT A NEW WAY OF INTEREST GROUP ORGANIZATION?

Unlike former mass marches, one woman's angry post on Facebook, the night after Donald J. Trump was elected, launched the Women's March on Washington. Trump had defeated Hillary Clinton, the first woman ever to run for president with the backing of a major political party. Clinton's loss sparked a movement that took off almost overnight. The idea of a massive march was put forward and soon women from around the nation and the world pledged to make it to Washington, D.C., or began to organize marches in major cities such as New York and Los Angeles, and cities, small towns, and villages across the planet in the largest sign of protest in American history.

G. Midford/Shutterstock

Individuals who have greater amounts of time or money available simply have lower transaction costs. Thus, according to one political scientist, "The flaw in the pluralist heaven is that the heavenly chorus sings with a strong upper-class bias."[16] Still, social media is now challenging this assumption as people are able to organize meetups online—as was the case with several "impromptu" protests by anti-Trump activists in 2016 and again in 2017 when, during the Women's March on Washington and in large and small cities and towns, millions marched or rallied around the globe to protest the election of Donald J. Trump and to advocate for women's rights. Later in 2017, President Trump's rejection of climate change and his removal of scientists from federal panels—leaving only industry leaders to examine rules and regulations concerning pollution and global warming—prompted concerned scientists to organize the March for Science. This march, and several others conducted in Washington, D.C., and across the nation early in the Trump administration, often started out with simple calls to action on Facebook—thus changing the way many new groups now form. The #MeToo/#TimesUp movement against sexual harassment also started out online, helped by celebrities sharing their own stories.

Money can also be raised via Facebook in ways never envisioned a decade ago. In response to the dramatic photos and videos of crying and distraught children separated from their parents at the U.S. border, a Facebook campaign to raise $1,500 ended up raising far more than originally envisioned. On June 16, 2018, a married Silicon Valley couple set up a fundraiser for the Refugee and Immigrant Center for Education and Legal Services, a Texas-based nonprofit. Within a week, over $20 million had been collected—the largest ever viral fundraiser movement on Facebook.

WHAT TYPES OF INTEREST GROUPS EXIST?

14.4 Identify the different types of political interest groups.

Political interest groups range from small to large, local to national, conservative to liberal, and partisan to nonpartisan. Generally, however, they share a goal of representing their members' interests in the bureaucracy, Congress, and even the courts.

Public Interest Groups

One political scientist defines public interest groups as organizations "that seek a collective good, the achievement of which will not selectively and materially benefit the membership or activists of the organization."[17] For example, upper- and middle-class women created many Progressive-era groups in an attempt to solve the varied problems of new immigrants and the poor. Today, civil liberties groups, environmental groups, good-government groups, peace groups, church groups, and groups that speak out for those who cannot (such as children, the mentally ill, or animals) are examples of public interest groups. Ironically, even though many of these groups are not well funded, they are highly visible and can actually wield more political clout than other better-funded groups.

Economic Interest Groups

The primary purpose of economic interest groups is to promote the financial interests of their members. Historically, the three largest categories of economic interest groups were business groups (including trade and professional groups such as the American Medical Association), labor organizations (such as the AFL-CIO), and organizations representing the interests of farmers. The influence of farmers and labor unions is on the decline, but big businesses such as General Electric and AT&T are spending increasingly large amounts contributing to campaigns and hiring lobbyists. This trend intensified after the Supreme Court's 2010 *Citizens United* v. *FEC* ruling, which overruled several precedents concerning campaign contributions and invalidated the laws of twenty-two states that had attempted to regulate campaign expenditures. In it, the Court decided that corporations and unions have the same free speech rights as individuals and thus cannot be banned from making independent political expenditures to fund political broadcasts in campaigns and elections under the First Amendment's free speech protections, as long as the expenditures are not coordinated with any candidate or their campaign. This decision was a huge blow to the McCain–Feingold Campaign Finance Act, a notable attempt to limit the influence of big money in elections. It also facilitated the creation of super PACs, as the Federal Election Commission took guidance from the decision and loosened contribution caps.

Groups that mobilize to protect particular economic interests generally are the most fully and effectively organized of all interest group types.[18] They exist to make profits and to obtain economic benefits for their members. To achieve these goals, however, they often find they must resort to political means rather than trust the operation of economic markets to produce favorable outcomes. Their leaders can also move in and out of the government sector. Several former partners at the powerful investment firm Goldman Sachs were members of President Trump's circle of advisers. Their work experience clearly informs their points of view. By contrast, President Joe Biden has looked to those with prior government experience to guide him.

Governmental Units

State and local governments—as well as intergovernmental associations, such as the Council of Local Governments—are becoming strong organized interests as they lobby the federal government to make certain they get their fair share of federal dollars in the form of block grants or pork projects. Most states, large cities, and even public universities retain lobbyists in Washington, D.C., to advance their interests or to keep them informed about relevant legislation. States seek to influence the amount of money allotted to them in the federal budget for projects such as building roads and schools, enhancing parks or waterways, or other public works projects.

political action committee (PAC)

Officially recognized fund-raising organization that represents interest groups and is allowed by federal law to make contributions directly to candidates' campaigns.

***Citizens United* v. FEC (2010)**

Supreme Court ruling that enabled corporations and unions to have the same political speech rights as individuals under the First Amendment. As part of this ruling, the Supreme Court found that the government may not prohibit corporations or unions from using their general treasury funds to support or denounce political candidates in elections.

Political Action Committees

In 1974, amendments to the Federal Election Campaign Act made it legal for businesses, labor unions, and interest groups to form **political action committees (PACs)**, officially registered fund-raising organizations that represent interest groups in the political process. Many elected officials also have leadership PACs to help raise money for themselves and other candidates. Unlike many other types of interest groups, PACs do not have formal members; they simply have contributors. *Citizens United v. FEC (2010)* is a landmark case in which the Supreme Court ruled that the Federal Election Commission Act's ban on corporate entities' or unions' use of independent expenditures, that is, those not in cooperation with a campaign, was unconstitutional. This decision gave corporations and unions even more power in elections.[19]

WHAT DO INTEREST GROUPS DO?

14.5 Analyze the methods and activities that interest groups use to influence political outcomes.

Just as members of Congress are assumed to represent the interests of their constituents in Washington, D.C., interest groups are assumed to represent the interests of their members to policy makers at all levels of government. In the 1950s, for example, the NAACP was able to articulate the interests of African Americans to national decision makers, even though as a group they had little or no electoral clout, especially in the South, where restrictions made many ineligible to vote. Without the efforts of

Scott Olson/Getty Images

Over the past decade, activism regarding the stagnation of working-class wages alongside the concentration of both new income and cumulative wealth among a small sliver of the highest earners has emerged in the United States. Labor unions have had an integral role in raising awareness of this issue. Here, members of the Service Employees International Union (SEIU) rally in support of the American Federation of State County and Municipal Employees (AFSCME) in Chicago.

civil rights groups, it is unlikely that either the courts or Congress would have acted as quickly to make race discrimination illegal. By banding together with others who have similar interests at a particular time, all sorts of individuals—from railroad workers to women to physical therapists to concerned parents to members of the LGBTQ community to mushroom growers—can advance their collective interests in Congress, statehouses, communities, and school districts. Gaining celebrity support or hiring a lobbyist to advocate those interests also increases the likelihood that issues of concern will be addressed and acted on favorably.

Interest groups, however, do have a downside. Because groups make claims on society, they can increase the cost of public policies. The elderly can push for more costly health care and Social Security programs; people with disabilities for improved access to public buildings and accommodations at work; industry for tax loopholes; and veterans for improved access to medical care and benefits that may take funds usually appropriated for other social programs. Many Americans believe that interest groups exist simply to advance their own selfish interests, with little regard for the rights of other groups or, more importantly, of people not represented by any organized group.

Whether good or bad, interest groups play an important role in U.S. politics. In addition to enhancing the democratic process by providing increased representation and participation, they raise public awareness about important issues, help frame the public agenda, and often monitor programs to guarantee effective implementation. Most often, they accomplish these goals through lobbying, electoral activities, or educational campaigns. The push for a national minimum wage of $15 is one such union-led effort at the local, state, and national levels. In the District of Columbia, for example, the minimum wage in 2018 was $13.25, as compared to the federal minimum of $7.25 an hour, last raised in 2009. In 2020 the District raised the minimum wage to $15 an hour—more than double that of the federal minimum.

Lobbying

Lobbying is at the top of most interest groups' agendas because it allows groups to effectively pursue their policy agendas by seeking to persuade political leaders to support the group's position. The exact origin of the term is disputed. In mid-seventeenth-century England, there was a room located near the floor of the House of Commons where members of Parliament would congregate and could be

lobbying
The activities of a group or organization that seeks to persuade political leaders to support the group's position.

approached by their constituents and others who wanted to plead a particular cause. Similarly, in the United States, people often waited outside the chambers of the House and Senate to speak to members of Congress as they emerged. Because they waited in the lobbies to argue their cases, by the nineteenth century they were commonly referred to as lobbyists. An alternate piece of folklore explains that when Ulysses S. Grant was president, he would frequently walk from the White House to the Willard Hotel on Pennsylvania Avenue just to relax in its comfortable and attractive lobby. Interest group representatives and those seeking favors from Grant would crowd into that lobby and try to press their claims. Soon they were nicknamed lobbyists.

Most politically active groups use lobbying to make their interests heard and understood by those in a position to influence or change governmental policies. Depending on the type of group and on the role it aims to play, lobbying can take many forms. You probably have never thought of the Boy Scouts or Girl Scouts as political. Yet when Congress began debating the passage of legislation dealing with discrimination in private clubs, representatives of both organizations testified in the hope of persuading Congress to allow them to remain single-sex organizations.

In 2020, the U.S. Chamber of Commerce ranked first in spending at $84 million. The National Association of Realtors was second at nearly $82 million[20] (see Figure 14.2).

LOBBYING CONGRESS A wide variety of lobbying activities target members of Congress: At the top is congressional testimony on behalf of a group, followed by individual letters or e-mails from interested constituents, campaign contributions, or the outright payment of money for votes. Of course, the last activity is illegal, but there exist numerous documented instances of money changing hands for votes.

Lobbying Congress and issue advocacy are skills that many people have developed over the years. In 1869, for example, women gathered in Washington, D.C., for the second annual meeting of the National Woman Suffrage Association and marched to Capitol Hill to hear one of their members (unsuccessfully) ask Congress to pass legislation that would enfranchise women under the terms of the Fourteenth Amendment. Practices such as these floor speeches are no longer permitted.

FIGURE 14.2 HOW MANY LOBBYISTS ARE THERE? HOW MUCH DO THEY SPEND?

In 2020, over 11,000 registered lobbyists attempted to influence public policy in Congress and the federal agencies. While this number is far lower than the all-time high of 14,820 in 2007, this large-scale lobbying effort is an expensive industry, spending nearly $3.5 billion in 2020.

SOURCE: OpenSecrets.org.

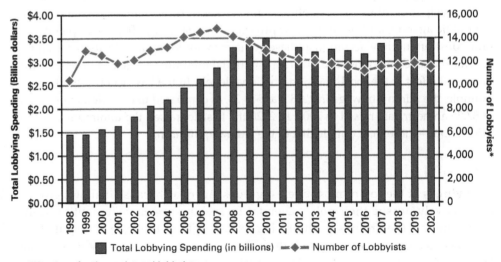

Total Lobbying Spending (in billions) ◆ Number of Lobbyists

*Number of active registered lobbyists

"*A very special interest to see you, Senator.*"

Joseph Farris/The New Yorker Collection/The Cartoon Bank

Today, many effective lobbyists are former members of Congress, staff aides, or other Washington insiders. These connections help them develop close relationships with senators and House members in an effort to enhance their access to the policy-making process. A symbiotic relationship between members of Congress, interest group representatives, and affected bureaucratic agencies often develops. Congressional representatives and their staff members, who face an exhausting workload and legislation they frequently know little about, often look to lobbyists for information. "Information is the currency on Capitol Hill, not dollars," said one lobbyist.[21] One aide reports: "My boss demands a speech and a statement for the *Congressional Record* for every bill we introduce or co-sponsor—and we have a lot of bills. I just can't do it all myself. The better lobbyists, when they have a proposal they are pushing, bring it to me along with a couple of speeches, a *Record* insert, and a fact sheet."[22]

Not surprisingly, lobbyists work most closely with representatives who share their interests.[23] A lobbyist from the Family Research Council, which advocates for traditional marriage and families as set forth by God in the Bible, would be unlikely, and indeed, foolhardy, to approach a Democratic female senator supported by the liberal EMILY's List, which supports only pro-choice Democratic women. It is much more effective for a group such as the Family Research Council to provide useful information for its supporters and to those who are undecided. Good lobbyists also can encourage members to file amendments to bills favorable to their interests. They also can urge their supporters in Congress to make speeches (often written by the group) and to pressure their colleagues in the chamber.

A lobbyist's effectiveness depends largely on his or her reputation for fair play and provision of accurate information. No member of Congress wants to look uninformed. As one member noted, "It doesn't take very long to figure out which lobbyists are straightforward and which ones are trying to snow you. The good ones will give you the weak points as well as the strong points of their case. If anyone ever gives me false or misleading information, that's it—I'll never see him again."[24] Many former members of Congress on both sides of the aisle have found extremely lucrative lobbying jobs in the private sector.

LOBBYING THE EXECUTIVE BRANCH As the executive branch has increasingly concerned itself with shaping legislation, lobbying efforts directed toward the president and the bureaucracy have gained in frequency and importance. Groups often begin their support by endorsing a particular candidate for president. If they bet on the winner, they often enjoy special consideration and extra attention from a grateful president. Groups often target one or more levels of the executive branch because so many potential access points exist, including the president, White House staff, and numerous levels of the executive branch bureaucracy. Groups try to work closely with the administration to influence policy decisions at their formulation and later implementation stages as well as to obtain appropriations from various departments and government entities. Bureaucrats often look to organized interests to help them implement rules, while interest groups may pressure bureaucrats to approach regulation with caution. Climate change deniers, for example, found a willing listener in Scott Pruitt, President Trump's first head of the Environmental Protection Agency. At their urging, Pruitt took the lead in rolling back several Obama-era rules that were written to promote clean air and water. These rules were then reversed by the Biden administration.

As with congressional lobbying, the effectiveness of a group often depends on its ability to provide decision makers with important information and a sense of where the public stands on the issue. The National Women's Law Center, for example, has been instrumental in seeing that Title IX, which Congress passed to mandate educational equity for women and girls, is always on the agenda of the Department of Education, which is charged with its enforcement.

Compared to his predecessors, Vice President Mike Pence's office saw a high number of lobbyists. During his first year in office, he personally saw more than double the number of lobbyists than the previous two vice presidents, Dick Cheney and Joe Biden. Among his frequent visitors were lobbyists for drug companies, energy firms, and those seeking tax breaks. In 2017 alone, 236 lobbyists reported that they contacted the vice president's office.

LOBBYING THE COURTS   The courts, too, have proved a useful target for interest groups.[25] Although you might think the courts decide cases affecting only the parties involved or they should be immune from political pressures, interest groups for years have recognized the value of lobbying the courts, especially the U.S. Supreme Court, and many political scientists view it as a form of political participation.[26]

Generally, interest group lobbying of the courts takes two forms: (1) direct sponsorship; or, (2) the filing of *amicus curiae* briefs. Sponsorship involves providing resources (financial, human, or otherwise) to shepherd a case through the judicial system, and the group may even become a named party, as in *Planned Parenthood of Southeastern Pennsylvania* v. *Casey* (1992). Interest groups may be parties to a case even when they are not named as the lead party. In *Zubik* v. *Burwell* (2016), seven cases from different lower courts were consolidated under one name. Little Sisters of the Poor and Priests for Life, lead parties in two of the seven cases, were not named. Sylvia Mathews Burwell was the secretary of the department of health and human services at the time.

When a case that a group is interested in, but not actually sponsoring, comes before the Court, the organization often will file an *amicus* brief—either alone or with other like-minded groups—to inform the justices of the group's policy preferences, generally offered in the guise of legal arguments. Over the years, as the number of both liberal and conservative groups viewing litigation as a useful tactic has increased, so has the number of briefs submitted to the courts. An interest group has sponsored or filed an *amicus curiae* brief in most of the major U.S. Supreme Court cases noted in this text.[27] Interest groups also file *amicus* briefs in lower federal and state supreme courts.

In addition to litigating, interest groups try to influence nominations to the federal courts. For example, they play an important part in judicial nominees' Senate confirmation hearings. In 2009, for example, 218 groups testified or prepared statements for or against the nomination of Sonia Sotomayor to the Supreme Court. The diversity of groups was astounding, from gun rights groups to pro-choice groups, women's groups, and Hispanic advocacy organizations.[28] In 2017, a conservative group,

Judicial Crisis Network, ran a $10 million multimedia campaign to rally support for the confirmation of Judge Neil Gorsuch to the Supreme Court. It also ran an ad in *Time* magazine thanking the two Democratic senators who broke ranks to vote for Gorsuch. In contrast, a liberal group, The Constitutionality Responsibility Project, was hastily formed to rally voters to contact their senators and urge them to vote "no" on Gorsuch's nomination.

The case of Judge Brett Kavanaugh's nomination to the Supreme Court in summer 2018 was initially similar to that of Justice Gorsuch's but for the fact that Kavanaugh's previous experience in the Bush administration, his role in Special Prosecutor Kenneth Starr's investigation of Bill Clinton, his writings on the law, and his judicial opinions made it clear that his appointment would move the Court farther to the right. Corporate lobbyists paid more than $15 million to run ads praising him. The Judicial Crisis Network chipped in another $6 million targeting Democratic senators up for reelection in states won by President Trump in large numbers. Even after Christine Blasey Ford testified before the Senate Judiciary Committee with accusations of sexual assault against Kavanaugh, the success of the pro-Kavanaugh groups was clear: On Election Day 2018, targeted Democratic Senators Claire McCaskill, Joe Donnelly, and Heidi Heitkamp, who voted against Kavanaugh, were all defeated at the polls, giving the Republicans a larger majority in the Senate which they lost in 2021, but not before President Trump was able to get a third conservative justice on the Court, Amy Coney Barrett, to replace the liberal Justice Ruth Bader Ginsburg.

GRASSROOTS LOBBYING   Interest groups regularly try to inspire their members to engage in grassroots lobbying, hoping that lawmakers will respond to those pressures and the attendant publicity.[29] In essence, the goal of many organizations is to persuade ordinary voters to serve as their advocates. In the world of lobbying, few things are more useful than a list of committed supporters. Radio and TV talk-show hosts, both conservative and liberal, try to stir up their listeners by urging them to contact their representatives in Washington, D.C. Other interest groups use petition drives and carefully targeted and costly TV advertisements pitching one side of an argument. It is also routine for interest groups to e-mail or text message their members and provide a direct Web link as well as suggested text that citizens can use to lobby their legislators. Social media can be a strong conduit for grassroots movements. The #MeToo movement largely started on Twitter and Facebook when thousands of women posted their stories of sexual harassment and assault. Subsequent news coverage of the public trials of sexual predators such as Olympic gymnast physician Larry Nassar, Bill Cosby, and Harvey Weinstein; the rash of firings of well-known media personalities such as Bill O'Reilly and Matt Lauer; and the resignations of several elected officials, including U.S. Democratic Senator Al Franken, helped to further invigorate the movement.

PROTESTS AND RADICAL ACTIVISM   A highly visible tactic used by some groups is nonviolent protest activity, such as that once used by the Southern Christian Leadership Council and also by the Black Lives Matter movement today. Although most groups opt for more conventional forms of lobbying and seek to influence policy through the electoral process, when these forms of interest group activities are unsuccessful, some groups (or individuals within groups) resort to more forceful measures to attract attention to their cause.

Legal, peaceful protests are now the norm among interest groups in the United States, but a minority of participants and groups within larger movements may rely on illegal protest activities and tactics that range from intimidation to terrorist violence. Intimidation tactics include publishing the names, contact information, and addresses of those groups or individuals believed to be engaging in wrongful activity and urging supporters to phone, e-mail, or protest outside of their homes. Some groups have faced federal terrorism charges for their illegal actions.

In other situations, overreaction by members of the police or individual protesters may result in violence and injuries at the site of an otherwise peaceful protest. Such was the case in Louisville, Kentucky, after police killed a Black woman, Breonna Taylor, at her apartment; and in Minneapolis, Minnesota, after police killed a Black man, George Floyd, during an arrest. Videos of convicted former police officer Derek Chauvin with his knee on Floyd's neck for more than nine minutes, as Floyd begged him to stop because he could not breathe, went viral on social media and hundreds of thousands took to the streets to protest the excessive use of violent and often deadly force by police against Black Americans. Some protesters got violent; the vast majority, however, were peaceful.

That was not the case in Charlottesville, Virginia, in the Unite the Right protest on August 11 and 12, 2017. Members of the alt-right, neo-Confederates, White nationalists, neo-Nazis, and members of the Ku Klux Klan marched to show their opposition to the removal of Confederate monuments. As protesters carried guns and chanted racist and anti-Semitic slogans, they clashed with counter-protesters, one of whom was killed and seventeen more participants injured.

Election Activities

In addition to trying to achieve their goals (or at least draw attention to them) by lobbying, many interest groups also become involved more directly in the electoral process. Interest groups recruit and endorse candidates, aid in get-out-the-vote campaigns, and rate office holders. The recent mid-term and presidential elections, for example, were the targets of significant fund-raising, a record of more than $14 billion by organized interests. Women candidates, in particular, smashed all previous records.

CANDIDATE RECRUITMENT AND ENDORSEMENTS Interest groups play an important role in helping to identify potential candidates for political office. Involvement in an interest group helps citizens to develop the skills necessary to be effective leaders, fundraisers, and communicators. In the aftermath of Hillary Clinton's loss to Donald J. Trump, existing liberal women's groups, as well as newly formed ones, started recruiting candidates to run for office at all levels. EMILY's List alone received over 34,000 requests for help from women interested in running for office. The so-called "Trump Bump" led groups to hold thousands of training sessions, both in person and online, to encourage women to seek office where, as legislators, they can advance women's issues. Organized interests may also believe that activists and members will be particularly effective advocates for their causes as candidates or elected officials. To further this goal, many groups also provide candidate training, make direct and indirect contributions to campaigns, help to hire campaign consultants, and fund some print and digital media.

Interest groups may also choose to endorse candidates who express views consistent with their policy positions. Candidate endorsements play a prominent role in focusing voters' attention on candidates who share their beliefs. Endorsements also may help to mobilize group members and provide much-needed volunteers and enthusiasm. They also might provide voters with reasons not to vote for a particular candidate. An NRA endorsement, for example, may lead gun control advocates to vote against an NRA supported candidate. Singer Taylor Swift's entry into the political fray had limited success. While voter registrations surged after she urged her followers to vote, none of the Democratic candidates she supported in Tennessee in 2020 won. By contrast, Georgian Stacey Abrams' efforts at Fair Fight to increase voter registration and turnout undoubtedly contributed to the wins of two Democratic senators. Their election gave Democrats the fifty votes they needed to control the Senate, as Vice President Kamala Harris can cast the tie-breaking fifty-first vote.

GETTING OUT THE VOTE Many interest groups believe they can influence public policy by putting like-minded representatives in office. To that end, many groups across the ideological spectrum launch massive get-out-the-vote efforts. These include identifying prospective voters and transporting them to the polls. Well-financed interest groups often cast a wider net, producing issue-oriented ads for newspapers, radio,

CAN A POLITICAL STAR CHANGE THE SHAPE OF THE ELECTORATE?
Georgia House of Representatives member Stacey Abrams, who formed the voting rights advocacy organization Fair Fight Action in 2018, was successful not only in promoting free and fair elections, but helped to register 800,000 voters in the state of Georgia. Her efforts at empowering people to use their voice and their vote undoubtedly led to Democratic wins in Senate and presidential elections.

TV, and social media designed to educate the public as well as increase voter interest in election outcomes. Planned Parenthood and the NRA do so at the local, state, and national level in every election cycle.

RATING THE CANDIDATES OR OFFICE HOLDERS Many ideological groups rate candidates to help their members (and the general public) evaluate the voting records of members of Congress. They use these ratings to help their members and other voters make informed voting decisions. The American Conservative Union (conservative) and Americans for Democratic Action (liberal)—two groups at ideological polar extremes—are just two examples of groups that routinely rate candidates and members of Congress based on their votes on key issues. Interest groups also rate judicial candidates. The American Bar Association long has rated presidential nominees to the federal courts. President George W. Bush looked to the conservative Federalist Society for guidance in his appointments. President Trump took a new approach. He relied on the Federalist Society for lists of pre-rated or vetted potential nominees for *all* vacancies on the federal bench. Thus, Bush looked to the Federalist Society to evaluate his nominees; Trump looked to it for pre-vetted nominees.

CAMPAIGN CONTRIBUTIONS Corporations, labor unions, and interest groups may give money to political candidates in a number of ways. Organized interests are allowed to form political action committees (PACs) to raise money for direct contributions to political candidates in national elections. PAC money plays a significant role in the campaigns of many congressional incumbents, often averaging more than half a House candidate's total spending (see Figure 14.3). PACs generally contribute to those who have helped them before and who serve on committees or subcommittees that routinely consider legislation of concern to that group. Super PACs contributed $615 million to the numerous presidential candidates during the primary season and the general election in 2020.

Some organized interests may also prefer to make campaign expenditures through industry PACs, leadership PACs, and super PACs, among others. Based on federal court decisions starting in 2010 with *Citizens United* v. *FEC* (2010), super PACs may raise unlimited funds since political speech is considered protected speech, but such funds may not be given to or spent in coordination with a candidate's campaign. This money may be used for issue advocacy, however, which may help a group's preferred candidate indirectly. These groups have been major players in recent elections.

FIGURE 14.3 HOW MUCH MONEY DO TOP PACS SPEND ON NATIONAL ELECTIONS?

Political action committees play an important role in national elections. The amount of money they spend and how it is allocated between Democrats and Republicans varies widely over interest group sectors, as shown in this illustration of spending through November 13, 2020, during the 2019–2020 election cycle.

SOURCE: Data from the Center for Responsive Politics, accessed November 14, 2020, www.opensecrets.org/overview/sectors.php.

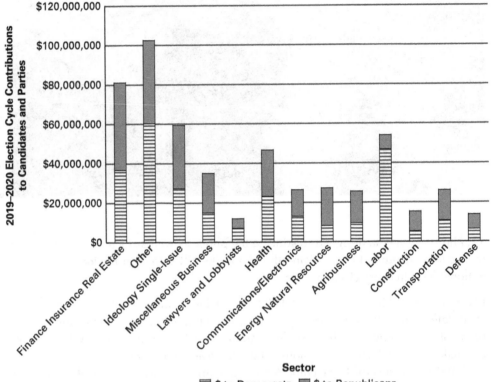

EDUCATIONAL CAMPAIGNS Interest groups may choose to raise awareness and sway voters to their viewpoints on key issues—especially when voters have a choice between a candidate sympathetic to a group's views and a candidate who is not. In these circumstances, interest groups often try to simplify or even oversimplify the issue with a slogan or biting campaign ad. Groups also identify issues that they believe are of particular interest to certain groups of voters. Many groups create nonprofit educational foundations to further their goals to allow supporters to make tax-deductible contributions.

WHAT MAKES INTEREST GROUPS SUCCESSFUL?

14.6 Evaluate the factors that affect the relative success of interest groups.

In early America, interest groups were largely *ad hoc* organizations formed in local communities. Following the advent of television, the first national political organizations began to take shape. Today, smartphones and social media platforms such as Facebook, Instagram, and Twitter have once again contributed to changes in the interest group system.

No longer does joining a group imply attending physical meetings or becoming a dues-paying or card-carrying member. Today, joining an interest group or participating in a social movement may be as simple as clicking a "like" button, signing an online petition, sharing on Facebook or Instagram, signing up for an e-mail listserv, or attending a meeting remotely, as has often been the case during the COVID-19 pandemic.

As a result, the way we understand interest groups and their role in American politics is also changing. Although groups still hold in-person marches and protests, the numbers of people attending these events pale in comparison to the number of supporters groups have online. Such was the case in 2011 with the Occupy Wall Street movement. Approximately 2,000 protesters gathered in New York City at the height of the movement, but tens of thousands were inspired to hold similar protests across the country, and millions liked the movement on Facebook or followed it on Twitter.

Interest groups are becoming more informal. Stalwart groups such as the Chamber of Commerce continue to play key roles in politics. But so, too, do nebulous interests organized around race, ethnicity, or class. During the 2016 elections, for example, candidates paid a great deal of attention to the "middle class." Though this group is based more on identity than formal membership, mobilizing a group of Americans around a shared goal and common policy objectives is precisely what interest groups have been doing since the nation's inception.

Despite these changes, all of the groups discussed in this chapter have one characteristic in common: they all want to shape the public agenda and advance their goals, whether by helping to elect candidates, maintaining the status quo, or obtaining favorable legislation or judicial rulings from national, state, and local governments.[30] For powerful groups, simply making sure that certain issues never get discussed may be the goal. In contrast, other groups succeed when an issue they care about becomes front-page news and citizens place pressure on government leaders to address it.

Groups succeed when they win legislation, court cases, or even elections individually or in coalition with other groups.[31] They also are successful when their leaders become elected officials or policy makers in any of the three branches of the government. For example, Representative Cori Bush (D–MO) is a Black Lives Matter activist. Jay Sekulow, the chief counsel at the American Center for Law and Justice and frequent advocate of conservative issues before the U.S. Supreme Court, was a member of President Trump's personal legal team, even defending him in his first impeachment trial.

Political scientists have studied several phenomena that contribute in varying degrees—individually and collectively—to particular groups' successes. These include leaders, funding and patrons, and a solid membership base.

Leaders

Interest group theorists frequently acknowledge the role of leaders in the formation, viability, and success of interest groups, while noting that leaders often vary from rank-and-file members on various policies.[32] Without the powerful pen of William Lloyd Garrison in the 1830s, who knows whether the abolition movement would have

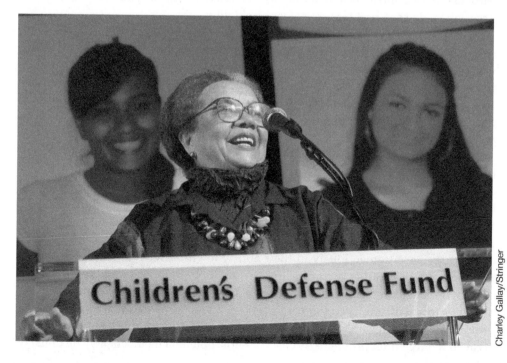

WHO ARE INTEREST GROUP LEADERS?

As president emerita of the Children's Defense Fund, Marian Wright Edelman continues to fight against child poverty and for better health care. Since founding the group in 1973, Edelman has been an active, public face for the cause she represents.

Charley Gallay/Stringer

been as successful? Other notable leaders include Frances Willard of the WCTU; the Reverend Martin Luther King Jr., who founded the Southern Christian Leadership Conference (now the Southern Leadership Conference); and Enrique Tarrio, chair of Proud Boys, a male-only group that supports many far-right ideas.

The role of an interest group leader is similar to that of an entrepreneur in the business world. Leaders of groups must find ways to attract members. As in the marketing of a new product, an interest group leader must offer something attractive to entice members to join. Potential members of the group must be convinced that the benefits of joining outweigh the costs. Union members, for example, must be persuaded that the union's winning higher wages and concessions for them will offset the cost of their union dues. Proud Boys must convince its members that they can successfully challenge election outcomes or breach Capitol security and take out their fury on institutions or government, as illustrated by their activities at the Capitol on January 6, 2021.

Funding and Patrons

Advertising, litigating, lobbying, and even protesting are expensive. Without financiers, few public interest groups could survive their initial start-up periods. To remain in business, many interest groups rely on membership dues, direct-mail solicitations, special events, and patrons. Charismatic leaders often are especially effective fundraisers and recruiters of new members. The Web has become a major source not only of campaigns but interest groups, too. Many now employ digital experts. In addition, governments, foundations, and wealthy individuals can serve as **patrons**, providing crucial start-up funds for groups, especially public interest groups.[33]

patron
A person who finances a group or individual activity.

Members

Organizations usually comprise three kinds of members. At the top are a relatively small number of leaders who devote most of their energies to the single group. The second tier of members generally is involved psychologically as well as organizationally. They are the workers of the group—they attend meetings, pay dues, and chair committees to see that things get done. In the bottom tier are the rank-and-file members who don't actively participate. They pay their dues and call themselves group members, but they do little more. Most group members fall into this last category. Their reasons for joining may be varied; some choose to participate because they feel a particular right is threatened, while others, such as lawyers who join the American Bar Association, do so in part for professional credibility.

Survey data have consistently revealed that group membership is drawn primarily from people with higher income and education levels.[34] Individuals who are wealthier can afford to belong to more organizations because they have more money and, often, more leisure time. Money and education also are associated with greater confidence that one's actions will bring results, a further incentive to devote time to organizing or supporting interest groups. These elites also are often more involved in politics and hold stronger opinions on many political issues.

People who do belong to groups often join more than one. Overlapping memberships can affect the cohesiveness of a group. Imagine, for example, that you are an officer in the College Republicans. If you call a meeting, people may not attend because they have academic, athletic, or social obligations. Divided loyalties and multiple group memberships frequently affect the success of a group, especially if any one group has too many members who simply fall into the dues-paying category.

Groups vary tremendously in their ability to enroll what are called potential members. As noted earlier, according to Mancur Olson, all groups provide a collective good.[35] If one union member at a factory gets a raise, for example, all other workers at that factory will, too. Therefore, those who don't join or work for the benefit of the group still reap the rewards of the group's activity. The downside of this phenomenon is called the **free rider problem**. As Olson asserts, potential members may be unlikely

free rider problem
Potential members who fail to join a group because they can get the benefit, or collective good, sought by the group without contributing the effort.

Jeffrey Isaac Greenberg 4+/Alamy Stock Photo

to join a group because they realize that they will receive many of the benefits the group achieves, regardless of their participation. Not only is it irrational for free riders to join any group, but the bigger the group, the greater the free rider problem. In a small group such as the National Governors Association, any individual's share of the collective good may be great enough to make it rational for him or her to join.

Groups attempt to overcome the free rider problem in numerous ways. One method used by many groups is providing a variety of material benefits to convince potential members to join. The American Automobile Association (better known as AAA), for example, offers roadside assistance and trip-planning services to its members. Similarly, AARP offers a wide range of discount programs to its members over the age of fifty. Many of those members do not necessarily support all of the group's positions but simply want to take advantage of its discounts. Other groups may overcome this problem by forming alliances that allow interests to work together to solve problems. Finally, patrons, be they large foundations such as the Koch Family Foundation or individuals such as wealthy financier George Soros, may also help to alleviate the free rider problem for public interest groups.[36] They make the costs of joining minimal because they contribute much of the group's necessary financial support.[37]

POLITICAL REFORM AND REALITIES: HOW ARE INTEREST GROUPS AND LOBBYISTS REGULATED?

14.7 Assess the effectiveness of regulations designed to control interest groups.

For the first 150 years of our nation's history, federal lobbying practices went unregulated. While the courts remain largely free of lobbying regulations, reforms have altered the state of affairs in Congress and the executive branch.

Regulating Congressional Lobbyists

In 1946, in an effort to limit the power of lobbyists, Congress passed the Federal Regulation of Lobbying Act, which required anyone hired to lobby any member of Congress to register and file quarterly financial reports. For years, few lobbyists actually filed these reports and numerous good-government groups continued to argue for the strengthening of lobbying laws.

By 1995, public opinion polls began to show that Americans believed the votes of members of Congress were available to the highest bidder. Thus, in late 1995,

Lobbying Disclosure Act

A 1995 federal law that employs a strict definition of lobbyist and establishes strict reporting requirements on the activities of lobbyists.

Congress passed the first effort to regulate lobbying since the 1946 act. The **Lobbying Disclosure Act** employed a strict definition of lobbyist (one who devotes at least 20 percent of a client's or employer's time to lobbying activities). It also required lobbyists to: (1) register with the clerk of the House and the secretary of the Senate; (2) report their clients and issues and the agency or house they lobbied; and (3) estimate the amount they are paid by each client. These reporting requirements made it easier for watchdog groups or the media to monitor lobbying activities, but they did little to reduce the influence of pressure groups in the Congress, where it is believed that some lobbyists are no longer registering.

In the wake of a variety of lobbying scandals, Congress attempted to remedy this problem by passing the **Honest Leadership and Open Government Act of 2007**. Among the act's key provisions were a ban on gifts and honoraria worth over fifty dollars to members of Congress and their staffs, tougher disclosure requirements, and longer time limits on moving from the federal government to the private lobbying sector. Many observers complained, however, that the law did not go far enough. In particular, many commentators were critical of the fact that the ban on gifts applied only to private lobbyists. Thus, state and local agencies and public universities, for example, are still free to offer tickets for football and basketball games, as well as to provide meals and travel.[38]

Honest Leadership and Open Government Act of 2007

Lobbying reform banning gifts to members of Congress and their staffs, toughening disclosure requirements, and increasing time limits on moving from the federal government to the private sector.

Regulating Executive Branch Lobbyists

Formal lobbying of the executive branch is governed by some restrictions in the 1995 Lobbying Disclosure Act as well as updates contained in the Honest Leadership and Open Government Act. Executive branch employees are also constrained by the 1978 Ethics in Government Act. Enacted in the wake of the Watergate scandal, this legislation attempted to curtail questionable moves by barring members of the executive branch from representing any clients before their agency for two years after leaving governmental service. Thus, someone who worked in air pollution policy for the Environmental Protection Agency and then went to work for the Environmental Defense Fund would have to wait two years before lobbying their old agency.

The Obama administration implemented reforms to bring congressional-style lobbying regulation to the executive branch. In regulations put into place on his first day on the job, Barack Obama limited aides leaving the White House from lobbying executive agencies within two years. He also banned members of the administration from accepting gifts from lobbyists. Via an executive order made in the early days of his administration, President Donald J. Trump announced an "ethics pledge" that banned people from lobbying those in the executive branch for whom they worked directly in the last two years, but allowed them to work elsewhere in the government immediately. He also reduced an Obama-era two-year ban on anyone contacting their former employers to one year. Even with this more generous standard, President Trump granted five times as many waivers of his executive order in his first four months than did President Obama, including waivers for several key members of his inner circle.

Regulating Judicial Branch Lobbyists

There are few formal regulations on interest group participation before the Supreme Court. Though interested parties must ask the Court for permission to file an *amicus curiae* brief, in practice, the great majority of these petitions are granted. In recent years, activists have called for reform to the case sponsorship and oral advocacy processes before the Court, but to no avail. Similarly, a number of nonprofit and good-government groups have suggested that additional restrictions are needed on groups' access to judges in "legal education" sessions—many of which are held at fancy resorts at little to no cost to the judges. Congress and the judiciary have also failed to put these regulations in place.

CONCLUSION AND REVIEW

What Are the Roots of American Interest Groups?

14.1 Explain the origins of interest groups in America.

An organized interest is a collection of people or groups with shared attitudes who make claims on government. Interest groups did not begin to emerge in the United States until the 1830s. From 1890 to 1920, the Progressive movement dominated.

How Did the Modern Interest Group State Develop?

14.2 Describe the beginnings of modern American interest groups.

The 1960s saw the rise of a wide variety of liberal interest groups. During the 1970s and 1980s, conservatives formed new groups to counteract those efforts. Business groups, corporations, and unions also established their presence in Washington, D.C., during this time.

Why Do Interest Groups Form?

14.3 Describe how interest groups form.

Political scientists approach the development of interest groups from a number of theoretical perspectives, including pluralist theory and the transactions approach. Interest groups can be classified in a variety of ways, based on their functions and membership.

What Types of Interest Groups Exist?

14.4 Identify the different types of political interest groups.

Several major categories of groups include public interest groups, business and economic groups, governmental units such as state and local governments, and political action committees.

What Do Interest Groups Do?

14.5 Analyze the methods and activities that interest groups use to influence political outcomes.

Interest groups often fill voids left by the major political parties and give Americans opportunities to make organized claims on government. The most common activity of interest groups is lobbying, which takes many forms. Groups routinely pressure members of Congress and their staffs, the president and the bureaucracy, and the courts; they use a variety of techniques to educate and stimulate the public to pressure key governmental decision makers. Interest groups also attempt to influence the outcome of elections. They may run their own candidates for office, rate elected officials, or form political action committees.

What Makes Interest Groups Successful?

14.6 Evaluate the factors that affect the relative success of interest groups.

Interest group success can be measured in a variety of ways, including a group's ability to get its issues on the public agenda, win key pieces of legislation in Congress or executive branch or judicial rulings, or back successful candidates. Several factors contribute to interest group success, including leaders and patrons, funding, and committed members.

Political Reform and Realities: How Are Interest Groups and Lobbyists Regulated?

14.7 Assess the effectiveness of regulations designed to control interest groups.

In 1995, Congress passed the Lobbying Disclosure Act, which required lobbyists to register with both houses of Congress. By 2007, a rash of scandals resulted in sweeping reforms called the Honest Leadership and Open Government Act, which dramatically limited what lobbyists can do. The executive branch is regulated by the 1978 Ethics in Government Act. Lobbying the judiciary is largely unregulated.

LEARN THE TERMS

Christian Coalition
Citizens United v. *Federal Election Commission (FEC)* (2010)
civic virtue
collective good
disturbance theory
free rider problem
Honest Leadership and Open Government Act of 2007

interest group
lobbying
Lobbying Disclosure Act
lobbyist
Moral Majority
National Rifle Association (NRA)
patron
pluralist theory
political action committee (PAC)

Progressive movement
public interest group
social capital
trade association
transactions theory

LEARN THE NAMES

Jerry Falwell
Pat Robertson

Geopix/Alamy Stock Photo

HOW DOES THE AFFORDABLE CARE ACT REFLECT THE POLICY-MAKING PROCESS?

Although first enacted a decade ago, the Affordable Care Act (known as the ACA or "Obamacare") remains controversial and continues to evolve. Here, Democratic presidential candidate Joe Biden speaks in June 2020 about his goal to "protect and build on" the ACA. Biden was vice president in 2010 and was involved with crafting the law and ensuring its passage by Congress.

CRITICAL THINKING QUESTION: *The Affordable Care Act (ACA) is an exceptionally complicated and contested law, yet it has endured for over a decade. What can the case of the ACA tell us about the nature of the making of social and economic policy in the United States?*

SOCIAL AND ECONOMIC POLICY

LEARNING OBJECTIVES

15.1   Trace the stages of the policy-making process.

15.2   Describe the scope of the federal budget, and analyze the problems associated with the national deficit and debt.

15.3   Assess the effectiveness of the monetary policy tools used by the federal government to manage the economy.

15.4   Describe current U.S. policy in health care.

15.5   Describe current U.S. policy in primary, secondary, and higher education.

15.6   Describe U.S. social welfare policy and programs.

15.7   Review ongoing challenges in U.S. social and economic policy making.

Affordable Care Act (ACA)
A 2010 law designed to ensure that nearly all Americans would have access to health care coverage, including those living in poverty.

The **Affordable Care Act**—also known as the ACA or "Obamacare"—was perhaps the most significant piece of legislation enacted by Congress over the last decade. Passed in 2010, the ACA largely accomplished what Democrats had sought since the days of President Harry Truman in the mid-twentieth century: the near-universal availability of health care throughout the country. Yet, the enactment of the ACA is a story of many challenges, compromises, and even near-death experiences, as well as a parable for the complexities of enacting major public policy changes in the United States.

Even with a staunchly committed president, House Speaker, and Senate majority leader, as well as substantial Democratic majorities in both houses of Congress, enactment of the ACA during the period 2009–2010 was far from assured. Some on the left advocated for a UK-style, government-run national health service; others preferred a "single-payer" system like that in Canada, where the government pays for all insurance costs. Many on the right saw the ACA as yet another example of overreach, overregulation, and excessive spending by "big government." Centrists argued in favor of a hybrid system, a view shared not only by President Barack Obama and Vice President Joe Biden, but also by 2012 Republican presidential nominee Mitt Romney, who as governor of Massachusetts had enacted a prototype of the ACA in his state. Any impulses toward comity and consensus were quickly sidelined, however, amidst partisan polarization. Fierce and unified opposition by Republicans and intense lobbying by entrenched insurance, health care, pharmaceutical, and other interest groups meant that the ACA barely made it through Congress.

The law was ultimately more modest in scope than some Democrats had desired—its major innovations were all incremental reforms. Still, some Republican governors refused to create insurance exchanges or to accept federal funding to expand Medicaid programs in their states. An inept rollout of the healthcare.gov Web site further soured opinions among an already skeptical public. And then two potent legal challenges began making their way up to the Supreme Court, with the law only narrowly surviving them.

Upon his election in 2016, President Donald J. Trump allied with Republican majorities in both houses of Congress that repeatedly committed themselves to "repeal and replace" Obamacare. And yet, a unified executive and legislative branch failed to repeal the ACA as a whole, although Republicans did manage to repeal the unpopular "individual mandate" that imposed a modest penalty on Americans who did not secure health insurance. A major problem for GOP officeholders is that while their supporters broadly endorse the "repeal" portion, there is no consensus about how to "replace" the ACA—especially some of provisions that are highly popular even among conservative voters. Despite Republicans' rhetoric, many of their proposals would amend the existing law rather than abolish it. For example, insurance companies would still be required to provide coverage for preexisting conditions and children could remain on their parents' insurance policies until age twenty-six.

The future of the ACA remains uncertain. Ironically, some of the law's most enduring detractors have been left-wing figures, such as U.S. Senator and presidential candidate Bernie Sanders, who have championed the original liberal vision of "Medicaid for All." Most Republicans remain uneasy with the law and aim to at least whittle away at its provisions.

In all, the ACA serves as a vivid example of the reality that once a major new public program becomes established in the United States—whether it be Social Security, Medicare, the Environmental Protection Agency, or the expansion of national security powers after the September 11, 2001, attacks—it eventually becomes understood to be part of the expected scope of government. Millions of Americans, including supporters of the Republican Party, have already come to rely on provisions of the ACA, suggesting that at least parts of many Republicans' least-favorite law are likely to remain in place. Two major events in November 2020 suggested that the ACA may indeed be safe for a while. Oral arguments at the Supreme Court for the latest challenge to the law suggested that the justices were unlikely to overturn the law. And of course, Joe Biden, an ardent supporter of the ACA, won the election to become the next president.

• • •

Public policy is an intentional course of action (or, sometimes, inaction) followed by government in dealing with some problem or matter of concern.[1] Individuals, groups, and even government agencies that do not comply with policies can face penalties of fines, loss of benefits, or even jail terms. The phrase "course of action" implies that policies develop or unfold over time. They involve more than a legislative decision to enact a law or a presidential decision to issue an executive order. Also important is how the law or executive order is carried out. The impact or meaning of a policy depends on whether it is vigorously enforced, enforced only in some instances, or not enforced at all. Government inaction, or the decision not to make policy, also defines public policy.

This chapter begins by discussing the policy-making process and examines how it has played out in five major areas of social and economic policy: monetary policy, fiscal policy, health, education, and social welfare. While myriad other policy areas exist, these five broad issue areas provide an overview of both the roots and reform of social and economic policy.

public policy
An intentional course of action or inaction followed by government in dealing with some problem or matter of concern.

WHAT ARE THE ROOTS OF THE POLICY-MAKING PROCESS?

15.1 Trace the stages of the policy-making process.

The Framers of the Constitution created a decentralized policy-making process with powers shared by Congress, the president, the courts, and the states. In addition, social forces, including public opinion toward the role and size of government and the divergent ideologies of political parties, constrain the development of government policies. In some areas, such as fiscal and monetary policy, the initiative usually takes place at the federal level. In areas such as health, education, and social welfare, policy making often begins at the state and local levels, where these "laboratories for democracy" set the stage for federal governmental action. The bureaucracy is also an important policy maker. Through a quasi-legislative process known as rule making, executive branch agencies formulate and implement policies in nearly every imaginable issue area. Rules, in fact, are the largest source of policy decisions made by the national government. Even the judicial branch, which the Framers thought would be largely powerless with regard to policy, has evolved into an important source of policy decisions. In recent years, the Supreme Court has made policy prescriptions in each of the domestic policy issue areas discussed in this chapter as well as in criminal justice, civil liberties, civil rights, and many other areas.

As issues evolve, which branch and level of government dominates can change over time. During the nineteenth century, the national government defined its economic role narrowly, although it did collect tariffs, fund public improvements, and encourage private development. Later, the federal government's involvement in domestic policy making shifted to include improvement of social and working conditions created by industrialization and an expanded focus on issues such as health care, welfare, education, and public safety. The Great Depression sparked clear changes in the federal government's role in fiscal, monetary, and other domestic policy making, specifically in the president's role in dominating that process. President Franklin Roosevelt's New Deal created the modern welfare state and the first entitlement programs: Social Security and Aid to Families with Dependent Children. From that point, the federal government has continued to expand its role in domestic policy. The federal government has tended to expand its reach further under Democratic administrations such as those of Lyndon Johnson and Barack Obama, but even Republican presidents, including Richard Nixon and George H. W. Bush, presided over expansions of the federal role in domestic policy. President Trump supported deregulation of business but even he did not reverse the overall trends of the past century. The Biden administration seems likely to represent a return to the conventional policies of the Democratic Party, albeit facing some unprecedented challenges stemming from the coronavirus pandemic and its economic fallout. An early sign of the ambitions of the Biden administration and a new Democratic majority in Congress was enactment in March 2021 of the landmark American Rescue Plan with $1.9 trillion in spending for COVID-related needs, economic stimulus, and poverty alleviation.

Theories of the Policy-making Process

Political scientists and other social scientists have developed many theories and models to explain the formation of public policies. These theories include elite theory, bureaucratic theory, special interest theory, and pluralist theory. According to elite theory, all societies are divided into elites and masses. The elites have power to make and implement policy, while the masses simply respond to the desires of the elites. Elite theorists believe an unequal distribution of power in society is normal and inevitable.[2] Elites, however, are not immune from public opinion, nor do they necessarily oppress the masses.

Bureaucratic theory dictates that all institutions, governmental and nongovernmental, have fallen under the control of a large and ever-growing bureaucracy that carries out policy using standardized procedures. This growing complexity of modern organizations has empowered bureaucrats, who become dominant as a consequence of their expertise and competence. Eventually, the bureaucrats wrest power from others, especially elected officials.

In contrast, according to special interest theory, narrow, specialized groups—not elites or bureaucrats—control the governmental process. Interest group theorists believe there are so many potential pressure points in the three branches of the national government, as well as at the state level, that interest groups can step in on narrow issues of particular concern to them.[3]

Finally, many political scientists subscribe to the pluralist perspective. This theory argues that political resources in the United States are scattered so widely that no single group or interest could ever gain monopoly control over any substantial area of policy.[4] Participants in every political controversy have the ability to weigh in; thus, each has some impact on how political decisions are made.

Which theory applies depends, in part, on the type of policy. Some policies are procedural in nature, incrementally changing existing policy, while others are substantive, involving bold revisions or innovation to change a policy outcome. Policy types can also be categorized as distributive, regulatory, or redistributive.[5] **Distributive policies** provide benefits to individuals, groups, communities, or corporations. These policies are the most common, and typically are the least controversial, form of federal action to solve public problems, providing tangible benefits to the recipient while costs are shared widely and not necessarily viewed as zero-sum. Examples include student loans, farm subsidies, and water projects. **Regulatory policies** limit the activities of individuals and corporations or prohibit certain types of unacceptable behavior. Land use regulations, for example, limit how property can be developed in order to protect the environment. These policies are typically more controversial because the costs are concentrated, in this case on developers, while the benefits are diffused, or shared by the larger community. **Redistributive policies** involve transferring resources from one group to assist another group. Most social welfare programs are intrinsically redistributive in nature, which is partly why they face considerable political opposition.

Although the policy-making process is often described in terms of stages or functional activities, the process is not necessarily sequential. One illustration of such a model is shown in Figure 15.1. This model can be used to analyze any of the issues

distributive policies
Public policies that provide benefits to individuals, groups, communities, or corporations.

regulatory policies
Public policies that limit the activities of individuals and corporations or prohibit certain types of unacceptable business practices.

redistributive policies
Public policies that transfer resources from one group to assist another group.

discussed in this book. Although models such as these can be useful, it is important to remember that they inevitably simplify the actual process. Moreover, models for analyzing the policy-making process do not always explain why public policies take the specific forms they do. Nor do models necessarily tell us who dominates or controls the formation of public policy.

Policy making typically can be regarded as a process of sequential steps:

1. *Agenda setting.* Government recognition that a problem is worthy of consideration for governmental intervention.
2. *Policy formulation.* Identification of alternative approaches to addressing the problems placed on the government's agenda.
3. *Policy adoption.* The formal selection of public policies through legislative, executive, judicial, and bureaucratic means.
4. *Policy implementation.* The actual funding and administration or application of public policies to their targets.
5. *Policy evaluation.* The determination of a policy's accomplishments, consequences, or shortcomings.

With this overview in mind, the chapter examines the various stages of the policy process or cycle.

FIGURE 15.1 WHAT ARE THE STAGES OF THE PUBLIC POLICY PROCESS?

One of the best ways to understand public policy is to examine the process by which policies are made. In this figure, the general process of policy making is broken down into five steps. Each step has distinguishing features, but it is important to remember that the steps often merge into one another in a less distinct manner.

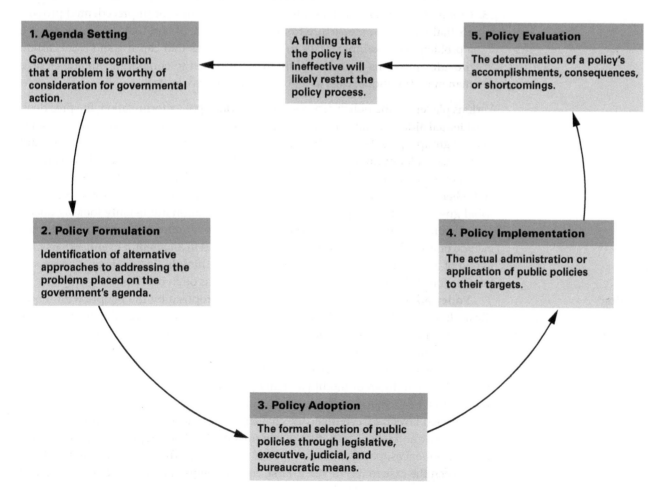

The Policy-making Cycle

systemic agenda

A set of of issues to be discussed or given attention; it consists of all public issues viewed as requiring governmental attention.

governmental (institutional) agenda

Problems to which public officials feel obliged to devote active and serious attention.

policy formulation

The crafting of proposed courses of action to resolve public problems.

An agenda is the set of issues to be discussed or given attention. Every political community—national, state, and local—has a **systemic agenda**. The systemic agenda is essentially a discussion agenda; it consists of all issues viewed as requiring public attention and as involving matters within the legitimate jurisdiction of governments.[6] A **governmental or institutional agenda**, in contrast, is much narrower. It includes only problems to which public officials feel obliged to devote active and serious attention. The movement of an issue from the systemic to the institutional agenda is known as *agenda setting*. John Kingdon has described this process as three streams—problems, policies, and politics—that must converge to create a policy window, or opportunity, for government action.[7]

Policy formulation is the crafting of proposed courses of action to resolve public problems. It has both political and technical components.[8] The political aspect of policy formulation involves determining generally what should be done to address a problem. The technical facet involves correctly stating in specific language what one wants to authorize or accomplish, to adequately guide those who must implement policy and to prevent distortion of legislative intent.

Policy formulation may take many forms:

1. *Routine formulation* is the process of altering existing policy proposals or creating new proposals within an issue area the government has previously addressed. For instance, the formulation of policy concerning government retirees is routine.

2. *Analogous formulation* handles new problems by drawing on experience with similar problems in the past or in other jurisdictions. What has been done in the past to cope with economic recession? How have other states dealt with child abuse or divorce law reform?

3. *Creative formulation* involves attempts to develop new or unprecedented proposals that represent a departure from existing practices and that will better resolve a problem. For example, plans to develop systems that capture and store carbon dioxide emissions represent a different approach to combating climate change than more traditional calls to reduce industrial activity itself.

Various players in the policy process may undertake policy formulation: the president, presidential aides, agency officials, specially appointed task forces and commissions, interest groups, private research organizations (or "think tanks"), and legislators and their staffs. Notably, under the U.S. federal system, the policy process is shared among the federal government; the fifty state governments; Washington, D.C., Puerto Rico, and other territorial governments; and thousands of city, county, and American Indian tribal governments. The people engaged in formulation are usually looking ahead toward policy adoption at their particular level of government. These individuals may include or exclude particular provisions of a proposal in an attempt to enhance its likelihood of adoption. To the extent that formulators think in this strategic manner, the formulation and adoption stages of the policy process often overlap.

policy adoption

The approval of a policy proposal by people with the requisite authority, such as a legislature.

Policy adoption is the approval of a policy proposal by the people with requisite authority, such as a legislature or chief executive. This approval gives the policy legal force. Because most public policies in the United States result from legislation, policy adoption frequently requires building a series of majority coalitions necessary to secure the enactment of legislation in Congress. To secure the needed votes, a bill may be watered down or modified at any point in the legislative process. Or the bill may fail to win a majority at one of them and die, at least for the time being. And even duly enacted laws may eventually be challenged in state and federal courts.

The slow and laborious nature of congressional policy adoption has some important consequences, particularly in times of partisan "gridlock" in Washington, D.C., as has been the case in recent years. First, complex legislation may require substantial periods of time to enact. Second, the legislation passed is often incremental, making only limited or marginal changes in existing policy. Third, there is no guarantee that even a program that has been authorized will always be fully funded through appropriations by Congress. Fourth, legislation is frequently written in general or ambiguous language, as in the Clean Air Act, which provided amorphous instructions to administrators in the Environmental Protection Agency to set air quality standards that would allow for an "adequate margin of safety" to protect the public health. Phrases such as "adequate margin" are highly subjective and open to a wide range of interpretations.[9] Language such as this may provide considerable discretion to the people who implement the law and leave them doubting its intended purposes.

Policy implementation is the process of carrying out public policies, most of which are implemented by administrative agencies. Some policies, however, are enforced in other ways. Voluntary compliance by businesses and individuals is one such technique. When grocers take out-of-date products off their shelves or when consumers choose not to buy food products after their expiration dates, voluntary compliance is at work. Implementation also involves the courts when they are called on to interpret the meaning of legislation, review the legality of agency rules and actions, and determine whether institutions such as prisons and mental hospitals conform to legal and constitutional standards.

policy implementation
The process of carrying out public policy.

Administrative agencies may be authorized to use a number of techniques to implement public policies within their jurisdictions. These techniques can be categorized as authoritative, incentive, capacity, or hortatory, depending on the behavioral assumptions on which they are based.[10]

1. *Authoritative techniques* for policy implementation rest on the notion that people's actions must be directed or restrained by government enforcement in order to prevent or eliminate activities or products that are unsafe, unfair, or otherwise contrary to the public and individual welfare.

2. *Incentive techniques* for policy implementation encourage people to act in their own best interest by offering payoffs or financial inducements for compliance with public policies. Such policies may provide tax deductions to encourage charitable giving or the purchase of alternative fuel vehicles, such as hybrid automobiles. Conversely, sanctions, such as high taxes, may discourage the purchase and use of products such as tobacco and liquor, and pollution fees may reduce the discharge of pollutants by making this action more costly to businesses.

3. *Capacity techniques* provide people with information, education, training, or resources that enable them to participate in desired activities. The assumption underlying these techniques is that people have an incentive or desire to do what is right but sometimes lack the capacity to act accordingly.

4. *Hortatory techniques* encourage people to comply with policy by appealing to their "better instincts" and thereby directing them to act in desired ways. In this instance, policy implementers assume that people decide how to act according to their personal values and beliefs.

Often, government will turn to a combination of authoritative, incentive, capacity, and hortatory approaches to reach its goals. For example, public health officials use all of these tools in their efforts to reduce tobacco use. These techniques include laws prohibiting smoking in public places, taxes on the sales of tobacco products, warning labels on packs of cigarettes, and anti-smoking commercials on TV. There is no easy formula that will guarantee successful policy implementation; in practice, many policies only partially achieve their goals.

Budgeting also influences policy implementation. When a policy is adopted, funding levels are recommended but must be finalized by another set of policy makers. Congress often separates the authorizations of new policies from the appropriations of funds so that debates over new policies do not delay or derail the national budgetary process. Whether a policy is well funded, poorly funded, or funded at all has a significant effect on its scope, impact, and effectiveness.

policy evaluation
The process of determining whether a course of action is achieving its intended goals.

Practitioners of **policy evaluation** seek to determine whether a course of action is achieving its intended goals. They may also try to determine whether a policy is being fairly or efficiently administered. Policy evaluation may be conducted by a variety of players, including congressional committees, presidential commissions, administrative agencies, the courts, university researchers, private research organizations, and the Government Accountability Office (GAO). The GAO, created in 1921, conducts hundreds of studies of government agencies and programs each year, either at the request of members of Congress or on its own initiative.

Evaluation research and studies can stimulate attempts to modify or terminate policies and thus restart the policy process. Legislators and administrators may formulate and advocate for amendments designed to correct problems or shortcomings in a policy. The evaluation process may also result in the termination of policies. Policies may also be terminated automatically through sunset provisions, or "expiration dates," that Congress can add to legislation.

The budgetary process also gives the president and the Congress an opportunity to review the government's many policies and programs, to inquire into their administration, to appraise their value and effectiveness, and to exercise some influence on their conduct.

Not all of the government's thousands of programs undergo full examination every year. But over a period of several years, most programs come under scrutiny. The demise of programs is relatively rare; more often, a troubled program is modified or allowed to limp along because it provides a popular service or is supported by a powerful organized interest group.

WHAT IS THE U.S. FISCAL POLICY?

15.2 Describe the scope of the federal budget, and analyze the problems associated with the national deficit and debt.

fiscal policy
The deliberate use of the national government's taxing and spending policies to maintain economic stability.

Fiscal policy is the deliberate use of the national government's taxing and spending policies to maintain economic growth and stability (see Figure 15.2 for breakdowns of federal spending for fiscal year 2020). Government spending, taxing, and borrowing are the principal tools used to expand or contract the economy as needed. Deficits or surpluses are the outcomes of these policy decisions. When government spending is not offset by tax revenue, the result is a deficit at the end of the fiscal year. If, however, tax revenue exceeds spending, the result is a government surplus.

national debt
The total amount owed by the federal government to its creditors, both domestic and international.

Economists argue that increased government spending stimulates economic growth, which can help the economy rebound from a recession. However, it also means that government is likely to run a deficit. The continuation of deficits long term, especially after the economy has recovered, can have adverse effects, including inflation and increased **national debt**. The national debt is the total amount owed by the federal government to its creditors, both domestic and international. Financing a large national debt reduces government savings and the amount of capital available for investment. As the debt grows, interest payments increase and must be offset by increases in tax revenues or decreases in spending. If investor confidence in the government's ability to manage its finances weakens, lenders will charge the government higher interest rates. High debt also reduces the government's ability to use taxes and spending to address fiscal crises in the future. The right combination of government spending and taxes is a constant source of debate, influenced by economic theory, history, politics, and public opinion.

The Foundations of Fiscal Policy

Prior to the 1930s, the U.S. government largely subscribed to a *laissez-faire* (literally "to allow to do" or "to leave alone") economic philosophy, which endorses a very limited role for government in the economy. In the late nineteenth and early twentieth century, Congress began to expand its oversight of new economic developments such as railroads and telecommunications. It also enacted antitrust laws to prevent large-scale monopolistic practices. But it was not until the New Deal—and President Franklin D. Roosevelt's response to the Great Depression—that the federal government played an increasingly interventionist role through financial reforms, agricultural policy, protection of laborers, and regulation of industry.

In the era of the Great Depression, British economist John Maynard Keynes revolutionized economic policy theory by arguing that spending by governments could prevent the worst impacts of **recession** and **depression** through increasing people's disposable income to encourage economic activity, even at the risk of running government deficits. This view represented a departure from *laissez-faire*, which suggested that if left alone, a free market would regulate itself. In contrast, proponents of **Keynesian economics** maintained that increasing demand would increase employment, stimulating a cycle of economic growth much faster than a free market would accomplish on its own.

The benefits of more immediate economic growth, they believed, outweighed the costs of government deficits in the short run. Governments could increase demand through increased government spending, tax cuts, or a combination of the two. Economists argued, however, that government spending would increase consumption and demand more directly than tax cuts. This is the case because people do not always spend their tax cuts; they often save the money or use it to pay down existing debt. The precise mix of government spending and taxes, however, is often dictated more by politics than economics.

laissez-faire
Economic philosophy that endorses a very limited role for government in the economy.

recession
A decline in the economy that occurs as investment sags, production falls off, and unemployment increases.

depression
A severe and long-lasting decline in the economy that occurs as investment sags, production falls off, and unemployment increases.

Keynesian economics
An economic approach first championed by economist John Maynard Keynes in the 1930s, who maintained that spending by government can stimulate economic growth much faster than a free market could on its own.

FIGURE 15.2   HOW DOES THE FEDERAL GOVERNMENT RAISE AND SPEND MONEY?

The federal government budget outlines how taxpayer revenues are raised and spent, summarizing the priorities of federal government policy making. These figures reflect federal government revenue inflows and expenditure outflows in fiscal year 2019. Total revenues were $3.5 trillion, while expenditures were $4.4 trillion, resulting in a deficit of $900 billion.

SOURCES: Data from the Congressional Budget Office: www.cbo.gov/publication/56324. Note that some small categories are not included in this chart, so figures do not sum to 100 percent.

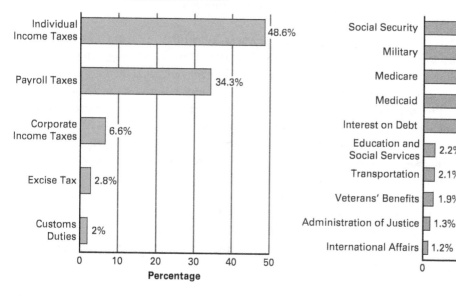

inflation

A rise in the general price levels of goods and services within an economy.

budget deficit

The economic condition that occurs when expenditures exceed revenues.

Budget deficits may have both positive and negative effects. Increases in government spending, if they remain in proportion to the overall economy, can stimulate economic activity. However, in the long term, running deficits year after year can have negative consequences. A high national debt such as this can stifle economic growth and cause **inflation**, a rise in the general price levels of an economy. The national debt accrues a huge burden of interest payments, which can divert attention and money from other governmental programs for years to come.

In the early 1960s, Democratic President John F. Kennedy, who was committed to getting the country moving again through the use of fiscal policy, brought economists to Washington, D.C., to study the issue. There emerged a consensus that greater government spending, even at the expense of an increase in the **budget deficit**, was needed to achieve full employment. This thinking is consistent with Keynesian economics; however, many conservatives opposed budget deficits as bad public policy. To appease these critics, the president's advisers decided that many Americans would find deficits less objectionable if they were achieved by cutting taxes rather than by increasing government spending. This decision resulted in adoption of the Revenue Act of 1964, which President Lyndon B. Johnson signed into law. The Act reduced personal and corporate income tax rates. The tax-cut stimulus contributed to the expansion of the economy throughout the remainder of the 1960s and reduced the unemployment rate to less than 4 percent, its lowest peacetime rate and what many people then considered essentially full employment.[11] The 1970s, however, were marred by the experience of so-called "stagflation" in which wages are stagnant but inflation increases due to outside factors, in this case the global price of oil.

During the 1980s President Ronald Reagan introduced "supply-side economics," which advanced the idea that deep cuts in the tax rates paid by high earners would stimulate new investment and economic growth. Therefore, *lower* tax rates would ultimately result in *higher* overall tax revenues by expanding the size of the economy and adding to the overall supply of jobs and goods for purchase. Likewise, under a related theory dubbed by its critics as "trickle-down economics," tax cuts targeted at the wealthy would create opportunities throughout the entire economy because the wealthy would then cause the private sector to grow and to create new and better-paying jobs. Reagan also endorsed cuts in spending on most nonmilitary programs and promoted an ideology of rolling back the level of government regulation of the economy. Despite the theory of supply-side economics, however, in practice the federal deficit expanded considerably during the Reagan era, due partly to lower tax revenues and partly to increased spending on defense.

After the Reagan era, there was a general turning away from supply-side economics to the more conventional view that tax revenues and government spending should be roughly on par, and that balanced budgets are to be desired. Indeed, for a brief time in the 1990s the federal budget was balanced. Early in the decade, this was due to President George H. W. Bush's willingness to endorse a tax increase; during the rest of the decade it was made possible through an accord struck between Democratic President Bill Clinton and a Republican-controlled Congress, facilitated by an era of peace (marked by scaled-down military spending following the end of the Cold War) and prosperity (caused in part because of the so-called dot.com boom). Such fiscal probity was fleeting, however, and was largely undone in the early 2000s by large tax cuts, the ever-growing costs of the wars in Iraq and Afghanistan, and the massive government spending required after 2008 to bail out failing financial institutions and provide stimulus spending for an economy mired in deep recession during the George W. Bush and Obama presidencies.

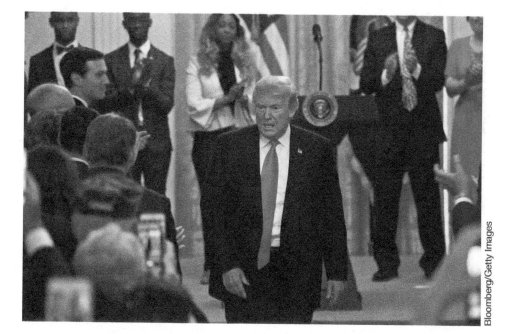

Bloomberg/Getty Images

HOW DO THE PARTIES DIFFER ON TAX CUTS?

In general, Democrats have historically favored higher federal taxation, especially on high earners and corporations. Republicans have preferred lower taxation, including President Trump, pictured here at an event in 2018 to mark the six-month anniversary of the Tax Cuts and Jobs Act.

A major economic development took place in December 2017, when President Trump signed the Tax Cuts and Jobs Act, which is in effect from January 1, 2018, to January 1, 2026. The bill lowered a number of tax brackets and amended the income thresholds at which the rates apply. Specifically, the bill decreases the top tax rate for high earners and ensures large tax cuts for corporations, with big business tax rates falling from 35 percent to 21 percent. The bill will increase the number of Americans who owe nothing in taxes from 44 percent to 47.5 percent, and generally under this plan most Americans will pay less in taxes until 2026.[12]

The National Deficit and Debt

While most of the fifty states are required by their state constitutions or laws to have a balanced budget—revenues must meet or exceed expenditures—this is not the norm for the federal government. The Constitution does not limit the annual deficit or the overall level of debt for the federal government. For most of the first 200 years of U.S. history, the federal government usually ran annual budget deficits only in times of war or economic downturns. As noted earlier, this pattern was broken in the 1980s, with peacetime deficits averaging $206 billion between 1983 and 1992. This increased the level of government debt from $789 billion in 1981 to $3 trillion in 1992.[13]

The federal government briefly ran surpluses again in the late 1990s, when the economy was experiencing an expansion due to the widespread use of the Internet and budget deals cut between Democratic President Bill Clinton and a Congress fully controlled by Republicans for the first time since the 1950s. However, a new pattern of extraordinary annual deficits resulted during the George W. Bush administration due to such factors as tax cuts, the wars in Iraq and Afghanistan, and expanded spending on homeland security.

In the fall of 2008, an economic recession and the collapse of the mortgage industry led to a cascading crisis that threatened the world's financial system. As the risk of a global economic depression grew, the federal government acted repeatedly to stimulate the economy and reinvigorate consumer spending through fiscal policy. Under both Presidents George W. Bush and Barack Obama, Congress enacted various

HOW HAS COVID-19 AFFECTED THE U.S. ECONOMY?

The COVID-19 pandemic devastated certain industries, among them commercial aviation as the number of Americans travelling both domestically and internationally plummeted amidst fears of infection aboard airplanes and in airports. In September 2020, the Association of Flight Attendants staged a rally in Chicago to urge Congress to provide further financial support to struggling airlines, and thereby to save their jobs.

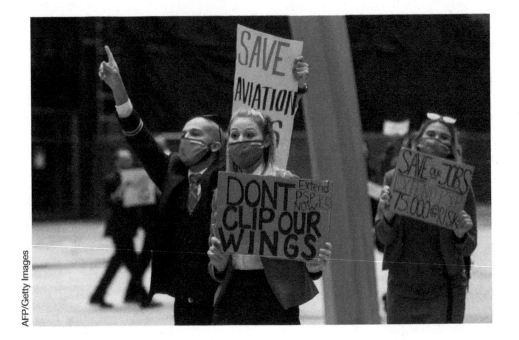

AFP/Getty Images

"bailout packages" for distressed banks, extended unemployment insurance, cut taxes, and raised spending. Prominent among these programs were the Troubled Assets Relief Program, which helped to stabilize American banks, and the American Recovery and Reinvestment Act, which authorized the more than $787 billion in spending on a variety of tax cuts and public works programs designed to stimulate the economy and to maintain and create jobs.[14]

In response to stubborn rates of unemployment, the federal government also extended and expanded unemployment benefits. However, in 2008 the federal government's debt also exceeded $10 trillion for the first time and in 2011 reached $14.2 trillion, which Congress had established by law as the limit on how much the U.S. government can borrow. By 2019, the national debt had increased to $22 trillion, more than 100 percent of **gross domestic product (GDP)**, or the total market value of all goods and services produced in a country during a year.[15]

gross domestic product (GDP)
The total market value of all goods and services produced in a country during a year.

The federal government's response to the economy—increased government spending plus tax cuts—fits the Keynesian model, and labor market indicators began to improve. The economy started to grow steadily by the third quarter of 2009, and employment increased. From a peak of 10.0 percent in October 2009, unemployment decreased to 8.1 percent by 2012, to 4.1 percent in 2017, and on to a low of 3.6 percent in January 2020. Immediately after this, however, unemployment rates temporarily quadrupled due to layoffs related to the COVID-19 pandemic. Concerns were widespread that a severe recession, or even a depression, might occur due to the suspension of economic activity during the early COVID period, including drastic contractions in industries including restaurants, entertainment, and aviation. As a result, the federal government enacted the $2.2 trillion Coronavirus Aid, Relief, and Economic Security (CARES) Act, which included a direct payment of $1,200 to many American households, an increase in unemployment pay for several months, and support for small businesses in order to avert further layoffs. As expected, however, the national debt also surged, reaching $26 trillion by the fall of 2020.[16] Nonetheless, some economic indicators continued to reflect economic optimism, the most notable being that on November 24, 2020, the Dow Jones Industrial Average stock market index exceeded 30,000 for the first time in its history, reacting to promising news about coronavirus vaccines alongside positive indicators about the transition to the Biden administration.

WHAT IS THE U.S. MONETARY POLICY?

15.3   Assess the effectiveness of the monetary policy tools used by the federal government to manage the economy.

Economic stability is also promoted through **monetary policy**, by regulating the nation's supply of money and influencing interest rates. The **Federal Reserve System** (informally, "the Fed"), especially its Board of Governors, handles much of the day-to-day management of monetary policy and is given a number of tools to aid its efforts.

The Federal Reserve System

Created in 1913 to adjust the money supply to the needs of agriculture, commerce, and industry, the Federal Reserve System comprises the Federal Reserve Board, the Federal Open Market Committee, the twelve Federal Reserve Banks in regions throughout the country, and other member banks.[17] Typically, the **Board of Governors** of the Federal Reserve System, a seven-member board that makes most economic decisions regarding interest rates and the supply of money, dominates this process. The board is designed to be politically independent.

The president appoints (subject to Senate confirmation) the seven members of the Board of Governors, who serve fourteen-year, overlapping terms. The president can remove a member who commits illegal activities, but this has never occurred. The president designates one board member to serve as chair for a four-year term, which runs from the midpoint of one presidential term to the midpoint of the next to ensure economic stability during a change of administrations. It also insulates monetary policy from being excessively influenced by political considerations. Federal Reserve chairs are among the most high-profile and powerful appointed officials in the nation, with wide-ranging influence over the U.S. economy. In 2017 President Trump nominated, and the Senate subsequently confirmed, Jerome Powell, one of the sitting governors appointed by President Obama, to be Fed chair for a four-year term.

The Tools of Monetary Policy

The primary monetary policy tools used by the Fed are open market operations, control of the discount rate, and the setting of reserve requirements for member banks. **Open market operations** are the buying and selling of government securities, or debt, by the Federal Reserve Bank. The Federal Open Market Committee meets periodically to decide on purchases or sale of government securities to member banks. When member banks buy long-term government bonds, they make dollar payments to the Fed and reduce the amount of money available for loans.

The Fed also influences interest rates through the **discount rate**, or the rate of interest at which it lends money to member banks. Lowering the discount rate encourages member banks to increase their borrowing from the Fed and extend more loans at lower rates. This practice expands economic activity, since more people should be able to qualify for car loans or mortgages if rates are lower. As a consequence of cheaper interest rates, more large durable goods (such as houses and cars) can be produced and sold.

Reserve requirements set by the Federal Reserve designate the portion of deposits that member banks must retain on hand. The reserves determine how much or how little banks can lend to businesses and consumers. When the Fed reduces the reserve requirements and allows banks to keep more funds on hand, it can free up additional money for loans and lower interest rates.

monetary policy
A form of government regulation in which the nation's money supply and interest rates are controlled.

Federal Reserve System
The organization in the United States tasked with such responsibilities as managing the money supply, stabilizing prices, moderating interest rates, and reducing unemployment.

Board of Governors
In the Federal Reserve System, a seven-member board that makes most economic decisions regarding interest rates and the supply of money; it is led by the Federal Reserve chair.

open market operations
The buying and selling of government securities by the Federal Reserve Bank.

discount rate
The rate of interest at which the Federal Reserve Board lends money to member banks.

reserve requirements
Government requirements that a portion of member banks' deposits be retained as backing for their loans.

In addition to these formal tools, the Fed can also use "moral suasion" to influence the actions of banks and other members of the financial community by suggestion, exhortation, and informal agreement. Because of its commanding position as a monetary policy maker, the media, economists, and market observers pay attention to verbal signals sent by the Fed and its chair with regard to economic trends and conditions.

During the economic crisis that began in 2008, monetary policy played a critically important function, in part because it can be easily implemented and has fewer long-term financial consequences than the deficit spending typified by fiscal policy. The Federal Reserve Board responded quickly to the economic slowdown, taking extraordinary action to lower interest rates and engaging in large open market operations and discount rate reductions to increase liquidity in the markets. The Fed also injected large-scale funds into the U.S. banking system by offering banks low-interest, one-month loans to ease the tightening credit conditions. It later took action to adjust mortgage lending rules and expand the commodities that U.S. markets could borrow against in order to increase the money supply in the market.

In addition to these traditional tools of monetary policy, the Fed has taken extraordinary measures designed to stimulate bank lending, including the purchase of mortgage-backed securities, credit easing, and quantitative easing (that is, increasing the amount of money in circulation). New regulations on capital leverage, risk management, and liquidity passed in the Dodd–Frank Wall Street Reform and Consumer Protection Act of 2010 attempt to reduce the risks associated with the international interconnectedness of large financial institutions.

Despite an ongoing economic recovery, the Fed continued to keep interest rates low in the hope of attracting borrowers who will inject money into the market. Among the factors the Fed considers are the interrelated variables of the unemployment rate and the inflation rate. By early 2018, the Fed had raised interest rates six times since the depths of the financial crisis, in small increments and following what Fed Chair Powell described as a "patient path." Concerned about a drop-off in investments due to the economic disruptions of the COVID-19 epidemic, however, the Fed decided in September 2020 to slash interest rates again, raising the expectation that they would remain low for the foreseeable future.

WHAT IS THE U.S. HEALTH POLICY?

15.4 Describe current U.S. policy in health care.

Under the U.S. system of federalism, states and localities traditionally had primary responsibility for public health issues, including public sanitation, clean water programs, immunization programs, and other activities designed to reduce the incidence of infectious and communicable diseases. However, the national government's involvement in health policy also extends to a range of policy areas. Many millions of people receive medical care through the medical branches of the armed forces and the hospitals and medical programs of the Department of Veterans Affairs and the Indian Health Service. In the 1960s, the government began funding health programs for senior citizens, poor people, and people with disabilities, known as Medicare and Medicaid, respectively. In a major expansion of the program, Medicare began to cover many costs of prescription drugs beginning in 2006. In 2010, the Democratic Congress passed, and President Barack Obama signed into law, the Affordable Care Act, which expanded the federal government's role in providing health insurance and in ensuring access to quality care. The federal government is also critical to the nation's response to public health challenges, including basic research, prevention of disease, and control of chronic illnesses.

Medicare and Medicaid

Medicare, which was created by Congress and Democratic President Lyndon B. Johnson in 1965, covers persons over age sixty-five without regard to income, medical history, or health status, as well as some younger people with disabilities. The program is administered by the Centers for Medicare and Medicaid Services in the federal **Department of Health and Human Services**. Today, Medicare provides health insurance coverage for more than 60 million Americans. Coverage includes many medical care services, including hospitalizations, doctor visits, prescription drugs, and other specialized care. In recent years, many liberal politicians have endorsed the idea of lowering the Medicare eligibility age or perhaps even making it universally available to everyone in the country.

Medicare costs made up nearly 15 percent of the federal budget in 2020, and the program also received support from payroll tax contributions (36 percent) and beneficiary premiums. Employees and employers share the cost of a 2.9 percent tax on the total amount of wages and salaries, with high-earning individuals earning paying slightly more. In 2020, Medicare benefit payments totaled $731 billion, up from $462 billion in 2008, a sign of an aging population.[18] **Medicaid**, a government program that subsidizes health insurance for poor people, and people with disabilities, was enacted in 1965, at the same time as Medicare. It provides health insurance coverage for low-income Americans who meet a set of eligibility requirements. To receive Medicaid benefits, citizens must meet minimum-income thresholds, have a disability, or be pregnant. As of 2020, Medicaid programs provided health- and long-term care coverage to more than 73 million low-income Americans, including nearly 7 million children.[19]

Unlike Medicare, which is financed and administered by the national government, Medicaid is a joint venture between the national and state governments. The hybrid nature of the program has caused tensions between federal- and state-level priorities and led to substantial state variation across states for the level of access to coverage and care for low-income Americans. The national government provides more than half of the funding necessary to administer Medicaid programs (depending on state per-capita income). This money is given to the states in the form of block grants. States then supplement the national funds with money from their own treasuries. They also are given the latitude to establish eligibility thresholds and the level of benefits available to citizens. The Affordable Care Act included provisions of a significant expansion of Medicaid to include all citizens and legal residents earning up to 133 percent of the poverty line; however, not all state governments chose to participate.

The Affordable Care Act

The Affordable Care Act (ACA) of 2010 marked the first truly major change in national health policy since the adoption of Medicare and Medicaid in 1965. A major priority of the Obama administration—to the point that its critics dubbed it "Obamacare"—the primary purpose of the ACA was to ensure that nearly all Americans would have access to health care coverage. This includes those living in poverty, who are eligible for special government subsidies. Other major features included allowing children to remain under their parents' health insurance coverage until age 26 and disallowing the long-standing practice of denying insurance coverage to individuals with preexisting conditions.

Medicare

The federal program established during Lyndon B. Johnson's administration that provides medical care coverage to elderly Social Security recipients.

Department of Health and Human Services

The cabinet-level department administering most federal social welfare and health-related policies and programs; it includes the National Institutes of Health (NIH), the Centers for Disease Control and Prevention (CDC), and the Food and Drug Administration (FDA).

Medicaid

A government program that subsidizes medical care for the poor and disabled.

The ACA established government-run health insurance exchanges financed by a number of taxes and fees, most notably an increase in the Medicare tax for individuals earning more than $200,000 per year. Americans had the option to buy into one of these exchanges or simply to retain their existing private health insurance. However, in one of its more controversial provisions, the ACA required by law that every American have some form of health insurance or else pay a fine. This "individual mandate" was necessary so that the overall pool of those purchasing health insurance would be large enough that the premiums of healthy people help to underwrite the costs of care to the smaller proportion of more seriously ill people.

In 2020, about nine out of ten Americans were estimated to have access to health insurance, closing one of the major gaps in health policy between the United States and other wealthy countries. However, many elements of the ACA have proven highly controversial. Some criticisms are ideologically based, arguing that the ACA was tantamount to a "government takeover" of the health care system and took control from the private sector. Others were practical, including higher-than-anticipated premiums and co-pays for some and the cost burdens placed on smaller businesses. Still other concerns were religious in nature, particularly objections by employers over requirements to provide access to birth control.

The ACA has been especially unpopular with state governments led by Republican governors and legislatures. These states believed that the Act is an infringement on states' reserved powers, and more than half of the states sued to block implementation of the policy. However, in 2012, the Supreme Court upheld the constitutionality of the individual mandate and again, in 2015, upheld the legal status of the health-insurance exchanges. Republican majorities in Congress and the Trump administration vowed to "repeal and replace" the ACA, but as with many government programs, the longer it is in place and the more people use its provisions, the harder it may be to completely eliminate. As a first step, the 2018 tax cut bill enacted by Congress repealed the individual mandate, creating uncertainty about the fiscal viability of the overall program moving forward, especially its ability to fully cover people with preexisting conditions. During the COVID-19 pandemic, Democrats argued for expansion of health coverage through the ACA, especially for those who lost employer-provided health coverage through layoffs and furloughs, which are unpaid leaves of absence for employees. The Trump administration and Republicans continued to consider the ACA a form of government overreach that had failed to contain spiraling health care costs, out-of-pocket expenses, high deductibles, and other costs borne by individuals.

Public Health

Government also plays a major role in curbing the spread of infectious disease and managing increases in chronic conditions. From HIV/AIDS and COVID-19 to drug abuse and obesity, public policy makers have attempted to use government power to fight threats to the nation's health. Among the government's tools are immunizations, education, advertisements, and regulations. For many contagious diseases, such as polio, measles, and chickenpox, the government requires immunization of young children if they are enrolled in day care, preschool, or elementary school. Public health officials also use vaccines in the adult population to manage the spread of diseases such as influenza (the flu). While not requiring citizens to receive flu shots, the government recommends that high-risk groups (infants, senior citizens) receive immunizations and subsidizes vaccines for low-income populations.

The national government also finances medical research, primarily through the National Institutes of Health (NIH). The National Cancer Institute; the National Heart, Lung, and Blood Institute; the National Institute of Allergy and Infectious Diseases; and the other NIH institutes and centers spend more than $40 billion annually on biomedical research. NIH scientists and scientists at universities, medical schools, and other research facilities receiving NIH research grants conduct the research. Another leading agency is the Centers for Disease Control and Prevention (CDC), which is tasked with the prevention and management of infectious disease, food- and water-borne pathogens, environmental health, occupational safety, injury prevention, and conditions such as obesity and diabetes. Likewise, the Food and Drug Administration plays an important regulatory role with regard to such substances as tobacco products, dietary supplements, pharmaceutical drugs, vaccines, food, cosmetics, and veterinary products.

An increasingly important area of public health involves interactions between humans and the environment. In response to alarm among scientists and an out-cry by the public, governments have increasingly taken steps to reduce the health problems associated with pollution by regulating industry. Starting in the 1970s, the United States initiated a large number of programs intended to stave off the harm-ful effects that pollution has on health and created the Environmental Protection Agency, which now serves as the primary environmental regulator in the country. These legislative accomplishments addressed myriad environmental concerns, most significantly water and air pollution. Still, many environment-related health threats persist, with one dramatic case being the discovery in the city of Flint, Michigan, of dangerously elevated levels of lead in the water supply, which is particularly danger-ous for children. This event spurred renewed focus on questions of "environmental justice," particularly considering that the residents of Flint were disproportionately low-income people of color.

The onset of the COVID-19 pandemic in 2020 laid bare both some of the strengths and weaknesses of the U.S. health care and public health systems, including the frequently not-well-coordinated roles of federal and state gov-ernments. A robust research agenda was initiated by the NIH, the nation's pre-mier set of biomedical research facilities, but the CDC, the flagship organization intended to promote public health, was widely viewed as providing technical support but not policy leadership.

Some aspects of health care, such as the requisitioning of ventilators to help patients with severe lung damage from coronavirus, proved more successful than initially feared. Other basic needs, such as personal protecting equipment (PPE) for health care workers, became snarled in inefficient supply chains unresponsive to the surge in nationwide demand. The federal government endorsed an "Operation Warp Speed" to hasten development of a safe and effective vaccine against coronavirus, even as plans remained unclear as to how the hundreds of millions of doses of vaccine would be delivered to the masses. Without a unified national agenda from Washington, D.C., implementation of public health measures became a patchwork of responses by individual states, counties, and cities. This reality allowed for not only local responses to specific epidemiological circumstances but also different strategies that sometimes conflicted with one another and were inconsistent across jurisdictional boundaries. The Biden administration indicated a different approach to the pandemic when President-elect Biden—who made a point of wearing a face mask throughout the campaign—undertook as his first act to appoint the members of a new coronavirus task force that heavily prioritized quick and efficient distribution of coronavirus vaccines as they became available.

HOW HAS GOVERNMENT RESPONDED TO THE PUBLIC HEALTH CHALLENGE OF COVID-19?

Caught off guard by the sudden onset of COVID-19, many public health agencies had to improvise to ensure that coronavirus testing could be scaled up while curbing additional spread of the virus in crowded health facilities. For example, Arlington County, Virginia, was one of many that set up outdoor testing sites in parking lots administered by workers in masks and PPE. Other new facilities had to be established late in 2020 to begin delivery of coronavirus vaccines.

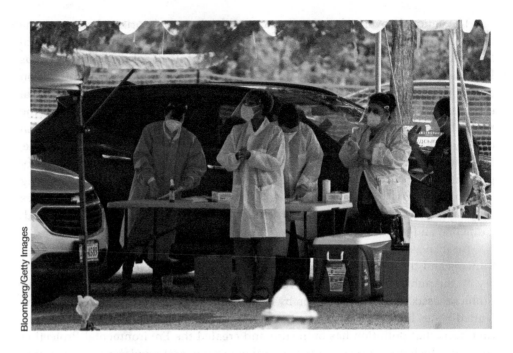

Bloomberg/Getty Images

WHAT IS THE U.S. EDUCATION POLICY?

15.5 Describe current U.S. policy in primary, secondary, and higher education.

Historically, the states have taken the lead in the field of public education. Following the Revolutionary War, reformers of that era, such as Benjamin Franklin, began to see education as a means of legitimizing democratic institutions in the minds of young people and of establishing social and political order in the United States. In 1852, Massachusetts passed the first compulsory education law, and by 1918 all states had similar laws. In the late nineteenth and early twentieth centuries, when immigration was at high levels, education again emerged on the governmental agenda as a tool for assimilating immigrants and for protecting social and political order. By the mid-twentieth century, the Cold War between the United States and the Soviet Union sparked new curriculum reforms focused on enhancing math and science programs.

At the same time, education policy making at the federal level shifted toward access and equality. The Supreme Court's landmark decision in *Brown* v. *Board of Education* (1954) ruled that separate educational facilities for Black and White students were inherently unequal. *Brown* established both the road map for racial desegregation in American schools and a national standard for equality of educational opportunity. As part of President Lyndon Johnson's War on Poverty, Head Start was initiated in 1964 to provide preschool to at-risk, low-income children, and the Elementary and Secondary Education Act of 1965 created Title I programs to improve educational opportunities for low-income K–12 students. These policies marked an important turning point in education policy. Enforcement of civil rights legislation—related to both race and gender, such as Title IX of the Education Amendments Act of 1972—required the national government to increasingly involve itself in directly in education.

Primary and Secondary Education

Policy making with regard to primary and secondary education in the United States represents an important example of the intertwining nature of American federalism, involving the active participation of the federal, state, and local governments, as well as many counties, American Indian tribal governments, and neighborhood school districts. As such, it highlights both the strengths of federalism, such as flexibility and grassroots participation, and the controversies, including the appropriate level of federal involvement and the allocation of a fair share of resources across lines of race, ethnicity, and socioeconomic status. Primary and secondary education also accounts for a modest proportion of overall federal government spending, but is the single largest budget item for state and local governments.

The most recent attempt at a major revision in the role of the federal government toward education was widely considered to have failed. The 2002 No Child Left Behind Act (NCLB) was designed to monitor student achievement in schools, paying special attention to disadvantaged student populations. The aim was to set high standards and establish measurable goals as a method of improving American education across states. However, disillusionment with NCLB grew over time, and in a rare show of bipartisan support in Congress, the law was replaced at the end of 2015 with the Every Student Succeeds Act (ESSA), which restores greater control to states over issues of accountability, teacher quality, and school improvement. ESSA also largely withdrew federal support for the **Common Core** State Standards Initiative, an ambitious plan to set nationwide standards for all primary and secondary school students that has been widely criticized for reinforcing a one-size-fits-all approach and overemphasizing rote learning over true comprehension.

Another area of controversy in educational policy has been the question of "school choice," which argues that if a child is attending a failing school, students and their parents should have the option to enroll at a more successful institution. In some cases, this may mean sending a child to another public school in the district or to a private school. One way to implement a school choice policy is through the use of **vouchers**, or certificates issued by the government that may be applied toward the cost of attending private or other public schools. The monetary value of these certificates usually correlates with the cost of educating a student in his or her local public school.

Parents may also choose to send their children to **charter schools**. Charter schools are semipublic schools founded by universities, corporations, or concerned parents. They have open admission and receive some support from the government; they may also receive private donations to increase the quality of education. The Trump administration, and in particular Education Secretary Betsy DeVos, tilted the support of the federal government toward charter schools, which they viewed as more effective vehicles for learning and as opportunities for parents to assert more control over their children's education.

Higher Education

Federal governmental policies toward higher education provide indirect support through funding of research grants and financial assistance to students. The federal government also funds academies for the U.S. Army, Navy, Air Force, Coast Guard, and Merchant Marine. Any school that receives federal funding (K–12 or higher education) must comply with Title IX of the Educational Amendment Acts of 1972, barring any discrimination on the basis of sex in admissions, student financial aid, or athletics.

The most prominent higher education policy focus in recent years has been on improving access to affordable higher education. In 2019, students graduated from higher education with an average debt of $37,000,[20] even though grants, based on financial need, do not require repayment. The Federal Direct Student Loan Program allows students and families to borrow money to pay for college, with repayment (with interest) deferred until a student graduates or leaves college. College work study programs, which provide part-time jobs to college students while enrolled in school, also rely on federal funding. Loans from private sources are also available to some students and families.

Common Core
A voluntarily adopted multi–state approach to setting standards that all students should achieve up through the high school level.

vouchers
Certificates issued by the government that may be applied toward the cost of attending private or other public schools.

charter schools
Semi-public schools that have open admission and receive some support from the government and may also receive private donations to increase the quality of education.

HOW DID TITLE IX CHANGE EDUCATION?

Title IX of the Education Amendments Act of 1972 greatly expanded educational and athletic opportunities for women. As a result of gender equity requirements, women's basketball programs have gained more prominence in recent years.

Over the past two decades, the overall level of higher education debt taken on by American students and their families has been rapidly increasing. Since 1989, inflation-adjusted tuition and fees more than doubled at four-year public institutions and increased by more than 50 percent at private four-year and public two-year colleges. Further, Americans on the whole have steadily been increasing the number of years of education that they complete. As a result, since 1989 the average debt levels of borrowers far outpaced both inflation and the increased earning potential created by such degrees. By 2019, outstanding student debt passed $1.5 trillion, collectively owed by nearly 50 million Americans. Education increases average lifetime incomes and contributes to the overall economy by increasing the level of job skills and, later, enhancing collection of tax revenue. All of this makes it a sound investment at both the personal and societal levels. However, some public policy analysts fear that a bubble in student debt could lead to widespread defaults and the need for a taxpayer bailout. A range of public policy responses have been considered, including expanding access to educational grants, cutting interest rates, and easing repayment terms. For example, the Department of Education's Pay As You Earn loan repayment plans caps student loan repayments at 10 percent of current discretionary monthly income.

Most recently, the disruptions caused by COVID-19 in schools at all levels all but ensure that local, state, and federal governments will have to find innovative ways to support education moving forward. This challenge is magnified the longer that restoring standard operating procedures in grammar schools, high schools, and colleges remains difficult or impossible. At the same time, COVID-19, like many crises, seems likely to accelerate certain underlying trends such as online education and distance learning, much as it is also doing in related areas such as employees working from home and health care providers using information technology to deliver "telemedicine," in which they engage patients remotely.

WHAT IS THE U.S. SOCIAL WELFARE POLICY?

15.6 Describe U.S. social welfare policy and programs.

Social welfare programs protect people against loss of income because of retirement, disability, unemployment, death, or absence of the family breadwinner. In 1780, for example, national legislation was passed to provide a pension to the widows of sailors. These programs, however, like many of the other issues discussed in this chapter, were not a priority for the federal government during much of its first 150 years. Beginning with the passage of the Social Security Act as a part of the 1930s New Deal, the government began to pay greater attention to this policy area. Today, the federal government administers a range of social welfare programs, so termed because they fall under the Constitution's goal to "promote the general welfare."

The Foundations of Social Welfare Policy

With the election of President Franklin D. Roosevelt in 1932, the federal government began to play a more active role in addressing the hardships and turmoil that grew out of the Great Depression. An immediate challenge facing the Roosevelt administration was massive unemployment, viewed as having a corrosive effect on the economic well-being and moral character of American citizens. An array of programs to put people back to work would, in Roosevelt's words, "eliminate the threat that enforced idleness brings to spiritual and moral stability."

A major legacy of the New Deal was the creation of the Social Security program. The intent of Social Security was to go beyond various "emergency" programs such as the Works Projects Administration and provide at least a minimum of economic security for all Americans. Passage of the **Social Security Act** in 1935 thus represented the beginning of a permanent welfare state in America and a dedication to the ideal of greater equity. The Act consisted of three major components: (1) old-age insurance (what we now call Social Security); (2) public assistance for the needy, aged, blind, and families with dependent children (known as SSI); and (3) unemployment insurance and compensation. Since that time, the program has expanded to include a much greater percentage of American workers. It has also become one of the most successful government programs. In the 1930s, poverty rates were highest among the elderly. Today, seniors aged sixty-five or older have the lowest rate of poverty among any age group in the United States. Still, changing demographics, most notably an aging population, present ongoing challenges to the maintenance of sufficient levels of support for seniors.

Social Security Act
A 1935 law that established old-age insurance; assistance for the needy, aged, blind, and families with dependent children; and unemployment insurance.

Social Welfare Programs Today

Modern social welfare programs help a wide variety of citizens to survive in cases of unintentional loss of income. They also help people with disabilities, low-income people, and elderly people to make ends meet and provide a minimally decent standard of living for themselves and their families. In 2020, the federal poverty threshold for a four-person family unit was $26,200 in most of the United States.[21]

Many social welfare programs are **entitlement programs**, government benefits which all citizens meeting eligibility criteria—such as age, income level, or unemployment—are legally entitled to receive. Unlike programs such as public housing, military construction, and space exploration, spending for entitlement programs is mandatory and places a substantial ongoing obligation on the federal budget.

Some of these are **non–means-tested programs** that provide cash assistance to qualified beneficiaries, regardless of income. Contributions are made by or on behalf of the prospective beneficiaries, their employers, or both. When a person becomes eligible for benefits, he or she is paid as a matter of right, regardless of wealth or unearned income. Sometime referred to as "social insurance" programs, these include programs for old age, survivors, and disability insurance (Social Security) and unemployment insurance. In contrast, **means-tested programs** require people to have incomes below specified levels to be eligible for benefits. Benefits of means-tested programs may come either as cash or in-kind benefits, such as help with finding employment or child care. Included in the means-tested category are the Supplemental Security Income program and the Supplemental Nutrition Assistance Program (SNAP, sometimes still

entitlement programs
Government benefits that all citizens meeting eligibility criteria—such as age, income level, or unemployment—are legally "entitled" to receive; these are also referred to as non-means-tested programs.

non–means-tested programs
Programs that provide cash assistance to qualified beneficiaries, regardless of income; among these are Social Security and unemployment insurance.

means-tested programs
Programs requiring beneficiaries to have incomes below specified levels to be eligible for benefits; among these are Social Security Insurance (SSI), Temporary Aid to Needy Families (TANF), and the Supplemental Nutrition Assistance Program (SNAP).

President Franklin Delano Roosevelt
is portrayed as Dr. New Deal trying
several remedies for an ailing Uncle
Sam; Congress is portrayed as a nurse
following the doctor's orders. The role
of the federal government in domestic
policy making was revolutionized
during the 1930s in response to
the social dislocations of the Great
Depression.

known as "food stamps"). Temporary Assistance for Needy Families (TANF) is also
means-tested, but the program is not an entitlement. States are given discretion to
determine TANF eligibility and benefits.

OLD AGE, SURVIVORS, AND DISABILITY INSURANCE   As mentioned earlier,
the Social Security program is a non–means-tested program that began as old-age
insurance, providing benefits only to retired workers. Its coverage was extended to
survivors of covered workers in 1939 and to people with permanent disabilities in
1956. Nearly all employees and most of the self-employed are now covered by Social
Security. Americans born before 1938 are eligible to receive full retirement benefits at
age sixty-five. The full retirement age gradually rises until it reaches sixty-seven for
persons born in 1960 or later. In 2020, the average monthly Social Security benefit for
retired workers was $1,503, with the maximum monthly benefit of $3,011 for workers
who retire the at the full retirement age of 66.[22]

Social Security is not, as many people believe, a pension program that collects
contributions from workers, invests them, and then returns them with interest to beneficiaries. Instead, current workers pay employment taxes that go directly toward providing benefits for retirees. In 2020, for example, a tax of 6.2 percent was levied on the
first $132,900 of an employee's wages and placed into the Social Security Trust Fund.
An additional 6.2 percent tax was levied on employers.[23]

As a result of this system, in recent years, it has become increasingly apparent
that the current Social Security system is on a collision course with itself. Americans
are living longer and having fewer children. And beginning in 2010, the exceptionally large age cohort of the Baby Boom generation (roughly speaking, those born in
the two decades immediately following World War II) began to retire. These factors,
taken together, skew the number of working Americans per retiree, and lead the
Social Security system toward financial insolvency unless Congress acts to update
the system.

UNEMPLOYMENT INSURANCE Unemployment insurance is a social insurance program financed by a payroll tax paid by employers. The program benefits full-time employees of companies of four or more people who become unemployed through no fault of their own. Unemployed workers who have been fired for professional faults or who have quit their jobs, or those who are unwilling to accept suitable employment, do not receive benefits.

State governments administer unemployment insurance programs. As a result, unemployment programs differ a great deal in levels of benefits (see Figure 15.3). For example, as of May 2020, average weekly benefit payments ranged from $190 in Oklahoma to up to $2,153 in Washington state. During the middle of 2020, the federal government began augmenting states' base rate of insurance as a cushion against unemployment caused by the COVID-19 pandemic.[24]

In January 2020, just before the start of the coronavirus-related spike in unemployment, the national unemployment rate stood at 3.6 percent, but differences were considerable across the country. In North Dakota, South Carolina, and Vermont, the unemployment rate was below 2.5 percent, while Alaska was at 6.0 percent; and Louisiana, Mississippi, and West Virginia were at or above 5.0 percent. Unemployment rates also varied quite a bit across races and by age. For example, the level of unemployment for African Americans has often been was significantly higher than the national average.

SUPPLEMENTAL SECURITY INCOME The Supplemental Security Income (SSI) program is a means-tested program that began under the Social Security Act as a government benefit for needy elderly or blind citizens. In 1950, Congress extended coverage to needy people who were permanently and totally disabled. The federal government,

---

FIGURE 15.3   HOW DO STATE UNEMPLOYMENT RATES VARY?

Rates of unemployment vary considerably across states, as does the duration of temporary unemployment insurance. This graphic shows the unemployment rate in each state (and Washington, D.C.) in January 2020, just prior to the start of a surge in unemployment related to the COVID-19 pandemic. The majority of states offer a half-year (26 weeks) of unemployment benefits, although in 2020 these were extended nationwide through the federal CARES Act and in 2021 through the American Rescue Plan.

SOURCE: National Council of State Legislatures, www.ncsl.org/research/labor-and-employment/state-unemployment-update.aspx.

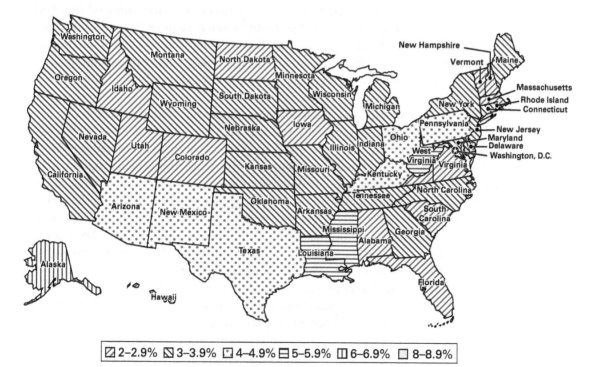

which provides primary funding for SSI, prescribes minimum national benefit levels. The states may also choose to supplement national benefits, and forty-six states take advantage of this option.

To be eligible for SSI, beneficiaries can have only a very limited income; the lower an individual's income, the higher the SSI payment. SSI beneficiaries may also have only a limited number of possessions. For example, the total of an individual's personal resources, excluding certain assets such as a home, cannot exceed $2,000.

FAMILY AND CHILD SUPPORT The Aid to Dependent Children program is a means-tested program first established as part of the Social Security Act in 1935. In 1950, it was broadened to include not only dependent children without fathers but also the mothers or other adults with whom dependent children were living. At this time, it was retitled the Aid to Families and Dependent Children (AFDC) program. As a result of this change and changes in the American family (including a rise in the birthrate to unwed mothers and a rise in the divorce rate), the family and child support rolls expanded significantly in the latter part of the twentieth century.

By the 1990s, the growth of this program began to attract widespread criticism from many conservatives and moderates, including Democratic President Bill Clinton. Critics pointed to the rising number of recipients and claimed that the AFDC program undermined family structures, encouraged dependency, and resulted in a semipermanent class of people dependent on welfare. In what is regarded as the biggest shift in social welfare policy in decades, a new family and child support program called Temporary Assistance for Needy Families (TANF) was created to replace AFDC. TANF switched the funding of welfare from an open-ended matching program to a block grant to the states, which were also given more flexibility in reforming their welfare programs toward work-oriented goals. The success of the TANF program has been widely debated. The total number of Americans receiving benefits has fallen, in part because states have found ways to minimize the number of TANF recipients. Little evidence supports the success of the program in job training or as a means of reducing economic and social inequality. Despite these shortcomings, the program has continued to operate.[25]

SUPPLEMENTAL NUTRITION ASSISTANCE PROGRAM The first attempt at this means-tested program (1939–1943), which is more commonly known as food stamps, was primarily an effort to expand domestic markets for farm commodities. Food stamps provided poor people with the ability to purchase more food, thus increasing the demand for American agricultural produce. Attempts to reestablish the program during the Eisenhower administration failed, but in 1961, a pilot program began under the Kennedy administration. It became permanent in 1964 and extended nationwide in 1974.

The method of delivering the food stamp benefit has changed dramatically over time. For much of the program's history, the benefit was administered as actual paper coupons—quite literally, food "stamps"—given to citizens who were eligible for relief. Today, the program is administered entirely using an electronic debt program, much like an ATM card. This change in administration necessitated a formal name change for the program—from food stamps to the Supplemental Nutrition Assistance Program (SNAP)—in 2008. Still, this benefit continues to be an important means of ensuring income security. In a typical month in 2019, nearly 40 million Americans received SNAP aid. In 2020, the average participant received about $125 worth of assistance per month, or not quite $1.40 per meal.[26] In addition to SNAP, the national government operates several other food programs for the needy. These programs include a special nutritional program for women, infants, and children, known as WIC; a school breakfast and lunch program; and an emergency food assistance program.

POLITICAL REFORM AND REALITIES: ONGOING CHALLENGES IN SOCIAL AND ECONOMIC POLICY MAKING

15.7 Review ongoing challenges in U.S. social and economic policy making.

Social and economic policy has a long and complex history in the United States, as has been discussed in this chapter. However, in each of the issue areas considered, public policy challenges have yet to be solved. Some Americans are not yet covered by health insurance, implementation of education reforms has not met goals for standards and performance, and income inequality remains at historically high levels. Innovative, bold solutions to problems, however, are difficult to achieve in a decentralized policy-making process. Ultimately, which group dominates the process varies by issue. The elite theory, bureaucratic theory, special interest theory, and pluralist theory are useful models for understanding the politics of domestic policy making. It is also important to understand that each stage of the policy-making process presents both opportunities and barriers to change. At the agenda-setting stage, rarely do all three streams—problems, policies, and politics—converge to open a policy window. In addressing education reform, for example, the competing values of local control versus national standards make it difficult to gain consensus on a solution. Policy often is formulated in the context of uncertainty. Policy makers do not always have complete information on the long-term costs and benefits of proposed policy solutions. As a result, incrementalism often describes the policy adoption stage. The exception is at times of crisis, such as that provoked by the 2008 financial crisis or the 2020 COVID-19 pandemic, in which governments engage in a flurry of improvisation to blunt the impact on the overall economy and the livelihoods of individual Americans.

At the implementation stage, policies can change shape as they are carried out day to day by the bureaucracy. As schools implemented new standards and changed the content and delivery of information to K–12 students, feedback from parents, teachers, and others led to calls for further reform. Policies also are constantly subject to challenge, in routine evaluations and budget allocations, or in constitutional challenges in the courts. Challenges to the Affordable Care Act have repeatedly jeopardized full implementation of Obama's health care initiative.

As new policy concerns rise, the policy-making cycle starts over again. At the same time, this process has limits. Political scientists have described an issue attention cycle in which problems are easier to address when a crisis or critical mobilizing event captures the public's attention. As the problem is addressed, or the shocking nature of the crisis fades, the public loses interest. Sometimes, realization dawns that no easy solution is possible, or that the costs outweigh benefits. Incremental steps toward solving the problem, or just the perception that something is going to be done, can also shift the public's attention to another issue. Once the intensity of public interest fades, comprehensive policy making is much more difficult to achieve.

The shift to a new presidential administration, particularly when the hand-off of power is from one party to another, is always a time for new directions. As president, Joe Biden has promised to return to many of the policy approaches and priorities of the Obama era. But no new presidency is ever simply a reversion to a former status quo. New challenges, typified by the coronavirus pandemic but not limited to it, will inevitably require novel approaches and altered directions for the work of government.

CONCLUSION AND REVIEW

What Are the Roots of the Policy-making Process?

15.1 Trace the stages of the policy-making process.

Public policy is an intentional course of action or inaction followed by government in dealing with some problem or matter of concern. A popular model used to describe the policy-making process views it as a sequence of stages that include agenda setting, policy formulation, policy adoption, policy implementation, and policy evaluation. Although this model can be useful, it is a simplification of the actual process, and it does not always explain why policies take the forms they do or who controls the formation of public policy. Approaches to explaining policy-making outcomes include elite, bureaucratic, special interest, and pluralist theories.

What Is the U.S. Fiscal Policy?

15.2 Describe the scope of the federal budget, and analyze the problems associated with the federal deficit and debt.

Fiscal policy is the deliberate use of the national government's taxing and spending policies to maintain economic stability and promote prosperity. Many factors influence fiscal policy, including concerns about unemployment, inflation, and the risk of recession or depression. The federal government has generally run a budget deficit, which can have negative consequences for the economy over the long term. The overall national debt has also been rising for more than three decades, which has been exacerbated in recent years due to the combined effects of tax cuts, increased military and national security spending, the 2008–2009 bailout and stimulus bills, and the federal response to the COVID-19 pandemic.

What Is the U.S. Monetary Policy?

15.3 Assess the effectiveness of the monetary policy tools used by the federal government to manage the economy.

Monetary policy is a form of government regulation through which the nation's money supply and interest rates are controlled. In 1913, the federal government created the Federal Reserve System ("the Fed"), which handles much of the day-to-day management of monetary

policy. It has a number of tools to aid its efforts, including open market operations, which involve the buying and selling of government securities by the Federal Reserve Bank in the securities market; control of the discount rate, or the rate of interest at which the Federal Reserve Board lends money to member banks; and the ability to set reserve requirements, or government requirements that a portion of member banks' deposits be retained as backing for their loans.

What Is the U.S. Health Policy?

15.4 Describe current U.S. policy in health care.

Government in the United States has a long history of involvement in the health of Americans. Beginning in the 1960s, the government began to fund health programs for senior citizens and poor people, known as Medicare and Medicaid, respectively. In 2010, after several failed attempts by prior administrations, the Democratic Congress passed and President Barack Obama signed the Affordable Care Act, expanding the national government's role in providing health insurance. The U.S. government also plays a prominent role in public health through agencies such as the National Institutes of Health, the Centers for Disease Control and Prevention, and the Food and Drug Administration. These and other agencies were faced with an extensive set of new challenges by the onset of the COVID-19 pandemic.

What Is the U.S. Education Policy?

15.5 Describe current U.S. policy in primary, secondary, and higher education.

Education policy in the United States has been a work in progress for more than two centuries, and reform has focused on social and political order, individual liberty, and social and political equality. Recent efforts at educational reform, including the No Child Left Behind program and the Common Core curriculum, have been controversial and had only limited impacts. Higher education is supported by the federal government in the form of grants and low-interest student loans. Due to rising costs, reforms have been made to limit the amount of debt students must repay.

What Is the U.S. Social Welfare Policy?

15.6 Describe U.S. social welfare policy and programs.

Social welfare programs protect people against loss of income. These programs also serve as automatic stabilizers, increasing government spending during economic crises. Social welfare policy was not a priority for the federal government until the 1930s, when it passed the Social Security Act. Today, the federal government administers a range of social welfare programs that fall into two major areas: non–means-tested and means-tested programs. Non–means-tested programs provide cash assistance to qualified beneficiaries regardless of income; they include old age, survivors, and disability insurance; and unemployment insurance. Means-tested programs require that people have incomes below specified levels to be eligible for benefits; they include Supplemental Security Income, family and child support, and the Supplemental Nutrition Assistance Program (food stamps).

Political Reform and Realities: Ongoing Challenges in Social and Economic Policy Making

15.7 Review ongoing challenges in U.S. social and economic policy making.

Policy making in the United States is a decentralized process that makes it difficult to pass comprehensive reform. Each of the domestic policy areas highlighted in this chapter illustrates the forces that create opportunities for and constraints on change. Each of the five stages of policy making—agenda setting, policy formulation, policy adoption, policy implementation, and policy evaluation—presents an additional hurdle for policies to survive. Often, it takes policy entrepreneurs or crises to elevate an issue to national attention and force governmental action. Still, most policy making takes place in a context of uncertainty. The nature of problems also constantly evolves, and the policy cycle repeats itself continuously. The issue attention cycle suggests, however, is that the country's attention does not stay focused on any one problem for very long.

LEARN THE TERMS

Affordable Care Act (ACA)
Board of Governors
budget deficit
charter schools
Common Core
Department of Health
   and Human Services
depression
discount rate
distributive policies
entitlement programs
Federal Reserve System
fiscal policy

governmental (institutional)
   agenda
gross domestic product (GDP)
inflation
Keynesian economics
laissez-faire
means-tested programs
Medicaid
Medicare
monetary policy
national debt
non–means-tested programs
open market operations

policy adoption
policy evaluation
policy formulation
policy implementation
public policy
recession
redistributive policies
regulatory policies
reserve requirements
Social Security Act
systemic agenda
vouchers

AFP/Getty Images

HOW DOES THE PRESIDENT LEAD ON FOREIGN POLICY?

President Ronald Reagan speaks in 1987 at the Brandenburg Gate in Berlin, near the Berlin Wall, issuing a challenge to Soviet leader Mikhail Gorbachev to "tear down this wall." Presidents have numerous powers that enable them to play the lead role on relations with other nations.

CRITICAL THINKING QUESTION: The United States has been the world's most powerful country for several decades. What opportunities and challenges does this present for the U.S. government and its citizens?

FOREIGN AND DEFENSE POLICY

LEARNING OBJECTIVES

16.1	Outline the major events and issues in the development of U.S. foreign and defense policy.
16.2	Describe the roles of government officials and of other influences on U.S. foreign and defense policy.
16.3	Evaluate major foreign and defense policy challenges now facing the United States.
16.4	Understand emerging challenges that are shaping U.S. foreign and defense policies in four key geographic regions.

I n the decade between 1991 and 2001, the United States experienced a unique "unipolar moment" in which it was the world's sole superpower. This era was a time in which it seemed possible that the major remaining challenges to capitalism, western democracy, and America's global leadership role had been swept aside. One essayist famously even termed it "the end of history" in the sense that the major ideological and political disagreements dividing the globe had been essentially resolved.[1]

This unipolar moment had been nearly a half century in the making. Since the end of World War II, the United States had led the democratic West in the long, tense stand-off known as the Cold War. Its principal adversary was the Union of Soviet Socialist Republics (also called the USSR or simply the Soviet Union) and its bloc of allies. For decades, there was deep uncertainty about which side would prevail—or even whether both sides, and much of the rest of the world, would be reduced to rubble in an exchange of nuclear weapons.

Then in November 1989, authorities in Communist-controlled East Germany permitted the opening of the Berlin Wall, which had long divided the two halves of Berlin and was the ultimate symbol of the post-World War II division of the European continent. The removal of the wall had been called for by U.S. President Ronald Reagan the prior year, and marked the culmination of a reform process in the USSR and its satellite states that had unexpectedly turned into a revolutionary process. Within a year, the two halves of Germany would go on to be reunified; just over two years later, the Soviet Union itself ceased to exist. Much of the democratic world felt a wave of both euphoria and relief that the Cold War was over.

The 1990s were a time of triumph for U.S. foreign and defense policy. The Soviet Union's principal successor state, Russia, sought integration rather than confrontation with the rest of the world. The NATO military alliance expanded into the former Soviet sphere of influence, and other regional conflicts began to be resolved in places such as South Africa, Nicaragua, and Northern Ireland. The United Nations authorized coordinated worldwide military action to reverse the occupation of the nation of Kuwait by neighboring Iraq. Globalization of trade relations expanded, and the then-nascent World Wide Web promised to bring the world closer, with English increasingly serving as a worldwide lingua franca.

But the unipolar moment would prove short-lived. The devastating terrorist attacks of September 11, 2001, jolted the United States into an awareness that it still had many ideological enemies and military threats from abroad. The subsequent American-led invasions of Iraq and Afghanistan proved the ability of the United States to topple enemy regimes but also revealed its inability to clearly "win the peace" that followed such incursions. Challengers old and new, such as Russia, China, and North Korea, became increasingly assertive on the world stage, even as U.S. allies in Europe and Japan struggled with their own economic and social problems. It soon became clear that while the twenty-first-century challenges facing U.S. foreign and defense policy would look quite different from those of the twentieth century, the world was not in fact any closer to the "end of history."

• • •

Although popular and governmental opinions on the role of the United States in the world have changed dramatically in the past two and a half centuries, many fundamental challenges remain the same. Should the United States, for example, isolate itself from other nations or become engaged in international conflicts? When do diplomatic solutions fall short, necessitating warfare? And how do economic policies at home and abroad affect these relationships?

Evaluating the potential strengths and weaknesses of U.S. foreign policy today starts with acquiring a broad understanding of the roots of past foreign and defense policies and the political forces that have shaped them. We must also look closely at the key issues confronting the United States as it attempts to address emerging issues in foreign and defense policy.

WHAT ARE THE ROOTS OF U.S. FOREIGN AND DEFENSE POLICY?

16.1 Outline the major events and issues in the development of U.S. foreign and defense policy.

Foreign and defense policy are two separate areas of policy making. **Foreign policy** relates to how one country (referred to as a state by political scientists) builds relationships with other countries to safeguard its national interests. **Defense policy** comprises the strategies a country uses to protect itself from its enemies. However, foreign policy and defense policy are interrelated. Countries use defense policy for many problems that are better addressed by well-planned foreign policy, and a failure to make good foreign policy can require the use of defense policy.

Like domestic, social, and economic policies, U.S. foreign and defense policies have evolved. Today, the United States is a powerful and influential presence on the world stage, but it was not always this way. Upon its founding, the United States was a weak country on the margins of world affairs, with an uncertain future. The historical roots of American foreign and defense policy are found in the period from the founding of the republic to the period leading up to its leadership in World War II and the Cold War. The importance of these early experiences comes into clearer focus when we consider three distinct pre-World War II periods: (1) isolation in the early republic, (2) the United States as an emerging power, and (3) World War I (1917–1918) and the interwar years (between World Wars I and II).

Isolationism in the Early Republic

Independence did not change the fundamental foreign policy problem faced by colonial America: steering a safe course between Great Britain and France, the two feuding giants of world politics in the late 1700s. For some Framers, the best course of action was to maintain a close relationship with one of these two powers. Alexander Hamilton, for example, became a champion of a pro-British foreign policy, whereas Thomas Jefferson was an early supporter of a pro-French foreign policy.

For other early political leaders, the best course of action was one of neutrality and relative **isolationism**, a national policy that did not mean avoiding participation in foreign affairs, but instead sidestepping "entangling alliances" with the major European powers. President George Washington articulated this neutrality position most forcefully. In his **Farewell Address**, he called for a policy that would "steer clear of permanent alliances with any portion of the foreign world."

The dual goals of isolationism and neutrality, however, did not guarantee the ability of the United States to always stay out of international conflicts. The United States fought an undeclared naval war in the 1790s with France because France was seizing U.S. ships that were trading with its enemies. Shortly thereafter, the United States fought the Barbary Wars against North African Barbary States, which had captured ships and held sailors for ransom.

Conflict with the British was not resolved after the American Revolution. In the early 1800s, the ongoing wars between France and Great Britain, British support for American Indian tribes opposing U.S. westward expansion, and the British naval practice of impressment (stopping U.S. ships to seize suspected deserters of the British Royal Navy, and sometimes seizing ships and cargo while forcing American sailors to serve on British ships) led to the War of 1812 between the United States and Great Britain.

After the 1815 defeat of French leader Napoleon Bonaparte at Waterloo, Europe was at peace for the first time in almost two decades. Europeans celebrated, but the United States feared that European powers would try to reestablish control in the

foreign policy
Area of policy making that encompasses how one country builds relationships with other countries in order to safeguard its national interest.

defense policy
Area of policy making that focuses on the strategies that a country uses to protect itself from its enemies.

isolationism
The U.S. policy of avoiding entangling alliances with foreign powers.

Farewell Address
When President George Washington left office, he wrote a letter, addressed to the People of the United States, warning them of the dangers to avoid in order to preserve the republic.

Western Hemisphere. To prevent this, President James Monroe issued the **Monroe Doctrine** in 1823. It warned European countries that the United States would view "any attempt on their part to extend their system to any portion of this hemisphere as dangerous to our peace and safety." It also promised to continue the American policy of noninterference in the internal concerns of European powers.

Monroe Doctrine
President James Monroe's 1823 pledge that the United States would oppose attempts by European states to reestablish their political control in the Western Hemisphere.

The United States as an Emerging Power

Throughout most of the nineteenth century, the United States gained territory, developed economically, and emerged as a world power. This process centered on four areas: (1) trade policy and commerce, (2) continental expansion and manifest destiny, (3) dominance over the Western Hemisphere, and (4) interests in Asia.

TRADE POLICY AND COMMERCE The neutrality articulated in Washington's Farewell Address made free trade a cornerstone of early American foreign policy. Reciprocity and most favored nation status were its guiding principles. Reciprocity meant that the U.S. government treated foreign traders in the same way that foreign countries treated American traders. Most favored nation status guaranteed that a country's imports into the United States would be given the lowest possible **tariffs**, or taxes on imported goods.

tariffs
Taxes on imported goods.

Increased global trade and competition following the end of the Napoleonic Wars led the United States to abandon the policies of reciprocity and most favored nation status. Beginning in 1816, Congress adopted the "American System" of trade protection by adding increasingly higher tariffs, sometimes as high as 100 percent of the value of the goods being imported.[2] High tariffs remained the American norm well into the twentieth century.

manifest destiny
Theory that the United States was divinely supported to expand across North America to the Pacific Ocean.

CONTINENTAL EXPANSION AND MANIFEST DESTINY During the nineteenth century, the United States acquired immense quantities of land in various ways. It forcibly took land from American Indians in wars against the Creek, Seminole, Sioux, Comanche, Apache, and other tribes. It bought territory from the French (the Louisiana Territory), Spanish (Florida), and Russians (Alaska). It also fought the 1846 Mexican War, conquering a large expanse of Mexican territory in the American Southwest and California.

HOW DID THE ROOSEVELT COROLLARY AFFECT AMERICAN FOREIGN POLICY?

In this political cartoon, President Theodore Roosevelt is shown policing Panama, carrying the "big stick" of military intervention proposed by the Roosevelt Corollary.

Manifest destiny is the summary phrase used to capture the logic behind American continental expansionism. According to this idea, the United States had a divinely supported obligation to expand across North America to the Pacific and "overspread the continent allotted by Providence for the free development of our multiplying millions."[3] Manifest destiny was viewed as natural and inevitable, far different from the colonial expansion of European states.

DOMINANCE OVER THE WESTERN HEMISPHERE The twentieth century began with a revision of the Monroe Doctrine. In what came to be known as the **Roosevelt Corollary** to the Monroe Doctrine, President Theodore Roosevelt asserted in 1904 that it was the responsibility of the United States to ensure stability in Latin America and the Caribbean. In accordance with this role, the United States would intervene with military force to punish wrongdoing and establish order in these nations when their own governments were incapable of doing so.

Roosevelt was particularly concerned with the Dominican Republic. It was deeply in debt, was plagued by

Bettmann/Getty Images

Roosevelt Corollary
Concept developed by President Theodore Roosevelt early in the twentieth century declaring that it was the responsibility of the United States to ensure stability in Latin America and the Caribbean.

growing domestic unrest, and faced the threat of hostile military action by France. Roosevelt blocked French action by taking over customs collection there in 1906. Later, the United States sent troops to other countries in the Americas, including Cuba, Haiti, Nicaragua, Panama, and Mexico.

Although these exercises of military power were significant in establishing regional dominance, the signature event of this period for American foreign policy was the acquisition of the Panama Canal Zone. The United States wished to build a canal through Panama, which was then part of Colombia, but when the Colombian government refused to approve the necessary treaty, the Roosevelt administration supported a Panamanian independence movement. When this movement achieved success, the U.S. government quickly recognized the independent state and signed an agreement granting the United States rights to a ten-mile strip of land connecting the Atlantic and Pacific Oceans. Construction of the Panama Canal began in 1904 and was completed in 1914, providing a way for ships to avoid the long and dangerous trip around South America to reach western U.S. territories.

Supporting Panamanian independence was not the only way the United States established its influence in Central America and the Caribbean. Beginning with the William H. Taft administration, the United States also began to use its economic power through so-called "dollar diplomacy." Dollar diplomacy was designed to make the United States the banker of the region, and to open up countries throughout all of Latin America to American investment.

INTERESTS IN ASIA   The 1898 Spanish-American War, fought between the United States and Spain over Spanish policies and presence in Cuba, gave the United States control over Cuba as well as other Spanish colonies such as Puerto Rico and the Philippines. As a result, the United States now had overseas colonies and a major stake in Asian affairs. The major problems confronting the United States in Asia were the disintegration of China and the rising power of Japan.

In 1898 and 1899, as European powers were extending their influence in China, the United States called on Russia, Germany, France, and Great Britain not to discriminate against other investors in their spheres of influence. While the United States could not force other countries to agree, the logic behind this Open Door Policy was consistent with long-standing American support for opening up foreign markets to U.S. investment.

In sharp contrast to the unilateral action taken on China, President Theodore Roosevelt sought to contain Japan through a series of international agreements. The most notable of these was the Taft-Katsura Agreement of 1905. This act recognized Japanese preeminence over Korea in return for a Japanese agreement to respect American control over the Philippines and Hawai'i.

World War I and the Interwar Years

World War I
A global military conflict from 1914 to 1918 across Europe and its overseas territories, in which the United States militarily intervened in 1917–1918.

League of Nations
A multilateral diplomatic organization that existed from 1920 to 1946 that sought, unsuccessfully, to prevent future wars; the United States never joined.

collective security
The idea that an attack on one country is an attack on all countries.

When **World War I** broke out in Europe in 1914, the United States remained neutral at first. It was a European war, and it seemed that no U.S. interests were directly involved. In addition, the United States population was largely composed of immigrants from many countries in Europe, and Americans were deeply divided about whom to support. As the war progressed, however, it became increasingly difficult to remain neutral. Under Germany's policy of unrestricted submarine warfare, German subs sank U.S. ships carrying cargo to Great Britain and France as well as a passenger liner, the *Lusitania*.

Finally, declaring that the United States was fighting "to make the world safe for democracy," President Woodrow Wilson led the nation into the war in 1917. Wilson also put forward a statement of American aims, the Fourteen Points. The fourteenth point called for the creation of a **League of Nations**, which was established at the Paris Peace Conference at the conclusion of the war. Its guiding principle was **collective security**, the idea that an attack on one country is an attack on all countries. Wilson failed, however, to build support at home, and the Senate voted against joining the League of Nations.

The period between the two world wars saw U.S. foreign policy dominated by isolationist sentiment. In 1928, support for disarmament led to the signing of the Kellogg-Briand Pact in which the United States, Japan, and the European powers (including Great Britain, France, and Germany) agreed to renounce war "as an instrument of national policy" and to resolve their disputes "by pacific means." In 1930, Congress passed the Smoot-Hawley Tariff Act, and other countries responded by raising their tariffs. By 1932, these higher tariffs, in conjunction with the Great Depression, caused world trade to drop to about one-third its former level.[4]

Belief in isolationism also led to the passage of four neutrality acts in the 1930s. Among their core provisions were arms embargoes and a prohibition on loans to countries involved in international conflicts. After Great Britain and France declared war on Nazi Germany in the late 1930s, however, President Franklin D. Roosevelt was able to soften these bans to enacting a "lend lease" policy to allow Great Britain to obtain American weapons in return for allowing the United States to lease British military bases.

World War II and Its Aftermath

The United States entered **World War II** in response to the Japanese bombing of Pearl Harbor in Hawai'i on December 7, 1941. For the first time since the War of 1812, the United States was attacked on its own territory, and began an unprecedented "total war mobilization" in which all sectors of the American economy and society were primed for battle. The war was fought by the Allied Powers (including the United States, the Soviet Union, Great Britain, and France) against the Axis Powers (including Nazi Germany, Italy, and Japan) in Europe, North Africa, Asia, and the Pacific. World War II was the most extensive and destructive conflict in all of human history. It brought about the mass death not only of military but also civilian populations caught in war zones, and also those targeted for genocide as part of the Holocaust and other crimes against humanity. It has shaped much of the subsequent course of human history, as could be seen from the opening vignette in this chapter focusing on the Berlin Wall.

World War II concluded in Europe first, in May 1945 with the unconditional surrender of the Nazis to the United States, Great Britain, the Soviet Union, and the Allies. World War II ended in the Pacific in August 1945, following the still-debated U.S. decision to destroy the Japanese cities of Hiroshima and Nagasaki using the unprecedented power of the newly developed atomic bomb.

World War II was a watershed in U.S. foreign policy. Prior to the war, isolationist sentiment dominated American thinking on world politics, but afterwards, internationalism emerged triumphant. In contrast to its earlier rejection of the League of Nations, the United States enthusiastically led in the creation of the **United Nations** (UN), establishing itself as a permanent member of the **UN Security Council**, along with Great Britain, France, China, and the Soviet Union. It also entered into security alliances with countries around the globe, with an implicit understanding that America's role was to be "the leader of the free world."

President Franklin D. Roosevelt took an activist role in World War II diplomacy, holding or attending several major conferences until he died in April 1945. The most consequential of these was the Yalta Conference, held in the Soviet Union in February 1945, to decide the future of Germany and Eastern Europe, and to discuss the development of the UN. The Yalta agreement opened the way for the Soviet Union to continue to occupy the eastern half of Europe, bringing down what British Prime Minister Winston Churchill later termed an **Iron Curtain** across the center of the continent.

In the belief that protectionist trade policies had led to the rise of dictators and the beginning of World War II, the United States moved to create a set of international economic organizations to encourage and manage global trade and finance. Collectively, they came to be known as the **Bretton Woods System**, which remain a powerful influence on the global economy. The **International Monetary Fund (IMF)** was

World War II

A global military conflict from 1939 to 1945 in Europe, Africa, Asia, and the Pacific region, in which the United States was engaged from 1941 to 1945.

United Nations

A multilateral diplomatic organization founded in 1945 and continuing today that is intended to promote peaceful resolution of international disputes and advance human development worldwide; the United States is a founding member.

UN Security Council

A principal part of the United Nations, charged with authorizing peacekeeping operations, international sanctions, and military action in order to maintain global peace and security.

Iron Curtain

A term used during the Cold War to describe the divide between the capitalist West and Communist East.

Bretton Woods System

International financial system devised shortly before the end of World War II that created the World Bank and the International Monetary Fund.

International Monetary Fund (IMF)

International governmental organization designed to stabilize international currency transactions.

HOW DID WORLD WAR II CHANGE U.S. FOREIGN POLICY?

World War II cemented America's role as a world power. Here President Franklin D. Roosevelt (seated at center) meets with British Prime Minister Winston Churchill (at left) and Soviet Premier Josef Stalin at Yalta in 1945 to plan the postwar settlement.

Keystone/Hulton Archive/Getty Images

World Bank

International governmental organization created to provide loans for large economic development projects.

General Agreement on Tariffs and Trade (GATT)

Post–World War II economic development treaty designed to help facilitate international trade negotiations and promote free trade.

World Trade Organization (WTO)

An international organization that replaced GATT in 1995 to supervise and expand international trade.

Cold War

The period of superpower rivalry and confrontation between the United States and the Soviet Union, lasting from the end of World War II to 1991.

containment

U.S. policy of opposing Soviet expansion and Communist revolutions around the world with military forces, economic assistance, and political influence.

deterrence

The military strategy of employing enormous force, including nuclear weapons, in order to prevent the outbreak or escalation of armed conflicts.

Truman Doctrine

U.S. anti-Communist policy initiated in 1947 that became the basis of U.S. foreign policy throughout the Cold War.

established to stabilize international currency transactions. In addition, the International Bank for Reconstruction and Development, also called the **World Bank**, was set up to help the world recover from the destruction of World War II and to help poorer countries prosper by providing loans for large economic development projects. Created in 1947, the **General Agreement on Tariffs and Trade (GATT)** had as its mission: the facilitation of international trade negotiations and promotion of free trade; in 1995, it evolved into the **World Trade Organization (WTO)**. This process occurred through negotiating "rounds" or multiyear international conferences.

The Cold War: Containment and Deterrence

The **Cold War** was the defining feature of the international system from the end of World War II in 1945 until the collapse of Communism in Eastern Europe and the Soviet Union in the late 1980s and early 1990s. It was a period of intense competition, hostility, tension, and the near outbreak of direct conflict between the Western powers (the United States, Great Britain, and Western Europe) and the Communist bloc states (Eastern Europe and the Soviet Union). However, the Cold War never escalated into direct and open warfare between the United States and the Soviet Union, which came to be known as the two "superpowers."

American foreign policy during the Cold War was organized around two key concepts. The first was **containment**, which held that the "the main element of any United States policy toward the Soviet Union must be that of a long-term, patient but firm and vigilant containment of Russian expansionist tendencies."[5] This meant that the United States would oppose Soviet expansion with military forces, economic assistance, and political influence.

The second concept was nuclear **deterrence**. From the 1950s through the 1980s, the United States and the Soviet Union developed large arsenals of nuclear weapons, whose sheer destructive capacity led many to believe would prevent both sides from ever actually using them. This drastically altered the traditional calculus of warfare by making it clear that neither side in an all-out nuclear exchange could prevail at a bearable cost, a condition referred to as "mutually assured destruction." This reality kept the Cold War from ever turning fully "hot."

March 1947 brought the enunciation of the **Truman Doctrine**, stating that the United States will provide economic assistance and military aid to countries fighting against Communist revolutions or political pressure. Three months later, the United States took a major action consistent with this political worldview. Secretary of State George Marshall announced that the United States would help finance Europe's economic recovery. All European states were invited to participate in the drafting of a European collective recovery plan known as the **Marshall Plan**. Importantly, the Soviet Union chose not to participate in this program and prevented its Eastern European "satellite states" from participating as well.

In 1949, the economic division of Europe was reinforced by its military partition with the establishment of the **North Atlantic Treaty Organization (NATO)**. This alliance, the first peacetime military treaty joined by the United States, is a collective security pact among the United States, Canada, and parts of Europe. In retaliation, the Soviet Union organized the Eastern European Communist regimes into the Warsaw Pact. This division of Europe was further established by the **Berlin Wall**, built by East Germany in 1961 to cut off Communist-controlled East Berlin from democratic West Berlin. The Warsaw Pact was disbanded by its members in 1991, but the NATO alliance continues as a significant force to the current day.

MILITARY CONFLICTS OF THE COLD WAR Cold War competition between the United States and the Soviet Union moved to Latin America in the late 1950s and early 1960s. The most intense confrontation involved the Communist regime installed in 1959 by the revolutionary Fidel Castro in Cuba, which was intensively opposed by Presidents Dwight D. Eisenhower and John F. Kennedy. In October 1962, the United States and Soviet Union directly confronted one another over the deployment of nuclear missiles in Cuba. Perhaps at no time was the world closer to a nuclear war than it was during this event, known as the **Cuban Missile Crisis**. In response, President Kennedy established a "quarantine" on Cuba: a naval blockade that prevented Soviet ships from landing in Cuba. The crisis ended after two weeks, when Soviet Premier Nikita Khrushchev agreed to remove the Soviet missiles. However, the incident provoked a half-century of tension between the United States and Cuba which only began to abate with the tentative reestablishment of diplomatic relations in 2015.

The Cold War also reached into Asia, anchored by the victory of Communists in 1949 after a long-running civil war in China. In the early 1950s, the United States fought the inconclusive **Korean War**, which left the Korean peninsula divided between a Communist regime in the North and a capitalist regime in the South. Likewise, the United States became embroiled in a civil war in the Southeast Asian country of Vietnam. The **Vietnam War** escalated in the 1960s under President Lyndon B. Johnson. American forces carried out sustained and massive bombing campaigns against the North, and U.S. ground troops began fighting in the South. The Vietnam War was an especially difficult one for the United States, fought in unfamiliar terrain with little chance of success. Casualties escalated quickly, and the American public soon turned against the war. The peace movement that emerged at this time in response to the war and the military draft significantly influenced public opinion, helping to bring about America's withdrawal from the war and the collapse of its South Vietnamese allies.

DÉTENTE When Richard M. Nixon became president in 1969, he declared it was time to move from "an era of confrontation" to "an era of negotiation" in relations with the Soviet Union.[6] The improvement in U.S.–Soviet relations was called **détente**. At its core was a series of negotiations that aimed to use linked rewards and punishments (rather than military power) to contain the Soviet Union. The greatest success of détente was in the area of arms control, most notably with the signing of the Strategic Arms Limitation Treaties (SALT I and SALT II), which limited the deployment of nuclear weapons. Another key element of détente was improved relations with China, which Nixon cemented by seeking the normalization of relations, including a visit to Beijing in 1972.

Marshall Plan
European collective recovery program, named after Secretary of State George C. Marshall, that provided extensive American aid to Western Europe after World War II.

North Atlantic Treaty Organization (NATO)
The first peacetime military treaty joined by the United States; NATO is a collective security pact that includes the United States, Canada, and parts of Europe.

Berlin Wall
A barrier built by East Germany in 1961 to prevent East German citizens from fleeing to the democratic West from Communist East Berlin.

Cuban Missile Crisis
The 1962 confrontation over the deployment of ballistic missiles in Cuba that nearly escalated into nuclear war between the United States and the Soviet Union.

Korean War
A civil war from 1950 to 1953 in which the United States supported the South Korean regime against Communist forces in North Korea.

Vietnam War
A civil war in which the United States supported the South Vietnamese regime against Communist forces in North Vietnam, which escalated through the 1960s before ending in 1975.

détente
The improvement in relations between the United States and the Soviet Union that occurred during the 1970s.

The greatest failure of détente, however, was an inability to establish agreed-upon rules to govern competition in the developing world. In Africa, Asia, and Latin America, the United States and Soviet Union each armed and supported competing sides in many civil wars. In Chile, Nixon used covert action to undermine the government of President Salvador Allende and reestablish a strongly pro-American regime. In many places, the United States subsequently experienced so-called "blowback" from its activities, most notably in Iran, where in 1979 the U.S.-supported ruling monarch, the Shah, was overthrown by a radical Islamist revolution. The new regime held fifty-two American hostages for over a year and began sponsoring terrorist activities in the Middle East and beyond.

THE END OF THE COLD WAR   During his one term as president (1977–1981), Jimmy Carter reoriented American foreign policy from the management of the Cold War to the promotion of **human rights**, which refers to the protection of people's basic freedoms and needs. This new emphasis began to slowly undermine the credibility of the Communist nations, which were only able to maintain control by ruthlessly suppressing all domestic dissent.

Republican President Ronald Reagan replaced Carter in the White House in January 1981 and took a more assertive stance, promising to reestablish American credibility and restore American military strength. The Reagan administration's commitment to combating Communism by providing military assistance to anti-Communist groups, such as in Nicaragua and El Salvador, became known as the **Reagan Doctrine**. In the Central Asian country of Afghanistan, the United States vehemently opposed the Soviet Union's 1979 invasion of that country, which supported a pro-Communist government in power. The Soviet occupation army grew but could never defeat the guerrilla forces, known as the mujahideen. American military aid contributed to the defeat of the Soviet Union and its eventual withdrawal (but also sowed seeds of later conflict with terrorists based in Afghanistan).

The Soviet retreat from Afghanistan was part of a larger change in Soviet politics and policy in the mid-1980s. After nearly two decades of economic and social stagnation within the Soviet Union, a new generation of leaders saw that the country's path was unsustainable. A new, more pragmatic Soviet leader, Mikhail Gorbachev, entered into nuclear arms control agreements with the United States and reduced foreign aid to Soviet allies. At home, Gorbachev also implemented a program of political openness and economic reform that were meant to strengthen Communism, but instead undermined the control of the Communist Party.

Once it became clear that the Gorbachev government would not intervene militarily, one Communist regime after another in Eastern Europe collapsed in the fall of 1989, with the most potent symbol being the opening of the Berlin Wall. Two years later, the Soviet Union itself collapsed and broke apart into fifteen separate countries. These developments left only the People's Republic of China as a major power under the control of a Communist Party. The China regime ruthlessly reasserted its claim to power by massacring student democracy protesters in Tiananmen Square in Beijing in the spring of 1989.

The Post–Cold War World

In a period of barely two years, the long-standing "bipolar" world split between the influence of the two superpowers was transformed. In the 1990s, it seemed for a time that the United States might lead the world in a unilateral and unchallenged way. George H. W. Bush, who became president in 1989, sought to navigate through this new, post–Cold War world. In 1990–1991, Bush was able to assemble a unified and overwhelmingly effective response to the invasion by Iraqi dictator Saddam Hussein of a neighboring country, Kuwait. Proclaiming that the end of the Cold War was ushering in a "new world order" unaffected by the superpower rivalry, Bush turned to

---

human rights
The protection of people's basic freedoms and needs.

Reagan Doctrine
The Reagan administration's commitment to ending Communism by providing military assistance to anti-Communist groups.

the United Nations, whose members voted to impose economic sanctions and authorized the use of force. During the ensuing **Gulf War**, the U.S.-led coalition was victorious in removing Iraqi forces from Kuwait after just six weeks.

Bush's successor in office, Bill Clinton, sought to define a clear role for the United States in world affairs now that a dismantled Soviet Union no longer posed a clear and present danger. The president chose to actively promote the expansion of democracy, open markets, and free trade throughout the world. Clinton secured Senate approval for the North American Free Trade Agreement (NAFTA), an agreement promoting free movement of goods and services among Canada, Mexico, and the United States. The United States also brought former Soviet allies into the NATO military alliance, while supporting their integration with Western Europe. Even in the 1990s, however, it became clear that there were limits to American power. In Somalia and Rwanda, the United States was unable to resolve civil conflicts that resulted in mass casualties, including a brutal genocide in Rwanda. Even on the continent of Europe, the United States and its allies were only belatedly able to halt "ethnic cleansing" amidst the collapse of the formerly Communist country of Yugoslavia.

In the late 1990s, a little-known radical Islamic terrorist group known as **al-Qaeda** began to attack vulnerable American targets overseas. The group vehemently objected to the intrusion of U.S. troops into Arab and Muslim countries. Its leadership, including founder Osama bin Laden, operated from safe havens in the wartorn nation of Afghanistan and neighboring Pakistan. The group adopted a decentralized organization with a range of affiliates and associates, making it difficult for the United States to counter, and giving it wide latitude to carry out its operations.

Gulf War

A military conflict from 1990 to 1991 in which a U.S.-led international coalition reversed the occupation of Kuwait by the armed forces of Iraq.

al-Qaeda

The Islamic terrorist organization responsible for the 9/11 terrorist attacks and numerous other actions against U.S. overseas interests.

September 11, 2001, and the War on Terror

On **September 11**, 2001, the vulnerability of even the American homeland was demonstrated to devastating effect. That morning, nineteen members of al-Qaeda simultaneously hijacked four U.S. commercial airliners and crashed two of them into the World Trade Center in New York City and one into the Pentagon near Washington, D.C., with the fourth crashing in an open field in Pennsylvania. Nearly 3,000 people lost their lives that day, the first time since Pearl Harbor that U.S. territory had been directly attacked. This shocking event challenged Americans' longstanding belief in

September 11

A terrorist plot carried out on September 11, 2001, that used hijacked civilian aircraft to attack the World Trade Center in New York and the Pentagon near Washington, D.C.

Thomas Nilsson/Getty Images

HOW DID THE SEPTEMBER 11 TERRORIST ATTACKS AFFECT AMERICAN FOREIGN POLICY?

The twin towers of the World Trade Center collapsed September 11, 2001, after they were struck by hijacked airplanes. The attacks caused thousands of deaths and injuries and resulted in the beginning of a long-running war on terrorism.

global war on terror

An international action, initiated by President George W. Bush after the 9/11 terrorist attacks, to weed out terrorist operatives throughout the world.

Afghanistan War

A military conflict begun in 2002 in which a U.S.-led international coalition invaded Afghanistan in order to depose the government and deny a safe haven to terrorists.

Iraq War

A military conflict from 2003 to 2011 in which a U.S.-led international coalition invaded Iraq and deposed its regime but proved unable to establish a stable new government.

their security at home and reinforced the reality that the world political order had never been as unipolar as some had hoped.

THE WAR IN AFGHANISTAN   In response, President George W. Bush declared a **global war on terror** to weed out terrorist operatives throughout the world. It demanded that the government of Afghanistan, which was led by an extremist group called the Taliban, expel Osama bin Laden and al-Qaeda and sever its ties with international terrorist groups. When this did not occur, the United States and its NATO allies in October 2001 began aerial strikes and, subsequently, ground assaults against terrorist facilities and Taliban military targets inside Afghanistan. The Taliban proved no match for this combination of air and ground power, and its last stronghold fell before the end of the year. However, the Taliban and al-Qaeda soon pursued a sustained insurgency against American troops and the new Afghan government. The **Afghanistan War** eventually became America's military conflict, continuing through the tenures of President Barack Obama and the term of President Donald J. Trump. The leader of al-Qaeda, Osama bin Laden eluded capture until May 2011, when he was killed in Pakistan by U.S. special forces.

THE WAR IN IRAQ   A broader foreign policy agenda emerged in President Bush's 2002 State of the Union Address. In this speech, Bush identified Iraq, North Korea, and Iran as an "axis of evil" that threatened American security interests. Claiming that Iraqi dictator Saddam Hussein was actively pursuing nuclear and other weapons of mass destruction, the administration moved toward war with Iraq. It also enunciated a new doctrine of "preemption," in which threats to American interests would not be allowed to grow, as had al-Qaeda, but proactively attacked by whatever means necessary. The **Iraq War** was also justified in terms of the need to secure access to oil supplies and the desire to topple dictatorships and foster democracy in the region.

Following a series of authorization negotiations with Congress, Operation Iraqi Freedom began on March 19, 2003, with a decapitation strike aimed at targets in Baghdad, Iraq's capital city. On April 9, Baghdad fell, and one month later, Bush declared the "mission accomplished." However, the Bush administration did not prepare for a long or contested occupation of Iraq, and forces opposing the new government and the presence of American troops launched a guerrilla war. By mid-2008, more than 4,000 U.S. military personnel and Department of Defense civilians had died in Iraq, and 30,000 had been wounded, prompting increased calls for an end to the war. Barack Obama came into the presidency in 2009 pledging to end the war in Iraq. An end to formal U.S. combat operations was announced in 2010, and the last U.S. combat forces left Iraq in December 2011, although small numbers of U.S. troops remain within the country.

However, internal violence in Iraq continued and, indeed, the larger Middle East entered a period of severe turmoil and strife that left the United States with little opportunity to act unilaterally, as it often had over prior decades. Supported by airstrikes by American and other NATO forces, rebels in Libya overthrew and killed its longtime dictator, Muammar Gaddafi, in 2011. However, Libya thereafter fell into civil strife, which included the murder of four Americans at the U.S. consulate in Benghazi the following year. Several other countries in the region, including Yemen, Egypt, and Lebanon, likewise experienced uprisings, chaos, and military crackdowns.

Most devastating has been the protracted civil war in Syria in which a half-million people are believed to have lost their lives, with as many as 10 million more being displaced and seeking refuge throughout the Middle East, North Africa, and Europe. The unprecedented outflows of population from Syria, Afghanistan, Libya, and elsewhere caused a humanitarian disaster and raised serious political tensions within the United States, European countries, and other nations about how to address the refugee crisis.

Likewise, the vacuum created by civil war and insurgency in Syria and Iraq allowed the proliferation of the most virulent new terrorist threat to face the United States since al-Qaeda—the Islamic State in Iraq and Syria, commonly known by the initials **ISIS** or, sometimes, ISIL. The presence of ISIS posed a major challenge to U.S. foreign and defense policies by destabilizing Syria, Iraq, and their immediate neighbors and promoting the proliferation of other terrorist groups from countries such as Libya, Nigeria, and Somalia. ISIS also directed or indirectly inspired supporters to mount violent mass-casualty massacres in the United States and other western nations.

It was partly on the strength of public sentiment for a stronger U.S. response to ISIS and other sponsors of global terrorism that Donald J. Trump won the presidency in 2016. Among Trump's first acts as president was to curtail the admission of refugees due partly to concerns about their potential to carry out terrorist attacks in the United States. He also curtailed all travel from a small group of countries where planning and activities for terrorism is particularly concentrated. By 2020, ISIS was forced out of the territory it once held, and its founder, Abu Bakr al-Baghdadi, died during a U.S. military raid, but the group retains an influence around the world by inspiring and radicalizing supporters. President Trump also took decisive action in ordering a drone strike that killed Qasem Soleimani, a top-ranking Iranian general widely believed to be behind a range of terrorist activities sponsored by the Iranian regime. Despite bellicose language and a small retaliatory strike from Iran, tensions between the United States and Iran did not escalate into further conflict. The November 2020 election of Obama-era Vice President Joe Biden to be the next president of the United States promises a return to a far more conventional American approach to defense and foreign policy issues. However, terrorism by its very nature is based on disruption and surprise, and every administration must remain vigilant against hostile actions by terrorists, foreign states, and other non-state actors.

ISIS

A terrorist organization that calls itself an Islamic State; controlled parts of Iraq and Syria and used that as a base to direct and inspire terrorist attacks abroad.

HOW DOES THE UNITED STATES MAKE FOREIGN AND DEFENSE POLICY DECISIONS?

16.2 Describe the roles of government officials and of other influences on U.S. foreign and defense policy.

The basic structure of foreign and defense policy decision making is laid out in the Constitution. The executive branch is the most powerful branch of government in the formulation and implementation of U.S. foreign and defense policy. Congress also influences and shapes policy through oversight, treaty ratification, appointments, appropriations, and war powers. The judiciary has a more limited role in foreign and defense affairs, usually addressing questions of executive authority. In addition, public opinion, political parties, and interest groups have important forms of influence.

The Constitution

When the Framers of the Constitution met in Philadelphia in 1787, they wanted a stronger national government in part to keep the United States out of European affairs and to keep Europe out of American affairs. As a result, they bequeathed the power to formulate and implement foreign policy to the national government rather than the states. In addition, many foreign and military powers not specified in the Constitution were, over time, asserted by the national government.

The Framers of the Constitution divided national authority for foreign and military policy functions between the president and Congress. The Framers named the president commander in chief of the armed forces but gave Congress power to fund and regulate the Army and Navy and to declare war. The president has authority to negotiate and sign treaties, but these take effect only after the Senate ratifies them by a two-thirds majority. Similarly, the president appoints ambassadors and other key foreign and military affairs officials, but the Senate grants advice and a majority of senators must give their consent to nominees. Ultimately, all such actions are subject to judicial review, although the judiciary tends to provide the elected branches with a great deal of latitude on foreign and military affairs.

The Executive Branch

The executive branch is the central place for creating and implementing U.S. foreign and defense policy, and within the executive branch, the president is the most important individual. Among executive departments, the Department of State is primarily responsible for diplomatic activity and the Department of Defense for military policy. Other parts of the executive branch, such as the National Security Council and the Central Intelligence Agency (CIA), provide additional resources for the president. The Department of Homeland Security focuses on the territory of the United States itself but also influences foreign and defense policy making.

THE PRESIDENT The president is preeminent in foreign and defense policy. As the Framers intended, presidents have greater access to and control over information than any other government official or agency, and presidents alone can act with little fear that their actions will be countermanded. As such, U.S. foreign policy tends to be discussed in terms of presidential action. Presidents have varied widely in their prior experience on these issues. At one end would be presidents such as Dwight D. Eisenhower, who led Allied forces during World War II, and George H. W. Bush, who headed the CIA, represented the United States at the United Nations and in China, and was vice president prior to being elected president. At the other end are many former state governors—such as Bill Clinton and George W. Bush—with little direct experience in foreign policy. Donald J. Trump was unprecedented in having never served in any military or political office prior to his election and in having his international experience largely limited to business and media enterprises. Trump's successor, Joe Biden, has deep experience in foreign affairs after eight years as vice president and decades before that in the U.S. Senate.

Fortunately, presidents are able to rely on an array of organizations and individuals located within the White House to help them make foreign policy. The most notable of these organizations is the **National Security Council**, led by the national security adviser, which brings together key foreign policy actors, including the vice president, the secretaries of state and of defense, intelligence officials, military leaders, and other presidential advisers. The organization's primary goal is to advise and assist the president on foreign and defense policy, particularly in crisis situations when speed in decision making is essential. Originally, the national security adviser was a neutral voice in the decision-making process, but today can be a significant player in the shaping of foreign policy. Prominent former national security advisers include Henry Kissinger, Colin Powell, and Condoleezza Rice, all of whom went on to become secretary of state. There was considerable turnover in the role during the Trump administration, with four different national security advisers in four years. In January 2021, Jake Sullivan became President Biden's national security adviser.

National Security Council

The agency within the White House, led by the national security adviser, which brings together key foreign policy actors to advise the president.

THE DEPARTMENTS OF STATE, DEFENSE, AND HOMELAND SECURITY According to tradition, the **Department of State**, the oldest of all Cabinet agencies, is the leading executive branch department responsible for formulation and implementation of U.S. foreign policy. The Department of State serves as a link between foreign governments and U.S. policy makers and as a source of advice on how to deal with problems. The position of secretary of state is one of the most prominent figures in any administration, and during the Obama years was held by two prominent former U.S. senators who had themselves been presidential contenders, Hillary Clinton and John Kerry. The State Department includes a large bureaucracy in Washington, D.C., and a diplomatic corps composed of ambassadors and lower-level officials in every country with which the U.S. has diplomatic relations, as well as numerous

Department of State

Chief executive branch department responsible for formulation and implementation of U.S. foreign policy.

intergovernmental organizations. In a characteristically unorthodox move, President Trump named as his first secretary of state fellow businessman Rex Tillerson, who was the chairman and CEO of the ExxonMobil oil and gas company. Tillerson maintained a lower public profile than many of his predecessors, had weaker connections with career civil servants within the State Department, and ultimately was replaced by President Trump in favor of then-CIA Director Mike Pompeo, who continued through the remainder of Trump's term. An unusually large number of ambassadorships and other positions within the State Department were left unfilled, and large cuts to the State Department budget were proposed, perhaps reflecting skepticism within the Trump administration about the usefulness of a large bureaucracy in the management of foreign policy. In January 2021, former Obama-era official Antony Blinken became secretary of state for the Biden administration.

Today, the Department of State's position of prominence has been challenged from many directions. Within the White House staff, the national security adviser may face competing viewpoints. Within each foreign country, the U.S. ambassador is often described as head of the "country team" that operates inside a U.S. embassy. In the U.S. embassy in Mexico, for example, this means not only coordinating Department of State officials but also individuals from the Departments of Defense, Agriculture, Commerce, Labor, and Homeland Security, as well as the Federal Bureau of Investigation, the Drug Enforcement Agency, and the U.S. Trade Representative.

The **Department of Defense** is the principal executive branch department responsible for formulation and implementation of U.S. military policy. It came into existence after World War II, when the War Department and the Navy Department were combined into a single agency for military affairs. The secretary of defense is the nation's chief civilian military official, subordinate only to the president. Still, within the department, numerous lines of potential disagreement exist. Among the most prominent are those between professional military officers and civilians working in the office of the secretary of defense, and between the separate branches of the armed services (including the Army, Navy, Air Force, and Marines) over missions, weapons, and priorities. In an innovation in 2020, the support of the Trump administration led to the founding of an additional service branch, the U.S. Space Force. To coordinate these branches, the president relies on the **Joint Chiefs of Staff**, a military advisory body. In 2019, then-secretary of the Army Mark Esper was promoted to secretary of defense, while army general Mark Milley became chairman of the Joint Chiefs. Former army general Lloyd Austin was named as secretary of defense in January 2021.

Department of Defense
Principal executive branch department responsible for formulation and implementation of U.S. defense and military policy.

Joint Chiefs of Staff
Military advisory body composed of top officials including the Army chief of staff, the Air Force chief of staff, the chief of naval operations, the Marine commandant, and the chief of space operations.

White House Photo/Alamy Stock Photo

HOW DOES THE PRESIDENT CONDUCT FOREIGN AND DEFENSE POLICY?

The president is invested with enormous authority over U.S. foreign and defense policy, serving as the nation's head of state, military commander in chief, and chief diplomat. Here, President Trump addresses the United Nations General Assembly in 2017.

Department of Homeland Security

Cabinet department created after the 9/11 terrorist attacks to coordinate domestic security efforts.

The **Department of Homeland Security**, the Cabinet department created after the 9/11 terrorist attacks in order to coordinate domestic security efforts, straddles the line between foreign and domestic policy making. The department brought together twenty-two existing agencies, approximately thirty newly created agencies or offices, and 180,000 employees into a single agency. Among its key units are the Transportation Security Administration (TSA), the organization responsible for aviation security; the Federal Emergency Management Agency (FEMA), the primary federal disaster relief organization; Customs and Border Protection; the U.S. Coast Guard; the Secret Service; and Immigration and Customs Enforcement (ICE).[7] In the first year and a half of the Trump administration, the position saw two secretaries and one acting secretary. In February 2021, former Obama-era official Alejandro Mayorkas was named as secretary of homeland security.

In addition to state, defense, and homeland security, the complexity of contemporary foreign policy problems has increased the importance of views held by other Cabinet-level departments such as treasury, justice, and commerce. In an interdependent global economy, these can also play critical roles, for example in the enforcement of economic sanctions against foreign countries.

THE INTELLIGENCE COMMUNITY The intelligence community is a term used to describe the agencies of the U.S. government that are involved in the collection and analysis of information, counterintelligence (the protection of U.S. intelligence), and covert action. The head of the intelligence community is the director of national intelligence, a position to which former CIA official Avril Haines was appointed in 2021. The most prominent branch is the **Central Intelligence Agency (CIA)**, which gathers and analyzes information about the activities of foreign countries and nonstate actors. Perhaps more famously, the CIA also carries out covert operations to advance American strategic interests—which has included even the toppling of foreign governments. During the Trump administration, the CIA was led by former U.S. Representative Mike Pompeo until President Trump nominated him to be the next secretary of state in 2018; Pompeo was succeeded as CIA director by his deputy, Gina Haspel. Under Biden, William J. Burns was approved by the Senate as Director of the CIA on March 9, 2021.

Central Intelligence Agency (CIA)

A U.S. government agency dedicated to intelligence gathering and covert operations.

Beyond the CIA, other key members of the intelligence community include the Bureau of Intelligence and Research in the Department of State, the Defense Intelligence Agency, the military service intelligence agencies, the National Security Agency in the Department of Defense, the Federal Bureau of Investigation in the Department of Justice, and the Department of Homeland Security. Coordinating these units can be difficult, since each has control over its own budget and they do not always share intelligence information with each other. Some branches have come under significant scrutiny and criticism for overstepping their established boundaries, such as the use of extreme interrogation measures by the CIA and the extensive and invasive monitoring of electronic communications by the NSA.

Congress

While the Constitution specifies several responsibilities for Congress, in practice it has much less influence over foreign and defense policy than does the president. Congress particularly tends to be deferential to the executive in times of war or threats to national security. For example, the attacks on September 11, 2001, prompted adoption of the USA PATRIOT Act, a law proposed by the Department of Justice and passed by Congress in October 2001. The law gave the government greater law enforcement authority to gather intelligence domestically, detain and deport immigrants, search business and personal records, and conduct wiretaps, although subsequent re-authorizations by Congress have revised some of the law's most controversial elements. In all, there is often greater agreement on foreign and military affairs in the United States across the branches of government than on most domestic issues. Nevertheless, the legislative branch does play a significant role in the policy process.

OVERSIGHT Congress conducts oversight by holding hearings that monitor agency activities, as well as the content and conduct of U.S. policy. Congress may also establish reporting requirements; for instance, the State Department must submit annual evaluations of other nations' human rights practices, and the president must notify Congress "in a timely fashion" of CIA covert actions. Members of Congress also engage in oversight of foreign and defense policy by visiting other countries, where they conduct "fact finding" missions and meet with political leaders, businesspeople, and even dissidents. Congressional oversight of a foreign-affairs issue marked a significant new chapter in December 2019 when the U.S. House of Representatives approved two articles of impeachment against President Trump alleging that he misused his foreign policy authority for personal political advantage in interactions with the president of Ukraine and that he also obstructed Congress's investigation of the matter.

TREATIES AND EXECUTIVE AGREEMENTS Additionally, the Constitution gives the Senate explicit power to approve treaties, although the Senate has rejected treaties only twenty times in U.S. history.[8] The most famous of these unapproved treaties was the international agreement to establish the League of Nations, which the Senate refused to approve in 1919. More recently, in 1999, the Senate rejected the Comprehensive Test Ban Treaty, which would prohibit testing of nuclear weapons among the countries that approve it. In more recent decades, a norm has also emerged in which both houses of Congress can act together to enact international agreements as ordinary laws, subject to approval by the president.

On many issues, presidents can avoid the involvement of Congress by drawing on their inherent constitutional authority to enter in to "executive agreements" with other countries. Although many executive agreements deal with routine foreign policy matters, a great many also involve major military commitments on the part of the United States. Among them are agreements allowing for military bases in the Philippines and defense in Saudi Arabia.

Even when a treaty or other agreement has been approved by Congress, the president retains the ability to withdraw the United States, an action that has been a hallmark of the foreign policy of the Trump administration. Among these have been arms control treaties with Russia and multilateral international agreements, including the Paris Climate Agreement, the Trans-Pacific Partnership trade arrangement, and a nuclear nonproliferation deal with Iran. The administration also withdrew U.S. participation in the UN Human Rights Council and the World Health Organization. Early in his tenure, President Biden restored U.S. participation in some of these agreements, and signaled intent to restore others.

APPOINTMENTS AND APPROPRIATIONS Another significant power wielded by Congress involves the Senate's authority to reject the president's nominees to high military and diplomatic offices. Although this power is rarely exercised in practice, the potential for rejection by the Senate can influence the nominations made by presidents. For example, due to Senate opposition in 2013, President Obama changed his plans to appoint Susan Rice as secretary of state, naming her instead to be national security adviser, a role that does not require confirmation. The need for Senate confirmation seems likely also to have dissuaded President Trump from making some unorthodox choices with regard to appointees to some high offices.

Congress also influences foreign and defense policy through its power to appropriate funds, and it can influence when and where the United States fights through its control of the budget. Although the power to go to war is shared by the executive and legislative branches of government, the power to appropriate funds belongs to the legislature alone. A significant problem faced by Congress in using budgetary powers to set the foreign policy agenda is that after the president publicly commits the United States to a high-profile course of action, it is very hard for Congress to intervene. For example, nothing came of discussion among Democrats in 2007 to halt the war in Iraq by cutting appropriations. Once U.S. troops were already involved in combat, any effort to cut funding was seen as a lack of support for American troops, who could be endangered by budget shortfalls. Figure 16.1 lays out changes in U.S. defense spending over the past eighty years.

FIGURE 16.1   HOW HAS DEFENSE SPENDING CHANGED OVER TIME?

This chart shows U.S. spending on national defense since 1940. Defense spending was at its highest levels during World War II and at its second highest in the post-9/11 period. Dollar amounts were adjusted for inflation to 2015 dollars.

SOURCE: U.S. Office of Management and Budget, Table 3.1—Outlays by Superfunction and Function: 1940–2021.

WAR POWERS   Under the Constitution, the president is commander in chief of the armed forces, but it is reserved to Congress to make a formal declaration of war. During most of American history, it did so for all major international hostilities, including the War of 1812, the Spanish-American War, the Mexican-American War, and the two World Wars. However, as the nature of war has evolved since World War II, this practice has lapsed—even though the United States has pursued sustained military engagements in Korea, Vietnam, the Persian Gulf, Afghanistan, and Iraq.

In 1973, Congress enacted the *War Powers Resolution*. This articulated a new norm that, absent a declaration of war, military actions by the president would need a vote of approval from both houses of Congress for actions lasting longer than sixty days. Under the resolution, the president can respond to an emergency, such as rescuing endangered Americans, but cannot engage in a prolonged struggle without congressional approval.

The War Powers Resolution is controversial and has not been an effective restraint on presidential military authority. No president has recognized its constitutionality, nor has any president felt obligated to inform Congress of military action. Most recently, President Obama employed technicalities to avoid going to Congress after the use of military airpower in Libya exceeded the time limit.

The Judiciary

The area of war powers remains perhaps the most potent and yet unsettled area of constitutional law, in part because of the unwillingness of the federal courts to intervene on such topics. The courts have generally regarded most disputes over foreign policy to be political in nature, and thus not subject to judicial rulings. They also recognize that courts have only limited institutional capabilities with which to analyze complex military and intelligence data.

On the relatively infrequent occasions in which the courts do intervene on foreign and military affairs, it is often to protect a core civil liberty. For instance, the federal courts have ruled on *habeas corpus* with respect to suspected terrorists who have been detained without trial at Guantanamo Bay, Cuba.

Interest Groups and Political Parties

Four types of interest groups are especially active in trying to influence foreign and defense policy decisions. Business groups are the first type that lobbies heavily on foreign policy issues. Particularly controversial is the lobbying carried out by defense industries, often in cooperation with the military, to try to maximize the appropriation of funds by Congress. These groups are often identified as part of the **military-industrial complex**, a term coined by President Dwight D. Eisenhower, who had been a five-star army general during World War II.

Ethnic interest groups are a second type of group heavily involved in foreign policy decision making. The American Israel Public Affairs Committee and the Cuban American National Foundation are among the two more influential groups. Periodically, TransAfrica has also emerged as an important foreign policy lobbying force for the Black community. A number of European American ethnic groups, among them Greeks, Armenians, and Irish, have advocated on behalf their ancestral homelands, as have newer groups centered on Americans with roots in India and Pakistan.

Foreign governments and companies are a third type of organized lobbying interest. The most common concerns of foreign governments are acquiring foreign aid and preventing hostile legislation from being passed. Turkey, for example, lobbied extensively to prevent Congress from passing resolutions labeling as genocide the deaths of Armenians at the hands of the Ottoman Empire around the time of World War I; nonetheless, the House of Representatives did so in 2019. Foreign companies also actively lobby to gain access to the American market and improve the terms under which their investments in the United States are made. During the Trump administration, concerns have been raised that the wide-ranging international business interests of the president and his family could lead to undue influence on foreign policy decision making.

Ideological–public interest groups are a fourth type of group active in foreign policy lobbying. This broad category encompasses think tanks such as the left-leaning Brookings Institution and the conservative Heritage Foundation, activist nongovernmental organizations such as Amnesty International and Greenpeace, and religious organizations. Opinions on major foreign policy issues such as military interventionism, free trade, and environmental agreements often vary widely on the basis of the political ideology held by these organizations. There are sharp differences between Democratic and Republican administrations with regard to which types of ideological–public interest groups are able to influence policy making, mostly notably on contentious issues such as the use of foreign aid for abortion services.

Foreign and military policy are also the subject of disagreement across party lines, with Republicans in recent decades typically assuming a more assertive, unilateral, and at times belligerent approach and Democrats often are more inclined toward diplomacy and the use of multilateral institutions. The Trump administration took what might be considered a third path between these two approaches, marked by relative isolationism. On the one hand, the administration has not

military-industrial complex
The network of political and financial relations formed by defense industries, the U.S. armed forces, and Congress.

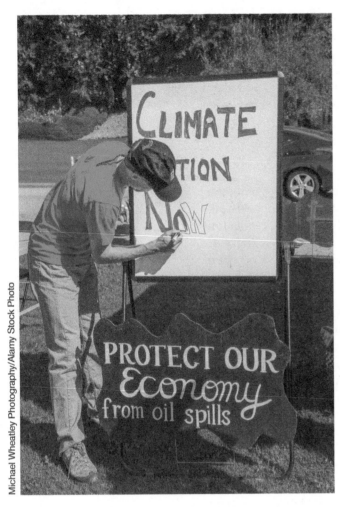

Michael Wheatley Photography/Alamy Stock Photo

undertaken significant armed incursions into foreign countries. On the other hand, the United States had ceded much of its traditional leadership role in multilateral institutions ranging from NATO to the United Nations to the World Trade Organization.

Another factor complicating the conduct of American foreign and defense policy is public opinion, which is often deeply divided over how to proceed on different issues. It can also be difficult to get citizens to devote attention to foreign policy. This is known as the "guns and butter" theory. Generally speaking, most citizens are more interested in domestic policy issues ("butter") because they have a greater impact on their everyday lives. Only in cases of emergency or times of crisis do citizens express significant concern over foreign policy issues ("guns"). This tendency complicates foreign policy making and can make it difficult for foreign policy issues to occupy space on the policy agenda. When they do, public opinion can sometimes shift suddenly in the direction of favoring harsh and excessive action, such as the support voiced for taking extreme action against ISIS.

WHAT ARE THE CONTEMPORARY CHALLENGES IN FOREIGN AND DEFENSE POLICY?

16.3 Evaluate major foreign and defense policy challenges now facing the United States.

Under the direction of the president and other government leaders, the foreign policy and military establishments must address a multitude of contemporary challenges in foreign and defense policy. This section begins by framing the international context within which the United States operates. Then, it highlights four specific issue areas: trade, terrorism, nuclear weapons, and global climate change. Foreign policy making was especially unconventional and even erratic under the Trump administration, making it even more difficult than usual to track ongoing developments in these areas.

The International Context

In the making of foreign and defense policy, the international context is crucially important—U.S. domestic laws and institutions do not extend beyond its borders, and so American policy makers must contend with the leaders of other countries, the realities of power rivalries among global competitors, and the role of nonstate actors, including multinational corporations, transnational nongovernmental organizations, political and religious social movements, organized crime, and terrorist groups.

The field of international relations is a complex one, but two main theories are usually applied to explain the behavior of countries and their foreign and defense policies. One perspective, known as **foreign-policy realism**, argues that nations first and foremost act to protect their core national interests, including the integrity of their territory, the safety of their citizens, the prosperity of their economies, and the welfare

HOW DOES PUBLIC OPINION INFLUENCE FOREIGN POLICY?

Input from citizens can have a significant impact on the conduct of U.S. foreign policy and government engagement with international affairs. Here, a man participates in an international rally at the U.S.–Canadian border, demanding action on runaway climate change and defending the area from new coal, oil, and LNG export projects. Although President Trump had announced his intention to withdraw the United States from the Paris Climate Agreement, President Biden quickly restored United States participation after he entered office.

foreign-policy realism

A perspective contending that the behavior of countries in the international arena is mainly intended to protect their economic and security interests.

TABLE 16.1 HOW DOES U.S. MILITARY SPENDING COMPARE WITH OTHER NATIONS?

Country	Dollars (billions)	% of World Total
1. United States	732	38
2. China	261	14
3. India	71.1	3.7
4. Russia	65.1	3.4
5. Saudi Arabia	61.9	3.2
6. France	50.1	2.6
7. Germany	49.3	2.6
8. United Kingdom	48.7	2.5
9. Japan	47.6	2.5
10. South Korea	43.9	2.3
Total	1800	100

SOURCE: Stockholm International Peace Research Institute Military Expenditure Database, 2020, www.sipri.org/databases/milex.

of their key allies. Realist approaches typically emphasize the role of force, including nuclear deterrence, conventional military power, coercive economic pressure, covert intelligence capabilities, and, increasingly, the threat of cyberattacks. As can be seen in Table 16.1, the U.S. places an extremely heavy priority on military spending when compared with other countries.

An alternate view, known as **foreign-policy idealism**, contends that the behavior of countries in the international arena is largely intended to advance the values and principles that motivate them, such as advancement of free-market capitalism, protection of human rights, and propagation of democratic norms. Idealists emphasize the skillful use of diplomacy, promote peaceful economic interdependence, and make use of multilateral international institutions such as the United Nations, the World Bank, and the International Monetary Fund.

Often, both realism and idealism can simultaneously motivate national behavior. For instance, the Iraq War was partly motivated by classic realist aims to eliminate a potential terrorist threat, to protect regional allies, and to secure access to supplies of oil from the Middle East. But the war was also framed as an opportunity to rid Iraq of a violent dictator, protect the human rights of Iraqis, and advance democratic goals throughout the larger Middle East. Although the United States was unable to secure a UN Security Council resolution authorizing the use of force, it did its best to assemble a multinational coalition and worked toward the return of sovereignty to the Iraqi people via free elections rather than attempting an open-ended occupation. The Trump administration largely embraces foreign policy realism, although in a form that critics often argue can be short-sighted in terms of investing in relations with its allies and in perpetuating the leading American role in multilateral organizations. Supporters of the Trump-era foreign policy contend that the president has done exactly what he said he would do, namely, put "America First" and leave other countries mostly to contend with their own concerns.

foreign-policy idealism

A perspective contending that the behavior of countries in the international arena is mainly intended to advance their values and principles.

Trade

Trade among nations has been a priority in international relations since antiquity. It can be a source of cooperation, competition, or conflict among countries. In the modern world, countries adopt one of three basic approaches in constructing their international trade policy: (1) protectionism, (2) strategic trade, or, (3) free trade. In practice, most countries use some elements of each approach.

protectionism

A trade policy wherein a country takes steps to limit the import of foreign goods through tariffs and subsidies to domestic firms.

TYPES OF TRADE POLICY   First, countries may engage in **protectionism**. In this trade policy, a country takes steps to limit the import of foreign goods. It may also provide domestic producers with subsidies to help them compete against foreign imports. The early American system was rooted in protectionist thinking, including during the Great Depression in the 1930s.

strategic trade policy

A trade policy wherein governments identify key industries that they wish to see grow and enact policies to support their development and success.

Second, countries may embrace a **strategic trade policy**. Under such a policy, governments identify key industries that they want to see grow. They then provide those industries with economic support through tax breaks, low-interest loans, and other benefits. In the United States, computers, aerospace, and biotechnology are sectors that have often been singled out for support.

free trade system

A system of international trade that limits government interference on the sale of goods and services among countries.

Finally, countries may choose to participate in an international **free trade system**. The hallmark of such a system is limited government involvement in international trade. Instead, goods and services cross borders according to supply and demand, as well as the principle of comparative advantage, in which countries sell goods they can produce most efficiently and buy from countries what they cannot. Creating and supporting a free trade system has been a major goal of U.S. trade policy since World War II.

Currently, the United States has trade relations with most countries in the world, but much of U.S. trade policy is defined by its relationship with China, with which trade has increased dramatically over the past three decades. In 1980, the year after the first U.S.–China bilateral trade agreement was signed, total trade (the value of imports and exports) was valued at $5 billion, but by 2017, it was $636 billion. That same year, the United States continued its longstanding and severe trade deficit with China, importing $506 billion from the Chinese while exporting only $130 million in goods to the Chinese.[9] This imbalance has been widely criticized within the United States, partly because some deem it responsible for the loss of domestic manufacturing jobs. Over time, China has pledged to reduce tariffs on agricultural and industrial products, limit agricultural subsidies, open its banking system to foreign banks, halt manipulations of the value of its currency, permit full trading rights to foreign firms, and respect intellectual property rights. The country's failure to fully meet these conditions has been a repeated source of conflict with the United States and others.

Donald J. Trump vociferously criticized Chinese trade policies as a presidential candidate in 2016, arguing that China had long taken advantage of the United States in such areas as violating intellectual property rights and conducting industrial espionage. In office, he initially took a more conciliatory posture, but by early 2018 he had initiated a series of more protectionist policies toward China, including significantly increased tariffs on imports from China. The Trump administration also sought to thwart China from achieving dominance in the telecommunications and information technology industries, especially the emerging 5G technology for cellular networks.

MAKING TRADE POLICY   Three broad policy options exist for the United States under a free trade approach. The first is to emphasize bilateral trade, or that between two nations. Bilateral agreements have a rich history in the United States and continue to be used today. President George W. Bush was able to gain congressional approval for bilateral trade agreements with Australia, Chile, and Singapore. Under President Obama, Congress approved long-stalled trade agreements with South Korea, Colombia, and Panama.

FIGURE 16.2 WHAT ARE THE MAJOR MARKETS FOR U.S. EXPORTS?

The United States exports more goods to Canada than any other country. China, Mexico, and Japan also account for large shares of U.S. exports. Presented are U.S. exports, in billions of dollars, to its top ten trading partners in 2019.

SOURCE: U.S. Census Bureau, Foreign Trade Statistics, www.census.gov/foreign-trade/statistics/highlights/top/top1912yr.html.

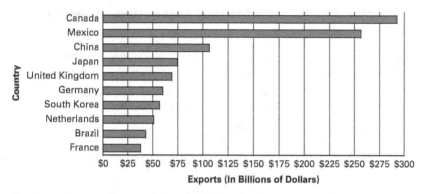

In an attempt to adapt to globalization and incorporate a greater number of trading partners, presidents have increasingly turned to regional trade agreements. Such agreements involve more than two but as few as three states. This was the case with the 1994 North American Free Trade Agreement (NAFTA), which further united the economies of Mexico, Canada, and the United States. NAFTA created the world's largest regional free trade area with a market, but was criticized for moving manufacturing jobs from the United States to Mexico, where labor is much cheaper. In 2019, NAFTA was updated to the **United States–Mexico–Canada Agreement (USMCA)**, which seems likely to boost the U.S. auto, dairy, and information technology industries while tightening certain labor and environmental standards. Figure 16.2 provides information about the United States's major trading parters in 2019.

A wide variety of concerns produce congressional opposition to bilateral and regional trade agreements. Among the most frequent are concerns for workers' rights, labor standards, environmental protection policies, and the health and safety of imports from other countries. Some congressional resistance is also spurred by the potential impact on specific industries in the particular states represented by these members of Congress, such as agriculture in Midwestern states. Presidents have sought to overcome congressional opposition and tried to stop legislators from inserting amendments to these agreements by obtaining what is known as fast-track authority. Congress has the option to give this power to the president for a specific period of time. It requires that Congress may vote on—but not amend—trade agreements concluded by the president, such as the USMCA.

Most modern trade agreements are concluded under a global free trade system. The best known (but not always the most successful) example of this system is the WTO, the international organization created in 1995 to replace the General Agreement on Tariffs and Trade (GATT) and to supervise and expand international trade. Like its predecessor, the WTO reaches agreements through negotiating rounds. The latest round of WTO talks began in 2001 and has involved more than 150 countries. However, the talks largely stalled as rich and poor countries found themselves in deep disagreement over free trade in agricultural products and clothing, protecting the environment, and intellectual property rights.

United States–Mexico–Canada Agreement (USMCA)

A 2019 free trade agreement that promotes movement of goods and services among Canada, Mexico, and the United States. It is a successor to the 1994 North American Free Trade Agreement (NAFTA).

Terrorism

Terrorism is violence designed to achieve political intimidation and instill fear and panic in a population. It is generally pursued for ideological, political, and/or religious goals, and deliberately disregards or directly targets the safety of noncombatants.

Terrorism is usually regarded as a tactic pursued by nongovernmental organizations, but governments may also engage in or support terrorism against either domestic or foreign enemies. Over time and in many different settings, terrorist activities have been used by insurgents against their own governments, by colonized peoples against their occupiers, and by people with grievances against outside countries, including the United States. Terrorism attacks the enemy through a series of largely independent and episodic strikes that, when added together, have an effect far greater than the sum of the individual actions.

TERRORISM AGAINST THE UNITED STATES   In recent years, most terrorist activities directly affecting the United States have been conducted by groups and individuals inspired by the concept of *jihad*, or holy war. A major goal has been to drive the United States out of the Middle East and to return this region to Muslim rule. Even before the devastating attacks of September 11, 2001, this wave of terrorist activity had produced a steady flow of assaults. These included bombings of the U.S. Marine barracks in Lebanon in 1983, the World Trade Center in 1993, American embassies in Kenya and Tanzania in 1998, and the *USS Cole* in port in Yemen in 2000.

Since 9/11, *jihad*-related terrorist activities within the United States have been limited but still have resulted in a number of civilian casualties. Prominent examples over the past decade include a massacre at an Army base in Fort Hood, Texas; the bombing of the Boston Marathon; and shootings at a public benefit center in San Bernardino, California, and in a gay nightclub in Orlando, Florida. Other potential attacks have been detected, deterred, and defended against by vigilance among citizens, by effective law enforcement techniques, and by U.S. intelligence and military capabilities abroad.

Terrorist activity is difficult to combat because it is planned and conducted with stealth and has a broad base of support in many parts of the world. Unlike in traditional warfare, it can also be difficult to define victory against nebulous groups and unknown individual who harbor terrorist inclinations and intentions. Some actors may have direct links to known organizations such as al-Qaeda or ISIS and can be detected through surveillance programs; others may be so-called "lone wolves" who are inspired by terrorist organizations but act on their own initiative, increasingly using low-tech and difficult-to-prevent means such as ramming vehicles into crowds of people. Another persistent concern is that terrorists might obtain a chemical, biological, or nuclear weapon of mass destruction and use it on the territory of a state that they regard as an enemy, or use radioactive materials to contaminate urban areas.

In recent years, the term "domestic terrorism" has also gained increased usage to describe the phenomenon of mass shootings and other violent acts in schools and

HOW DOES TERRORISM CHALLENGE THE UNITED STATES?

Terrorists rely on shock, horror, and the element of surprise to attack enemies, such as the United States and its allies, that they would have no hope of defeating through conventional military means. The terrorist group known as the Islamic State in Iraq and Syria (ISIS) sought to provoke a public response by uploading disturbing video footage of hostages, such as captured American journalist David Cawthorne Haines in 2014, pictured here. Although ISIS has been on the wane in recent years, it and other terrorist organizations pose a continuing threat to the territory and interests of the United States and its allies.

EyePress News/SIPA/AP Images

other public setting. Critics on the political left have adopted this term to apply to gun violence motivated by White supremacist ideology, while some on the right have applied it to the property damage and loss of life associated with rioting in urban areas. Still others find this a misleading, and even inflammatory, misapplication of the term "terrorism" to acts covered by ordinary criminal law.

Nuclear Weapons

Since the American bombings of the Japanese cities of Hiroshima and Nagasaki in 1945, the existence, proliferation, and potential use of nuclear weapons has been a central concern of U.S. foreign policy. The potential for a catastrophic exchange of nuclear weapons between the United States and the Soviet Union was the defining fear of the Cold War. However, nuclear weapons were never again used after 1945, and the overall number of operational warheads has declined since its peak during the late Cold War. Still, there are estimated to be more than 10,000 warheads remaining under the control of nine countries.[10] In addition to the five UN Security Council members (the United States, Russia, Britain, France, and China), the less stable and more conflict-prone countries of India, Pakistan, North Korea, and Israel also possess nuclear arms. Over the past year, political rhetoric from the United States, North Korea, and Russia has increasingly implied—or outright threatened—the possible use of nuclear weapons. Even if such language was mainly bluster, it defied long-term trends away from even invoking that possibility.

This proliferation raises the ongoing risk not only of direct military confrontation, but also that warheads or other nuclear materials could come under the control of terrorist groups. Their mere existence also adds anxiety and uncertainty to international relations, such as when unstable and unpredictable North Korea has periodically threatened to use nuclear weapons against its regional neighbors and even against Washington, D.C. Other countries, most notably Iran, have created global tensions merely through their pursuit of nuclear capabilities. All of these concerns pose major ongoing challenges for U.S. foreign and defense policy. Several strategies traditionally have been in place to limit arms proliferation: disarmament, arms control, defense, and counterproliferation.

DISARMAMENT   Disarmament takes the very existence of weapons as a cause for conflict and hopes to secure peace through eliminating them. The earliest nuclear disarmament proposals, following World War II, aimed to place all aspects of nuclear energy production and use under international control, but such aspirations foundered under the pressure of the Cold War. In the 1990s, a number of countries unilaterally chose to pursue disarmament, including the former Soviet countries of Belarus, Kazakhstan, and Ukraine, as well as South Africa, which was rapidly democratizing at that time. In 2009, President Obama publicly endorsed disarmament as a goal, but to little avail, and today the prospects for moving toward the abolition of nuclear arsenals seem slim.

ARMS CONTROL   A second strategy is arms control. This approach takes the existence of conflict between countries as a given in world politics and attempts to find ways of reducing the chances that those conflicts will become deadly. Decreasing the numbers and types of weapons at the disposal of policy makers is one approach. All but one of the world's major nuclear arms control agreements have been made between the United States and the Soviet Union (and its principal successor state, Russia), as they possess the largest numbers of these weapons. This regime of arms control has achieved considerable success, considering that stockpiles of operational nuclear warheads have declined more than six-fold since the mid-1980s. However, nuclear arms control efforts were significantly set back in 2018 when both the United States and Russia suspended their cooperation on the Intermediate-Range Nuclear Forces (INF) Agreement, a remnant of the end of the Cold War era. The following year, the United States officially withdrew, alleging that Russia had been violating INF and also noting that the treaty's value had eroded because China was not a signatory.

Also significant is the Nuclear Non-proliferation Treaty (NPT) of 1968, which has been joined by nearly every member of the United Nations. The NPT commits those countries that do not already have nuclear weapons not to develop them, while those that do have them commit to pursuing disarmament and to sharing technologies for the use of nuclear energy for peaceful purposes. However, the few non parties to the treaty include the nuclear-armed states of India, Pakistan, and Israel, which limits its practical scope. The limitations of the NPT were also made evident when North Korea withdrew in 2003 and then, despite multiple rounds of diplomatic negotiations, went on to test both nuclear weapons and long-range missiles.

The possibility of preemptive American action against the North Korean nuclear weapons program remains a possibility, curtailed in part by the horrifying potential toll of death and destruction in South Korea and Japan, two close U.S. allies, that would likely take place during the opening days of any such conflict. Analysts of North Korea's nuclear capabilities believe that it is expanding its capacity to place nuclear weapons onto long-range ballistic missiles. It already has the ability to reach American allies, armed forces bases abroad, and possibly territories in the Pacific Ocean. In fact, it may be because North Korean leader Kim Jong-un felt secure in his country's capabilities that he undertook a process of peacebuilding with South Korea and the United States in 2018, including a brief summit meeting with President Trump. Since then, nuclear tensions with North Korea have entered into abeyance, with neither major advances nor clear-cut regressions taking place. Still, the opaque nature of the North Korean regime, and persistent rumors about ill health and prolonged disappearances from public on the part of Kim, have kept the Korean peninsula a tense region of the world.

DEFENSE A third strategy is defense. Essentially, this goal encourages the creation of a system to block or intercept attacks from other countries, particularly by developing the capability to strike down nuclear-armed missiles while they are still over the territory of the country that is undertaking the launch. Such a system was the animating vision of the **Strategic Defense Initiative (SDI)**, introduced by the Reagan administration in 1983. Although SDI was actually far beyond what was technologically possible at the time, or even today, it is credited by some for increasing pressure on the Soviet Union and hastening the end of the Cold War. More recently, the United States has undertaken long-term plans to deploy a limited system of long-range missile interceptors positioned within U.S. territories, on Navy vessels, and within the territory of NATO allies. Such moves by the United States have drawn sharp protests from countries such as China and Russia, and have likely accelerated those countries' efforts to build weapons that can counteract any defensive measures that the United States may develop as well as methods to destroy satellites and other infrastructure that would be used to guide a defensive system.

COUNTERPROLIFERATION A final strategy embraced by many countries today is counterproliferation. This involves the use, or at least threat, of preemptive military action against a threatening country or terrorist group. One of the major rationales for the 2003 invasion of Iraq by a U.S.-led multinational coalition was to eliminate the nuclear and other weapons of mass destruction alleged to exist there. More recently, the threat of such a preemptive attack—combined with crippling economic sanctions—led to a diplomatic breakthrough with Iran in 2015. Under the terms of the wide-ranging Joint Comprehensive Plan of Action, the Iranian regime agreed to dismantle its existing nuclear facilities and submit to invasive international inspections in exchange for the lifting of economic sanctions and its reintegration into the world financial system. From the outset, however, the Trump administration accused Iran of breaching its responsibilities, and the president withdrew from the agreement in 2018. Since then, the agreement has continued a fragile existence among Iran and other signatories to the treaty, either waiting to collapse entirely or else be comprehensively renegotiated.

Global Climate Change

The issue of global climate change has been on the global political agenda since at least 1994, with the establishment of the United Nations Framework Convention on Climate Change (UNFCCC). In 1997, President Bill Clinton signed the Kyoto Protocol. This landmark multilateral agreement codified an international consensus that rising levels of "greenhouse gas emissions" are causing a dangerous increase in the Earth's temperature. Some remaining skeptics, particularly among conservatives in the United States, argue either that climate change is not a serious threat or that it is simply a naturally occurring phenomenon. However, over the past two decades, a robust body of scientific evidence has demonstrated that climate-warming trends over the last century have been caused primarily by human industrial activities.

One report by the U.S. National Aeronautics and Space Administration (NASA) identified a range of potentially disastrous effects from global temperature increases, including warming oceans and sea-level rise, shrinking ice sheets and glacial retreat, decreased snow cover, and ocean acidification.[11] Such changes could increase the incidence of catastrophic droughts, floods, hurricanes, heat waves, crop failures, and health problems among both human and animal populations. These impacts are likely to be greatest on the poorest countries with the fewest resources—ironically, the very ones that have benefitted the least from the mass industrialization in wealthier countries that led to climate change. According to the Intergovernmental Panel on Climate Change, some risks of damaging climate change occur at just 1° or 2°C above preindustrial levels; an increase of global mean temperature of 4°C or more above preindustrial levels could cause disastrous consequences.[12] The submersion of highly populated coastal areas, mass flows of refugees, increased border conflict, widespread starvation, and even the disappearance of several small island nations are all among the potential politically destabilizing impacts of global climate change.

In response to such threats, the Obama administration designated a new Global Climate Change Initiative as one of three priority U.S. development initiatives, released a Climate Action Plan, and struck bilateral accords with India, Brazil, and China.[13] These advances involving the world's two largest "emitters" provided momentum for the Paris Climate Agreement. This historic framework brought together 196 developed and developing countries to resolve to bring down global greenhouse gas emissions "as soon as possible," to retain an existing target of keeping global warming below 2°C while aspiring to 1.5°C, and to aim for no further net increases in emissions from human activities after 2050.[14]

Reflecting the priorities of his political party and his base of support, President Trump largely halted efforts at international cooperation on climate change, including withdrawing from the Paris Agreement. Climate change also was downgraded, or even eliminated, as a priority by a range of federal agencies. However, with increasing evidence of wildfires, hurricanes, floods, and other damaging weather-related disasters, global efforts against climate change continue. Most countries remain engaged with the Paris Agreement, and many U.S. states, cities, and private institutions signaled their intention to advance its goals even without the participation of the U.S. federal government. Then in 2021, President Biden returned the U.S. to the agreement and appointed former U.S. secretary of state John Kerry as a cabinet-level special presidential envoy for climate.

POLITICAL REFORM AND REALITIES: A GLOBAL SYSTEM IN FLUX

16.4 Understand emerging challenges that are shaping U.S. foreign and defense policies in four key geographic regions.

The United States remains a dominant power in world politics, with the world's largest economy and its strongest military. It has many allies and provides economic and military aid to many countries around the globe. At the same time, however, the lengthy wars in

Iraq and Afghanistan, the ongoing challenges posed by al-Qaeda and ISIS, domestic political gridlock, and other social, political, and economic factors have demonstrated some of the limits of American power. This concluding section considers emerging challenges facing the United States and the Trump administration with regard to four critical world regions: China, Russia, Europe, and the Middle East and North Africa (MENA) region.

China

The tremendous economic growth and global influence of China is leading it to become a challenger to the United States in some areas, but also its most logical partner in others. Both countries benefit from trade and globalization, both want to limit the spread of nuclear weapons, and both are served by reining in countries such as Iran and North Korea that threaten peace and stability. There is still considerable tension and mistrust as well. China depends on the U.S. market to sell exports and fuel its economic growth. The United States borrows heavily from China, which finances growing U.S. budget deficits by purchasing American Treasury bonds. This type of interaction creates a potentially unhealthy mutual dependency for economic prosperity, especially as China's rate of growth has slowed in recent years. Worsening tensions over tariffs and trade imbalances have contributed to a so-called "trade war" mentality between the two countries under the Trump administration.

At the same time, China is modernizing its navy, missiles, aircraft, cyber warfare capabilities, and anti-satellite weapons. In a move deemed provocative by many of its neighbors, China has even constructed artificial islands in the South China Sea and claimed sovereignty over them—giving it a stronger foothold for military action and a tighter grip on a major transit route for global trade. In response, the United States has begun deploying more military forces in the Pacific and also strengthened its partnerships with India, Japan, South Korea, and other Asian countries that serve as regional counterweights to China in the Asia–Pacific region.

In early 2020, the sudden global spread of the novel coronavirus from its point of origin in Wuhan, China, became a serious challenge for the Chinese regime and made the country a focus of escalating hostility on the part of the U.S. government. Major accusations by the United States included that China failed to contain the virus early on and also failed to share data with other countries on a timely basis, allowing the COVID-19 pandemic to spread worldwide and cause huge loss of life, economic losses, and social disruption. To underscore his point, Trump took to referring to the coronavirus as "the China virus," a provocative phrase to use in reference to a country that is acutely conscious of its image in the world.

In all, the Trump administration has undertaken an aggressive stance toward China, in both words and deeds, but not a stance so extreme to cause the Chinese–American relationship to turn toward armed conflict or deteriorate beyond repair. What seems clear is that relations between the two countries will increasingly determine how peaceful or dangerous the world becomes, and quite possibly also how prosperous it is.

Russia

Russia has begun to aggressively reassert the great-power status that it lost in the early 1990s with the collapse of the Soviet Union. Strongman President Vladimir Putin first consolidated power domestically by crushing terrorist threats from the Caucasus region; he then took control of Russian television and some other media and began to use heavy-handed tactics to suppress political dissent. Long propelled by high oil prices, Putin has cannily used his leverage to attempt to reestablish a zone of influence in neighboring countries that had been part of the Russian Empire and the Soviet Union. A global decline in the price of oil somewhat curtailed Putin's latitude for action, but Russia remains a continuing geopolitical rival for the United States and its allies.

HOW IS CHINA ASSERTING ITSELF ON THE WORLD STAGE?
China has increasingly been claiming a larger role in not only the world economy but also with regard to military affairs. This image shows an artificial island being created by China in a heavily trafficked and legally contested region of the South China Sea, underscoring the country's assertion of power in the region and globally.

Where possible, Putin uses economic means, including promotion of a "Eurasian Economic Community" as a counterweight to the European Union (EU). But Putin also has not hesitated to use military means, including outright invasions of former Soviet republics Georgia and Ukraine and an intervention in Syria to prop up his ally Bashar al-Assad. His show of force has even included the use of Russian naval and air forces to skirt the boundaries of former Soviet countries in the Baltic region that are now NATO and EU members.

Russian–American relations are widely considered to have sunk to the lowest point since the Cold War, with an ever-diminishing number of diplomatic, economic, cultural, and other connections. Behavior by the United States has been inconsistent, with some firm actions taken against Russia, such as expelling diplomats from the country, but seemingly little will on the part of President Trump to confront Russia. Indeed, President Trump's uncharacteristically passive demeanor during a 2018 summit meeting with Putin in Helsinki, Finland, raised further concerns about his resolve to confront Russian aggression, as did his stated desire in 2020 to reinstate Russia as a member of the G-7 group of major democratic countries.

Overshadowing much of the U.S.–Russia relationship since the 2016 presidential election have been persistent questions of how, and in what ways, agents of the Russian government may deliberately have intervened to spread misinformation, sow confusion, and perhaps damage the candidacy of Hillary Clinton, who was perceived by Russia as being particularly hostile toward it. A number of U.S. intelligence agencies have asserted that such electoral interference was conducted by Russia, but President Trump himself largely avoided the issue other than to deny collusion between his campaign and Russia, which is under active investigation by the Justice Department. As evidence has continued to grow regarding manipulation of social media by Russians to disrupt the internal politics of the United States and other democracies, this issue remains a complicated and potentially explosive subject, particularly if Russia is eventually found to have meddled in the 2020 presidential election.

Europe

At the same time that China and Russia have been strengthening, America's most enduring allies in Europe have lately lurched from crisis to crisis in both the political and economic realms. This poses a challenge for the United States, whose global standing is tied to that of Europe, which forms the core of the NATO military alliance, constitutes the world's largest economic bloc, and is a key U.S. trading partner.

WHO ARE AMERICA'S KEY FOREIGN ALLIES?

Since World War II, the United States has led the NATO military alliance. Two key American partners are its oldest ally, France, and its one-time enemy in both of the world wars, Germany. Above, President Trump met with French President Emmanuel Macron, left, and German Chancellor Angela Merkel at the 2017 summit of the G20, a group of leading global powers.

European Union

An organization with political institutions that join twenty-seven countries in Europe into a union that promotes free trade, a central bank, flow of labor and capital, and a common currency among most members.

A cornerstone of European peace, prosperity, and democracy has been the **European Union (EU)**, which promotes cooperation rather than conflict among the nations on the once-war-torn continent.

In recent years, however, the EU has faced severe challenges. Several countries, including Greece, Spain, Portugal, Italy, and Ireland, have run the risk of defaulting on their loans. This has undermined the euro, the common currency shared by seventeen EU nations, and required numerous bailouts by Europe's richer countries, whose citizens are often resentful. At the same time, a crisis caused by massive flows of refugees from Syria, Iraq, and other conflict zones has escalated tensions within the EU and threatened the viability of its much-valued open borders and free flow of populations. Another challenge has been the emergence of illiberal nationalist governments in such countries as Hungary and Poland that have undermined the consensus of democratic values underpinning the Union.

Also damaging has been series of terrorist attacks, especially in France and Belgium, against which police and intelligence communities were proven unable to respond in an effective or coordinated fashion. The closing of borders in response to the COVID-19 pandemic also reversed decades of integration among Europeans, although hopes persisted that such closures would be temporary measures easily reversed once the pandemic abates. Perhaps most existentially threatening for the European Union has been the so-called "Brexit" process in 2020 when the United Kingdom became the first country to withdraw from EU membership. Cumulatively, these crises have emboldened anti-EU political parties across the continent, laid bare the limits of the EU's ability to govern collectively, and even threatened the long-term viability of the EU itself. This all matters greatly to the United States, as Europe remains the most important American strategic ally in global affairs, despite President Trump's periodic expressions of disdain for the NATO Alliance.

The Middle East and North Africa (MENA) Region

The United States also faces myriad foreign and defense policy challenges created by events in the world's most volatile area: the Middle East and North Africa (MENA) region. Following the U.S.-led invasions of Afghanistan in 2002 and Iraq in 2003, and a series of short-lived popular uprisings in several Arab countries beginning in 2010, almost the entire MENA region was destabilized. Certainly, hopes of a democratic awakening have been mostly dashed: some MENA countries have devolved into chaos and civil war, such as Libya, Yemen, and Syria, while others have undergone harsh crackdowns, such as Egypt, Turkey, and Bahrain. Tensions between the two major branches of Islam have also escalated, with a Sunni coalition led by Saudi Arabia increasingly at odds with a Shia bloc led by Iran for regional predominance. Such grave developments are only somewhat offset by a few success stories, such as the consolidation of democracy in Tunisia, a domestic liberalization process within Saudi Arabia, and the establishment of diplomatic relations between Israel and the United Arab Emirates.

The United States has numerous key interests in the MENA region, including support for allies such as Turkey and Israel, protection of the global supply of oil, and the need to thwart terrorist forces originating in the region. For every step forward for U.S. policy, such as the nuclear deal with Iran and efforts to bring peace to Syria, new threats have emerged, including the proliferation of ISIS and periodic flare-ups in the Israeli–Palestinian conflict. Indeed, no other region of the world so exemplifies both the continuing power of the United States and its sharp limitations as an actor in the world.

CHALLENGES AHEAD FOR THE UNITED STATES   In conclusion, the United States faces no existential military threats such as those posed by the Soviet Union during the Cold War. The United States remains the planet's most potent military power, backed by the world's largest economy, and it has on the whole managed the steady emergence of China as a rival power. At the same time, the United States faces turbulence and conflict in nearly every corner of the world and a range of persistent threats requiring ongoing vigilance and determination. Indeed, the year 2020 also dramatically underscored the inability of any country to act unilaterally and the continuing need for international cooperation. The immediate response to the COVID-19 pandemic was often nationalism and isolationism, even as it became clear that the long-term scientific, medical, and epidemiological response to the disease would demand robust worldwide cooperation. Yet COVID-19 may ultimately pale in comparison to the international upheavals caused by global climate change, a truly unprecedented challenge for a planet that remains more divided than united and at least as confrontational as cooperative.

As president, Joe Biden seems likely to represent a return to a more conventional U.S. foreign policy, placing priority on repairing damaged relationships with allies and returning the United States to multilateral frameworks such as the Paris Climate Accords, the World Health Organization, and the UN Human Rights Council. Yet, as every U.S. president learns at some point, despite their potent political authority and their nation's military and economic might, they must confront a complicated world as it really is, not as they might wish it to be.

CONCLUSION AND REVIEW

What Are the Roots of U.S. Foreign and Defense Policy?

16.1 Outline the major events and issues in the development of U.S. foreign and defense policy.

For most of the nation's first century, foreign and defense policy largely involved trade and commerce, isolationism with regard to Europe, and expansion across North America. As U.S. economic interests expanded, the United States intervened more and more overseas, especially in Latin America and Asia. The United States' status as a world power was cemented by its entry into, and subsequent victories in, World Wars I and II. During the Cold War, U.S. foreign and defense policy was focused on its confrontation with the Soviet Union. The September 11, 2001, terrorist attacks marked a new direction in American foreign policy, as the United States pursued a war on terrorism both at home and overseas.

How Does the United States Make Foreign and Defense Policy Decisions?

16.2 Describe the roles of government officials and of other influences on U.S. foreign and defense policy.

The basic structure of foreign and defense policy decision making is laid out in the Constitution. The executive branch of government dominates foreign and defense policy. The president is preeminent, with the Departments of State, Defense, and Homeland Security also playing important roles, along with the intelligence community. Congress also influences and shapes policy through oversight, approval of treaties and appointments, appropriations, and the War Powers Resolution. Four types of interest groups are also especially active in trying to influence foreign and defense policy decisions; these groups include the military-industrial complex, ethnic interest groups, foreign governments and companies, and ideological–public interest groups. Political parties and public opinion also influence the shape of U.S. foreign and defense policies.

What Are the Contemporary Challenges in Foreign and Defense Policy?

16.3 Evaluate major foreign and defense policy challenges now facing the United States.

The United States faces major challenges in foreign and defense policy during the twenty-first century. These include trade, terrorism, nuclear weapons, and global climate change. In terms of trade, the United States operates within a global free trade system but runs an overall trade imbalance of more imports than exports. Although terrorism may have at least temporarily receded as the most high-profile threat to American interests, it poses enduring dangers. The threat of nuclear weapons has receded somewhat since the end of the Cold War, but rogue nations and terrorist organizations still raise serious concerns. Global climate change threatens political, economic, and social stability around the globe, yet the world's leaders have been hard-pressed to find effective collective solutions.

Political Reform and Realities: A Global System in Flux

16.4 Understand emerging challenges that are shaping U.S. foreign and defense policies in four key geographic regions.

The United States remains a dominant power in world politics, with the world's largest economy and its largest military, but faces challenge on many fronts. China is America's single most significant economic partner, but also the greatest potential threat to U.S. global supremacy, and Russia has also reasserted itself on the world stage. At the same time, Europe and the European Union are under growing duress, and the Middle East and North Africa (MENA) region is embroiled in conflict and turmoil. These and other new challenges, including the COVID-19 pandemic and global climate change, pose threats, and in some cases also opportunities, for the United States today and in the years ahead.

LEARN THE TERMS

Afghanistan War
al-Qaeda
Berlin Wall
Bretton Woods System
Central Intelligence Agency (CIA)
Cold War
collective security
containment
Cuban Missile Crisis
defense policy
Department of Defense
Department of Homeland Security
Department of State
détente
deterrence
European Union
Farewell Address
foreign policy
foreign-policy idealism
foreign-policy realism

free trade system
General Agreement on Tariffs and
    Trade (GATT)
global war on terror
Gulf War
human rights
International Monetary Fund
    (IMF)
Iraq War
Iron Curtain
ISIS
isolationism
Joint Chiefs of Staff
Korean War
League of Nations
manifest destiny
Marshall Plan
military-industrial complex
Monroe Doctrine
National Security Council

North Atlantic Treaty Organization
    (NATO)
protectionism
Reagan Doctrine
Roosevelt Corollary
September 11
strategic trade policy
tariffs
Truman Doctrine
UN Security Council
United Nations
U.S.–Mexico–Canada Agreement
    (USMCA)
Vietnam War
World Bank
World Trade Organization
    (WTO)
World War I
World War II

THE DECLARATION OF INDEPENDENCE

In Congress, July 4, 1776
The Unanimous Declaration
of the Thirteen United States of America

When in the Course of human events it becomes necessary for one people to dissolve the political bands which have connected them with another, and to assume, among the powers of the earth, the separate and equal station to which the Laws of Nature and of Nature's God entitle them, a decent respect to the opinions of mankind requires that they should declare the causes which impel them to the separation.

We hold these truths to be self-evident, that all men are created equal, that they are endowed by their Creator with certain unalienable Rights, that among these are Life, Liberty and the pursuit of Happiness. That to secure these rights, Governments are instituted among Men, deriving their just powers from the consent of the governed. That whenever any Form of Government becomes destructive of these ends, it is the Right of the People to alter or to abolish it, and to institute new Government, laying its foundation on such principles and organizing its powers in such form, as to them shall seem most likely to effect their Safety and Happiness. Prudence, indeed, will dictate that Governments long established should not be changed for light and transient causes; and accordingly all experience hath shewn that mankind are more disposed to suffer, while evils are sufferable, than to right themselves by abolishing the forms to which they are accustomed. But when a long train of abuses and usurpations, pursuing invariably the same Object evinces a design to reduce them under absolute Despotism, it is their right, it is their duty, to throw off such Government, and to provide new Guards for their future security. —Such has been the patient sufferance of these Colonies; and such is now the necessity which constrains them to alter their former Systems of Government. The history of the present King of Great Britain is a history of repeated injuries and usurpations, all having in direct object the establishment of an absolute Tyranny over these States. To prove this, let Facts be submitted to a candid world.

He has refused his Assent to Laws, the most wholesome and necessary for the public good.

He has forbidden his Governors to pass Laws of immediate and pressing importance, unless suspended in their operation till his Assent should be obtained; and when so suspended, he has utterly neglected to attend to them.

He has refused to pass other Laws for the accommodation of large districts of people, unless those people would relinquish the right of Representation in the Legislature, a right inestimable to them and formidable to tyrants only.

He has called together legislative bodies at places unusual, uncomfortable, and distant from the depository of their Public Records, for the sole purpose of fatiguing them into compliance with his measures.

He has dissolved Representative Houses repeatedly, for opposing with manly firmness his invasions on the rights of the people.

He has refused for a long time, after such dissolutions, to cause others to be elected; whereby the Legislative Powers, incapable of Annihilation, have returned to the People at large for their exercise, the State remaining in the mean time exposed to all the dangers of invasion from without, and convulsions within.

He has endeavored to prevent the population of these States; for that purpose obstructing the Laws of Naturalization of Foreigners; refusing to pass others to encourage their migration hither, and raising the conditions of new Appropriations of Lands.

He has obstructed the Administration of Justice, by refusing his Assent to Laws for establishing Judiciary powers.

He has made Judges dependent on his Will alone, for the tenure of their offices, and the amount and payment of their salaries.

He has erected a multitude of New Offices, and sent hither swarms of Officers to harass our people, and eat out their substance.

He has kept among us, in times of peace, Standing Armies without the Consent of our legislatures.

He has affected to render the Military independent of and superior to the Civil power.

He has combined with others to subject us to a jurisdiction foreign to our constitution, and unacknowledged by our laws, giving his Assent to their Acts of pretended Legislation:

For quartering large bodies of armed troops among us:

For protecting them, by a mock Trial, from punishment for any Murders which they should commit on the Inhabitants of these States:

For cutting off our Trade with all parts of the world:

For imposing Taxes on us without our Consent:

For depriving us in many cases, of the benefits of Trial by Jury:

For transporting us beyond Seas to be tried for pretended offences:

For abolishing the free System of English Laws in a neighboring Province, establishing therein an Arbitrary government, and enlarging its Boundaries so as to render it at once an example and fit instrument for introducing the same absolute rule into these Colonies:

For taking away our Charters, abolishing our most valuable Laws, and altering fundamentally the Forms of our Governments:

For suspending our own Legislatures, and declaring themselves invested with power to legislate for us in all cases whatsoever.

He has abdicated Government here, by declaring us out of his Protection and waging War against us.

He has plundered our seas, ravaged our Coasts, burnt our towns, and destroyed the lives of our people.

He is at this time transporting large Armies of foreign Mercenaries to compleat the works of death, desolation and tyranny, already begun with circumstances of Cruelty and perfidy scarcely paralleled in the most barbarous ages, and totally unworthy the Head of a civilized nation.

He has constrained our fellow Citizens taken Captive on the high Seas to bear Arms against their Country, to become the executioners of their friends and Brethren, or to fall themselves by their Hands.

He has excited domestic insurrections amongst us, and has endeavored to bring on the inhabitants of our frontiers, the merciless Indian Savages, whose known rule of warfare, is an undistinguished destruction of all ages, sexes and conditions.

In every stage of these Oppressions We have Petitioned for Redress in the most humble terms: Our repeated Petitions have been answered only by repeated injury: A Prince, whose character is thus marked by every act which may define a Tyrant, is unfit to be the ruler of a free people.

Nor have We been wanting in attention to our British brethren. We have warned them from time to time of attempts by their legislature to extend an unwarrantable jurisdiction over us. We have reminded them of the circumstances of our emigration and settlement here. We have appealed to their native justice and magnanimity; and we have conjured them by the ties of our common kindred to disavow these usurpations, which would inevitably interrupt our connections and correspondence. They too have been deaf to the voice of justice and consanguinity. We must, therefore, acquiesce in the necessity, which denounces our Separation, and hold them, as we hold the rest of mankind, Enemies in War, in Peace Friends.

We, therefore, the Representatives of the United States of America, in General Congress, Assembled, appealing to the Supreme Judge of the world for the rectitude of our intentions, do, in the Name, and by Authority of the good People of these Colonies, solemnly publish and declare, That these United Colonies are, and of Right ought to be Free and Independent States; that they are Absolved from all Allegiance to the British Crown, and that all political connection between them and the State of Great Britain, is and ought to be totally dissolved: and that as Free and Independent States, they have full power to levy War, conclude Peace, contract Alliances, establish Commerce, and to do all other Acts and Things which Independent States may of right do. And for the support of this Declaration, with a firm reliance on the protection of Divine Providence, we mutually pledge to each other our Lives, our Fortunes and our sacred Honor.

JOHN HANCOCK

New Hampshire
Josiah Bartlett
William Whipple
Matthew Thornton

Massachusetts
Samuel Adams
John Adams
Robert Treat Paine
Elbridge Gerry

Rhode Island and Providence Plantations
Stephen Hopkins
William Ellery

Connecticut
Roger Sherman
Samuel Huntington
William Williams
Oliver Wolcott

New York
William Floyd
Philip Livingston
Francis Lewis
Lewis Morris

New Jersey
Richard Stockton
John Witherspoon
Francis Hopkinson
John Hart
Abraham Clark

Pennsylvania
Robert Morris
Benjamin Rush
Benjamin Franklin
John Morton
George Clymer
James Smith
George Taylor
James Wilson
George Ross

Delaware
Caesar Rodney
George Read
Thomas McKean

Maryland
Samuel Chase
William Paca

Thomas Stone
Charles Carroll

Virginia
George Wythe
Richard Henry Lee
Thomas Jefferson
Benjamin Harrison
Thomas Nelson, Jr.
Francis Lightfoot Lee
Carter Braxton

North Carolina
William Hooper
Joseph Hewes
John Penn

South Carolina
Edward Rutledge
Thomas Heyward, Jr.
Thomas Lynch, Jr.
Arthur Middleton

Georgia
Button Gwinnett
Lyman Hall
George Walton

THE CONSTITUTION OF THE UNITED STATES OF AMERICA

We the People of the United States, in Order to form a more perfect Union, establish Justice, insure domestic Tranquility, provide for the common defence, promote the general Welfare, and secure the Blessings of Liberty to ourselves and our Posterity, do ordain and establish this Constitution for the United States of America.

ARTICLE I

Section 1

All legislative Powers herein granted shall be vested in a Congress of the United States, which shall consist of a Senate and House of Representatives.

Section 2

The House of Representatives shall be composed of Members chosen every second Year by the People of the several States, and the Electors in each State shall have the Qualifications requisite for Electors of the most numerous Branch of the State Legislature.

No person shall be a Representative who shall not have attained to the Age of twenty five Years, and been seven Years a Citizen of the United States, and who shall not, when elected, be an Inhabitant of that State in which he shall be chosen.

Representatives and direct Taxes shall be apportioned among the several States which may be included within this Union, according to their respective Numbers which shall be determined by adding to the whole Number of free Persons, including those bound to Service for a Term of Years, and excluding Indians not taxed, three fifths of all other Persons. The actual Enumeration shall be made within three Years after the first Meeting of the Congress of the United States, and within every subsequent Term ten Years, in such Manner as they shall by Law direct. The Number of Representatives shall not exceed one for every thirty Thousand, but each State shall have at Least one Representative; and until such enumerations shall be made, the State of New Hampshire shall be entitled to chuse three, Massachusetts eight, Rhode-Island and Providence Plantations one, Connecticut five, New-York six, New Jersey four, Pennsylvania eight, Delaware one, Maryland six, Virginia ten, North Carolina five, South Carolina five, and Georgia three.

When vacancies happen in the Representation from any State, the Executive Authority thereof shall issue Writs of Election to fill such Vacancies.

The House of Representatives shall chuse their speaker and other Officers; and shall have the sole Power of Impeachment.

Section 3

The Senate of the United States shall be composed of two Senators from each State chosen by the Legislature thereof, for six Years; and each Senator shall have one Vote.

Immediately after they shall be assembled in Consequence of the first Election, they shall be divided as equally as may be into three Classes. The Seats of the Senators of the first Class shall be vacated at the Expiration of the second year, of the second Class at the Expiration of the fourth Year, and of the third Class at the Expiration of the sixth Year, so that one third may be chosen every second Year and if Vacancies happen by Resignation, or otherwise, during the Recess of the Legislature of any State, the Executive thereof may make temporary Appointments until the next Meeting of the Legislature, which shall then fill such Vacancies.

No Person shall be a Senator who shall not have attained to the Age of thirty Years, and been nine Years a Citizen of the United States, and who shall not, when elected, be an Inhabitant of that State for which he shall be chosen.

The Vice President of the United States shall be President of the Senate, but shall have no Vote, unless they be equally divided.

The Senate shall chuse their other Officers, and also a President pro tempore, in the Absence of the Vice President, or when he shall exercise the Office of President of the United States.

The Senate shall have the sole Power to try all Impeachments. When sitting for that Purpose, they shall be on Oath or Affirmation. When the President of the United States is tried, the Chief Justice shall preside: And no Person shall be convicted without the Concurrence of two thirds of the Members present.

Judgment in Cases of Impeachment shall not extend further than to removal from Office, and disqualification to hold and enjoy any Office of honor, Trust or Profit under the United States; but the Party convicted shall nevertheless be liable and subject to Indictment, Trial, Judgment and Punishment, according to law.

Section 4

The Times, Places and Manner of holding Elections for Senators and Representatives, shall be prescribed in each State by the Legislature thereof; but the Congress may at any time by Law make or alter such Regulations, except as to the Places of chusing Senators.

The Congress shall assemble at least once in every Year, and such Meeting shall be on the first Monday in December, unless they shall by Law appoint a different Day.

Section 5

Each House shall be the Judge of the Elections, Returns and Qualifications of its own Members, and a Majority of each shall constitute a Quorum to do business; but a smaller Number may adjourn from day to day, and may be authorized to compel the Attendance of absent Members, in such Manner, and under such Penalties as each House may provide.

Each House may determine the Rules of its Proceedings, punish its Members for disorderly Behaviour, and with the Concurrence of two thirds, expel a Member.

Each House shall keep a Journal of its Proceedings, and from time to time publish the same, excepting such Parts as may in their judgment require Secrecy; and the Yeas and Nays of the Members of either House on any question shall, at the Desire of one fifth of those present, be entered on the Journal.

Neither House, during the Session of Congress, shall, without the Consent of the other, adjourn for more than three days, nor to any other Place than that in which the two Houses shall be sitting.

Section 6

The Senators and Representatives shall receive a Compensation for their Services, to be ascertained by Law, and paid out of the Treasury of the United States. They shall in all Cases, except Treason, Felony and Breach of the Peace, be privileged from Arrest during their Attendance at the Session of their respective Houses, and in going to and returning from the same; and for any Speech or Debate in either House, they shall not be questioned in any other Place.

No Senator or Representative shall, during the Time for which he was elected, be appointed to any civil Office under the Authority of the United States, which shall have been created, or the Emoluments whereof shall have been encreased during such time; and no Person holding any Office under the United States, shall be a Member of either House during his Continuance in Office.

Section 7

All Bills for raising Revenue shall originate in the House of Representatives; but the Senate may propose or concur with Amendments as on other Bills.

Every Bill which shall have passed the House of Representatives and the Senate, shall, before it become a Law, be presented to the President of the United States; If he approve he shall sign it, but if not he shall return it, with his Objections to that House in which it shall have originated, who shall enter the Objections at large on their Journal, and proceed to reconsider it. If after such Reconsideration two thirds of that House shall agree to pass the Bill, it shall be sent, together with the Objections, to the other House, by which it shall likewise be reconsidered, and if approved by two thirds of that House, it shall become a Law. But in all such Cases the Votes of both Houses shall be determined by Yeas and Nays, and the Names of the Persons voting for and against the Bill shall be entered on the Journal of each House respectively. If any Bill shall not be returned by the President within ten Days (Sundays excepted) after it shall have been presented to him, the Same shall be a Law, in like Manner as if he had signed it, unless the Congress by their Adjournment prevent its Return, in which Case it shall not be a Law.

Every Order, Resolution, or Vote to which the Concurrence of the Senate and House of Representatives may be necessary (except on a question of Adjournment) shall be presented to the President of the United States; and before the Same shall take Effect, shall be approved by him, or being disapproved by him, shall be repassed by two thirds of the Senate and House of Representatives, according to the Rules and Limitations prescribed in the Case of a Bill.

Section 8

The Congress shall have Power To lay and collect Taxes, Duties, Imposts and Excises, to pay the Debts and provide for the common Defence and general Welfare of the United States; but all Duties, Imposts and Excises shall be uniform throughout the United States;

To borrow Money on the credit of the United States;

To regulate Commerce with foreign Nations, and among the several States, and with the Indian Tribes;

To establish a uniform Rule of Naturalization, and uniform Laws on the subject of Bankruptcies throughout the United States;

To coin Money, regulate the Value thereof, and of foreign Coin, and fix the Standard of Weights and Measures;

To provide for the Punishment of counterfeiting the Securities and current Coin of the United States;

To establish Post Offices and post Roads;

To promote the Progress of Science and useful Arts, by securing for limited Times to Authors and Inventors exclusive Right to their respective Writings and Discoveries;

To constitute Tribunals inferior to the supreme Court;

To define and punish Piracies and Felonies committed on the high Seas, and Offences against the Law of Nations;

To declare War, grant Letters of Marque and Reprisal, and make rules concerning Captures on Land and Water;

To raise and support Armies, but no Appropriation of Money to that Use shall be for a longer Term than two Years;

To provide and maintain a Navy;

To make Rules for the Government and Regulation of the land and naval Forces;

To provide for calling forth the Militia to execute the Laws of the Union, suppress Insurrections and repel Invasions;

To provide for organizing, arming, and disciplining, the Militia, and for governing such Part of them as may be employed in the Service of the United States, reserving to the States respectively, the Appointment of the Officers, and the Authority of training the Militia according to the discipline prescribed by Congress;

To exercise exclusive Legislation in all Cases whatsoever, over such District (not exceeding ten Miles square) as may, by Cession of particular States, and the Acceptance of Congress, become the Seat of the Government of the United States, and to exercise like Authority over all Places purchased by the Consent of the Legislature of the State in which the Same shall be for the Erection of Forts, Magazines, Arsenals, dock-Yards, and other needful Buildings;

—And To make all Laws which shall be necessary and proper for carrying into Execution the foregoing Powers, and all other Powers vested by this Constitution in the Government of the United States, or in any Department or Officer thereof.

Section 9

The Migration or Importation of such Persons as any of the States now existing shall think proper to admit, shall not be prohibited by the Congress prior to the Year one thousand eight hundred and eight, but a Tax or duty may be imposed on such Importation, not exceeding ten dollars for each Person.

The Privilege of the Writ of *Habeas Corpus* shall not be suspended, unless when in Cases of Rebellion or Invasion the public Safety may require it.

No Bill of Attainder or *ex post facto* Law shall be passed.

No Capitation, or other direct, Tax shall be laid, unless in Proportion to the Census or Enumeration herein before directed to be taken.

No Tax or Duty shall be laid on Articles exported from any State.

No Preference shall be given by any Regulation of Commerce or Revenue to the Ports of one State over those of another: nor shall Vessels bound to, or from, one State, be obliged to enter, clear, or pay Duties in another.

No money shall be drawn from the Treasury, but in Consequence of Appropriations made by Law; and a regular Statement and Account of the Receipts and Expenditures of all public Money shall be published from time to time.

No Title of Nobility shall be granted by the United States: And no Person holding any Office of Profit or Trust under them, shall, without the Consent of the Congress, accept of any present, Emolument, Office, or Title, of any kind whatever, from any King, Prince, or foreign State.

Section 10

No state shall enter into any Treaty, Alliance, or Confederation; grant Letters of Marque and Reprisal; coin Money; emit Bills of Credit; make any Thing but gold and silver Coin a Tender in Payment of Debts; pass any Bill of Attainder, *ex post facto* Law, or Law impairing the Obligation of Contracts, or grant any Title of Nobility.

No State shall, without the Consent of the Congress, lay any Imposts or Duties on Imports or Exports, except what may be absolutely necessary for executing its inspection Laws: and the net Produce of all Duties and Imposts, laid by any State on Imports or Exports, shall be for the Use of the Treasury of the United States, and all such Laws shall be subject to the Revision and Control of the Congress.

No State shall, without the Consent of Congress, lay any Duty of Tonnage, keep Troops, or Ships of War in time of Peace, enter into any Agreement or Compact with another State, or with a foreign Power, or engage in War, unless actually invaded, or in such imminent Danger as will not admit of delay.

ARTICLE II

Section 1

The executive Power shall be vested in a President of the United States of America. He shall hold his Office during the Term of four Years, and, together with the Vice President, chosen for the same Term, be elected as follows.

Each State shall appoint, in such Manner as the Legislature thereof may direct, a Number of Electors, equal to the whole Number of Senators and Representatives to which the State may be entitled in the Congress; but no Senator or Representative, or Person holding an Office of Trust of Profit under the United States, shall be appointed an Elector.

The Electors shall meet in their respective States, and vote by Ballot for two Persons, of whom one at least shall not be an Inhabitant of the same State with themselves. And they shall make a List of all the Persons voted for, and, of the Number of Votes for each; which List they shall sign and certify, and transmit sealed to the Seat of the Government of the United States, directed to the President of the Senate. The President of the Senate shall, in the Presence of the Senate and House of Representatives, open all the Certificates, and the Votes shall then be counted.

The Person having the greatest Number of Votes shall be the President, if such Number be a Majority of the whole Number of Electors appointed; and if there be more than one who have such Majority, and have an equal Number of Votes, then the House of Representatives shall immediately chuse by Ballot one of them for President; and if no Person have a Majority, then from the five highest on the List the said House shall in like Manner chuse the President. But in chusing the President, the Votes shall be taken by States, the Representation from each State having one Vote; A quorum for this Purpose shall consist of a Member or Members from two thirds of the States, and a Majority of all the States shall be necessary to a Choice. In every Case, after the Choice of the President, the Person having the greatest Number of Votes of the Electors shall be the Vice President. But if there should remain two or more who have equal Votes, the Senate shall chuse from them by Ballot the Vice President.

The Congress may determine the Time of chusing the Electors, and the Day on which they shall give their Votes; which Day shall be the same throughout the United States.

No Person except a natural born Citizen, or a Citizen of the United States, at the time of the Adoption of this Constitution, shall be eligible to the Office of President; neither shall any Person be eligible to that Office who shall not have attained to the Age of thirty five Years, and been fourteen Years a Resident within the United States.

In Case of the Removal of the President from Office, or of his Death, Resignation, or Inability to discharge the Powers and Duties of the said Office, the Same shall devolve on the Vice President, and the Congress may by Law provide for the Case of Removal, Death, Resignation or Inability, both of the President and Vice President, declaring what Officer shall then act as President, and such Officer shall act accordingly, until the Disability be removed, or a President shall be elected.

The President shall, at stated Times, receive for his Services, a Compensation, which shall neither be encreased nor diminished during the Period for which he shall have been elected, and he shall not receive within that Period any other Emolument from the United States, or any of them.

Before he enter on the Execution of his Office, he shall take the following Oath or Affirmation:— "I do solemnly swear (or affirm) that I will faithfully execute the Office of President of the United States, and will to the best of my Ability, preserve, protect and defend the Constitution of the United States."

Section 2

The President shall be Commander in Chief of the Army and Navy of the United States, and of the Militia of the several States, when called into the actual Service of the United States; he may require the Opinion, in writing, of the principal Officer in each of the executive Departments, upon any Subject relating to the Duties of their respective Offices, and he shall have Power to grant Reprieves and Pardons for Offences against the United States, except in Cases of Impeachment.

He shall have Power, by and with the Advice and Consent of the Senate, to make Treaties, provided two thirds of the Senators present concur; and he shall nominate, and by and with the Advice and Consent of the Senate, shall appoint Ambassadors, other public Ministers and Consuls, Judges of the supreme Court, and all other Officers of the United States, whose Appointments are not herein otherwise provided for, and which shall be established by Law: but the Congress may by Law vest the Appointment of such inferior Officers, as they think proper, in the President alone, in the Courts of Law, or in the Heads of Departments.

The President shall have Power to fill up all Vacancies that may happen during the Recess of the Senate, by granting Commissions which shall expire at the End of their next Session.

Section 3

He shall from time to time give to the Congress Information of the State of the Union, and recommend to their Consideration such Measures as he shall judge necessary and expedient; he may, on extraordinary Occasions, convene both Houses, or either of them, and in Case of Disagreement between them, with Respect to the Time of Adjournment, he may adjourn them to such Time as he shall think proper; he shall receive Ambassadors and other public Ministers; he shall take Care that the Laws be faithfully executed, and shall Commission all the Officers of the United States.

Section 4

The President, Vice President and all civil Officers of the United States, shall be removed from Office on Impeachment for, and Conviction of, Treason, Bribery, or other High Crimes and Misdemeanors.

ARTICLE III

Section 1

The judicial Power of the United States, shall be vested in one supreme Court, and in such inferior Courts as the Congress may from time to time ordain and establish. The Judges, both of the supreme and inferior Courts, shall hold their Offices during good Behaviour, and shall, at stated Times, receive for their Services, a Compensation, which shall not be diminished during their Continuance in Office.

Section 2

The judicial Power shall extend to all Cases, in Law and Equity, arising under this Constitution, the Laws of the United States, and Treaties made, or which shall be made, under their Authority;—to all Cases affecting Ambassadors, other public Ministers and Consuls;—to all Cases of admiralty and maritime Jurisdiction;—to Controversies to which the United States shall be a Party;—to Controversies between two or more States;—between a State and Citizens of another State;—between Citizens of different States;—between Citizens of the same State claiming Lands under Grants of different States,—and between a State, or the Citizens thereof, and foreign States, Citizens or Subjects.

In all Cases affecting Ambassadors, other public Ministers and Consuls, and those in which a State shall be Party, the supreme Court shall have original Jurisdiction. In all the other Cases before mentioned, the supreme Court shall have appellate Jurisdiction, both as to Law and Fact, with such Exceptions, and under such Regulations as the Congress shall make.

The Trial of all Crimes, except in Cases of Impeachment, shall be by Jury; and such Trial shall be held in the State where the said Crimes shall have been committed; but when not committed within any State, the Trial shall be at such Place or Places as the Congress may by Law have directed.

Section 3

Treason against the United States, shall consist only in levying War against them, or in adhering to their Enemies, giving them Aid and Comfort. No Person shall be convicted of Treason unless on the Testimony of two Witnesses to the same overt Act, or on Confession in open Court.

The Congress shall have Power to declare the Punishment of Treason, but no Attainder of Treason shall work Corruption of Blood, or Forfeiture except during the Life of the Person attainted.

ARTICLE IV

Section 1

Full Faith and Credit shall be given in each State to the public Acts, Records, and judicial Proceedings of every other State. And the Congress may by general Laws prescribe the Manner in which such Acts, Records and Proceedings shall be proved, and the Effect thereof.

Section 2

The Citizens of each State shall be entitled to all Privileges and Immunities of Citizens in the several States.

A Person charged in any State with Treason, Felony, or other Crime, who shall flee from Justice, and be found in another State, shall on Demand of the executive Authority of the State from which he fled, be delivered up, to be removed to the State having Jurisdiction of the Crime.

No Person held to Service or Labour in one State under the Laws thereof, escaping into another, shall, in Consequence of any Law or Regulation therein, be discharged from such Service or Labour, but shall be delivered up on Claim of the Party to whom such Service or Labour maybe due.

Section 3

New States may be admitted by the Congress into this Union; but no new State shall be formed or erected within the Jurisdiction of any other State; nor any State be formed by the Junction of two or more States, or Parts of States, without the Consent of the Legislatures of the States concerned as well as of the Congress.

The Congress shall have Power to dispose of and make all needful Rules and Regulations respecting the Territory or other Property belonging to the United States; and nothing in this Constitution shall be so construed as to Prejudice any Claims of the United States, or of any particular State.

Section 4

The United States shall guarantee to every State in this Union a Republican Form of Government, and shall protect each of them against Invasion; and on Application of the Legislature, or of the Executive (when the Legislature cannot be convened) against domestic Violence.

ARTICLE V

The Congress, whenever two thirds of both Houses shall deem it necessary, shall propose Amendments to this Constitution, or, on the Application of the Legislatures of two thirds of the several States, shall call a Convention for proposing Amendments, which, in either Case, shall be valid to all Intents and Purposes, as Part of this Constitution, when ratified by the Legislatures of three fourths of the several States, or by Conventions in three fourths thereof, as the one or the other Mode of Ratification may be proposed by the Congress; Provided that no Amendment which may be made prior to the Year One thousand eight hundred and eight shall in any Manner affect the first and fourth Clauses in the Ninth Section of the first Article; and that no State, without its Consent, shall be deprived of its equal Suffrage in the Senate.

ARTICLE VI

All Debts contracted and Engagements entered into, before the Adoption of this Constitution, shall be as valid against the United States under this Constitution, as under the Confederation.

This Constitution, and the Laws of the United States which shall be made in Pursuance thereof; and all Treaties made, or which shall be made, under the Authority of the United States, shall be the supreme Law of the Land; and the Judges in every State shall be bound thereby, any Thing in the Constitution or Laws of any State to the Contrary notwithstanding.

The Senators and Representatives before mentioned, and the Members of the several State Legislatures, and all executive and judicial Officers, both of the United States and of the several States, shall be bound by Oath or Affirmation, to support this Constitution; but no religious Test shall ever be required as a Qualification to any Office or public Trust under the United States.

ARTICLE VII

The Ratification of the Conventions of nine States, shall be sufficient for the Establishment of this Constitution between the States so ratifying the Same.

Done in Convention by the Unanimous Consent of the States present the Seventeenth Day of September in the Year of our Lord one thousand seven hundred and Eighty seven and of the Independence of the United States of America the Twelfth. IN WITNESS whereof We have hereunto subscribed our Names,

G. WASHINGTON,
Presid't. and deputy from Virginia

Attest

WILLIAM JACKSON,
Secretary

Articles in addition to, and amendment of the Constitution of the United States of America, proposed by Congress and ratified by the Legislatures of the several states, pursuant to the Fifth Article of the original Constitution.

(The first ten amendments were passed by Congress on September 25, 1789, and were ratified on December 15, 1791.)

DELAWARE
George Read
Gunning Bedford, Jr.
John Dickinson
Richard Basset
Jacob Broom

MASSACHUSETTS BAY
Nathaniel Gorham
Rufus King

CONNECTICUT
William Samuel Johnson
Roger Sherman

NEW YORK
Alexander Hamilton

NEW JERSEY
William Livingston
David Brearley

William Paterson
Jonathan Dayton

PENNSYLVANIA
Benjamin Franklin
Thomas Mifflin
Robert Morris
George Clymer
Thomas FitzSimons
Jared Ingersoll
James Wilson
Gouverneur Morris

NEW HAMPSHIRE
John Langdon
Nicholas Gilman

MARYLAND
James McHenry
Daniel of St. Thomas Jenifer
Daniel Carroll

VIRGINIA
John Blair
James Madison, Jr.

NORTH CAROLINA
William Blount
Richard Dobbs Spaight
Hugh Williamson

SOUTH CAROLINA
John Rutledge
Charles Cotesworth Pinckney
Charles Pinckney
Pierce Butler

GEORGIA
William Few
Abraham Baldwin

AMENDMENT I

Congress shall make no law respecting an establishment of religion, or prohibiting the free exercise thereof; or abridging the freedom of speech, or of the press; or the right of the people peaceably to assemble, and to petition the Government for a redress of grievances.

AMENDMENT II

A well regulated Militia, being necessary to the security of a free State, the right of the people to keep and bear Arms, shall not be infringed.

AMENDMENT III

No Soldier shall, in time of peace be quartered in any house, without the consent of the Owner, nor in time of war, but in a manner to be prescribed by law.

AMENDMENT IV

The right of the people to be secure in their persons, houses, papers, and effects, against unreasonable searches and seizures, shall not be violated, and no warrants shall issue, but upon probable cause, supported by Oath or affirmation, and particularly describing the place to be searched, and the persons or things to be seized.

AMENDMENT V

No person shall be held to answer for a capital, or otherwise infamous crime, unless on a presentment or indictment of a Grand Jury, except in cases arising in the land or naval forces, or in the Militia, when in actual service in time of War or public danger; nor shall any person be subject for the same offence to be twice put in jeopardy of life or limb; nor shall be compelled in any criminal case to be a witness against himself, nor be deprived of life, liberty, or property, without due process of law; nor shall private property be taken for public use, without just compensation.

AMENDMENT VI

In all criminal prosecutions, the accused shall enjoy the right to a speedy and public trial, by an impartial jury of the State and district wherein the crime shall have been committed, which district shall have been previously ascertained by law, and to be informed of the nature and cause of the accusation; to be confronted with the witnesses against him; to have compulsory process for obtaining witnesses in his favor, and to have the assistance of counsel for his defence.

AMENDMENT VII

In Suits at common law, where the value in controversy shall exceed twenty dollars, the right of trial by jury shall be preserved, and no fact tried by a jury, shall be otherwise re-examined in any Court of the United States, than according to the rules of the common law.

AMENDMENT VIII

Excessive bail shall not be required, nor excessive fines imposed, nor cruel and unusual punishments inflicted.

AMENDMENT IX

The enumeration in the Constitution, of certain rights, shall not be construed to deny or disparage others retained by the people.

AMENDMENT X

The powers not delegated to the United States by the Constitution, nor prohibited by it to the States, are reserved to the States respectively, or to the people.

AMENDMENT XI

(Ratified on February 7, 1795)

The Judicial power of the United States shall not be construed to extend to any suit in law or equity, commenced or prosecuted against one of the United States by Citizens of another State, or by Citizens or Subjects of any Foreign State.

AMENDMENT XII

(Ratified on June 15, 1804)

The Electors shall meet in their respective states, and vote by ballot for President and Vice-President, one of whom, at least, shall not be an inhabitant of the same state with themselves; they shall name in their ballots the person voted for as President, and in distinct ballots the person voted for as Vice-President, and they shall make distinct lists of all persons voted for as President, and of all persons voted for as Vice-President, and of the number of votes for each, which lists they shall sign and certify, and transmit sealed to the seat of the government of the United States, directed to the President of the Senate;

The President of the Senate shall, in the presence of the Senate and House of Representatives, open all the certificates and the votes shall then be counted;

The person having the greatest number of votes for President, shall be the President, if such number be a majority of the whole number of Electors appointed; and if no person have such majority; then from the persons having the highest numbers not exceeding three on the list of those voted for as President, the House of Representatives shall choose immediately, by ballot, the President. But in choosing the President, the votes shall be taken by states, the representation from each state having one vote; a quorum for this purpose shall consist of a member or members from two-thirds of the states, and a majority of all the states shall be necessary to a choice. And if the House of Representatives shall not choose a President whenever the right of choice shall devolve upon them, before the fourth day of March next following, then the Vice-President shall act as President, as in the case of the death or other constitutional disability of the President.

The person having the greatest number of votes as Vice-President, shall be the Vice-President, if such number be a majority of the whole number of Electors appointed, and if no person have a majority, then from the two highest numbers on the list, the Senate shall choose the Vice-President; a quorum for the purpose shall consist of two-thirds of the whole number of Senators, and a majority of the whole number shall be necessary to a choice. But no person constitutionally ineligible to the office of President shall be eligible to that of Vice-President of the United States.

AMENDMENT XIII

(Ratified on December 6, 1865)

Section 1

Neither slavery nor involuntary servitude, except as a punishment for crime whereof the party shall have been duly convicted, shall exist within the United States, or any place subject to their jurisdiction.

Section 2

Congress shall have power to enforce this article by appropriate legislation.

AMENDMENT XIV

(Ratified on July 9, 1868)

Section 1

All persons born or naturalized in the United States, and subject to the jurisdiction thereof, are citizens of the United States and of the State wherein they reside. No State shall make or enforce any law which shall abridge the privileges or immunities of citizens of the United States; nor shall any State deprive any person of life, liberty, or property, without due process of law; nor deny to any person within its jurisdiction the equal protection of the laws.

Section 2

Representatives shall be apportioned among the several States according to their respective numbers, counting the whole number of persons in each State, excluding Indians not taxed. But when the right to vote at any election for the choice of electors for President and Vice President of the United States, Representatives in Congress, the Executive and Judicial officers of a State, or the members of the Legislature thereof, is denied to any of the male inhabitants of such State, being twenty-one years of age, and citizens of the United States, or in anyway abridged, except for participation in rebellion, or other crime, the basis of representation therein shall be reduced in the proportion which the number of such male citizens shall bear to the whole number of male citizens twenty-one years of age in such State.

Section 3

No person shall be a Senator or Representative in Congress, or elector of President and Vice President, or hold any office, civil or military, under the United States, or under any State, who, having previously taken an oath, as a member of Congress, or as an officer of the United States, or as a member of any State legislature, or as an executive or judicial officer of any State, to support the Constitution of the United States, shall have engaged in insurrection or rebellion against the same, or given aid or comfort to the enemies thereof. But Congress may by a vote of two-thirds of each House, remove such disability.

Section 4

The validity of the public debt of the United States, authorized by law, including debts incurred for payment of pensions and bounties for services in suppressing insurrection or rebellion, shall not be questioned. But neither the United States nor any State shall assume or pay any debt or obligation incurred in aid of insurrection or rebellion against the United States, or any claim for the loss or emancipation of any slave, but all such debts, obligations and claims shall be held illegal and void.

Section 5

The Congress shall have power to enforce, by appropriate legislation, the provisions of this article.

AMENDMENT XV

(Ratified on February 3, 1870)

Section 1

The right of citizens of the United States to vote shall not be denied or abridged by the United States or by any State on account of race, color, or previous condition of servitude.

Section 2

The Congress shall have power to enforce this article by appropriate legislation.

AMENDMENT XVI

(Ratified on February 3, 1913)

The Congress shall have power to lay and collect taxes on incomes, from whatever source derived, without apportionment among the several States, and without regard to any census or enumeration.

AMENDMENT XVII

(Ratified on April 8, 1913)

The Senate of the United States shall be composed of two Senators from each State, elected by the people thereof, for six years; and each Senator shall have one vote. The electors in each State shall have the qualifications requisite for electors of the most numerous branch of the State legislatures.

When vacancies happen in the representation of any State in the Senate, the executive authority of such State shall issue writs of election to fill such vacancies: Provided, That the legislature of any State may empower the executive thereof to make temporary appointments until the people fill the vacancies by election as the legislature may direct.

This amendment shall not be so construed as to affect the election or term of any Senator chosen before it becomes valid as part of the Constitution.

AMENDMENT XVIII

(Ratified on January 16, 1919)

Section 1

After one year from the ratification of this article the manufacture, sale, or transportation of intoxicating liquors within, the importation thereof into, or the exportation thereof from the United States and all territory subject to the jurisdiction thereof for beverage purposes is hereby prohibited.

Section 2

The Congress and the several States shall have concurrent power to enforce this article by appropriate legislation.

Section 3

This article shall be inoperative unless it shall have been ratified as an amendment to the Constitution by the legislatures of the several States, as provided in the Constitution, within seven years from the date of the submission hereof to the States by the Congress.

AMENDMENT XIX

(Ratified on August 18, 1920)

The right of citizens of the United States to vote shall not be denied or abridged by the United States or by any State on account of sex.

Congress shall have power to enforce this article by appropriate legislation.

AMENDMENT XX

(Ratified on February 6, 1933)

Section 1

The terms of the President and Vice President shall end at noon on the 20th day of January, and the terms of Senators and Representatives at noon on the 3d day of January, of the years in which such terms would have ended if this article had not been ratified; and the terms of their successors shall then begin.

Section 2

The Congress shall assemble at least once in every year, and such meeting shall begin at noon on the 3d day of January, unless they shall by law appoint a different day.

Section 3

If, at the time fixed for the beginning of the term of the President, the President elect shall have died, the Vice President elect shall become President. If a President shall not have been chosen before the time fixed for the beginning of his term, or if the President elect shall have failed to qualify, then the Vice President elect shall act as President until a President shall have qualified; and the Congress may by law provide for the case wherein neither a President elect nor a Vice President elect shall have qualified, declaring who shall then act as President, or the manner in which one who is to act shall be selected, and such person shall act accordingly until a President or Vice President shall have qualified.

Section 4

The Congress may by law provide for the case of the death of any of the persons from whom the House of Representatives may choose a President whenever the rights of choice shall have devolved upon them, and for the case of the death of any of the persons from whom the Senate may choose a Vice President whenever the right of choice shall have devolved upon them.

Section 5

Sections 1 and 2 shall take effect on the 15th day of October following the ratification of this article.

Section 6

This article shall be inoperative unless it shall have been ratified as an amendment to the Constitution by the legislatures of three-fourths of the several States within seven years from the date of its submission.

AMENDMENT XXI

(Ratified on December 5, 1933)

Section 1

The eighteenth article of amendment to the Constitution of the United States is hereby repealed.

Section 2

The transportation or importation into any State, Territory, or possession of the United States for delivery or use therein of intoxicating liquors, in violation of the laws thereof, is hereby prohibited.

Section 3

This article shall be inoperative unless it shall have been ratified as an amendment to the Constitution by conventions in the several States, as provided in the Constitution, within seven years from the date of the submission hereof to the States by the Congress.

AMENDMENT XXII

(Ratified on February 27, 1951)

Section 1

No person shall be elected to the office of the President more than twice, and no person who has held the office of President, or acted as President, for more than two years of a term to which some other person was elected President shall be elected to the office of the President more than once. But this article shall not apply to any person holding the office of President when this article was proposed by the Congress, and shall not prevent any person who may

be holding the office of President, or acting as President, during the term within which this Article becomes operative from holding the office of President or acting as President during the remainder of such term.

Section 2

This article shall be inoperative unless it shall have been ratified as an amendment to the Constitution by the legislatures of three-fourths of the several States within seven years from the date of its submission to the States by the Congress.

AMENDMENT XXIII

(Ratified on March 29, 1961)

Section 1

The District constituting the seat of Government of the United States shall appoint in such manner as the Congress may direct:

A number of electors of President and Vice President equal to the whole number of Senators and Representatives in Congress to which the District would be entitled if it were a State, but in no event more than the least populous State; they shall be in addition to those appointed by the States, but they shall be considered, for the purposes of the election of President and Vice President, to be electors appointed by a State; and they shall meet in the District and perform such duties as provided by the twelfth article of amendment.

Section 2

The Congress shall have power to enforce this article by appropriate legislation.

AMENDMENT XXIV

(Ratified on January 23, 1964)

Section 1

The right of citizens of the United States to vote in any primary or other election for President or Vice President, for electors for President or Vice President, or for Senator or Representative in Congress, shall not be denied or abridged by the United States or any State by reason of failure to pay any poll tax or other tax.

Section 2

The Congress shall have power to enforce this article by appropriate legislation.

AMENDMENT XXV

(Ratified on February 10, 1967)

Section 1

In case of the removal of the President from office or of his death or resignation, the Vice President shall become President.

Section 2

Whenever there is a vacancy in the office of the Vice President, the President shall nominate a Vice President who shall take office upon confirmation by a majority vote of both Houses of Congress.

Section 3

Whenever the President transmits to the President pro tempore of the Senate and the Speaker of the House of Representatives his written declaration that he is unable to discharge the powers and duties of his office, and until he transmits to them a written declaration to the contrary, such powers and duties shall be discharged by the Vice President as Acting President.

Section 4

Whenever the Vice President and a majority of either the principal officers of the executive departments or of such other body as Congress may by law provide, transmit to the President pro tempore of the Senate and the Speaker of the House of Representatives their written declaration that the President is unable to discharge the powers and duties of his office, the Vice President shall immediately assume the powers and duties of the office as Acting President.

Thereafter, when the President transmits to the President pro tempore of the Senate and the Speaker of the House of Representatives his written declaration that no inability exists, he shall resume the powers and duties of his office unless the Vice President and a majority of either the principal officers of the executive department or of such other body as Congress may by law provide, transmit within four days to the President pro tempore of the Senate and the Speaker of the House of Representatives their written declaration that the President is unable to discharge the powers and duties of his office. Thereupon Congress shall decide the issue, assembling within forty-eight hours for that purpose if not in session. If the Congress, within twenty-one days after receipt of the latter written declaration, or, if Congress is not in session, within twenty-one days after Congress is required to assemble, determines by two-thirds vote of both Houses that the President is unable to discharge the powers and duties of his office, the Vice President shall continue to discharge the same as Acting President; otherwise, the President shall resume the powers and duties of his office.

AMENDMENT XXVI

(Ratified on July 1, 1971)

Section 1

The right of citizens of the United States, who are eighteen years of age or older, to vote shall not be denied or abridged by the United States or by any State on account of age.

Section 2

The Congress shall have power to enforce this article by appropriate legislation.

AMENDMENT XXVII

(Ratified on May 7, 1992)

No law, varying the compensation for the services of the Senators and Representatives, shall take effect until an election of Representatives shall have intervened.

Appendix III

THE FEDERALIST PAPERS

The Federalist Papers, essays initially released alone and serially by proponents of the U.S. Constitution, provide us with firsthand views of the Framers' intentions. John Jay, James Madison, and Alexander Hamilton were engaged in the writing of the Constitution, and they used *The Federalist Papers* to help persuade citizens to support ratification of that document. Jay was later named the first chief justice of the Supreme Court of the United States, Madison served as the nation's fourth president, and Hamilton (prevented from seeking the presidency by his birth in the British West Indies) was the first secretary of the treasury. Annotated below are three of the most often read and cited of the essays.

FEDERALIST NO. 10

November 22, 1787

James Madison

To the People of the State of New York:

Controlling factions, or groups of like-minded citizens united in a common interest adverse to the interests of the community, was a major concern of the Framers. In *Federalist No. 10*, James Madison argues that one of the best ways to check the power of faction is to create a republican form of government.

Among the numerous advantages promised by a well constructed Union, none deserves to be more accurately developed than its tendency to break and control the violence of faction. The friend of popular governments, never finds himself so much alarmed for their character and fate, as when he contemplates their propensity to this dangerous vice.

He will not fail therefore to set a due value on any plan which, without violating the principles to which he is attached, provides a proper cure for it. The instability, injustice and confusion introduced into the public councils, have in truth been the mortal diseases under which popular governments have every where perished; as they continue to be the favorite and fruitful topics from which the adversaries to liberty derive their most specious. The valuable improvements made by the American Constitutions on the popular models, both ancient and modern, cannot certainly be too much admired; but it would be an unwarrantable partiality, to contend that they have as effectually obviated the danger on this side as was wished and expected.

Complaints are every where heard from our most considerate and virtuous citizens, equally the friends of public and private faith, and of public and personal liberty, that our governments are too unstable; that the public good is disregarded in the conflicts of rival parties; and that measures are too often decided, not according to the rules of justice, and the rights of the minor party, but by the superior force of an interested and over-bearing majority. However anxiously we may wish that these complaints had no foundation, the evidence of known facts will not permit us to deny that they are in some degree true. It will be found indeed, on a candid review of our situation, that some of the distresses under which we labor, have been erroneously charged on the operation of our governments; but it will be found, at the same time, that other causes will not alone account for many of our heaviest misfortunes; and particularly, for that prevailing and increasing distrust of public engagements, and alarm for private rights, which are echoed from one end of the continent to the other. These must be chiefly, if not wholly, effects of the unsteadiness and injustice, with which a factious spirit has tainted our public administrations.

By a faction I understand a number of citizens, whether amounting to a majority or minority of the whole, who are united and actuated by some common impulse of passion, or of interest, adverse to the rights of other citizens, or to the permanent and aggregate interests of the community.

There are two methods of curing the mischiefs of faction: the one, by removing its causes; the other, by controlling its effects.

There are again two methods of removing the causes of faction: the one by destroying the liberty which is essential to its existence; the other, by giving to every citizen the same opinions, the same passions, and the same interests.

It could never be more truly said than of the first remedy, that it is worse than the disease. Liberty is to faction, what air is to fire, an aliment without which it instantly expires. But it could not be a less folly to abolish liberty, which is essential to political life, because it nourishes faction, than it would be to wish the annihilation of air, which is essential to animal life, because it imparts to fire its destructive agency.

The second expedient is as impracticable, as the first would be unwise. As long as the reason of man continues fallible, and he is at liberty to exercise it, different opinions will be formed. As long as the connection subsists between his reason and his self-love, his opinions and his passions will have a reciprocal influence on each other; and the former will be objects to which the latter will attach themselves. The diversity in the faculties of men from which the rights of property originate, is not less an insuperable obstacle to a uniformity of interests. The protection of these faculties is the first object of Government. From the protection of different and unequal faculties of acquiring property, the possession of different degrees and kinds of property immediately results: and from the influence of these on the sentiments and views of the respective proprietors, ensues a division of the society into different interests and parties.

The latent causes of faction are thus sown in the nature of man; and we see them everywhere brought into different degrees of activity, according to the different circumstances of civil society. A zeal for different opinions concerning religion, concerning Government and many other points, as well of speculation as of practice; an attachment to different leaders ambitiously contending for pre-eminence and power; or to persons of other descriptions whose fortunes have been interesting to the human passions, have in turn divided mankind into parties, inflamed them with mutual animosity, and rendered them much more disposed to vex and oppress each other, than to cooperate for their common good. So strong is this propensity of mankind to fall into mutual animosities, that where no substantial occasion presents itself, the most frivolous and fanciful distinctions have been sufficient to kindle their unfriendly passions, and excite their most violent conflicts. But the most common and durable source of factions, has been the various and unequal distribution of property. Those who hold, and those who are without property, have ever formed distinct interests in society. Those who are creditors, and those who are debtors, fall under a like discrimination. A landed interest, a manufacturing interest, a mercantile interest, a monied interest, with many lesser interests, grow up of necessity in civilized nations, and divide them into different classes, actuated by different sentiments and views. The regulation of these various and interfering interests forms the principal task of modern Legislation, and involves the spirit of party and faction in the necessary and ordinary operations of Government.

No man is allowed to be a judge in his own cause, because his interest would certainly bias his judgment, and, not improbably, corrupt his integrity. With equal, nay with greater reason, a body of men, are unfit to be both judges and parties, at the same time; yet, what are many of the most important acts of legislation, but so many judicial determinations, not indeed concerning the rights of single persons, but concerning the rights of large bodies of citizens, and what are the different classes of legislators, but advocates and parties to the causes which they determine? Is a law proposed concerning private debts? It is a question to which the creditors are parties on one side, and the debtors on the other. Justice ought to hold the balance between them. Yet the parties are and must be themselves the judges; and the most numerous party, or, in other words, the most powerful faction, must be expected to prevail. Shall domestic

manufactures be encouraged, and in what degree, by restrictions on foreign manufactures? are questions which would be differently decided by the landed and the manufacturing classes; and probably by neither, with a sole regard to justice and the public good. The apportionment of taxes on the various descriptions of property, is an act which seems to require the most exact impartiality; yet, there is perhaps no legislative act in which greater opportunity and temptation are given to a predominant party, to trample on the rules of justice. Every shilling with which they over-burden the inferior number, is a shilling saved to their own pockets.

It is in vain to say, that enlightened statesmen will be able to adjust these clashing interests, and render them all subservient to the public good. Enlightened statesmen will not always be at the helm. Nor, in many cases, can such an adjustment be made at all, without taking into view indirect and remote considerations, which will rarely prevail over the immediate interest which one party may find in disregarding the rights of another, or the good of the whole.

The inference to which we are brought, is, that the *causes* of faction cannot be removed; and that relief is only to be sought in the means of controlling its *effects*.

If a faction consists of less than a majority, relief is supplied by the republican principle, which enables the majority to defeat its sinister views by regular vote. It may clog the administration, it may convulse the society, but it will be unable to execute and mask its violence under the forms of the Constitution. When a majority is included in a faction, the form of popular government on the other hand enables it to sacrifice to its ruling passion or interest, both the public good and the rights of other citizens. To secure the public good, and private rights, against the danger of such a faction, and at the same time to preserve the spirit and the form of popular government, is then the great object to which our enquiries are directed. Let me add that it is the great desideratum, by which alone this form of government can be rescued from the opprobrium under which it has so long labored, and be recommended to the esteem and adoption of mankind.

By what means is this object attainable? Evidently by one of two only. Either the existence of the same passion or interest in a majority at the same time, must be prevented; or the majority, having such co-existent passion or interest, must be rendered, by their number and local situation, unable to concert and carry into effect schemes of oppression. If the impulse and the opportunity be suffered to coincide, we well know that neither moral nor religious motives can be relied on as an adequate control. They are not found to be such on the injustice and violence of individuals, and lose their efficacy in proportion to the number combined together; that is, in proportion as their efficacy becomes needful.

From this view of the subject, it may be concluded, that a pure Democracy, by which I mean, a Society, consisting of a small number of citizens, who assemble and administer the Government in person, can admit of no cure for the mischiefs of faction. A common passion or interest will, in almost every case, be felt by a majority of the whole; a communication and concert results from the form of Government itself; and there is nothing to check the inducements to sacrifice the weaker party, or an obnoxious individual. Hence it is, that such Democracies have ever been spectacles of turbulence and contention; have ever been found incompatible with personal security, or the rights of property; and have in general been as short in their lives, as they have been violent in their deaths. Theoretic politicians, who have patronized this species of Government, have erroneously supposed, that by reducing mankind to a perfect equality in their political rights, they would, at the same time, be perfectly equalized and assimilated in their possessions, their opinions, and their passions.

A republic, by which I mean a government in which the scheme of representation takes place, opens a different prospect, and promises the cure for which we are seeking. Let us examine the points in which it varies from pure democracy, and we shall comprehend both the nature of the cure and the efficacy which it must derive from the union.

The two great points of difference, between a democracy and a republic, are, first, the delegation of the government, in the latter, to a small number of citizens, elected by the rest; secondly, the greater number of citizens, and greater sphere of country, over which the latter may be extended.

The effect of the first difference is, on the one hand, to refine and enlarge the public views, by passing them through the medium of a chosen body of citizens, whose wisdom may best discern the true interest of their country, and whose patriotism and love of justice, will be least likely to sacrifice it to temporary or partial considerations. Under such a regulation, it may well happen, that the public voice, pronounced by the representatives of the people, will be more consonant to the public good, than if pronounced by the people themselves, convened for the purpose. On the other hand the effect may be inverted. Men of factious tempers, of local prejudices, or of sinister designs, may by intrigue, by corruption, or by other means, first obtain the suffrages, and then betray the interest of the people. The question resulting is, whether small or extensive republics are most favorable to the election of proper guardians of the public weal, and it is clearly decided in favor of the latter by two obvious considerations.

In the first place, it is to be remarked that, however small the republic may be, the representatives must be raised to a certain number, in order to guard against the cabals of a few; and that however large it may be, they must be limited to a certain number, in order to guard against the confusion of a multitude. Hence, the number of representatives in the two cases not being in proportion to that of the constituents, and being proportionally greatest in the small republic, it

follows, that if the proportion of fit characters be not less in the large than in the small republic, the former will present a greater option, and consequently a greater probability of a fit choice.

In the next place, as each Representative will be chosen by a greater number of citizens in the large than in the small Republic, it will be more difficult for unworthy candidates to practise with success the vicious arts, by which elections are too often carried; and the suffrages of the people being more free, will be more likely to center on men who possess the most attractive merit, and the most diffusive and established characters.

It must be confessed, that in this, as in most other cases, there is a mean, on both sides of which inconveniences will be found to lie. By enlarging too much the number of electors, you render the representatives too little acquainted with all their local circumstances and lesser interests; as by reducing it too much, you render him unduly attached to these, and too little fit to comprehend and pursue great and national objects. The Federal Constitution forms a happy combination in this respect; the great and aggregate interests being referred to the national, the local and particular, to the state legislatures.

The other point of difference is, the greater number of citizens and extent of territory which may be brought within the compass of Republican, than of Democratic Government; and it is this circumstance principally which renders factious combinations less to be dreaded in the former, than in the latter. The smaller the society, the fewer probably will be the distinct parties and interests composing it; the fewer the distinct parties and interests, the more frequently will a majority be found of the same party; and the smaller the number of individuals composing a majority, and the smaller the compass within which they are placed, the more easily will they concert and execute their plans of oppression. Extend the sphere, and you take in a greater variety of parties and interests; you make it less probable that a majority of the whole will have a common motive to invade the rights of other citizens; or if such a common motive exists, it will be more difficult for all who feel it to discover their own strength, and to act in unison with each other. Besides other impediments, it may be remarked, that where there is a consciousness of unjust or dishonorable purposes, communication is always checked by distrust, in proportion to the number whose concurrence is necessary.

Hence it clearly appears, that the same advantage, which a Republic has over a Democracy, in controlling the effects of faction, is enjoyed by a large over a small Republic—is enjoyed by the Union over the States composing it. Does this advantage consist in the substitution of Representatives, whose enlightened views and virtuous sentiments render them superior to local prejudices, and to schemes of injustice? It will not be denied, that the Representation of the Union will be most likely to possess these requisite endowments. Does it consist in the greater security afforded by a greater variety of parties, against the event of any one party being able to outnumber and oppress the rest? In an equal degree does the increased variety of parties, comprised within the Union, increase this security? Does it, in fine, consist in the greater obstacles opposed to the concert and accomplishment of the secret wishes of an unjust and interested majority? Here, again, the extent of the Union gives it the most palpable advantage.

The influence of factious leaders may kindle a flame within their particular States, but will be unable to spread a general conflagration through the other States: a religious sect, may degenerate into a political faction in a part of the Confederacy but the variety of sects dispersed over the entire face of it, must secure the national Councils against any danger from that source: a rage for paper money, for an abolition of debts, for an equal division of property, or for any other improper or wicked project, will be less apt to pervade the whole body of the Union, than a particular member of it; in the same proportion as such a malady is more likely to taint a particular county or district, than an entire State.

In the extent and proper structure of the Union, therefore, we behold a Republican remedy for the diseases most incident to Republican Government. And according to the degree of pleasure and pride, we feel in being Republicans, ought to be our zeal in cherishing the spirit, and supporting the character of Federalists.

PUBLIUS

FEDERALIST NO. 51

February 6, 1788

James Madison

To the People of the State of New York:

Federalist No. 51 is one of the most widely cited of all The Federalist Papers. In it, James Madison carefully explains how the structure of the new government helps to protect citizens' individual liberties. He contends that the Constitution contains two main protections: a system of checks and balances, and a federal system of government that divides power between state and national governments. Perhaps the most famous line of this paper is "Ambition must be made to counteract ambition."

To what expedient then shall we finally resort for maintaining in practice the necessary partition of power among the several departments, as laid down in the Constitution? The only answer that can be given is, that as all these exterior provisions are found to be inadequate, the defect must be supplied, by so contriving the interior structure of the government, as that its several constituent parts may, by their mutual relations, be the means of keeping each other in their proper places. Without presuming to undertake a full development of this important idea, I will hazard a few general observations, which may perhaps place it in a clearer light, and enable us to form a more correct judgment of the principles and structure of the government planned by the convention.

In order to lay a due foundation for that separate and distinct exercise of the different powers of government, which to a certain extent, is admitted on all hands to be essential to the preservation of liberty, it is evident that each department should have a will of its own; and consequently should be so constituted, that the members of each should have as little agency as possible in the appointment of the members of the others. Were this principle rigorously adhered to, it would require that all the appointments for the supreme executive, legislative, and judiciary magistracies, should be drawn from the same fountain of authority, the people, through channels, having no communication whatever with one another. Perhaps such a plan of constructing the several departments would be less difficult in practice than it may in contemplation appear.

Some difficulties however, and some additional expense, would attend the execution of it. Some deviations therefore from the principle must be admitted. In the constitution of the judiciary department in particular, it might be inexpedient to insist rigorously on the principle; first, because peculiar qualifications being essential in the members, the primary consideration ought to be to select that mode of choice, which best secures these qualifications; secondly, because the permanent tenure by which the appointments are held in that department, must soon destroy all sense of dependence on the authority conferring them.

It is equally evident that the members of each department should be as little dependent as possible on those of the others, for the emoluments annexed to their offices. Were the executive magistrate, or the judges, not independent of the legislature in this particular, their independence in every other would be merely nominal.

But the great security against a gradual concentration of the several powers in the same department, consists in giving to those who administer each department, the necessary constitutional means, and personal motives, to resist encroachments of the others. The provision for defense must in this, as in all other cases, be made commensurate to the danger of attack. Ambition must be made to counteract ambition.

The interest of the man must be connected with the constitutional right of the place. It may be a reflection on human nature, that such devices should be necessary to control the abuses of government. But what is government itself but the greatest of all reflections on human nature? If men were angels, no government would be necessary. If angels were to govern men, neither external nor internal controls on government would be necessary. In framing a government which is to be administered by men over men, the great difficulty lies in this: you must first enable the government to control the governed; and in the next place, oblige it to control itself. A dependence on the people is no doubt the primary control on the government; but experience has taught mankind the necessity of auxiliary precautions.

This policy of supplying by opposite and rival interests, the defect of better motives, might be traced through the whole system of human affairs, private as well as public. We see it particularly displayed in all the subordinate distributions of power; where the constant aim is to divide and arrange the several offices in such a manner as that each may be a check on the other; that the private interest of every individual, may be a sentinel over the public rights. These inventions of prudence cannot be less requisite in the distribution of the supreme powers of the state.

But it is not possible to give to each department an equal power of self defense. In republican government the legislative authority, necessarily, predominates. The remedy for this inconveniency is, to divide the legislature into different branches; and to render them by different modes of election, and different principles of action, as little connected with each other, as the nature of their common functions, and their common dependence on the society, will admit. It may even be necessary to guard against dangerous encroachments by still further precautions. As the weight of the legislative authority requires that it should be thus divided, the weakness of the executive may require, on the other hand, that it should be fortified. An absolute negative, on the legislature, appears at first view to be the natural defense with which the executive magistrate should be armed. But perhaps it would be neither altogether safe, nor alone sufficient. On ordinary occasions, it might not be exerted with the requisite firmness; and on extraordinary occasions, it might be prefidiously abused.

May not this defect of an absolute negative be supplied, by some qualified connection between this weaker department, and the weaker branch of the stronger department, by which the latter may be led to support the constitutional rights of the former, without being too much detached from the rights of its own department? If the principles on which these observations are founded be just, as I persuade myself they are, and they be applied as a criterion, to the several state constitutions, and to the federal constitution, it will be found, that if the latter does not perfectly correspond with them, the former are infinitely less able to bear such a test.

There are moreover two considerations particularly applicable to the federal system of America, which place that system in a very interesting point of view.

First. In a single republic, all the power surrendered by the people, is submitted to the administration of a single government; and usurpations are guarded against by a division of the government into distinct and separate departments. In the compound republic of America, the power surrendered by the people, is first divided between two distinct governments, and then the portion allotted to each, subdivided among distinct and separate departments. Hence a double security arises to the rights of the people. The different governments will control each other; at the same time that each will be controlled by itself.

Second. It is of great importance in a republic, not only to guard the society against the oppression of its rulers; but to guard one part of the society against the injustice of the other part. Different interests necessarily exist in different classes of citizens.

If a majority be united by a common interest, the rights of the minority will be insecure. There are but two methods of providing against this evil: the one by creating a will in the community independent of the majority, that is, of the society itself; the other by comprehending in the society so many separate descriptions of citizens, as will render an unjust combination of a majority of the whole, very improbable, if not impracticable. The first method prevails in all governments possessing an hereditary or self appointed authority. This at best is but a precarious security; because a power independent of the society may as well espouse the unjust views of the major, as the rightful interests, of the minor party, and may possibly be turned against both parties. The second method will be exemplified in the federal republic of the United States. While all authority in it will be derived from and dependent on the society, the society itself will be broken into so many parts, interests and classes of citizens, that the rights of individuals or of the minority, will be in little danger from interested combinations of the majority. In a free government, the security for civil rights must be the same as for religious rights. It consists in the one case in the multiplicity of interests, and in the other, in the multiplicity of sects. The degree of security in both cases will depend on the number of interests and sects; and this may be presumed to depend on the extent of country and number of people comprehended under the same government.

This view of the subject must particularly recommend a proper federal system to all the sincere and considerate friends of republican government. Since it shows that in exact proportion as the territory of the union may be formed into more circumscribed confederacies or states, oppressive combinations of a majority will be facilitated, the best security under the republican form, for the rights of every class of citizens, will be diminished; and consequently, the stability and independence of some member of the government, the only other security, must be proportionally increased. Justice is the end of government. It is the end of civil society.

It ever has been, and ever will be pursued, until it be obtained, or until liberty be lost in the pursuit. In a society under the forms of which the stronger faction can readily unite and oppress the weaker, anarchy may as truly be said to reign, as in a state of nature where the weaker individual is not secured against the violence of the stronger; and as in the latter state even the stronger individuals are prompted by the uncertainty of their condition, to submit to a government which may protect the weak as well as themselves; so, in the former state, will the more powerful factions or parties be gradually induced by a like motive, to wish for a government which will protect all parties, the weaker as well as the more powerful. It can be little doubted, that if the state of Rhode Island was separated from the confederacy, and left to itself, the insecurity of rights under the popular form of government within such narrow limits, would be displayed by such reiterated oppressions of factious majorities, that some power altogether independent of the people would soon be called for by the voice of the very factions whose misrule had proved the necessity of it. In the extended republic of the United States, and among the great variety of interests, parties and sects which it embraces, a coalition of a majority of the whole society could seldom take place on any other principles than those of justice and the general good; and there being thus less danger to a minor from the will of the major party, there must be less pretext also, to provide for the security of the former, by introducing into the government a will not dependent on the latter; or in other words, a will independent of the society itself. It is no less certain than it is important, notwithstanding the contrary opinions which have been entertained, that the larger the society, provided it lie within a practicable sphere, the more duly capable it will be of self government. And happily for the *republican cause*, the practicable sphere may be carried to a very great extent, by a judicious modification and mixture of the *federal principle*.

PUBLIUS

FEDERALIST NO. 78

May 28, 1788

Alexander Hamilton

To the People of the State of New York:

Federalist No. 78 is the first of six *Federalist Papers* that discusses the judicial branch. Alexander Hamilton's analysis focuses on several points. Among these are the method of judicial selection, tenure in office, and the scope of judicial authority. This piece is perhaps best known for its defense of lifetime terms for judges, as well as its declaration that the judiciary would be the "least dangerous branch."

We proceed now to an examination of the judiciary department of the proposed government.

In unfolding the defects of the existing Confederation, the utility and necessity of a federal judicature have been clearly pointed out. It is the less necessary to recapitulate the considerations there urged, as the propriety of the institution in the abstract is not disputed; the only questions which have been raised being relative to the manner of constituting it, and to its extent. To these points, therefore, our observations shall be confined.

The manner of constituting it seems to embrace these several objects: 1st. The mode of appointing the judges. 2d. The tenure by which they are to hold their places. 3d. The partition of the judiciary authority between different courts, and their relations to each other.

First. As to the mode of appointing the judges; this is the same with that of appointing the officers of the Union in general, and has been so fully discussed in the two last numbers, that nothing can be said here which would not be useless repetition.

Second. As to the tenure by which the judges are to hold their places: this chiefly concerns their duration in office; the provisions for their support; the precautions for their responsibility.

According to the plan of the convention, all judges who may be appointed by the United States are to hold their offices *during good behavior*; which is conformable to the most approved of the State constitutions and among the rest, to that of this State. Its propriety having been drawn into question by the adversaries of that plan, is no light symptom of the rage for objection, which disorders their imaginations and judgments. The standard of good behavior for the continuance in office of the judicial magistracy, is certainly one of the most valuable of the modern improvements in the practice of government. In a monarchy it is an excellent barrier to the despotism of the prince; in a republic it is a no less excellent barrier to the encroachments and oppressions of the representative body. And it is the best expedient which can be devised in any government, to secure a steady, upright, and impartial administration of the laws.

Whoever attentively considers the different departments of power must perceive, that, in a government in which they are separated from each other, the judiciary, from the nature of its functions, will always be the least dangerous to the political rights of the Constitution; because it will be least in a capacity to annoy or injure them. The Executive not only dispenses the honors, but holds the sword of the community. The legislature not only commands the purse, but prescribes the rules by which the duties and rights of every citizen are to be regulated. The judiciary, on the contrary, has no influence over either the sword or the purse; no direction either of the strength or of the wealth of the society; and can take no active resolution whatever. It may truly be said to have neither *force* nor *will*, but merely judgment; and must ultimately depend upon the aid of the executive arm even for the efficacy of its judgments.

This simple view of the matter suggests several important consequences. It proves incontestably, that the judiciary is beyond comparison the weakest of the three departments of power[1]; that it can never attack with success either of the other two; and that all possible care is requisite to enable it to defend itself against their attacks. It equally proves, that though individual oppression may now and then proceed from the courts of justice, the general liberty of the people can never be endangered from that quarter; I mean so long as the judiciary remains truly distinct from both the legislature and the Executive. For I agree, that "there is no liberty, if the power of judging be not separated from the legislative and executive powers."[2] And it proves, in the last place, that as liberty can have nothing to fear from the judiciary alone, but would have every thing to fear from its union with either of the other departments; that as all the effects of such a union must ensue from a dependence of the former on the latter, notwithstanding a nominal and apparent separation; that as, from the natural feebleness of the judiciary, it is in continual jeopardy of being overpowered, awed, or influenced by its co-ordinate branches; and that as nothing can contribute so much to its firmness and independence as permanency in office, this quality may therefore be justly regarded as an indispensable ingredient in its constitution, and, in a great measure, as the citadel of the public justice and the public security.

The complete independence of the courts of justice is peculiarly essential in a limited Constitution. By a limited Constitution, I understand one which contains certain specified exceptions to the legislative authority; such, for instance, as that it shall pass no bills of attainder, no ex-post-facto laws, and the like. Limitations of this kind can be preserved in practice no other way than through the medium of courts of justice, whose duty it must be to declare all acts contrary to the manifest tenor of the Constitution void. Without this, all the reservations of particular rights or privileges would amount to nothing.

Some perplexity respecting the rights of the courts to pronounce legislative acts void, because contrary to the Constitution, has arisen from an imagination that the doctrine would imply a superiority of the judiciary to the legislative power. It is urged that the authority which can declare the acts of another void, must necessarily be superior to the one whose acts may be declared void. As this doctrine is of great importance in all the American constitutions, a brief discussion of the ground on which it rests cannot be unacceptable.

There is no position which depends on clearer principles, than that every act of a delegated authority, contrary to the tenor of the commission under which it is exercised, is void. No legislative act, therefore, contrary to the Constitution, can be valid. To deny this, would be to affirm, that the deputy is greater than his principal; that the servant is above his master; that the representatives of the people are superior to the people themselves; that men acting by virtue of powers, may do not only what their powers do not authorize, but what they forbid.

If it be said that the legislative body are themselves the constitutional judges of their own powers, and that the construction they put upon them is conclusive upon the other departments, it may be answered, that this cannot be the natural presumption, where it is not to be collected from any particular provisions in the Constitution. It is not otherwise to be supposed, that the Constitution could intend to enable the representatives of the people to substitute their *will* to that of their constituents. It is far more rational to suppose, that the courts were designed to be an intermediate body between the people and the legislature, in order, among other things, to keep the latter within the limits assigned to their authority. The interpretation of the laws is the proper and peculiar province of the courts. A constitution is, in fact, and must be regarded by the judges, as a fundamental law. It therefore belongs to them to ascertain its meaning, as well as the meaning of any particular act proceeding from the legislative body. If there should happen to be an irreconcilable variance between the two, that which has the superior obligation and validity ought, of course, to be preferred; or, in other words, the Constitution ought to be preferred to the statute, the intention of the people to the intention of their agents.

Nor does this conclusion by any means suppose a superiority of the judicial to the legislative power. It only supposes that the power of the people is superior to both; and that where the will of the legislature, declared in its statutes, stands in opposition to that of the people, declared in the Constitution, the judges ought to be governed by the latter rather than the former. They ought to regulate their decisions by the fundamental laws, rather than by those which are not fundamental.

This exercise of judicial discretion, in determining between two contradictory laws, is exemplified in a familiar instance. It not uncommonly happens, that there are two statutes existing at one time, clashing in whole or in part with each other, and neither of them containing any repealing clause or expression. In such a case, it is the province of the courts to liquidate and fix their meaning and operation. So far as they can, by any fair construction, be reconciled to each other, reason and law conspire to dictate that this should be done; where this is impracticable, it becomes a matter of necessity to give effect to one, in exclusion of the other. The rule which has obtained in the courts for determining their relative validity is, that the last in order of time shall be preferred to the first. But this is a mere rule of

---

[1]The celebrated Montesquieu, speaking of them, says: "Of the three powers above mentioned, the judiciary is next to nothing."—"Spirit of Laws," vol. 1, page 186.

[2]Idem, page 181.

construction, not derived from any positive law, but from the nature and reason of the thing. It is a rule not enjoined upon the courts by legislative provision, but adopted by themselves, as consonant to truth and propriety, for the direction of their conduct as interpreters of the law. They thought it reasonable, that between the interfering acts of an *equal* authority, that which was the last indication of its will should have the preference.

But in regard to the interfering acts of a superior and subordinate authority, of an original and derivative power, the nature and reason of the thing indicate the converse of that rule as proper to be followed. They teach us that the prior act of a superior ought to be preferred to the subsequent act of an inferior and subordinate authority; and that accordingly, whenever a particular statute contravenes the Constitution, it will be the duty of the judicial tribunals to adhere to the latter and disregard the former.

It can be of no weight to say that the courts, on the pretense of a repugnancy, may substitute their own pleasure to the constitutional intentions of the legislature. This might as well happen in the case of two contradictory statutes; or it might as well happen in every adjudication upon any single statute. The courts must declare the sense of the law; and if they should be disposed to exercise *will* instead of *judgment*, the consequence would equally be the substitution of their pleasure to that of the legislative body. The observation, if it prove any thing, would prove that there ought to be no judges distinct from that body.

If, then, the courts of justice are to be considered as the bulwarks of a limited Constitution against legislative encroachments, this consideration will afford a strong argument for the permanent tenure of judicial offices, since nothing will contribute so much as this to that independent spirit in the judges which must be essential to the faithful performance of so arduous a duty.

This independence of the judges is equally requisite to guard the Constitution and the rights of individuals from the effects of those ill humors, which the arts of designing men, or the influence of particular conjunctures, sometimes disseminate among the people themselves, and which, though they speedily give place to better information, and more deliberate reflection, have a tendency, in the meantime, to occasion dangerous innovations in the government, and serious oppressions of the minor party in the community. Though I trust the friends of the proposed Constitution will never concur with its enemies,[3] in questioning that fundamental principle of republican government, which admits the right of the people to alter or abolish the established Constitution, whenever they find it inconsistent with their happiness, yet it is not to be inferred from this principle, that the representatives of the people, whenever a

momentary inclination happens to lay hold of a majority of their constituents, incompatible with the provisions in the existing Constitution, would, on that account, be justifiable in a violation of those provisions; or that the courts would be under a greater obligation to connive at infractions in this shape, than when they had proceeded wholly from the cabals of the representative body. Until the people have, by some solemn and authoritative act, annulled or changed the established form, it is binding upon themselves collectively, as well as individually; and no presumption, or even knowledge, of their sentiments, can warrant their representatives in a departure from it, prior to such an act. But it is easy to see, that it would require an uncommon portion of fortitude in the judges to do their duty as faithful guardians of the Constitution, where legislative invasions of it had been instigated by the major voice of the community.

But it is not with a view to infractions of the Constitution only, that the independence of the judges may be an essential safeguard against the effects of occasional ill humors in the society. These sometimes extend no farther than to the injury of the private rights of particular classes of citizens, by unjust and partial laws. Here also the firmness of the judicial magistracy is of vast importance in mitigating the severity and confining the operation of such laws. It not only serves to moderate the immediate mischiefs of those which may have been passed, but it operates as a check upon the legislative body in passing them; who, perceiving that obstacles to the success of iniquitous intention are to be expected from the scruples of the courts, are in a manner compelled, by the very motives of the injustice they meditate, to qualify their attempts. This is a circumstance calculated to have more influence upon the character of our governments, than but few may be aware of. The benefits of the integrity and moderation of the judiciary have already been felt in more States than one; and though they may have displeased those whose sinister expectations they may have disappointed, they must have commanded the esteem and applause of all the virtuous and disinterested. Considerate men, of every description, ought to prize whatever will tend to beget or fortify that temper in the courts: as no man can be sure that he may not be to-morrow the victim of a spirit of injustice, by which he may be a gainer to-day. And every man must now feel, that the inevitable tendency of such a spirit is to sap the foundations of public and private confidence, and to introduce in its stead universal distrust and distress.

That inflexible and uniform adherence to the rights of the Constitution, and of individuals, which we perceive to be indispensable in the courts of justice, can certainly not be expected from judges who hold their offices by a temporary commission. Periodical appointments, however regulated, or by whomsoever made, would, in some way or other, be fatal to their necessary independence. If the power of making them was committed either to the Executive or

---

[3] Vide "Protest of the Minority of the Convention of Pennsylvania," Martin's Speech, etc.

legislature, there would be danger of an improper complaisance to the branch which possessed it; if to both, there would be an unwillingness to hazard the displeasure of either; if to the people, or to persons chosen by them for the special purpose, there would be too great a disposition to consult popularity, to justify a reliance that nothing would be consulted but the Constitution and the laws.

There is yet a further and a weightier reason for the permanency of the judicial offices, which is deducible from the nature of the qualifications they require. It has been frequently remarked, with great propriety, that a voluminous code of laws is one of the inconveniences necessarily connected with the advantages of a free government. To avoid an arbitrary discretion in the courts, it is indispensable that they should be bound down by strict rules and precedents, which serve to define and point out their duty in every particular case that comes before them; and it will readily be conceived from the variety of controversies which grow out of the folly and wickedness of mankind, that the records of those precedents must unavoidably swell to a very considerable bulk, and must demand long and laborious study to acquire a competent knowledge of them. Hence it is, that there can be but few men in the society who will have sufficient skill in the laws to qualify them for the stations of judges. And making the proper deductions for the ordinary depravity of human nature, the number must be still smaller of those who unite the requisite integrity with the requisite knowledge. These considerations apprise us, that the government can have no great option between fit character; and that a temporary duration in office, which would naturally discourage such characters from quitting a lucrative line of practice to accept a seat on the bench, would have a tendency to throw the administration of justice into hands less able, and less well qualified, to conduct it with utility and dignity. In the present circumstances of this country, and in those in which it is likely to be for a long time to come, the disadvantages on this score would be greater than they may at first sight appear; but it must be confessed, that they are far inferior to those which present themselves under the other aspects of the subject.

Upon the whole, there can be no room to doubt that the convention acted wisely in copying from the models of those constitutions which have established *good behavior* as the tenure of their judicial offices, in point of duration; and that so far from being blamable on this account, their plan would have been inexcusably defective, if it had wanted this important feature of good government. The experience of Great Britain affords an illustrious comment on the excellence of the institution.

PUBLIUS

501(c) group   Interest group whose primary purpose is not electoral politics.

527 political committee   Organization created with the primary purpose of influencing electoral outcomes; the term is typically applied only to freestanding interest groups that do not explicitly advocate for the election of a candidate.

abolitionist   A supporter, especially in the early nineteenth century, of ending the institution of slavery.

Abraham Lincoln   Sixteenth president of the United States, the first elected Republican president, who served from 1861 to 1865. Lincoln, who led the Union during the Civil War, was assassinated in 1865 by a Confederate sympathizer, John Wilkes Booth.

affirmative action   Policies designed to give special attention or compensatory treatment to members of a previously disadvantaged group.

Affordable Care Act (ACA)   A 2010 law designed to ensure that nearly all Americans would have access to health care coverage, including those living in poverty.

Afghanistan War   A military conflict begun in 2002 in which a U.S.-led international coalition invaded Afghanistan in order to depose the government and deny a safe haven to terrorists.

agenda setting   The process of forming the list of issues to be addressed by government.

Alexander Hamilton   A key Framer who envisioned a powerful central government, co-authored *The Federalist Papers*, and served as the first secretary of the treasury. He was killed by Vice President Aaron Burr in a duel.

al-Qaeda   The Islamic terrorist organization responsible for the 9/11 terrorist attacks and numerous other actions against U.S. overseas interests.

Alien and Sedition Acts   Laws passed in 1798 that allowed the imprisonment and deportation of aliens considered dangerous and criminalized false statements against the government.

American Dream   An American ideal of a happy, successful life, which often assumes wealth, a house, and a better life for one's children.

Americans with Disabilities Act (ADA)   A law enacted by Congress in 1990 designed to guarantee accommodation and access for people with a wide range of disabilities.

amicus curiae   "Friend of the court"; *amici* may file briefs or even appear to argue their interests orally before the court.

Andrew Jackson   Seventh president of the United States serving from 1829 to 1837 as a Democratic Republican. He became a national hero for leading American troops to victory over the British in the War of 1812's Battle of New Orleans. He depended on the labor of enslaved people for his plantation and was responsible for removing Indians across the South to Oklahoma.

Andrew Johnson   Seventeenth president of the United States, a Republican, who served from 1865 to 1869. Johnson had served as Abraham Lincoln's vice president and became president after Lincoln's assassination.

Anne Hutchinson   Seventeenth-century political leader and thinker who supported religious liberty.

Anti-Federalists   Those who favored strong state governments and a weak national government; opposed ratification of the U.S. Constitution.

appellate court   Court that generally reviews only findings of law made by lower courts.

apportionment   The process of allotting congressional seats to each state according to its proportion of the population, following the decennial census.

aristocracy   A government in which a small group of individuals govern for the perceived good of all.

Article I   Vests all legislative powers in the Congress and establishes a bicameral legislature, consisting of the Senate and the House of Representatives; it also sets out the qualifications for holding office in each house, the terms of office, the methods of selection of representatives and senators, and the system of apportionment among the states to determine membership in the House of Representatives. Its numbering as Article I and the extensive attention to its powers make it clear that the Congress was to be the most important political actor in the new government.

Article II   Vests the executive power, that is, the authority to execute the laws of the nation, in a president of the United States; section 1 sets the president's term of office at four years, explains the Electoral College, states the qualifications for office, and describes a mechanism to replace the president in case of death, disability, or removal from office.

Article III   Establishes a Supreme Court and defines its jurisdiction.

Article IV   Mandates that states honor the laws and judicial proceedings of other states. Article IV also includes the mechanisms for admitting new states to the union. *See also* "full faith and credit clause."

Article V Specifies how amendments can be added to the Constitution.

Article VI Contains the supremacy clause, which asserts the basic primacy of the Constitution and national law over state laws and constitutions. *See also* "supremacy clause."

Article VII Sets forth the procedures for the newly minted U.S. Constitution to be ratified by the states.

Articles of Confederation The compact between the thirteen original colonies that created a loose league of friendship, with the national government drawing its powers from the states.

Baker v. *Carr* **(1962)** Supreme Court case ruling that issues presented by redistricting are within its jurisdiction to review.

Barack Obama The first Black president of the United States, a Democrat, who served as forty-fourth president from 2009 to 2017. Senator from Illinois from 2005 to 2008; member of the Illinois Senate from 1997 to 2004.

Barron v. *Baltimore* **(1833)** Supreme Court ruling that, before the Civil War, limited the applicability of the Bill of Rights to the federal government and not to the states.

Benjamin Franklin A brilliant inventor and senior statesman at the Constitutional Convention who urged colonial unity as early as 1754, twenty-two years before the Declaration of Independence.

Berlin Wall A barrier built by East Germany in 1961 to prevent East German citizens from fleeing to the democratic West from Communist East Berlin.

Bernie Sanders Longest serving independent in the United States Congress. Ran for the Democratic Party nomination for president in 2020 and against Hillary Clinton in the 2016 Democratic presidential primary; senator from Vermont since 2007; first elected to the House of Representatives in 1991.

bicameral legislature A two-house legislature.

Bill of Rights The first ten amendments to the U.S. Constitution, which largely guarantee specific rights and liberties.

bill A proposed law.

Bipartisan Campaign Reform Act (BCRA) Passed in 2002, this act amended the Federal Election Campaign Act of 1971 with several provisions designed to end the use of nonfederal, or "soft money" (money raised outside the limits and prohibitions of federal campaign finance law) for activity affecting federal elections.

Black Lives Matter (BLM) An organized movement for racial justice in America advocating for nonviolent protest and civil disobedience. It began in 2013, after a police officer was acquitted of killing Trayvon Martin, a Black teenager. Subsequent deaths of Black men at the hands of police officers have sparked continued protests.

block grant A large grant given to a state by the federal government with only general spending guidelines.

Board of Governors In the Federal Reserve System, a seven-member board that makes most economic decisions regarding interest rates and the supply of money; it is led by the Federal Reserve chair.

Bretton Woods System International financial system devised shortly before the end of World War II that created the World Bank and the International Monetary Fund.

brief A document containing the legal written arguments in a case filed with a court by a party prior to a hearing or trial.

Brown v. *Board of Education* **(1954)** U.S. Supreme Court decision holding that school segregation is inherently unconstitutional because it violates the Fourteenth Amendment's guarantee of equal protection of the law.

budget deficit The economic condition that occurs when expenditures exceed revenues.

bureaucracy The government agencies, institutions, and personnel that implement and administer laws and programs.

Burger Court The period in Supreme Court history during which Warren Burger served as chief justice (1969–1986).

Cabinet The formal body of presidential advisers who head the fifteen executive departments. Presidents often add others to this body of formal advisers.

Cabinet departments Major administrative units with responsibility for a broad area of government operations. Departmental status usually indicates a permanent national interest in a particular governmental function, such as defense, commerce, or agriculture.

Calvin Coolidge Thirtieth president of the United States, a Republican, who served from 1923 to 1929.

campaign consultant A private-sector professional who sells to a candidate the technologies, services, and strategies required to get that candidate elected.

campaign manager The individual who travels with the candidate and coordinates the campaign.

candidate-centered politics Politics that focus on the candidates, their particular issues, and their character, rather than party affiliation.

categorical grants Grants that appropriate federal funds to states for a specific purpose.

census Mandated under Article 1, section 2, of the Constitution, the census provides data necessary to appoint representatives among the states for the House of Representatives and to redistrict legislative districts.

Central Intelligence Agency (CIA) A U.S. government agency dedicated to intelligence gathering and covert operations.

Cesar Chavez Labor organizer who, with Dolores Huerta, founded the United Farm Workers Union (UFW) in the 1960s.

charter schools Semi-public schools that have open admission and receive some support from the government and may also receive private donations to increase the quality of education.

charter   A document that, like a constitution, specifies the basic policies, procedures, and institutions of local government. Charters for local governments must be approved by state legislatures.

checks and balances   A constitutionally mandated structure that gives each of the three branches of government some degree of oversight and control over the actions of the others.

Christian Coalition   A religious interest group founded in 1989 to advance conservative Christian principles and traditional values in American politics.

citizen journalists   Ordinary individuals who collect, report, and analyze news content.

Citizens United v. FEC **(2010)**   Supreme Court ruling that enabled corporations and unions to have the same political speech rights as individuals under the First Amendment. As part of this ruling, the Supreme Court found that the government may not prohibit corporations or unions from using their general treasury funds to support or denounce political candidates in elections.

civic virtue   The tendency to form small-scale associations for the public good.

civil liberties   The personal guarantees and freedoms that the government cannot abridge by law, constitution, or judicial interpretation.

civil rights   The government-protected rights of individuals against arbitrary or discriminatory treatment by governments or individuals.

Civil Rights Act of 1964   Wide-ranging legislation passed by Congress to outlaw segregation in public facilities and discrimination in employment, education, and voting; created the Equal Employment Opportunity Commission.

civil service system   The merit system by which many federal bureaucrats are selected.

Civil War   The military conflict from 1861 to 1865 in the United States between the Northern forces of the Union and the Southern forces of the Confederacy. Over 600,000 Americans lost their lives during this war.

closed primary   A primary election in which only a party's registered voters are eligible to cast a ballot.

cloture   Mechanism requiring the vote of sixty senators to cut off debate.

Cold War   The period of superpower rivalry and confrontation between the United States and the Soviet Union, lasting from the end of World War II to 1991.

collective good   Something of value that cannot be withheld from a nonmember of a group, for example, a tax write-off or a better environment.

collective security   The idea that an attack on one country is an attack on all countries.

Common Core   A voluntarily adopted multi-state approach to setting standards that all students should achieve up through the high-school level.

communications director   The person who develops the overall media strategy for the candidate.

concurrent powers   Powers shared by the national and state governments.

concurring opinion   A type of judicial opinion issued by a minority of judges on a court who agree with the outcome of a case but wish to express different legal reasoning.

confederation   Type of government in which the national government derives its powers from the states; a league of independent states.

conference committee   Special joint committee created to reconcile differences in bills passed by the House and Senate.

congressional review   A process whereby Congress can nullify agency regulations within a sixty-day window by passing a joint resolution of legislative disapproval. The president's approval of the resolution or a two-thirds majority vote in both houses to overrule a presidential veto is also required.

conservative   One who favors limited government intervention, particularly in economic affairs.

constitution   A document establishing the structure, functions, and limitations of a government.

constitutional (or Article III) courts   Federal courts specifically created by the Constitution of the United States or by Congress pursuant to its authority in Article III.

containment   U.S. policy of opposing Soviet expansion and Communist revolutions around the world with military forces, economic assistance, and political influence.

content regulations   Limitations on the substance of the mass media.

contrast ad   Ad that compares the records and proposals of the candidates, with a bias toward the candidate sponsoring the ad.

cooperative federalism   The intertwined relationship between national, state, and local governments that began with the New Deal; often referred to as marble-cake federalism.

Crispus Attucks   An African American and first American to die in what became known as the Boston Massacre in 1770.

critical election   An election that signals a party realignment through voter polarization around new issues and personalities.

Critical Period   The chaotic period from 1781 to 1789 after the American Revolution during which the former colonies were governed under the Articles of Confederation.

crossover voting   Participation in the primary election of a party with which the voter is not affiliated.

Cuban Missile Crisis   The 1962 confrontation over the deployment of ballistic missiles in Cuba that nearly escalated into nuclear war between the United States and the Soviet Union.

Declaration of Independence   Document drafted largely by Thomas Jefferson in 1776 that proclaimed the right of the American colonies to separate from Great Britain.

deep background   Information provided to a journalist that will not be attributed to any source.

defense policy   Area of policy making that focuses on the strategies that a country uses to protect itself from its enemies.

delegate   Role played by representative who votes the way his or her constituents would want, regardless of personal opinions; may refer to an elected representative to Congress or a representative to the party convention.

democracy   A system of government that gives power to the people, whether directly or through elected representatives.

Department of Defense   Principal executive branch department responsible for formulation and implementation of U.S. defense and military policy.

Department of Health and Human Services   The cabinet-level department administering most federal social welfare and health-related policies and programs; it includes the National Institutes for Health (NIH), the Centers for Disease Control and Prevention (CDC), and the Food and Drug Administration (FDA).

Department of Homeland Security   Cabinet department created after the 9/11 terrorist attacks to coordinate domestic security efforts.

Department of State   Chief executive branch department responsible for formulation and implementation of U.S. foreign policy.

depression   A severe and long-lasting decline in the economy that occurs as investment sags, production falls off, and unemployment increases.

détente   The improvement in relations between the United States and the Soviet Union that occurred during the 1970s.

deterrence   The military strategy of employing enormous force, including nuclear weapons, in order to prevent the outbreak or escalation of armed conflicts.

digital-native   News publishers originally founded on the Web.

Dillon's Rule   A premise articulated by Judge John F. Dillon in 1868 that states that local governments do not have any inherent sovereignty and instead must be authorized by state governments that can create or abolish them.

direct incitement test   Test articulated by the Supreme Court in *Brandenburg* v. *Ohio* (1969) holding that the First Amendment protects advocacy of illegal action unless imminent lawless action is intended and likely to occur.

discharge petition   Petition that gives a majority of the House of Representatives the authority to bring an issue to the floor in the face of committee inaction.

discount rate   The rate of interest at which the Federal Reserve Board lends money to member banks.

dissenting opinion   A type of judicial opinion issued by a minority of judges on a court who disagree with the outcome of a case and wish to explain their legal reasoning.

distributive policies   Public policies that provide benefits to individuals, groups, communities, or corporations.

disturbance theory   The theory that interest groups form as a result of changes in the political system.

divided government   The political condition in which different political parties control the presidency and at least one house of Congress.

Dolores Huerta   Labor organizer who, with Cesar Chavez, founded the United Farm Workers Union (UFW) in the 1960s.

Donald J. Trump   The forty-fifth president, a Republican, elected in 2016, serving only one term; first candidate elected without prior political or military experience; an experienced businessman.

double jeopardy clause   Part of the Fifth Amendment that protects individuals from being tried twice for the same offense in the same jurisdiction.

Dred Scott   Named plaintiff in major Supreme Court case in which the court concluded enslaved people were property—not persons.

Dred Scott v. Sandford (1857)   Supreme Court decision that ruled the Missouri Compromise unconstitutional and denied citizenship rights to enslaved Black people. *Dred Scott* heightened tensions between the pro-slavery South and the abolitionist North in the run-up to the Civil War.

dual federalism   The belief that having separate and equally powerful levels of government is the best arrangement, often referred to as layer-cake federalism.

due process clause   Clause contained in the Fifth and Fourteenth Amendments; over the years, it has been construed to guarantee a variety of rights to individuals.

due process rights   Protections drawn from the Fourth Amendment and the Bill of Rights. Due process may be procedural, ensuring fair treatment, or substantive, protecting fundamental rights.

Dwight D. Eisenhower   The thirty-fourth president of the United States (1953–1961). Also like Gorge Washington, he served as the Supreme Commander of the Allied Expeditionary Force in Europe during World War II.

Earl Warren The fourteenth chief justice of the United States who served from 1953 to 1969 and led the Court through an important liberal phase; previously a Republican governor and vice presidential nominee.

Edmund Burke British political philosopher of the eighteenth century who articulated the view that elected representatives should act as "trustees" and use their own best judgment when voting.

Eighteenth Amendment A 1913 amendment that created the nationwide prohibition on alcoholic beverages; it was repealed in 1933 by the Twentieth Amendment.

Eighth Amendment Part of the Bill of Rights that states: "Excessive bail shall not be required, nor excessive fines imposed, nor cruel and unusual punishments inflicted."

Eleanor Roosevelt First Lady of the United States from 1933 to 1945. Roosevelt championed human rights throughout her life and served as the United States's first delegate to the United Nations General Assembly and later chaired the UN's Commission on Human Rights.

elector Member of the Electoral College.

Electoral College The system established by the Constitution through which the president is chosen by electors from each state, which has as many electoral votes as it has members of Congress.

electorate Individuals who are eligible to vote.

Elena Kagan An associate justice of the Supreme Court, appointed by President Barack Obama in 2009 while she was serving as solicitor general in his administration.

Eleventh Amendment An amendment adopted in 1789 protecting states from being sued in federal court by a citizen of a different state or country.

Elizabeth Cady Stanton Leading nineteenth century feminist, suffragist, and abolitionist who, along with Lucretia Mott, organized the Seneca Falls Convention. Stanton later founded the National Woman Suffrage Association (NWSA) with Susan B. Anthony.

Emancipation Proclamation President Abraham Lincoln issued this proclamation on January 1, 1863, in the third year of the Civil War. It freed all enslaved people in states that were in active rebellion against the United States.

Engel v. Vitale **(1962)** Court case in which the recitation of a brief, nondenominational prayer drafted by the school board was unconstitutional because it violated the First Amendment's religious establishment clause.

Enlightenment A philosophical movement in eighteenth-century Europe; its adherents advocated liberty and tolerance of individual differences, decried religious and political abuses, and rejected the notion of an absolute monarch.

entitlement programs Government benefits that all citizens meeting eligibility criteria—such as age, income level, or unemployment—are legally "entitled" to receive; these are also referred to as non-means-tested programs.

enumerated powers The powers of the national government specifically granted to Congress in Article I, section 8, of the Constitution.

Equal Pay Act of 1963 Legislation that requires employers to pay men and women equal pay for equal work.

equal protection clause Section of the Fourteenth Amendment that guarantees that all citizens receive "equal protection of the laws."

Equal Rights Amendment (ERA) Proposed amendment to the Constitution that states, "Equality of rights under the law shall not be denied or abridged by the United States or any state on account of sex."

equal time rule The rule that requires broadcast stations to sell air time equally to all candidates in a political campaign if they choose to sell it to any.

establishment clause The first clause of the First Amendment; it directs the national government not to sanction an official religion.

European Union An organization with political institutions that join twenty-seven countries in Europe into a union that promotes free trade, a central bank, flow of labor and capital, and a common currency among most members.

ex post facto **law** Law that makes an act punishable as a crime even if the action was legal at the time it was committed.

exclusionary rule Judicially created rule that prohibits police from using illegally seized evidence at trial.

executive agreements Formal international agreements entered into by the president that do not require the advice and consent of the U.S. Senate.

Executive Office of the President (EOP) A mini-bureaucracy created in 1939 to help the president oversee the executive branch bureaucracy.

executive order Rule or regulation issued by the president that has the effect of law. All executive orders must be published in the *Federal Register*.

executive privilege An implied presidential power that allows the president to refuse to disclose information regarding confidential conversations or national security to Congress or the judiciary.

exit polls Polls conducted as voters leave selected polling places on Election Day.

Farewell Address When President George Washington left office, he wrote a letter, addressed to the People of the United States, warning them of the dangers to avoid in order to preserve the republic.

Federal Election Campaign Act (FECA) Passed in 1971, this is the primary law that regulates political campaign spending and fundraising. The law originally focused on increased disclosure of contributions for federal campaigns.

Federal Election Commission (FEC)   An independent regulatory agency founded in 1975 by the U.S. Congress to regulate the campaign finance legislation in the United States.

Federal Register   The official journal of the U.S. government, including all federal rules and public notices so that citizens and organization can follow proposed changes and comply with rule changes.

Federal Reserve System   The organization in the United States tasked with such responsibilities as managing the money supply, stabilizing prices, moderating interest rates, and reducing unemployment.

federal system   System of government in which the national government and state governments share power and derive all authority from the people.

federalism   The distribution of constitutional authority between state governments and the national government, with different powers and functions exercised by both.

Federalist No. 10   A *Federalist Paper* penned by Alexander Hamilton setting out his beliefs in the limited powers of the judicial branch of government.

Federalist No. 78   A *Federalist Papers* essay authored by Alexander Hamilton that covers the role of the federal judiciary, including the power of judicial review.

Federalists   Those who favored a stronger national government and supported the proposed U.S. Constitution; later became the first U.S. political party.

Fifteenth Amendment   One of three major amendments ratified after the Civil War; specifically enfranchised newly freed men who had been enslaved.

Fifth Amendment   Part of the Bill of Rights that imposes a number of restrictions on the federal government with respect to the rights of persons suspected of committing a crime. It provides for indictment by a grand jury and protection against self-incrimination, and prevents the national government from denying a person life, liberty, or property without the due process of law. It also prevents the national government from taking property without just compensation.

fighting words   Words that "by their very utterance inflict injury or tend to incite an immediate breach of peace." Fighting words are not subject to the restrictions of the First Amendment.

filibuster   A formal way of halting Senate action on a bill by means of long speeches or unlimited debate.

finance chair   The individual who coordinates the financial business of the campaign.

First Amendment   Part of the Bill of Rights that imposes a number of restrictions on the federal government with respect to civil liberties, including freedom of religion, speech, press, assembly, and petition.

first lady   The designation provided to the wife of a president or, at the state level, of a governor; no specific analogue exists for a male spouse.

fiscal policy   The deliberate use of the national government's taxing and spending policies to maintain economic stability.

foreign policy   Area of policy making that encompasses how one country builds relationships with other countries in order to safeguard its national interest.

foreign-policy idealism   A perspective contending that the behavior of countries in the international arena is mainly intended to advance their values and principles.

foreign-policy realism   A perspective contending that the behavior of countries in the international arena is mainly intended to protect their economic and security interests.

Fourteenth Amendment   One of three major amendments enacted after the Civil War, extending the "privileges and immunities of citizenship" and "equal protection of the law" to all U.S. citizens. None of these rights or liberties could be taken without the "due process" of law.

Fourth Amendment   Part of the Bill of Rights that protects people from unreasonable searches and seizures of their persons, houses, papers, and effects without a warrant from a judge, among other guarantees. Items found pursuant to an illegal search are to be prevented from use at trial according to what is called the exclusionary rule.

framing   The process by which a news organization defines a political issue and consequently affects opinion about the issue.

Franklin D. Roosevelt (FDR)   Thirty-second president, a Democrat, who served from 1933 to 1945. FDR's leadership took the United States through the Great Depression and World War II.

Frederick Douglass   A formerly enslaved person born in the early 1800s who became a leading abolitionist, writer, and suffragist.

free exercise clause   The second clause of the First Amendment; it prohibits the U.S. government from interfering with a citizen's right to practice his or her religion.

free rider problem   Potential members who fail to join a group because they can get the benefit, or collective good, sought by the group without contributing the effort.

free trade system   A system of international trade that limits government interference on the sale of goods and services among countries.

front-loading   The tendency of states to choose an early date on the nomination calendar.

full faith and credit clause   Section of Article IV of the Constitution that ensures judicial decrees and contracts made in one state will be binding and enforceable in any other state.

fundamental freedoms   Those rights defined by the Court as essential to order, liberty, and justice and therefore entitled to the highest standard of review.

Furman v. Georgia (1972)   Supreme Court decision that ended capital punishment in the United States based on the fact that it was applied in an arbitrary manner within and across the states that had a death penalty and could be considered cruel and unusual punishment in violation of the Eighth Amendment.

General Agreement on Tariffs and Trade (GATT)   Post–World War II economic development treaty designed to help facilitate international trade negotiations and promote free trade.

general election   Election in which voters decide which candidates will actually fill elective public offices.

George Gallup   One of the earliest developers of scientific methods for public opinion polling and a proponent for a strong role for the voice of the public in politics and government.

George Washington   Widely considered the "Father of the Nation," he was the commander of the revolutionary armies; served as the presiding officer of the Constitutional Convention and as the United States' first president from 1789 to 1797.

gerrymandering   The drawing of congressional districts to produce a particular electoral utcome without regard to the shape of the district.

get-out-the-vote (GOTV)   A push at the end of a political campaign to encourage supporters to go to the polls.

Gibbons v. Ogden (1824)   Supreme Court ruling that upheld broad congressional power to regulate interstate commerce. The Court's broad interpretation of the Constitution's commerce clause paved the way for later rulings upholding expansive federal powers.

Gideon v. Wainwright (1963)   Unanimous Supreme Court decision that criminal defendants who cannot afford an attorney are guaranteed one by the Sixth Amendment.

global war on terror   An international action, initiated by President George W. Bush after the 9/11 terrorist attacks, to weed out terrorist operatives throughout the world.

government   The formal vehicle through which policies are made and affairs of state are conducted.

government corporations   Businesses established by Congress to perform functions that private businesses could provide, such as the U.S. Postal Service and Amtrak. Often established when the financial incentives for private industry to provide services are minimal.

governmental (institutional) agenda   Problems to which public officials feel obliged to devote active and serious attention.

grand jury   A group of citizens charged with determining whether enough evidence exists for a case to go to trial. Guaranteed by the Fifth Amendment.

grandfather clause   Voter qualification provision in many southern states that allowed only those citizens whose grandfathers had voted before Reconstruction to vote unless they passed a wealth or literacy test.

Great Compromise   The final decision of the Constitutional Convention to create a two-house legislature, with the lower house elected by the people and powers divided between the two houses; also made national law supreme.

Great Depression   A severe global economic downturn marked by mass unemployment and poverty that began in the United States in 1929 and persisted to some degree until the end of the 1930s.

Great Society   Reform program begun in 1964 by President Lyndon B. Johnson that was a broad attempt to combat poverty and discrimination through urban renewal, education reform, and unemployment relief.

Green New Deal   A program to accelerate the transition from fossil fuels to clean, renewable energy with the goal of generating 100 percent of the nation's electricity from these sources within ten years.

Gregg v. Georgia (1976)   Supreme Court decision that found Georgia's new statutory requirements specifying a range of crimes that could be considered for possible death sentences to be acceptable.

gross domestic product (GDP)   The total market value of all goods and services produced in a country during a year.

Gulf War   A military conflict from 1990 to 1991 in which a U.S.-led international coalition reversed the occupation of Kuwait by the armed forces of Iraq.

Harriet Tubman   Born as an enslaved person in Maryland in the early 1820s, Tubman escaped to freedom and became a conductor on the Underground Railroad. She led more than seventy people to freedom in the North, served in the Union during the Civil War, and championed women's suffrage.

Harry S Truman   The thirty-third president, a Democrat, who served from 1945 until 1953. Truman became president when Franklin D. Roosevelt died in office; he led the United States through the end of World War II and the start of the Cold War.

Hatch Act   The 1939 act to prohibit civil servants from taking activist roles in partisan campaigns. This act prohibited federal employees from making political contributions, working for a particular party, or campaigning for a particular candidate.

Help America Vote Act (HAVA)   A federal law passed in 2002 that addresses issues of voting systems and voter access that were identified following the 2000 election. It established minimum election administration standards for states and units of local government with responsibility for the administration of federal elections and for other purposes related to the Act.

Herbert Hoover   Thirty-first president of the United States, a Republican, who served from 1929 to 1933 during the start of the Great Depression.

Honest Leadership and Open Government Act of 2007   Lobbying reform banning gifts to members of Congress and their staffs, toughening disclosure requirements, and increasing time limits on moving from the federal government to the private sector.

human rights   The protection of people's basic freedoms and needs.

impeachment   The power delegated to the House of Representatives in the Constitution to charge the president, vice president, or other "civil officers," including federal judges, with "Treason, Bribery, or other high Crimes and Misdemeanors." This is the first step in the constitutional process of removing government officials from office.

implied powers   The powers of the national government derived from the enumerated powers and the necessary and proper clause.

incorporation doctrine   An interpretation of the Constitution holding that the due process clause of the Fourteenth Amendment requires state and local governments to guarantee the rights stated in the Bill of Rights.

incumbency   Already holding an office.

independent executive agencies   Governmental units that closely resemble a Cabinet department but have narrower areas of responsibility and perform services rather than regulatory functions.

independent expenditures   Spending for campaign activity that is not coordinated with a candidate's campaign.

independent regulatory commission   An entity created by Congress outside a major executive department that regulates a specified interest or economic activity.

inflation   A rise in the general price levels of goods and services within an economy.

inherent powers   Powers that belong to the president because they can be inferred from the Constitution.

initiative   An election that allows citizens to propose legislation or state constitutional amendments by submitting them to the electorate for popular vote.

inoculation ad   Advertising that attempts to counteract an anticipated attack from the opposition before the attack is launched.

interagency councils   Working groups created to facilitate coordination of policy making and implementation across a host of governmental agencies.

interest group   A collection of people or organizations that tries to influence public policy.

intermediate standard of review   A standard of review in which the Court determines whether classifications serve an important governmental objective and are substantially related to serving that objective. Gender-related legislation automatically accorded this level of review.

International Monetary Fund (IMF)   International governmental organization designed to stabilize international currency transactions.

Iraq War   A military conflict from 2003 to 2011 in which a U.S.-led international coalition invaded Iraq and deposed its regime but proved unable to establish a stable new government.

Iron Curtain   A term used during the Cold War to describe the divide between the capitalist West and Communist East.

iron triangles   The relatively ironclad relationships and patterns of interaction that occur among agencies, interest groups, and congressional committees or subcommittees.

ISIS   A terrorist organization that calls itself an Islamic State, controlled parts of Syria and Iraq and used that as a base to direct and inspire terrorist attacks abroad.

isolationism   The U.S. policy of avoiding entangling alliances with foreign powers.

issue networks   The loose and informal relationships that exist among a large number of actors who work in broad policy areas.

James Madison   A key Framer often called the "Father of the Constitution" for his role in conceptualizing the federal government. Co-authored *The Federalist Papers*; served as secretary of state; served as the fourth U.S. president from 1809 to 1817.

Jay Court   Named after the first chief justice of the United States.

Jean-Jacques Rousseau   Swiss-born philosopher, writer, and political theorist who influenced the French Revolution and the formation of modern governments.

Jerry Falwell   A Southern Baptist minister who, in 1978, founded the conservative religious interest group the Moral Majority.

Jim Crow laws   Laws enacted by southern states that required segregation in public schools, theaters, hotels, and other public accommodations.

Joe Biden   Elected 46th president of the United States, a Democrat, who ran against President Donald J. Trump in 2020. Vice President from 2009 to 2016; Delaware senator from 1973 to 2009.

John C. Calhoun   A politician and political theorist from South Carolina who supported slavery and states' rights in the pre-Civil War era and served as vice president from 1825 to 1832.

John F. Kennedy   The thirty-fourth president, a Democrat, who served from 1961 to 1963 and marked a generational shift in U.S. politics at the height of the Cold War. He was assassinated on November 22, 1963.

John Jay   A member of the Founding generation who was the first chief justice of the United States. A diplomat and co-author of *The Federalist Papers*.

John Locke   An English philosopher and physician, widely regarded as one of the most influential of Enlightenment thinkers and commonly known as the "Father of Liberalism."

John Marshall The longest-serving Supreme Court chief justice, Marshall served from 1801 to 1835. Marshall's decision in *Marbury* v. *Madison* (1803) established the principle of judicial review.

Joint Chiefs of Staff Military advisory body composed of top officials including the Army chief of staff, the Air Force chief of staff, the chief of naval operations, the Marine commandant, and the chief of space operations.

joint committee Standing committee that includes members from both houses of Congress set up to conduct investigations or special studies.

judicial activism A philosophy of judicial decision making that posits judges should use their power broadly to further justice.

judicial implementation How and whether judicial decisions are translated into actual public policies affecting more than the immediate parties to a lawsuit.

judicial restraint A philosophy of judicial decision making that posits courts should allow the decisions of other branches of government to stand, even when they offend a judge's own principles.

judicial review Power of the courts to review acts of other branches of government and the states.

Judiciary Act of 1789 Legislative act that established the basic three-tiered structure of the federal court system.

Judiciary Act of 1801 A partisan effort by Federalists to pack the court with Federalist judges. It also reduced the size of the Supreme Court from six to five to limit incoming President Thomas Jefferson's ability to appoint state's rights–minded Democratic-Republicans.

jurisdiction Authority vested in a particular court to hear and decide the issues in a particular case. Original jurisdiction is the jurisdiction of courts that hear a case first, usually in a trial. These courts determine the facts of a case. Appellate jurisdiction is the power vested in particular courts to review and/or revise the decision of a lower court.

Keynesian economics An economic approach first championed by economist John Maynard Keynes in the 1930s, who maintained that spending by government can stimulate economic growth much faster than a free market could on its own.

Korean War A civil war from 1950 to 1953 in which the United States supported the South Korean regime against Communist forces in North Korea.

Korematsu v. U.S. (1944) Supreme Court ruling that upheld the authority of the U.S. government to require mass interment of people of Japanese ancestry in the United States during World War II.

laissez-faire Economic philosophy that endorses a very limited role for government in the economy.

Lawrence v. Texas (2003) Supreme Court ruling that anti-sodomy laws violated the constitutional right to privacy.

League of Nations A multilateral diplomatic organization that existed from 1920 to 1946 that sought, unsuccessfully, to prevent future wars; the United States never joined.

League of United Latin American Citizens (LULAC) An activist group founded in 1929 to combat discrimination against, and promote assimilation among, Americans of Hispanic origin.

legislative courts Courts established by Congress for specialized purposes, such as the Court of Appeals for Veterans Claims.

Lemon v. Kurtzman (1971) The Supreme Court created a three-part test for examining the constitutionality of religious establishment issues.

"Letter from Birmingham City Jail" Document written by the Reverend Martin Luther King Jr., carefully setting out four key steps to nonviolent protest: (1) fact finding; (2) negotiation; (3) self-purification; and (4) direct action.

LGBTQ community A minority group based on sexual orientation and gender identity that includes lesbian, gay, bisexual, transgender, and queer (LGBTQ) people.

libel False written statement that defames a person's character.

liberal One who favors greater government intervention, particularly in economic affairs and in the provision of social services.

libertarian One who believes in limited government interference in personal and economic liberties.

lobbying The activities of a group or organization that seeks to persuade political leaders to support the group's position.

Lobbying Disclosure Act A 1995 federal law that employs a strict definition of lobbyist and establishes strict reporting requirements on the activities of lobbyists.

lobbyist Interest group representative who seeks to influence legislation that will benefit their organization or client through political and/or financial persuasion.

logrolling Vote trading; voting to support a colleague's bill in return for a promise of future support.

Lucretia Mott Leading nineteenth century feminist, suffragist, and abolitionist who, along with Elizabeth Cady Stanton, organized the Seneca Falls Convention.

Lyndon B. Johnson (LBJ) Thirty-sixth president of the United States, a Democrat, who served from 1963 to 1969. LBJ led the nation during the Civil Rights era and the Vietnam War.

mandate A command, indicated by an electorate's votes, for the elected officials to carry out a party platform or policy agenda.

manifest destiny   Theory that the United States was divinely supported to expand across North America to the Pacific Ocean.

Mapp v. Ohio **(1961)**   Court ruling that made the "fruits" of all searches conducted illegally inadmissible in court.

Marbury v. Madison **(1803)**   Case in which the Supreme Court first asserted the power of judicial review by finding that part of the congressional statute extending the Court's original jurisdiction was unconstitutional.

margin of error   A measure of the accuracy of a public opinion poll within statistical parameters.

Marshall Plan   European collective recovery program, named after Secretary of State George C. Marshall, that provided extensive American aid to Western Europe after World War II.

Martin Luther King Jr.   A Baptist minister, proponent of nonviolence, and the most prominent leader of the civil rights movement of the 1950s and 1960s. He was assassinated on April 4, 1968.

mass media   The entire array of organizations through which information is collected and disseminated to the general public.

matching funds   Donations to presidential campaigns whereby every dollar raised from individuals in amounts less than $251 is matched by the federal treasury.

Mayflower Compact   Document agreed to by the men on the Mayflower, creating an agreement to set up a government and be subject to its rules and laws.

McCulloch v. Maryland **(1819)**   Supreme Court ruling that upheld the power of the national government and denied the right of a state to tax the federal bank, using the Constitution's supremacy clause. The Court's broad interpretation of the necessary and proper clause paved the way for later rulings upholding expansive federal powers.

McCutcheon v. FEC **(2014)**   2014 Supreme Court ruling that declared Section 441 of the Federal Election Campaign Act (FECA) unconstitutional. Section 441 imposed limits on any individual's total political contributions (to federal candidates, parties, or political action committees) in a two-year period.

McDonald v. City of Chicago **(2010)**   Supreme Court decision that the Second Amendment, which guarantees a citizen's right to "keep and bear arms," applies to state and local governments.

McGirt v. Oklahoma **(2020)**   A 5–4 decision of the Supreme Court recognizing that broken treaties did not allow Oklahoma to prosecute individuals who commit serious criminal offenses on tribal lands. The Court found that nearly one-half of Oklahoma is legally owned by several Indian tribes.

means-tested programs   Programs requiring beneficiaries to have incomes below specified levels to be eligible for benefits; among these are Social Security Insurance (SSI), Temporary Aid to Needy Families (TANF), and the Supplemental Nutrition Assistance Program (SNAP).

media effects   The influence of news sources on public opinion.

Medicaid   A government program that subsidizes medical care for the poor and disabled.

Medicare   The federal program established during Lyndon B. Johnson's administration that provides medical care to elderly Social Security recipients.

mercantilism   An economic theory designed to increase a nation's wealth through the development of commercial industry and a favorable balance of trade.

merit system   A system of employment based on qualifications, test scores, and ability, rather than party loyalty.

Mexican American Legal Defense and Educational Fund (MALDEF)   An organization modeled on the NAACP Legal Defense and Educational Fund that works to protect the civil rights of Americans of Mexican and other Hispanic heritage.

midterm election   An election that takes place in the middle of a presidential term.

military-industrial complex   The network of political and financial relations formed by defense industries, the U.S. armed forces, and Congress.

Miranda **rights**   Statements required of police that inform a suspect of his or her constitutional rights protected by the Fifth Amendment, including the right to an attorney provided by a court if the suspect cannot afford one.

Miranda v. Arizona **(1966)**   Landmark Supreme Court ruling holding that the Fifth Amendment requires individuals arrested for a crime to be advised of their right to remain silent and to have counsel present.

moderate   A person who takes a relatively centrist or middle-of-the-road view on most political issues.

monarchy   A form of government in which power is vested in hereditary kings and queens who govern the entire society.

monetary policy   A form of government regulation in which the nation's money supply and interest rates are controlled.

Monroe Doctrine   President James Monroe's 1823 pledge that the United States would oppose attempts by European states to reestablish their political control in the Western Hemisphere.

Montesquieu   The French baron and political theorist who first articulated the concept of separation of powers with checks and balances.

Moral Majority   A conservative religious interest group credited with helping to mobilize conservative evangelical Christian voters from its founding in 1978 through the presidency of Ronald Reagan (1981–89).

muckraking A form of journalism, in vogue in the early twentieth century, devoted to exposing misconduct by government, business, and individual politicians.

NAACP Legal Defense and Educational Fund (LDF) The legal arm of the NAACP that successfully litigated the landmark case of *Brown* v. *Board of Education* and a host of other key civil rights cases.

Nancy Pelosi A California Democrat, Pelosi is the first woman Speaker of the House. She served from 2007 to 2011 when Democrats took control of Congress and again in the 116th and 117th Congresses when Democrats flipped the House. She served as House Minority Whip from 2002 to 2003.

narrowcasting Targeting media programming at specific populations within society.

National Association for the Advancement of Colored People (NAACP) An important rights organization founded in 1909 to oppose segregation, racism, and voting rights violations targeted against African Americans.

national convention A party meeting held in the presidential election year for the purposes of nominating a presidential and vice presidential ticket and adopting a platform.

national debt The total amount owed by the federal government to its creditors, both domestic and international.

National Organization for Women (NOW) The leading activist group of the women's rights movement, especially in the 1960s and 1970s.

national party platform A statement of the general and specific philosophy and policy goals of a political party, usually promulgated at the national convention.

National Rifle Association (NRA) The major gun-rights lobbying group in the United States, which opposes gun control and advances an expansive interpretation of the Second Amendment.

National Security Council The agency within the White House, led by the national security adviser, which brings together key foreign policy actors to advise the president.

necessary and proper clause The final paragraph of Article I, section 8, of the Constitution, which gives Congress the authority to pass all laws "necessary and proper" to carry out the enumerated powers specified in the Constitution; also called the "elastic clause."

negative ad Advertising on behalf of a candidate that attacks the opponent's character or platform.

New Deal The political program enacted by President Franklin D. Roosevelt in the 1930s that greatly expanded the role of the federal government in order to combat the effects of the Great Depression.

New Jersey Plan A framework for the Constitution proposed by a group of small states; it called for a one-house legislature with one vote for each state, a Congress with the ability to raise revenue, and a Supreme Court appointed for life.

New Jersey v. *T.L.O.* **(1985)** Supreme Court case that decided that public school officials can search a student's items without violating the Fourth Amendment.

New York Times Co. v. *U.S.* **(1971)** Supreme Court decision that the U.S. government could not block the publication of secret Department of Defense documents illegally furnished to the *Times* by anti-war activists. Also called the *Pentagon Papers* case.

news leaks The intentional disclosure of confidential information often made by an anonymous source whose goal is to make the information public.

news media Media providing the public with new information about subjects of public interest.

Nineteenth Amendment Amendment to the Constitution passed in 1920 that guaranteed women the right to vote.

Ninth Amendment Part of the Bill of Rights that makes it clear that enumerating rights in the Constitution or Bill of Rights does not mean that others do not exist.

non–means-tested programs Programs that provide cash assistance to qualified beneficiaries, regardless of income; among these are Social Security and unemployment insurance.

North Atlantic Treaty Organization (NATO) The first peacetime military treaty joined by the United States; NATO is a collective security pact that includes the United States, Canada, and parts of Europe.

nullification The belief in the right of a state to declare void a federal law.

Obergefell v. *Hodges* **(2015)** Supreme Court ruling that held that same-sex couples have a fundamental right to marry under the Constitution.

off the record Information provided to a journalist that will not be released to the public.

oligarchy A form of government in which the right to participate depends on the possession of wealth, social status, military position, or achievement.

on background Information provided to a journalist that will not be attributed to a named source.

on the record Information provided to a journalist that can be released and attributed by name to the source.

open market operations The buying and selling of government securities by the Federal Reserve Bank.

open primary A primary election in which party members, independents, and sometimes members of the other party are allowed to participate.

Oregon Employment Division v. *Smith* (1990)   Supreme Court decision that a state could deny unemployment to American Indian employees who tested positive for peyote, which was categorized as an illegal drug, even though it was part of an age-old religious ceremony of the Native American Church. The Court found that this was not a violation of the free exercise clause.

pardon   An executive grant providing restoration of all rights and privileges of citizenship to a specific individual charged with or convicted of a crime.

partisanship   Prejudice in favor of a particular cause; bias.

partisan polarization   The presence of increasingly conflicting and divided viewpoints between the Democratic and Republican parties.

party identification   Citizen's attachment to a political party based on issues, ideology, past experience, or upbringing, which tends to be a reliable indicator of likely voting choices.

party realignment   Dramatic shifts in partisan preferences that drastically alter the political landscape.

party unity   When a major political party is in agreement about their politics, policies, and/or leadership.

Pat Robertson   A Southern Baptist minister and television evangelist who ran for president in 1988, and in 1989 founded the conservative religious interest group the Christian Coalition.

patron   A person who finances a group or individual activity.

patronage   Jobs, grants, or other special favors that are given as rewards to friends and political allies for their support.

Plessy v. *Ferguson* (1896)   Supreme Court case that challenged a Louisiana statute requiring that railroads provide separate accommodations for Blacks and Whites; the Court found that separate-but-equal accommodations did not violate the equal protection clause of the Fourteenth Amendment.

pluralist theory   The theory that political power is distributed among a wide array of diverse and competing interest groups.

plurality opinion   A type of judicial opinion, the reasoning of which is agreed to by fewer than a majority of judges on a court; although it resolves the particular case, the opinion does not establish a binding precedent.

pocket veto   If Congress adjourns during the ten days the president has to consider a bill passed by both houses of Congress, the bill is considered vetoed without the president's signature.

policy adoption   The approval of a policy proposal by people with the requisite authority, such as a legislature.

policy coordinating committees   Committees created at the sub-Cabinet level to facilitate interactions between agencies and departments to handle complex policy problems.

policy evaluation   The process of determining whether a course of action is achieving its intended goals.

policy formulation   The crafting of proposed courses of action to resolve public problems.

policy implementation   The process of carrying out public policy.

political action committee (PAC)   Officially recognized fundraising organization that represents interest groups and is allowed by federal law to make contributions directly to candidates' campaigns.

political activism   Activism that attempts to influence the political process through protests, boycotts, buycotts, and picketing.

political ideology   The coherent set of values and beliefs about the purpose and scope of government held by groups and individuals.

political machine   A party organization that recruits voter loyalty with tangible incentives and is characterized by a high degree of control over member activity.

political participation   Activism that attempts to influence the political process through commonly accepted forms of persuasion, such as voting or contacting elected officials.

political party   An organized group that may include office holders, candidates, activists, and voters who pursue their common interests by gaining and exercising power through the electoral process.

political socialization   The process through which individuals acquire their political beliefs and values.

politico   An elected representative who acts as a trustee or as a delegate, depending on the issue.

politics   The study of who gets what, when, and how—or how policy decisions are made.

poll tax   Tax levied in many southern states and localities that had to be paid before an eligible voter could cast a ballot.

pollster   A campaign consultant who conducts public opinion surveys.

population   The entire group of people whose attitudes a researcher wishes to measure.

pork   Legislation that allows representatives to bring money and jobs to their districts in the form of public works programs, military bases, or other programs.

pork barrel   Legislation that allows representatives to bring money and jobs to their districts in the form of public works programs, military bases, or other programs.

positive ad   Advertising on behalf of a candidate that stresses the candidate's qualifications, family, and issue positions, with no direct reference to the opponent.

precedent   A prior judicial decision that serves as a rule for settling subsequent cases of a similar nature.

president   The chief executive officer of the United States, as established by Article II of the Constitution of the United States.

presidential coattails   When successful presidential candidates carry into office congressional candidates of the same party in the year of their election.

Presidential Succession Act   A 1947 law enacted by Congress that provides for the filling of any simultaneous vacancy of the presidency and vice presidency.

press briefing   A relatively restricted session between a press secretary or aide and the press.

press conference   An unrestricted session between an elected official and the press.

press release   A document offering an official comment or position.

press secretary   The individual charged with interacting and communicating with journalists on a daily basis.

primary election   Election in which voters decide which of the candidates within a party will represent the party in the general election.

prior restraint   Constitutional doctrine that prevents the government from prohibiting speech or publication before the fact; generally held to be in violation of the First Amendment.

Progressive Era (1890–1920)   A period of widespread activism to reform political, economic, and social ills in the United States.

progressive federalism   A pragmatic approach to federalism that views relations between national and state governments as both coercive and cooperative.

Progressive movement   A broad group of political and social activists from the 1890s to the 1920s who opposed corruption in government, supported regulation of monopolies, and sought improvement of socioeconomic conditions.

proportional representation   A voting system that apportions legislative seats according to the percentage of the vote won by a particular political party.

prospective judgment   A voter's evaluation of a candidate based on what he or she pledges to do about an issue if elected.

protectionism   A trade policy wherein a country takes steps to limit the import of foreign goods through tariffs and subsidies to domestic firms.

public funds   Donations from general tax revenues to the campaigns of qualifying presidential candidates.

public interest group   An organization that seeks a collective good that if achieved will not selectively and materially benefit group members.

public opinion   What the public thinks about a particular issue or set of issues at any point in time.

public opinion polls   Interviews or surveys with samples of citizens that are used to estimate the feelings and beliefs of the entire population.

public policy   An intentional course of action or inaction followed by government in dealing with some problem or matter of concern.

push polls   Polls taken for the purpose of providing information on an opponent that would lead respondents to vote against that candidate.

random sampling   A method of poll selection that gives each person in a group the same chance of being selected.

rational basis standard of review   A standard of review in which the Court determines whether any rational foundation for the discrimination exists. Legislation affecting individuals based on age, wealth, or mental capacity is generally given this level of review.

Reagan Doctrine   The Reagan administration's commitment to ending Communism by providing military assistance to anti-Communist groups.

reapportionment   The reallocation of the number of seats in the House of Representatives after each decennial census.

recall   An election in which voters can remove an incumbent from office prior to the next scheduled election.

recession   A decline in the economy that occurs as investment sags, production falls off, and unemployment increases.

Reconstruction   The period from 1865 to 1877 after the Civil War, in which the United States militarily occupied and dominated the eleven former states of the Confederacy.

redistributive policies   Public policies that transfer resources from one group to assist another group.

redistricting   The process of redrawing congressional districts to reflect increases or decreases in seats allotted to the states, as well as population shifts within a state.

referendum   An election whereby the state legislature submits proposed legislation or state constitutional amendments to the voters for approval.

regulations   Rules governing the operation of all government programs that have the force of law.

regulatory policies   Public policies that limit the activities of individuals and corporations or prohibit certain types of unacceptable business practices.

republic   A government rooted in the consent of the governed; a representative or indirect democracy.

Reno v. *ACLU* **(1997)**   Supreme Court ruling that found a federal law prohibiting transmission of pornography via the Internet to minors was unconstitutionally broad and violated the First Amendment.

reserve requirements   Government requirements that a portion of member banks' deposits be retained as backing for their loans.

reserved powers   Powers reserved to the states by the Tenth Amendment that lie at the foundation of a state's right to legislate for the public health and welfare of its citizens.

retrospective judgment   A voter's evaluation of a candidate based on past performance on a particular issue.

Reynolds v. *United States* **(1878)**   Supreme Court ruling that plural marriages could be banned by federal law and that prohibiting such practices did not violate the free exercise clause of the Constitution.

Richard M. Nixon   The thirty-seventh president, a Republican, who served from 1969 to 1974. Nixon advocated détente during the Cold War and resigned rather than face impeachment and likely removal from office due to the Watergate scandal.

right of rebuttal   The rule that requires broadcast stations to give individuals the right to have the opportunity to respond to personal attacks made on a radio or TV broadcast.

right to privacy   The right to be left alone; a judicially created principle encompassing a variety of individual actions protected by the penumbras cast by several constitutional amendments, including the First, Third, Fourth, Ninth, and Fourteenth Amendments.

Roe v. *Wade* **(1973)**   Supreme Court ruling that found that a woman's right to an abortion was protected by the right to privacy that could be implied from specific guarantees found in the Bill of Rights applied to the states through the Fourteenth Amendment.

Roger B. Taney   Supreme Court chief justice who served from 1835 to 1864. Taney supported slavery and states' rights in the pre–Civil War era.

Roger Williams   Seventeenth-century religious and political leader who was expelled by Puritans in Massachusetts and then established the colony of Providence Plantations that later became Rhode Island.

Ronald Reagan   Fortieth president of the United States, a Republican, who served from 1981 to 1989. Reagan led the nation through the end of the Cold War, and his leadership led to a national shift toward political conservatism.

Roosevelt Corollary   Concept developed by President Theodore Roosevelt early in the twentieth century declaring that it was the responsibility of the United States to ensure stability in Latin America and the Caribbean.

Rosa Parks   A leading civil rights activist of the twentieth century. Parks was most notably involved with the Montgomery Bus Boycott.

rule making   A quasi-legislative process resulting in regulations that have the characteristics of a legislative act.

rule of law   The set of principles and ideals that posit that all people and institutions are subject to the law that is fairly applied and enforced.

Rule of Four   At least four justices of the Supreme Court must vote to consider a case before it can be heard.

runoff primary   A second primary election between the two candidates receiving the greatest number of votes in the first primary.

sample   A subset of the whole population selected to be questioned for the purposes of prediction or gauging opinion.

sampling error   Errors resulting from the size or the quality of a survey sample.

Samuel Adams   A founder of the Committees of Correspondence, a key way colonists communicated with each other.

Sandra Day O'Connor   An associate justice of the Supreme Court from 1981 to 2005 who was appointed by President Ronald Reagan as the first woman to serve on the Court.

Santa Fe Independent School District v. *Doe* **(2000)**   Supreme Court decision that even nondenominational prayers made part of public-school gatherings violate the establishment clause of the First Amendment.

Schenck v. *U.S.* **(1919)**   Supreme Court ruling that upheld the federal Espionage Act, which outlawed resistance against the draft or distributing anti-war leaflets, saying they presented a "clear and present danger" to the conduct of war.

secession   A unilateral assertion of independence by a geographic region within a country. The eleven southern states making up the Confederacy during the Civil War seceded from the United States.

secular realignment   The gradual rearrangement of party coalitions, based more on demographic shifts than on shocks to the political system.

sedition laws   Laws that make it illegal to speak or write any political criticism that threaten to diminish respect for the government, its laws, or public officials. State sedition laws were overturned as a result of the 1925 *Gitlow* Supreme Court decision.

select (or special) committee   Temporary committee appointed for a specific purpose.

selective incorporation A judicial doctrine whereby most, but not all, protections found in the Bill of Rights are made applicable to the states via the Fourteenth Amendment.

senatorial courtesy A process by which presidents generally allow senators from the state in which a judicial vacancy occurs to block a nomination by simply registering their objection.

Seneca Falls Convention The first major feminist meeting, held in New York State in 1848, which produced the historic "Declaration of Sentiments," calling for voting rights for women.

seniority Time of continuous service on a committee.

separate-but-equal doctrine The central tenet of the *Plessy* v. *Ferguson* decision that claimed that separate accommodations for Blacks and Whites did not violate the Constitution. This doctrine was used by southern states to pass widespread discriminatory legislation at the end of the nineteenth century.

separation of powers A way of dividing the power of government among the legislative, executive, and judicial branches, each staffed separately, with equality and independence of each branch ensured by the Constitution.

September 11 A terrorist plot carried out on September 11, 2001, that used hijacked civilian aircraft to attack the World Trade Center in New York and the Pentagon near Washington, D.C.

Seventeenth Amendment Amendment to the U.S. Constitution that made senators directly elected by the people, removing their selection by state legislatures.

Shaw v. Reno **(1993)** Supreme Court ruled that while race can be considered in drawing district lines, it cannot be the overriding reason.

Shays's Rebellion A rebellion in which an army of 1,500 disgruntled and angry farmers led by Daniel Shays marched to Springfield, Massachusetts, and forcibly restrained the state court from foreclosing mortgages on their farms.

Shelby County v. Holder **(2013)** Court ruled that preclearance of election changes cannot be applied to just certain states previously found to curtail or inhibit minority voting, thus overruling a key provision of the Voting Rights Act.

signing statements Occasional written comments attached to a bill signed by the president.

Sixteenth Amendment Amendment to the U.S. Constitution that authorized Congress to enact a national income tax.

Sixth Amendment Part of the Bill of Rights that sets out the basic requirements of procedural due process for federal courts to follow in criminal trials. These include speedy and public trials, impartial juries, trials in the state where the crime was committed, notice of the charges, the right to confront and obtain favorable witnesses, and the right to counsel.

slander Untrue spoken statements that defame the character of a person.

social capital Cooperative relationships that facilitate the resolution of collective problems.

social conservative One who believes that the government should support and further traditional moral teachings.

social contract theory The belief that governments exist based on the consent of the governed.

Social Security Act A 1935 law that established old age insurance; assistance for the needy, aged, blind, and families with dependent children; and unemployment insurance.

solicitor general The fourth-ranking member of the Department of Justice; responsible for handling nearly all appeals on behalf of the U.S. government to the Supreme Court.

Speaker of the House The only officer of the House of Representatives specifically mentioned in the Constitution; the chamber's most powerful position; traditionally a member of the majority party.

spoils system The practice that allows the firing of public-office holders of a defeated political party to be replaced by loyalists of the newly elected party.

standards of review The levels of deference the Court gives governments to craft policies that make distinctions on the basis of personal characteristics. These standards stem from the Court's need to ensure that laws do not undermine the Fourteenth Amendment's equal protection clause.

standing committee Committee to which proposed bills are referred; continues from one Congress to the next.

stare decisis In court rulings, a reliance on past decisions or precedents to formulate decisions in new cases.

statist One who believes in extensive government control of personal and economic liberties.

strategic trade policy A trade policy wherein governments identify key industries that they wish to see grow and enact policies to support their development and success.

stratified sampling A variation of random sampling; the population is divided into subgroups and weighted based on demographic characteristics of the national population.

straw poll Unscientific survey used to gauge public opinion on a variety of issues and policies.

strict constructionist An approach to constitutional interpretation that emphasizes interpreting the Constitution as it was originally written and intended by the Framers.

strict scrutiny A heightened standard of review used by the Supreme Court to determine the constitutional validity of a challenged practice. Legislation affecting the fundamental freedoms of speech, assembly, religion, and the press as well as suspect classifications are automatically accorded this level of review.

substantive due process Judicial interpretation of the Fifth and Fourteenth Amendments' due process clauses. Protects citizens from arbitrary or unjust state or federal laws.

suffrage movement The drive for voting rights for women that took place in the United States in the nineteenth and early twentieth centuries until ratification of the Nineteenth Amendment in 1920.

super PAC Political action committee established to make independent expenditures.

superdelegate Delegate to the Democratic Party's national convention that is reserved for a party official and whose vote at the convention is unpledged to a candidate.

supremacy clause Portion of Article VI of the Constitution mandating that national law is supreme over (that is, supersedes) all other laws passed by the states or by any other subdivision of government.

Susan B. Anthony Nineteenth century feminist, suffragist, and founder of the National Woman Suffrage Association with Elizabeth Cady Stanton. Anthony later formed the National American Woman Suffrage Association (NAWSA) which along with the National Woman's Party (NWP) helped to ensure ratification of the Nineteenth Amendment.

suspect classifications Category or class, such as race or a fundamental freedom, that triggers the highest standard of scrutiny from the Supreme Court.

symbolic speech Symbols, signs, and other methods of expression generally considered to be protected by the First Amendment.

systemic agenda A set of issues to be discussed or given attention; it consists of all public issues viewed as requiring governmental attention.

tariffs Taxes on imported goods.

Tenth Amendment The final part of the Bill of Rights that defines the basic principle of American federalism in stating that the powers not delegated to the national government are reserved to the states or to the people.

Terry v. Ohio **(1968)** Supreme Court decision that the Fourth Amendment is not violated if a police officer, acting on a reasonable suspicion, stops someone that they suspect is armed and dangerous and about to commit a crime.

The Federalist Papers A series of eighty-five political essays written by Alexander Hamilton, James Madison, and John Jay in support of ratification of the U.S. Constitution.

Thirteenth Amendment One of three major amendments ratified after the Civil War; specifically bans slavery in the United States.

Thomas Hooker A minister who believed that Puritans were too narrow-minded. He founded the colony of Connecticut where all men were given the right to vote, regardless of religious views or property qualifications.

Thomas Jefferson Principal drafter of the Declaration of Independence; second vice president of the United States; third president of the United States from 1801 to 1809. Co-founder of the Democratic-Republican Party created to oppose Federalists.

Thomas Paine The influential writer of *Common Sense*, a pamphlet that advocated for independence from Great Britain.

Three-Fifths Compromise Agreement reached at the Constitutional Convention stipulating that three-fifths of the total number of enslaved people in each state was to be counted for purposes of determining population for representation in the U.S. House of Representatives.

Thurgood Marshall A leading civil rights lawyer and the first head of the NAACP's Legal Defense and Educational Fund. Marshall was the first African American appointed to the Supreme Court and served on the Court from 1967 until 1991.

Title IX Provision of the Education Amendments of 1972 that bars educational institutions that receive federal funds from discriminating against female students.

totalitarianism A form of government in which power resides in leaders who rule by force in their own self-interest and without regard to rights and liberties.

tracking polls Continuous surveys that enable a campaign or news organization to chart a candidate's daily or weekly rise or fall in support.

trade association A group that represents a specific industry.

transactions theory The theory that public policies are the result of narrowly defined exchanges or transactions among political actors.

trial court Court of original jurisdiction where cases begin.

Truman Doctrine U.S. anti-Communist policy initiated in 1947 that became the basis of U.S. foreign policy throughout the Cold War.

Trustee A lawmaker who listens to their constituents, weighs their beliefs, and ultimately uses their own judgment as they vote.

turnout The proportion of the voting-age public that casts a ballot.

Twenty-Fifth Amendment Adopted in 1967; establishes procedures for filling vacancies in the office of president and vice president as well as providing procedures to deal with the disability of a president.

Twenty-Second Amendment Adopted in 1951; prevents presidents from serving more than two terms, or more than ten years if they attain office via the death, resignation, or removal of their predecessor.

U.S. v. Nixon (1974) Supreme Court ruling on power of the president; holds that no absolute constitutional executive privilege allows a president to refuse to comply with a court order to produce information needed in a criminal trial.

UN Security Council A principal part of the United Nations, charged with authorizing peacekeeping operations, international sanctions, and military action in order to maintain global peace and security.

undue burden test A standard set by the Supreme Court, in the *Casey* case in 1992, that narrowed *Roe* v. *Wade* and allowed for greater regulation of abortion by the states.

unified government The political condition in which the same political party controls the presidency and Congress.

United Nations A multilateral diplomatic organization founded in 1945 and continuing today that is intended to promote peaceful resolution of international disputes and advance human development worldwide; the United States is a founding member.

United States–Mexico–Canada Agreement (USMCA) A 2019 free trade agreement that promotes movement of goods and services among Canada, Mexico, and the United States. It is a successor to the 1994 North American Free Trade Agreement (NAFTA).

veto The formal, constitutional authority of the president to reject bills passed by both houses of Congress, thus preventing them from becoming law without further congressional action.

vice president An officer created by Article II of the Constitution of the United States to preside over the U.S. Senate and to fill any vacancy in the office of president due to death, resignation, removal, or (since 1967) disability.

Vietnam War A civil war in which the United States supported the South Vietnamese regime against Communist forces in North Vietnam, which escalated through the 1960s before ending in 1975.

Virginia Plan A proposed framework for the Constitution favoring large states. It called for a bicameral legislature, which would appoint executive and judicial officers.

voter canvass The process by which a campaign reaches individual voters, either by door-to-door solicitation or by telephone.

vouchers Certificates issued by the government that may be applied toward the cost of attending private or other public schools.

War Powers Resolution Passed by Congress in 1973; limits the president in the deployment of troops overseas to a sixty-day period in peacetime (which can be extended for an extra thirty days to permit withdrawal) unless Congress explicitly gives its approval for a longer period.

Warren Court The period in Supreme Court history during which Earl Warren served as chief justice (1953–1969), noted for its many rulings expanding civil liberties and civil rights.

Warren E. Burger Fifteenth Chief Justice of the United States. Served from 1969 to 1986. Was a well-known critic of the liberal Warren Court and moved the Court to the right on key civil rights and civil liberties issues.

Watergate A scandal in the early 1970s involving a break-in at the Democratic National Committee offices in the Watergate office complex. The involvement of members of the Nixon administration and subsequent coverup attempts led to President Richard Nixon's resignation from office and jail sentences for some members of his administration.

William H. Rehnquist Served first as an associate justice and chief justice from 1972 until 2005. He was a strong supporter of states' rights within the federal system.

William Penn Quaker leader and supporter of religious tolerance who founded Pennsylvania.

winner-take-all system An electoral system in which the party that receives at least one more vote than any other party wins the election.

Wisconsin v. Yoder (1972) Supreme Court ruling that a state compulsory school attendance law violated the free exercise clause as it applied to the Amish, who believed education beyond the eighth grade was harmful to their children who they did not want to be further exposed to the influences outside their insular community.

World Bank International governmental organization created to provide loans for large economic development projects.

World Trade Organization (WTO) An international organization that replaced GATT in 1995 to supervise and expand international trade.

World War I A global military conflict from 1914 to 1918 across Europe and its overseas territories, in which the United States militarily intervened in 1917–1918.

World War II A global military conflict from 1939 to 1945 in Europe, Africa, Asia, and the Pacific region, in which the United States was engaged from 1941 to 1945.

writ of *certiorari* A request for the Supreme Court to order up the records from a lower court to review the case.

yellow journalism A form of newspaper publishing, in vogue in the late nineteenth century, that featured pictures, comics, color, and sensationalized news coverage.

Youngstown Sheet & Tube v. Sawyer (1952) After President Truman seized the nation's steel mills as part of his conduct of the Korean War, the Court ruled that without legislative approval, the president had no constitutional authority under his aggregated powers.

Endnotes

Chapter 1

1. Susan A. MacManus, *Young* v. *Old: Generational Combat in the 21st Century* (Boulder, CO: Westview, 1995), 3.
2. Ashley Turner, "More young adults in the US are dying from heart failure, study finds," CNBC, published May 6, 2019.
3. Holly Hedegaard, Arialdi M. Miniño, and Margaret Warner, "Drug Overdose Deaths in the United States, 1999–2017," NCHS Data Brief No. 329, November 2018, https://www.cdc.gov/nchs/products/databriefs/db329.htm.
4. _____ ibid.
5. Reid Wilson. "CDC: Blacks, Hispanics dying of COVID-19 at disproportionality high rates." *THE HILL* (posted October 16, 2020). https://thehill.com/policy/healthcare/521404-blacks-hispanics-dying-of-covid-19-at-disproportionately-high-rates
6. Gina Kolata, "Rise in Deaths for U.S. Whites in Middle Age," *New York Times* (November 3, 2015): A1; Sabrina Tavernise, "Sweeping Pain as Suicides Hit a 30-Year High," *New York Times* (April 22, 2016): A1; Jared Keller, The U.S. Suicide Rate is at its highest in a half century." *Pacific Standard* (posted December 4, 2018).
7. Peter Monseau, "The Muslims of Early America," *New York Times* (February 9, 2015): A17.
8. Paul O'Donnell, "For Some, the US Embassy's Move to Jerusalem Fulfills Divine Prophecy," Religion New Service, May 14, 2018, https://religionnews.com/2018/05/14/some-christians-and-jews-hail-embassy-move-to-jerusalem-as-key-to-a-biblical-plan/
9. Lydia Saad, "Americans, in Theory, Think Larger Families Are Ideal," *Gallup News*, July 6, 2018.
10. Juliana Menasce Horowitz, Nikki Graf and Gretchen Livingston, "Marriage and Cohabitation in the U.S." Pew Research Center (posted November 6, 2019). https://irpcdn.multiscreensite.com/af750ddb/files/uploaded/marriage%20and%20cohabitation%202019.pdf
11. U.S. Census Bureau Releases 2018 Families and Living Arrangements Tables, November 14, 2018.
12. *Obergerfell* v. *Hodges*, 576 U.S. ____ (2015); 2015 U.S. LEXIS 4250.
13. James B. Gimpel and Kimberly A. Karnes, "The Rural Side of the Urban-Rural Gap," *PS: Political Science and Politics* (July 2006): 467–72.
14. Matt Stevens. "Americans are skeptical of government, trusting less in each other, study finds." *The Buffalo News*, July 23, 2019: A2.

Chapter 2

1. See Richard B. Bernstein with Jerome Agel, *Amending America* (New York: New York Times Books, 1993), 138–40.
2. *Oregon* v. *Mitchell*, 400 U.S. 112 (1970).
3. Bernstein with Agel, *Amending America*, 139.

4. For an account of the early development of the colonies, see D. W. Meining, *The Shaping of America*, vol. 1: *Atlantic America, 1492–1800* (New Haven, CT: Yale University Press, 1986).
5. For an excellent chronology of the events leading up to the writing of the Declaration of Independence and the colonists' break with Great Britain, see Calvin D. Lonton, ed., *The Bicentennial Almanac* (Nashville, TN: Thomas Nelson, 1975).
6. See Garry Wills, *Inventing America: Jefferson's Declaration of Independence* (New York: Random House, 1978). Wills argues that the Declaration was signed solely to secure foreign aid for the ongoing war effort.
7. See Gordon S. Wood, *The Creation of the American Republic, 1776–1787*, reissue ed. (New York: Norton, 1993).
8. John Fiske, *The Critical Period of American History* (Boston: Houghton Mifflin, 1988).
9. Charles A. Beard, *An Economic Interpretation of the Constitution of the United States*, reissue ed. (Mineola, NY: Dover, 2004).
10. Quoted in Richard N. Current, et al., *American History: A Survey*, 6th ed. (New York: Knopf, 1983), 170.
11. John Patrick Diggins, "Power and Authority in American History: The Case of Charles A. Beard and His Critics," *American Historical Review* 86 (October 1981): 701–30; and Robert Brown, *Charles Beard and the Constitution: A Critical Analysis of An Economic Interpretation of the Constitution* (Princeton, NJ: Princeton University Press, 1956).
12. Wood, *The Creation of the American Republic*.
13. *Chiafalo* v. *Washington*, 591, U.S. _____ (2020).
14. Quoted in Current, et al., *American History*, 168.
15. Bernard Bailyn, *The Ideological Origins of the American Revolution* (Cambridge, MA: Belknap Press, 1967).
16. Richard E. Neustadt, *Presidential Power: The Politics of Leadership from FDR to Carter* (New York: Macmillan, 1980), 26.
17. Federal Republicans favored a republican or representative form of government (do not confuse this term with the modern Republican Party, which came into being in 1854). Ultimately, the word *federal* referred to the form of government embodied in the new Constitution, and *confederation* referred to a "league of states," as under the Articles, and later was applied in the "Confederacy" of 1861–1865 that governed the southern states.
18. See Ralph Ketcham, ed., *The Anti-Federalist Papers and the Constitutional Debates* (New York: New American Library, 1986).
19 See Herbert J. Storing, *What the Anti-Federalists Were For* (Chicago: University of Chicago Press, 1981), for a fuller discussion of Anti-Federalist views.
20. See Jane J. Mansbridge, *Why We Lost the ERA* (Chicago: University of Chicago Press, 1986).
21. Katherine Tully-McManus. "House action on Equal Rights Amendment sets up legal fights." *Roll Call* (posted February 12, 2020).

22. *Marbury* v. *Madison*, 5 U.S. 137 (1803).
23. See, for example, the speech by Attorney General Edwin Meese III before the American Bar Association, July 9, 1985, Washington, D.C. See also Antonin Scalia and Amy Gutman, eds., *A Matter of Interpretation: Federal Courts and the Law* (Princeton, NJ: Princeton University Press, 1998).
24. See, for example, the speech by Associate Justice William J. Brennan Jr. at Georgetown University Text and Teaching Symposium, October 10, 1985, Washington, DC.
25. *Riley* v. *California*, 573 U.S. 373 (2014).
26. *Carpenter* v. *U.S.*, 585 *U.S.* _____ *(June 22, 2018)*, 136 S. Ct. 2206 (2018).

Chapter 3

1. *Missouri* v. *Holland*, 252 U.S. 416 (1920).
2. John Mountjoy, "Interstate Cooperation: Interstate Compacts Make a Comeback," Council of State Governments, www.csg.org.
3. *McCulloch* v. *Maryland*, 17 U.S. 316 (1819).
4. *Gibbons* v. *Ogden*, 22 U.S. 1 (1824).
5. For more on *Gibbons*, see Thomas H. Cox, *Gibbons v. Ogden: Law and Society in the Early Republic* (Athens, OH: Ohio University Press, 2010).
6. *Barron* v. *Baltimore*, 32 U.S. 243 (1833).
7. For more on *Barron*, see Brendan J. Doherty, "Interpreting the Bill of Rights and the Nature of Federalism: *Barron* v. *City of Baltimore.*" *Journal of Supreme Court History* 32 (2007): 211–28.
8. *Dred Scott* v. *Sandford*, 60 U.S. 393 (1857).
9. *Pensacola Telegraph* v. *Western Union*, 96 U.S. 1 (1877).
10. John O. McGinnis, "The State of Federalism," Testimony before the Senate Government Affairs Committee, May 5, 1999.
11. Jeff Shesol, *Supreme Power: Franklin Roosevelt* vs. *the Supreme Court* (New York: W. W. Norton, 2010).
12. *NLRB* v. *Jones and Laughlin Steel Co.*, 301 U.S. 1 (1937).
13. *Wickard* v. *Filburn*, 317 U.S. 111 (1942).
14. Peter Harkness, "What Brand of Federalism Is Next?" *Governing* (January 2012), http://www.governing.com/columns/potomac-chronicle/gov-col-what-brand-of-federalism-is-next.html.
15. *New State Ice Co.* v. *Liebmann*, 285 U.S. 262 (1932).
16. Beth Duff-Brown. "Federalism Meets the COVID-19 Pandemic: Thinking Globally, Acting Locally." *SLS Blogs* (posted April 6, 2020). Jennifer Selin. 220. "How the Constitution's federalist framework is being tested by COVID-19," Brookings (posted June 8). Sheila R. Foster, "As COVID-19 Proliferates Mayors Take Response Lead, Sometimes in Conflict with Governors," *Georgetown Law*, https://www.law.georgetown.edu/salpal/as-covid-19-proliferates-mayors-take-responselead-sometimes-in-conflicts-with-their-governors/.
17. Candace McCowan. "New Jersey tightens restrictions as coronavirus cases, hospitalizations surge." *Abc7NJ* (posted November 13, 2020).
18. Jessica M. Vaughan and Bryan Griffith. "Map: Sanctuary Cities, Counties, and States." Center for Immigrations Studies posted and updated October 26, 2020.
19. Linda Greenhouse, "The Rehnquist Court and Its Imperiled States' Rights Legacy," *New York Times* (June 12, 2005): A3.
20. *Shelby County* v. *Holder*, 571 U.S. 529 (2013).
21. *Arizona* v. *United States*, 567 U.S. 387 (2012) and *National Federation of Independent Business* v. *Sebelius*, 567 U.S. 519 (2012).

Chapter 4

1. The absence of a bill of rights led Mason to refuse to sign the proposed Constitution, noting that he "would sooner chop off his right hand than put it to the Constitution as it now stands." Quoted in Eric Black, *Our Constitution: The Myth That Binds Us* (Boulder, CO: Westview, 1988), 75.
2. Quoted in Jack N. Rakove, "Madison Won Passage of the Bill of Rights but Remained a Skeptic," *Public Affairs Report* (March 1991): 6.
3. *Barron* v. *Baltimore*, 32 U.S. 243 (1833).
4. *Allgeyer* v. *Louisiana*, 165 U.S. 578 (1897).
5. *Gitlow* v. *New York*, 268 U.S. 652 (1925).
6. *Near* v. *Minnesota*, 283 U.S. 697 (1931). For more about *Near*, see Fred W. Friendly, *Minnesota Rag: The Dramatic Story of the Landmark Case That Gave New Meaning to Freedom of the Press* (New York: Random House, 1981).
7. *Palko* v. *Connecticut*, 302 U.S. 319 (1937).
8. *Benton* v. *Maryland*, 395 U.S. 784 (1969).
9. *Cantwell* v. *Connecticut*, 310 U.S. 296 (1940).
10. *Lemon* v. *Kurtzman*, 403 U.S. 602 (1971).
11. *Engel* v. *Vitale*, 370 U.S. 421 (1962).
12. *Abington School District* v. *Schempp*, 374 U.S. 203 (1963).
13. *Lee* v. *Weisman*, 505 U.S. 577 (1992).
14. *Santa Fe Independent School District* v. *Doe*, 530 U.S. 290 (2000).
15. *Widmar* v. *Vincent*, 454 U.S. 263 (1981).
16. *Mitchell* v. *Helms*, 530 U.S. 793 (2000).
17. *Zelman* v. *Simmons-Harris*, 536 U.S. 639 (2002); *Espinoza* v. *Montana Department of Revenue*, 591 U.S. ____ 2020).
18. *Rosenberger* v. *University of Virginia*, 515 U.S. 819 (1995); *Christian Legal Society* v. *Martinez*, 561 U.S. 661 (2010).
19. *McCreary County* v. *ACLU of Kentucky*, 545 U.S. 844 (2005).
20. *The American Legion* v. *American Humanist Society*, 588 U.S. ____ (2019).
21. *Reynolds* v. *United States* 98 U.S. 145 (1878).
22. *U.S.* v. *Seeger*, 380 U.S. 163 (1965).
23. *Wisconsin* v. *Yoder*, 406 U.S. 205 (1972).
24. *O'Lone* v. *Estate of Shabazz*, 482 U.S. 342 (1987).
25. *Our Lady of Guadalupe School* v. *Morrissey-Berru*, 591 U.S. ____ (2020).
26. *Employment Division* v. *Smith*, 494 U.S. 872 (1990).
27. The Religious Freedom Restoration Act (RFRA) of 1993 and the Religious Land Use and Institutionalized Persons Act (RLUIPA) of 2000 are two noteworthy examples.
28. *Gonzales* v. *O Centro Espirita Beneficente União do Vegetal*, 546 U.S. 418 (2006).
29. *Burwell* v. *Hobby Lobby Stores*, 573 U.S. 682 (2014).
30. *The Little Sisters of the Poor Saints Peter and Paul Home* v. *Pennsylvania*, consolidated with *Trump* v. *Pennsylvania*, 591 U.S. ____ (2020).
31. *Ex parte Merryman*, 17 F. Cas. 144 (C.C.D. Md. 1861).
32. *Schenck* v. *U.S.*, 249 U.S. 47 (1919).
33. *Ex parte McCardle*, 74 U.S. 506 (1869).
34. *Brandenburg* v. *Ohio*, 395 U.S. 444 (1969).
35. *New York Times Co.* v. *U.S.*, 403 U.S. 713 (1971).
36. *Nebraska Press Association* v. *Stuart*, 427 U.S. 539 (1976).
37. John Bolton, *The Room Where It Happened: A White House Memoir* (New York: Simon and Schuster, 2020); Mary L. Trump, *Too Much and Never Enough: How My Family Created the World's Most Dangerous Man* (New York: Simon and Schuster, 2020).
38. Associated Press, "John Bolton: Judge Rejects Trump Bid to Bar Ex-adviser's Book," BBC News, June 29, 2020;

"Appeals Court Lifts Restraint Against Trump Book Publisher," *Los Angeles Times*, July 1, 2020.

39. *Abrams* v. *U.S.*, 250 U.S. 616 (1919).
40. *Stromberg* v. *California*, 283 U.S. 359 (1931).
41. *Tinker* v. *Des Moines Independent Community School District*, 393 U.S. 503 (1969).
42. *Morse* v. *Frederick*, 551 U.S. 393 (2007).
43. *R.A.V.* v. *City of St. Paul*, 505 U.S. 377 (1992).
44. *Virginia* v. *Black*, 538 U.S. 343 (2003).
45. Nina Burleigh, "Fightin' Words," *Newsweek* (June 3, 2016), 24–33; David L. Hudson, "Hate Speech and Campus Speech Codes," *Freedom Forum Institution*, March 2017.
46. *Minnesota Voters Alliance* v. *Mansky*, 585 U.S. ___ (2018).
47. *Chaplinsky* v. *New Hampshire*, 315 U.S. 568 (1942).
48. *New York Times Co.* v. *Sullivan*, 376 U.S. 254 (1964).
49. *Hustler Magazine* v. *Falwell*, 485 U.S. 46 (1988).
50. *Chaplinsky* v. *New Hampshire*, 315 U.S. 568 (1942).
51. *Miller* v. *California*, 413 U.S. 15 (1973).
52. *Reno* v. *ACLU*, 521 U.S. 844 (1997).
53. *U.S.* v. *Haymond*, 588 U.S. (2019).
54. *DeJonge* v. *Oregon*, 229 U.S. 353 (1937).
55. *John Doe #1* v. *Reed*, 561 U.S. ____ (2010).
56. *U.S.* v. *Miller*, 307 U.S. 174 (1939).
57. *D.C.* v. *Heller*, 554 U.S. 290 (2008).
58. *Heller* v. *District of Columbia*, civil action 08-1289 (2010).
59. *McDonald* v. *City of Chicago*, 561 U.S. ____742 (2010).
60. *Terry* v. *Ohio* 392 U.S. 1 (1968).
61. *Fernandez* v. *California*, ____ 571 U.S. ____ (2014), 134 S.Ct. 1126 (2014).
62. *Carpenter* v. *U.S.*, 585 U.S. ____ (2018).
63. *Carroll* v. *U.S.*, 267 U.S. 132 (1925).
64. *U.S.* v. *Arvizu*, 534 U.S. 266 (2002).
65. *South Dakota* v. *Neville*, 459 U.S. 553 (1983).
66. *Arizona* v. *Gant*, 556 U.S. 332 (2009).
67. *United States* v. *Jones*, 564 U.S. ____ (2012).
68. *Collins* v. *Virginia*, 584 U.S. __ (2018).
69. *U.S.* v. *Sokolov*, 490 U.S. 1 (1989).
70. Evan Hill, et al., "How George Floyd Was Killed in Police Custody," *New York Times*, May 3, 2020.
71. Jose A. Del Real, Robert Samuels, and Tim Craig, "How the Black Lives Matter Movement Went Mainstream," *Washington Post*, June 9, 2020.
72. *Hester* v. *U.S.*, 265 U.S. 57 (1924).
73. *Michigan* v. *Tyler*, 436 U.S. 499 (1978).
74. *New Jersey* v. *T.L.O.*, 469 U.S. 325 (1985).
75. *Counselman* v. *Hitchcock*, 142 U.S. 547 (1892).
76. *Brown* v. *Mississippi*, 297 U.S. 278 (1936).
77. *Lynum* v. *Illinois*, 372 U.S. 528 (1963).
78. *Miranda* v. *Arizona*, 384 U.S. 436 (1966).
79. *Rhode Island* v. *Innis*, 446 U.S. 291 (1980).
80. *Arizona* v. *Fulminante*, 499 U.S. 279 (1991).
81. *Puerto Rico* v. *Sanchez Valle* (2016).
82. *Weeks* v. *U.S.*, 232 U.S. 383 (1914).
83. *Mapp* v. *Ohio*, 367 U.S. 643 (1961).
84. *Stone* v. *Powell*, 428 U.S. 465 (1976).
85. *Powell* v. *Alabama*, 287 U.S. 45 (1932).
86. *Johnson* v. *Zerbst*, 304 U.S. 458 (1938).
87. *Gideon* v. *Wainwright*, 372 U.S. 335 (1963).
88. *Argersinger* v. *Hamlin*, 407 U.S. 25 (1972).
89. *Rothgery* v. *Gillespie County*, 554 U.S. 191 (2008).
90. *Rompilla* v. *Beard*, 545 U.S. 374 (2005).
91. *Hernandez* v. *Texas*, 347 U.S. 475 (1954).
92. *Batson* v. *Kentucky*, 476 U.S. 79 (1986).
93. *J. E. B.* v. *Alabama*, 511 U.S. 127 (1994).
94. *Maryland* v. *Craig*, 497 U.S. 836 (1990).
95. Jess Bravin and Sadie Gurman, "U.S. Executes First Federal Inmate Since 2003," *Wall Street Journal*, July 14, 2020.
96. *Hallinger* v. *Davis*, 146 U.S. 314 (1892).
97. *O'Neil* v. *Vermont*, 144 U.S. 323 (1892).
98. *Montgomery* v. *Louisiana*, ____ 577 U.S. (2016), 136 S.Ct. 718 (2016).
99. *Furman* v. *Georgia*, 408 U.S. 238 (1972).
100. *Gregg* v. *Georgia*, 428 U.S. 153 (1976).
101. *McCleskey* v. *Kemp*, 481 U.S. 279 (1987).
102. *McCleskey* v. *Zant*, 499 U.S. 467 (1991).
103. *Baze* v. *Rees*, 553 U.S. 35 (2008).
104. *Atkins* v. *Virginia*, 536 U.S. 304 (2002); *Roper* v. *Simmons*, 543 U.S. 551 (2005).
105. Haley Fuchs, "Supreme Court, 5–4, Lifts Block on Federal Execution," *New York Times*, July 14, 2020.
106. *Skinner* v. *Switzer*, 562 U.S. 521 (2011).
107. *House* v. *Bell*, 547 U.S. 518 (2006).
108. *Olmstead* v. *U.S.*, 277 U.S. 438 (1928).
109. *Griswold* v. *Connecticut*, 381 U.S. 481 (1965).
110. *Eisenstadt* v. *Baird*, 410 U.S. 113 (1972).
111. *Burwell* v. *Hobby Lobby Stores*, 573 U.S. 682 (2014).
112. *The Little Sisters of the Poor Saints Peter and Paul Home* v. *Pennsylvania*, consolidated with *Trump* v. *Pennsylvania*, 591 U.S. ____ (2020).
113. Amy Howe, "Opinion Analysis: Court Rejects Challenge to Exemptions from Birth Control Mandate," SCOTUS Blog (blog), July 8, 2020.
114. *Roe* v. *Wade*, 410 U.S. 113 (1973).
115. *Beal* v. *Doe*, 432 U.S. 438 (1977); *Harris* v. *McRae*, 448 U.S. 297 (1980).
116. *Webster* v. *Reproductive Health Services*, 492 U.S. 490 (1989).
117. *Planned Parenthood of Southeastern Pennsylvania* v. *Casey*, 505 U.S. 833 (1992).
118. *Gonzalez* v. *Carhart*, 550 U.S. 124 (2007).
119. *Whole Woman's Health* v. *Hellerstedt*, 579 U.S. ____ (2016), 136 S.Ct. 2292 (2016).
120. *June Medical Services L. L. C. ET AL.* v. *Russo*, 591 U.S. ____ (2020).
121. *Bowers* v. *Hardwick*, 478 U.S. 186 (1986); *Lawrence* v. *Texas*, 539 U.S. 558 (2003).
122. *Bostock* v. *Clayton County, Georgia*, 590 U.S. ____ (2020).
123. Mike Jordan Laskey, "For Catholics, Wearing a Mask Is an Expression of True Freedom," *National Catholic Reporter*, June 25, 2020, https://www.ncronline.org/news/coronavirus/young-voices/catholics-wearing-mask-expression-true-freedom.
124. Mansee Khurana, "The Right to Worship: Church and State Clash over Religious Services in the Coronavirus Era," NBC News, May 9, 2020, https://www.nbcnews.com/politics/politics-news/right-worship-church-state-clash-over-religious-services-coronavirus-era-n1201626.
125. Kim Fields, "Wearing a Face Mask: Does It Infringe on Personal Freedoms?" KTVB7, July 6, 2020, https://www.ktvb.com/article/news/local/208/university-of-idaho-law-professor-masks-versus-personal-freedom/277-087e4e8d-c25c-4b8a-bacc-8353466f3350.
126. "Freedom Foundation Lawsuit Alleges Mask Order Violated Free Speech," Freedom Foundation (Press Release), July 7, 2020, https://www.freedomfoundation.com/press-release/freedom-foundation-lawsuit-alleges-mask-order-violates-free-speech/#:~:text=Freedom%20Foundation%20Lawsuit%20Alleges%20Mask%

20Order%20Violates%20Free%20Speech,-Press&
text=%E2%80%9CI'm%20glad%20to%20see,because%20
of%20the%20First%20Amendment.%E2%80%9D.

127. "U.S. Current Trend: Anti-Mask Laws, COVID-19, and the First Amendment," International Center for Not for Profit Law, April 2020, https://www.icnl.org/post/analysis/anti-mask-laws-covid-19-and-the-first-amendment.

128. "U.S. Current Trend: Anti-Mask Laws, COVID-19, and the First Amendment."

129. "U.S. Current Trend: Anti-Mask Laws, COVID-19, and the First Amendment."

130. Dalton Bennett, et al., "The Crackdown Before Trump's Photo Op," *Washington Post*, June 8, 2020.

131. Dalton Bennett, et al., "The Crackdown Before Trump's Photo Op."

132. Aaron C. Davis, et al., "Officials Familiar with Lafayette Square Confrontation Challenge Trump Administration Claim of What Drove Aggressive Expulsion of Protesters," *Washington Post*, June 14, 2020.

133. Mikela Lefrak, "Witnesses in House Hearing Decry Forced Removal of Protesters Near Lafayette Square," WAMU American University Public Radio, June 29, 2020, https://wamu.org/story/20/06/29/witnesses-in-house-hearing-decry-forced-removal-of-protesters-near-lafayette-square/.

134. Kevin Johnson, et al., "Federal Officers May Be Sent to Chicago, Elsewhere," *USA TODAY*, July 21, 2020, 3A.

135. "Coronavirus: Armed Protesters Enter Michigan Statehouse," BBC News, May 1, 2020, https://www.bbc.com/news/world-us-canada-52496514.

136. "COVID-19, Digital Surveillance, and Privacy: Fourth Amendment Considerations," Congressional Research Service, April 16, 2020, https://crsreports.congress.gov/product/pdf/LSB/LSB10449.

137. "COVID-19, Digital Surveillance, and Privacy: Fourth Amendment Considerations."

138. William Cooper, "Imprisonment During a Pandemic? That's Cruel and Unusual Punishment," *Sun Sentinel,* April 19, 2020, https://www.sun-sentinel.com/opinion/commentary/fl-op-com-cooper-covid-19-cruel-unusual-punishment-20200419-gfvnfnfvtngf3gclohq7f5ii5e-story.html.

Chapter 5

1. Kate Clifford Nelson, *Harriet Tubman: Bound for the Promised Land.* N.Y: One World (2004).

2. *Dred Scott* v. *Sandford*, 60 U.S. 393 (1857).

3. *Civil Rights Cases*, 109 U.S. 3 (1883).

4. *Plessy* v. *Ferguson*, 163 U.S. 537 (1896).

5. Jack Greenberg, *Judicial Process and Social Change: Constitutional Litigation* (St. Paul, MN: West, 1976), 583–86.

6. *Williams* v. *Mississippi*, 170 U.S. 213 (1898); and *Cummins* v. *Richmond County Board of Education*, 175 U.S. 528 (1899).

7. *Missouri ex rel. Gaines* v. *Canada*, 305 U.S. 337 (1938).

8. *McLaurin* v. *Oklahoma State Regents*, 339 U.S. 637 (1950).

9. Megan Henney, "How much money is Nancy Pelosi worth?" *FOX Business*, Published July 17, 2020.

10. *Sweatt* v. *Painter*, 339 U.S. 629 (1950).

11. *Brown* v. *Board of Education*, 347 U.S. 483 (1954).

12. Gerald Rosenberg, *The Hollow Hope: Can Courts Bring about Social Change?* 2nd ed. (Chicago: University of Chicago Press, 2008).

13. Quoted in Juan Williams, *Eyes on the Prize: America's Civil Rights Years, 1954–1965*, revised ed. (New York: P Penguin Books, 2013).

14. Michael McCann, "Reform Litigation on Trial," *Law and Social Inquiry* 17(1992): 715–43.

15. *Brown* v. *Board of Education II*, 349 U.S. 294 (1955).

16. Quoted in Williams, *Eyes on the Prize*, 37 p. 17–23, 25.

17. *Cooper* v. *Aaron*, 358 U.S. 1 (1958).

18. *Heart of Atlanta Motel* v. *U.S.*, 379 U.S. 241 (1964).

19. Jo Freeman, *The Politics of Women's Liberation* (New York: Longman, 1975), p. 57.

20. Betty Friedan, *The Feminine Mystique* (New York: Dell, 1963).

21. *Meritor Savings Bank* v. *Vinson*, 477 U.S. 57 (1986).

22. *Hishon* v. *King & Spalding*, 467 U.S. 69 (1984).

23. *Oncale* v. *Sundowner Offshore Services, Inc.*, 523 U.S. 75 (1998).

24. *Johnson* v. *Transportation Agency*, 480 U.S. 616 (1987).

25. *Davis* v. *Monroe County Board of Education*, 526 U.S. 629 (1999).

26. *Jackson* v. *Birmingham Board of Education*, 544 U.S. 167 (2005).

27. Alixandra B. Yanus and Karen O'Connor, "To Comply or Not to Comply: Evaluating Compliance with Title IX of the Educational Amendments of 1972," *Journal of Women, Politics & Policy* 37 (2016): 341–358.

28. *Hernandez* v. *Texas*, 347 U.S. 475 (1954).

29. Dennis Romero, "A Chicano renaissance? A new Mexican-American generation embraces the term," *NBC News* (posted July 16, 2018).

30. Erin Duffy, "Resident Population of California in 2018 by Race and Ethnicity." *statista* (posted October 16, 2019).

31. *White* v. *Register*, 412 U.S. 755 (1973).

32. P. R. "How Shelby County v. Holder upended voting rights in America." VOX - *Huntsville Tribune* (posted June 25, 2019).

33. *San Antonio Independent School District* v. *Rodriguez*, 411 U.S. 1 (1973).

34. *Edgewood Independent School District* v. *Kirby*, 777 S.W. 2d 391 (Texas 1989).

35. "MALDEF Pleased with Settlement of California Public Schools Inequity Case, *Williams* v. *California*," August 13, 2004, www.maldef.org

36. Michelle Hackman, "DHS Couldn't Track How Many Immigrant Children It Separated From Families, Report Says," *Wall Street Journal* (posted November 27, 2019).

37. *Department of Homeland Security* v. *Regents of the University of California*, 591 (Decided June 18, 2020).

38. Dee Brown, *Bury My Heart at Wounded Knee: An Indian History of the American West* (New York: E Holt, Rinehart & Winston, 1970).

39. Emily Chertoff, "Occupy Wounded Knee: A 71-Day Siege and a Forgotten Civil Rights Movement," *The Atlantic* (posted October 23, 2012).

40. Ibid.

41. *McGirt* v. *Oklahoma*, 591 U.S. (2020).

42. Jack Healy, "For Oklahoma tribe, Vindiction at Long Last, *New York Times* (posted July 11, 2020).

43. *Yick Wo* v. *Hopkins*, 118 U.S. 356 (1886).

44. *Ozawa* v. *U.S.*, 260 U.S. 178 (1922).

45. *Trump* v. *Hawaii*, 585 U.S. _____ (2018).

46. David Inoue and Sarah Baker, "President Trump has Dishonored Our Nation's History with Concentration Camps," Japanese American Citizens League statement June 23, 2020.

47. Tracy Jan, "Asian American Doctors and Nurses Are Fighting Racism and the Coronavirus, Washington Post (posted May 19, 2020).

48. Ibid.

49. Diane Helene Miller, *Freedom to Differ: The Shaping of the Gay and Lesbian Struggle for Civil Rights* (New York: New York University Press, 1998).

50. Sarah Brewer, et al., "Sex and the Supreme Court: Gays, Lesbians, and Justice," in Craig A. Rimmerman, Kenneth D. Wald, and Clyde Wilcox, eds., *The Politics of Gay Rights* (Chicago: University of Chicago Press, 2000), 377–408.

51. Evan Gerstmann, *The Constitutional Underclass: Gays, Lesbians, and the Failure of Class-Based Equal Protection* (Chicago: University of Chicago Press, 1999).

52. Hallie Jackson and Courtney Kube, "Trump's controversial transgender military policy goes into effect," OUT POLITICS AND POLICY (posted April 12, 2018).

53. *Lawrence v. Texas*, 539 U.S. 558 (2003).

54. Joan Biskupic, "Court's Opinion on Gay Rights Reflects Trends," *USA Today* (July 18, 2003): 2A.

55. *United States v. Windsor*, 570 U.S. 12 (2013).

56. *Obergefell v. Hodges*, 575 U.S. ____ (2015).

57. *Bostock v. Clayton County*, 591 U.S. ____ (2020).

58. David Pfeiffer, "Overview of the Disability Movement: History, Legislative Record and Political Implications," *Policy Studies Journal* (Winter 1993): 724–42; and "Understanding Disability Policy," *Policy Studies Journal* (Spring 1996): 157–74.

59. American Association of People with Disabilities, www.aapd.com.

60. *Korematsu v. U.S.*, 323 U.S. 214 (1944). This is the only case involving race-based distinctions applying the strict scrutiny standard where the Court has upheld the restrictive law.

61. *Trump v. Hawaii*, 589 U.S. ____ (2018).

62. *Grutter v. Bollinger*, 539 U.S. 306 (2003).

63. *Gratz v. Bollinger*, 539 U.S. 244 (2003).

64. *Fisher v. University of Texas*, 579 U.S. ____ (2016).

65. Scott Jaschick, "Judge Upholds Harvard's Admissions Policies." *Inside Higher Ed*, posted October 7, 2019. On appeal to full circuit court, 2020, as *Students for Fair Admissions v. Harvard*.

66. *Reed v. Reed*, 404 U.S. 71 (1971).

67. *Craig v. Boren*, 429 U.S. 190 (1976).

68. *Rostker v. Goldberg*, 453 U.S. 57 (1981).

69. *Nebbia v. New York*, 291 U.S. 502 (1934).

Chapter 6

1. Charles S. Bullock III, "House Careerists: Changing Patterns of Longevity and Attrition," *American Political Science Review 66* (December 1972): 1295–1300.

2. Richard F. Fenno Jr., "U.S. House Members in Their Constituencies: An Exploration," *American Political Science Review* 71 (September 1977): 883–917.

3. Richard F. Fenno Jr., *Home Style: House Members in Their Districts* (New York: Longman, 2009), 32; and Judy Schneider and Michael L. Koempel, *Congressional Deskbook 2005–2007: 109th Congress* (Alexandria, VA: Capital Net, 2005).

4. Conversation with Karen O'Connor, July 2015.

5. Hedrick Smith, *The Power Game* (New York: Ballantine Books, 1989), 108.

6. "Life in Congress: The Member Perspective, A Joint Research Report by the Congressional Management Foundation and the Society for Human Resource Management,"

accessed May 30, 2016, at www.congressfoundation.org/storage/documents/CMF_Pubs/life-in-congress-the-member-perspective.pdf.

7. Ryan Grim and Sabrina Siddiqui, "Call Time for Congress Shows How Fundraising Dominates Bleak Work Life," *Huffington Post*, January 9, 2013, accessed May 30, 2016, at www.huffingtonpost.com/2013/01/08/call-time-congressional-fundraising_n_2427291.html.

8. Casey Burgat, Charles Hunt, and Trey Billing, "Everything You Wanted to Know About the 2018 Midterm House Elections in 8 Charts." *Leg Branch*, November 7, 2018, www.legbranch.org/2018-11-7-f78na713u8z7f2qszuude67s4feln9/.

9. Megan Henney, "How much money is Nancy Pelosi worth? *Fox Business* (published July 17, 2020).

10. Warren E. Miller and Donald Stokes, "Constituency Influence in Congress," *American Political Science Review* 57 (March 1963): 45–57.

11. Gary W. Cox and Jonathan N. Katz, "Why Did the Incumbency Advantage in U.S. House Elections Grow?" *American Journal of Political Science* 40 (May 1996): 478–97; Kenneth N. Bickers and Robert M. Stein, "The Electoral Dynamics of the Federal Pork Barrel," *American Journal of Political Science* 40 (November 1996): 1300–26; "2010 Overview: Incumbent Advantage," www.opensecrets.org; and Scott Ashworth and Ethan Bueno de Mesquita, "Electoral Selection, Strategic Challenger Entry, and the Incumbency Advantage," *Journal of Politics* 70 (October 2008): 1006–25.

12. Dan Hopkins, "Being an Incumbent Isn't as Fun as It Used to Be," October 29, 2014, https://fivethirtyeight.com/features/being-an-incumbent-isnt-as-fun-as-it-used-to-be/.

13. Alex Guillen and David Cohen, "2018 midterms: Incumbents who lost," POLITICO, November 11, 2018, www.politico.com/story/2018/11/06/2018-midterm-election-results-incumbents-967438.

14. "How to Rig an Election," *The Economist* (April 25, 2002): 51–54.

15. In *Davis v. Bandemer*, 478 U.S. 109 (1986), the Court found that gerrymandering was not a political question but was unable to determine a standard by which to judge constitutionality.

16. *Harris v. Arizona Independent Redistricting Commission*, 578 U.S. _____ (2016).

17. *Reynolds v. Sims*, 377 U.S. 533 (1964).

18. *Thornburg v. Gingles*, 478 U.S. 30 (1986).

19. *Shaw v. Reno*, 509 U.S. 630 (1993).

20. *LULAC v. Perry*, 548 U.S. 399 (2006).

21. *Shaw v. Reno*, 509 U.S. 630 (1993).

22. *Rucho v. Common Cause*, 585 U.S. _____ (2019); and Pete Williams, "Supreme Court Allows Gerrymandering in North Carolina, Maryland, Setting Back Reform Efforts," *NBC News*, June 27, 2019, www.nbcnews.com/politics/supreme-court/supreme-court-allows-gerrymandering-north-carolina-maryland-n1014656.

23. "What Is the Democratic Caucus?" www.dcaucusweb.house.gov.

24. Barbara Hinckley, *Stability and Change in Congress*, 3rd ed. (New York: Harper and Row, 1983), 166.

25. David R. Mayhew, "Supermajority Rule in the U.S. Senate," *PS: Political Science and Politics* 36 (January 2003): 31–36.

26. Barbara Sinclair, "The Struggle over Representation and Law-making in Congress: Leadership Reforms in the

27. Woodrow Wilson, *Congressional Government: A Study in American Politics* (Cambridge, MA: Riverside Press, 1885).

28. Roger H. Davidson, "Congressional Committees in the New Reform Era: From Combat to the Contract," in Thurber and Davidson, eds., *Remaking Congress*, 28.

29. Christopher Deering and Steven S. Smith, *Committees in Congress*, 3rd ed. (Washington, DC: CQ Press, 1997).

30. Wilson, *Congressional Government*.

31. "The Mysteries of the Congressional Review Act," *Harvard Law Review* 122 (June 2009): 2163–83.

32. Cindy Skrzycki, "Reform's Knockout Act, Kept Out of the Ring," *Washington Post* (April 18, 2006): D1.

33. Quoted in Stewart M. Powell, "Lee Fight Signals Tougher Battles Ahead on Nomination," *Commercial Appeal* (December 21, 1997): A15.

34. Jonathan Miller, "Part Unity on Congressional Votes Takes a Dive: CQ Vote Studies," *Roll Call*, February 28, 2019, www.rollcall.com/2019/02/28/party-unity-on-congressional-votes-takes-a-dive-cq-vote-studies/.

35. Shawn Zeller, "2019 vote studies: Pelosi sets record holding caucus in line," *Roll Call*, March 4, 2020, www.rollcall.com/2020/03/04/2019-vote-studies-pelosi-sets-record-holding-caucus-in-line/.

36. John W. Kingdon, *Congressmen's Voting Decisions*, 3rd ed. (Ann Arbor: University of Michigan Press, 1989). See also Lee Sigelman, Paul J. Wahlbeck, and Emmett H. Buell Jr., "Vote Choice and the Preference for Divided Government: Lessons of 1992," *American Journal of Political Science* 41 (July 1997): 879–94.

37. Barbara S. Romzek and Jennifer A. Utter, "Congressional Legislative Staff: Political Professionals or Clerks?" *American Journal of Political Science* 41 (October 1997): 1251–79; and Michael T. Heaney, "Brokering Health Policy: Coalitions, Parties, and Interest Group Influence," *Journal of Health Politics, Policy, and Law* 31 (October 2006): 887–944.

Chapter 7

1. "Two Hundred Years of Presidential Funerals," *Washington Post* (June 10, 2004): C14; and Sarah Barns, "Deadly Serious," *The Sun* (posted February 6, 2018).

2. Gail Russell Chaddock, "The Rise of Mourning in America," *Christian Science Monitor* (June 11, 2004): 1.

3. Richard E. Neustadt, *Presidential Power and the Modern Presidency* (New York: Free Press, 1991).

4. Edward S. Corwin, *The President: Office and Powers, 1787–1957*, 4th ed. (New York: New York University Press, 1957), 5.

5. Dan Mangan, "Trump Wins Appeal in Case Where Democrats Sued Him for Allegedly Violating Emoluments Clause," CNBC, Feb. 7, 2020, www.cnbc.com/2020/02/07/trump-wins-appeal-of-emoluments-clause-lawsuit-by-democrats.html; and *Blumenthal* v. *Trump*, cert. denied, USSC, October 13, 2020.

6. Quoted in Corwin, *The President*, 11.

7. Reynolds Holding, "Executive Privilege Showdown," *Time* (March 21, 2007): 21–24.

8. J. David Alvis, "The Contested Removal Power, Heritage Foundation, June 2019, www.heritage.org/political-process/report/the-contested-removal-power.

9. Adrienne Cobb, "Tracking Turnover in the Trump Administration: Year Three," *FORENSIC NEWS*, January 27. 2020, https://forensicnews.net/2020/01/27/tracking-turnover-in-the-trump-administration-year-three/.

10. Ibid.

11. Benjamin I. Page and Mark P. Petracca, *The American Presidency* (New York: McGraw-Hill, 1983), 262.

12. "Treaties," United States Senate Web site, www.senate.gov.

13. Ana Swanson and Emily Cochrane, "Trump Signs Trade Deal with Canada and Mexico, *New York Times*, January 29, 2020, www.nytimes.com/2020/01/29/business/economy/usmca-trump.html.

14. Katie Rogers and Apoorva Mandavilli, "Trump Administration Signals Formal Withdrawal From WHO." *New York Times*, July 7, 2020, www.nytimes.com/2020/07/07/us/politics/coronavirus-trump-who.html.

15. D. Roderick Kiewiet and Mathew D. McCubbins, "Presidential Influence on Congressional Appropriations Decisions," *American Journal of Political Science* 32 (August 1988): 713–36.

16. Julie Hirschfeld Davis and Gardiner Harris, "Obama Issues Reductions of Sentences in Drug Cases," *New York Times* (July 14, 2015): A11.

17. Peter Baker, Maggie Haberman, and Sharon LaFraniere. "Trump Commutes Sentence of Roger Stone in Case He Long Denounced," *New York Times*, July 10, 2020, www.nytimes.com/2020/07/10/us/politics/trump-roger-stone-clemency.html.

18. Quoted in Neustadt, *Presidential Power*, 9.

19. Quoted in Paul F. Boller Jr., *Presidential Anecdotes* (New York: Penguin Books, 1981), 78.

20. Lyn Ragsdale and John Theis III, "The Institutionalization of the American Presidency, 1924–1992," *American Journal of Political Science* 41 (October 1997): 1280–1318.

21. Quoted in Benjamin I. Page and Mark P. Petracca, *The American Presidency* (New York: McGraw-Hill, 1983), 57.

22. Alfred Steinberg, *The First Ten: The Founding Presidents and Their Administrations* (New York: Doubleday, 1967), 59.

23. Alisha Haridasani Gupta, "Jill Biden is a Teacher: And She's Not About the Change That," *The New York Times*, Published online on December 9, 2020; updated December 11, 2020.

24. Ibid.

25. Neustadt, *Presidential Power*, 1–10.

26. Kernell, Samuel H. *Going Public: New Strategies of Presidential Leadership*, 2nd ed. (Washington, DC: CQ Press, 1993).

27. Tom Rosenstiel, *Strange Bedfellows: How Television and Presidential Candidates Changed American Politics* (New York: Hyperion Books, 1992).

28. Morgan Gstalter. "The Five Trump Communications Directors Who Have Come and Gone," *The Hill*, Post, March 8, 2019, https://thehill.com/homenews/administration/433248-trump-has-had-five-communications-directors-heres-who-has-come-and-gone.

29. Brandice Canes-Wrone and Kenneth W. Shotts, "The Conditional Nature of Presidential Responsiveness to Public Opinion," *American Journal of Political Science* 48 (October 2004): 690–706.

30. See Louis Fisher, *Constitutional Conflicts Between Congress and the President*, 5th ed. (Lawrence: University Press of Kansas, 2007).

31. Franklin D. Roosevelt, Press Conference, July 23, 1937.

32. Lyndon B. Johnson, *The Vantage Point* (New York: Holt, Rinehart and Winston, 1971), 448.

33. See Cary Covington, J. Mark Wrighton, and Rhonda Kinney, "A 'Presidency-Augmented' Model of Presidential Success on House Roll Call Votes," *American Journal of Political Science* 39 (November 1995): 1001–24; and Wayne P. Steger, "Presidential Policy Initiation and the Politics of Agenda Control," *Congress & the Presidency* 24 (Spring 1997): 102–14.

34. Quoted in Thomas E. Cronin, *The State of the Presidency*, 2nd ed. (Boston: Little, Brown, 1980), 169.

35. CRFB, "Appropriations Watch: FY 2021." *Committee for a Responsible Budget* (posted December 28, 2020).

36. Jason L. Riley, "What Trump Can Learn from James Carville," *Wall Street Journal*, June 11, 2019, www.wsj.com/articles/what-trump-can-learn-from-james-carville-11560294122.

37. *Youngstown Sheet and Tube* v. *Sawyer*, 343 U.S. 579 (1952).

38. "Executive Order on Regulatory Relief to Support Economic Recovery," Whitehouse.gov. Issued May 19, 2020.

39. Charlie Savage, "Are Signing Statements Constitutional?" *Boston Globe* (April 30, 2006): A4.

40. Joyce Green. "Presidential Signing Statements: 2001–present," coherentbabble.com, accessed July 23, 2020.

41. Ibid.

Chapter 8

1. Julie Pace and Hannah Fingerhut, "AP–NORC Poll: Trump Approval Remains Steady During Pandemic," *AP*, May 21, 2020, https://apnews.com/article/b99efa86389b74313a7f9b182cacaa7d.

2. Harold D. Lasswell, *Politics: Who Gets What, When and How* (New York: McGraw-Hill, 1938).

3. Clyde Wayne Crews Jr., "How Many Federal Agencies Exist? We Can't Drain the Swamp Until We Know," *Forbes Magazine*, July 5, 2017, www.forbes.com/sites/waynecrews/2017/07/05/how-many-federal-agencies-exist-we-cant-drain-the-swamp-until-we-know/#5aeedde01aa2.

4. Mark Landler, *Alter Egos: Hillary Clinton, Barack Obama, and the Twilight Struggle Over America* (New York: Random House, 2016).

5. *Humphrey's Executor* v. *U.S.*, 295 U.S. 602 (1935).

6. John F. Duffy, "The Death of the Independent Regulatory Commission and the Birth of a New Independence," www.law.georgetown.edu/faculty/documents/duffy_paper.pdf.

7. Neil Vigador and Charlie Savage, "What is the Hatch Act? Explaining Why Trump Was Urged to Fire Kellyanne Conway," *New York Times*, June 6, 2019, www.nytimes.com/2019/06/13/us/hatch-act.html.

8. David Osborne and Ted Gaebler, *Reinventing Government: How the Entrepreneurial Spirit is Transforming the Public Sector*, (Reading, MA: Addison-Wesley, 1992), 20–21.

9. Ibid.

10. Joe Davidson, "Fill-ins are running agencies as Senate dawdles on confirmations," *Washington Post*, January 24, 2020: A22.

11. David Osborne and Peter Plastrik, *BANISHING BUREAUCRACY: The Five Strategies for Reinventing Government*, reprint ed. (New York: Plume, 1998).

12. "Demographics of Federal Workforce Summarized," *FEDweek*, February 24, 2016, www.fedweek.com/issue-briefs/demographics-of-federal-workforce-summarized/.

13. Ibid. 17

14. Courtney Bublé, "Watchdog Finds Serious Staffing and Leadership Problems at State Department," *Government Executive*, January 23, 2020, www.govexec.com/oversight/2020/01/watchdog-finds-serious-staffing-and-leadership-problems-state-department/162621/.

15. Richard L. Hermann, "Federal Political Appointments Under the Radar," *Legal Career View* (posted February 17, 2017).

16. Federal Soup Staff, "14 percent of feds eligible to retire now," *Federal Soup*, June 18, 2018. https://federalsoup.com/articles/2018/06/18/14-percent-of-feds-eligible-to-retire-now.aspx?admgarea=RETIREMENT&m=1.

17. Dareh Gregorian, "Help Wanted: Trump Administration Riddled with Vacancies," NBC News, March 28, 2019, www.nbcnews.com/politics/donald-trump/help-wanted-trump-administration-riddled-vacancies-n983036.

18. H. H. Gerth and C. Wright Mills, *From Max Weber* (New York: Oxford University Press, 1958).

19. Jennifer Steinhaver, "Veterans' Groups Compete with Each Other, and Struggle with the V.A.," *New York Times*, January 4, 2019, www.nytimes.com/2019/01/04/us/politics/veterans-service-organizations.html.

20. Michael Lipsky, *Street-Level Bureaucracy: Dilemmas of the Individual in Public Services, 30th Anniversary Expanded Edition* (New York: Russell Sage Foundation, 2010).

21. Steven J. Balla and William T. Gormley, *Bureaucracy and Democracy: Accountability and Performance*, 4th ed., Washington, D.C.: CQ Press, 2018; and Cornelius M. Kerwin and Scott R. Furlong, *Rulemaking: How Government Agencies Write Law and Make Policy*, 4th ed. (Washington, DC: CQ Press, 2011).

22. Richard Wolfe, "Supreme Court upholds but limits agency powers," *USA Today* (June 27, 2019: 2A).

23. Quoted in Arthur Schlesinger Jr., *A Thousand Days* (Greenwich, CT: Fawcett Books, 1967), 377.

24. Joe Davidson, "Fill-ins are Running Agencies as Senate Dawdles on Confirmations," *Washington Post* (January 24, 2020: A22).

25. Brandon Rottinghaus and Adam L. Warber, "Unilateral Orders as Constituency Outreach: Executive Orders, Proclamations, and the Public Presidency," *Presidential Studies Quarterly* 45 (June 2015): 289–309.

26. Irene Murphy, *Public Policy on the Status of Women* (Lexington, MA: Lexington Books, 1974).

27. Amelia Thomson-DeVeaux, "Should Judges Pay Attention to Trump's Tweets?" *FiveThirtyEight* (posted February 4, 2019).

28. Kathryn Dunn Tempas, "Tracking Turnover in the Trump Administration," *Brookings*, October 2020, www.brookings.edu/research/tracking-turnover-in-the-trump-administration/.

29. Jeremy Herb, "5 Takeaways from a Combative Barr Hearing." *CNN Politics*, July 29, 2020, www.cnn.com/2020/07/28/politics/barr-hearing-highlights/index.html.

30. Ibid.

31. Rosemary O'Leary, *Environmental Change: Federal Courts and the EPA* (Philadelphia: Temple University Press, 1995).

Chapter 9

1. Bernard Schwartz, *The Law in America* (New York: American Heritage, 1974), 48.

2. Julius Goebel Jr., *History of the Supreme Court of the United States, vol. 1: Antecedents and Beginnings to 1801* (New York: Macmillan, 1971), 206.

3. Damon Winter. "The Impeachment Inquiry goes Public." *The New York Times,* Nov. 22, 2019.

4. Quoted in Goebel, *History of the Supreme Court,* 280.

5. *Chisholm* v. *Georgia,* 2 U.S. 419 (1793).

6. *Fletcher* v. *Peck,* 10 U.S. 87 (1810); *Martin* v. *Hunter's Lessee,* 14 U.S. 304 (1816); and *Cohens* v. *Virginia,* 19 U.S. 264 (1821).

7. *McCulloch* v. *Maryland,* 17 U.S. 316 (1819).

8. *Marbury* v. *Madison,* 5 U.S. 137 (1803).

9. *Marbury* v. *Madison,* 5 U.S. 137 (1803).

10. David W. Neubauer, *Judicial Process: Law, Courts, and Politics* (Pacific Grove, CA: Brooks/Cole, 1991), 57.

11. Sheldon Goldman and Elliot E. Slotnick, "Clinton's First Term Judiciary: Many Bridges to Cross," *Judicature* (May/June 1997): 254–5.

12. Betsy Palmer, "Evolution of the Senate's Role in the Nomination and Confirmation Process," *CRS Report RL 31498* (March 29, 2005).

13. Quoted in Judge Irving R. Kaufman, "Charting a Judicial Pedigree," *The New York Times* (January 24, 1981): A23.

14. "Judicial vacancies during Trump's first term," BALLOTPEDIA. Accessed March 20, 2020.

15. Quoted in Lawrence Baum, *The Supreme Court,* 3rd ed. (Washington, DC: CQ Press, 1989), 108.

16. Lee Epstein, Andrew D. Martin, Kevin M. Quinn, and Jeffrey A. Segal. "Circuit Effects: How the Norm of Federal Judicial Experience Biases the Supreme Court," *University of Pennsylvania Law Review* 157 (2008): 833–80.

17. See Barbara A. Perry, *A Representative Supreme Court? The Impact of Race, Religion, and Gender on Appointments* (New York: Greenwood, 1991). Clarence Thomas was raised a Catholic but attended an Episcopalian church at the time of his appointment, having been barred from Catholic sacraments because of his remarriage. He again, however, is attending Roman Catholic services.

18. Shane Goldmacher, Eliana Johnson, and Josh Gerstein, "How Trump got to yes on Gorsuch." *Politico.* Posted February 1, 2017.

19. David Kravets, "Supreme Court says live streaming 'adversely affects' oral arguments." arsTECHNIA. Posted October 4, 2017.

20. Adam Liptak, "Virus Pushes a Staid Supreme Court into Revolutionary Changes." *The New York Times.* Posted May 3, 2020; updated May 12, 2020.

21. David G. Savage, "From hospital bed, Ginsburg challenges Trump plan to limit Obamacare's birth-control coverage." *Los Angeles Times.* Posted May 6, 2020.

22. Stephen L. Wasby, *The Supreme Court in the Federal Judicial System,* 4th ed. (Chicago: Nelson-Hall, 1988), 194.

23. Wasby, *The Supreme Court in the Federal Judicial System,* 199. Much of this change occurred as the result of an increase in state criminal cases, of which nearly 100 percent concerned constitutional questions.

24. Paul Wahlbeck, et al., "Ghostwriters on the Court? A Stylistic Analysis of U.S. Supreme Court Opinion Drafts," *American Politics Research* 30 (March 2002): 166–92. Wahlbeck et al. note that "between 1969 and 1972—the period

during which the justices each became entitled to a third law clerk... the number of opinions increased by about 50 percent and the number of words tripled."

25. Richard A. Posner, *The Federal Courts: Crisis and Reform* (Cambridge, MA: Harvard University Press, 1985), 114; Todd Peppers and Clare Cushman, eds. *Of Courtiers and Kings: More Stories of Supreme Court Law Clerks and Their Justices* (Charlottesville: University of Virginia Press, 2016).

26. "Retired Chief Justice Warren Attacks Freund Study Group's Composition and Proposal," *American Bar Association Journal* 59 (July 1973): 728.

27. Rebecca Mae Salokar, *The Solicitor General: The Politics of Law* (Philadelphia: Temple University Press, 1992), 3.

28. See, for example, Lawrence Baum, *The Supreme Court,* 4th ed. (Washington, DC: CQ Press, 1992), 106.

29. Richard C. Cortner, *The Supreme Court and Civil Liberties* (Palo Alto, CA: Mayfield, 1975), vi.

30. *Brown* v. *Board of Education,* 347 U.S. 483 (1954); *Planned Parenthood of Southeastern Pennsylvania* v. *Casey,* 585 U.S. 833 (1992); and *Grutter* v. *Bollinger,* 539 U.S. 306 (2003).

31. *Obergefell* v. *Hodges,* 576 U.S. 644 (2015)

32. Nina Totenberg, "Record Number of Amicus Briefs Filed in Same-Sex Marriage Case." *NPR,* April 14, 2015.

33. Gregory A. Caldeira and John R. Wright, "Amicus Curiae Before the Supreme Court: Who Participates, When and How Much?" *Journal of Politics* 52 (August 1990): 803.

34. *U.S.* v. *Nixon,* 418 U.S. 683 (1974).

35. Linda Greenhouse, "With O'Connor Retirement and a New Chief Justice Comes an Awareness of Change," *The New York Times* (January 28, 2006): A10.

36. Donald L. Horowitz, *The Courts and Social Policy* (Washington, DC: Brookings Institution, 1977), 538.

37. Ben Johnson and Logan Struther, "The Supreme Court hasn't followed public opinion for 50 years. Why would it start now?" *The Washington Post.* October 17, 2018.

38. Timothy R. Johnson and Andrew D. Martin, "The Public's Conditional Response to Supreme Court Decisions," *American Political Science Review* 92 (June 1998): 299–309.

39. *U.S.* v. *Nixon,* 418 U.S. 683 (1974).

40. Kalvis Golde, "Recent polls show confidence in Supreme Court, with caveats." *SCOTUSblog.* Posted October 22, 2019.

41. Gallup, *Supreme Court In Depth: Topics A to Z.* N.D.

42. *Boumediene* v. *Bush,* 553 U.S. 723 (2008).

43. *Arizona* v. *United States,* 567 U.S. (2012).

44. "Supreme Court Cases Overruled by Subsequent Decision." www.gpoaccess.gov/constitution/pdf/con041.pdf.

45. *Trump* v. *Hawai'i,* 585 U.S. _____ (2018).

46. See, for example, *Colegrove* v. *Green,* 328 U.S. 549 (1946).

47. *Baker* v. *Carr,* 369 U.S. 186 (1962).

48. Kevin T. McGuire, "Public Schools, Religious Establishments, and the U.S. Supreme Court: An Examination of Policy Compliance," *American Politics Research* 37 (2009): 50–74.

49. Charles Johnson and Bradley C. Canon, *Judicial Policies: Implementation and Impact,* 2nd ed. (Washington, DC: CQ Press, 1998), ch. 1.

50. *Reynolds* v. *Sims,* 377 U.S. 533 (1964).

51. *Mississippi University for Women* v. *Hogan,* 458 U.S. 718 (1982).

52. Robert Barnes, "With a wave of major rulings, Roberts and Supreme Court emerge as powerful counterweight to Trump and Congress." *The Washington Post.* Posted July 10, 2020.

53. _____ ibid.
54. *Trump* v. *Vance* & *Trump* v. *Mazars*. S. Ct., July 9, 2020.
55. _____ ibid
56. Robert Barnes, "With a wave of major rulings, Roberts and Supreme Court emerge as powerful counterweight to Trump and Congress." *The Washington Post*. Posted July 10, 2020.
57. Robert Barnes, "If it wasn't the Roberts Court already, it is the Roberts court now." *The Washington Post*. Posted June 28, 2018.

Chapter 10

1. Hans Spier, "Historical Development of Public Opinion," *American Journal of Sociology* 55 (Jan. 1950), 376.
2. William T. Bianco and David T. Canon, "Public Opinion," *American Politics Today*, 3rd ed. (New York: Norton, 2013).
3. Alan M. Winkler, "Public Opinion," in Jack Greene, ed., *The Encyclopedia of American Political History* (New York: Charles Scribner's Sons, 1988).
4. W.E.B. Du Bois, *The Philadelphia Negro*. Philadelphia: University of Pennsylvania Press, 1899.
5. Walter Lippmann, Public Opinion. NY: Harcourt, 1922.
6. Don D. Walker, "Woodrow Wilson and Walter Lippman: A Narrative Historical Imagery," *Western Political Quarterly* 12(December 4, 1959): 939–47; Henry A. Turner, "Woodrow Wilson and Public Opinion," *Public Opinion Quarterly*, 21 4 (Winter, 1957–1958): 506–520.
7. *Literary Digest* 125 (November 14, 1936): 1.
8. Robert S. Erikson, Norman R. Luttbeg, and Kent L. Tedin, *American Public Opinion: Its Origin, Contents, and Impact* (New York: Wiley, 1980), 28.
9. Diane J. Heith, "Staffing the White House Public Opinion Apparatus 1969–1988," *Public Opinion Quarterly* 62 (Summer 1998): 165.
10. Francis J. Connolly and Charley Manning, "What 'Push Polling' Is and What It Isn't," *Boston Globe* (August 16, 2001): A21.
11. *Mobile Fact Sheet*, Pew Research Center. Posted June 12, 2019.
12. Kyley McGeeny, "Pew Research Center will call 75% cellphones for surveys in 2016," Pew Research Center, January 5, 2016.
13. Steven Shepard, "Pew: Phone Polling in Crisis Again." Posted February 27, 2019.
14. Michael Schulson. "In Fallout Over Polls, 'Margin of Errors' Gets New Scrutiny." *UNDARK*, Nov. 23, 2020.
15. This discussion draws heavily from Terence Ball and Richard Dagger, *Political Ideologies and the Democratic Ideal*, 5th ed. (New York: Longman, 2004).
16. Ball and Dagger, *Political Ideologies and the Democratic Ideal*, 2.
17. Isaiah Berlin, *The Crooked Timber of Humanity: Chapters in the History of Ideas* (New York: Vintage, 1992), 1.
18. William Safire, *Safire's New Political Dictionary* (New York: Random House, 1993), 144–5.
19. Jack C. Plano and Milton Greenberg, *The American Political Dictionary*, 9th ed. (Fort Worth, TX: Harcourt Brace, 1993), 16.
20. Philip E. Converse, "The Nature of Belief Systems in Mass Publics," in David E. Apter, ed., *Ideology and Discontent* (New York: Free Press, 1964), 206–21.
21. Lydia Saad, "U.S. Conservatism Down Since Start of 2020," Gallup. Posted July 27, 2020.
22. Richard Dawson and Kenneth Prewitt, *Political Socialization*, 2nd ed. (Boston: Little, Brown, 1977), 33.
23. Nicholas J. G. Winter, *Dangerous Frames: How Ideas About Race and Gender Shape Public Opinion* (Chicago: University of Chicago Press, 2008).
24. "2012 American Values Survey," Pew Research Center, www.people-press.org/values-questions/.
25. Jacqueline Alemany, "Power up: There's been a dramatic shift in public opinion about police treatment of black Americans," *Washington Post*. Posted June 9, 2020.
26. Karlyn Bowman, "What do Blacks and Whites Think about Local Policing?," *AEI*. Posted July 16, 2020.
27. Susan A. MacManus, *Young* v. *Old: Generational Combat in the 21st Century* (Boulder, CO: Westview, 1995).
28. Jan W. van Deth, Simone Abendschon, and Meike Vollmar, "Children and Politics: An Empirical Reassessment of Early Political Socialization," *Political Psychology* 32 (2011): 147–74.
29. James Simon and Bruce D. Merrill, "Political Socialization in the Classroom Revisited: The Kids Voting Program," *Social Science Journal* 35 (1998): 29–42.
30. "Daily Media Use Among Children and Teens Up Dramatically from Five Years Ago," Kaiser Family Foundation, January 21, 2010, www.kff.org/entmedia/entmedia012010nr.cfm.
31. Fairleigh Dickinson University Public Mind Poll, May 3, 2012, http://publicmind.fdu.edu/2012/confirmed/.
32. Jon Cohen, "'I'm going to keep pushing.' Anthony Fauci tries to make the White House listen to facts of the pandemic," *Science*. Posted March 22, 2020.
33. Roderick P. Hart, *The Sound of Leadership: Presidential Communication in the Modern Age* (Chicago: University of Chicago Press, 1989).
34. Mona Kleinberg, "Importance of Political Knowledge for Effective Citizenship," *Public Opinion Quarterly* 83 (Summer 2019): 338–362.
35. National Geographic-Roper Public Affairs Poll, December 17, 2005–January 20, 2006, www.nationalgeographic.com.
36. Kathleen Dolan, "Do Women and Men Know Different Things? Measuring Gender Differences in Political Knowledge," *Journal of Politics* 73 (2011): 97–107.
37. Joy K. Dow, "Gender Differences in Political Knowledge: Distinguishing Characteristics-Based and Returns-Based Differences," *Political Behavior* 31 (2009): 117–36.
38. Andrew Kohut, "But What Do the Polls Show? How Public Opinion Surveys Came to Play a Major Role in Policymaking and Politics," Pew Research Center Publications, October 14, 2009, http://pewresearch.org/pubs/.
39. Quoted in Kohut, "But What Do the Polls Show?"

Chapter 11

1. This conception of a political party was originally put forth by V. O. Key Jr. in *Politics, Parties, and Pressure Groups* (New York: Crowell, 1958).
2. John H. Aldrich, *Why Parties? The Origin and Transformation of Party Politics in America* (Chicago: University of Chicago Press, 1995).
3. By contrast, Great Britain did not develop truly national, broad-based parties until the 1870s.
4. See *Historical Statistics of the United States: Colonial Times to 1970*, part 2, series Y-27-28 (Washington, DC: Government Printing Office, 1975), based on unpublished data

prepared by Walter Dean Burnham. See also Harold W. Stanley and Richard G. Niemi, *Vital Statistics on American Politics 2009–2010* (Washington, DC: CQ Press, 2009), for contemporary turnout figures.

5. On the subject of party realignment, see Walter Dean Burnham, *Critical Elections and the Mainsprings of American Politics* (New York: Norton, 1970); Kristi Andersen, *The Creation of a Democratic Majority* (Chicago: University of Chicago Press, 1979); and John R. Petrocik, "Realignment: New Party Coalitions and the Nationalization of the South," *Journal of Politics* 49 (May 1987): 347–75.

6. See, for example, V. O. Key Jr., "A Theory of Critical Elections," *Journal of Politics* 17 (February 1955): 3–18.

7. For a discussion of secular realignment in the South, see Jeffrey M. Stonecash, "Class and Party: Secular Realignment and the Survival of Democrats Outside the South," *Political Research Quarterly* 53:4 (2000): 731–52.

8. Josh Putnam, "2016 Republican Delegate Allocation by State," Frontloading HQ, http://frontloading.blogspot.com/p/2016-republican-delegate-allocation-by.html.

9. John Green and Paul S. Herrnson, eds., *Responsible Partisanship: The Evolution of American Political Parties Since the 1950s* (Lawrence: University Press of Kansas, 2003).

10. Cornelius P. Cotter, et al., *Party Organizations in American Politics* (Pittsburgh: University of Pittsburgh Press, 1989).

11. Daniel Hopkins, *The Increasingly United States: How and Why American Political Behavior Nationalized* (Chicago, IL: University of Chicago Press, 2018), https://press.uchicago.edu/ucp/books/book/chicago/I/bo27596045.html.

12. For an analysis of the parties' role in recruiting candidates, see Paul S. Herrnson, *Congressional Elections: Campaigning at Home and in Washington* (Washington, DC: CQ Press, 1995).

13. See David E. Price, *Bringing Back the Parties* (Washington, DC: CQ Press, 1984), 284–88.

14. Nate Silver, "Republicans Were More United Than Ever Under John Boehner," *FiveThirtyEight*, September 28, 2015, http://fivethirtyeight.com/datalab/republicans-were-more-united-than-ever-under-john-boehner/.

15. Sidney M. Milkis, *The President and the Parties: The Transformation of the American Party System Since the New Deal* (New York: Oxford University Press, 1993).

16. Lazaro Gamio and Dan Keating, "How Trump Redrew the Electoral Map, from Sea to Shining Sea," *Washington Post*, November 9, 2016, www.washingtonpost.com/graphics/politics/2016-election/election-results-from-coast-to-coast/.

17. Karen M. Kaufmann and John R. Petrocik, "The Changing Politics of American Men: Understanding the Sources of the Gender Gap," *American Journal of Political Science* 43 (July 1999): 864–87.

18. William H. Flanigan and Nancy H. Zingale, *Political Behavior of the American Electorate*, 12th ed. (Washington, DC: CQ Press, 2010).

19. "Trends in Party Identification of Religious Groups," Pew Forum on Religion and Public Life, February 2, 2012, www.pewforum.org/Politics-and-Elections/Trends-in-Party-Identification-of-Religious-Groups.aspx.

20. This section draws on Morris Fiorina, *Culture War? The Myth of a Polarized America* (New York: Longman, 2011); Morris P. Fiorina and Samuel J. Abrams, "Political Polarization in the American Public," *Annual Review of Political Science* 11 (2008): 563–88; and Alan I. Abramowitz and

21. Kyle L. Saunders, "Is Polarization a Myth?," *Journal of Politics* 70 (2008): 542–55.

21. Alan I. Abramowitz and Steven Webster, "The Rise of Negative Partisanship and the Nationalization of U.S. Elections in the 21st Century," *Electoral Studies* 41 (2016): 12–22.

22. Alan Abramowitz, *The Polarized Public? Why American Government Is So Dysfunctional* (Pearson, 2012).

23. Samuel J. Abrams and Morris P. Fiorina, *Disconnect: The Breakdown of Representation in American Politics* (University of Oklahoma Press, 2009).

24. Samuel J. Abrams and Morris P. Fiorina, "'The Big Sort' That Wasn't: A Skeptical Reexamination," *PS: Political Science and Politics*, 45:2 (April 2012): 203–10.

25. Barbara Sinclair, *Party Wars: Polarization and the Politics of National Policy Making* (University of Oklahoma Press, 2006).

26. Pew Research Center, "A Deep Dive Into Party Affiliation," April 7, 2015, www.people-press.org/2015/04/07/a-deep-dive-into-party-affiliation/.

Chapter 12

1. Paul Allen Beck, *Party Politics in America*, 8th ed. (New York: Longman, 1998); David Adamany, "Cross-Over Voting and the Democratic Party's Reform Rules," *American Political Science Review* 70 (1976): 536–41; Ronald Hedlund and Meredith W. Watts, "The Wisconsin Open Primary: 1968 to 1984," *American Politics Quarterly* 14 (1986): 55–74; Gary D. Wekkin, "The Conceptualization and Measurement of Crossover Voting," *Western Political Quarterly* 41 (1988): 105–14; Gary D. Wekken, "Why Crossover Voters Are Not 'Mischievous' Voters," *American Politics Quarterly* 19 (1991): 229–47; Todd L. Cherry and Stephan Kroll, "Crashing the Party: An Experimental Investigation of Strategic Voting in Primary Elections," *Public Choice* 114 (2003): 387–420.

2. Of these ten states, South Dakota is the only state outside the South to hold a runoff primary. A runoff is held only if no candidate receives at least 35 percent of the vote. See "Statutory Election Information of the Several States," *The Green Papers*, www.thegreenpapers.com/slg/sei.phtml?format=sta.

3. Shaun Bowler, et al., eds., *Citizens as Legislators: Direct Democracy in the United States* (Columbus: Ohio State University Press, 1998).

4. For a more in-depth discussion of initiative, referendum, and recall voting, see Larry J. Sabato, Howard R. Ernst, and Bruce Larson, *Dangerous Democracy? The Battle over Ballot Initiatives in America* (Lanham, MD: Rowman and Littlefield, 2001); David S. Broder, *Democracy Derailed: Initiative Campaigns and the Power of Money* (New York: Harcourt, 2000).

5. Howard R. Ernst, "The Historical Role of Narrow-Material Interests in Initiative Politics," in Larry J. Sabato, Howard R. Ernst, and Bruce Larson, eds., *Dangerous Democracy?*

6. Seth Masket, "The Recall Is the New Normal," *Pacific Standard Magazine*, September 17, 2013, www.psmag.com/politics-and-law/recall-election-now-thing-permanent-campaign-election-66344.

7. Joshua Spivak, "The 21st Century Recall—Cheaper, Faster, Easier," *Politico* (March 18, 2011): 19.

8. Elaine Ciulla Kamarck and Kenneth M. Goldstein, "The Rules Matter: Post-Reform Presidential Nominating Politics,"

in L. Sandy Maisel, ed., *The Parties Respond: Changes in American Parties and Campaigns* (Boulder, CO: Westview, 1994), 174.

9. M. W. Wagner and M. Gruszczynski, "Who Gets Covered? Ideological Extremity and News Coverage of Members of the U.S. Congress, 1993 to 2013," *Journalism & Mass Communication Quarterly*, 95:3 (2018): 670–90, https://doi.org/10.1177/1077699017702836.

10. Hunt Alternatives Fund, "Media Coverage of Women Candidates," *Political Parity*, www.politicalparity.org/wp-content/uploads/2017/10/Parity-Research-Women-Media.pdf.

11. Jeremey Zilber and David Niven, "Stereotypes in the News: Media Coverage of African-Americans in Congress," *The Harvard International Journal of Press/Politics*, 5:1 (2000): 32-49; *Project MUSE*, muse.jhu.edu/article/28432; O. Ward. "Seeing Double: Race, Gender, and Coverage of Minority Women's Campaigns for the U.S. House of Representatives," *Politics & Gender*, 12:2 (2016): 317–43; doi:10.1017/S1743923X16000222; N. Terkildsen and D. F. Damore, "The Dynamics of Racialized Media Coverage in Congressional Elections," *The Journal of Politics*, 61 (1999): 680–99.

12. James M. Snyder and David Strömberg, "Press Coverage and Political Accountability," *Journal of Political Economy*, 118:2 (2010): 355–408.

13. George Serra, "What's in It for Me? The Impact of Congressional Casework on Incumbent Evaluation," *American Politics Quarterly* 22 (1994): 403–20.

14. Glenn R. Parker and Suzanne L. Parker, "Correlates and Effects of Attention to District by U.S. House Members," *Legislative Studies Quarterly* 10 (May 1985): 223–42.

15. Jamie L. Carson, "Strategy, Selection, and Candidate Competition in U.S. House and Senate Elections," *Journal of Politics* 67 (2005): 1–28.

16. Gary W. Cox and Jonathan N. Katz, "Why Did the Incumbency Advantage in U.S. House Elections Grow?" *American Journal of Political Science* 40 (May 1996): 478–97.

17. Sunhil Ahuja, et al., "Modern Congressional Election Theory Meets the 1992 House Elections," *Political Research Quarterly* 47 (1994): 909–21; and Paul S. Herrnson, *Congressional Elections: Campaigning at Home and in Washington*, 2nd ed. (Washington, DC: CQ Press, 1998).

18. Gary C. Jacobson and Michael A. Dimock, "Checking Out: The Effects of Bank Overdrafts on the 1992 House Elections," *American Journal of Political Science* 38 (1994): 601–24; and Herrnson, *Congressional Elections*.

19. See "Candidates and Nominations," in Paul S. Herrnson, *Congressional Elections: Campaigning at Home and in Washington*, 4th ed. (Washington, DC: CQ Press, 2004), 35–68.

20. Run for Something, "The Candidate Experience," January 2019, runforsomethingaction.net/survey-findings.

21. Peter Hamby, "Review: 'Double Down,' on the 2012 election," *Washington Post* (November 1, 2013).

22. James N. Druckman and Lawrence R. Jacobs, *Who Governs? Presidents, Public Opinion, and Manipulation* (Chicago: University of Chicago Press, 2015).

23. M. P. Wattenberg, "The Declining Relevance of Candidate Personal Attributes in Presidential Elections," *Presidential Studies Quarterly*, 46 (2016): 125–39, doi:10.1111/psq.12254.

24. Dennis W. Johnson, *No Place for Amateurs: How Political Consultants Are Reshaping American Democracy* (New York: Routledge, 2001).

25. Robert S. Erikson and Christopher Wlezien, *The Timeline of Presidential Elections: How Campaigns Do and Do Not Matter* (Chicago: University of Chicago Press, 2012).

26. Thomas E. Patterson, "News Coverage of the 2016 Presidential Primaries: Horse Race Reporting Has Consequences," Harvard Kennedy School working paper, December 2016.

27. Diana C. Mutz, "Effects of Horse-Race Coverage on Campaign Coffers: Strategic Contributing in Presidential Primaries," *Journal of Politics* 57 (November 1995): 1015–42.

28. Alon Zoizner, "The Consequences of Strategic News Coverage for Democracy: A Meta-Analysis," *Communication Research*, 2018; Johanna Dunaway and Regina G. Lawrence, "What Predicts the Game Frame? Media Ownership, Electoral Context, and Campaign News," *Political Communication*, 2015; Meredith Conroy, "Gender Bias and Mainstream Media," chapter within the book *Masculinity, Media, and the American Presidency*, 2015; David Nicolas Hopmann, Adam Shehata, and Jesper Strömbäck, "Contagious Media Effects: How Media Use and Exposure to Game-Framed News Influence Media Trust," *Mass Communication and Society*, 2015.

29. See "Media, Old and New," in Johnson, *No Place for Amateurs*, 115–47.

30. Emily Schultheis, "Campaigns Picking Up on Mobile Ads," *Politico* (November 29, 2011): 21–22.

31. Jody C. Baumgartner and Jonathan S. Morris, "MyFaceTube Politics: Social Networking Sites and Political Engagement of Young Adults," *Social Science Computer Review* 28 (2010): 24–44.

32. Five liberal Democratic U.S. senators, including George McGovern of South Dakota, were defeated in this way in 1980, for example.

33. Wesleyan Media Project, "Pro-Clinton Ads Dominate Airwaves," https://mediaproject.wesleyan.edu/sept-2016/.

34. Center for Responsive Politics, www.opensecrets.org/.

35. *McConnell* v. *FEC*, 540 U.S. 93 (2003).

36. *FEC* v. *Wisconsin Right to Life, Inc.*, 551 U.S. 449 (2007).

37. *Davis* v. *FEC*, 554 U.S. 729 (2008).

38. *Citizens United* v. *FEC*, 558 U.S. 50 (2010).

39. Herrnson, *Congressional Elections*, 133.

40. Center for Responsive Politics, www.opensecrets.org/.

41. *Buckley* v. *Valeo*, 424 U.S. 1 (1976).

42. Center for Responsive Politics, www.opensecrets.org/.

43. Steven T. Engel and David J. Jackson, "Wielding the Stick Instead of Its Carrot: Labor PAC Punishment of Pro-NAFTA Democrats," *Political Research Quarterly* 51 (September 1998): 813–28.

44. Janet M. Box-Steffensmeier and J. Tobin Grant, "All in a Day's Work: The Financial Rewards of Legislative Effectiveness," *Legislative Studies Quarterly* 24 (November 1999): 511–23.

45. Campaign Finance Institute, "501(c) Groups Emerge as Big Players Alongside 527s," www.cfinst.org. Information also drawn from www.opensecrets.org/527s/types.php.

46. Federal Election Commission, "Public Funding of Presidential Elections," published in August 1996 (updated February 2016), www.fec.gov/pages/brochures/pubfund.shtml#anchor688095.

47. CNN, 2020 election results, www.cnn.com/election/2020/exit-polls/president/national-results.

48. Steven J. Rosenstone and John Mark Hanson, *Mobilization, Participation, and Democracy in America* (New York: Macmillan, 1993).

49. Bernard Fraga, *The Turnout Gap: Race, Ethnicity, and Political Inequality in a Diversifying America* (Cambridge University Press, 2018).

50. CNN, 2020 election results, www.cnn.com/election/2020/exit-polls/president/national-results.

51. CNN, 2020 election results, www.cnn.com/election/2020/exit-polls/president/national-results.

52. CNN, 2020 election results, www.cnn.com/election/2020/exit-polls/president/national-results.

53. Karlo Bakkios Marcelo, et al., "Young Voter Registration and Turnout Trends," www.civicyouth.org. Estimates of young voter registration vary widely in large part because they are often based on polling numbers, and these numbers are subject to overreporting as well as difficulties in reaching and surveying this demographic group.

54. Center for Information and Research on Civic Learning and Engagement, "Growing Voters: A Profile of the Youngest Eligible Voters in 2020," July 13, 2020, https://circle.tufts.edu/latest-research/growing-voters-profile-youngest-eligible-voters-2020.

55. Neil Visalvanich, "When Does Race Matter? Exploring White Responses to Minority Congressional Candidates," *Politics, Groups, and Identities*, 5:4 (2017): 618–41, doi:10.1080/21565503.2016.1146152.

56. Adam J. Berinsky and Gabriel S. Lenz, "Education and Political Participation: Exploring the Causal Link," *Political Behavior*, 33:3 (2011): 357–73, web.mit.edu/berinsky/www/files/edu.pdf.

57. See, for example, Brennan Center for Justice, "Automatic Voter Registration and Modernization in the States," July 12, 2016, www.brennancenter.org/analysis/voter-registration-modernization-states.

58. See, for example, Barry C. Burden, et al., "Election Laws, Mobilization, and Turnout: The Unanticipated Consequences of Election Reform," *American Journal of Political Science* 58:1 (2014): 95–109.

59. See for example, David C. Wilson and Paul R. Brewer, "The Foundations of Public Opinion on Voter ID Laws: Political Predispositions, Racial Resentment, and Information Effects," *Public Opinion Quarterly*, 77:4 (2013): 962–84, doi:10.1093/poq/nft026.

60. See for example, Paul Gronke, et al., "Convenience Voting," *Annual Review of Political Science* 11 (2008): 437–455.

61. See for example, U.S. Vote Foundation, "The Future of Voting: End-to-End Verifiable Internet Voting," 2015, www.usvotefoundation.org/sites/default/files/E2EVIV_full_report.pdf.

62. "Beyond Chads: Voting Technology Catches Up," *Washington Post*, November 2, 2016, www.washingtonpost.com/sf/brand-connect/beyond-chads-voting-technology-catches-up/.

63. James Madison Center for Civic Engagement, "Ranked Choice Voting," https://www.jmu.edu/civic/RCV.shtml.

Chapter 13

1. "The Personal News Cycle: How Americans Choose to Get Their News," American Press Institute, March 17, 2014, www.americanpressinstitute.org/publications/reports/survey-research/personal-news-cycle/single-page/.

2. See Mitchell Stephens, *A History of News: From the Drum to the Satellite* (New York: Viking, 1989).

3. See Shelley Ross, *Fall from Grace* (New York: Ballantine, 1988), Chapter 12.

4. Richard L. Rubin, *Press, Party, and Presidency* (New York: Norton, 1981), 38–39.

5. Stephen Bates, *If No News, Send Rumors* (New York: St. Martin's, 1989), 185.

6. See Doris A. Graber, *Mass Media and American Politics*, 3rd ed. (Washington, DC: CQ Press, 1989), 12; Thomas C. Leonard, *The Power of the Press: The Birth of American Political Reporting* (New York: Oxford University Press, 1986), Chapter 7.

7. Darrell M. West, *The Rise and Fall of the Media Establishment* (Boston: Bedford/St. Martin's, 2001).

8. Elizabeth Grieco, "U.S. Newspapers Have Shed Half of Their Newsroom Employees Since 2008," Pew Research Center, April 20, 2020, www.pewresearch.org/fact-tank/2020/04/20/u-s-newsroom-employment-has-dropped-by-a-quarter-since-2008/.

9. See, for example, Matthew Gentzkow, Jesse M. Shapiro, and Michael Sinkinso, "The Effect of Newspaper Entry and Exit on Electoral Politics," *American Economic Review* 101 (December 2011): 2980–3018, www.aeaweb.org/articles.php?doi.

10. Meghan E. Rubado and Jay T. Jennings, "Political Consequences of the Endangered Local Watchdog: Newspaper Decline and Mayoral Elections in the United States," *Urban Affairs Review* (April 2019).

11. "How Public Is Public Radio?," Fairness and Accuracy in Reporting, www.fair.org.

12. "The Personal News Cycle," March 2014, American Press Institute, www.americanpressinstitute.org/wp-content/uploads/2014/03/AP_NORC_API-Personal-News-Cycle_Topline_March-18-Release.pdf.

13. "State of the Media 2015: Network News Fact Sheet," Pew Research Center, April 29, 2015, www.journalism.org/2015/04/29/network-news-fact-sheet/.

14. Rick Kissell, "Cable News Ratings: CNN on the Rise in 2015; Fox News Channel Remains Dominant," *Variety*, variety.com/2015/tv/news/cable-news-ratings-cnn-top-gainer-fox-news-channel-dominant-1201666151/. See also: Pew Research Center, "State of the News Media 2015," www.journalism.org/2015/04/29/cable-news-fact-sheet/.

15. Amy Mitchell, Mark Jurkowitz, J. Baxter Oliphant, and Elisa Shearer, "Americans Who Mainly Get Their News on Social Media Are Less Engaged, Less Knowledgeable," Pew Research Center, July 30, 2020, www.journalism.org/2020/07/30/americans-who-mainly-get-their-news-on-social-media-are-less-engaged-less-knowledgeable/.

16. Emily A. Vogels, Andrew Perrin, and Monica Anderson, "Most Americans Think Social Media Sites Censor Political Viewpoints," Pew Research Center, August 19, 2020, www.pewresearch.org/internet/2020/08/19/most-americans-think-social-media-sites-censor-political-viewpoints/.

17. Monica Anderson and Brooke Auxier, "55% of U.S. Social Media Users Say They Are 'Worn Out' by Political Posts and Discussions," Pew Research Center, August 19, 2020, www.pewresearch.org/fact-tank/2020/08/19/55-of-u-s-social-media-users-say-they-are-worn-out-by-political-posts-and-discussions/.

18. Peter Hamby, "Did Twitter Replace the Boys on the Bus?," Joan Shorenstein Center on the Press, Politics and Public

Policy Discussion Paper Series #D-80, September 2013, shorensteincenter.org/wp-content/uploads/2013/08/d80_hamby.pdf.

19. Ann Friedman, "Should All Journalists Be on Twitter," Columbia Journalism Review, October 9, 2014, www.cjr.org/realtalk/journalists_using_twitter.php?page=all.

20. Wesley Donehue, "The Danger of Twitter, Facebook Politics," CNN.com (April 24, 2012): www.cnn.com/2012/04/24/opinion/donehue-social-media-politics/index.html.

21. "Buzz in the Blogosphere: Millions More Bloggers and Blog Readers," Nielsen Media Research, March 8, 2012, blog.nielsen.com/nielsenwire/online_mobile/buzz-in-the-blogosphere-millions-more-bloggers-and-blog-readers/.

22. Henry Farrell and Daniel W. Drezner, "The Power and Politics of Blogs," *Public Choice* 134 (2008): 15–30.

23. Radio and Television Correspondents Association, rtcacaphill.org/board/.

24. John R. Hibbing and Elizabeth Theiss-Morse, *Congress as Public Enemy: Political Attitudes Toward American Political Institutions* (New York: Cambridge University Press, 1995).

25. Karen Aho, "Broadcasters Want Access, but Will They Deliver Serious Coverage?"*Columbia Journalism Review* 5 (September/October 2003): www.cjr.org.

26. Matthew P. Hitt and Kathleen Searles, "Media Coverage and Public Approval of the U.S. Supreme Court," *Political Communication* 35:4 (2018), 566–586, doi:10.1080/10584609.2018.1467517.

27. Michael A. Zilis, Justin Wedeking, and Alexander Denison, "Hitting the 'Bullseye' in Supreme Court Coverage: News Quality in the Court's 2014 Term," *Elon Law Review* 9:2 (May 14, 2017).

28. Tony Mauro, "A Gun Case in Need of Some Explaining: But Because of Our Reclusive Court, Today's Argument Is All We'll Get," *USA Today* (March 2, 2010): www.usatoday.com.

29. Benjamin I. Page, et al., "What Moves Public Opinion?," *American Political Science Review* 81 (March 1987): 23–44.

30. Thomas E. Nelson, et al., "Media Framing of a Civil Liberties Conflict and Its Effect on Tolerance," *American Political Science Review* 92 (September 1997): 567–83.

31. Shanto Iyengar and Donald R. Kinder, *News That Matters*, reprint ed. (Chicago: University of Chicago Press, 1989).

32. The Knight Foundation survey conducted by Dan Weaver of Indiana University found that 36 percent of journalists identify as Democrats, while 18 percent identify as Republicans, 33 percent say they do not identify with any party, and 13 percent identify with another party. The Pew Center found that most journalists self-identify as moderates (54 percent), but 34 percent say they are liberal and 7 percent say they are conservative. Dan Weaver, *The American Journalist of the 21st Century: U.S. News People at the Dawn of a New Millennium* (Mahwah, NJ: Erlbaum, 2007); "How Journalists See Journalists," Pew Center on Press and Politics, Washington, DC, 2004, people-press.org/files/legacy-pdf/214.pdf.

33. See, for example, the classic study by CBS and the *New York Times* in the 1980s: Michael J. Robinson and Margaret A. Sheehan, *Over the Wire and on TV: CBS and UPI in Campaign '80* (New York: Russell Sage Foundation, 1983). In a comparison of press coverage of the first 100 days of the presidencies of Bill Clinton and George W. Bush, the Pew Project for Excellence in Journalism found that coverage was nearly identical—about half of printed stories were neutral, a quarter were positive, and a quarter negative. In comparison, 42 percent of stories were positive toward President Obama during his first 100 days, 38 percent were neutral, and 20 percent were negative. "Obama's First 100 Days: How the President Fared in the Press vs. Clinton and Bush," Pew Research Center's Project for Excellence in Journalism, April 28, 2009, www.journalism.org/2009/04/28/obamas-first-100-days/.

34. Timothy Groseclose and Tom Milyo, "A Measure of Media Bias," *Quarterly Journal of Economics* 120 (2005): 1191–1237.

35. John McIver, "Shoptalk/Commentary: How Incumbent Presidents Fare in Newspaper Endorsements," *Editor and Publisher*, November 6, 2012, www.editorandpublisher.com/Columns/Article/Shoptalk-Commentary-How-Incumbent-Presidents-Fare-in-Newspaper-Endorsements#sthash.jkcAwjYj.dpuf.

36. See, for example, Stephen Ansolabehere, Rebecca Lessem, and James M. Snyder Jr., "The Orientation of Newspaper Endorsements 1940–2002," *Quarterly Journal of Political Science* 1:4 (October 2006): 393–404.

37. See, for example, Matthew Gentzkow and Jesse M. Shapiro, "Political Slant of United States Daily Newspapers," 2005 (ICPSR 26242), www.icpsr.umich.edu/icpsrweb/ICPSR/studies/26242.

38. Eric Alterman, *What Liberal Media? The Truth About Bias and the News* (New York: Basic Books, 2003).

39. "Silenced: Gender Gap in the 2012 Election Coverage," The Fourth Estate, www.4thestate.net/female-voices-in-media/infographic.

40. Girish Gulati, et al., "News Coverage of Political Campaigns," in Lynda Kaid, ed., *The Handbook of Political Communication Research* (New York: Lawrence Erlbaum, 2004).

41. Thomas E. Patterson, "News Coverage of the 2016 National Conventions: Negative News, Lacking Context," Shorenstein Center on Media, Politics and Public Policy, September 21, 2016, www.shorensteincenter.org/news-coverage-2016-national-conventions/.

42. R. M. Perloff, "A Three-decade Retrospective on the Hostile Media Effect," *Mass Communication and Society* 18:6 (2015): 701–29.

43. Megan Brenan, "Americans' Trust in Mass Media Edges Down to 41%," Gallup, September 26, 2019, news.gallup.com/poll/267047/americans-trust-mass-media-edges-down.aspx.

44. Amy Mitchell, Jeffrey Gottfried, Michael Barthel, and Elisa Shearer, "The Modern News Consumer: New Attitudes and Practices in the Digital Era," Pew Research Center, July 7, 2016, www.journalism.org/2016/07/07/the-modern-news-consumer/.

45. *New York Times Co. v. U.S.*, 403 U.S. 713 (1971).

46. Vivek Wadhwa, "Social Media's Role in Politics," *Washington Post* (January 25, 2012): www.washingtonpost.com/national/on-innovations/social-medias-role-in-politics/2012/01/25/gIQAQvZgdQ_story.html Google, "Take Action," https://www.google.com/takeaction/.

47. "Dan Rather: Corporate Media Is 'in Bed' with Washington," *Huffington Post*, May 20, 2012, www.huffingtonpost.com/2012/05/20/dan-rather-cbs-news-corporate-media_n_1531121.html?ref=fb&src=sp&comm_ref=false.

48. "Partisanship and Cable News Audiences," Pew Research Center for the People and the Press, October 30, 2009, www.pewresearch.org/.

49. Shanto Iyengar and Kyu S. Hahn, "Red Media, Blue Media: Evidence of Ideological Selectivity in Media Bias," *Journal of Communication* 59 (2009): 19–39.

50. Cass R. Sunstein, *Republic.com 2.0* (Princeton, NJ: Princeton University Press, 2009).

51. David Brock and Ari Rabin-Havit, *The Fox Effect: How Roger Ailes Turned a Network into a Propaganda Machine* (New York: Anchor Books, 2012).

52. Preetam Kaushik, "Tomorrow's Internet: A World of Hyper-Personalized Tribes?," *Wired*, www.wired.com/insights/2014/03/todays-internet-world-hyper-personalized-tribes/.

53. Rachel Smolkin, "What the Mainstream Media Can Learn from Jon Stewart," *American Journalism Review* (June/July 2007): www.ajr.org/article.asp?id=4329.

54. Matthew A. Baum and Angela Jamison, "The Oprah Effect: How Soft News Helps Inattentive Citizens Vote Consistently," *Journal of Politics* 68 (2008): 946–59.

55. Donald L. Jorand and Benjamin I. Page, "Shaping Foreign Policy Opinions: The Role of TV News," *Journal of Conflict Resolution* 36 (June 1992): 227–41.

56. Philip E. Tetlock, *Expert Political Judgment: How Good Is It? How Can We Know?* (Princeton, NJ: Princeton University Press, 2006).

57. Kelly Kaufhold, Sebastian Valenzuela, and Homero Gil de Zuniga, "Citizen Journalism and Democracy: How User-Generated News Use Relates to Political Knowledge and Participation," *Journalism and Mass Communication Quarterly* 87 (2010): 515–29.

Chapter 14

1. Robert D. Putnam, "Bowling Alone: America's Declining Social Capital," *Journal of Democracy* 6 (1995): 650–65; and Putnam, *Bowling Alone: The Collapse and Revival of American Community* (New York: Simon and Schuster, 2000).

2. Everett Carll Ladd, quoted in Richard Morin, "Who Says We're Not Joiners," *Washington Post* (May 2, 1999): B5.

3. Alixandra B. Yanus and Adam Chamberlain, "The Effect of 'Do Everything' on Unity in Diversity: A Neopluralist Examination of the Women's Temperance Union." *Polity* (2021)

4. Quoted in Grant McConnell, "Lobbies and Pressure Groups," in Jack Greene, ed., *Encyclopedia of American Political History*, vol. 2 (New York: Macmillan, 1984), 768.

5. Lee Epstein, *Conservatives in Court* (Knoxville: University of Tennessee Press, 1985).

6. "Facts Matter," VOTE SMART, Accessed March 25, 2020.

7. Jack L. Walker, "The Origins and Maintenance of Interest Groups in America," *American Political Science Review* 77 (June 1983): 390–406.

8. Peter Steinfels, "Moral Majority to Dissolve: Says Mission Accomplished," *New York Times* (June 12, 1989): A14.

9. Sarah Pulliam Bailey, "Joe Biden reportedly denied Communion at a South Carolina church because of his stance on abortion," *Washington Post*, Posted October 29, 2019. https://www.washingtonpost.com/religion/2019/10/29/joe-biden-reportedly-denied-communion-south-carolina-church-over-his-stance-abortion/.

10. "Business Roundtable: About Us," January 2014, Business Roundtable, http://businessroundtable.org/about.

11. John Brehm and Wendy Rahn, "Individual-Level Evidence for the Causes and Consequences of Social Capital," *American Journal of Political Science* 41 (July 1997): 999.

12. Mark Schneider, et al., "Institutional Arrangements and the Creation of Social Capital: The Effects of Public School Choice," *American Political Science Review* 91 (March 1997): 82–93.

13. Nicholas Lemann, "Kicking in Groups," *Atlantic Monthly* (April 1996), NEXIS.

14. David B. Truman, *The Governmental Process: Political Interests and Public Opinion* (New York: Knopf, 1951), ch. 16.

15. Mancur Olson, *The Logic of Collective Action: Public Goods and the Theory of Groups* (Cambridge, MA: Harvard University Press, 1965).

16. E. E. Schattschneider, *The Semisovereign People* (New York: Holt, Rinehart and Winston, 1960), 35.

17. Jeffrey M. Berry, *Lobbying for the People: The Political Behavior of Public Interest Groups* (Princeton, NJ: Princeton University Press, 1977), 7.

18. Berry, *Lobbying for the People*, 7.

19. *Citizens United* v. *FEC*, 558 U.S. 310 (2010).

20. Karl Evers-Hillstrom, "Lobbying spending reaches $3.4 billion in 2018, highest in 8 years," OpenSecrets.org. Posted January 25, 2019. 2020 data from OpenSecrets, "Lobbying Data Summary." Accessed March 10, 2021.

21. Michael Wines, "For New Lobbyists, It's What They Know," *New York Times* (November 3, 1993): B14.

22. Quoted in Kay Lehman Schlozman and John T. Tierney, *Organized Interests and American Democracy* (New York: Harper and Row, 1986), 85.

23. Ken Kollman, "Inviting Friends to Lobby: Interest Groups, Ideological Bias, and Congressional Committees," *American Journal of Political Science* 41 (April 1997): 519–44.

24. Quoted in Norman J. Ornstein and Shirley Elder, *Interest Groups, Lobbying and Policy Making* (Washington, DC: CQ Press, 1978), 77.

25. Some political scientists speak of "iron rectangles," reflecting the growing importance of a fourth party, the courts, in the lobbying process.

26. Clement E. Vose, "Litigation as a Form of Pressure Group Activity," *Annals* 319 (September 1958): 20–31.

27. Paul M. Collins Jr., *Friends of the Supreme Court* (New York: Oxford University Press, 2008).

28. Amy Harder and Charlie Szymanski, "Sotomayor in Context: Unprecedented Input from Interest Groups," *National Review* (August 5, 2009): www.nationaljournal.com.

29. Robert A. Goldberg, *Grassroots Resistance: Social Movements in Twentieth Century America* (Belmont, CA: Wadsworth, 1991).

30. Ken Kollman, *Outside Lobbyists: Public Opinion and Interest Group Strategies* (Princeton, NJ: Princeton University Press, 1998); and Karen O'Connor, *Women's Organizations' Use of the Courts* (Lexington, MA: Lexington Books, 1980).

31. Marie Hojnacki, "Interest Groups' Decisions to Join Alliances or Work Alone," *American Journal of Political Science* 41 (January 1997): 61–87.

32. Lee Ann Banaszak, *Why Movements Succeed or Fail: Opportunity, Culture, and the Struggle for Woman Suffrage* (Princeton, NJ: Princeton University Press, 1996); Frank R. Baumgartner and Beth L. Leech, *Basic Interests: The Importance of Groups in Politics and in Political Science* (Princeton, NJ: Princeton University Press, 1990); Nancy E. McGlen, et al., *Women, Politics, and American Society*, 5th ed. (New York: Longman, 2010); Robert H. Salisbury, "An Exchange Theory of Interest Groups," *Midwest Journal of Political Science* 13 (1969): 1–32; and Jack Walker, *Mobilizing Interest Groups*

in America: Patrons, Professions, and Social Movements (Ann Arbor: University of Michigan Press, 1991).

33. Walker, *Mobilizing Interest Groups in America*.

34. Schattschneider, *The Semisovereign People*, 35.

35. Olson, *The Logic of Collective Action*.

36. Leslie Wayne, "And for His Next Feat, Billionaire Sets Sights on Bush," *New York Times* (May 31, 2004): A14.

37. Walker, "The Origins and Maintenance of Interest Groups," 390–406.

38. Richard Simons, "Bush Signs Bill to Tighten Lobbying Rules," *Los Angeles Times* (September 15, 2007): A13.

Chapter 15

1. This discussion draws on James E. Anderson, *Public Policy-making: An Introduction*, 2nd ed. (Boston: Houghton Mifflin, 1994), 5.

2. Thomas R. Dye, *Who's Running America?* (Englewood Cliffs, NJ: Prentice Hall, 1976).

3. David B. Truman, *The Governmental Process* (New York: Knopf, 1951).

4. Robert Dahl, *Who Governs?* (New Haven, CT: Yale University Press, 1961).

5. Theodore J. Lowi, "American Business, Public Policy Case Studies, and Political Theory," *World Politics* XVI (July 1964): 677–715.

6. Roger W. Cobb and Charles D. Elder, *Participation in American Politics: The Dynamics of Agenda-building*, 2nd ed. (Baltimore, MD: Johns Hopkins University Press, 1983), 85.

7. John W. Kingdon, *Agendas, Alternatives, and Public Policies*, 2nd ed. (New York: Harper Collins, 1995).

8. Charles O. Jones, *An Introduction to the Study of Public Policy*, 3rd ed. (Monterey, CA: Brooks/Cole, 1984), 87–89.

9. R. Frank, "Health Issues in the Clean Air Act," *Environmental Health Perspectives* 53 (1983): 241–246.

10. This discussion draws on Anne Schneider and Helen Ingram, "Behavioral Assumptions of Policy Tools," *Journal of Politics* 52 (May 1990): 510–29.

11. James D. Savage, *Balanced Budgets and American Politics* (Ithaca, NY: Cornell University Press, 1988), 176–79.

12. U.S. Congress, Tax Cuts and Jobs Act (December 22, 2017), www.congress.gov/bill/115th-congress/house-bill/1/text/eh.

13. "The Debt Limit: History and Recent Increases," Congressional Research Service, www.senate.gov/CRSReports/crs-publish.cfm?pid='0E%2C*P%5C%3F%3D%23%20%20%20%0A.

14. "American Recovery and Reinvestment Act," U.S. Congress, February 17, 2009, www.congress.gov/bill/111th-congress/house-bill/1/text.

15. "What Is the National Debt Today?" Peter G. Peterson Foundation, www.pgpf.org/national-debt-clock.

16. Ibid.

17. "About the Fed," U.S. Federal Reserve, www.federalreserve.gov/aboutthefed.htm.

18. Kaiser Family Foundation, "Medicare," www.kff.org/state-category/medicare/.

19. "May 2020 Medicaid and CHIP Enrollment Highlights," Medicaid.gov, www.medicaid.gov/medicaid/program-information/medicaid-and-chip-enrollment-data/report-highlights/index.html.

20. "Student Debt Rising Worldwide," Yale Global Online, https://yaleglobal.yale.edu/content/student-debt-rising-worldwide#:~:text=The%20average%20student%20loan%20debt%20is%20%2437%2C000%20in,for%20students%20from%20rural%20areas%20and%20developing%20nations.

21. "Federal Poverty Guidelines," U.S. Department of Health and Human Services, https://aspe.hhs.gov/2020-poverty-guidelines.

22. "Retirement Benefits," U.S. Social Security Administration, www.ssa.gov/benefits/retirement/.

23. Ibid.

24. "This is the Average Unemployment Insurance Payment in Every U.S. State," CNBC, www.cnbc.com/2020/07/23/average-unemployment-insurance-payment-in-each-us-state.html

25. "Temporary Assistance for Needy Families," U.S. Department of Health and Human Services, www.acf.hhs.gov/ofa/programs/tanf.

26. "A Quick Guide to SNAP Eligibility and Benefits," Center on Budget and Priorities, www.cbpp.org/research/food-assistance/a-quick-guide-to-snap-eligibility-and-benefits.

Chapter 16

1. Francis Fukuyama, *The End of History and the Last Man* (New York: Free Press, 1992).

2. Alfred E. Eckes Jr., *Opening America's Market: U.S. Foreign Trade Policy Since 1776* (Chapel Hill: University of North Carolina Press, 1995).

3. John L. O'Sullivan, writing in 1845, quoted in Julius W. Pratt, "The Ideology of American Expansion," in Avery Craven, ed., *Essays in Honor of William E. Dodd* (Chicago: University of Chicago Press, 1935), 343–44.

4. Charles P. Kindleberger, *The World in Depression, 1929–1939* (Berkeley: University of California Press, 1986).

5. Mr. X., "The Sources of Soviet Conduct," *Foreign Affairs* (July 1947): 566–82. Mr. X was later revealed to be U.S. ambassador and diplomat George Kennan.

6. Richard M. Nixon, Inaugural Address, January 20, 1969, Public Papers of the Presidents of the United States (Washington, DC: Government Printing Office).

7. "History," Department of Homeland Security, www.dhs.gov/history.

8. *Congress A to Z*, 4th ed. (Washington, DC: CQ Press, 2003).

9. United States Census Bureau, www.census.gov/foreign-trade/balance/c5700.html.

10. "Doomsday and the history of nuclear weapons," *The Economist* (January 28, 2016), www.economist.com/blogs/graphicdetail/2016/01/daily-chart-21.

11. NASA Global Climate Change: Climate change, "How Do We Know?," www.climate.nasa.gov/evidence/.

12. "Climate Change 2014: Impacts, Adaptation, and Vulnerability," IPCC (Intergovernmental Panel on Climate Change), www.ipcc.ch/report/ar5/wg2/.

13. White House: The President's Climate Action Plan, www.whitehouse.gov/sites/default/files/image/president27sclimateactionplan.pdf.

14. Fiona Harvey, "Paris Climate Change Agreement: The World's Greatest Diplomatic Success," *The Guardian* (December 14, 2015), www.theguardian.com/environment/2015/dec/13/paris-climate-deal-cop-diplomacy-developing-united-nations.

501(c) groups, 313
527 political committees, 312–313
2020 elections, 290, 329

A

AAPD (American Association of People with Disabilities), 129
abolitionists, 103, 104–105
abortion
    right to privacy and, 92–93
    Roberts Court, 239–240
Abrams, Stacey, 371
ACA (Affordable Care Act), 379, 380–381, 393–394
activism, 365, 369–370
ADA (Americans with Disabilities Act), 128–129
Adams, John, 21, 24
Adams, Samuel, 21
Administrative Procedures Act, 206
AFDC (Aid to Families and Dependent Children), 402
affirmative action, 130–131
Affordable Care Act, 14
    RFRA (Religious Freedom Restoration Act), 76
Afghanistan War, 416
AFL (American Federation of Labor), 357
    CIO (Congress of Industrial Organizations) and, 360
age
    aging population, 10–11
    party identification and, 279, 280*f*
    voting and, 318–319
agenda setting in news media, 340–341
"Ain't I a Woman?" (Sojourner Truth), 105
Alexander VI (Pope), 2
Alien and Sedition Acts, 77
Alito, Samuel A., 225*t*
al-Qaeda, 415
amendments to Constitution, 19–20, 40. *See also* specific
    amendments
    Article V, 36
    Civil Rights Era, 40
    Civil War Amendments, 103–104
    Civil War Era, 40
    Corrections Era, 40
    cultural change and, 43
    formal methods of amending, 41–42
    Founding Era, 40
    implications, 41
    informal methods, 42–43
    judicial interpretation, 42–43
    Progressive Era, 40
    requirements, 41
    social change and, 43
    Susan B. Anthony Amendment, 110
    technological change and, 43
    voting rights, 18
American Dream, 13
American Independent Party, 282

American Indian Law Center, 124
American Indians, 123–125
    governing structure, 46
    peyote use, free exercise clause, 76
    tribe sovereignty, 47
amicus curiae, 111, 231–232
ANES (American National Election Studies), 245–246
Anthony, Susan B., 106, 354
Anti-Federalists, 37–38
appellate courts, 220
appellate jurisdiction, federal courts, 216*f*
appointments, foreign and defense policy, 421
appointments by president, 171–172
apportionment, 136–137
appropriations, foreign and defense policy, 421
aristocracy, 48
arms control, nuclear weapons, 429
Article I of Constitution, 34–36, 136
Article II of Constitution, 35
Article III of Constitution, 36, 220
Article IV of Constitution, 36
Article V of Constitution, 36
Article VI of Constitution, 36
Article VII of Constitution, 36
Articles of Confederation, 6, 25, 32, 136
    compared to the Constitution, 35*t*
    Critical Period, 26
    executive branch, 168
Asians and Pacific Island Americans, 125–127
assemblies, colonies, 5
ATP (American Trends Panel), 246
Attucks, Crispus, 21, 22
authoritative techniques, policy implementation, 385

B

Baker v. *Carr*, 143
balance of power, 161–162
balanced budget, 186
ballot measures, 293
banking
    government and, 54–55
    McCulloch v. *Maryland*, 54–55
Barrett, Amy Coney, 15, 42, 224, 225*t*
Barron v. *Baltimore*, 53
    Bill of Rights and, 55
Baxter, Leone, 304
BCRA (Bipartisan Campaign Reform Act), 309
Beard, Charles A., 28
Berlin Wall, 406, 413
bicameral legislature, 34, 136
Biden, Jill, 181
Biden, Joe, 16, 36, 278
    ACA (Affordable Care Act), 379
    Electoral College win, 296*f*
    Trump debate, 305

Bill of Rights, 39, 71
  Barron v. *Baltimore* and, 55
  colonies, 6
  criminal defendants, 84–90
  due process rights, 84
  fundamental freedoms, 72
  incorporation doctrine, 71
  Ninth Amendment and, 71
  right to privacy, 90–94
  selective incorporation, 72, 73
  substantive due process, 71
  Tenth Amendment and, 71
  Warren Court, 72
bills, 137
  path to law, 152*f*
birth control, right to privacy and, 91–92
Black Americans, party identification, 278
Black Codes, 106
Black Lives Matter plaza, 7*f*
BLM (Black Lives Matter), 6, 315
  hate speech concerns, 80
block grants, 64
blogs, 336–337
Board of Governors, Federal Reserve System, 391
Booker, Corey, 142
Bork, Robert H., 227
Boston Massacre, 21, 22
Boston Tea Party, 22
Bowser, Muriel, 7
branches of government, 33
Brandeis, Louis, 62, 90
Brandenburg v. *Ohio*, 78
Brennan Jr., William J., 91
Bretton Woods System, 411
Breyer, Stephen A., 225*t*
briefs, 221
Brooks, Preston, 135
Brown v. *Board of Education*, 112–113, 396
Brown v. *Board of Education II*, 113–114
budget
  balanced, 186
  budget deficit, 388
  Congress and, 155–156
  national debt, 389–390
  national deficit, 389–390
  president and, 186–187
Budget and Accounting Act of 1921, 155
bureaucracy, 191. *See also* federal bureaucracy
bureaucrats, 200–203
Burger, Warren, 87
Burger Court, *Miranda* rights, 87
Burke, Edmund, 142
Burke, Tarana, 118
Burr, Aaron, 31
Burwell v. *Hobby Lobby*, 91
Bush, Barbara, 166
Bush, Cori, 140
Bush, George H. W., 166

C

Cabinet, 172, 180
  departments, 197, 197*f*
  resignations under Trump, 210
  role, 190
  secretaries, 197–198
Cabot, John, 2
Calhoun, John C., 55
Calvert, George, 4
campaign consultant, 303
campaigns, 302–303. *See also* elections
  501(c) groups, 313
  527 political committees, 312–313
  advertisements, 307–308
  BCRA (Bipartisan Campaign Reform Act), 309
  candidate, 300–301
  Citizens United v. *FEC*, 309
  communications staff, 303
  contribution limits 2019–2020, 309
  conventions and, 304–305
  debates and, 304–305
  FEC (Federal Election Commission), 309
  FECA (Federal Election Campaign Act), 308–309
  finance regulation, 308–310
  financing changes, 310*f*
  funding sources, 310–314, 371
  GOTV (get-out-the-vote), 303
  independent expenditures, 313
  individual donors, 312
  matching funds, 314
  McCutcheon v. *FEC*, 309
  media and, 305–308
  PACs (political action committees), 311–312
  personal savings funding, 311
  pollsters, 303
  press secretary, 303
  public funds, 314
  voter canvass, 303
candidate traits, voting and, 319–320
candidate-centered politics, 265
capacity techniques, policy implementation, 385
Capitol insurrection, 16, 156, 162–163
CARES (Coronavirus Aid, Relief, and Economic Security) Act, 390
Carter, Jimmy, 166
Carter, Roslyn, 166
categorical grants, 63–64
caucuses, presidential elections, 294
Cawthorn, Madison, 140
CBO (Congressional Budget Office), 161
CCC (Civilian Conservation Corps), 59
CDC (Centers for Disease Control and Prevention), 395
census, House of Representatives, 295
chairperson, national party, 269
charter schools, 397
charters, 52
Chauvin, Derek, 370
Chavez, Cesar, 120
checks and balances, 32–34, 33*f*
China, foreign and defense policy and, 432
Chisolm v. *Georgia*, 218
Christian Coalition, 359
Churchill, Winston, 412
CIA (Central Intelligence Agency), 420
CIO (Congress of Industrial Organizations), 360
citizen journalists, 351–352
Citizens United v. *FEC*, 309, 364
civic organizations, voting and, 319

civic virtue, interest groups and, 362
civil disobedience, 114
civil liberties, 69. *See also* Bill of Rights
    abortion and, 92–93
    birth control and, 91–92
    COVID-19 and, 94–98
    criminal defendants, 84–90
    Fifth Amendment, 85–87
    First Amendment, 73–82
    Fourth Amendment, 84–85, 87
    LGBTQ issues, 93–94
    Muslim travel ban, 70
    right to privacy and, 90–94
    roots, 70–73
    Second Amendment, 82–83
    Sixth Amendment, 88–90
civil rights, 69, 103. *See also* racial discrimination
    abolition, 104–105
    American Indians, 123–125
    Americans with disabilities, 128–129
    Asians and Pacific Island Americans, 125–127
    Brown v. Board of Education, 112–113
    Brown v. Board of Education II, 113–114
    Chavez, Cesar, 120
    Cooper v. Aaron, 113
    equal protection clause, 129–131
    ERA (Equal Rights Amendment), 119–120
    freedom rides, 115
    Hernandez v. Texas, 120
    Hispanic Americans, 120–123
    Huerta, Dolores, 120
    Johnson, Lyndon B., 116
    Kennedy, John F., 115
    legal tests, 110–113
    LGBTQ community, 127–128
    Little Rock Central High School, 113–114
    lunch counter protests, 115
    lynching of Black people, 109
    Montgomery bus boycott, 114
    NAACP LDF, 111
    origins, 103–108
    Parks, Rosa, 114
    Progressive Era, 108–113
    school desegregation, 113–114
    SCLC (Southern Christian Leadership Conference), 115
    separate-but-equal doctrine, 108
    sit-ins, 115
    SNCC (Student Nonviolent Coordinating Committee), 115
    women's rights, 104–105
Civil Rights Act of 1866, 106
Civil Rights Act of 1875, 107
Civil Rights Act of 1964, 116
    March on Washington for Jobs and Freedom, 116
    same-sex marriage, 128
    Title VII, 117
Civil Rights Cases, Supreme Court, 107
Civil Rights Era, constitutional amendments, 40
Civil Service, 201–202
Civil Service Reform Act, 193
civil service system, 193
Civil War, 57–59, 61f
Civil War Amendments, 40, 103, 105–106
Clark, Kenneth, 112
Clark, Mamie, 112

climate change, foreign and defense policy, 431
Clinton, Bill, 166, 186
Clinton, Hillary, 166, 362
closed primary, 292
cloture, 154
Coercive Acts, 22
Cold War, 407, 412
    post-Cold War environment, 414–415
collective good, interest groups, 362
colonial settlers, 3–4
    diversity among, 6
    Mayflower, 4
    Mayflower Compact, 4
    Penn's Woods, 4
    Pennsylvania, 4
    pre-1700, 4f
    Providence Plantations, 4
    religion and, 3–4
colonies
    Bill of Rights, 6
    government, 5
    local government, 5–6
    Proprietary, 5
    Royal, 5
colonists, 3
Columbus, Christopher, 1, 2
Comey, James, 172
commander in chief, 174
commerce, Congress and, 55
commerce regulation, 194
Committee of Five, 24
committees (Congress), 148
    117th Congress, 150t
    chairs, 150–151
    conference committee, 149
    discharge petition, 149
    joint committee, 149
    membership, 151
    select (special) committee, 149
    seniority, 151
    standing committees, 149
Committees of Correspondence, 21, 22
Common Core standards, 397
Common Sense (Paine), 23
communications director, 303
concurrent powers, 51, 51f
concurring opinion, Supreme Court, 235
confederacy. *See also* Articles of Confederation
    Iroquois Confederacy, 46
    Iroquois League of Nations, 2
Confederate monuments, 58
confederate system, 49f
confederation, 47
conference committee, 149
Congress. *See also* House of Representatives; Senate
    American people and, 162–163
    Articles of Impeachment, 156
    caucuses and, 160
    commerce and, 55
    committee system, 148–151
    constituents and, 159–160
    court appointments, 158
    daily activities, 139t

Congress (*continued*)
　decision making, 158–161
　delegate theory, 142
　demographics, 139–142
　diversity in, 140–142
　executive and, 161–162
　federal bureaucracy and, 210–211
　First Continental Congress, 135–136
　foreign and defense policy, 420–422
　impeachment, 138, 158
　incumbency, 143
　interest groups and, 160
　judiciary and, 162
　legislative branch and, 33
　lobbying, 366–367
　lobbyists and, 160
　members' net worth, 139
　news media and, 339
　opinions of Americans, 162*f*
　organization, 145–151, 145*f*
　oversight hearings, 157
　PACs (political action committees), 160
　partisan composition (117th), 146*f*
　political parties and, 158–159
　politicos, 142
　pork, 156
　powers, 138*t*
　redistricting, 143–145
　representation of the people, 138–142
　staff, 160–161
　support agencies, 160–161
　Tenure of Office Act, 161
　trustee theory, 142
　War Powers Resolution, 156–157
Congress of the Confederation, 37
Congressional Budget Act of 1974, 155
congressional elections, 297–300
congressional powers
　budgetary, 155–156
　law-making, 151–154
　oversight, 156–158
congressional review, 157
Congressional Review Act of 1996, 156, 157
Connecticut Constitution, 4
conservative political ideology, 252–253, 254*f*
　interest groups, 359–360
　news audiences, 349*f*
　social conservative, 253
constituents, congressional decisions and, 159–160
constitution, 28
Constitution, U.S. *See also* amendments to Constitution
　amendment methods, 41–42
　amendments, 19–20, 36, 40, 451–455
　approval, 32
　Article I, 34, 136, 445–447
　Article II, 35, 447–448
　Article III, 36, 448–449
　Article IV, 36, 449
　Article V, 36, 449
　Article VI, 36, 449–450
　Article VII, 36, 450
　checks and balances, 32
　Civil War Amendments, 103–104

　compared to Articles of Confederation, 35*t*
　concurrent powers, 51
　as economic document, 28
　federalism and, 49–53
　foreign and defense policy, 417–418
　government by the people, 32
　interstate relations, 52
　local governments, 52–53
　necessary and proper clause, 34
　origins, 20–25
　powers denied, 51–52
　ratification, 37–39
　separation of powers, 32, 33–34
　state powers, 50–51
　writing of, 27–32
Constitutional Convention
　bill of rights discussion, 70
　Committee on Unfinished Portions, 31
　Electoral College, 31
　Great Compromise, 30, 136
　impeachment, 31
　judiciary and, 214–219
　New Jersey Plan, 29
　removal of president, 31
　slavery, 30–31, 102
　Three-Fifths Compromise, 30–31
　Virginia Plan, 29
constitutional courts (Article III courts), 220
constitutional monarchy, 48
containment, Cold War, 412
contrast ads, campaigns, 307
Coolidge, Calvin, 59
Cooper v. *Aaron*, 113
cooperative federalism, 59–61, 61*f*
coronavirus pandemic. *See* COVID-19
Corrections Era, constitutional amendments, 40
Cosby, William, 69
counterproliferation, nuclear weapons, 430
counties, 52
court appointments, 158
courts of appeals, 221, 222*f*
COVID-19, 7
　2020 elections and, 290
　ACA expansion, 394
　CARES Act, 390
　civil liberties and, 94–98
　economy and, 390
　Eighth Amendment and, 98
　ethnicity, deaths and, 11
　federalism and, 62
　First Amendment and, 95–97
　Fourth Amendment and, 97–98
　free exercise clause and, 95–96
　freedom of assembly and, 96–97
　freedom of expression and, 96
　governors' powers change, 62
　insurance coverage and, 14
　public health policy, 395–396
　relief package, 186–187
　response, 208
　Second Amendment and, 97
　Supreme Court hearings, 234
　symbolic speech and, 96

voting and, 43
WHO (World Health Organization) withdrawal, Trump, 173
criminal defendants' rights, 84
bail, 89–90
cruel and unusual punishment, 89–90
double jeopardy, 87
due process rights, 84, 88
exclusionary rule, 87
habeas corpus, 84
jury trials and, 88–89
Miranda v. *Arizona*, 86–87
right to counsel, 88
searches and seizures, 84–85
self-incrimination, 85–87
wrongful conviction, 90
critical elections, party realignment and, 265
Critical Period, 26
crossover voting, 292
The Crown v. *Zenger*, 68, 69
CRS (Congressional Research Service), 161
cruel and unusual punishment, 89–90
CSO (Community Service Organization), 120
Cuban Missile Crisis, 413

D

da Verrazzano, Giovanni, 2
DACA (Deferred Action for Childhood Arrivals), 122–123
DADT (Don't Ask, Don't Tell), 127
Daughters of Liberty, 21
Davis, Jefferson, 58
Dawes Act, 123
de Soto, Hernando, 2
death penalty, 89–90
Declaration of Independence, 24, 442–444
Liberty Bell, 25
"men" terminology, 103
Declaration of Rights and Resolves, 23
defense policy. *See* foreign and defense policy
delegate theory of representation, 142
delegates to national party convention, 268
democracy, 6, 48
Democratic Party, delegates to national convention, 268
Democratic-Republican party, 263
Department of Agriculture, 197*f*
Department of Commerce, 197*f*
Department of Defense, 197*f*, 419
Department of Education, 197*f*
Department of Energy, 197*f*
Department of Health and Human Services, 197*f*, 393
Department of Homeland Security, 420
Department of Housing and Urban Development, 196, 197*f*
Department of Justice, 197*f*
Department of Labor, 197*f*
Department of State, 197*f*, 418–419
Department of the Interior, 197*f*
Department of the Treasury, 197*f*
Department of Transportation, 197*f*
Department of Veterans Affairs, 197*f*
depression, 387
détente, 413–414
deterrence, Cold War, 412
devolution revolution, 61*f*

digital media, 335
blogs, 336–337
podcasts, 336
social media, 335–336
digital-native news outlets, 330
Dillon, John F., 52
Dillon's Rule, 52
direct incitement test, 78
disarmament, nuclear weapons, 429
discharge petition, 149
dissenting opinion, Supreme Court, 235
distributive policies, 382
district courts, 220, 222*f*
disturbance theory, interest groups, 362
divided government, 156
Divine Right of the king, 5
Dixiecrats, 282
DOMA (Defense of Marriage Act), 127–128
domestic terrorism, 428
double jeopardy, 87
Douglass, Frederick, 104
Drake, Sir Francis, 2
Dred Scott v. *Sandford*, 56–57
Missouri Compromise and, 105
Du Bois, W.E.B., 109
dual federalism, 61*f*
Dred Scott v. *Sandford*, 56–57
federal–state relationship evolution, 61*f*
nullification and, 55–56
DuBois, W.E.B., *The Philadelphia Negro*, 244
due process clause, 71
due process rights, 84
Dutch New Netherland Company, 3
Dutch West India Company, 3

E

East India Company, 21
economic interest groups, 363–364
economic policy
challenges, 403
fiscal policy, 386–390
monetary policy, 391
regulatory policies, 382
Edelman, Marian Wright, 373
education
party identification and, 281*f*
political socialization and, 256–257
voting and, 316
education policy
Brown v. *Board of Education*, 396
charter schools, 397
Common Core, 397
higher education, 397–398
No Child Left Behind Act, 397
primary education, 396–397
secondary education, 396–397
Title IX (Educational Amendment Acts), 397–398
vouchers, 397
EEOC (Equal Employment Opportunity Commission), 196
Eighteenth Amendment, 83, 453
Eighth Amendment, 89–90, 451
Eisenhower, Dwight D., 19

elections. *See also* campaigns; voting
  congressional, 297–300
  general, 292
  initiative, 292
  interest group activities, 370–372
  midterm, 299
  polling, 246*f*
  primary, 292
  recall elections, 293
  reelection rates, 298*f*
  referendum, 292
  voting patterns, 314–320
Electoral College, 31, 295–297
  Article II and, 35
  reform, 321–322
electoral process
  front-loading, 320–321
  nominee selection, 321*f*
  reform, 320–325
electorate, 291
Eleventh Amendment, 218, 451
Ellsworth, Oliver, 219
Emancipation Proclamation, 105
Emoluments Clause, 168–169
Engel v. *Vitale*, 74
English settlement in Americas, 3
entitlement programs, 399
enumerated powers, 34, 50, 51*f*
EOP (Executive Office of the President), 182
Equal Pay Act of 1963, 118–119
equal protection clause, 103
  affirmative action, 130–131
  Fourteenth Amendment, 106
  intermediate standard of review, 131
  rational basis standard of review, 131
  standards of review, 129–131
  strict scrutiny, 130
  suspect classifications, 130
equal time rule, media, 346
equality, Progressive Era, 108–113
ERA (Equal Rights Amendment), 41, 119–120
Era of Good Feelings, 263
Espionage Act, 78
establishment clause, 73, 74–75
  Santa Fe Independent School District v. *Doe*, 74
  school prayer, 74–75
  state property, 75
ethnic composition of nation, 9–10
ethnicity
  COVID-19 deaths and, 11
  early settlers, 3
  federal justices, 226
  party identification and, 278–279
  voting and, 317–318
EU (European Union), foreign and defense policy, 434
Europe, foreign and defense policy and, 433–434
European colonialism, 1
European explorers, 2
ex post facto laws, 52, 84
exclusionary rule, 87
executive agreements, 173
  foreign and defense policy, 421
  Supreme Court and, 215

executive branch, 33
  checks on judicial branch, 33*f*
  checks on legislative branch, 33*f*
  foreign and defense policy, 418–420
  inherent powers, 35
executive orders, 33, 187–188
  Supreme Court, 215
executive power, Article II and, 35
executive privilege, 170
exit polls, 249

F

Facebook, 336
false information
  Russian government and, 14
  Trump, Donald J., 14
Falwell, Jerry, 359
family, political socialization and, 256–257
Farewell Address (George Washington), 408
Faubus, Orval, 113
Fauci, Anthony, 62, 157, 257
FDR. *See* Roosevelt, Franklin D.
FEC (Federal Election Commission), 309
FECA (Federal Election Campaign Act), 308–309
federal bureaucracy, 191–192. *See also* bureaucracy
  administrative adjudication, 207
  Administrative Procedures Act, 206
  agencies, regions, 203*f*
  agency accountability, 207
  Cabinet departments, 197
  commerce regulation, 194
  congressional control, 210–211
  controlling, 207–211
  Department of Housing and Urban Development, 196
  EEOC (Equal Employment Opportunity Commission), 196
  executive control, 208–210
  federal executive branch employees, 195*f*
  Federal Register, 206
  FTC (Federal Trade Commission), 194
  government corporations, 199
  ICC (Interstate Commerce Commission), 194
  independent executive agencies, 198
  independent regulatory commissions, 198–199
  interagency councils, 205
  iron triangles, 204, 204*f*
  issue networks, 204
  judicial control, 211
  organization, 196–199
  pandemic response, 208
  PCCs (policy coordinating committees), 205
  policymaking, 205–207
  public opinion, 192*f*
  regulation creation, 206*f*
  regulations, 205
  rule making, 205
  Sixteenth Amendment, 194–195
  U.S. Department of Commerce and Labor, 194
  Weber, Max, on, 203–204
  world wars and, 195–196
federal court system
  appellate courts, 220
  appellate jurisdiction, 216*f*
  constitutional courts (Article III courts), 220
  courts of appeals, 216*f*, 221

district courts, 216*f*, 220
   judge selection, 222–228
   legislative courts, 220
   original jurisdiction, 216*f*
   Supreme Court, 216*f*, 221–222
   trial courts, 220
federal deficit, 186
federal employees, 201–202, 202*f*
federal executive branch, employees, 195*f*
federal grants
   block grants, 64
   categorical grants, 63–64
   programmatic (earmark) grants, 64
federal judges. *See also* Supreme Court
   committee hearings, 228
   confirmation process, 226–228
   as of December 2020, 225*t*
   demographics, 223*f*, 224
   impeachment, 215
   interest group lobbying, 227–228
   investigation, 227
   nomination, preferences, 224–226
   Senate Judiciary Committee, 226–227
   senatorial courtesy, 223
Federal Open Market committee, 391
Federal Register, 206
Federal Reserve Banks, 391
Federal Reserve Board, 391
Federal Reserve System, 391
federal system, 47–48, 49*f*
   charters, 52
   concurrent powers, 51, 51*f*
   creation, 48–49
   enumerated powers, 51*f*
   federal grants for states, 63*f*
   interstate relations, 52
   national powers, 51*f*
   power distribution, 51*f*
   powers denied, 51–52
   reserved powers, 51*f*
   sanctuary cities/counties/states, 64*f*
   state powers, 51*f*
federalism, 32
   Barron v. *Baltimore* and, 55
   Civil War and Reconstruction, 61*f*
   Constitution and, 49–53
   cooperative, 59–61, 61*f*
   coronavirus pandemic and, 62
   devolution revolution, 61*f*
   dual federalism, 55–59, 61*f*
   Gibbons v. *Ogden* and, 54–55
   Great Society, 61*f*
   Marshall court and, 53–55
   McCulloch v. *Maryland* and, 53–55
   national government growth, 59–61
   national intervention, economy, 61*f*
   New Deal, 61*f*
   new federalism, 61*f*
   progressive federalism, 61*f*, 62
   Roosevelt, Franklin D., 60
   Supreme Court and, 65
The Federalist Papers, 38
   Federalist No. 10, 214, 456–459
   Federalist No. 51, 459–461

Federalist No. 68, 31
   Federalist No. 78, 215, 461–464
   judicial review, 219
Federalist Party, 263
Federalists
   versus Anti-Federalists, 37
   interest groups and, 355
   ratification of Constitution, 37–38
FHA (Federal Housing Administration), 59
Fifteenth Amendment, 106, 107–108, 452–453
Fifth Amendment, 85–87, 451
fighting words, 80
filibuster, 154
finance chair, 303
First Amendment, 73–82, 451
   COVID-19 and, 95–97
   Engel v. *Vitale*, 74
   establishment clause, 73, 74–75
   free exercise clause, 73, 75–77
   freedom of assembly, 81–82
   freedom of petition, 81–82
   freedom of speech, 77–78
   freedom of the press, 77–78
   Lemon v. *Kurtzman*, 74
   protected speech and press, 78–80
   school prayer, 74–75
First Continental Congress, 23, 135–136
first ladies, 181
   Biden, Jill, 181
   Kennedy, Jacqueline, 181
   Obama, Michelle, 181
   Roosevelt, Eleanor, 181
   Trump, Melania, 181
   Wilson, Edith Bolling Galt, 181
fiscal policy, 386
   budget deficit, 388
   depression and, 387
   inflation, 388
   Keynesian economics, 387
   laissez-faire philosophy, 387
   national debt and, 386
   national deficit, 389–390
   recession and, 387
   supply-side economics, 388
   Tax Cuts and Jobs Act, 389
Floyd, George, 6, 85, 370
   racial injustice movement, 95
Ford, Betty, 166
Ford, Gerald, 166
foreign allies, Second Continental Congress and, 24–25
foreign and defense policy, 408
   Afghanistan War, 416
   al-Qaeda, 415
   appointments, 421
   appropriations, 421
   Berlin Wall, 413
   Bretton Woods System, 411
   China and, 432
   CIA (Central Intelligence Agency), 420
   climate change, 431
   Cold War, 407, 412
   collective security, 410
   Congress and, 420–422
   Constitution and, 417–418

foreign and defense policy (*continued*)
   containment, 412
   Cuban Missile Crisis, 413
   decision-making process, 417–424
   defense spending, 422*f*
   Department of Defense, 419
   Department of Homeland Security, 420
   Department of State, 418–419
   détente, 413–414
   deterrence, 412
   Europe and, 433–434
   executive agreements, 421
   executive branch, 418–420
   export markets, 427*f*
   foreign-policy idealism, 425
   foreign-policy realism, 424–425
   Gaddafi, Muammar, 416
   GATT (General Agreement on Tariffs and Trade), 412
   global war on terror, 416
   government and, 7
   Gulf War, 415
   human rights, 414
   Hussein, Saddam, 415
   IMF (International Monetary Fund), 411–412
   interest groups and, 423–424
   Iraq War, 416
   Iron Curtain, 411
   ISIS, 417
   isolationism, 408
   Joint Chiefs of Staff, 419
   judiciary and, 422–423
   Korean War, 413
   League of Nations, 410
   manifest destiny, 409
   Marshall Plan, 413
   MENA (Middle East and North Africa) region, 434–435
   military-industrial complex, 423
   Monroe Doctrine, 409
   NAFTA (North American Free Trade Agreement), 415
   National Security Council, 418
   NATO (North Atlantic Treaty Organization), 413
   nuclear weapons, 429–430
   Operation Iraqi Freedom, 416
   Osama bin Laden, 416
   Panama Canal Zone, 410
   political parties and, 423–424
   Reagan Doctrine, 414
   Roosevelt Corollary, 410
   Russia and, 432–433
   SALT (Strategic Arms Limitation Treaties), 413
   September 11 attacks, 415–416
   spending, 422*f*
   Taliban, 416
   terrorism, 427–429
   trade policy, 426–427
   treaties, 421
   Truman Doctrine, 412–413
   UN Security Council, 411
   unipolar moment in history, 407
   United Nations, 411
   U.S. as emerging power, 409–410
   Vietnam War, 413
   War on Terror, 415–416
   War Powers Resolution, 422
   western hemisphere dominance by U.S., 409–410
   World Bank, 412
   World War I, 410
   World War II, 411–412
   WTO (World Trade Organization), 412
foreign-policy idealism, 425
foreign-policy realism, 424–425
Founding Era, constitutional amendments, 40
Founding Fathers, 28. *See also* Framers
Fourteenth Amendment, 71, 106, 108, 452
Fourth Amendment, 84–85, 97–98, 451
fourth estate, 330
Framers
   amendments, 19–20
   motives, 28–29
   occupations, 29*f*
framing, news media, 341
Franken, Al, 118
Franklin, Benjamin, 20, 23, 24
free exercise clause, 73
   Amish children in school, 76
   COVID-19 and, 95–96
   marriage, 75
   Oregon Employment Division v. *Smith*, 76
   Reynolds v. *United States*, 75
   RFRA (Religious Freedom Restoration Act), 76
   school prayer, 74–75
   Wisconsin v. *Yoder*, 76
free rider problem, 375
Free Soil Party, 282
freedmen, 107
freedom of assembly, 81–82
   COVID-19 and, 96–97
freedom of expression, COVID-19 and, 96
freedom of petition, 81–82
freedom of religion, 73
   Engel v. *Vitale*, 74
   establishment clause, 74–75
   Lemon v. *Kurtzman*, 74
freedom of speech and the press. *See also* protected speech and press
   Alien and Sedition Acts, 77
   Brandenburg v. *Ohio*, 78
   Civil War and, 77–78
   direct incitement test, 78
   Espionage Act, 78
   New York Times Co. v. *U.S.*, 78
   Pentagon Papers, 78
   prior restraint, 77
   rights curtailment, 78
   Schenck v. *U.S.*, 78
   slavery, 77–78
   symbolic speech, 79
   Trump, Donald, attempts to bar publication, 79
   unprotected speech and press, 80–81
   World War I and, 78
freedom rides, 115
French and Indian War, 20
front-loading, 320–321
FTC (Federal Trade Commission), 194
Fugitive Slave Act, 102

full faith and credit clause, Article IV, 36
fundamental freedoms, 72
Furman v. *Georgia*, 89

G

G20, 434
Gaines, Lloyd, 110
Gallup, George, 243
Gallup polls, 242, 245
GAO (Government Accountability Office), 161, 386
Garfield, James A., 193, 194
Garner, Tyron, 94
Garrison, William Lloyd, 103, 109
    The Liberator, 104
GATT (General Agreement on Tariffs and Trade), 412
GDP (gross domestic product), 390
gender
    Black women voters, 278
    electoral outcomes and, 320
    federal justices, 226
    party identification and, 277f, 278
    voting and, 318–319
general elections, 292
gerrymandering, 143, 144f
G.I. Bill, 196
Gibbons v. *Ogden*, 53–55
Gideon v. *Wainwright*, 88
Giffords, Gabrielle, 140
Ginsburg, Ruth Bader, 15, 42, 131, 235
Gitlow, Benjamin, 71
Gitlow v. *New York*, 71
global war on terror, 416
Golden Age of political parties, 264
Gompers, Samuel, 357
Gorbachev, Mikhail, 406
Gore, Al, 186
Gorsuch, Neil, 15, 42, 224, 225t
GOTV (get-out-the-vote), 303
government, 2
    aristocracy, 48
    Aristotle on, 48
    common defense and, 7
    democracy, 48
    domestic tranquility, 6–7
    functions, 5–8
    general welfare, 7–8
    justice and, 6
    liberty, 8
    monarchy, 48
    number in U.S., 52f
    oligarchy, 48
    by the people, 32
    post-Civil War, 58
    revenues, 387f
    skepticism about, 14
    spending, 387f
    totalitarianism, 48
government corporations, 199
governmental (institutional) agenda, policy-making, 384
governmental authority, 49f
governmental units, interest groups, 364
grand jury, 85
grandfather clause, 108
grassroots lobbying, 369

Great Binding Law, Iroquois Confederacy, 47
Great Compromise, 30, 136
Great Depression, 195
    Roosevelt, Franklin D. and, 60
Great Society, 61f, 63, 196
Green New Deal, 140, 243
Green Party, 282
Gregg v. *Georgia*, 89
Griswold, Roger, 134
gross domestic product (GDP). *See* GDP (gross domestic product)
group identity, party identification and, 277
Guiteau, Charles J., 194
Gulf War, 415
gun laws, shootings and, 83

H

Haaland, Deb, 141
habeas corpus, 84
Hamilton, Alexander, 31, 190
    The Federalist Papers, 38
    judicial review, 219
Harlan, John Marshall, 79, 108
Harris, Kamala, 16, 62, 180, 278, 296f
Hatch Act, 200
hate speech, 79–80
    R.A.V. v. *City of St. Paul*, 79
HAVA (Help America Vote Act), 324
Hayes, Rutherford B., 193
health policy, 392
    ACA (Affordable Care Act), 393–394
    Department of Health and Human Services, 393
    Medicaid, 393
    Medicare, 393
    public health, 394–396
Hernandez v. *Texas*, 120
high Court. *See* Supreme Court
higher education policies, 397–398
Hiroshima bombing, 429
Hispanic Americans' civil rights, 120
    Chavez, Cesar, 120
    Chicano Movement, 121
    DACA (Deferred Action for Childhood Arrivals), 122–123
    Hernandez v. *Texas*, 120
    Huerta, Dolores, 120
    LULAC (League of United Latin American Citizens), 120
    MALDEF (Mexican American Legal Defense and Educational Fund), 121
    NHLA (National Hispanic Leadership Agenda), 122
    Puerto Rico residents, 122
    Saenz, Thomas, 121
    UnidosUS, 121
    voting rights, 121
Hispanic population, 9
Honest Leadership and Open Government Act of 2007, 376
Hooker, Thomas, 4
Hoover, Herbert, 59
hortatory techniques, policy implementation, 385
House of Representatives
    apportionment, 136–137
    Article I and, 34

House of Representatives (*continued*)
    careerists, 136
    compared to Senate, 138*t*
    Democratic whip, 147
    demographics compared to general public, 141*f*
    leadership, 147–148
    majority leader, 147
    membership requirements, 136
    minority leader, 147
    nonvoting members, 137
    organization, 145*f*
    reapportionment, 295
    Republican whip, 147
    Speaker of the House, 147
    term length, 137
    whips, 147–148
Huerta, Dolores, 120
human rights, 414
Hussein, Saddam, 414
Hutchinson, Anne, 4, 5*f*
Hyde, Henry, 92

I

ICC (Interstate Commerce Commission), 194
ideological interest groups, 359–360
IMF (International Monetary Fund), 411–412
immigrants
    Hispanic Americans, 122–123
    population growth, 9*f*
immigration, 9–10
    Roberts Court, 240
    Trump, Donald J., and, 9, 122–123
impeachment, 138, 158, 170
    Clinton, Bill, 158
    Constitutional Convention, 31
    federal judges, 215
    Johnson, Andrew, 158
    Nixon, Richard M., 158
    Supreme Court and, 215
    Trump, Donald J., 156, 158
    Tyler, John, 158
implied powers, 50
    necessary and proper clause and, 35
incentive techniques, policy implementation, 385
incorporation doctrine, 71
incumbency in Congress, 143
    advantage, 297
Indigenous People's Day, 1
indigenous peoples of Americas, 2–3
    tribal distribution, 3*f*
industries, confidence in, 14*f*
inflation, 388
infotainment, 349–351
inherent powers, 35, 177
initiatives, 292, 293
inoculation ads, campaigns, 308
institutions, confidence in, 14*f*
interagency councils, 205
interest groups, 160, 355
    activities, 364–372
    associations, 360
    business groups, 357–358, 360
    Citizens United v. FEC, 364

civic virtue and, 362
    collective good, 362
    conservative, 359–360
    corporations, 360
    disturbance theory, 362
    economic interest groups, 363–364
    educational campaigns, 372
    election activities, 370–372
    Federalist and, 355
    foreign and defense policy, 423–424
    free rider problem, 375
    funding, 374
    governmental units, 364
    ideological, 359–360
    leaders, 373–374
    lobbying and, 365–370
    lobbyists, 357
    members, 374–375
    NRA (National Rifle Association), 360
    organized labor, 357, 360–361
    origins, 355–358
    PACs (political action committees), 364
    patrons, 374
    pluralist theory, 362
    Progressive Era and, 357–358
    Public Citizen interest group, 359
    public interest groups, 357, 358–361, 363
    reasons for, 361–363
    regulation, 375–376
    religious, 359–360
    social capital and, 361
    successful, 372–375
    trade associations, 357–358
    transactions theory, 362
    WCTU (Women's Christian Temperance Union), 356
    Women's March on Washington, 362
intermediate standard of review, 131
Internet, government regulation, 346
interstate relations, 52
Iraq War, 416
Iron Curtain, 411
iron triangles, 204, 204*f*
Iroquois Confederacy, 46, 47
Iroquois League of Nations, 2
ISIS (Islamic State in Iraq and Syria), 417, 428
isolationism, 408
issue networks, 204

J

Jackson, Andrew, 103, 177, 263–264
Jackson, Stonewall, 58
Jacksonian democracy, 263–264
Jamestown settlement, 3
    Puritans, 3–4
    slavery and, 102
Japanese Americans during WWII, 126
Jay, John, 38, 217
    The Federalist Papers, 38
Jay Court, 217
Jefferson, Thomas, 24, 190, 296
Jim Crow laws, 106, 107
    Civil Rights Cases, 107
Johnson, Andrew, 57, 106

Johnson, Lyndon B., 64
    civil rights and, 116
Joint Chiefs of Staff, 419
joint committee, 149
Judd, Ashley, 118
judicial activism, Supreme Court, 235
judicial branch, 33, 214. *See also* Supreme Court
    amendments to Constitution, 42–43
    Article III and, 36
    checks on executive branch, 33*f*
    checks on legislative branch, 33*f*
    federal bureaucracy and, 211
    judicial system creation, 216–218
judicial implementation, 238–239
judicial restraint, Supreme Court, 235
judicial review, 218–219
judicial system
    circuit courts, 217
    colonies, 5
    creation, 216–218
    federal court system structure, 216*f*
    grand jury, 85
    state court system structure, 216*f*
judiciary
    constitutional foundations, 214–219
    foreign and defense policy, 422–423
Judiciary Act of 1789, 216–217
Judiciary Act of 1801, 218
jurisdiction, Supreme Court, 215
jury trials, 88–89
justice, government and, 6
justiciable question, 143

K

Kagan, Elena, 224, 225*t*, 230
Kavanaugh, Brett, 15, 42, 224, 225*t*
Kelly, Mark, 140
Kennedy, Anthony, 15, 224
Kennedy, Jacqueline, 181
Kennedy, John F., 115
    Nixon debate, 305
Keynes, John Maynard, 387
Keynesian economics, 387
Kidman, Nicole, 118
King Jr., the Reverend Martin Luther, 114
    "Letter from a Birmingham City Jail," 115
Knox, Henry, 190
Kohut, Andrew, 259
Korean War, 413
Korematsu v. *U.S.*, 126

L

labor unions, 357, 360–361
    Clayton Act, 357
    membership, 361*f*
laissez-faire philosophy, 387
Lane, George, 129
Latinx, 9*n*
    voting rights, 121
Lauer, Matt, 118
law-making, 137, 151–152
    bill path to law, 152*f*
    bills, 137, 152*f*

cloture, 154
committee referral, 152–153
filibuster, 154
final approval, 154
floor debate, 153–154
pocket veto, 154
president and, 153, 185
veto, 154
Lawrence, John Geddes, 94
Lawrence v. *Texas*, 94, 127
LBJ. *See* Johnson, Lyndon B.
League of Nations, 173
Lee, Richard Henry, 23
Lee, Robert E., 58
legislative branch, 33
    Article I and, 34–35
    bicameral, 34, 136
    checks on executive branch, 33*f*
    checks on judicial branch, 33*f*
    Congress and, 33
    enumerated powers, 34
    president and, 33
legislative courts, 220
Lemon v. *Kurtzman*, 74
"Letter from Birmingham City Jail" (King), 115
LGBTQ rights
    civil rights, 127–128
    DOMA (Defense of Marriage Act), 127–128
    right to privacy, 93–94
    Roberts Court, 240
libel, 80
liberal political ideology, 253, 254*f*
    news audiences, 349*f*
The Liberator (Garrison), 104
Libertarian Party, 282
libertarians, 253, 254*f*
liberty, government and, 8
Liberty Bell, 25
Liberty Party, 282
Lilly Ledbetter Fair Pay Act of 2009, 118
Lincoln, Abraham, 57, 178
    Emancipation Proclamation, 105
    funeral, 167
    on Harriet Beecher Stowe, 105
Lippmann, Walter, 244
Literary Digest, 244
Livingston, Robert, 24
Lobby Disclosure Act, 376
lobbying, 365–370
lobbyists, 160, 357
    numbers, 366*f*
    regulation, 375–376
local government
    charters, 52
    colonies, 5–6
    counties, 52
    municipalities, 52–53
    special districts, 53
    towns, 53
Locke, John, 24, 243
Lodge, Henry Cabot, 173
logrolling, 160
LULAC (League of United Latin American Citizens), 120

lynching of Black people, 109
Lyon, Matthew, 134
Lyon, Phyllis, 128

M

Macron, Emmanuel, 434
Madison, James, 38
    The Federalist Papers, 38
MALDEF (Mexican American Legal Defense and
        Educational Fund), 121
Maloney, Carolyn, 41
mandate, 291
manifest destiny, 409
Mapp v. Ohio, 87
Marbury, William, 218
Marbury v. Madison, 218–219
March on Washington for Jobs and Freedom, 116
margin of error, 250
marriage
    DOMA (Defense of Marriage Act), 127–128
    free exercise clause, 75
    Obergefell v. Hodges, 12, 128
Marshall, John, 53, 218–219
Marshall, Thurgood, 111
Marshall Court
    Bill of Rights, limiting, 55
    Marbury v. Madison, 218–219
    national power, 53–55
Marshall Plan, 413
Martin, Del, 128
Mason, George, 70
mass media, 330
mass shootings, 83
Masterpiece Cakeshop v. Colorado Civil Rights Commission, 73
matching funds, campaigns, 314
Mayflower, 4
Mayflower Compact, 4, 135
McConnell, Mitch, 15, 159
McCorvey, Norma, 92
McCulloch v. Maryland, 50, 53
    national power and, 53–54
    necessary and proper clause, 219
McCutcheon v. FEC, 309
McDaniel, Ronna Romney, 270
McDonald v. City of Chicago, 83
McGirt v. Oklahoma, 125
McLaurin, George, 111
means-tested programs, 399
media
    campaigns and, 305–308
    digital media, 335–337
    mass media, 330
    news media, 329, 330
    ownership, 345–346
    political socialization and, 257
    print media, 331–333
Medicaid, 393
Medicare, 393
MENA (Middle East and North Africa) region, foreign and
        defense policy, 434–435
mercantilism, 20
merit system, 193
Merkel, Angela, 434

#MeToo movement, 118
midterm elections, 299
military-industrial complex, 423
Miller v. California, 80
minor parties in system, 282t
Minutemen, 23
Miranda, Ernesto, 86
Miranda rights, 87
Miranda v. Arizona, 86–87
Missouri Compromise, 104
    Dred Scott v. Sandford and, 105
moderate political ideology, 253
monarchy, 48
Mondale, Walter, 180
monetary policy
    discount rate, 391
    Federal Reserve System and, 391
    open market operations, 391
    reserve requirements, 391
Monroe, James, 409
Monroe Doctrine, 409
Montesquieu, 32
Montgomery bus boycott, 114
Moral Majority, 359
Morrill Anti-Bigamy Act, 76
Mott, Lucretia, 105, 354
muckraking, 332
municipalities, 52–53

N

NAACP (National Association for the Advancement of
        Colored People), 108
    founding, 109
NAACP LDF (Legal Defense and Educational Fund), 111
NAFTA (North American Free Trade Agreement),
        173, 415
Nagasaki bombing, 429
NAM (National Association of Manufacturers), 357–358
narrowcasting, 348–349
national debt, 386, 389–390
national deficit, 389–390
National Firearms Act, 83
national party committee, 269
national powers, 51f
    state power balance, 61–65
National Security Council, 418
National Woman's Party, 354
NATO (North Atlantic Treaty Organization), 413
NAWSA (National American Woman Suffrage
        Association), 109
necessary and proper clause, 34–35, 137, 219
negative ads, campaigns, 307
New Amsterdam, 3
New Deal, 59, 61f, 399, 400
new federalism, 61f
New Green Deal, public awareness, 243f
New Jersey Plan, 29
New Jersey v. T.L.O., 85
New Netherlands, 3
New York Times Co. v. U.S., 78
news. See also media
    2020 elections, 329
    consumption changes, 335f

digital-native, 330
muckraking, 332
political news sources, 334*f*
Progressive movement and, 332
radio news, 333
social media and, 329
TV news, 333–334
yellow journalism, 331, 332
news leaks, 337
news media, 329, 330. *See also* press
2020 elections, 329
agenda setting, 340–341
audience political identification, 349*f*
on background information, 344
bias in, 341–343
citizen journalists, 351–352
Congress and, 339
consolidation, 347–348
content regulation, 346–347
deep background information, 344
equal time rule, 346
experts and, 351
fourth estate, 330
framing, 341
government regulations, 345–347
influence, 340–341
infotainment, 349–351
Internet regulation, 346
journalistic standards, 344–345
narrowcasting, 348–349
news leaks, 337
off the record information, 344
ownership, 347–348
ownership regulation, 345–346
partisanship and, 343*f*
politics, covering, 337–340
president and, 338–339
press briefings, 337
press conferences, 337
press releases, 337
prior restraint, 345
public confidence and, 343–344
pundits and, 351
on the record information, 344
right of rebuttal, 346
SOPA (Stop Online Piracy Act), 347
Supreme Court and, 339–340
Newsom, Gavin, 128
NHLA (National Hispanic Leadership Agenda), 122
Niagara Movement, 109
NIH (National Institutes of Health), 395
Nineteenth Amendment, 109–110, 453
Ninth Amendment, 71, 451
Nixon, Richard M., 155, 170
Kennedy debate, 305
No Child Left Behind Act, 397
no-knock warrants, 85
non–means-tested programs, 399
Northwest Ordinance, 123
NOW (National Organization for Women), 117
NPT (Nuclear Nonproliferation Treaty), 430
NRA (National Recovery Administration), 59

NRA (National Rifle Association), 83, 360
nuclear weapons, foreign and defense policy, 429–430
NWP (National Woman's Party), 109–110
NWSA (National Woman Suffrage Association), 106

O
Obama, Barack, 299
progressive federalism and, 62
Obama, Michelle, 181
Obamacare. *See* ACA (Affordable Care Act)
Obergefell v. *Hodges*, 12, 128
obscenity, 80–81
Ocasio-Cortez, Alexandria, 140
Occupy Wall Street, hate speech concerns, 80
O'Connor, Sandra Day, 224, 230
oligarchy, 48
Olive Branch Petition, 23
Omar, Ilhan, 140
OMB (Office of Management and Budget), 186
open primary, 292
Operation Iraqi Freedom, 416
Oregon Employment Division v. *Smith*, 76
organized labor, 357, 360–361
original jurisdiction, federal courts, 216*f*
Osama bin Laden, 416
Osoff, Jon, 140
oversight function of Congress, 156–158

P
PACs (political action committees), 159, 160, 311–312, 364
election spending, 372*f*
super PACs, 313
Paine, Thomas, 23
Common Sense, 23
Panama Canal Treaty, 173
Panama Canal Zone, 410
pandemic response. *See* COVID-19
pardons, presidential, 175–176
Trump, Donald J., 176
Parks, Rosa, 114
Partial Birth Abortion Ban Act, 93
parties, 158–159
partisan polarization, 283, 285*f*
ACA (Affordable Care Act), 380
causes, 283–284
consequences of, 285–286
partisan tribalism, 262
partisanship, 134, 262
political news and, 343*f*
party identification, 276
age and, 279, 280*f*
Black Americans, 278
education and, 281*f*
ethnicity and, 278–279
gender and, 277*f*, 278
geography and, 278
group identity and, 277
pluralists and, 277
political socialization and, 277
race and, 278–279
religion and, 280, 281*f*

party identification (*continued*)
  social and economic factors, 279, 280*f*
  voting and, 315–316
party realignment, 265
  secular realignment, 266
patronage, 193
patrons, interest groups, 374
PCCs (policy coordinating committees), 205
Pearl Harbor attack, 195
Pelosi, Nancy, 139, 147
  ERA (Equal Rights Amendment), 41
Pence, Mike, 180
Pendleton Act, 193
Penn, William, 4
Penn's Woods, 4
Pennsylvania, 4
Pentagon Papers, 78
Perez, Thomas, 270
Pew Research Center, 246
The Philadelphia Negro, 244
Planned Parenthood of Southeastern Pennsylvania v. *Casey*, 93
Plessy, Homer, 108
Plessy v. *Ferguson*, 108
  legal tests, 110–113
  Truman, Harry, 111
pluralists, party identification and, 277
plurality opinion, Supreme Court, 235
pocket veto, 154
podcasts, 336
polarization. *See* partisan polarization
policy. *See also* monetary policy
  distributive policies, 382
  education policy, 396–398
  federal bureaucracy and, 205–207
  fiscal policy, 386–390
  foreign and defense policy, 408–431
  health policy, 392–395
  monetary policy, 391
  public policy, 381
  redistributive policies, 382
  regulatory policies, 382
  social welfare, 398–402
  Supreme Court role, 237–240
  trade policy, 409
policy adoption, policy making, 384
policy formation, policy–making, 384
policy implementation, policy making, 385
policy-making process, 381–382
  adoption, 384
  evaluation, 386
  formation, 384
  governmental agenda, 384
  implementation, 385
  stages, 383*f*
  systemic agenda, 384
  theories, 382–383
political activism, 314
political ideology, 251. *See also* political socialization
  classifying, 254*f*
  conservatives, 252–353
  evaluation, 251
  explanation, 251
  liberals, 253
  libertarians, 253–254

moderates, 253
opinion formation, 254–258
orientation, 251
political program, 251
statists, 253–254
urban–rural differences, 266*f*
political machine, 264
political news, 334*f*
political participation, 314
political parties, 262
  American Independent Party, 282
  campaign funding and, 311
  candidate-centered politics, 265
  Congress and, 158–159
  Democratic-Republican party, 263
  development, 263
  Era of Good Feelings, 263
  Federalist Party, 263
  foreign and defense policy, 423–424
  Free Soil Party, 282
  functions, 271–276
  Golden Age, 264
  Green Party, 282
  informal groups, 270–271
  Jacksonian democracy, 263–264
  Libertarian Party, 282
  Liberty Party, 282
  linkage and, 275–276
  minor parties, 281–283
  modern era, 265
  national committee, 269
  national convention, 268
  national party organization, 267–269, 267*f*
  national party platform, 273
  organization, 267–271
  organizing government, 273–275
  partisan tribalism, 262
  partisanship, 262
  party realignment, 265
  population migration and, 265
  Progressive/Bull Moose Party, 282
  Prohibition Party, 282
  proportional representation, 283
  Reform Party, 282
  Republican Party, 264
  running candidates for office, 271–273
  secular realignment, 266
  southern strategy, 266
  state and local party organization, 267*f*, 269–270
  taxes, differences, 389
  unity and, 275–276
  urban–rural differences, 266*f*
  Whig Party, 264
political reform, 320–325
political socialization, 254
  demographic characteristics, 254–256
  education and, 256–257
  family and, 256–257
  leaders and, 257–258
  mass media and, 257
  opinion makers and, 257–258
  party identification and, 277
  peers and, 256–257
  political knowledge and, 258

politico, 142
politics, 13
  news media coverage, 337–340
  science and, 257
poll taxes, voting and, 108
polling, 242. *See also* public opinion
  ANES (American National Election Studies),
    245–246
  conducting, 247–251
  data analysis, 249–250
  Du Bois, W.E.B., 244
  exit polls, 249
  Gallup, George, 245
  intensity of opinion, 252
  lack of interest, 251
  Literary Digest, 244
  margin of error, 250
  Pew Research Center, 246
  phone banks, 248
  population, 247–248
  presidential elections, 246*f*
  public opinion, 243
  Public Opinion (Lippmann), 244
  push polls, 247
  respondents, 248–249
  samples, 244, 247–248
  sampling error, 250
  straw poll, 244
  survey design, 247
  survey errors, 250
  tracking polls, 248, 249*f*
  Truman *vs.* Dewey election, 245
pollsters, 303
Ponce de Leon, Juan, 2
population
  age, 10–11
  political parties and, 265
  polling, 247–248
  representation and, 10*f*
population growth of nation, 8–9*f*
pork, 156
positive ads, campaigns, 307
post-Civil War Reconstruction, 264
power distribution in federal system, 51*f*
precedent, Supreme Court, 222
president, 167
  appointee removal, 171
  appointment power, 171–172
  budgetary process, 186–187
  Cabinet, 172
  changes in power, 176–179
  chief law enforcer, 175
  chief of state, 175
  commander in chief, 174, 175
  congressional elections and, 299
  constitutional powers, 171–176
  empathy and, 16
  executive agreements, 173
  executive orders, 187–188
  executive privilege, 170
  expansion of power, 177–178
  foreign and defense policy and, 418
  former presidents gathering, 169
  funeral, 167

  impeachment, 170
  inherent powers, 35, 177
  law-making role, 153
  leadership, 182–184
  legislative branch and, 33
  legislative implementation, 186–187
  legislative process and, 175
  lying in state, 167
  media, modern, and, 167
  modern presidency, 179
  news media and, 338–339
  pardoning power, 175–176
  party leader, 175
  personality, 182–184
  pocket veto, 154
  policy making and, 185–189
  power to persuade, 183
  proclamations, 187–188
  public opinion, 167–168, 184–185
  public outreach, 183
  public policy and, 175
  qualifications, 169–170
  rules of succession, 170–171
  signing statements, 188
  State of the Union, 172
  terms of office, 169–170
  treaty power, 172–173
  veto, 154, 173–174
  War Powers Resolution, 156–157, 174
  White House Correspondents' Dinner, 184
presidential coattails, 299
presidential elections
  caucuses, 294
  Electoral College, 295–297
  electors, 295
  nomination process, 294–295
  polling, 246*f*
  proportional representation primary, 294
  reapportionment, 295
  winner-take-all primary, 294
presidential establishment, 179
  Cabinet, 180
  EOP (Executive Office of the President), 182
  first ladies, 181
  vice president, 179–180
  White House staff, 182
presidential power, Roberts Court, 240
Presidential Succession Act, 170–171
press. *See also* news media
  presidency and, 338–339
  public figures and, 337–338
press briefings, 337
press conferences, 337
press releases, 337
press secretary, 303
Pressley, Ayanna, 140
primary education policies, 396–397
primary elections, 292, 294
print media, 331–333
prior restraint, 345
  freedom of speech, 77
  protected speech and press, 78
proclamations, 187–188
programmatic (earmark) grants, 64, 156

Progressive Era, 108, 264
   Constitutional amendments, 40
   interest groups and, 357–358
   women's group, 109
progressive federalism, 61f, 62
Progressive movement
   interest groups, 357
   journalism and, 332
Progressive/Bull Moose Party, 282
Prohibition Party, 282
proportional representation, 283
Proprietary colonies, 5
prospective judgment, 319
protected speech and press
   hate speech, 79–80
   New York Times Co. v. U.S., 78
   Pentagon Papers, 78
   prior restraint and, 78–79
   symbolic speech, 79
   Trump, Donald, attempts to bar publication, 79
protests, 14–15
   freedom of assembly, 81–82
   lobbying and, 369–370
Providence Plantations, 4
Public Citizen interest group, 359
public funds, campaigns, 314
public health policy, 394–396
public interest groups, 357, 358–361, 363
public opinion, 242, 243. *See also* polling
   effects, 258–259
   Literary Digest, 244
   The Philadelphia Negro, 244
   polls, 243
   of president, 184–185
Public Opinion (Lippmann), 244
public policy, 381
public trust in government, 276f
pundits, 351
Puritan settlers, 3–4
push polls, 247
Putin, Vladimir, 432

Q

Quadafi, Moamar, 416
Quartering Act, 21

R

race
   early settlers, 3
   federal justices, 226
   party identification and, 278–279
   voting and, 317–318
racial composition of nation, 9–10
racial discrimination
   Black Codes, 106
   Civil Rights Act of 1866, 106
   Civil Rights Act of 1875, 107
   Fifteenth Amendment, 106
   Fourteenth Amendment, 106, 108
   Jim Crow laws, 106, 107
   legal tests, 110–113
   Montgomery bus boycott, 114

Plessy, Homer, 108
Plessy v. Ferguson, 108
racial segregation
   Brown v. Board of Education, 112–113
   Brown v. Board of Education II, 113–114
   Cooper v. Aaron, 113–114
   Montgomery bus boycott, 114
   public trains, 108
   school desegregation, 113–114
   separate-but-equal doctrine, 108
radio news, 333
Randolph, Edmund, 190
Randolph, Jennings, 19
ratification of Constitution
   Anti-Federalists and, 37–38
   Bill of Rights, 39
   Federalists and, 37–38
   support for, 39
rational basis standard of review, 131
R.A.V. v. City of St. Paul, 79
Reagan, Ronald, 64, 167, 406
Reagan Doctrine, 414
reapportionment, 295
recall elections, 293, 294
recession, 387
Reconstruction (Civil War), 57, 107
   federalism and, 61f
Reddit, 336
redistributive policies, 382
redistricting congressional districts, 143–145
Reed v. Reed, 131
referendums, 292, 293
Reform Party, 282
regional growth/expansion, 12–13
regulations, 205, 206f
regulatory policies, 382
Rehnquist, William H., 65
Rehnquist Court, *Miranda* rights, 87
religion. *See also* freedom of religion
   Article VI, 36
   federal justices, 226
   interest groups, 359–360
   party identification and, 280, 281f
   preferences, 12f
   Puritan settlers, 3–4
   Roberts Court, 240
   separation of church and state, 36
   voting and, 319
religious beliefs among population, 11
Reno v. ACLU, 81
representation, population and, 10f
republic, 6
Republican Party
   Black Americans and, 263
   delegates to national convention, 268
   formation, 264
reserved powers, 50, 51f
retrospective judgment, 319
Revere, Paul, 21, 22
Revolutionary War, 6
Reynolds v. United States, 75
RFRA (Religious Freedom Restoration Act), 76
right of rebuttal, 346

right to counsel, 88
right to privacy, 90
    abortion, 92–93
    birth control, 91–92
    Burwell v. *Hobby Lobby*, 91
    Griswold v. *Connecticut*, 91
    LGBTQ issues, 93–94
    Roe v. *Wade*, 92
Roberts Jr., John G., 225*t*
Roberts Court
    decisions, 239–240
    Miranda rights, 87
Robertson, Pat, 359
Roe v. *Wade*, 92
Roosevelt, Eleanor, 117, 181
Roosevelt, Franklin D., 59, 179, 412
    federalism and, 60
    New Deal, 59
Roosevelt Corollary, 410
Rose, Charlie, 118
Rousseau, Jean-Jacques, 24, 32
royal colonies, 5
royal governors, 168
rule making, federal bureaucracy, 206*f*
Rule of Four, Supreme Court, 230
Russia, foreign and defense policy and, 432–433
Russian government, involvement in elections, 15

S

SALT (Strategic Arms Limitation Treaties), 413
same-sex marriage
    DOMA (Defense of Marriage Act), 127–128
    Obergefell v. *Hodges*, 12, 128
samples, polling, 244, 248, 250
sanctuary cities/counties/states, 64*f*
Santa Fe Independent School District v. *Doe*, 74
Scalia, Antonin, 15
Schenck v. *U.S.*, 78
school districts, 53
school prayer, 74–75
school shootings, 14–15, 83
Schumer, Chuck, 159
SCLC (Southern Christian Leadership Conference), 115
Scott, Dred, 56
Scott, Tim, 142
SDI (Strategic Defense Initiative), nuclear weapons, 430
searches and seizures, 84–85, 87
secession, 57
Second Amendment, 82–83, 451
    COVID-19 and, 97
    D.C. v. *Heller*, 83
    McDonald v. *City of Chicago*, 83
    school shootings and, 83
    state gun laws, 82
    U.S. v. *Miller*, 83
Second Continental Congress, 23
    Articles of Confederation, 25–27
    Committee of Five, 24
    Declaration of Independence, 24
    foreign allies, 24–25
secondary education policies, 396–397
secular realignment, 266
sedition laws, 71

segregation, Jim Crow laws, 106
select (special) committee, 149
selective incorporation, 72, 73
Senate
    Article I and, 34
    cloture, 154
    compared to House of Representatives, 138*t*
    leadership, 148
    majority leader, 148
    membership requirements, 136
    minority leader, 148
    organization, 145*f*
    president pro tempore, 148
    presiding officer, 148
    term length, 137
    vice president, 148
senatorial courtesy, 158
    federal judges, 223
Seneca Falls Convention, 105
separate-but-equal doctrine, 108
    legal tests, 110–113
    McLaurin, George, accommodations, 112
separation of church and state, 36. *See also* establishment
        clause; First Amendment; free exercise clause
separation of powers, 32
    checks and balances, 33*f*
    executive branch, 33
    judicial branch, 33
    legislative branch, 33
September 11 attacks, 415–416
seriatim opinions, 218–219
Sessions, Jeff, 64
Seven Years' War, 20
Seventeenth Amendment, 59, 453
Seventh Amendment, 451
sex discrimination
    Civil Rights Act of 1964, 117
    Equal Pay Act of 1963, 118–119
sexual harassment
    Civil Rights Act of 1964, 117
    lawsuits, 117–118
    #MeToo movement, 118
    #TimesUp movement, 118
Shaw v. *Reno*, 144
Shays, Daniel, 27
Shays's Rebellion, 27
Shelby County v. *Holder*, 65
Sherman, Robert, 24
signing statements, 188
sit-ins, 115
Sixteenth Amendment, 58–59, 194–195, 453
Sixth Amendment, 88–89, 451
size growth of nation, 8–9
skepticism about government, 14
slander, 80
slavery
    abolitionists, 103
    auctions, 102
    Black Codes and, 106
    Constitutional Convention, 30–31, 102
    Douglass, Frederick, 104
    Emancipation Proclamation, 105
    freedmen, 107

slavery (*continued*)
  Fugitive Slave Act, 102
  Jamestown Colony, 102
  legal, 102
  Missouri Compromise, 104
  Thirteenth Amendment, 105–106
  Tubman, Harriet, 102
  Underground Railroad, 101, 102
  Virginia Colony, 102
SNAP (Supplemental Nutrition Assistance Program), 399, 402
SNCC (Student Nonviolent Coordinating Committee), 115
social capital, interest groups and, 361
social conservative, 253
social contract theory, 24
social media, 335–336
  Facebook, 336
  news and, 329
  Reddit, 336
  regulation, 344
  Twitter, 336
social movements, voting and, 315
Social Security, 400
Social Security Act, 399
social welfare policy
  AFDC (Aid to Families and Dependent Children), 402
  challenges, 403
  child support, 402
  entitlement programs, 399
  means-tested programs, 399
  New Deal, 399, 400
  non–means-tested programs, 399
  SNAP (Supplemental Nutrition Assistance Program), 399, 402
  Social Security, 400
  Social Security Act, 399
  SSI (Supplemental Security Income), 401–402
  TANF (Temporary Assistance for Needy Families), 402
  unemployment insurance, 401
  Works Projects Administration, 399
socioeconomics
  party identification and, 279, 280*f*
  voting and, 316
Sojourner Truth, 104
  "Ain't I a Woman?," 105
solicitor general, federal court cases and, 231
Sons of Liberty, 21
SOPA (Stop Online Piracy Act), 347
Sotomayor, Sonia, 225*t*
southern strategy, 266
Speaker of the House, 147
special districts, 53
spoils system, 193
SSA (Social Security Administration), 59
SSI (Supplemental Security Income), 401–402
Stalin, Josef, 412
Stamp Act, 20, 21
standards of review, 129–131
standing committees, 149
Stanton, Elizabeth Cady, 105, 106, 354
stare decisis, 222
state court system, 216*f*
State of the Union, 172

state powers, 50–51, 51*f*
states
  death penalty, 90
  federal grants, 63*f*
  gun laws, 82
  interstate relations, 52
statists, 253, 254*f*
Stowe, Harriet Beecher, 105
straw poll, 244
strict scrutiny, 73, 130
  undue burden test, 93
Stromberg v. *California*, 79
substantive due process, 71
succession, president, 170–171
suffrage, 104
  Black men, 106–108
  NAWSA (National American Woman Suffrage Association), 109
  NWP (National Woman's Party), 109–110
  NWSA (National Woman Suffrage Association), 106
  Susan B. Anthony Amendment, 110
Sugar Act, 20, 21
Sumner, Charles, 135
super PACs, 313
superdelegates, national party convention, 268
supply-side economics, 388
supremacy clause, Article VI, 36
Supreme Court, 221–222
  Alito, Samuel A., 225*t*
  amicus curiae, 231–232
  Article III and, 36
  Barrett, Amy Coney, 14, 42, 224, 225*t*
  Brandeis, Louis, 62
  Breyer, Stephen A., 225*t*
  cases, 228–235, 229*f*
  cert pool, 230
  chamber, 213
  Civil Rights Cases, 107
  clerks, 231
  closed conference, 234
  concurring opinions, 235
  courts of appeals and, 232
  COVID-19 and, 234
  dissenting opinions, 235
  docket contents, 229
  early court, 217–218
  executive agreements and, 215
  executive orders, 215
  federalism and, 65
  Ginsburg, Ruth Bader, 14, 42, 235
  Gorsuch, Neil, 14, 42, 224, 225*t*
  influences on decisions, 235–237
  interest groups and, 232
  Jay, John, 217
  Jay Court, 217
  judicial activism, 235
  judicial ideology and, 235
  judicial implementation, 238–239
  judicial philosophy and, 235
  judicial power, 215
  judicial restraint, 235
  judicial review, 218–219
  jurisdiction, 215

justices as of December 2020, 225*t*
Kagan, Elena, 224, 225*t*, 230
Kavanaugh, Brett, 14, 42, 224, 225*t*
Kennedy, Anthony, 14, 224
Marshall, John, 53
Marshall, Thurgood, 111
Marshall Court, 53–55
news media and, 339–340
O'Connor, Sandra Day, 224, 230
opinions, 234–235
oral arguments before, 233–234
originalists, 235
plurality opinions, 235
policymaking and, 237–240
precedent, 222
presidential impeachment and, 215
public opinion and, 236–237
Rehnquist, William H., 65
Rehnquist Court, 65
Roberts Jr., John G., 225*t*
Roberts Court, 65, 239–240
Rule of Four, 230
Scalia, Antonin, 14
solicitor general and, 231
Sotomayor, Sonia, 225*t*
standards of review, 129–131
stare decisis, 222
strict constructionist, 235
strict scrutiny, 73
Taney, Roger, 78
tenure, 215
Thomas, Clarence, 225*t*
types of cases, 215
Warren, Earl, 65, 72, 113
Warren Court, 72
writ of *certiorari*, 229–230
Susan B. Anthony Amendment, 110
suspect classifications, 130
Sweatt, H. M., 111
symbolic speech, 79
COVID-19 and, 96
Stromberg v. *California*, 79
Tinker v. *Des Moines Independent Community School District*, 79
systemic agenda, policy-making, 384

T

Taliban, 416
Taney, Roger, 78
TANF (Temporary Assistance for Needy Families), 402
tariffs, 409
Tax Cuts and Jobs Act, 389
taxes
political party differences, 389
Sixteenth Amendment, 58–59
Taylor, Breonna, 6, 370
Tea Act, 22
Tea Party, 28
Tennessee v. *Lane*, 129
Tenth Amendment, 32, 50, 71, 451
Tenure of Office Act, 161
term limits, Twenty-Second Amendment, 170

terrorism
domestic terrorism, 428
foreign and defense policy, 427–429
Terry v. *Ohio*, 84
the Enlightenment, 6–7
Third Amendment, 451
Thirteenth Amendment, 105–106
Thomas, Clarence, 225*t*
Three-Fifths Compromise, 30–31, 102
Thurmond, Strom, Civil Rights Act of 1964, 116
Tillerson, Rex, 172
#TimesUp movement, 118
Tinker v. *Des Moines Independent Community School District*, 79
Title IX (Educational Amendment Acts), 118, 397–398
Title VII of Civil Rights Act of 1964, 117
Tlaib, Rashida, 140
totalitarianism, 48
towns, 53
Townshend Acts, 21
tracking polls, 248, 249*f*
trade policy, 409
export markets, 427*f*
free trade system, 426
protectionism and, 426
strategic trade policy, 426
USMCA (U.S.-Mexico-Canada Agreement), 427
transactions theory, interest groups, 362
treaties
foreign and defense policy, 421
president and, 172–173
Treaty of Versailles, 173
trial courts, 220
Truman, Harry S., 111
Truman Doctrine, 412–413
Trump, Donald J., 13
ACA (Affordable Care Act), 380
adviser turnover, 209–210
appointee removal, 171–172
approval ratings, 185
attempts to bar publications, 79
Biden debate, 305
cabinet appointments, 209
China virus, 432
Chinese trade policies, 426
congressional review and, 157
COVID-19 and, 188
election challenges, 290
fake news claims, 168
false claims, 14
foreign policy, 168
immigration, 9, 122–123
impeachment, 156, 158
inherent powers and, 35
pardons, 176
re-election failure, 16
sexual harassment and, 117
Twitter and, 183, 257–258
War Powers Resolution, 174
whitening of federal courts, 224
WHO withdrawal, 173
Women's March on Washington, 362
Trump, Melania, 181
trustee theory of representation, 142

Tubman, Harriet, 101, 102
    Moses nickname, 103
TV news, 333–334
Twelfth Amendment, 451–452
Twentieth Amendment, 453–454
Twenty-Fifth Amendment, 171, 455
Twenty-Fourth Amendment, 454
Twenty-Second Amendment, 170, 454
Twenty-Seventh Amendment, 455
Twenty-Sixth Amendment, 455
Twenty-Third Amendment, 454
Twitter, 336

U

UN Security Council, 411
Uncle Tom's Cabin (Stowe), 105
Underground Railroad, 101, 102
undue burden test, 93
unemployment insurance, 401
unemployment rate by state, 401*f*
unified government, 159
unitary system, 49*f*
United Nations, 173, 411
unprotected speech and press, 80–81
U.S. Civil Service, 201–202
U.S. Department of Commerce and Labor, 194
U.S. v. Miller, 83
U.S. v. Nixon, 170
USMCA (U.S.-Mexico-Canada Agreement), 427

V

veto, 154, 173–174
vice president, 169
    Gore, Al, 186
    Harris, Kamala, 180
    Mondale, Walter, 180
    Pence, Mike, 180
    presidential establishment and, 179–180
    as senatorial tie breaker, 170
Vietnam War, 413
    War Powers Resolution and, 174
Villard, Oswald Garrison, 109
Virginia House of Burgesses, 6, 135
Virginia Plan, 29
voter canvass, 303
voting. *See also* elections
    age and, 318–319
    ballot types, 324
    candidate traits and, 319–320
    civic organizations and, 319
    coronavirus pandemic and, 43
    crossover voting, 292
    education and, 316
    ethnicity and, 317–318
    gender and, 318–319
    grandfather clause, 108
    hacking, 43
    issues and, 319–320
    party identification and, 315–316
    patterns, 314–320
    political activism and, 314

political participation, 314
    prospective judgment, 319
    race and, 317–318
    registration reform, 322
    religion and, 319
    retrospective judgment, 319
    social movements and, 315
    socioeconomics and, 316
    turnout, 314–315
voting age, 19
voting restrictions, 108
voting rights, 8, 18, 104. *See also* suffrage
    American Indians, 124
    Black people, 106–108
    Hispanics, 121
    Nineteenth Amendment, 109–110
    NWSA (National Woman Suffrage Association), 106
Voting Rights Act of 1965, redistricting and, 144
vouchers for schools, 397

W

War on Terror, 415–416
War Powers Resolution, 156–157, 174, 422
Warnock, Raphael, 142
Warren, Earl, 65, 72, 113
Warren Court, 72
Washington, George, 28, 168, 176–177
    army commander in chief, 23
    Farewell Address, 408
    funeral, 167
Watergate, 170
Weber, Max, 203–204
Webster v. Reproductive Health Services, 93
Weinstein, Harvey, 118
Whig Party, 264
whips, 147–148
Whitaker, Clem, 304
White House Correspondents' Dinner, 184
White House staff, 182
White privilege, 10
Whitmer, Gretchen, 97
WHO (World Health Organization), Trump's withdrawal, 173
Whole Woman's Health v. Hellerstedt, 93
Williams, Roger, 4
Wilson, Edith Bolling Galt, 181
Wilson, Woodrow, 173
winner-take-all system, 283, 294
Wisconsin v. Yoder, 76
Witherspoon, Reese, 118
women
    ERA (Equal Rights Amendment), 42
    National Woman's Party, 354
    suffragettes, 42
    white, wearing of, 42
Women's March on Washington, 14
women's rights, 104–105, 354
    Anthony, Susan B., 106
    Equal Pay Act of 1963, 118
    ERA (Equal Rights Amendment), 119–120
    Lilly Ledbetter Fair Pay Act of 2009, 118

Mott, Lucretia, 105
NAWSA (National American Woman Suffrage Association), 109
NOW (National Organization for Women), 117
NWP (National Woman's Party), 109–110
NWSA (National Woman Suffrage Association), 106
Seneca Falls Convention, 105
sexual harassment, 117
Sojourner Truth, 104
Stanton, Elizabeth Cady, 105
Susan B. Anthony Amendment, 110
Title IX, 118
Works Projects Administration, 399
World Bank, 412
World War II, 411–412
world wars
    federal bureaucracy and, 195–196
    foreign and defense policy, 410
writ of *certiorari*, 229–230
writ of *mandamus*, 219
wrongful conviction, 90
WTO (World Trade Organization), 412

Y
yellow journalism, 331, 332
Yick Wo v. *Hopkins*, 125
Youngstown Sheet & Tube v. *Sawyer*, 187

Z
Zenger, John Peter, 69
Zuckerberg, Mark, 344